SIMON SCHAMA

Belonging

The Story of the Jews

1492–1900

VINTAGE

3 5 7 9 10 8 6 4 2

Vintage
20 Vauxhall Bridge Road,
London SW1V 2SA

Vintage is part of the Penguin Random House group of companies
whose addresses can be found at global.penguinrandomhouse.com.

Penguin
Random House
UK

First published in the UK by The Bodley Head in 2017
First published by Vintage in 2018

penguin.co.uk/vintage

A CIP catalogue record for this book is available from the British
Library

ISBN 9780099590064

Printed and bound in Great Britain by Clays Ltd, Elcograf S.p.A.

Penguin Random House is committed to a sustainable future for our
business, our readers and our planet. This book is made from Forest

For Moses and Franklin who also belong to this story

Inside the brand-new museum
there's an old synagogue.
Inside the synagogue
is me.
Inside me
my heart.
Inside my heart
a museum.
Inside the museum
a synagogue,
inside it
me,
inside me
my heart,
inside my heart
a museum

Yehuda Amichai, 'Poem Without an End'

CONTENTS

I

C O U L D   I T   B E   N O W ?

I. David

Sometime, somewhere, between Africa and Hindustan, lay a river so Jewish it observed the Sabbath. According to the ninth-century traveller Eldad the Danite, for six days of the week the Sambatyon pushed a heavy load of rocks along its sandy course. On the seventh day, like the Creator fashioning the universe, the river rested. Some writers described the Sambatyon shrivelling overnight into a dry bed. Others swore that the river was waterless: a moving road of stone, its rocks tumbling and grinding against each other so abrasively that its sound, a low thunder, like 'a tempest at sea', could be heard a mile away.[1] The eccentric behaviour of the Sambatyon would not be stopped by anything except its own unnatural laws. It was said that were a man to take a bag of its sand and pour it into a glass vessel he would witness the full force of the mystery. Come sunset and the end of the Sabbath, the white grains which had lain inert during the day of rest would stir, shake and spray themselves against the walls of the bottle as if frantic to rejoin the mother stream. Should an intrepid traveller use the Sabbath as an opportunity to ford the stony bed he would, Eldad warned, be thwarted, for 'as soon as Sabbath begins, fire surrounds the river on the far bank, the flames remaining lit until the next evening when the Sabbath ends. Thus no human being can reach the river for a distance of half a mile for the fire consumes all that grows there.'[2]

In 1480, Eldad's *Letters* were published in Mantua, so one of the very earliest printed Hebrew texts was a journey into the imagination. But the limits of the world were shifting with every caravel sailing

around the coasts of Africa and north-east to the Indies. The most
fanciful thing could turn out to be true. And there was another
pressing reason to hope that an intrepid traveller might find the
Sambatyon. On the far side of its banks were said to dwell four
of the Lost Tribes of Israel, the people who had been carried away
by the conquering Assyrians in the eighth century BCE. All that was
known of the location of their ultimate exile was that it was somewhere orientally remote, since the Assyrians had ruled a vast realm
stretching from the coast of Yemen to the shores of the Caspian. But
find the Sambatyon and you would find the Israelites, preserved in
exile like insects in amber. Everything about them was miraculous.
They rode about on elephants in a countryside free from noxious
creatures. 'There is nothing unclean among them ... no wild beasts,
no flies, no fleas, no lice, no foxes, no scorpions, no serpents, no dogs
...' They lived in handsome, towered dwellings; dyed their clothes
vermilion; kept no servants, but tilled the fruitful land themselves.
Pomegranates without limit were theirs to harvest; succulently pulpy
figs, honey to the bite, dropped from the trees. Their land was kosher
Cockayne.

Even those who suspected that Eldad's story was, in every sense,
far-fetched, longed to know more, for the discovery of the river, and
beyond it these lost Israelites, could signal what every Jew yearned
for. Tradition had it that the appearance of the liberating prince from
the house of David, the true Messiah, the Redeemer of Jerusalem, the
Rebuilder of the Temple, would be heralded by the rediscovery of
the Lost Tribes of Israel, with the tribe of Reuben in their vanguard.
When Constantinople fell to the Turks in 1453, it was rumoured that
the Sambatyon had stopped running altogether, and that the Lost
Tribes were preparing to rejoin the world, if, indeed, they had not
already done so. Rabbi Obadiah of Bertinoro, no gullible fool, staying
in Jerusalem in 1487, made sure to ask freed slaves there whether they
had news of the Sambatyon and the people beyond. 'The Jews of
Aden', he wrote to his brother, 'relate all this with a certain confidence
as if it were well known and no one ever doubted the truth of their
assertions.'[3] The first Hebrew book of learned geography, Abraham
Farissol's *Iggeret Orhot Olam*, the Cosmic Itinerary, had a passage on
the whereabouts of the river, which it located somewhere in Asia.[4]

Reunion with the Lost Tribes of Israel became a consuming obsession for Christians as well as Jews. For the former there were reasons strategic and reasons apocalyptic to want the story of the Sambatyon and the Tribes to be true, and they both converged in a Hebrew moment. If the Israelites dwelled somehow *beyond* the limits of the Muslim world, whether in Africa or Asia, contact with them offered the opportunity to launch an attack on the Turks from the rear. Jews had already been sent by the king of Portugal to find the realm of Prester John, said to be a Christian king powerful in those faraway lands and close to the Lost Tribes. A holy alliance was within reach. The Last Days would be hastened: the long-prophesied battle of titanic antagonists, Gog and Magog, would be joined. Skulls would crack; hosannas would sound; the earth would bubble with blood. Divinely appointed warriors, magnificently arrayed, spears glittering, would go forth to battle the legions of the Antichrist. Following their victory a Christian golden age would commence. Led by the lost Israelites, the rest of the Jews would at last see the error of their ways and troop in their multitudes to the font. Christ would return, radiant in numinous majesty. Glory be to God.

And then, around the festival of Hanukkah in 1523, a small, dark man, his bony frame taut from habitual fasting, fetched up in Venice and declared himself to be David, 'son of King Solomon and brother to King Joseph', ruler of the tribes of Reuben, Gad and half Manasseh.[5] On meeting this ambassador from the dominion of the Lost Tribes some years later, the much-travelled learned geographer Giambattista Ramusio, who thought him genuine, described David as 'very thin and spare like the Jews of Prester John'.[6] The Reubenite himself encouraged the view that he had indeed come from that long-sought-after place where black Jews and Christians were territorial neighbours while warring with each other. The 'ambassador' maintained that others of the missing tribes – those of Simeon and Benjamin – were dwellers by the Sambatyon River, while his own kingdom was in the neighbouring wilderness of Habor. Still further off were the rest of Israel's lost people. So could this Jewish David be the long-expected one, carrying on his meagre frame the news that Jews and Christians alike wanted to hear?

At the turn of the sixteenth century, following the trauma of the expulsions from Spain and Portugal, messianic yearnings had been felt throughout European Jewry. In 1502 in Adriatic Istria, Asher Laemmlein Reutlingen, a pious and entranced master of Kabbalah, had declared that if the Jews atoned for their transgressions, the Messiah would appear within six months. The Church would collapse of its own accord (he imagined it physically, towers and spires crumbling to the ground), and Jerusalem would be liberated in time for the next Passover to be celebrated in the reclaimed city of David. In Jewish communities in northern Italy, southern Germany and beyond, fast days were proclaimed in response to Laemmlein's appeal. At least one man who should have known better, the father of the historian David Gans, in far-off Prague, believed so fervently in the prophecies of Laemmlein that he demolished his matzo oven. But the acts of mass repentance failed to impress the Almighty, for no redeemer showed up as prophesied. Dispirited, Father Gans was obliged to bake his unleavened bread in someone else's oven.

But while it lasted, the Laemmlein craze had the most powerful impact on the communities of northern Italy where there was a high concentration of German Jews who had fled persecution in Bavaria and Franconia. The disappointment dampened but did not extinguish messianic expectations; Laemmlein had just been the wrong man in the wrong year. The astronomer-astrologer Bonet de Lattes, who was also chief rabbi of Rome (and physician to popes Alexander VI and Leo X), went back to the ring-dial he had invented to calculate the altitude of stellar and solar bodies by night as well as day, and arrived at 1505 as the correct year when Jupiter and Saturn would be in Messiah-auspicious alignment. Another anticlimax ensued, but Bonet de Lattes had inaugurated a series of popular annual almanacs marrying up astrological and theological predictions about the timing of the Great Appearance. So when David Ha-Reuveni, the little warrior prince, showed up in Venice in 1523 in his dark silk, there was much excited poring over astral signs. In Ferrara, Farissol, working on his book, revisited the mythic geography of Israelite exile. The 'wilderness of Habor' where King Joseph ruled was indeed one of the places identified in the Books of Kings and Chronicles as the destination of the deported tribes. Farissol was convinced this must be in Asia. Others twisted 'Habor' into 'Khaibar', the ancient city in the Arabian Hejaz where Jews had lived before the coming of Islam. But a rough location for the coming climactic battle sufficed: somewhere between the horn of Africa and the mountains of India. At any rate, there could be no doubt that the wars of the Ottoman sultan, Suleyman the Magnificent, and the Holy Roman Emperor, Charles V, would one day end in messianic conflict. That day was close. A Jerusalem Jew had written that the king of Poland himself (though why he should have known this is mysterious) had reported that the Sambatyon was now so calm that four of the Lost Tribes had already waded through it, and another five were preparing to make the crossing. A great reunion of lost and found Jews was surely at hand. So when David spoke in a strange, sometimes unintelligible, semi-stammering Hebrew clotted with Arabic, this previously unheard accent seemed, excitingly, to belong to some remote place. He was the bearer of something ancient, immemorial, thrown, by God's design, into modern time.

From the outset David aimed high. In Venice he announced that he wished to have an audience with Pope Clement VII. The precondition of the grand Reubenite strategy which would free the Holy Land from the grip of the Turks was that those two inveterate foes, Charles V and Francis I, the king of France, should make peace. Only the Pope could bring that about, so David had set off for Rome to give the Pope the benefit of his strategic advice.

But if that was the case he certainly took the long way round. From the wilderness of Habor and its Ethiopian hinterland, he said, he had made his way into Arabia, but then, for unexplained reasons, had turned back south up the Nile. Where the river flowed between high gorges, in a magnificently barbaric African kingdom, David had seen people eating camels, wolves and other humans while the women covered their loins with nothing but a scanty drop of gold mesh. Further on in his journeyings, he had been given a pair of lion cubs who went everywhere with him and were his special delight until the Turks, who now ruled Egypt, took them from him. Turning downstream once more, he had then journeyed north-east to Palestine where his mission was sanctioned by miracles. In the cave of the Patriarchs at Hebron, as he prayed, the murk was lit by a sudden shaft of radiant light as if the sun had broken through the stone. In Jerusalem, the crescent atop the Dome of the Rock responded to his presence by changing direction from west to east, as if it were a weathercock. Fortified by these Signs he turned south-west again to the Mediterranean, camel-riding for days along the shore until he reached Alexandria and the ship that at last had brought him to Venice and its Jews.

To begin with David lodged with the ship's captain. But then, by his own account – a narrative preserved in the Bodleian Library only in a nineteenth-century facsimile copy (the original written by his personal scribe Solomon Cohen) – he was approached by Venetian Jews who stood behind him while he was praying. This would have been in a private apartment, a room smelling of the stewpot and mildew, its narrow windows, set high on the back wall, looking onto one of the little canals which were the moat of the Jews. The patricians who had established the ghetto in 1516, seven years before David's arrival, continued to forbid the construction of synagogues, even in the small patch of Venice where the Jews were cooped. The first Ashkenazi synagogue would not be built until 1528.[7]

Before 1516, most of the Ashkenazim had plied their trade as pawn-brokers or as sellers of *strazzarie* – 'rags', as second-hand clothes were called – in the city, but then were obliged to return to lodgings at Mestre on the mainland, or even further afield in Padua or Verona. For all Venice's vaunted independence from the authority of pope and emperor, the Serenissima was still the Christian Republic of St Mark and it didn't care to have Jews around overnight. It was at night, after all, when the seductive Jewish women who obsessed Venetians lured Christians into acts of profanity. Beneath bridges and arches, you never could quite see who was who, and patrician lads might find themselves siring little Jews if they didn't look out. So the Jews, women and men both, were required to wear the badges of their race, and they needed to be kept at bay.

And yet. As it had been for centuries through Christian Europe, those who most despised the Jews acknowledged they were good for some things – money for the hard-up especially. (Shakespeare was not wrong about that.) After the city had been overrun by the soldiers of the League of Cambrai, against which Venice had fought a doomed war, the need for money, whether you were a patrician or a pedlar, had become acute. The Jews could furnish it at interest rates far below those charged by Gentile lenders. They could supply cash to the poor in return for pawns, and the republic would benefit from the tax which the Jews had to pay for the privilege of being there at all. In fact the Jews had quickly become *so* useful that the rulers of Venice began to worry they might be lured away to the competing Adriatic port of Ancona by terms more favourable than the fifteen-day renewable licences that were the current norm.

Let them stay, then, but under strict regulation within a small area to which they would be confined. Come sunset, gates would be shut and locked; bridges barred; bells rung. Boats would patrol the miniature island to see that no one exited, unless they were doctors expressly called by Gentile patients. A convenient site for this purpose came to mind. The 'Gheto Novo' had been the republic's copper foundry and the area around it the dumping ground for its waste. Shacks had grown up on its perimeter and in them lived some of the foundry workers. When work for the growing fleets of the Venetian Stato da Mar outgrew the foundry's capacity and it was moved to the Arsenale, the site was left as an empty patch of land. Weeds covered the junkyard. Young patricians came to shoot bolts from their crossbows, trap quail, plot mischief, talk about girls. Bleachers and dyers stretched their fabric over the open space and squatted in the huts abandoned by the departed foundry workers. Then, as happens with commercial societies short of space, developers pounced. Patricians and their counting men saw that money could be made by building low-rent accommodation for cloth workers. Tenements rose around three sides of an open courtyard, the dimensions of which have not much changed from then to now. As soon as the executive Council of Ten made its decision to permit Jewish residence (in the first instance for five years) on condition of their confinement, the tenants of the high-walled buildings were swiftly moved out. At the same time, *all* Jews in Venice were required to evacuate whatever premises they had been living in (many near the Rialto), and move immediately into the ghetto, at rents exorbitantly higher than those charged to the old occupants. There was to be no bargaining and no appeal.

It was in one of those ghetto rooms that men watching the little man bob and sway after his own style got curious and asked the question Jews always ask when a stranger prays with them: 'And where might you be from?' One of the curious was an artist, Moses of Castellazzo, so intrigued by David, the emissary of King Joseph, that he took him to his own lodgings in the ghetto and allowed him to stay through the freezing winter of 1523–4.[8] Moses of Castellazzo was then in his fifties and, in so far as a Jewish artist could be, a great success, inside and outside the community of Jews. Some said he had come from the German world of the Ashkenazim, but a Castellazzo dynasty was famous in Egypt and North Africa. Moses' illustrations for the Hebrew Bible featured scenes and stories from the 'rewritten Bibles', picturesque *midrashic* additions to the canon. In 1521, two years before David's arrival, Moses had made woodcut illustrations for a picture Bible of the kind increasingly popular in the Yiddish-speaking world. The original is lost but a contemporary pen-and-ink copy vividly reveals both Moses' immersion in augmented scripture and the demand for those unauthorised stories: exactly the kind of cultural appetite that would have been receptive to the sudden appearance of a 'brother of the king of Habor'.[9] Instead of Abraham making ready to sacrifice his son Isaac, Moses of Castellazzo chose a scene of the patriarch recovering from his own circumcision as an adult – a moment that would have had immediate, painful resonance for the many Spanish *conversos* who, once in Venice, had returned to the Judaism of their ancestors and marked their commitment with the bloody cut. Many of Moses' scenes are dramas of life among the Gentiles. Restored to favour in Pharaoh's Egypt, Joseph does something no Jew in the dominions of Venice or anywhere else was permitted: he rides a horse, led by a groom, and is enthroned before kneeling supplicants. A Tower of Babel illustration features a building scene straight out of busy Venice, men carrying hods of bricks, ladders and pulleys, a campanile reaching to the sky.

Moses of Castellazzo did more than illustrate the sacred books of the Jews. As a jobbing portraitist he was commissioned to create likenesses on medallions as well as on panel or canvas. This kind of work took him well beyond the ghetto – sometimes even to the courts of Ferrara and Mantua. Though locked and barred at night, the ghetto should not be imagined as an urban prison: by day its residents were free to come and go, and Gentile customers and clients could do likewise. The Jews were in demand as they always were, even by cultures that despised them; in demand as physicians (allowed to attend medical school at the University of Padua); in demand as musicians, entertainers and dancing masters; very much in demand as sellers of fabrics and cloth in the ten stores permitted to them around Venice. For what had begun as the rag trade had developed into much fancier cloth and garments patronised by the patricians and their ladies throughout the city.

Once housed by Moses of Castellazzo, the exotic newcomer would have had entrée, first, to the grander Jews who dominated the community, above all the house of Meshullam (originally from Padua) for whom the word *banche* meant not just as it usually did, pawnbroker, but the real thing; and then also to Christians who had heard the rumours of this prince from the Lost Tribes and, however sceptical, needed to see and hear him for themselves. Little to nothing is known about how David spent that first winter in Venice. Though much questioned he must have been convincing enough to raise the money needed for the next step in his unveiling to the Christian as well as Jewish world – and the promotion of his grand design. That would be an audience with the Pope.

The adventure swiftly progressed from improbable to astonishing. The elders of the Venice ghetto had connections in Rome. It would have been impossible for Rabbi Meshullam not to have known the banker Daniele of Pisa, who counted cardinals, nobles and popes among his clientele. One of those aristocrats of the Church was Cardinal Egidio Antonini of Viterbo who, like many humanists of his generation, was a Kabbalist. For Christian Hebraists like Antonini, within the dense symbolic and numerological maze of the Kabbalah lay the prophecy of a new *Christian* golden age. That the Jews could not see this was but another symptom of their spiritual myopia. Once an exegetical companionship was established, with rabbis and clerics poring over the minutiae together, Jewish teachers would become disciples of Christian masters and be brought to the saving light.

Antonini's own ventures into Kabbalism were not some dilettante flirtation, but the product of long, intense, scrupulous study of the Hebrew texts, made possible by the fact that living in his palazzo in Viterbo was one of the great masters of that discipline: Rabbi Elijah Levita Bahur. Like so many learned but impoverished Jews, Elijah Bahur had come into contact with Christian humanists at Padua where he had been hired to teach Hebrew to sons of rich and often noble families from all over northern Italy, and to copy Hebrew texts for their study. As a grammarian who spent much time pondering irregular verbs and nouns (and writing about them), Elijah was in particular demand. His own style of language teaching was Kabbalistic: there was no word which, beside its surface meaning, did not also carry, in the numbers associated with its letters, some deeper significance. Elijah divided his own book on grammar into the fifty-two chapters corresponding to the numbers made up by his own name. The more fanciful this became, the more Christian scholars like Egidio Antonini, hunting for illumination, loved it. So when in 1514 the troops of the anti-Venetian alliance the League of Cambrai overran the republic's inland territories and subjected Padua to the customary rapine and destruction, the cardinal offered the rabbi a shelter. It seems likely that Elijah lost his library of Hebrew works. This is why he must have been retrospectively grateful to have spent so much time copying works for young Christian patrons who now held the only surviving versions. The refuge Antonini offered Elijah was not just that of his library in Rome, but a lodging for himself, his wife and children. Elijah and his family moved in and remained at the palazzo for thirteen years, and doubtless would have been there still longer had it not been for the catastrophe of the sack of Rome by mutinous imperial troops in 1527.

It was extraordinary, the cardinal and the rabbi in the closest residential proximity, so close in fact that pious Jews in the city pulled at their beards and muttered disapprovingly. But the friendship secured real benefits. In 1518, Pope Leo X licensed a Hebrew printing press to be established in Viterbo. Henceforth Elijah's grammatical speculations could be circulated, and much else too. This in turn drew the community of Kabbalists, both Christian and Jewish, even closer.

Antonini was now convinced about the convergence of the two fateful histories; that somehow the Jews and their Hebrew books would be instrumental to the inauguration of the new Christian golden age. Like all his learned contemporaries he was not doing this from some early version of cultural pluralism. It was all designed to speed conversion. But his humanist sensibilities had been offended by the coarseness of the coercion that had taken place in Spain and Portugal; the stench of burning books and Jews. It was inconceivable, then, that

Antonini, with all his Jewish contacts and companions, would not have consulted Elijah and other learned men of the Roman Jewish community, in particular Rabbi Joseph Ashkenazi and his physician Joseph Sarphati, about the credibility of David Ha-Reuveni. Their verdict, and therefore his, must have overcome the scepticism which was certainly voiced in Rome when David arrived in the city in the early spring of 1524. No impostors succeed without a predisposition on the part of their audience to want to believe. It made no difference that David repeatedly denied he was any sort of Messiah but merely 'the son of King Solomon of righteous memory'; the emissary of his older brother King Joseph, the great commander of the Jews who had slain forty men in one day. A warrior-prophet come from the east, from the Lost Tribes, resembling a Jew from the land of Prester John was *exactly* what Christians and Jews alike were looking for in 1524.

Jews were ready to believe. On the basis of reading the historical signs – the Ottoman conquest of Egypt and the rise of Martin Luther – the Jerusalem Kabbalist Abraham Eliezer Halevi had concluded that 1524 was destined to be the year of a great messianic alteration and had sent letters to that effect to all the major Jewish communities in Italy.[10] And anyone familiar with the Kabbalistic texts would have known that they singled out the tribe of Reuben as the first to lead Jews towards the ultimate confrontation with their enemies. So there would be a new Israelite–Presterite army battling the 'Ishmaelites', beginning, according to Halevi, in Arabia. There would be a reunion with the Lost Tribes. Jerusalem would be liberated.

The swarthy little man, then, was treated more like a Moses than a David; the liberator from oppression. The older Italian communities were often the first reception centres of destitute Jews coming from Spain and Portugal, who could not easily be brought out of traumatic anxiety. Entire cities like Ancona and Pesaro, Ferrara, Mantua and Venice itself had been transformed by the arrival of the Sephardim. Given everything they had gone through, the expelled brought with them a suspicion of the impermanence of asylums. The king of Portugal had offered his realm as just such a shelter, but it had rapidly turned into another prison of extortion, coercion and enforced conversion.[11] For the moment, many of the Italian princely states, the Venetian republic and even the papacy itself had resisted the imposition of a full and unsparing Inquisition and were in the business of attracting rather than expelling their Jews. But for all the occasional and genuine affinity between learned Christians and Jews, the latter were never free of a sense of helplessness at the hands of the Gentiles. If one picture of that relationship was the companionship of cardinal and rabbi, the other would be Jews, some of them aged, forced to run naked through the muddy streets of Rome at carnival time while pelted with rotten oranges.

So a new Moses claiming to restore their dignity would always find a receptive audience among the Roman Jews. Michelangelo's biographer Giorgio Vasari describes the Jews of Rome 'flocking on Saturday afternoons' to the Church of St Peter in Chains (notwithstanding it was the Sabbath), to see the heroic figure of Moses carved in 1513 for the unfinished tomb of Pope Julius II. Never mind the horns – a confusion between *qeren*, Hebrew for horns, and *kareyn*, the word for the effulgence on Moses' face when coming down from Mount Sinai a second time with the tablets of the Law – Michelangelo's Moses would indeed have been as Vasari characterised him, both 'prince and saint'. If the Jews stopped well short of 'adoring [Moses] as a figure more divine than human', as Vasari claimed – for that would have been a gross violation of the Second Commandment – there is no doubt that they were ready for some sort of charismatic leader.

David Ha-Reuveni, the Prince of Habor, son of 'King Solomon of righteous memory', in no wise resembled Moses. But he knew how to play the role he had invented for himself, and he must also have known when he concocted his story that the tribe of Reuben had been given a vanguard role in whatever messianic army would achieve the redemption of Jerusalem. He was versatile with his Bible prototypes. Assuming the role of a latter-day Mordecai, he made a point of entering the city gates of Rome on the eve of the feast of Purim, when Jews would have been on the streets and in their houses performing plays celebrating their escape from destruction by the wicked Haman. David's narrative, written by his secretary Solomon Cohen, records him buying a Purim 'skipping hoop' to join in the festivities.

From mysterious exotic to potential liberator; David, Prince of Habor, became the talk of Jewish Rome. A vocal minority always thought he was a fraud, but the well connected, beginning with the Pope's banker, Rabbi Daniele of Pisa, bought the act entirely. A white horse was provided for the Moses-Mordecai, along with a retinue of servants including the 'Cantor', the 'Arab Jew Shua' and, indispensably, the scribe Solomon Cohen who would tell the story to future generations. The grandees of Jewish Rome competed to accommodate him, and took offence at being slighted in the pecking order. Meanwhile David's habit of fasting took on ostentatious asceticism. The trances into which he would fall on the fourth or fifth day of such self-deprivation were widely taken to be the sign of someone in communion with the heavenly world. His appearance was the studied persona of an oriental mystic: black silk indoors, over which, outdoors, a white headpiece, wound like a scarf, fell in folds down the length of his body. Scoffers giggled that the get-up made the man look like a woman, but there were not many of those in 1524.

Mounted on his Arab mare, David rode all the way to the Vatican as was right and proper for a Reubenite prince. There he was received by Cardinal Egidio, who had with him two prime notables: the physician Joseph Sarphati and one 'Rabbi Ashkenaz'. In addition, Daniele of Pisa, who was powerful enough to have organised the Jewish community into a council responsible for the affairs of Jews, had summoned a selection of the best informed to look David over. None of them uttered a word of doubt, a remarkable thing for a gathering of Jewish notables. It seemed that he truly was a prince of the Lost Tribes, the awaited vindicator of Israel.

Once he had passed muster with the Jewish notables, David was received by Pope Clement VII who regarded him with the careful eye of the Medici. It seems likely that a master storyteller like David would have been aware of the last time, in the year 1280, a Jew in the grip of messianic aspirations – the Kabbalist Abraham Abulafia – demanded an audience with a pope. Told that Nicholas III had retired to his elegant summer retreat at Soriano nel Cimino near Viterbo, and was unavailable, Abulafia was undeterred by both that information and the threat to arrest and execute him should he proceed. Bent on having a discussion of 'Judaism in general', with an eye to disabusing the Pope of slanders and prejudices, and even (it has been suggested) imagining he could attempt the Pope's conversion to Judaism, he made his way to Soriano nel Cimino. Abulafia was prepared to risk martyrdom, but death took the wrong party, for when he arrived at the Pope's residence he was told that Nicholas had suddenly and inexplicably died. It was probably a stroke, but Abulafia, ever the messianic mystic, took the event to be a divine visitation.

David Ha-Reuveni's reception by Clement VII was less dramatic but still momentous. With Daniele of Pisa acting as interpreter, and no less than three cardinals looking on, he told his story, made his appeal, and asked the Pope to effect a reconciliation between the king of France and the Habsburg emperor without which the prospect of a great campaign to free the Holy Land was doomed. Hearing him out, Clement failed to rise to the invitation. Alas, he said, if only such a fateful reconciliation were his to accomplish, but regrettably this was not the case. Besides, might it not be that David and his brother King Joseph were looking in the wrong direction for their strategy; should they not look to maritime rather than land power, in which case to the young king of Portugal, João III, whose ships 'were more accustomed to sail the great ocean every year', and whose far-flung Afro-Asian empire was much closer to the country of Prester John and his own tribes? Making contact with that Christian lord of East Africa had long been a royal Portuguese plan. And in India, Goa had been established as a fortress port of religion as well as trade in 1512. The Pope told his visitor he would be happy to provide letters of persuasion for King João to support David's ambitions, and for Prester John as well.

Disappointed with the Pope's caution, David had no choice but to accept what was offered. But it took an entire year before those letters were actually supplied, along with a ship to take him to Lisbon. In the meantime he was treated like royalty both in Rome and beyond. He moved into a spacious apartment, paid for by the Pope, with a private custom-built synagogue lit by thirty lamps. The rich and the rabbinical fell over each other to have David Ha-Reuveni in their houses, although he seems also to have been pursued around the city by the plague, and from time to time succumbed to stomach ailments so crippling that he thought his last hours had come. The Jews of Rome, of all kinds and conditions, flocked to set eyes on their prom-ised liberator. Travelling north, his train of servants, carriages and horsemen growing ever longer, David went first to Viterbo to see his benefactor and patron the cardinal, then onward into Tuscany, where he was welcomed by another Jewish reception committee. In Pisa he stayed months (for the Pope's promised letters had still not arrived) with Rabbi Yechiel Nissim, famous far and wide for his piety and learning. But this orthodoxy was no bar to Yechiel's wife Diamante (the daughter of Meshullam of Venice) and her mother Sarah entertaining David with performances on harp, lute and flute, along with the dancing which, even in devout Jewish households in Renaissance Italy, was celebrated rather than banned.

The mission to the king of Portugal outfitted itself with trappings befitting its messianic ambitions. From Naples, Benvenida – the wife of Samuel Abravanel (himself the brother of Isaac who had faced down the king and queen of Spain in a last hopeless attempt to prevent the expulsion in 1492) – sent David a magnificent silk banner (all bona fide princes had to have them) to be unfurled as the sign of his divine appointment. On a field of white, the Ten Commandments were written in two columns of 'antique' golden thread. Benvenida also knew how a prince of the Jews ought to appear before the jumped-up monarch of Portugal whose father had presumed to tear them away from the Law of Moses, and gave David a great gown in the Turkish manner, reaching to the ground, worked with heavy gold brocade. Yechiel's mother slipped gold signet rings on David's fingers and offered matriarchal advice not to be 'angry or hastily wrathful' to the man notorious, as he himself conceded, for a low boiling point. When he finally arrived at Livorno to take ship, David also received from Pope Clement an imposing shield, a long gown of red damask and a velvet black cap to set it off. With every showy costume the little man from somewhere or other in the east seemed to grow taller, finally emerging on the dockside of Livorno as a true David. Half the crew was Jewish. Banners, pennants, horses, servants, and the sheaf of papal letters written on parchment were all loaded. A fanfare of trumpets accompanied his boarding. Behold, the Redeemer of Israel.

II. Solomon

Portugal was waiting for him. From his ambassadors in Rome the young King João III had heard about David of the Lost Tribes and his mission to launch a Judaeo-Christian offensive against the Turks. The envoys disagreed about the Jew's plausibility, but an endorsement from Pope Clement carried weight. Papers of safe conduct were supplied. King and court remained wary. Whether or not this little man with big pretensions was a fraud, there was a risk that the *converso* New Christians might, under sway of sudden belief, revert to their old religion and depart Portugal en masse. It was, after all, a mere two generations since João's father King Manuel had imposed conversion, expelling any unwilling to submit. Concerned to minimise an exodus (perhaps with a sense that the vizier of the sultan Bayezid had been right to jibe that Spain's expulsion of the Jews had been a gift to the Ottomans), a promise had been made to refrain from any investigation of the converts' beliefs for twenty years. That had had the desired effect of retaining a large 'Marrano'* population of New Christians, though not of preventing outbreaks of violence against them, the most horrifying in Lisbon at Easter 1506, when two thousand were slaughtered in three days. The ostensible cause was a vocal comment made by a New Christian in church to the effect that a miraculous illumination on the face of the Saviour on the cross might have been a mere effect of candlelight. This was enough to have him dragged by the hair and beaten to death. Incited by Dominican friars who were in the habit of calling the New Christians 'Jews', local mobs together with foreign seamen in Lisbon murdered as many New Christians as they could get their hands on. On Easter Sunday alone five hundred were dragged from hiding places to have their throats cut. So many corpses lay in the streets that extra carts of firewood had to be brought into the city to burn them on vast pyres that filled the port with the smoking stench. The plague had taken King Manuel out of Lisbon but none of his officers made much of an effort to stop the massacre. Eventually the principal Dominican malefactors were condemned and executed, but the memory of the terror lingered on in the *converso* community. The enthusiasm of King João III to import the Inquisition into Portugal did not make them sanguine about a future in the kingdom.

---

* As the Old Christians derisively called New Christians, alluding to their suspiciously conspicuous consumption of, or secret abstinence from, pig meat – either way, a tip-off.

The worry that the New Christians might leave the country, taking with them all their assets of treasure and commercial connections with the east, prompted the Portuguese Crown to issue a series of edicts restricting their movements and forbidding their exit, notwithstanding the fact they were supposed to be treated in the same fashion as other Christians. But the very nature of New Christian economic activities – financing and operating the trade in pepper and spices which had turned the obscure maritime backwater into a great pan-continental empire – meant that constraints on the movement of men and money could not be absolute or the trade would dry up. All these considerations weighed with the young king and his advisers. Even if they were of 'the Hebrew race', the New Christians went to Mass, married in church and baptised rather than circumcised their children. Was closer scrutiny really necessary? Perhaps taking a look at the Jew Reuveni might give them an answer. If he stirred up the New Christians, then the friars were right: a Jew was always a Jew, however many paternosters they could parrot.

Then again, suppose, just suppose, that this David *was* the long-awaited envoy from the land of Prester John, eager to prosecute a war against the Turks as soon as he had the guns. What then? Of all the monarchs of Europe, the king of Portugal was the one most likely to take this possibility seriously. It had been ten years since the priest Francisco Alvares had left Lisbon with the Ethiopian envoy Matheus to try and find Pêro da Covilhã, an earlier envoy sent to Prester John. After endless mishaps Alvares and Matheus had actually reached Ethiopia in 1520, and had been reunited with Covilhã, but the Portuguese court at home was as yet none the wiser about this momentous meeting. As far as they could see, Islam was everywhere triumphant: in India, Africa and the Balkans. But the Jews were incomparable in their knowledge of the Orient. Years before, it had been two Jews, a cobbler and a rabbi, who had found Covilhã in Cairo and had relayed the crucial maritime knowledge which had led Portuguese fleets to the riches of the Coromandel coast. If there was even a chance that David Ha-Reuveni was serious, and the Medici Pope seemed to think so, then at the very least he should be given a hearing.

But the expectations of the Portuguese court were as nothing compared with the excitement of the New Christians, who, even as they knew they would be playing into the hands of watchful inquisitors, could not contain themselves. Nevertheless, to show themselves overwelcoming to the exotic Jew would be madness, for João had introduced a network of spies, run by a New Christian Enrique Nunes, charged with snooping into the domestic lives of *converso* families and reporting on anything suspicious. Ever since the trauma of the Lisbon massacre, they were scrupulous in the discreet management of their double life. But for many it was still a double life and there were ways to maintain their old identity without giving too much away to Nunes' spies. Since it was all but impossible for the enforcers of conformity to spot abstinence from food, fasting became one way of expressing secret solidarity. Candles might be lit on Friday night, for, after all, candlelight was nothing special in the Iberian world of the sixteenth century. It was just that these candles might be quickly blessed. The braver might mark the Sabbath with a slight but significant change of clothing, though they knew the sartorial police of the Inquisition and their own informing neighbours would be on the look out. The most daring act of all would be to cook an overnight stew, the Portuguese version of the *adafina*, since the toothsome aroma drifting into the street could give the game away. This systematic caution gave the New Christians every incentive to ignore David or even reject him outright. But it is impossible to read the narratives of 1526 and not think that the vast majority were helplessly caught up in the excitement.

When the Reubenite appeared on a mule, riding into Tavira, the New Christians of the town came out to greet him in throngs, jamming the roads and streets, all caution thrown to the wind. Similar scenes were repeated in Beja and Evora. The mule gave way to a fine mount. Travelling north, the retinue became longer. Doors were thrown open, notables of the towns begged him on bended knee to stay overnight. Men, women and children lined up to kiss his hand. Marranos were seized with sudden visions of armies trooping through the sky, standards unfurling. When an indignant priest confronted David with accusations that his sort had killed the true King of the Jews, he was impulsively thrown out of a second-storey window for his temerity. David played his devotees like a harp. 'Some were of stout heart because they believed in me with a perfect faith, as Israel believed in our Master Moses, on whom be peace! And I said to them in every place we came to that I am the son of King Solomon and that I have not come to you with a sign or a miracle or a mystery but as a man of war as I have been from my youth till now and I have come to help your king and to help you and to go in the way he shall lead me to the land of Israel.'

By the time David reached Almeida, where the king had moved to avoid the plague in Lisbon, he rode as an Israelite *fidalgo*: with a long baggage train of mules, a following of fifty servants, liveried and all conspicuously armed, and an additional cavalcade of fifteen horses. Aware of the impression made by Benvenida Abravanel's banner, David had ordered four more to be made, embroidered in Hebrew, replete with the mysterious signs and numbers that conveyed the great mystery and power of his mission.

For a brief moment it was unclear who was the sovereign. João opened his doors to David only to hear from him that he was too fatigued from riding and fasting for a conversation. This was not a tactful start. During the period between audiences, one of David's Marrano hosts, an Arabic speaker who had been in Ethiopia at the command of the king (and thus might have been either the rabbi or the cobbler), spoke to David of the volcanic island on which Jewish children had been dumped by João II, 'near to a tribe that eats human flesh', and imperilled always by scaly *'lagartos'* – alligators. David's familiarity with Africa was also tested by someone at the court who had been in Morocco. But the Jew passed all these tests with flying colours. He steadfastly repeated his mission and his message. He had come, he explained, to seek guns and artificers. Although his people, thirty times 10,000, were true warriors, they had only the sword, the lance and the bow. Guns were needed to match the firepower of the Muslims. When a 'judge' asked the leading question as to what David's intentions were regarding the Jews of the western European lands, 'I replied that we shall first take the Holy Land and its surroundings and [only] then will our captains of the host go forth west and east to gather the dispersed of Israel.' David even foresaw that it would be a Muslim lord who would accept the inevitable and realise that bringing the Jews back to Jerusalem (like Cyrus the Persian) would give him honour that would endure through all posterity. Despite the liberation of Jerusalem being exactly the mission of a Messiah, David made sure to repudiate the title. He was, he said, just a sinning warrior.

Came the day of the second – longer – audience. A great banqueting table had been laid in the open air before the palace at Almeida. David Ha-Reuveni had been fasting for days on end – his record was six – and he soberly took in the ewers, the cups and plate of gold and silver. The centrepiece was a ram, its horns painted with gold. David marvelled and turned the dish aside. Before João spoke to him, there was one further test. A captain who had been taken prisoner in India was asked by João if it was true that there were Jewish kings in the east; and were there truly black and brown Jews in the lands David came from? *Sim.* Yes. It was always yes. Everything seemed on the point of success. David would be given a fleet of eight warships, four thousand guns and artificers to instruct the Reubenite army.

But then, just like that, the wind of his fortune shifted direction as abruptly as the crescent on the Dome of the Rock. Four of the most ardent New Christian Davidians were thrown in prison. With a marked change of tone João summoned David to the queen's chamber and accused him of coming to Portugal to Judaise: 'the Marranos pray with thee and read books day and night and thou hast made for them a synagogue'. Forgetting Sarah of Pisa's advice, David flew off the handle so fiercely that João, taken aback, momentarily relented, renewing his promises. But the auspicious moment had passed. Reuveni was summoned four more times in two days, the questioning getting progressively more inquisitorial. Something specific, something personal had happened and David was about to find out what it was. The king accused David of ruining his kingdom, of encouraging Marranos to bow to him and kiss his hand. The king then revealed to David the reason for his sharp change of attitude: he had learned, he said, that a high official of the judiciary, who was also secretary-scribe at court, had been circumcised by David. Was this true? The Reubenite angrily denied the charge. He had not come to convert, he protested, but had no control over Marranos who came to him of their own accord since his house was open to all, New or Old Christian. As for this circumcision, 'God forbid; it is not true.'

The moment could hardly have been more dramatic. However else the New Christians contrived to preserve their attachment to Judaism, they stopped short of circumcision. For this to have happened to someone in the circle of the court, close to the king, was a shocking act of defiance. The New Christian secretary-scribe was Diogo Pires.

Strictly speaking, David was telling the truth when he told João he had not circumcised Pires. In fact, Pires had come in secret to David and begged him to perform the act of covenant. When he had been indignantly rebuffed, Pires had done it to himself. Spellbound by David, whom he had seen at court, Pires had been overcome by violent dreams in which he had been circumcised. Knowing this would be a disaster for his mission, contradicting all the assurances he had given the king, David upbraided Pires for even thinking of such a thing. Supposing David was protesting too much, and that once the deed was done they would be reconciled, Pires whetted his knife. 'That night I performed the circumcision by myself, [and] though I felt great pain and distress and fainted for the blood flowed like a surging spring, the Merciful One the Healer healed in an unbelievably short time.'[12] When he woke from his bloody swoon, he had become Shelomo Molkho the Jew, his new name so close to 'Solomon the king'. If he hoped for understanding and welcome from David he was quickly disabused, but it made no difference to Solomon, for now he was 'sealed with the signet of my Creator'.

More elaborate visions followed. An old man with a long white beard crooked his finger, beckoning Solomon to come and see the ruins of Jerusalem. Along the way to the holy city he encountered three trees growing from a single root, while in their branches perched doves, some white as snow, some grey as ash. Troops of furious horsemen appeared, bent on destroying the tree, hurling balls of fire, swinging blades of steel. They in turn were followed by ravening birds which tore at the living flesh of doves and men alike, and were set to consume Solomon himself when he woke.

Enough! David Ha-Reuveni did not want this new ally. But the damage had been done, irreparably for his mission. To King João the reverted Solomon was the clearest sign that David's presence was pernicious. Where one New Christian had gone, and he a favoured man at the court, multitudes would surely follow. João wanted the little Jew out of Portugal, and without ships, guns or artificers. Since you have spoken of it, the king said, go and see my brother-in-law, the emperor Charles, or return to the Pope in Rome. The king promised papers of safe conduct, though David characteristically took umbrage. *Paper* letters of safe conduct would be unseemly when Pope Clement had provided *parchment*, a sign of trust. Disarmed again by the Jew's temerity, João replied that, regrettably, we don't do that in Portugal, but from love of your person I shall order them rewritten on parchment.

David and Solomon went their separate ways. In a fit of unforgiving vexation, David told the unwanted proselyte that since he had dreamed of Jerusalem, he might as well get himself there. And set off at once: 'be not seen here or they will burn or slay thee'. Solomon duly journeyed all the way to the Ottoman Empire, precisely the route most likely to enrage the Catholic authorities, and into the dominions of David's avowed foe. In Salonika, the most populous of the Jewish communities of Turkey, Solomon Molkho studied Torah, Talmud and Kabbalah and astounded his teachers with the speed and breadth of his Jewish learning. Even the great rabbi Joseph Karo, the writer of the code of observance the *Shulkhan Arukh* (*Set Table*), marvelled at the adept's immersion in the sacred texts. That someone recently so ignorant should now be such a prodigy was, many thought, itself a sign. Such a modest marvel must have been invested with a gift. It was a 'regeneration' which corresponded exactly to the Kabbalistic prescription of creating a new soul within the old husk.

For his part, David began a procrastinating retreat through Portugal, back the way he had come, outstaying the two months the king had given him to exit. But the Reubenite could not quite abandon the fantastic vision he still had of himself. Downcast though he was, he now turned his misfortune to good purpose, convinced that he might yet grow great by self-dispossession. In one town, then, he gave his hosts his fine-chased parade armour and swords; in another he bestowed on the lady of the house the diamond-studded gold rings he had received in Italy. Elsewhere he parted with his silken gowns and robes; the St Francis of the Jews. At one point he even sent João a fine horse he had bought, along with all its trappings – a lofty gesture which implied the two men were peers. Along the route, the Marranos still came to see him, kissed his hand, wept when he left. Be not downcast, he told the *conversos* of Beja, there still have to be great wars before Jerusalem is taken, but it will surely come to pass and the Redeemer will come unto Zion. He went back to riding mules and finally trudged into Faro on foot in the pouring rain, to board, with Solomon Cohen and one other servant, a mouldering ship. The indignities were not yet over. Unfavourable winds forced the vessel into a Spanish harbour and put David in the hands of officers and magistrates who were unimpressed by his papers. He was thrown into jail, his men roughed up, and once released wandered through southern Spain, ministering to former Muslims in Granada who themselves had been made destitute by an earthquake that had hit five years earlier.

Misfortune steeled him. God was testing him. Perhaps he would find other Christian benefactors? The one destination the king of Portugal had not offered David was France, so naturally he made his way there only to be arrested in 1528 and languish in prison for two years before being released by order of King Francis. But among the possessions the French had taken from him were the parchment letters he had carried everywhere, together with his precious flags. An attempt to restore them by whatever means available would lead to his undoing. From France David returned to Italy in 1530, and undeterred by his misfortunes he resolved to get an audience with Charles V, then preparing for his imperial coronation in Bologna. There were still scenes of crowd-rejoicing at his appearance in cities like Venice and Mantua, but there were also multiplying doubters, especially among those for whom Solomon Molkho, not David, had become the true Hope of Israel. The respected rabbi of Sabbioneta, Azriel Diena, was as hostile to David as he was enthusiastic about Solomon.

As David's star declined, so Solomon's ascended, to the point where the acolyte began to outshine the master. Solomon started to believe that David had been the prophetic forerunner but that he himself was appointed the true Messiah. And Solomon had one great gift denied David: that of an eloquent tongue. In Salonika he took to preaching *derashot* – sermons on the Torah in which he expounded deeper and broader wisdoms of the faith. His reputation as a marvel spread so fast and so far that Christians as well as Jews came to hear him. He continued to have the extravagant visions of a latter-day prophet, and as his fame grew and Jews were heard to remark that perhaps Solomon was not just the advance guard but the man himself, he took less trouble to contradict them. He took to flying pennants in the style he had seen David display, and wearing coats embroidered on the back with Kabbalistic letters, names and numbers. He was fast becoming a magus: a messianic prince-magician, given to strange chants and incomprehensible utterances that he said would bring down the

Church. Notwithstanding this, and his notorious apostasy, when he came to Rome in 1529, Pope Clement initially protected him from the Inquisition. He seemed to have prophesied – as 'the destruction of Edom' – the year in which Rome would be sacked: 1527. Now he lived with the beggars on a bridge over the Tiber and predicted the river would flood, as it duly did in October 1530. That might have been an easy call, but Solomon also prophesied in the synagogue that there would be an earthquake in Portugal and this too duly came to pass on 26 January 1531.

The sack of Rome by mutinous soldiers of the imperial army – three days of horrifying rapine and destruction – had left the Pope traumatised and impotent, his Medici reason sacrificed to catastrophic visions. This may explain why, when Solomon dared to come to Rome, abandoning the safety of the Ottoman Empire, Clement was drawn to him with an intensity that had been absent from his dealings with David Ha-Reuveni. If David had left Portugal in the guise of a dispossessed ascetic, Solomon outdid him by sitting with his beggar's bowl at the gates of Rome for the thirty days required of a true Jewish penitent. This was the kind of gesture that had appealed across the boundaries of the two religions. As a sign of his esteem, Clement took the extraordinary step of allowing Solomon to print his sermons in the most Christian city, embattled with the Lutheran heresy. But hating Protestants did not preclude loving this particular Jew. The two instincts may even have been mysteriously connected.

This was all the more startling because, technically and legally, Solomon was himself a heretic Christian who had not only committed the unforgivable sin of relapsing into Judaism but spent the rest of his life aggressively Judaising. This made him prime bait for the Inquisition, and once informed on, he was surrendered to its ordeals. There was nothing his papal protector and patron could do about that. The excruciating rigours were put upon Solomon and he was condemned. Offered, as was standard practice, the possibility of being saved by turning back to the Christian fold, he defiantly rejected the invitation. The pyre was stacked and kindled and Solomon Molkho was burned upon it.

But that very afternoon a visitor to the papal apartments was surprised to see Solomon walking through the rooms, not a hair on his head showing the least sign of scorch. Clement had switched martyrs, substituting some pathetic creature for his friend Solomon the Jew.

Was this not enough for the prophet? Might he not now depart quietly back to the safety of the Ottoman lands, where he had so many Jewish friends, audiences for his homilies, people who would listen to him and read him? Apparently not. But no writer of the fantastic could devise an ending more extraordinary than the one Prince David and Solomon the king wrote for themselves. Their paths crossed once more in Italy, probably sometime in 1532 when both might have been expected to be looking for refuge rather than yet more opportunities to promote the grand design of Jewish redemption. Despite his ordeals in prisons, or possibly because of them, David had recovered his self-belief, enough to ask for and receive an audience with Federico Gonzaga, the Duke of Mantua, a city with a large, culturally lively community. What he did not know was that one of the Jewish families he believed to be an ally as well as host had betrayed him to Gonzaga. While staying with Abraham Portaleone, the brother of one of the most famous Jewish physicians of Italy, and wanting to boost his credentials with Charles V and with the Pope, David had letters for both of them, purportedly written by his brother King Joseph but in fact rewritten by a local scribe to whom he said he would teach the art of making the documents appear old and worn. Outraged, Portaleone reported the forgery to the duke's court, which then passed the news on to the Mantuan ambassador at the papal Curia, and thence to the emperor. From that point on, there could be no doubt that David was an impostor.

For the moment this was not made common knowledge. Back in Venice, the place where he had first revealed himself to the Jewish and Gentile worlds, David still had reason to suppose he could carry off his act. The government of the republic commissioned one of its sharpest minds, the geographer Ramusio, to examine David on his itinerary and origins, and the conversation was reported by another shrewd observer, the patrician Marin Sanudo. David had changed his story to fit his more modest circumstances. Instead of seeking weapons for a military campaign he now said he was merely prophesying the great battle to come. In any event Ramusio and Sanudo both seem to have taken it all in.

In 1532, Solomon Molkho travelled to Regensburg in Bavaria where Charles V had convened the Imperial Diet. Some sources have Hareuveni accompanying him but this now seems doubtful. At any rate Molkho had consulted the planetary alignments and concluded that this was definitely the prime moment to move the messianic timetable along. He would urge the emperor to mobilise German Jews against the sultan. Rabbi Josel of Rosheim, experienced at negotiating with bishops, kings and dukes and accountable to the emperor himself was present at Regensburg and knew that only bad things would come from such foolishness. A tide of belligerence was sweeping across the German lands, on both the Lutheran and Catholic sides; and it was best not to provoke the Emperor. It seems likely that the rabbi knew in advance that Molkho was walking into a baited trap.

But he was not listening. Molkho came to Regensburg as if at the height of his powers banners flying, carrying the Pope's shield and a a great sword 'sanctified by the names of God in Hebrew'. He may have been moved by the city's Jewish history. It had been the most ancient Jewish community in Bavaria until, in February 1519 following the death of the protective Emperor Maximilian I, it had been liquidated after the Jews had been forced to demolish the interior of their own synagogue with the church built on its ruins consecrated to the Virgin. Many of the Regensburg Jews had made their way to Venice where Reuveni would have met them and heard their dreadful story. Molkho did, in fact get his audience with Charles who, for two hours, listened to his fantastic exhortations to make war against the Turks with a Jewish-Israelite army. Two Mantuan chroniclers report that attempts were even made to convert the Emperor himself. In this whole astonishing story, the most unlikely scene of all was perhaps this; a prophet appearing in robes sewn with the magically rearranged letters of God's name, before the imperial sovereign of Catholic Christendom, embattled with both Turks and Protestants, trying to persuade Charles that the way to repair his fortunes would lie with him becoming a Jew. The temerity makes no sense unless Solomon, like David, had come to believe that the course of Jewish history had arrived at a moment when its persecutors would become the instruments of redemption. Though most of this messianism was a delusion, there were indeed some among the rulers and councillors of Christendom who thought that the long epic of the Jewish story was somehow raveled up with the fate of Christianity. It would not be the last time this was the case.

Solomon told himself that while the emperor was not about to follow him in the act of adult circumcision, the audience had gone reasonably well and that he had been granted right of residence in Regensburg. He was mistaken. His customary eloquence had fallen short of its mark. Words, every kind of word – mystical, magical, rational, scriptural, strategic, prophetic, rhetorical, spiritual – all of them failed utterly. Whatever impact the self-appointed embodiments of Jewish destiny made on Charles, in the end, the great Habsburg listened to his horrified councillors. These Jews were not only preposterous, they were dangerous. So instead of being allowed to stay in Regensburg, Solomon was taken in heavy chains to a prison cell, ending up in Mantua where the Inquisition got a second chance to convict him as a heretic and Judaiser. He was 'relaxed' to the temporal authority which this time made sure that the right person was burned. This was another Jewish destiny Solomon embraced as if it was preordained, joining his history to generations of those who had died by a persecuting church while 'Sanctifying the Name'. Since David Ha-Reuveni could not be accused of being a lapsed Christian, he was for a while spared the same fate; but there was no doubt that he had violated the ban on Judaising. Six years late, he too was burned at the stake in Spain by the Inquisition.

Something endured: in the histories that were beginning to be written by the Italian rabbis Azariah de Rossi and Joseph Ha-Cohen. Both David and especially Solomon, whose ultimate end moved countless numbers of pious and learned Jews to include him in the Jewish martyrology, were seen as bringing apostates back to the Torah. The Reubenite moment became the first since the expulsion from Spain and the introduction of the Inquisition when Jews and New Christians sensed a common identity. And some of Solomon's startling, prophetic writings survive, including *The Beast of the Reed*, foretelling the fall of Rome, a fragment of an extraordinary poem which still gives a sense of the high pitch of his fervour. Even among the more sceptical Ashkenazim of the north, his memory survived its final debacle in objects which became Jewish relics. One of the embroidered robes and a banner made the long journey to a city which had by no means done with Jewish prophecy and magic: Prague, the first destination of printed Kabbalistic texts. They were first identified in the Pinkas Synagogue in 1628, but were later removed to the Zidovske (Jewish) Museum in the Maisel Synagogue. There, encased in their own climate-controlled display, protected by fibre-optic cables and light-absorptive paint from the damage of ultraviolet and infrared rays, the robe and the banner wait and wait and wait for the liberating Messiah.

2

IN TRANSIT

I. *Caminho Difícil*

Always it began in darkness, in the hours between midnight and dawn, when the last dockside patrols had ended and the guards were snoring or whoring. Like small night animals emerging from burrows, whispering cloaked figures would come to the quays on the Tagus River carrying only what they needed for the two-week voyage to Antwerp: a cooking pot, a mattress, hard biscuits, a little oil, a chest of clothes. The most reliable member of the family, not always father, would keep the purse of gold pieces close – many more ducats than they would have needed had they not been New Christians. But they were people called Gomes, Dias, Lopes, people who knew they had once been Cohen, Levi, Benveniste, and they needed to be out of Portugal before they were caught in the snapping jaws of the Inquisition.

For a number of them, this was not the beginning of the flight from terror. Some had come to Lisbon from deep in Spain, across the mountain frontier. They had heard of great merchants, forced converts like themselves, who had got rich in the pepper trade and, Moses-like, had opened a path in the sea. God willing, their wandering would not take forty years, but they had some idea when they loaded their carts that the way, by land and water, would be long and hard. They were not wrong about that.

Although the Holy Office was not finally licensed to begin its investigations in Portugal until 1536, it had been expected for five years before that. In anticipation of its arrival, those who were bound to be its principal suspects, the forced converts of 1497, began to make their moves. The Portuguese New Christians, who following their

conversion had been spared the Inquisition, could not shake off the
terror that it might ensnare them, and now imagined its reappearance
in the form of a diabolical monster. The most eloquent of all the
emigrants, Samuel Usque, marshalled his inner Daniel when speaking
of the Inquisition as a tusked serpent, 'an amalgam of hard steel and
deadly poison ... rising into the air on a thousand wings with its black
venom and poisonous pinions and treading the ground with a thousand
feet of destruction'.[1] Where to run to, now that the king of Portugal
had barred the way and made emigration illegal for the Christians he
still called Jews? Wringing of hands and prayers of conveyance to the
Promised Land would accomplish little. What was needed was an
actual place of safety, somewhere the candles could be snuffed out at
night without fearing a heavy hand laid on the bodies of their sleeping
children. Venice? The Inquisition would come there too. Ferrara, to
its south-west, where the Este duke offered some respite from the
hounding, was a possibility. Hebrew books were printed there. From
Ferrara it was not so many miles as the crow flies to Pesaro and
Ancona. But safety dictated they take the less conspicuous, less
patrolled route over the mountains to the Adriatic. Step by step, little
by little, always looking over their shoulders, they could find their
way to the protection of the sultan in the east. The rumour that the
Turk was actually welcoming Jews might even be true.

They were desperate but not alone. In Lisbon and Antwerp a
consortium of pepper and spice merchants, the richest of the
Portuguese New Christians, had contributed to a saving fund to help
them on their way and see them through the worst. The solidarity
of Jews, rich with poor, the safe with the insecure, is now a truism of
their history; but this was the first time it had been systematically
organised and by those who could not openly call themselves Jews at
all but went to church, crossed themselves, and sank to their knees
to receive the body and blood of Christ. That rescue chest was
rumoured to be so full that Emperor Charles himself could hardly
wait to get his hands on it, were he ever able to prove it existed. If
he could unmask those he called *falsos cristianos*, the money would
be within his grasp. But the hard money was the least of it. The
princes of the pepper trade who made up the rescue committee had
turned their commercial intelligence into a transcontinental highway
of escape: a chain of ships, river ferries, lodgings, wagons, drivers and

riders extending from the Portuguese Atlantic coast to the English ports, then on across the Channel to Flanders, down through France and the Rhineland, over the Alpine passes, into the Po Valley. If they then eluded the guards posted in Lombardy expressly to detect, arrest and deal violently with them, they might be able to reach the safety of Ferrara. Some might stop there; others move on through the Apennines to Pesaro and Ancona, then over the Adriatic to Ragusa (now Dubrovnik), and finally into the realm of Suleyman the Magnificent where they would at last be free to do all those things they had had to deny themselves in Portugal. The women would plunge into the ritual baths, the men would be circumcised. They would assemble for prayer, rack their brains for half-remembered phrases and tunes; the chant of the Torah reading would ring out, and even amid their devotions they would, God forgive them, find their mouths moistening at the prospect of the Sabbath stew. They would allow themselves to feel, provisionally, at home.

Along the way to this Turkish destination, they would all be in the hands of men called 'the Conductors' hired by the Antwerp rescuers. They trusted those men with their purses, their stooped grandparents, and their babes in arms. What choice did they have? At no stage, though, was there a guarantee of safety. Even at the Tagus dockside some were betrayed and dragged away. To evade the police on the city wharves, many of the fugitives loaded themselves and their belongings into small boats further upstream, and were rowed, as quietly as could be managed, towards the Flanders-bound ships moored at the mouth of the river. Should the master of the ship be unscrupulous he might extort more than the agreed fare, however exorbitant, and rob them of the pearls they had brought to exchange for money in London or Antwerp. On-board piracy flourished in the 1530s and 40s.

Samuel Usque saw them emerge from the little ships in Antwerp, sallow with seasickness and fear, often despoiled of their purse. The rescuers would then provide lodging and a subsistence float, converting whatever had survived the shipboard depredations – a hidden necklace, a silver amulet – into bills of exchange that could be cleared in Ferrara or Venice. The travellers would be told where to find secret synagogues but warned in the strongest terms never to attract attention, least of all by rowdy behaviour and arguments. The Jews, baptised or not,

were seldom the quietest people in the world. And they were instructed
by their temporary guardians in Flanders to avoid the slightest show
of ostentation: no earrings, no fine lace or brocade pulled out from the
chest on Sabbath. *Especially* not on the Sabbath. That would attract
the thieves, and the thieves would talk to the police. They knew these
officers. There was no Inquisition in Flanders, and the men of the
local margrave and the burgomaster turned a blind eye to the affairs
of the 'Portuguese', for without them Antwerp would be just another
Flemish port. But the regent, the sister of Charles V, was eager to
sniff out heresy and extort money from the Jews. As far as brother
and sister were concerned, that's what the New Christians were: Jews
once, Jews now, Jews till they burned and the soot of their bones had
been taken by the wind.

Once the migrants were in a condition to be moved on, groups of
twenty or so would board covered wagons or rudimentary carriages,
prepaid by the rescuers. They would have with them instructions on
the route to take, where to find their contact for successive legs of the
journey, places they might safely stop overnight. One such instruction
has survived (thanks to the Inquisition, which pounced on it and,
doubtless after liquidating the network, stored the evidence in its
archive). Thus we know that the travellers from Antwerp made their
way south to Cologne where they looked for 'the Inn of the Vier
Escara'.[2] There they were to make contact with the conductor, Pero
Tonnellero. His posting was the Rhine journey upriver to Mainz (Basel
was another much-used transit point) in rented boats. They would
sleep aboard to save money and limit the possibility of exposure and
arrest. Again, the instruction was given not to raise voices (which
suggests how often it was disobeyed), though having been cooped up
together for so long and over such distances, it was hard to avoid
outbursts. 'Under all circumstances you are to behave like respectable
people avoiding all quarrels and arguments that may occur.' At Mainz
in the 'Inn with the sign of the Fish', another conductor would help
them find the wagons they would need for the onward and upward
route south-east along the Swiss lakes. Beyond Mainz or Basel, where
the Swiss lakeland rose into hills, they would see from across the
pasture and water the towering peaks of the Alps, glittering with
ominous light. Once more they were put in the hands of muleteers
and horse handlers who knew what was called the *caminho difícil*, the

difficult road. As many as possible would time the mountain crossings for summer; at the summits, though, it was always winter. The roads shrank into tracks, and the ascents and descents were so steep that the travellers had to get out and walk, their palms skinned from clutching at the rock wall or using the sinewy bushes sprouting from them to hoist their bodies up. Trudging and clambering was punctuated by stooping to recover sacks and bundles fallen from the carts. Usque, who had evidently experienced the Alpine crossings first-hand, wrote of 'many dying from helplessness and exposure. Women were widowed when they were about to give birth on those cold and merciless roads.'[3]

Once down into the Po Valley, yet more ordeals awaited, this time human and thus even more terrifying. Paranoid about the escape of those of 'the Judaic fallacy' to the Turks, along with their capital, merchandise and commercial knowledge, Charles V had established an office of 'Marrano affairs' at Antwerp, armed with exceptional powers of arrest, detention and interrogation, which in practice invariably meant torture and robbery. Its chief officer was Cornelis Schepperus but its most enthusiastic enforcer was his deputy Johannes Vuysting, who at Pavia and Milan (both in the Habsburg Duchy of Milan) posted roadblocks on the descents from the passes. Families would be dragged from their wagons, screamed at and told they were 'Jewish dogs', beaten up, hauled off to prison, tortured to reveal the identity of conductors and fugitives and their connections in Antwerp and Lisbon, and robbed of all their possessions. Captains, contacts and escort riders found guilty of abetting the escape would be sentenced to death. Pulling a cross from the wagon or an image of the Virgin fooled no one. Vuysting operated as a licensed gangster, extorting as much money as he could from the terrified crypto-Jews (always reputed to be loaded with hidden treasures even when they pleaded poverty). The rough treatment tended to speed things up a bit, especially when dished out to the elderly and the very young, and then, hey presto, that little purse of gems would magically materialise. Vuysting's greed would undo him, but his rapacity was just one version of the cupidity which went all the way up the chain from his captains on the passes to the avid emperor himself.

The fact that we know all this from the Inquisition archives means that many failed to reach Ferrara or the Adriatic. The miracle, one

wrought by the Antwerp Rescuers, is that many did survive and moved
on towards the Adriatic ships. Through their privations and moments
of panic, the travellers must have invoked the blessing bestowed on
them on their departure from Antwerp by the most powerful and
richest organiser of the escape route, the greatest of the pepper lords,
Diogo Mendes, who had once been Benveniste: 'The blessing Abraham
gave to Isaac and Isaac to Jacob I give you … may we meet each other
again in the Promised Land.'[4]

II. Sisters

In the dog days of summer 1537, a twin-masted caravel beat a laborious
course north from Portugal to Bristol. Instead of hugging the
French coast, the ship sailed farther out into the whipping Atlantic
westerlies, slowing its progress. But reports of pirates given liberty
by the king of France made the wider tack prudent, not least because
aboard were two sisters who were among the richest women in
Europe. Both were young and, as far as the world knew, New
Christians of good standing.[5] The elder, Beatriz de Luna, had been
married at eighteen (and widowed at twenty-four) to the spice king
Francisco Mendes of the house of Affaitati and Mendes. Francisco
was more than twice the age of his wife, and master of vaults, ships,
warehouses, men and millions. From the two ends of its business –
Lisbon and Antwerp – the house could make and break stupendous
fortunes, deliver fiscal mercy or drive a hard bargain for chronically
depleted princely treasuries. Thus, so it flattered itself, Affaitati and
Mendes could make the difference between peace and war, victory
and defeat. The firm amassed silver and pearls, onyx and rubies,
peppercorns and cinnamon, hard specie and bills of exchange.
Imposing warehouses lining the quays of the Tagus and the Scheldt
were packed with the pellets and scrolls of their aromatic inventory.
Ships plied back and forth across the oceans of the world on their
commission, even when the charters under which they sailed were
officially royal. This particular caravel taking the women north had
been chartered in Antwerp by Diogo Mendes, brother-in-law twice

over – for he was not only the brother of Beatriz's deceased husband Francisco, but also the intended match for her younger sister Brianda. For this house, endogamy, the arrangement known as a 'market marriage', was safety. In such dynasties, losses, opportunities, property and capital were best kept in the family.

You couldn't be too careful, not if you were Marrano. Potentially lethal suspicions lingered, even though Francisco Mendes and Beatriz de Luna had been conspicuously married in high Catholic style at the altar of Lisbon Cathedral. No matter that thereafter they made a great show of attending Mass, or that their daughter, named Brianda after her aunt, had been ceremoniously baptised. The Dominicans and those who listened to them – sailors, stevedores, sellers of pies and indulgences, the king himself – still called all the Marranos 'Jews'. Somewhere, behind locked doors, far from the grandiose public festivities, a nuptial contract or *ketubah*, written in Aramaic, would have been read out as tradition and *halakha* religious laws dictated, before witnesses, the reader's voice discreetly muffled, hurriedly rolling through the many clauses.

For those who kept asking, the voyage to Flanders had perfectly innocent explanations. Beatriz and Brianda were accompanied by their nephews João and Bernardo Micas, the sons of Samuel Micas, physician to the late King Manuel and a professor, first of 'moral philosophy' (which could mean Christian theology) and subsequently of medicine, at Lisbon University. With that impeccable background the boys could plausibly be bound for studies at the Catholic University of Louvain. It was perfectly natural, too, for the sisters' brother-in-law, Gonçalo, to be going to Antwerp to meet his brother and counterpart, Diogo, the manager of operations in the Flemish port. In 1512 the house of Mendes had opened its first office and warehouse in Antwerp. Francisco, the senior brother, had sent Diogo there to manage the pepper and spice business and he had gone into temporary partnership with a Cremonese, GianCarlo Affaitati. Before long, other New Christians had followed Diogo to Flanders. Manuel Serrão, Gabriel Negro and many more were brought into the syndicate and got rich fast. Portuguese caravel sailings had undercut the price of goods going the land route across Asia and thence by ship to Venice. The exotic goods landed at Lisbon, but were shipped from Antwerp for re-export to a world all at once greedy for them.

Who knows why alterations of taste happen and become fixed habit, why bourgeois, patrician and aristocratic consumers – who for generations had been accustomed to the tainted tang of spoiling meat and the dryness of stale bread and pastry – should suddenly have made the shift from treating exotic spice as a culinary luxury to an indispensable necessity? Asian spices, including pepper and cloves, had been present in the European (as well as Middle Eastern) diet for centuries, often, like Sri Lankan cinnamon, traded by Jews. But the length of time it took to get the merchandise from source to market – across the Indian Ocean, across the Persian Gulf, up the land routes north or across the Mediterranean – made them almost prohibitively expensive to all but the aristocracy, and the more volatile spices like cinnamon were hard to preserve in prime condition. Yet once pepper had entered the staple diet of the middle classes, there was no going back to unpeppered food. Eating underwent its renaissance. Sweetmeats, kickshaws and sugarloaves (for the Marranos were also importing from their first cane plantations on the Atlantic islands – São Tomé, Madeira and the Azores) became common fare. Pasties and tarts, loaves and puddings, all were transformed by a hit of sugar and spice. The whimwham, the posset, the custard and the cake all wanted dusting – so much toothsome power in a sprinkling of pulverised grains and pellets. East met west when cumin seeds or cloves studded a plain hard golden cheese and made it fragrant. A dish of beans would get a dusting of nutmeg (as it still does in Antwerp and Amsterdam, where any kind of green beans are known as *sperziebonen*); the torture of a throbbing tooth would ebb after a drop or two of oil of cloves.

All this was brought to European palates by GianCarlo Affaitati and Diogo Mendes, along with other partners they took on for one-off ventures. Together, this community was known in Antwerp, as if by complicit code, as the 'Portuguese Nation'. Its merchants became so rich so quickly that in both Lisbon and Antwerp whole streets were set aside for their warehouses and residences (sometimes the same building), invariably faced in stony grandeur. They commanded prominent space in the brand-new colonnaded Bourse, the first stock exchange in the world, opened in 1531 to raise capital on commercial ventures, and trade in bonds, promissory notes, futures and bills of exchange. The grandiose district of Kipdorp – the avenue of their commercial realm – was known as 'Portuguese'. Diogo's house was an urban palace set in formal gardens, a commercial court with a household of sixty – cousins and aunts, clerks and secretaries, servants and cooks (most of them Portuguese) bustling around inside. Imagine pictures and maps, marble floors, sandalwood cabinets, coffered ceilings, wall tapestries and Turkish rugs, swags of brocaded damask.

The Antwerp New Christians, who had sewn up this first truly global trade, sat at the centre of a perfect commercial feedback loop. Like the Fuggers of Augsburg, the Mendes family had first dealt in Tyrolean silver and copper, even though they lived further from the mines. But unlike the Germans they also had a network of Asian suppliers in place. Letters preserved in the medieval hoard of the Cairo Geniza paint a picture of Jews well established on the Coromandel coast of India, since at least the twelfth century, with long reach into the interior.[6] In the medieval centuries, the trading routes lay across the Indian Ocean to the Persian Gulf and then on by land to Egypt and the Mediterranean. But once the Portuguese fleets showed up, the mercantile wiring became global, and the most globally dispersed but culturally tight community was perfectly placed to take maximum advantage. Once again for the Jews and their convert descendants, the misfortune of dispersion was turned into a trading opportunity. The Mendes family in particular were well positioned to make a business of the interlocking parts where finance met commerce. The family firm was flush with the capital required to float seasonal fleets: the bullion which was all that Indian traders would take in return for their spices. When Malabar pepper was unloaded at Lisbon, it was officially the property of the royal monopoly, but what use was that when buyers were urgently needed and the Crown of Portugal was not in the marketing business? A maritime empire did not come cheap, especially when forts and warehouses were needed to protect its footholds in a bitterly embattled region of Hindu rajas and Muslim princes, and the Crown was chronically hard-pressed for funds. Affaitati and Mendes were there to take the cargo off its hands. Sometimes an advance would be tendered; at other times, the Crown had to wait for sales to be made in Antwerp before receiving its share of the receipts. One way or the other, proceeds from the pepper and spice trade came to constitute a full quarter of the Portuguese Crown's revenue. But the commercial firm which handled the merchandise dictated the terms of trade, paying low, shipping the bulk to Flanders, selling high and pocketing the substantial difference. Since another benefit of dealing directly with the Crown was that it had been granted a monopoly, the syndicate could manipulate prices by with-holding merchandise from the international mart. Profits would then be converted into the hard bullion required for further sailings, and so the fleet of good fortune sailed on and on into what must have seemed a perpetual eastern sunrise.

Seen from Old Christian courts and exchequers, these arrangements were a decidedly mixed blessing. Regular infusions of New Christian loans paid for armies which, as the sack of Rome had dramatically demonstrated, might otherwise help themselves to what they thought was their due and commit embarrassing enormities while they were at it. But it rankled with the emperor, Charles V, perennially strapped for cash though he was, always to be robbing Peter to pay Paul – or rather, contracting with New Christians to pay off the Germans. Everything was connected to everything else in an endless chain of debt which somehow always led back to those New Christians, their oversized houses and warehouses, their ships, their stacks of silver, gold and pearls, their rooms full of obliging paper; their power, in the sight of Old Christians, at once urgently needed and insolently threatening. Trapped in this maze of ambition and expenditure, cred-itors and debtors alike were powerful and powerless, forever making connections and separations. Cupidity led princes to turn a blind eye to the suspect practices of New Christians. Attacks of piety and the fulminations of friars periodically returned them to militancy. Then there would be accusations, arrests, confiscations, veiled and not so veiled threats, despite there being no Inquisition in the Netherlands. But life could be made difficult enough for these jumped-up Jew-plutocrats that they would cough up another cartload of gold to get back to business as usual. It was common extortion wearing the mask of zeal.

In Portugal, Charles's brother-in-law João III wanted to push the racket to its logical conclusion. If he could finally persuade the Farnese Pope, Paul III (none too keen on the idea), to extend the Inquisition into his realm, the richest Portuguese New Christians would be unmasked as Judaising heretics and would forfeit their property as well as their persons. At the same time, João was only too well aware that this would be a one-time killing. Thus he agonised over which way would serve him best: the confiscation of the Mendes fortune, or its indefinite perpetuation in his service. Without them, his constantly overburdened exchequer would be at the mercy of the far more exacting Germans and Italians. When all was said and done, perhaps the thing was to keep them close and watch them carefully. Thus a royal edict issued in 1532 forbade New Christians, on pain of death, from leaving the kingdom even to travel to the Azores or the islands off the African Atlantic coast. Any Christians assisting their exit, especially sea captains, were also liable for a death sentence should they be discovered. Five years later, in 1537, Charles and his sister Marie, formerly the regent of Hungary and now governor of the Habsburg Netherlands, in one of their periodic swings between hard and soft lines of approach to the Marrano business, allowed resumed emigration from Portugal to Flanders. But the leaders of the New Christian community were not so naive as to suppose this rediscovered pragmatism would last. Seize the moment, then. Get the young women out of Lisbon before the emperor or the king changed their mind, or, worse, before the Inquisition took them and their great estate.

The renewed permission for Portuguese New Christians to travel to Antwerp was granted only on condition of there being no question whatsoever of their taking themselves or their merchandise much further east into the realm of the enemy Ottoman Turk. The mere idea of such a thing turned Charles apoplectic. But that was, of course, exactly the long-term destination planned by the Mendes brothers as the Inquisition closed in. A cat-and-mouse game ensued. Charles and Marie could not help but respond to the anxieties of the Christian Flemish mercantile community themselves (trading in cloth and other bulk commodities for which the New Christians were not competitors) that to lose the pepper, spice and sugar empire would be an economic catastrophe. But for the rulers there was also their Christian duty to consider, especially if the pepper merchants really were heretic Jews on the loose. Every so often, the sword held above their notoriously stiff necks would be lowered until a tidy sum was offered to take it away again. It was extortion, but it was royal racketeering for God.

Every so often they enjoyed doing this. After the preposterous, insolent Jewish 'emissary' the self-appointed Messiah, Solomon Molkho, had appeared before Charles as he presided over the Imperial

Diet in Regensburg, he probably decided that he had had enough of the shameless pretences of the *falsos cristianos*. Diogo Mendes' house was searched and Hebrew literature discovered, identified as a Book of Psalms. The charges could not have been more serious: practising Judaism in secret; proselytising the return of others from Christianity; 'lese-majesty against God and the emperor'; a suddenly offensive trade monopoly; and, most ominous of all, abetting the escape of Jews to Ottoman-ruled Salonika. Diogo denied everything except trading with Turkey and assisting Jews who had made it to Venice and Ancona.

Battling Protestants and Turks on two fronts, Charles V was in no mood for casuistry. But where Diogo's protests of innocence cut little ice, alarms that were sounded in his brother-in-law's realm of Portugal inclined Charles to think again. Diogo had been arrested before current shipments of spices had been sold at market in Antwerp, and thus also before the Portuguese Crown, living from payday to payday, could receive its share of the proceeds. The money supply had frozen with immediately drastic consequences for Charles, whose capacity to wage war would be compromised by any inability to meet obligations to the Fuggers in a timely fashion. The knock-on from the arrest of a New Christian merchant as powerful as Diogo could be the disarming of the empire.

Charles's family saw this more clearly than the emperor himself, not least because they would be first to feel the drying up of funds. Frantic representations were made to Charles from João III and his queen, Caterina, another of Charles's sisters. In the first instance they were made at the behest of the senior partner and brother in Lisbon, Francisco, who was doing everything he could to secure the release of his brother in Antwerp. João wrote to the emperor, calling Francisco, his Marrano favourite, 'the most important, the most considerable and best supplied merchant known today' who 'in every respect has always served and so satisfactorily that I am most beholden to him and I have reason to rejoice in bestowing kindness and favours upon him'.[7] Both the king and queen begged the emperor to use his influence to ensure that Diogo and his 'rights' were treated with respect and equity and that a proper, impartial investigation was made. The implication was that the charges of Judaising were groundless, which in some senses was true, and in others not. It was a surprising moment:

the Portuguese king, whose eagerness to introduce the Inquisition into his realm was well known, doing everything he could on behalf of an accused Marrano who, in these letters, was given not just his New Christian name but also his ancient Jewish family name of Benveniste. João knew all about Diogo Mendes, but being cash poor, needs must. Others among the royal fraternity of the strapped chipped in, notably Henry VIII of England, still a good Catholic in 1532, whose government also depended on regular loans from the banking side of the house of Mendes. Thomas Cromwell, who had encountered Diogo and the 'Portuguese Nation' in his Antwerp days, became Chancellor of the Exchequer in 1533 and shared the general consternation about the potential collapse of the firm.

So Charles relented. The price exacted by Marie and the emperor (as greedy as he was sanctimonious) for releasing Diogo was a cool 50,000 gold ducats, paid up front. It was naked ransom and it worked. Diogo was freed before he was ever thrown into jail, but within the family circle the shock of his arrest – the sense that the most powerful of them could still be struck down at a minute's notice, made destitute overnight, perhaps dispatched to the hangman or the stake – would never be forgotten. In Lisbon, Francisco began to think the unthinkable: might it not be more prudent for firm and family to move its assets and its people, little by little, to a safer place – Venice, perhaps, or (unspoken, because of the lethal risks) even further east, out of Christendom altogether? Even as tentative a design as this was fraught with peril. The most serious charges that could be laid against the New Christians, worse than Judaising, was aiding and abetting the Turks. And what more effective aid could there be than the migration east of one of the greatest fortunes in the world? But in his prudently navigating mind, Francisco was already in transit. It was now 1534 and he felt (with reason, as it turned out) mortality coming on fast. Detailed provisions needed to be made. As was possible under Portuguese law, half his immense estate was to be left to his twenty-four-year-old widow; a further two-thirds of the remainder to their daughter Brianda. The rest was to be used for a funeral on a scale commensurate with Francisco's wealth and power. By the time of that funeral some months later, everything was in place for the move should the worst happen and the freshly funded

King João, liberated from having to go cap in hand to the Marranos, renewed his efforts to bring the Inquisition to Portugal.

Whether that would now happen depended on the pressure Charles V could bring to bear on Pope Paul III. Like Clement VII, Paul was in no hurry to lean on the New Christians who had been good to him and his treasury. But an impatient emperor was a threatening emperor, and Charles's sense of himself as the universal Christian warrior was becoming more grandiose with every campaign. In 1535 he had won a great naval victory off the North African coast over the navy of Hayreddin Barbarossa, a hitherto lethal war fleet custom-built in the dockyards of Constantinople on orders from the sultan. The spectacular prize of Tunis, or what was left of it after the sack, was taken for the Christians and the euphoria put the emperor into full crusading mode. The prospect of inaugurating the Christian golden age, perhaps even retaking Jerusalem, stirred within him. Imperial pressure was applied in Rome to deliver the Portuguese New Christians. And finally, sensing unspoken but ominous threats, Paul III assented. On 23 May 1536, the Holy Office of the Inquisition was formally established in Portugal. Four years later Lisbon would witness, with the usual festive enthusiasm, its first auto-da-fé. Burnings of the flesh of the living, the bones of the dead, and even effigies of those sentenced in absentia, would take place at regular intervals all the way into the eighteenth century. Effigy-burning might have been seen as a pointless mummery were it not for the fact that it authorised the confiscation of property.

The Mendes plan of cautionary emigration had already been set in motion when another kind of alarming news accelerated it. To ensure that, whatever happened to the Mendes family at the hands of the Portuguese Inquisition, their estate would lie within his reach, João III suggested – strongly – to Francisco's widow Beatriz that her daughter, the little heiress Brianda, should be brought to court, to be raised by Queen Caterina as her ward and married to someone of impeccably Old Christian and noble stock. In that event, the lingering stain of the new New Christian would be cleansed from the dynasty. Even while pretending to be flattered, the Mendes family were badly rattled. Quite apart from an aversion to this irreversible Christianisation, there was the material side to think of. Marriages within the clan had always been the best strategy to control their shared fortune.

It was one thing for a Mendes to marry another New Christian in church to keep up the outward form; another thing entirely to go to the altar with an Old Christian of ancient family. There was nothing for it now. The little girl, her mother and her aunt – the Mendes women – had to be got out of Portugal, and fast.

At sea in the summer winds of 1537, those Marrano sisters travelled between harbours and identities. In company they were Beatriz and Brianda de Luna; but below deck, when no outsiders were around to hear, they called themselves by the Jewish names they would eventually embrace: Gracia and Reyna. Loyalty to names, however heavily disguised, mattered deeply in the world of the Marranos. As well as the fact that before being baptised 'Mendes' in Spain, the forebears of the Benveniste family had also been rabbis, the greatest of them Sheshet ben Isaac ben Joseph – a byword for learned piety – Arabist, physician, interpreter of Talmud, Torah and philosophy. The great-grandfather of Francisco, Diogo and Gonçalo, Abraham Benveniste, had risen all the way to be 'Rab de la Corte' or Court Rabbi of Castile, responsible to the Crown for the Jewish communities of the kingdom, apportioning and collecting taxes, and for managing the finances of the entire realm. His descendant Beatriz de Luna was possibly named for the great Toledan noble, Alvaro de Luna, who had been protector and benefactor to the Jews and who had himself fallen from grace.

The eminence of the Benvenistes meant that in 1492, the year of the expulsion, they might have been among the six hundred eminent families granted generous terms of settlement in Portugal (while more than 100,000 of their co-religionists were permitted to stay for just six months).[8] This had not spared them from the Portuguese forced conversion of 1497, but the very fact of coercion, coupled with King Manuel's promise to leave the New Christians alone for twenty years, meant that the double allegiance of the Marranos persisted. A sausage made from pale chicken meat would pass itself off as pork (and is still known today in Lisbon as '*marrano*' sausage). Minute adjustments to dress might be made on Friday night. The bolder might find a way to celebrate Purim, the feast of Esther, with sweetmeats and Judaeo-Spanish Ladino song. None of this added up to Judaism, but it did represent some sort of stubbornly retained version of Jewish life. Through the centuries which followed – and in circumstances which might be less, or more, constrained than those in which the Mendes/de Luna women now found themselves as they bucketed around on the Atlantic swells – countless quasi-Jews, sometime Jews, lukewarm Jews, nostalgic Jews, indeterminately observant or unobservant Jews cut off, by choice or against their will, from the injunctions of the Torah, would live through the chapters of the Jewish story. Beatriz-Gracia, who had seen her husband Francisco's body laid to rest amidst the rites of the church, would herself not rest until he was reinterred on the Mount of Olives looking down on Jerusalem.

The journey made by Beatriz-Gracia and Brianda-Reyna from Lisbon to London, and from Calais to Antwerp, is not to be measured in miles alone. For whatever the women and their nephews knew about their Jewish history while leading the life of New Christians, they were about to be initiated into a world which fully and dangerously embraced it: the undercover existence of the rescuers and the conductors. Geographically close, the London and Antwerp communities coexisted in a push–pull relationship. When the screws tightened in Flanders, people and capital moved back to the Thames; when there was trouble in England, as there would be in 1542, the flow was reversed. When the de Luna sisters arrived in London, they found the double life they would already have known in Lisbon.[9] By day and in business dealings with merchants, courtiers and impecunious nobles, the tiny community of about seventy were publicly and necessarily 'Portuguese' since a statute dating from the reign of Henry IV, *De haeretico comburendo*, specified the death sentence for any Christian practising Judaism.[10] So as in Lisbon, while they married strictly within their community, they had an initial ceremony in a parish church. In the spirit of this double life Gonsalvo Anes, who became Dunstan Anes or 'Ames', had a surname which commonly meant 'son of John' in Portuguese but to those in the know also alluded to the *'anusim'*, as forced converts were known in Judaism. Under Elizabeth I the family name became Amis; Dunstan, a high-class grocer, had a coat of arms registered with the College of Heralds and was described as 'Purveyor and Merchant' to the queen's household.[11] But their position was always precarious. In 1542, a number of 'Portuguese' merchants were arrested on suspicion of being secret Jews, and although none were executed, their property was confiscated. And yet, despite the precautions, on Friday nights caped figures knocked on the door

of Luis Lopes's house near the Tower of London. In the secret, improvised synagogue, candles were lit, and murmured blessings recited.

When the sisters arrived, the English Marranos were being protected
by the most pragmatic embodiment of Tudor government: Thomas
Cromwell, a City man to his marrow. He had first encountered the
'Portuguese' in Antwerp, to which he came (for the second time) in
around 1514, two years after the Mendes family had established their
firm there. He had shaken their hands, exchanged contracts, been
hospitably entertained in their houses, and observed that they had the
best doctors, books and food. Trading connections were naturally
formed. Raw English wool went to Flanders and was finished into
broadcloth; pepper came back and entered the meaty diet. As he and
his royal master Henry became more ambitious, the 'Portuguese'
could do service. Who actually paid for the Field of the Cloth of Gold
where Henry VIII outdid even the Valois François I in chivalric ostentation and wrestling? Not the burghers of Norwich or the gentry of
Devon, that's for sure. The same was true of the infant Royal Navy,
the beginnings of a merchant fleet, the forts and the parade armour.
And in the end, Jewish money, which had paid for the building of so
many of the greatest abbeys and monasteries of England, became
available to the government commanding their destruction.

The 'Portuguese' link was needed in ways theological as well as
financial, so it helped that some of those men of business and medicine in Bristol, Southampton and London were apparently also rabbis
with learned connections abroad. The case Henry VIII was building
for his divorce from Catherine of Aragon was based on his reading
of the Torah's prohibition on marrying a brother's widow. There was
indeed such a ban to be found in Leviticus 18:16; but, as is the way of
the Torah, the king, his chancellor Thomas More and Cromwell
discovered that there was also an apparently contradictory injunction
in Deuteronomy 25:5 actually *requiring* marriage to the widow of a
dead brother when that union had produced no children. And this,
exasperatingly, had been the case with Catherine and Arthur, Henry's
older brother. Converted New Christians seemed just the people to
be helpful in such perplexing circumstances, and through them, rabbis
were mobilised to deliver the judgements which would oblige royal
necessity. But when the Tudor emissary who had been sent to Venice
to recruit such opinions managed to find willing parties he was also

faced, embarrassingly, with local rabbis of an adamantly opposite view. The last thing a clandestine London community wanted was a Talmudic debate with implications for the royal divorce, so it tried to keep clear of the interpretation wars.

Beatriz and Brianda were about to discover the rescuers. One of them – a merchant and rabbi, the one-eyed Antonio de la Ronha, described as 'master in theology' (meaning ministering to the community) – had been arrested in Antwerp in the sweep of 1532 that had caught Diogo Mendes in its trap. Instead of being chastened, Ronha had come to London where he became another dependable link in the chain of emigration. When things became perilous in Antwerp, another foot soldier in this underground army, Cristoforo Fernandez, stationed himself in the English ports – Southampton and Bristol as well as London – to warn travellers bound for Flanders that it would be unsafe to proceed. Disembarked in England and safely conveyed to London, they would then be housed and sheltered by the local rescuers. Alarming though he might have been to behold, Ronha secured whatever valuables they had been able to bring from Portugal and realised their value in bills of exchange that could be cleared in Antwerp.

The fact that the de Luna sisters stayed in London a while (exactly how long is difficult to reconstruct, but certainly several months) suggests that although the ban on emigration to Antwerp had been rescinded, the situation remained hazardous. Beatriz and Brianda would have crossed the Channel to Calais and then travelled by closed coach to Antwerp. Once safely arrived they would have had to conduct themselves as impeccably virtuous Christian *senhoras*. Unlike in London, however, they could come out of the shadows in the Flemish port. There they discovered another community that had learned to live simultaneously two different but overlapping lives. They would have seen Hebrew books printed by the Christian Daniel Bomberg, the production of which could, if necessary, be justified by the constant interest of Old Christian theologians and philosophers. But where walls did not have ears, they would have learned that Bomberg too was on the inside of the rescuers' world. Other men dwelling in two cultures would have shown up at the Mendes house, perhaps when matzot were being secretly baked or meat delivered from a kosher slaughterer: Diogo Pires, 'Pyrrhus Lusitanus', the poet and translator;

and a circle of physicians who were the intermediaries between Christian and Jewish worlds.[12] The most eminent of the doctors was 'Amatus Lusitanus', physician to the governor Marie. As the *converso* João Rodrigues de la Castela Branco, he had graduated from Salamanca University, but like so many others had anticipated the arrival of the Inquisition in Portugal by coming to live in Antwerp. There he began to publish, and worked on the anatomical studies of the vascular system that would culminate in identifying the venous valves. In Antwerp, where there were botanical gardens, he was also in a position to incorporate into his pharmacopoeia plants coming from Asia and America including pepper, cinnamon and ginger. It was assumed that the doctor was as good a Christian as the Mendes clan, though those wanting clues might have wondered if he did not now call himself 'Amatus Lusitanus' because his family name had once been Habib, 'well beloved'.

The question, as always, was whether financial indispensability to the Habsburgs would guarantee their immunity from close scrutiny. The scare of 1532 suggested not, but they had survived it. Seven years later, in 1539, all seemed well. Brianda and Diogo married ostentatiously in the great cathedral church of Our Dear Lady. Their daughter Beatriz, born a year later and named after her aunt, was publicly and formally baptised. In recognition of his particular services to the Crown and the city, Diogo and his household were granted the significant concession of worshipping in a private house chapel. For the moment no one enquired too closely about the exact nature of the prayers, which was just as well, since evidence later extracted by the Inquisition makes it clear that it was in fact a dual-purpose synagogue where Jewish prayers, known by the Hebrew word *tefillah*, were recited in Spanish. The Mendes women were even given access to the Carmelite convents, a gesture which could have signified their interest in devotional piety, but was much more likely (as the records of the Inquisition again attest) to open contact with girls sent by *converso* families.

No one thought this would last – for the Jews, safe havens are always provisional. That cautionary pessimism was not misplaced. In 1549 the New Christians would be expelled from the city whose immense riches they had made. A half-century of religious violence, war siege and massacre would follow which gave any Jews watching from afar no satisfaction, even though the fall of yet another empire

48 BELONGING

would as usual be added to the prophetic texts of Jeremiah, Daniel
and the rest. Some of the great luminaries of the Mendes world would
get out while they could. Amatus Lusitanus moved to the more hospitable climate of Ferrara, where he would perform public anatomies
on twelve cadavers and publish his great work of vascular medicine.
Then he would proceed along the rescuer route – to Venice, Pesaro,
Ancona and finally Salonika, where he composed and published his
moving rewrite of the Hippocratic oath, commanding physicians to
treat the poor alike with the rich before dying himself of the plague
in 1568.

His initial move from Antwerp took place in 1540, the year that the
community was shaken by another scare. One of the conductors,
Gaspar Lopes, a kinsman of Diogo, was caught by the Milanese interrogators and had turned informer under torture, betraying the network
to the Inquisition. The usual cash crisis moved Marie and Charles to
look the other way (doubtless to the fury of the Holy Office); but the
alarm was so acute that Diogo took the precaution of summoning
rescuers (including Antonio de la Ronha) from London, to a secret
meeting in Antwerp to discuss emergency contingencies. It was
apparent that Beatriz, now thirty, had been taken into confidence and
was judged to be a capable steward of her and her daughter's considerable portion of the Mendes estate.

This trust was not unusual for *converso* widows, who by both
rabbinic and Gentile law could be considered the owners of legacies
(including their dowry) bequeathed by a predeceased husband. What
was extraordinary in Beatriz's case was that she should be trusted by
the Mendes men to be the steward of so immense a fortune, perhaps
as much as 600,000 ducats of capital in the family as a whole. What
we will never know is the precise relationship between Beatriz and
her brother-in-law. Some historians believe it was she, rather than her
younger sister, for whom Diogo was originally intended, though as
Henry VIII could have attested, the fact of young Brianda would have
levitically ruled this out. But something odd began to happen between
the sisters at this point (if not before). Until very recently, the older
and the younger have been portrayed, in keeping with Renaissance
images of the virtuous and wanton woman, as opposites. Since there
is a long tradition (beginning with the writers she commissioned to
tell her story) of canonising Beatriz-Gracia as the embodiment of *eshet*

chayil, the priceless 'woman of worth', it followed therefore that Brianda was the other kind, described in most histories as prettier, more wilfully impulsive and even vindictive (although this may say more about the need for a Jewish fairy tale of two sisters – one wise and plain, the other beautiful and bad – than the reality).[13]

Rather than becoming husband and wife, Beatriz and Diogo became partners in the other sense: joint masters of one of the greatest fortunes in the world. Diogo would have initiated her in the cautionary nature of their bookkeeping (secret accounts and property; bills of exchange that could be cleared at ongoing staging posts across Europe; invisible ink when needed; coded languages for some entries – all of which would be resorted to in later centuries by other dynasties of Jewish financiers).

So when, in 1543, in his turn Diogo Mendes became deathly ill, it was his sister-in-law and not his wife to whom he entrusted the responsibility of administering not just his own estate but also that of his three-year-old daughter. A cool customer this Diogo, passing over one de Luna for his marriage and then reversing things for the legacy, in direct violation, moreover, of the prenuptial agreement made with his wife. Perhaps he regretted his earlier choice. It has long been assumed that he judged his wife unfit to be entrusted with the estate and that he had good reason for this. But whatever was wrong with Brianda, the third brother Gonçalo never saw it, for when he came to make his own will prior to dying in 1545, he was perfectly happy to bequeath half of his estate equally between the two sisters. However one looked at it, Diogo's decision was a stinging humiliation for Brianda, his widow. She was now, in effect, a pensioner or ward of her older sister. Brianda would not take the indignity lying down.

Beatriz, on the other hand, was reborn as the executrix of the estate, which made her the wealthiest woman in Europe. Only too aware of this, Charles and Marie – who were forever trying to square their need to keep the house of Affaitati and Mendes sweet enough to stay put along with their money with an equal urge to hunt down heretics – seized on a way to use her wealth for their own benefit. For the moment the hoard was theirs as it had to be put in a holding escrow pending settlement of what was legitimately owed to the overlords. But at some point those obligations would be discharged. Neither of the two widows, whatever their show of Christian piety, would be likely to accept marriage to someone from inside the imperial circle, but perhaps Beatriz's daughter, now on the verge of her nubile years, could be matched with an Old Christian of unquestioned imperial loyalty. A candidate was found in Francisco d'Aragon, an illegitimate son of the emperor himself and thus completely dependent on the Habsburgs for his fortune. Once concluded, the marriage would make the young Brianda's huge portion of the Mendes riches available to the imperial coffers, which as ever were emptied as fast as they were filled. And surely even the obstinate Mendes would not turn away from a family connection with the Habsburgs!

They did. Beatriz had rejected already the advances of the Portuguese dynasty of the Aviz; the incomparably grander Habsburgs met with the same rebuff. Imperial connection meant less than the integrity of her clan, the secret bond of her Jewish house. Aware that an outright snub was perilous, Beatriz procrastinated. When Marie asked for an interview to raise the matter of Beatriz's eligible daughter, she was told (many times) that, regrettably, she was indisposed. The indisposition seemed incurable: 'The mother excuses herself on the pretext of illness,' Marie wrote to her brother, 'and she might well do it again.'[14] In exasperation, other kinds of pressure were applied. Suddenly the screws were turned on the Antwerp New Christians and on the escape network. New arrivals were arrested, imprisoned and tortured. The Mendes family took even greater risks, hiding fugitives behind the doors of their own heavily guarded house. For her part, worried about a general exodus of the Portuguese New Christians from Antwerp, Marie held back from re-imprisoning members of the Mendes clan themselves. But everything was on a razor's edge.

Time to go. Beatriz had taken over the management of security for the family business and was already liquidating the Antwerp business with discreet urgency. Negotiable inventory was being packed in chests and sent to Bavaria to be warehoused and guarded by business partners. A map of outstanding debts that could be collected en route as the family migrated was drawn up. Numerous departments of operation were removed, in diverse forms to diverse places, to be reconstituted as commercial paper, specie or inventory wherever it was the Mendes clan would settle. When the time came to make the move in the spring of 1545, Beatriz had already established a custom of annual trips to the spa at Aix-la-Chapelle (Aachen), so that another excursion would not appear out of the ordinary. When it became apparent to the imperial government that the Mendes family were travelling not north but south – first to Besançon, then to Lyons and through the Rhône Valley, the obvious route into Italy – Marie was infuriated both by her own naivety but still more by what she regarded as their unconscionable bad faith. The crypto-Jews had revealed themselves to be what she had suspected all along: members of the tribe of deception. Marie believed that the ingratitude even extended to making loans to the Habsburgs' arch-enemy, the French Crown, a rumour that was not entirely without substance.

The Mendes family were exposed and proclaimed Jews. Diogo was posthumously declared to have been a Judaiser all along. Their property and assets (including debts owed to them) could now be immediately confiscated. Beatriz and Brianda were summoned to appear before a tribunal. But by the time these orders were published, the sisters and their daughters were already in Venice, safely beyond Habsburg reach. What Beatriz had calculated, along with her nephew João Micas – who as a twelve-year-old had made the sea journey from Lisbon in 1537, and was now a young man with his own share of the family's formidable intelligence – was that even if it reached out to take them, Habsburg vengeance could always be bought off. The only question was the price. Astonishingly, and with the reckless courage that would be his mark in a long and prodigious career, João volunteered to go and argue the case with Marie in Brussels. The first meeting did not go well. João claimed that contrary to public accusations, his aunts were living in Venice as 'good Christians', not as Jews. Their only mistake was to travel from Antwerp without proper authorisation. And when it came down to it, they were subjects of the king of Portugal, not the emperor. But these were quibbles. João knew the nub of it: how much?

The effrontery is less breathtaking when one knows that João Micas had been a student friend of Prince Maximilian of Austria and Bohemia. The personal connection remained strong enough to open doors to his Habsburg kinsman, Charles V. At a second meeting with Marie, João – exerting what was already becoming a considerable diplomatic talent, half charm, half veiled threat – managed to knock down the price for immunising Beatriz from accusations of being a crypto-Jew to 30,000 ducats. The agreement irked Marie, who thought her brother had been tricked into a bad bargain. But there was another round of campaigning against the Protestant German powers in the offing, and 30,000 ducats was 30,000 ducats. Whatever could be squeezed out of the Mendes clan and converted into arquebuses, cannon and cavalry could make the difference between victory and defeat. Just one more battle, thought the emperor (as he always did), and the reign of Christ would be gloriously at hand and all this sordid gameplaying would be a thing of the past.

Lodged in Venice unmolested, the sisters had no intention of being confined to the ghetto, even if more spacious accommodation was available in the extension confusingly known as 'Ghetto Vecchio' (because the foundry on which it sat was older). The Ghetto Vecchio had been authorised for Jews coming to Venice from the Turkish lands, thus known as 'Levantine' – a signal that the republic was rapidly expanding its commercial dealings with the Muslim empire. But the de Luna sisters were not yet ready to stand forth as Jews. The red or yellow hats required of their co-religionists were definitely not Mendes style. Moreover, the legal status of their movable capital depended on continuing the Christian masquerade. Maintaining for the moment their Christian identity, Beatriz moved the family into the most spectacular residence imaginable: the recently rebuilt Palazzo Gritti, situated at the majestic curve of the Grand Canal.

For a time the two women may have lived under the same roof, but before long the bad feeling engendered by Diogo's legacy deteriorated into an outright feud. Suspecting that her sister might try and overturn the will, Beatriz acted pre-emptively. In the spring of 1546, she initiated proceedings in the courts of Venice to reaffirm her custody over her sister's and niece's estate.[15] This turned out to be a mistake. A year later a legal decision annulled the will, returning personal assets to Brianda while leaving Beatriz in charge of the family business. Beatriz was now ordered to deposit the enormous sum of 300,000 ducats with the Venetian treasury, some of which was to remain in trust for her niece until she reached the age of eighteen.

It was not over. Before the funds could be taken, Beatriz, always a step ahead of her sister, planned to move to a place where the disagreeable Venetian ruling could be appealed and overturned. This new destination was the city state of Ferrara, sixty miles south-west of Venice, ruled by the Este dynasty whose duke, Ercole II, had made his prospective hospitality abundantly clear. For the Mendes-Benvenistes, whenever life became too difficult to stay in one place, there would always be another ruler ready to extend a warm welcome to their millions. And the Este dynasty had long invested in welcoming displaced Jews – whether living openly or as halfway Marranos. The Este hoped that the Jews would turn their city on the Po into the Antwerp of north Italy, the transit point for trade with the Adriatic coast, and transform a backwater into a modern commercial centre to rival Florence. As early as 1493, Duke Ercole I had welcomed twenty-one families, victims of the expulsion from Spain the year before.[16] They were given rights of unlimited residence and free worship, a liberal hospitality which existed nowhere else in Christian Europe. In 1538 Ercole II, whose wife Renée of France was a Protestant (and who tested the boundaries of her husband's tolerance by inviting Jean Calvin to the court), issued letters patent extending those rights. But he had gone well beyond providing a refuge for uprooted Jews. He made it clear that should any New Christians in Ferrara wish to revert to Judaism, his laws would not stand in their way, neither would those newly reverted Jews be molested by the Inquisition. There was already a synagogue in Ferrara for Ashkenazi Jews from Germany; another for the Sephardim from Spain and Portugal followed, all officially protected from the conversionary harangues of intruding friars which disrupted Jewish worship elsewhere in Latin Christian Europe. Just beyond the city walls, as Jewish law required, the Este family had authorised the one site which gave the Jews a sense of repose: their cemetery (the scene of the opening of Giorgio Bassani's heart-shaking homage to the fate of Ferrara's Jews, *The Garden of the Finzi-Continis*).

Ercole, whose mother was Lucrezia Borgia, presented himself as a politique humanist and a patron of the arts which flourished at his court. It was in keeping with his showy reasonableness, as well as economic self-interest, that he made a point of receiving Jews who had suffered from less enlightened rulers. In 1540 he took in Jews who had been expelled from Habsburg Milan. Sephardim who had been expelled from Naples were subsequently settled in Ferrara, including Samuel Abravanel and his wife Benvenida, who had made the elaborate banner for David Ha-Reuveni's unhappy venture in Portugal. After Samuel's death his widow ran the family fortune with as much force and care as Beatriz Mendes. Extolled as another paragon of womanly strength and virtue, Benvenida had responsibility for more than the Abravanel money and merchandise, for she was also the custodian of her father-in-law Don Isaac Abravanel's great library, taken from Spain to Portugal and then carried further east, the core of its treasures miraculously preserved. As such, Benvenida Abravanel was the last link in a chain of direct memory extending from the tragedy of 1492, Don Isaac's futile pleading and indignant confrontation with Ferdinand and Isabella, all the way to the perils and possibilities of the mid-sixteenth century. There was something culturally magnificent about the likes of the Abravanels which flattered Ercole's own sense of natural aristocracy.

The coming together of New Christians with thick-and-thin Jews was never straightforward. In Venice those who lived inside the ghetto and those Marranos who did not existed in separate worlds, even if they all ended up some day in the same cemetery on the Lido. Suspicion and outright hostility, a backlog of recrimination, coloured the attitude of some of the Orthodox against the selective reversion of the converts. The men could demonstrate their *tshuva*, their return, in the most dramatic way by undergoing adult circumcision. The circumciser who would be most sympathetic to the ordeal was someone who had gone through it himself, such as the Marrano Gabriel Henriques who, post-op, became the Jew Joseph Saralvo. Goldsmith and virtuoso *mohel*, the inexhaustible Saralvo was said to have circumcised eight hundred males in Ferrara alone, a record of such enthusiastic Judaising that it attracted attention from the Portuguese Inquisition who, in 1578, when the Counter-Reformation was barging even into tolerant Ferrara, pressured Duke Alfonso Este to have him arrested and taken to Rome where he was duly burned alive on the Campo de' Fiori, the only publicly martyred *mohel* in Jewish history.[17]

Understandably, many of those shedding their names and their Christianity flinched from this drastic operation. João Micas and his brother Bernardo would not be circumcised until they got to Constantinople. Many in Ferrara preferred to return to Judaism step by cautious step – not least because their daily business dealings with the Gentiles were altogether easier as Gomes than as Levi. And the Ferrara press was unique in publishing sacred books which took account of this spiritual halfway house. The printer-publisher Abraham Usque (who had once been Duarte Pinhel) and the typographer Yom

Tob Atias (once Jeronimo de Vargas) could be expected to be sympathetic, but they were also wonderfully creative. Daily prayer books, *siddurim*, containing the essential prayers – the daily affirmation of God's oneness, the *shema*; the prayer over the deceased, Kaddish, which remained the defining mark of Jewish identity – were printed in Ladino using Latin characters; then in Ladino but with Hebrew characters; and finally in Hebrew alone. Those books could thus constitute a graduated course in religious reacquaintance. When in 1549 the 'Portuguese Nation' in Antwerp was given one month to exit the Netherlands for good, those of their kin who had already made it safely to Ferrara must have congratulated themselves on their timing.

In the same spirit of graduated re-immersion in Judaism, Usque and Atias published the first Jewish Bible in Ladino.[18] Judaeo-Spanish translations had been available in Spain itself but, before the Ferrara Bible, only using Hebrew characters. Two generations out from Iberia, many of the forcibly converted had lost their familiarity with Hebrew altogether. The response of the Jewish community could have been a shrugging 'too bad, so go learn it', but the Usque–Atias answer was more considerate, better designed to make a connection with historical reality and the vitality of daily language. The issue was simple, and it is one which for another half-millennium has not gone away: whether people of Jewish descent would be lost to Judaism or whether a way could be found to welcome them back without compromising the core of texts and beliefs; to change the manner of Judaism without leaving the matter. The most severe would resist any translation whatsoever, especially since the Ladino used in the Ferrara Bible was a poeticised style, neither the conversational tongue of everyday life (for that would indeed be shocking) nor a flat-footed transcription from the Hebrew. But then Jews of all stripes were grappling with challenges of translation, and not only in religion. Another Usque, Salomon, took it on himself while living in Ancona to translate Petrarch, the very epitome of Italian poetic style, into Spanish. Some copies of the print run of the Ferrara Bible contained a dedication to the eulogised benefactor Ercole II Este, and were meant (despite the Judaeo-Spanish) for the use of non-Hebrew-reading Gentiles who wanted the flavour of the Jewish Bible; others bore a fulsome dedication to Gracia Nasi, as Beatriz was now called, protector of the uprooted, the destitute and the terrorised.

The date of publication – 1553 – could not have been more significant. The Council of Trent, where Counter-Reformation severities were being discussed and formalised, had been meeting for eight years. The Farnese Pope Paul III, who had been anxious to spare Jews from expulsion and New Christians from the Inquisition, despite all the pressure coming from Charles V, had died in 1549 and was succeeded first by the scandal-beset gay Pope Julius III, then the three-week papacy of Marcellus II, and finally by the uncompromisingly militant Carafa Pope Paul IV. The medieval demonising of the Talmud as the true and wicked Bible of Jewish errors got a new lease of life. In August 1553, a Council of Cardinals proscribed the Talmud as blasphemous and ordered it burned.[19] Other Hebrew books were to be subject henceforth to inspection and censorship. A month later, on the first day of Rosh Hashanah, the Jewish New Year, copies of the Talmud were carted to an enormous pyre on the Campo de' Fiori and burned; a moment so traumatic that it was commemorated afterwards in Rome by an annual fast. Other Italian cities were ordered to follow. Confiscations and burnings took place in Bologna, Ravenna, Florence, Mantua, Urbino, and even in tolerant Ferrara and in Venice, the centre of Hebrew printing.

Christian convergence based on Hebraism was on the retreat. With every year that passed, the gamble of a secret Jewish identity was becoming more perilous. Shockingly, both Mendes sisters were prepared to use these renewed fears to get their own way with the family fortune. In 1551, suspecting (correctly) that Beatriz was planning to move the entirety of the assets to Constantinople, Brianda had denounced her sister to the Venetian authorities. Beatriz made the counterclaim that since one Tristan da Costa, a New Christian but notorious secret Jew, was living under Brianda's roof in Venice, she too must be a Judaiser. The two contentious women were summoned to appear together before the Council of Ten, where vicious claims and counterclaims were lodged. There were enough grounds for believing Beatriz was up to something for guards to be placed at her house to prevent a departure. But all Beatriz had to do was to wait it out. Two years later in 1553, the year of the Rosh Hashanah Talmud burnings, she made her move, together with her daughter, along the route her family had planned for so many others: first to Ancona, securing capital assets on the way, then to Ragusa on the other side of the Adriatic and finally, with active help from the sultan's people, to Constantinople.

Brianda and her daughter stayed in Venice, ostensibly living a Christian life. But the girl Beatriz was now thirteen, the nubile age. Her mother was no fool (and had never been). She knew very well that her daughter's attractiveness as a match for chronically overspending patricians was her safety net against overzealous investigations in Venice. And yet when push came to shove and one of them actually got serious, Brianda – as was the family habit – panicked that this would end up alienating the family fortune, never mind the Jewish destiny to which she no less than her sister was deeply and secretly attached. So Brianda hatched an extraordinary escapade, something straight out of *commedia dell'arte*. Her personable nephew João Micas, now in his mid-twenties, would let it be known that he was passionately smitten with the teenage beauty, and had become desperate enough to elope with her. He would then marry her in a Christian ceremony, and claim (or enact) the irreversible consummation which in the most dramatically incontestable way would close off the possibility of her being married to anyone else. Matrimony by consummation was in fact a Talmudically approved possibility, so that what then happened was a reverse Romeo and Juliet, Jewish style, in which a parent was the orchestrator rather than the dupe of the illicit romance. The actors were primed and actually played it out. Eluding the gaze of the servants, Beatriz slipped out of the palazzo at night, stepping down into a gondola which was poled through the black canal waters by her suitor's brother Bernardo. It is probably too much to hope the boys were wearing masks, but capes, low-brimmed hats and swords were in order. Spirited out of Venice, the couple were arrested in Faenza. But João must have talked his way out of trouble, for instead of being imprisoned the couple were taken to Ravenna where some sort of actual union did take place, either openly and before witnesses or else in a private consummation.

Brianda, the drama queen, gave it everything she had, playing the distraught mother to the hilt, frantically appealing for the return of her abducted daughter. The authorities in Ravenna duly returned the runaway bride to Venice while the bridegroom João was formally banished by the magistrates of the republic on pain of being 'hanged between the two pillars of San Marco' should he dare return. Scarcely conducting himself like a fugitive, João went straight to the Pope in Rome to have the marriage upheld, without success, which may have been the idea all along.

What the thirteen-year-old girl thought about the whole madcap business we will never know. Was she married or not? Was João (should she call him Joseph?) her benefactor, or the man who had taken her maidenhood for the sake of some incomprehensible family plot? Was she Beatriz or was she Gracia? Was she a Christian or a Jew, or somehow both? Back in Venice, it seems very likely that she and her mother continued, at whatever risk, to live their double life as secret Jews, and in 1555 were hauled before the Council of Ten for 'Judaising'. They were interrogated along with the New Christian Tristan da Costa, Brianda's major-domo, physician and steward. Mother and daughter then did something extraordinary. After so many years of temporising and pretence, and after da Costa himself, trying to protect them, had sworn that while he was indeed a secret Jew the two women were unimpeachable Christians, Brianda and her daughter not only admitted but declared with great passion that they were in fact Jews, that they wished to live by the 'Law of Moses', and wanted only to go to the ghetto and live alongside their fellow Jews. This was an astonishing reversal of the usual Mendes subterfuges, a moment of truth. There must, however, have been some sort of prior agreement with the Venetians, for while the statement left no choice but to convict them, the sentence was banishment rather than anything more draconian – and this at a time when autos-da-fé were beginning again in the papal territories. 'And now, gentlemen,' Brianda is reported to have said with her customary disconcerting bluntness, 'what about the money?'

Amazingly the money went with her, back to Ferrara. There, mother and daughter openly embraced their Jewish names and identity. When the beautiful, mercurial, clever mother died the following year, it was as Reyna Benveniste.

Two years later, in 1558, the midnight gondolier Bernardo Micas showed up in Ferrara where the motherless teenager – now called Gracia La Chica, Little Gracia – was still living. Bernardo had come from Constantinople where he had ended his journey along with his brother João and their aunt Beatriz-Gracia. The two men had been circumcised and had reverted to their ancestral Jewish family name of Nasi. Bernardo Micas, now Samuel Nasi, courted the eighteen-year-old whom five years earlier he had helped abduct. The incident relegated to the past, Samuel and Gracia were married in 1559 in a Jewish rite. To mark the occasion, Ferrara's renowned medallist and Master of the Dies, Pastorino Pastorini, made single-face medals of the couple's profiles. Only that of the bride, called in Hebrew by her Jewish name, survives.

Still, it was unclear where the newly-weds would live. The condition of Brianda and her daughter returning to Ferrara was that they remain there for at least six years. Evidently as good a diplomat as his brother, Samuel Nasi managed to talk his way into an exit. The couple sailed for Constaninople that summer of 1559, and did not come back.

The women and the men of the family had endured the terrors of prison, the endless comings and goings in boats and closed carriages, the encounters with armed and brutal men all for this: to keep guard over the Mendes-Benveniste money which, whether self-interest or altruism, they had come to think of as a Shield of Israel. Whatever their differences, the sisters would have shared an understanding that God had preserved their good fortune for something other than patrician self-indulgence; that it was the capital of *tzedaka*: righteous care, the word conveying both charity and, from a cognate root, *tzedek*, justice. On them depended the fate of countless others less fortunate: converts who lived in terror of being called out as heretics and dragged before the torturing interrogators for a telling change of dress on Saturdays or refraining from food on a fast day. On them depended the possibility of a way out, a new exodus. On them, too, depended the self-declared Jews – forever intimidated, abused, publicly humiliated, marked with badges of identity; penned into ghettos, brutalised, imprisoned without cause; robbed, sent packing into the storm with barely the clothes on their backs. If not them, who else? Who else could open the doors of the profligate rulers of Christian Europe? Who else had the brass to deal with courts lay and ecclesiastical; to look kings and popes in the eye knowing the glitter of their regalia was bought and paid for with New Christian gold? Who else knew so well how to play for time, take the risks, to be ready to be off, always one step ahead of those who wished the Jews harm? And they knew all this because of necessity and upbringing. João Micas, who in Constantinople would become Joseph Nasi, councillor to the sultan, was after all a graduate of the University of Louvain, a hothouse of Catholic piety. Like all those dwelling in many worlds at once he understood the Christian universe from the inside out: its theology and philosophy, its rites and genuflections, its images and sprinklings, the lives of saints, the canon of miracles and martyrs. But when they could, Marranos like João Micas donned the habits of Jewish life as though they had never taken them off: the *aggadah* and the precepts of countless generations of sages and teachers, the beautiful calendar of feast and fast; the Sabbath stew and the Passover matzot; the poetry of the liturgy and the cantillation of the Torah. To live with all this gave them peerless cultural versatility even as it put them, again and again, in mortal peril.

A touching passage in the Talmud requires aspiring proselytes to receive a solemn warning that were they to become Jewish they would be throwing in their lot with a people whose sufferings were legion and which were not likely to end any time soon, not until all Jews became unswerving in their observance of the Torah commandments. If, after this stern caution, they persisted, then they ought not to be denied. None could then say that they hadn't been warned. Marranos returning to the ancestral faith might not have needed the cautionary advice. Could it possibly be worse, many of them might have wondered, seeing the Inquisition remorselessly hunting down the faintest trace of 'Judaising'? Yes it could, was the reply. But come, all the same.

This was the tragic welcome delivered by the first Jewish history book proper (rather than a genealogy of the generations of the pious) to have been written since Josephus. Samuel Usque's *Consolação as Tribulações de Israel* (*Consolation for the Tribulations of Israel*) appeared from Abraham Usque's (not necessarily a relation) and Yom Tob Atias's busy Ferrara press in 1553, the year of Talmud-burning. The long, intensely moving work was written neither in Hebrew nor Judaeo-Spanish but Portuguese, since, as its title page announced, it was meant first and foremost for the returning 'Gentlemen of the Portuguese Diaspora'. Like its primary readers, it is a cultural hybrid – Bible rehash, *midrashic* free interpretation of scripture, adulterated Josephus – but also, more improbably, a Renaissance pastoral. Its three characters, who meet in the kind of picnic arcadia not much frequented by Jews, are 'Ycabo' – the patriarch Jacob who is the principal narrator of his 'children's' sufferings – 'Numeo' the comforter and 'Zicareo' the visionary (thinly disguised versions of the prophets Nahum and Zechariah). As a sweetener, Usque sets them down in an Edenic landscape, rendered as if he had immersed himself in Dante, Petrarch and Virgil, a Jewish *Eclogues* in which 'blackbirds murmur, the nightingales trill enchanting airs and the tunes of fledgelings flitting to the grove for shelter against the oppressive heat, filled the whole place with melody'.[20] It's a balmy paradise, where the flocks graze and their shepherds wind down both before supper and after – by wrestling, competitive slingshots summoning their inner David, and 'pitching the bar' until they 'fall asleep their faces looking up at the star-studded sky'.

This can't last. The sky darkens. Enter the hunters. All this will have been familiar to any Sephardi who had looked at a Passover Haggadah in which hounds and hunters pursue the hapless Jewish quarry to their doom.[21] So it is here. A heron tries to escape the attack of falcons and hawks but, after a mighty battle of birds, falls victim to its predators: the heron song of the Jews. A quick skip through scripture and successive empires are doing their worst; acts of annihilation effacing the miracles of earlier Israelite history. 'The Babylonians made us vomit up in blood the pure water we had drunk from the desert rock [of Horeb in Exodus 17]. They pulled from our entrails now covered in gall, the sweet manna and tender quail on which we had fed.' Redemption is reversed. Ordeal after ordeal ensues, although Usque is enough of a literary entertainer to know how to deliver wonder as well as terror. The Holy of Holies in the Temple is described with all the happy fastidiousness of a Renaissance interior decorator: its doorless entrance fashioned like 'human shoulders', above it clusters of grapes 'the size of a man', and the veil-curtain fifty-five cubits long covering the Holy of Holies made from 'byssus a very white linen variegated with violet, the colour of the sky; and with crimson and purple'.[22]

Whether written as Renaissance poesy or scriptural lament and Jewish history, Usque's pages are a gripping read, even if Tribulation outweighs Consolation by some distance, to the point where Usque's tale of uninterrupted woe becomes the template for the 'lachrymose history' of which the great American historian of the Jews, Salo Baron, understandably complained. But this did not prevent it from being swiftly and widely circulated among the half-hidden, half-exposed community of the Marranos. Even if it was a lament it was a beautiful one, not without a grain of hope, and in any event it gave the wanderers some sense of how their own experience was organically attached to the millennia-long story of the Jews. In 1558, one Thomas Fernandes confessed to the Inquisition, which had accused him of being a secret observant Jew in Bristol, and he received from Simaõ Roiz, the surgeon and New Christian, 'a printed book which spoke of the troubles which the sons of Isaac suffered, scattered as they were over the kingdoms and cities where they wandered, but that they must not lose confidence nor be discouraged for the Lord would deliver them and send the Messiah to them and they must live in hope and the said confessant believes the book was sent from Italy to the ports of England'.[23]

Usque knew all about the travelling world of the quasi-Jews and the Mendes-Benveniste sisters whose own peregrinations he tracked, and for whom he worked in both Antwerp and Ferrara. Like them he was of the families who had come from Spain – perhaps from Huesca in the north-east, hence the unusual name – and been forcibly converted in 1497. His narrative of children torn from the arms of their parents and sent to the island of São Tomé to be devoured by 'giant lizards' (the alligators) was partly an exaggeration, but it has the terror of the small boy he might have been himself, shuddering at the story. At the heart of his martyrologies of ordinary Jews is the destruction of families: the couple who hang themselves rather than be converted, their burial-party themselves impaled on spears; the desperate who threw themselves from windows and whose bodies were burned (itself a desecration) in sight of the laggards who were hesitating over their conversion and baptism; among the two thousand dead in Lisbon, the young girls who are raped and killed, the infants whose heads are smashed against walls (not for the last time in our story).

When that 'wild monster' the Inquisition finally makes its way to Portugal, Usque, like the Mendes sisters, goes to England and evidently learns of their prejudices enough to make him deliver an English version of anti-Semitic atrocities. Not content with sticking to the real history of mass executions, mob rampages and expulsion, Usque invents a passage of inspired fantasy. The king of England erects two pavilions on the seashore. One contains a cross; the other the Scrolls of the Law. Jews are genially invited to choose. Naturally most opt for the Sefer Torah, but the entry to the pavilion is wide enough to admit only one of them at a time. On entering they are immediately beheaded by a concealed swordsman. A back curtain parts and the separated head and trunk are thrown into the sea.[24]

Though he uses all kinds of sources, Jewish and Gentile, relatively reliable and quite fantastic, the secret of Usque's readability is that he writes as if he were a personal witness to the medieval tragedies, the slaughters and the suicides, a Jewish history that flows through his veins. Seemingly he carried this history in his own wanderings which closely tracked those of the Mendes family who employed him. After England he went to Antwerp where he worked as some sort of factotum for the unpredictable Brianda. In Ancona he called himself a merchant and got into a row with two swordsmiths who failed to supply, as pledged, a thousand swordblades.[25] A Jew with an arsenal! When they were finally delivered, Usque judged them to be of such poor quality he took them to court. In Ferrara he went to work again for Brianda, who had him imprisoned in a dispute over back wages. Enter the 'Good Sister' Beatriz-Gracia, who liberated Usque from incarceration, although only after he agreed to sign a document for the 'Crazy Sister' – a condition he bitterly resented. Such is the graphic picture Usque paints of the sudden (and temporary, as it would turn out) expulsion of the Marranos from Ferrara at the end of 1549 – when they were held to be carriers of the plague that had arrived in the city – of the old, weak and infants having to leave their homes in the dead of night, that it seems likely he experienced this latest ordeal himself. The *Consolation* was dedicated to 'the very illustrious Lady Doña Gracia Nasi', who by that time was living in great splendour in Galata overlooking the Golden Horn, but who without any doubt would have secured a copy. She had already taken control of the story of the two sisters and had become in her own mind, and in the minds of all those who wrote of her, the ultimate Jewish Woman of Worth, or as Usque called her in a flight of inspired poetic fancy, 'the heart in the body of our people'.

Gracia is the sixth blessing listed by Numeo/Nahum, who does his best towards the end of the book to balance suffering with benedictions. And Usque is also perhaps the first in a vernacular language to ask directly what will also occur to many subsequent generations of innocently afflicted Jews. Why us? Why all this sorrow? Why all this hatred? The answers, already long since given by the biblical prophets and reiterated by the sages of the Talmud and after, amount to the coldest possible comfort. This has happened to the Jews because of their stiff-necked transgressions, their errant iniquities and idolatries from the golden calf to the hubris of Herod. The devastations and torments have been inflicted by those empires chosen by God for His punishing instrument.

But then Usque in the voice of Numeo the comforter says something quite new in Jewish literature. The heart of our tragedy, he says, our exile, the punishment laid on us to wander the earth in terror and dismay, is actually a blessing in (admittedly heavy) disguise. For by 'scattering you among all peoples He made it impossible for the world to destroy you, for if one kingdom rises against you in Europe to inflict death upon you, another in Asia allows you to live ... If the Spaniards burn you in Spain and banish you the Lord wills for you to find someone in Italy who welcomes you and lets you live in freedom.'[26] This too, the comfort of the diaspora, would also echo down the following centuries. And to another endlessly reiterated question, 'When will it stop? When will deliverance and the messianic deliverer appear?', Usque has another modern reply: it must stop soon because God has run out of countries to send you to. You have reached the ends of the earth, whether on the edge of the Iberian peninsula, in the African desert or on the Asian shores. Soon even amid the troubles it will be time to turn back, inwards from the perimeter of the earth to its centre, to Jerusalem and its wasteland which will be restored if not to the bucolic idyll with which the book began then to a place of 'tall and beautiful cedars, fragrant and delicate acacias, the myrtle and the blessed olive ... an abundance of camels shall cover you and the dromedaries of Midian and Ephah shall come from Sheba bringing gold and incense'.[27]

Pending this marvel, think on other consolations and blessings: 'the safe and placid port' of Ferrara where 'you could doff the heavy cloak you wore and deck your soul in its true and natural garb'; also Ottoman Turkey 'like a broad and expansive sea which our Lord has opened with the rod of his mercy as Moses did for you in the Exodus from Egypt ... there the gates of freedom are always wide open so that you may practise your Judaism ... there you may restore your true character, transform your nature'.[28] These, the reader would have noticed, are the places where Doña Gracia Nasi has gone, and for Usque she is the greatest of the living blessings: she is Miriam, Deborah, Esther and Judith; no mere paragon of the domestic hearth but the epitome of the strong Jewish woman, courageous, resourceful and wise. She has been the ultimate rescuer, the saviour of the uprooted, the wanderers, those dispossessed of their religion, their families, their everything.

The modern Jewish matriarch who many times later would be the difference between life and death first makes her mark in these pages of Usque and in the person of Beatriz-Gracia. But she is not just the tender, womanly healer of Jewish woes and fears. She is to be reckoned with, she is strength personified (and that, in whatever ways it took, had certainly been her hallmark all along), the very eagle prophesied by Moses which 'hovering over her young and spreading her outstretched wings bears and carries them aloft'. And she is something else too. Usque had described the sorrows of Jewish history as akin to living in a perpetual winter, while elsewhere others enjoyed the blessings of spring. Gracia, the Messiah in skirts, on the other hand, was the source of warmth. For she was, perpetually, 'a beautiful summer'.[29]

3

THE ENTERTAINER

The magic began when the candles in the wall sconces were snuffed out and those concealed in the wings were lit. Leone the Jew, the producer of enchantment, made sure to do this slowly, fading out the prattle of the streets and markets. Dimness stopped the craning of necks, the social ogling. Workaday Mantua disappeared into the darkness.[1] All eyes were now on whatever scene appeared on the stage, the light bright enough to make out the action but prone to tremble when a rogue draught caught the lamps. Most often it fell on the scene of an empty piazza, with the colonnaded facade of a monumental building standing at the far end. Rows of houses led onto this open square from each flank of the stage, painted according to the laws of theatrical perspective set out by Sebastiano Serlio, tallest where they were closest to the proscenium, tapering down to the backdrop, giving the illusion of long, narrow streets. From one of the wings, or striding through the darkened hall itself and up onto the platform, would come a speaking prologue, large with rhetoric, pleading the cause of the play and the indulgence of the genteel audience. As soon as he was done, and sometimes even before, actors would emerge stage right and left from doorways speaking both to each other and to everyone in the house. They would stand at a particular bias to the proscenium so as to be both voluble and audible, shifting their weight as emphasis required. Leone de Sommi Portaleone, or Leone Ebreo, or Leone the Jew, as the court called him – actor, producer and everything else – would stand in the wings or at the back of the hall, catching the first ha-ha hee-hee or gauging the thickness of the attentive silence, and then would try to relax a little as the play began to work its spell.[2]

If he had had his way, Leone would have installed his plays in a purpose-built chamber, or better yet a whole building. In 1567, established as one of the masters of spectacle in Mantua, he had petitioned Duke Guglielmo and the court for permission to find and fit out 'a room' for plays, a permanent theatre where the actors would be professionals, paid from the door takings – an unheard-of idea. Permission not granted. Such an establishment, the authorities thought, would be a magnet for the disorderly, a year-round carnival of riot. Nine years later in 1576, James Burbage, with the help of funds provided by his brother-in-law John Brayne, created just such a theatre on the site of a former monastery in Shoreditch, beyond the walls and jurisdiction of the City of London. Paying customers, the penny kind and the twopenny kind, tramped through the fields to its doors, and commercial theatre began its mighty, beautiful life.

Burbage's theatre would not have suited the Mantuan, for it was open to the elements, its performances confined by the hours of daylight. As Leone made clear in the third of his *Quattro Dialoghi*, a work devoted to the details of stagecraft, he wanted to manipulate mood and emotion through carefully calibrated lighting effects, and he needed the darkness of a controlled interior for his magic box to work its power. But there was only so much he could ask for. He was still Leone Ebreo. Favours had been granted to this particular Jew. He no longer had to wear the yellow patch on his coat or a red hat; the court would cluck with wonder at his productions, ask for more and try not to mind when told there would be no performances on Sabbaths and Jewish fasts and festivals. But there were always moments when Leone was reminded of the disadvantage, when the well-meaning smilers would insist how much easier matters might be were he to accept baptism. That had been the way for Guglielmo of Pesaro, the greatest of choreographers and Isabella d'Este's own dancing master. Yet Leone was a member of the Portaleone family. His great-great-grandfather had been doctor to the Stupor Mundi, Emperor Frederick II, but had remained steadfastly devout. Leone would do no less. He would bite on the occasional humiliation and spit it out again. In 1562 Cesare Gonzaga, his patron, a man of generous spirit and sharp mind, had assumed Leone would be a full, founding member of the Accademia degli Invaghiti (Academy of the Besotted) he had just created, one of thirty lovers and practitioners of the fine arts. The academy had been honoured not just with a papal dispensation but with the additional distinction of elevating each of its members to a

knighthood. And this was a difficulty since an unbaptised Jewish knight
was an unthinkable absurdity. Seven years before, Paul IV had expressly
forbidden any Christian to address a Jew or Jewess as *signor* or *signora*,
much less *cavaliere*. But Gonzaga knew there was no one to rival Leone
Ebreo in Mantua for the skill of his productions, so he contrived to
make him *scrittore academico*, an aggrandised secretary; and Leone,
with whatever misgivings and affront to his dignity, settled for that.

Leone de Sommi is the first unapologetically Jewish showman we
know anything about. The Roman comedian Alitorus, the Zero Mostel
of Nero's theatre, was adored for his exuberance by the emperor's
wife Poppaea, but ridiculed by the high minds of Roman tragedy –
Seneca and Juvenal – and even by the writers of comedies like Plautus
and Petronius who used grotesque caricatures of Jews in their stock
cast of characters. The fact that Poppaea, a legend of unquenchable
libido, favoured him and his comically circumcised *verpus* was cause
for more offstage sniggering. Though Leone would make a spirited
if imaginative case that Moses had been the first tragedian, anticipating
in the drama of Job the classically agonised hero, victimised by
torments over which he had no control, rabbinical Judaism had long
treated drama as an abomination. (This anathema had a long life.
When my father, who wanted more than anything else to live his life
in the theatre, made the mistake of asking his father for his blessing,
he was informed that a thespian Schama would be unwelcome under
the family roof. Arthur bowed before the patriarch's severity and spent
a lifetime regretting his submission.)

There was and still is, however, one exception to the rabbinical
hostility: *Purim shpils*, the plays of Purim. The festival, celebrating
Queen Esther's deliverance of the Jews of Persia from a plot to exterminate them, and wreaking revenge on the villain Haman, is Jewish
carnival. Almost anything goes. For one day in the early springtime
month of Adar, all austerity, including forbiddingly plain dress, is set
aside. Drinking, dancing and singing are non-stop (albeit still separated
by gender); children don fancy dress, most often as characters from
the *megillah*, the scroll book of Esther. When, during the synagogue
reading of the book, the name of the villain Haman occurs, it is
drowned out by wooden rattles. For unnumbered centuries too,
throughout the Jewish world, there were the plays, the *shpils*,
performed by keen amateurs, with the Esther story at the centre but

often with licence to embroider beyond the biblical text or even adding improvised playlets from the rich repertoire of Jewish disaster. The play tradition almost certainly goes back to the medieval centuries. The earliest surviving written text is a Yiddish poem written by the Polish Jew Gumprecht of Szczebrzeszyn: the town's name itself a tongue-twisting joke among the Ashkenazim of Venice, where it was published in 1555. And Purim plays were becoming popular with non-Jews. In 1530 a Venetian troupe played the Esther drama before an audience of patricians, and it became common for Christians to visit the ghetto to see springtime performances. Dramas of Jewish revenge, especially when they featured an irresistible but dangerous Jewess (probably but not certainly acted by males), often found an appreciative audience. The Gonzaga court at Mantua actually commissioned a performance of Judith and Holofernes from a Jewish troupe, even though a story featuring the beheading of a Babylonian general who has just been lulled into post-coital slumber by the seductive Jewish heroine seems an inauspicious choice for a wedding party, unless somehow the bride was being compared to the drop-dead virago. The groom may have left the candles burning that night.

More often the demand was for Jewish comedy. Two *ebrei istrioni*, Jewish ham actors – 'Solly and Jacob', probably the first double act we know of – had been booked by the marquis Federico Gonzaga for an earlier wedding celebration in 1520. A year later the *ebrei istrioni* (and you bet they were) became a regular feature of life in Mantua, performing every year before the ducal court. There is no mystery as to where the Jewish urge to perform, especially in comedy, came from.[3] For centuries Jews had been the butt of ridicule, much of it malignant. In paintings and on wooden sculptures of the Passion carried in procession, they had been represented as repellent grotesques. In the anti-Semitic farces, known as *giudate*, of the Roman carnival, they were made to perform humiliating parodies of the games: the healthy saddled up on the lame and ran races for the howling amusement of the crowd. In the early sixteenth century the *giudate* had been banned by popes like Leo X and Clement VII who were more sympathetic to the Jews and more nervous of inciting riot; but by the later part of the century, in the newly phobic atmosphere ushered in by the Counter-Reformation – when Jews were enclosed in specified districts, and identifying hats and badges were enforced – the dehumanising *giudate* were restored. Tragedy tomorrow, comedy tonight!

It was time, then, for Jews to be the authors, rather than the objects, of that comedy, to become the entertainers rather than the entertainment. But they could only do this if, ghetto or no ghetto, they were prepared to enter the cultural world surrounding them. That is exactly what began to happen in sixteenth-century Italy in city states like Ferrara, Mantua and Venice, and in centres of Christian Kabbalism where Jews were not treated as cultural lepers. A momentous two-way transaction was happening, an anticipation of what would happen to German Jews in the eighteenth and nineteenth centuries. As Christian scholars and theologians were learning Hebrew, Jews were mastering Latin and Italian. Once they had done so, the hard-edged realism of Renaissance enquiry made Jewish questioning at once more omnivorous in its scope and more bravely sceptical. In Ferrara, Azariah de Rossi (later befriended and championed by Leone) spent a lifetime of study soaking up a universe of learning, much of it derived from non-Jewish sources. His *Me'or Enayim* (*The Light of the Eyes*) – which rested on no less than 250 such works, including classical archaeology, history and philosophy – subjected some of the more extravagant passages of the Talmud to erudite modern scepticism. To continue to believe, with the rabbis and sages, that the emperor Titus had actually died from the bite of a gnat said to have entered his brain as divine punishment for the destruction of Jerusalem was, Rossi stated, to believe in nothing more than a puerile fable. There were many other such tarnished links that needed to be extracted from the great chain of Jewish wisdom.

This did not sit well with guardians of that same tradition for whom the coexistence of far-fetched anecdote alongside biblical interpretation and judgements of law was completely unproblematic. Life was just such a mishmash, disobedient to the uniformity of genres so beloved of the classicists. So they attacked the defensiveness, the cultural cringe. What business did Jews have deferring to the classical philosophers, pagan or Christian, asking their permission to take their own sacred texts seriously? There had been a similar response to the philosopher Moses Maimonides' efforts to reconcile classical reasoning with Jewish tradition three centuries earlier, when his critics accused him of adulterating the purity of Judaism from a misguided sense that it might learn something from pagan Greek philosophy.

These questions, put with renewed force at the beginning of modern Jewish history in the sixteenth century, have never gone away. Is Judaism a self-sufficient or an open culture? Is it heedless of time or marked by history? Were Torah, Bible, Talmud, and the myriad interpretative texts obsessively commenting on them and being in turn commented upon, enough unto themselves for leading an authentically Jewish life? Is that life necessarily diluted and compromised by immersion in Gentile culture, or deepened and enriched by it?

It was in this precious but deceptive Italian dawn, before the militant Counter-Reformation restarted its persecutions, that these perennial questions developed practical implications for how Jews lived their lives: what they read, how they dressed, what they ate, to whom they spoke and in what language, what work they undertook. To satisfy the demand for Jewish physicians, Jews had been admitted to medical schools at Padua, Pisa, Perugia, Siena, Pavia and Ferrara. But once there, many took advantage of their new freedom to study eye-opening philosophy, law and even theology. Very often they returned to their communities irreversibly curious, and intellectually voracious. Mantua was no exception and it was there that one of its leading families, the Provenzalis, became divided over such matters. One of their ancestral patriarchs, Jacob ben David of Naples, was among the most implacable critics of all secular learning, and in Mantua, Rabbi Moses Provenzali would berate Azariah de Rossi's flirtation with alien histories. But his brother, Rabbi David Provenzali, and his son, Abraham (needless to say, a doctor himself), took the opposite view. In 1566 they would publish a prospectus for a new kind of school the whole point of which was to reconcile Jewish and non-Jewish learning, to open young Jewish minds to other intellectual worlds without sacrificing core traditions. Students would pursue Talmud studies and learn Hebrew calligraphy but they would also be taught Latin and Italian, rhetoric and astronomy, mathematics and logic, and given a grounding in medicine. Even in this last discipline, the reforming Provenzalis were ambitious. The pre-meds would, as a matter of course, do clinical training by attending on Christian as well as Jewish doctors, a scandal unheard of in more conservative quarters. Who knew what they might pick up from such associations!

It was the expansive Rabbi David, not the severe Rabbi Moses, to whom the Portaleone family sent the young Leone ('Judah' in his rabbinical and family circles) for his early education. So the Hebrew calligraphy he mastered and practised as an apprentice Torah scribe would not have been an end in itself. There was not much chance Judah de Sommi was going to spend his life as a round-backed mole, blinking at the text. Hebrew letters were not just functional; they were also magic. The *Sefer Yetzirah*, one of the earliest mystical Jewish writings, and beloved of Kabbalists (of which there were many in Mantua), had God Himself creating the substance of the universe from those letters. An early seventeenth-century work by a relative, Abraham Portaleone (a doctor, what else?), describes his kinsman Leone inventing a new process for making ink, perhaps from walnuts rather than gall.[4] His Hebrew letters would be darker, harder, somehow more potent and enduring.

It was not enough. Poetic urges stirred. At twenty, Judah – well on his way to becoming Leone – turned literary gallant, writing *Magen Nashim* (*The Shield of Women*), in which he took it on himself, in fifty stanzas, to defend the power and glory of the other sex. The literary jousting between champions and detractors of women, invariably by men, had become a time-honoured genre in Hebrew as in many other languages. Leone went through the usual canon of biblical heroines only to swerve suddenly into modern reflections, explicitly insisting that it was unnecessary to be forever invoking Deborah and Ruth since there were many contemporary paragons, not just of womankind but Jewish courage and thoughtful virtue – the peerless Benvenida Abravanel, for example, the maker of David Ha-Reuveni's great banner and the steward of her deceased husband's estate. In the spirit of the tired game, Leone was himself challenged by Joseph Fano, who nudgingly accused his opponent of writing all this poetic pap merely to curry favour with the ladies and ingratiate himself with the court, both of which were probably true. But Fano faded while Leone shone for a reason that had nothing to do with the latter's argument and everything to do with the form in which he expressed it: Italian *ottava rima* stanzas interspersed between the Hebrew verses. The boy could write both! The modern sort among Mantuan Jews noticed. His father's friend Reuven Sullam, one of the producers of the annual play of the Jewish troupe, loved it. Reuven's wife, Hannah de Rieti (daughter of the revered Rabbi Yechiel Nissim of Pisa), loved it so much she insisted the dual-language poem be published. Overcome by gratitude Leone dedicated the finished work to her – a tribute bordering on the flirtatious.

Put all this together and you can see what the more open-minded set of north Italian Jews saw in young Judah-Leone: a future star, a writer, maybe even an actor who would be a credit to the local company, someone who would make the Christians sit up and see just what spirited, brilliant Jews could do – make them laugh, cry, *think*! And Leone himself was now so struck by the intoxicating possibility of leading a literary life that was still somehow an unimpeachably Jewish one, that he wrote something absolutely unprecedented: a full-on Hebrew comedy. Not simply some sort of *Purim shpil* either, but a true theatre piece, the first Jewish play.

Though we cannot be sure that *Tsahot Bedihuta Deidushin (A Comedy of Betrothal)* was ever performed, it certainly ought to have been. There was a ready-made audience for it in Mantua, the city accustomed to Jewish actors. If it was performed it would have been in one of the more spacious private houses, of which there were many, and it may well have been accompanied by instrumental and vocal music and dance.[5] Unlike most of the other plays in the eleven volumes of his drama that were lost (along with four volumes of poetry) in a fire at Turin University in 1904, the manuscript survived. It opens with the usual allegorical overture composed to flatter the audience. Wisdom – dressed, Leone specifies, in colourful costume (not the sombre clothes associated with the Jewish sages) – makes it clear that the play which follows is the answer to all those who sneered at the incapacity of the Jews' language, lacking the qualities needed for literature. This, Wisdom says, is beside the point, for that which other languages prize as a diadem is naught but 'the glitter of a shoe buckle to us'. But we will show you anyway.

Ostensibly set in ancient Sidon, the play turns on the old, universal obsessions: love, marriage and money. Aware that crude stereotypes of the grasping Jew had already figured in Gentile plays, Leone recaptures the mercenary wife and the shyster lawyer for Jewish writing, and it is funnier, fiercer and sadder. The plot is not a masterpiece but no worse than many run-of-the-mill comedies of its type. Boy and girl (Yedidiah and Beruria) are madly in love and the betrothal contract has been drawn up and signed. Happily ever after beckons. But then the boy's well-off father Sholom, travelling abroad on business as Jews must, dies, and it is discovered to general horror that he has left everything not to son and presumptive heir but to his enslaved servant, Shovel.

The father of the bride is caught in anguished dilemma. On the one hand the marriage would doom his daughter to a life of difficulty; on the other hand a prenup is a prenup. His wife, Deborah, however, is quite clear about what must be done. 'The pauper is as good as dead,' she briskly declares. When her husband protests that this would violate the contract she does a bit of overacting which may not sound altogether unfamiliar to Jewish ears: 'Before I would give her to such a man I would strangle her with my own hands or drown her in the sea.'

Miserable, the fired suitor seeks help from 'Master Chamdan' (Master Greedy) who is, naturally, a lawyer and a Rabbi – not just your average attorney, but a shrewd scrutiniser of Talmudic loopholes. Smelling a percentage of the dowry he comes up with a plan resting on a very broad interpretation of *nissuin*, the second stage in any marriage (the first being the betrothal). *Nissuin* involves a finalising ceremony beneath the *huppah* canopy, followed by a time in which bride and groom are left alone in each other's company. The strong implication is that this will be the moment of consummation marking the full accomplishment of the union. Master Greedy's idea, not entirely at odds with the Talmud, is that since the betrothal contract was the true engagement, all that needs completing is this act of sexual coupling. So, he counsels, run away, elope, just do it. Why should she mind? You already belong to each other. Then any scheme of the mother-in-law to exchange bridegrooms will be too late.

This duly happens, offstage, though the happy Yedidiah delivers a testimony of endearing First Time anxiety: 'At that very moment my loins trembled lest I lose my soul or be damned for pleasure and excess for my bliss was exceeding my wildest imaginings.' Although the object of his affections trembled along with him, Yedidiah is tried for rape before the Jewish equivalent of all those counts, dukes and kings who in Renaissance drama adjudicate wrongs, correct misunderstandings, unmask the disguised, confound the villains and ensure last-act happy-ever-after. In Leone's Jewish show this solemnising figure is the wise rabbi, Amitai – the truth speaker. Because the original betrothal remained valid (notwithstanding the misfortune of the vanished legacy) and because the fiancée seemed anything but reluctant to consummate the match, Yedidiah is judged not guilty. Then comes the twist which anyone half awake in the audience would have grasped as soon as the fine print of the bequest was examined. Despite being disinherited, Yedidiah had been allowed to take just one item from his father's estate. Duh. The forehead is slapped. Yedidiah chooses ... the slave! ... thus making the fortune of jumped-up Shovel his own. Happy ever after. Except for Shovel, that is, who appears in the last act divested of his fancy clothes and back in slave dress, commenting bitterly if understandably on the caprices of fortune.

This is a bald summary. Within the statutory five acts of the classical repertoire, Leone develops subplots and subplots of subplots with an overstuffed cast to match: cheekily truth-telling servants – male and female – banterers, teeth-gnashers, buffoons, rogues on the make, spineless nebbishes, the lot. It's a lovely play and a genuine weave of Jewish tradition and Italian comedy; but the hybrid didn't take. True Jewish drama would have to wait another two and a half centuries to come to fruition – and then it would reappear in Yiddish, not Hebrew.

Although *A Comedy of Betrothal* didn't inaugurate a new genre of Jewish performance literature, it did make its author. Doubtless helped by Reuven Sullam, Leone de Sommi invented, for the first time, the career of the Jewish showman, the *maestro degli spettacoli*. And unlike many who would follow him, the two parts of Leone's identity remained indivisible. Instead of abandoning the community for the stage, he became its spokesman to the Gonzaga court and its government. When kosher butchers in Mantua were accused of exploiting Lent to raise prices for Gentiles who fancied a leg of mutton it was Leone who argued that the accusation was unjust. When the local guild of silkworkers and vendors tried to shut out Jews from the trade, Leone contested the case.

None of this made him less of a daring producer-impresario. Around 1565 – during the time he was dreaming of a permanent space for his theatre, a professional company and paying customers – Leone wrote his *Quattro Dialoghi*. The dialogue form he chose is the only conventional thing about the work, and even then the figure of Veridico, the Truth-Teller, is self-evidently Leone's own voice. There had been and there would be many other works on the theatre, but Leone's was the first – and for centuries the only – book to ground all the poetic and philosophical ruminations on drama in the concrete details of staging a play. There are the usual bows in the direction of Aristotle, but what makes the book an anticipation of the modern theatre to come is Leone's naturalism. It is true that it coexists with his designs for illusion and enchantment and his bows towards conventional rustic pastorals – the usual nymph and shepherd numbers – but in almost every aspect of the stagecraft he outlines in the third and fourth dialogues, Leone wants to naturalise and humanise the play. The effect to aim at, he explains, is to trick the audience into believing that 'the episodes re-enacted for them seem real', much as they might happen in the street or in their house. This unforced naturalism, the uncanny sense that the play is an extension of life rather than separated from it, restores the possibility of surprise – a crucial element of dramatic tension, for if the spectator knows in advance how everything will unfold 'it will all seem too obvious and a foolish lie'. So the actors must not speak in lofty, stilted, indeed actorish tones, but conversationally as they would in daily life. That way, the impact when the plot soars or swoops into extreme passions is all the more powerful for its following the spoken encounters of credible fellow men and women. To achieve this, what happens between the lines, the body language of gesture and facial expression, is almost as important as the text itself. That this was not asking for something beyond the reach of most actors had been proven by Leone's favourite star, Flaminia the Roman, who personified all his favourite qualities of unforced naturalism: 'because she is so incredible on stage it seems to those listening to her that they are seeing true episodes unfold before their eyes for she changes her gestures, voice and colour with every change of circumstance'. Evidently her greatest fan, Leone might have felt that Flaminia was being denied full credit in Mantua for her transforming performances because of the catfight she was having with her rival Vincenza, who happened to be the mistress of the duke.

To read Leone is to listen to the voice of a true actor-manager-director – the ancestor of the Garricks, Reinhardts and Brookses – and to have a palpable sense of his working routine. Showtime is not all candlelit glory, he says; much of it depends on the grind. If you want it to work, overlook nothing. Take care with that first, most critical decision – the choice of play – or you might live to rue the results of an impulsive decision. Cast the actors widely and wisely, 'for actually it is more important to have good actors than a good play ... how many times we have seen an awful play succeed with the audience if it is well acted, as opposed to a good play badly acted?'[6] A lovely passage has the cast called for a first read-through: 'I make them all read the play, even the little children who have parts in it are taught the plot or at least those parts of it in which they are involved, burning into their minds the particular qualities of the character they must imitate.'⁷ Then, Leone says, let them go away, memorise and internalise the script before the rehearsals begin. This will all sound routinely familiar to any modern director, but it is stunning to see it spelled out in the middle of the sixteenth century. The archive of Renaissance English drama has nothing like it.

At every stage Leone is thinking 'How will this go down with the audience?' Soliloquies which go on forever are asking too much of audiences, and besides are ridiculously out of keeping with normal behaviour. Make sure that the only 'house lights' throughout the performance are a few candles set at the back of the hall, so that the stage illumination is all the more concentrated. Design the scenery with the utmost attention to perspective so that an entire city can be inferred from the slice of it seen on stage. Don't make perspective so sharp that when an actor moves upstage he will immediately seem like a giant in a town of midget housing. Why don masks which freeze a character's personality so ritually that they preclude changes of mood and temper, registered in facial expression? Body language, after all, is as important as the spoken text. Avoid jarring costume anachronisms. Don't dress figures from antiquity in the clothes of the sixteenth century: use the abundant evidence of classical friezes and sculpture to get that classical style right. Don't be trapped by colour convention. Why should old men always have to wear white, and prostitutes yellow? Use your imagination; be colourful, and think about the relationship between the bodies of the actors (which, he adds, should always be slim) and what they would wear. In a countryside play 'cover the performer's legs and arms with flesh-coloured tights and if the performer is young and handsome, it would not be inappropriate to leave the arms and legs bare but never the feet ... he must have a light shirt and over it two animal skins ... as for the nymphs they should have dresses well decorated ... with sleeves, and it's my custom to add a little starch to them so that when jewellery is tied on them or beautifully coloured silk girdles, the dress will swell and balloon in a way that will be an exquisite eyeful'.⁸

If the play calls for it, go for broke with stage effects, props and extras. You are performing a pastoral? Deck the stage with flowers and little trees, bring on the rabbits and the birds and don't worry where they might scamper or hop. Bring the audience right into the countryside. Get your hovels and hermitages right; have the actors walk through meadows up to their knees in wild flowers.

This is Leone the drama king speaking, but his showmanship wasn't confined to the play itself. His productions were expected to provide musical interludes, including dance numbers choreographed by Leone and rehearsed by the great Jewish dance master Isaachino (Little Ike) Masserano. Then there was the food, served in an adjoining hall in the cold months, or al fresco in palace gardens in spring and summer. (Theatre picnics did not begin at Glyndebourne.) Being Leone, this was never going to be a matter of conventional catering. Instead it was an opportunity to go immersive, the courses and the waiters themed to the action of the play. If there was a faintly monastic theme, diners would find themselves suddenly surrounded by boys dressed as monks delivering basketloads of bursting fruit to a fake prioress, who would then elaborately bless the fare (and invite the diners to join in) before the audience got anything to eat. If the play had a nautical theme, a fish course was brought in nets by pungent fishermen dressed in exactly the right kind of bandanas and leggings. These immersive interludes could get very weird indeed. Live animals brought in by nimble-footed dancers (more actor-waiters) would run and trot around the audience to make a kind of petting zoo – before previously cooked versions of their kin would be brought to the table. Watch out for a blast of the horn as it would herald hunters, bringing their game. On the lap of one guest would be dumped 'the head of a wild boar, to another a hare, to yet others the carcass of a deer, and so on'.[9]

Jews like Leone and Masserano used their status in a pleasure-addicted place like Mantua to be champion and conscience for their community. When trouble threatened, Leone had direct access to the duke. He was the first such head of a community I know of who was neither rabbi nor doctor. He was simply the showman who was also a good Jew, and in 1585, drawing on his own funds, he did what many good Jews do: built a new synagogue for the expanding community. To all appearances, Jewish Mantua was thriving even if its citizens still had to endure the indignity of a yellow badge. A census of 1588 records the sheer diversity of its walks of life, always a sign of communal health: milliners and printers, porters and servants, goldsmiths and dyers, leather-goods vendors and actors, tavern keepers and doctors, sellers of silk and binders of books. A whole new district of Jews settled south of the ancient centre and prospered. It all seems a world away from the cramped ghettos where, officially at least, the Jews were restricted to moneylending and the rag trade.

But this first nursery of modern Jewish creativity, like many that would follow, was also a fool's paradise. Twenty years after Leone's death in 1592, in his mid-sixties, Duke Guglielmo's son Vincenzo, who had praised the showman to the skies and exempted him from wearing the yellow patch, and who employed the Jewish composer Salomone Rossi and his sister, the opera singer 'Madama Europa', imposed a ghetto on the Jews of Mantua.[10] The achievement of natural cultural harmony between Jews and their Gentile patrons had always been vulnerable to long-inherited prejudices and passions.

Beyond Mantua, in the second half of the sixteenth century, the obstacles to a shared culture had become grimly formidable. Paul IV's papal bull of July 1555, *Cum nimis absurdum*, proclaimed at the very outset of his pontificate, had begun by stating that the Jews had been condemned to 'perpetual servitude' on account of their collective guilt. Notwithstanding this, and exploiting the indulgence of Christians, they had had the temerity to dwell amongst them, even in the best parts of cities and in the vicinity of churches! Paul was tapping an ancient but, since the Black Death, intense paranoia about the bodily contamination of Jews. Indistinguishable from Christians, their women in particular would corrupt the bodies of youths and men, and – so it was alleged – spread syphilis, an especially foul Jewish plot. Hence the need to force them to wear the yellow hat (previously it had been red, and not all Jews had been required to wear it). Any kind of inter-course that might pollute Christians was now forbidden. So Jews were no longer allowed to sell food to Christians; nor to employ them as wet nurses (apparently mammary contamination could be a two-way process). Jewish doctors were forbidden to practise on Christian patients lest they introduce something sinister into their bodies, and nor could Jews employ Christians as house servants. Instead of accepting their subjection they had insolently attempted to dominate those same Christians, so now they needed, literally, putting in their place. Thus was born the ghetto of Rome, originally called the *serraglie*, and in almost every respect more brutal than its predecessor in Venice. About four thousand Roman Jews were summarily ordered to abandon houses and neighbourhoods in which they had lived for generations in Ripa and Trastevere. (The community of Roman Jews long predated Christianity.) They were herded into an area one mile square that would be choked with filthy mud every spring when the Tiber flooded. In a hideous anticipation of the ghettos of Nazi Europe, the Jews were ordered by the Pope to police their own confinement. Land and all other forms of fixed property were forbidden to them. Henceforth their only living was to be made from pawnbroking, moneylending and rag dealing. No Christian was ever to address them as any sort of social superior.

Needless to say the ferocity of those restrictions, beginning with the ban on Jewish doctors, proved difficult to enforce. When Paul IV died in 1559, his passing was greeted with rejoicing by Jews, hopeful that his successor would rescind the bull. Pius IV did in fact relax some of the harshest constraints, but the walled ghetto itself, with its gates closing at dusk, remained. And so did the spirit of the edict which was determined to impose the most dehumanising degradation on Jews, the better to persuade them that their lives would be transformed in every way once they had seen the error of their ways and accepted baptism.[11] The memory of twenty-five Marranos burned before a vast crowd in Ancona in 1556 for 'Judaising' became an instant and permanent history in the canon of Jewish martyrdom. The less fanatical Pius IV was followed by the militantly Judaeophobic Pius V, who in 1569 expelled the Jews from every city in the papal territories other than ghettoised Rome itself and terrorised Ancona.

Paul IV's adamant conviction that his papacy was inaugurating the long-awaited moment of mass Jewish conversion was inherited by virtually all the princes and popes during the following century, who committed themselves to making life as unbearable as possible the better to persuade the Jews of their error. A wave of expulsions ensued – in Habsburg Milan, the Republic of Genoa and Medici Florence.

There were places this new wave of refugees could go to. In Tuscany, Livorno became their new home of settlement and trade, and stayed that way right through to the Fascist years. Pitigliano, on its tufa outcrop in the Tuscan maremma, had an older Jewish settlement courtesy of the local mercenary *condottiere* rulers, but in the sixteenth century became likewise reinforced by incomers from the expulsions and persecutions. The exquisite synagogue built at that time now stands as yet another memorial to a population that endured through the centuries until war and genocide overtook it.

As the Inquisition had been operating in Venice since 1547, Mantua and Ferrara stood virtually alone as places where Jews and Gentiles could, if they chose, share the same physical space and culture. But in November 1570 Ferrara was struck by a terrifying earthquake that levelled half of the beautiful city. Aftershocks – about two thousand of them – continued for months. Duke Alfonso II asked Pope Pius V for help in rebuilding Ferrara but was told the calamity had been visited on him and his city because he had indulged the Jews. More would be in store unless he took the kind of measures against them that were in force in Rome and the Papal States. This Alfonso declined to do, rejecting as an absurdity any notion that the natural disaster was in any sense connected with Ferrara's Jews.

In Mantua, despite the flourishing of Leone's theatre, the Gonzaga dynasty was not such a reliable defender of the Jews against heavy conversionary pressure. Though Leone was left alone, and continued to produce play after play until his death, another Jew in the cultural circle of the Gonzaga court, Abramino Levi dall'Arpa – harpist and singer – was the target of a sustained and vicious conversion campaign.[12] 'Little Abraham' belonged to a multi-generational dynasty of musicians and singers, founded by his grandfather Abramo Levi dall'Arpa, who was the first to be favoured by the Gonzaga family. Leone may have had trouble persuading classicists that Moses was the first tragedian, but the cult of David as the composer of the Psalms and sovereign of the lyre and the harp was well established in Renaissance Italy. The Gonzaga court might have seen in the Levi virtuosi some sort of reincarnation of biblical musicians, but David, of the stock of Jesse, also figured as the ancestor of Christ. It was more proper then that latter-day psalmists and harpists should be Christians, not wretchedly obstinate Jews. Abramino seems to have been close enough to the hunchback Duke Guglielmo, or at any rate enough of a perennial fixture, to invite this conversionary pressure. Riding to one of the duke's al fresco banquets where he was to be part of the entertainment, Abramino was subjected to strenuous arguments from the duke's barber and archer and accompanying priest on the obtuseness of Judaism and the necessity of salvation through Christ's passion. Remaining non-committal Abramino was later taken into the organ loft of the church where the duke's infant grandson was being baptised, and treated to another Pauline harangue on why baptism had made circumcision redundant and pernicious. The campaign became so intense that at one point Abramino's uncle Samuel and the great Jewish sage of Mantua Judah Moscato, fearing the worst, rushed over to the harpist's house to stiffen his resolve. The strategies broadened. Believing that eating at a Christian table would mark an irreversible step to conversion, Abramino was plied with fare, all dutifully reported by the campaigners: 'ricotta salata, macaroni cheese, fruit pie ... pancakes all cooked at court .., this suggests an inclination to become a Christian'.[13] But aside from the kitchen and the tableware (for the most orthodox admittedly a problem) there was nothing in this menu at odds with the dietary laws of kashrut at all. So once again the conversioneers were disappointed. Exasperated, Guglielmo turned ugly, rounding up not just his harpist but the uncle Samuel and even Judah Moscato, and subjected them to the persuasion of the rack. Abramino continued to resist, but when he heard the excruciating moans of his elderly uncle coming from the neighbouring cell he finally surrendered and was baptised. All this took place in 1587, and by August Guglielmo was dying at his country estate at Goito. It was said that in his final hours he asked for Abramino, now called Bernardino (a name chosen by the duke), to play for him so that his chords would be the last thing he heard before expiring. As Bernardino he appears again in the archives of the new duke, Vincenzo, but also as 'Abramino Ebreo', his original name, in 1593 in a letter written by the duke's secretary. Once a Jew ...

Although Duke Vincenzo was handsomely Michelangelesque, unlike his hunchbacked father, what he did inherit was the Gonzaga strain of dangerous unpredictability. Initially Vincenzo was all benevolence towards the Jews, defying the papal – imperial campaign of mass conversion by specifying that no Jewish children could be baptised without the consent of at least one of their parents. No pressure seems to have been put on the composer-performer Salomone Rossi to abandon the faith to which, as much as Leone before him, he felt uncompromisingly committed. Indeed Salomone would go on to write music for both chapel and synagogue, his *Hashirim Asher Lishlomo* (the *Songs of Solomon*, a play on his own name as well as the biblical book) being the first polyphonic music composed for the Jewish liturgy – and, as we shall see, fiercely controversial for exactly that reason.[14]

But these were difficult times for the princelings of the smaller city states. Attempting to hold their own amid the mightier powers of the empire, the Gonzaga and the Este courts needed a different kind of Jewish genius. In Abraham Colorni, called by the priest and writer Tomaso Garzoni 'one of the most famous of all living Italians', they certainly got one. If Leone was prized as the master of one kind of enchantment, Colorni, about twenty years younger, was the conjurer of another kind of magic: the lethal kind.[15] He was not the first Italian Jew to become famous for his weapons. In the late fifteenth century Salomone da Sesso, who worked primarily for the Este family, was admired and envied as the great maker of ceremonial swords and daggers, many of them exquisitely engraved with mythological scenes. But da Sesso was an artist; Colorni was a technologist of death. He first appears in the early 1570s working for the Este court as inventor of all kinds of weaponry that even Leonardo had never dreamed of: an automatic arquebus capable of getting off ten shots before reloading; deceptive musical instruments that could be played in a military band before being converted at a trice into guns; collapsible bridges that could be thrown across rivers (nearly four centuries before the Bailey Bridge); an armed wheelchair for gouty or otherwise disabled commanders, and much much more. The Este family were sufficiently impressed with the prototype machine guns that they ordered two thousand of them, and there is some strong evidence that many were made, although no specimens seem to have survived.

For the little Italian courts, there was something even more potent than these startlingly innovative arms, and that was the wizard who had created them. Colorni's greatest invention was himself: magician, alchemist and, not least, prestidigitator, the artist of sleight of hand. The Jews of Italy were famous as designers and makers of playing cards – and this was the golden age of gambling. It was Abraham Colorni who invented card tricks that deceived the eye and astonished the mind. He became, then, the entertainer who was also a master of dark, inaccessible knowledge, the Kabbalist as gunsmith. And the fact that he remained unswervingly Jewish all his life only added to the Colorni-lore, as Jews had for centuries been thought to be the custodians of esoteric wisdom. One of the arcana which Colorni declared he had mastered was escapology, so that when the Poles captured the brother of the Holy Roman Emperor Rudolf II (himself a great enthusiast and practitioner of alchemy and the occult), Alfonso took great pride in dispatching Colorni to contrive the escape. Whether this would actually have put Colorni's powers on the spot will never be known, since the archduke was liberated in a peace settlement; but such was the emperor's admiration for the Jew that he kept him in Prague for the better part of a decade. There, amid a community strong in Kabbalah, Colorni worked on new methods for the extraction of saltpetre and the manufacture of gunpowder at exactly the time when the Christian empire was attempting to prevent central Europe from being engulfed by the formidably armed Turks. To Rudolf's delight Colorni could do macro and micro, and came up with hitherto unimagined systems of ciphers and cryptography, some of which he published in his manual of the art of secret writing, *Scotographia*. To his admirers he was more than the contriver of mechanical and intellectual wonders: he was somehow a Jewish magus, a role Colorni was more than happy to exploit with a second book called *Solomon's Key*, in knowing reference to the ancient obsession with the secret Masonic knowledge said to have built the First Temple. Even the most rational minds bought into this wizardry – if, that is, we call Napoleon Bonaparte rational, for among his library on St Helena was the French translation of the work of the magical Jew.

Perhaps in his oceanic fastness, Napoleon was hoping to learn something about the art of escape. Colorni was loaned – it was said for a few days – by Rudolf to another devotee of the mysteries, Duke Frederick of Württemberg at Stuttgart. But just as Rudolf had stopped his house wizard from returning to Ferrara or Mantua, Frederick kept Colorni. Sulking, the conjurer went on a magic strike and was imprisoned for his insolent failure to generate marvels on demand. The cell was in Frederick's most impregnable fortress. Flatteringly to the great Colorni, guards were posted at every conceivable place of egress. And of course, as if made of vapour, Colorni vanished. Once the Württembergers had got over their astonished admiration, a hue and cry was sounded. Frederick, who was not amused by this demonstration of Colorni's escapology, dispatched men to the ends of Europe to track him down, but Colorni was already back in the city of his birth, amid the Jews of musical Mantua. For some years he had been signalling his wish to return by sending Duke Vincenzo all sorts of gadgetry and inventions, including musical instruments that could be played in the court concerts where his co-religionists Salomone Rossi and Madama Europa were so admired. He died in Mantua in 1597 of a fever, always a residential hazard in a city surrounded by lakes and marshes.

Three years later, another Jew became famous for magic in Mantua, but this time the reputation was entirely tragic. On 22 April 1600, a Sabbath morning when good Jews were going to Leone de Sommi's synagogue, the seventy-seven-year-old Judith Franchetta was burned alive as a witch. She had been accused of casting spells on a formerly Jewish nun of the order of St Vincent in an attempt to have her revert to Judaism. Thousands came to see the burning of the Jewish witch including Duke Vincenzo himself and his second wife Eleanora de Medici, accompanied by an Austrian archduchess. This too was Jewish entertainment.

Children found themselves places on the balustrades, the crowd in the square so packed that one could not turn one's head: about ten to twelve thousand. Judith the Jewess had her limbs bound by ropes to a wooden stake ... this was set alight by three Jews who came to comfort her. Two of them hurried away [as the flames spread] but the third who was old was so engrossed in his task that he almost stayed with her in the flames and would have died had not others pulled him down and away tugging at the lower parts of his body. The ropes holding her hands burned through and she held up her right hand to try and protect her face while she was still alive. But this availed her little for she swiftly fell into the fire and so expired.[16]

Two years later, in 1602, in liberal Mantua, seven Jews accused on a trumped-up charge of 'mockery' at the expense of Christianity were tortured and hanged and the flesh of their corpses shredded as they were dragged over the cobbles by horses. Ten years after that, Mantua became the latest Italian city to herd its yellow-badge-wearing Jews into a ghetto.

4

THE TIME OF THE
NIGHTINGALE

There was a time when Jewish catering opened doors. Every Friday afternoon, following Muslim prayers but before the Jewish Sabbath, a caravan of confections from the villa of the Great Jew in Pera was delivered to Topkapi Palace.[1] Seated upon silk cushions, the yellow-haired sultan, Selim II, awaited with keen anticipation the delicacies brought to him on Chinese porcelain: pigeon dainties baked in rose water and sugar; goose livers chopped with Corinth raisins and the spices which were, after all, the Jew's to command; also some items preserved in the kitchen of culinary nostalgia, from the ancient Turkic days of tents and flocks and racing ponies; the sour yogurts and *yufka*, the unleavened bread that was wrapped around a pilaf. In the new style there was an array of *zeytinyagli* dishes, named for the olive oil (another Jewish import trade) in which they were cooked and served cold – a corrective, the physicians said, to the black bile that would come on in the humid summers.

It was no light matter to take food from a Jew. The palace, and for that matter the whole Ottoman Empire, was built around catering. The first obligation of a sultan was the state feeding of the people, beginning with his palace servants (five thousand of them in the mid-sixteenth century), the army and, in times of difficulty, the common people. Public soup kitchens were a standard institution of Ottoman cities, so much so that one of the signs of Jewish philanthropy became the establishment and funding of similar kitchens for their own communities. The kitchens of Topkapi Palace were built to cope with great feasts, especially on dynastic occasions like circumcisions, but every time an ambassador was received he was treated to a banquet often laid out beneath the colonnaded gateways separating the courtyards. From the decks of boats and ships on the Golden Horn or the Bosphorus, the skyline silhouette of Topkapi was dominated by the ten domed buildings and chimneys of the royal kitchens, as prominent as the palace mosques and almost as sacred, for they symbolised the tender care the sultan had for the sustenance of his subjects.[2] The *khans* – the vast storehouses surrounding the Grand Bazaar, packed with wheat and rice – were vigilantly policed and regulated, as were the prices at which the grain could be sold. Within the palace, the sultan's cooks, more than a thousand of them, were organised like an army. But then the army, or at least the elite Yeniceri Christian-born slave soldiers, was organised around the provision of food. Hunger could be quite as deadly as musket shot. The relationship between sword and stomach was recognised in the names of ranks. Regimental colonels were called *corbaci*, 'the soup-servers', and wore spoons as a point of honour, tucked into their toque-like high headgear, woven by Jewish artisans in Salonika. Junior officers were *ousta* – cooks – and cadet recruits were assigned the honoured tasks of providing cooking fuel and doing the washing-up. Sensibly, the most prized possession of each *orta*, or battalion, was not its trench gun or cannon but the great cauldron: benevolent provider of soup and rice. The first sign of Janissary disaffection (which occurred at regular intervals) would be turning their noses up at the sultan's food. When grievances spilled over into outright rebellion, the insurrection was known as 'overturning the cauldron'.

Allegiance of the wider realm turned on the state of the public stomach. But inside the immense palace establishment – a city state in itself – loyalties also came and went as they were fed. The food-state at Topkapi was a masterwork of division of labour: separate kitchens for the palace pages, the five thousand other servants, and a single great kitchen, the *kusane*, for the sultan alone. Each were commanded by a chief cook, the *agha* (the same name for a military commander), often a eunuch who supervised the many departments: ice and snow keepers for the sherbets, poultry men, yogurters, copperers, confectioners, grill-men, bakers who specialised in the sesame-studded ring breads called *semit*, picklers, and preservers of *bastourma* (dried meat).

There were, then, a multitude of people for the Great Jew to offend with his movable feasts. But Selim II was indifferent to the rumours and threats. The sultan's plumpness was itself a form of propaganda, for it was fitting that the ruler should display his fleshly prosperity to the world. It was a more serious matter, however, to be known in the Grand Bazaar as 'Selim the Sot', for the implication was that the true gift of the Jew was the wine delivered along with the food, and that the sultan's weakness for malmsey, muscat and malvasia, the green wine of Gallipoli and Aegean red '*tipico*' vinified in the Spanish style, or the honeyed vino de Candia from Crete, had made him captive to Joseph the Jew. That the Quran forbade imbibing no one could dispute. Equally, no one could pretend that the wine poetry of the bibbing writers had not been one of the splendours of Arabic and Persian literature. Each sultan had taken a different view of policing abstention from alcohol. Selim's father Suleyman had been uncompromisingly severe, forbidding not just the wine but even the trade that served Unbelievers. Whole rows of wine shops in Galata – the colony largely inhabited by foreigners like the Genoese, on the north shore of the Golden Horn, constructed as an Italian home away from home with piazzas and campaniles – had been ruined by the decree. The more permissive Selim had restored the wine trade for non-Muslims, and for a steep asking price had given the Great Jew the *muqata'as*, the franchise of its monopoly. Don Joseph also farmed the customs revenues even as he exported Mediterranean wine to Moldavia and Poland, where the nobility could not get enough of it.

This Great Jew had once been the beardless twelve-year-old João Micas on the Bristol-bound caravel in 1537 with his aunts, Beatriz and Brianda de Luna. Now he was Duke of Naxos, master of an Aegean empire of castles and islands – lord of Milos, Paxos, Paros, Antiparos, Andros, Santorini (which itself produced potent wines from its volcanic soil) – and was known among his own people as Don Joseph Nasi, the prince. He had had the ear of Suleyman's grand vizier Rüstem Pasha, and now, attired in sable-trimmed silk, accompanied by his two mounted guards he could proceed through the outer gate of Bab-I-Ali, dismount and walk, without his arms being secured by gatekeepers, over pavements inlaid with gems past the stables and the royal bakery, between flanking columns of immobile statuesque turbaned cavalry astride caparisoned horses, into the Council Hall. There he would come before a rippling sea of gold cloth; young slave pages, their heads shaved save for a 'squirrel tail' lock hanging down their neck; a hundred deaf mutes who stood with hawks on their gloved wrists; another hundred burly dwarves sporting scimitars as big as themselves. The golden sea was utterly silent, a flat calm with the only movement that of light glittering on the costumes. If there was anything to be said it was done by sign language – *ixarette*, the second language of the court. An actual word, even whispered, would be met by a sharp rebuke from a ceremonial baton. The sultan himself would likewise attempt to resemble a living statue, occasionally making a motion with his soft plump hand or toying with a diamond the size of a quail's egg, which nested on his middle finger.

It was on days of audience (four times a week) that the Great Jew got to give actual advice, either through the grand vizier or directly to the sultan in the Chamber of Petitions (more gold, on the ceilings, the walls and the throne) within the third Inner Court of the palace. There he could venture opinions on war and diplomacy; the man-oeuvres of the Catholic kings; the tactics of the Venetians; the prospects of the rebels in Flanders; the health of revenues and the condition of the mint.

Back at what he styled 'our palace of the Belvedere', Don Joseph would closet himself in his *studiolo*, the equal of any Venetian patrician, or wander into the study reserved for scribes and illuminators working on Hebrew manuscripts. Slippered servants and slaves, their baggy pants catching breezes from the Golden Horn, followed him as he walked through the pleasure gardens. From the balustraded terrace he would observe his *cayiq* boats, on their way to inspect ships' cargoes at the entry to the Bosphorus. In his name as well as that of the sultan, they would search the holds, scrutinise inventories, receive fees, and add charges should they be warranted. This was not a way of acquiring popularity, either for the Great Jew or the sultan who favoured him; but Selim was unconcerned by the buzzing of the bazaar. He remained convinced that in the lethal succession struggle with his brother Bayezid, he would not have prevailed without the heavily funded friendship of Joseph Nasi. The Jew was a man who could be depended on to keep the cauldrons warm and full. So the weekly deliveries from the Jew's villa pandered simultaneously to Selim's appetite and his fear. The food could be counted on to be free from the poisons his many enemies might have smuggled into the kitchens. And should that misfortune overtake him there was always the other Jew, Moses Hamon, his physician, said to have the most comprehensive cabinet of antidotes in the empire.

Hamon was, in his own right, a marvel: rabbinical scholar, patron of learning, publisher of Hebrew and Ladino texts, and owner of one of the great libraries of the Levant, as well as master physician. Born in Granada, he had been two years old when that last enclave of Muslim sovereignty in Spain had fallen to the Castilian 'crusade' in 1492. But Moses had grown up fluent in Arabic as well as Castilian, Ladino and Persian. Since the reign of Mehmed II, the Conqueror of Constantinople, and possibly even earlier, there had been an Ottoman tradition of Jews as physicians to the sultans, because unlike Muslims who might be in the pay of the disaffected, or Christians who would have much to revenge, they were believed to be safe as well as wise. The first of the Jewish physicians to the Ottomans had been Giacopo of Gaeta, who had become Hekim Yakub Pasha. But the Hamons had stayed loyal to their religion. Moses' father Yosef Hamon had been one of the first Jewish notables to arrive in Constantinople from Spain in 1493 and had served Bayezid II, Selim I and Suleyman. They tended to their aches and pains, the seasonal fluxes of their appetites and desires, and rode with the sultans on campaigns to act as surgeon should the need arise. For the royal doctors the formal Muslim ban on Jews riding horses was waived. By the time of Suleyman there were forty-one Jewish doctors in Topkapi, as against twenty-one Muslims – so many that a special guild had to be founded to organise them.[3] With direct personal access to the sultan, Yosef Hamon became an unofficial representative of the Sephardim in Constantinople while Moses felt entitled to direct Suleyman's attention to miscarriages of justice affecting Jews. There were always acts of petty extortion by local officials, and occasionally monstrous libels, imported from Christendom, would bubble up accusing Jews of murdering small children for the blood allegedly needed to bake Passover matzot.[4]

It had been on Moses Hamon's initiative that feelers had first been put out to make the biggest Marrano catch of all: bringing the House of Mendes to Turkey. The doctor was himself related to Francisco Mendes and had been treated as part of the grandly extended family. A *caus* or special imperial representative had been sent to Venice, briefed by Hamon, to see how this might be accomplished with the least risk. Discretion was essential since the woman who would be known in Constantinople as 'La Senyora', Doña Gracia Benveniste, was then still Beatriz Mendes or Beatriz de Luna, pretending to lead a virtuous Catholic life. Even when Brianda, in her fit of pique, told the Venetian government that her Judaising sister had intended all along to move to Turkey, Gracia managed a great show of indignation. Nonetheless, in the spring of 1553, she arrived in the sultan's city. Andres Laguna, a Spanish prisoner of the Turks, reported that 'a Portuguese lady calling herself Doña Beatriz Mendes, very rich, entered Constantinople with forty horsemen and four triumphal chariots, filled with ladies and serving women. The household she had brought with her was nothing short of that befitting a duke of Spain ... Respects were paid to her at court. While she was still living in Venice she had already arranged with the Grand Turk that she required no special privileges except that her household might wear Venetian dress with stomachers and coifs. This she obtained and would certainly have got more had she asked for it.'[5] The troop of horsemen which so astonished Laguna had been needed since Gracia had taken the overland route from Ragusa, a vassal state of the Turks, and the land between was a paradise for brigands. But there is also no doubt that Doña Gracia wanted to make a spectacular public *grande entrée* into the city as if she were indeed some sort of queen. Another witness easily galled at the presumption of the Jews, Hans Dernschwam, the agent of the Augsburg bankers the Fuggers, described her as 'an old lady' (she was just forty-three) living 'in extravagance, with many servants, two of them from the Netherlands'.[6] Gracia had indeed brought two of the women whose mistress she had been two decades before in Antwerp.

Moses Hamon had hoped that a reward for the careful management of this last move of Doña Gracia and her family would be the marriage of his son (Yosef, a doctor, of course) to her daughter Reyna, the richest heiress in Constantinople. But as ever, the Mendes-Benvenistes were concerned to consolidate, not divide their fortune, which meant there could be only one ideal husband for Reyna and that was Joseph Nasi himself. The fact that he had also once married the bride's cousin, Brianda's daughter Gracia La Chica, in the runaway to Ravenna was no impediment to the match, for that escapade had been a Christian ceremony and thus of no valid standing in Jewish law. The party at the palatial villa was a great event in the life of the city, sumptuous enough to win admiration from the French ambassador who made sure he was there.

Only the very grandest and richest of Jews lived in Galata, dressing and conducting themselves more as Italians than Turks. The majority of the 50,000 lived in crowded districts on each side of the Golden Horn; some in Hasköy, also on the northern side but altogether less fashionable than the villas of Galata; far more in the busy streets of Eminönü, Sirkeci, Tahtakale and Mahmud Pasha on the south-western side. There they resided in modest wooden firetraps never free of kitchen smells or animals. In Constantinople there were a few court-yard blocks of the kind expressly built for the textile artisans of Salonika and Sarajevo: multi-storey tenements which quickly decayed. But more often the simplest Jewish dwellings were single- or two-room affairs: one for work, the other for everything else. Jewish Constantinople was a world of artisans – tinsmiths and copper-beaters, dyers and tanners, pearl-stringers and printers, bakers, sword-cutlers, gunsmiths, razor and mirror makers, enamellists and tailors. But there were also Jews who roughed it further afield: fishermen, sheep and cattle drovers bringing in animals and raw wool from the Balkans and Anatolian angora named for Ankara; and humble home bases for the pedlars in soap, knives and buttons. Above them was a substantial class of whole-salers, retailers and merchants trading as they had throughout the Muslim world in an extraordinary range of commodities. There were goldsmiths, gold refiners and assayers, jewellers in precious and semi-precious gems, rug merchants, traders in the soft mohair fabric known as *suf*, and the woven or silky wool known as *atlas*. In the Grand Bazaar they laid out satins and silks, necklaces and armlets. In other parts of the bazaar and outside it, alongside Muslim shop owners Jews sold cheese and spices, salt herring and medicinal herbs.

But they were a community divided by language, custom and historical memory. Some thousands, speaking Yevanic Greek as their daily tongue, were the descendants of Jews who had lived in Byzantine Constantinople, often in those same districts. By conspicuously with-holding support from the Byzantine governor during the Ottoman siege and conquest in 1453 (or at least perceived as being neutral if not pro-Turkish) they had avoided the fate of being treated as captive slaves. The most influential account of Jewish response to the fall of Constantinople was the Cretan Rabbi Elia Capsali's history of the Ottomans, written in Candia, still a Venetian possession in 1523.[7] Capsali is a beautiful writer but at the dawn of Jewish historiography it was natural for him to make his story a second coming of the Books of Nehemiah and Ezra. Thus Mehmed becomes a new Cyrus, who is chosen by God to be the instrument of His punishment on the brutal and oppressive Greeks. The Ottoman lord, on the other hand, 'invites' the Jews of conquered Byzantium – in the Balkans and islands – to come to his new capital and prosper there, 'every man under his vine and fig tree'. Jews had no choice in the matter. Instead of a benevolent invitation they were summarily uprooted in their hundreds and thousands and forcibly resettled in Constantinople.[8] Often they had to meet deadlines for their removal after which they could be punished by death. This *surgun*, as it was called, was routine practice in the Ottoman Empire and in the long run the outcome was to create a thriving, richly heterogeneous community in Constantinople. But that doesn't mean it was not deeply unsettling if not actually traumatic at the time. Capsali writes the story as if it were the exact obverse of the Iberian expulsions, but if you were a Salonika Jew ordered to move to Rhodes after its conquest in 1523, or a Hungarian Jew in Buda in 1526 taken off as 'useful colonists' in Turkish boats and planted God knows where, you would have been hard put to tell the difference. Under one sultan (though only one), Bayezid II, to whom Capsali attributes an 'invitation' to the Iberians, it was not clear what kind of a welcome Jews would get. Bayezid reimposed the old Islamic ban on the repair of damaged synagogues or the construction of new ones, along with many other of the more repressive conditions imposed on Jews such as clear identification through dress.

Under his successors, Selim I and Suleyman the Magnificent, those restrictions were again relaxed, though under Ottoman law the *surgun* immigrants to the city did not have free movement should they wish to live elsewhere. But the Romaniot Jews – from their many places of origin: Anatolia, Wallachia, Albania, Thrace, the islands – built their synagogues and the institutions of their respective communities. The custom of autonomous self-government for all these separate communities meant that, as they settled in, the Judaeo-Greek speakers largely kept their own company, their own synagogues, were subject only to their own Jewish courts, cooked after their own fashion and sang their own music. Often, too, they disagreed on crucial matters of family law and custom; whether or not for example a betrothed couple should be allowed, even expected to have sex, and live together *before* the wedding feast, the canopy ceremony and the reading of the nuptial contract. A majority of rabbis in the Romaniot community deemed the *kiddushin*, the betrothal, the constitutive act of the marriage. Once wedding gifts or *sivlonot* had been formally presented, the couple were free to couple. Inevitably problems arose when the fiancée had been deserted (possibly pregnant) by her intended, and when those partners were from different communities of custom, sparks flew.[9]

Those differences within the Romaniot community took on a different order of seriousness when something like 50,000–60,000 Sephardim arrived in two waves – the first after 1492, and the second, the result of the Portuguese escape network through Italy, after 1530.[10] This was a population speaking Portuguese or Ladino, and, in the case of those who had spent a generation or two in the havens of Ferrara, Venice and Mantua, Italian as well. Though the Greek communities had been well aware of the cultural splendour of Spanish Jewry and respected its learning, at close quarters they felt somewhat differently. To many of the Greek speakers, the Sephardim gave themselves intolerable airs of cultural superiority only reinforced by the new access they had to the Ottoman court and their legal treatment as *kendi gelen* – those who had come of their free will. For a generation or two they even dressed differently, affecting the Spanish *caperone* woollen topcoat and refusing the yellow hat officially required of Jews.[11] Like the Romaniots, the various Sephardim kept alive the particular character of their places of origin so that there were Cordoba synagogues, Granada synagogues, Toledo synagogues, Catalan and Provençals, and each of them subdivided yet again into once-and-for-all-time Jews and the incoming Marranos.

Precisely because of its expansive hospitality to so many kinds of Jews, the Ottoman Empire thus became one of the places where the age-old question of Jewish identity became most intensely tested and debated. For centuries, Karaites, who repudiated all post-biblical authority which they said had been usurped from the Torah by rabbis and Talmudic sages, had insisted they were the only true Jews, the followers of the Law of Moses. In return they had been marginalised by everyone else as fraudulent or heretical Jews. But in Egypt, Mesopotamia and North Africa, their numbers and influence were still strong. Added now to the Karaite–rabbinic schism was the pressing argument about the standing of Marranos who had lived for generations within the Church. What was the validity of their marriages? Was circumcision mandatory? Responsa judgements from various rabbis flew as usual in several directions, different Jews regarding as final the judgements that corresponded to their own prejudices. There were noble and significant attempts to bring some degree of unity to all these divisions. In 1547, a polyglot Pentateuch, with columns in Judaeo-Greek, Ladino and Hebrew, was published in Constantinople by Eliezer ben Gershom Soncino. It was his family which had pioneered printed Hebrew texts, and from their original base in the Lombard town of Soncino had transported their movable type to Fano, Brescia and Salonika, ending up in Constantinople, publishing in each of the stops on the way. As well as books of the Talmud and Bible, there were Soncino editions of Petrarch and the favourite reading of Charles V, the chivalric-Gothic romance of *Amadis of Gaul*. For a while, beginning in 1504, Jewish presses were the only ones operating in the Ottoman lands for they had been permitted on condition there would be no dangerous editions in Arabic. And it was to the presses that those rabbis turned when they wanted to bring the Babel of Jews together in a core of common practice. This at any rate was the ambition of Joseph Karo, who had been born in Portugal and ended up in Salonika. He managed the impossible by distilling down his enormous compilation of law and observance, the *Bet Yosef*, into the digest of Jewish laws he called *Shulkhan Arukh*. It was intended to create an uncontentious conformity over many differing traditions and practices, and to a remarkable extent it succeeded. To this day (or at any rate to mine in the 1950s) Jewish children are summoned to sit at that table and chew on its offerings.

These rabbinical gestures of harmony were all well and good but they had to contend with the stories that Romaniot and Sephardi Jews told about their respective pasts, and those had a quite different colour to them. Even though the Greek speakers had been forcibly uprooted, they had stayed within their old world of the Levant where they had lived for centuries. And like Capsali they were capable after a generation or two of seeing their transplantations and passages as historically benign. They were all about continuity. The Sephardim, who through the whole of the sixteenth century were numerically the minority, had the poets' and historians' hand which set down the Jewish story as *gerush*: a cycle of exiles and uprootings of which the Roman dispersion was merely the first, and the Iberian expulsions merely the most recently traumatic. The first Sephardi synagogue built in the Ottoman Empire, in the town of Bursa, was called the Gerush.[12] If Jewish history had a noble and transcendent meaning then it must be about *gerush*: disruption and wandering. Even the two Jewish vernaculars operated in contrasting ways. Romaniot Greek was the language of continuity; Ladino – a Spanish tongue spoken and written in Turkey! – was by definition the language of yearning for a lost home. They were, as Yosef Yerushalmi put it, living an exile within an exile.[13]

There were moments when this divided sensibility could do actual damage. Not long after she had reached Constantinople Doña Gracia learned of the effect of Paul IV's bull *Cum nimis absurdum* on the New Christians of Ancona, most of whom had taken advantage of the free-port status trading with the Levant to follow the example of their brethren there and revert to Judaism. But the ferocity of the papal edict now put those Ancona Jews into the hands of the Inquisition as lapsed heretics. One of the Marrano victims of the auto-da-fé had been the agent of the Mendes-Benvenistes in Ancona, Yacobo Mosso. Horrified and indignant, Doña Gracia launched the first campaign of organised counter-attack in Jewish history since the rebellions against Rome. But La Senyora's methods were, as befitted her long history managing men and money, economic. Acting with astonishing confidence as a self-appointed authority, she proposed a total boycott of the port of Ancona, knowing full well that its existence as a trading entrepôt depended on business with the east. Having established this plan of attack, she then demanded of the rabbis in Constantinople (summoning many of them to the villa for a talking-to), Salonika, Adrianople (now Edirne) and all centres of Jewish life within the Ottoman world that they read out its terms in synagogues and order their congregations to heed the ban. Merchants were not being asked to abandon their enterprises but rather divert them to Pesaro, further down the coast but outside the jurisdiction of the papal authorities.

Taken aback by this imperial fiat from La Senyora, the majority of rabbis nevertheless did what they were told but not all of them liked it. The Romaniot–Greek community in particular felt that the battle taken up by Doña Gracia was a Sephardi fight. In private, they often had serious reservations about the sometime New Christians. There was muttering at the high-handedness which boded ill for the campaign to punish Ancona, since it would succeed only if watertight. For two years, Doña Gracia managed this. Wharves and warehouses at Ancona emptied; its trading economy evaporated. Suleyman himself, prompted by Moses Hamon and Doña Gracia, sent a letter to the Pope, implying the dire consequences should personal immunities and property not be restored to the 'Levantines'. Were the Pope to see his way to doing this, the sultan promised, then Christian merchants trading in his realms would in turn receive the most generous treatment. If not, it was suggested, then not. Major opponents of the ban within the Jewish community – who themselves felt victimised by the campaign and who had tired already of being told their compliance was a duty to the memory of the martyred Marranos – began to recruit powerful spokesmen, including Rabbi Joshua Soncino. By 1558 the campaign was being sabotaged at both ends and finally collapsed.

It was a bitter pill for La Senyora to swallow. There were limits to her undefined authority after all. Like many self-appointed Jewish philanthropic grandees before and after, she almost certainly felt badly used. When funds are needed to ransom captives of pirates they come to me, she complained. When they need money for hospitals, for a yeshiva, for a new edition of the Talmud, they come to me. When I need them, what do I get? At the same time she was building synagogues in Constantinople, Salonika and Smyrna (now Izmir). For those she laid down an absolute condition that all Jews would be welcomed within, irrespective of language, background and liturgical customs. One of those synagogues associated with La Senyora, damaged many times by fires, earthquakes and brutal wars, can still be found in a narrow street behind the Izmir fish market. A low door opens onto a perfectly beautiful garden courtyard planted with fig and lemon trees. The interior, gracefully restored, principally by American funds, is a song of cream, blue and gold, vaulting Moorish arches and cushioned seating set around the perimeter in the Sephardi style. But it is the women's gallery, painted with delicate pastorals – deer leaping over low hills, the statutory birds a-flutter and a-twitter – which bear the stamp of its patroness, or at least an acknowledgement of her generosity. In Istanbul in the old Jewish quarter of Balat there is another synagogue, the Ahira, which has also survived the trials of time and history. Though the present structure is eighteenth century, its reading dais, known in Sephardi communities as the *tevah*, is claimed as much older, a survivor from the time of the nightingales. Fashioned in the form of a collective memory, the *tevah* is shaped like the rounded stern of a caravel, or perhaps Noah's ark (*tevah* also means ark). The lectern itself is set high, as if the reader of the Torah were a helmsman (which in many ways of course he was), sails filled with billowing hope.

Her body would end its days in Constantinople, but there was yet another journey preoccupying Doña Gracia's mind. In 1553, as she and her daughter were making their way to Turkey, the bones of her long-dead husband, Francisco Mendes, removed from their Christian tomb in Lisbon and brought to Venice, were being sent to Jerusalem for reinterment. This too had been one of her elaborate deceptions. Gracia had received permission from the Portuguese Church on the grounds that she wished to pay devotional respects to his remains in Venice. But the true destination was the Mount of Olives.

Palestine had been conquered from the Mamluks in 1516, exciting expectations of redemption and return among the Jewish communities in the Ottoman Empire. Eulogising Selim I, who had delivered Palestine, Elia Capsali had told Jews that 'we are living in the time of nightingale song and the voice of the turtle dove will be heard in the Land of Israel'.[14] But it was when Suleyman undertook the rebuilding of Jerusalem's walls in the 1530s that the greatest of the sultans seemed to shine as a second Cyrus for the Jews: restorer and redeemer. There were new Nehemiahs involved in this transformation, too, no longer cup-bearers to the king but mint-masters to the sultan. Confusingly there were not one but two Jews called Abraham Castro, one based in Damascus and Tripoli, the other in Cairo and Alexandria, both of whom were crucial to supplying revenue credits for the rebuilding of the walls and the tiling of the Dome of the Rock, and who were both in Jerusalem (where one of them had property) to oversee the project to completion.[15] What the Castros and Suleyman's chief builder in Jerusalem, Mehmed Calebi al-Naqqash, created between 1535 and 1538 is the 'Old City' we know today: the glowing girdle of limestone walls; the seven gates (some of which began in biblical and classical times); the thirty-odd towers and firing slits; the two great mosques seated on their platforms; the tiles for the facade of the Dome of the Rock supplied and applied at this time, and the western enclosing wall of Herod's Temple preserved.[16] At that moment around 10 per cent of Jerusalem's population – perhaps 1,600 souls – was Jewish, many of them artisans, and the possibility of a new Jewish age dawning in the city attracted many more. But the central significance of Jerusalem to Islam created obstacles for any sustained kind of renaissance there. The Muslim religious authorities were suspicious, and the Beduin population scattered through the Judaean hills was acutely suspicious. There were always rumours that Jewish adventurers, carriers of the sultan's money bags, might seek to usurp the city and desecrate the holy places.[17]

There was, however, another place in Palestine which radiated almost as intense a mystique of Jewish redemption as Jerusalem itself but without quite the same level of risk, and that was Galilee. It was, after all, the crucible of rabbinical Judaism following the destruction of the Second Temple. The editing of the Mishnah had begun in Sepphoris, and the court known as the Sanhedrin had relocated to Tiberias, both in the second century CE. The hills and the lake were imbued in the poetic imagination of Judaism as the site of rebirth, palms growing by the waterside. In the early sixteenth century there was virtually nothing left of Tiberias save ruins, rubble and the remains of an ancient synagogue, albeit with spectacular carvings of both five- and six-pointed stars on the masonry. It was to Safed, twenty-five miles north-west, up in the hills, that a generation of Kabbalist teachers took themselves in the 1540s, hoping for a greater degree of protection against Beduin violence, now that Ottoman authority was asserting itself again in both Jerusalem and Damascus.

In a very few years, Safed's streets and houses, tumbling over the pretty hills, became populated by ardent young Kabbalists wanting nothing to do with the longer-settled Arabic-speaking Musta'arabi Jews, but instead attaching themselves to the new sages like Moses Cordovero, the prolific author of *The Palm of Deborah* and *The Pomegranate Orchard*. Both books were edited anthologies of the classic

Kabbalist treatises together with new guides to the meditative steps needed to make the ascent to illumination. As usual a spurious tomb was made the focus of the cult, this one a few miles away from the centre of Safed at Meron, said to be the resting place of Shimon bar Yochai, imagined as the founding Kabbalist in the second century CE. The *Sefer Yetzirah*, the Book of Creation, could indeed have been composed in the second or third century but the great, systematic texts of Kabbalah – the *Bahir* and the *Zohar* – had been put together by Moses of Leon and others in the later thirteenth century. But there is no doubt at all that they continued to exert an extraordinary spell over generation after generation of Jews for whom the scholastic interrogation of Talmudic law and the interpretation of the overt text of the Bible would never be enough.

If you were young (or even old) in the Mediterranean world in the nightingale time of expectation, how could you not immerse yourself in the ten *sefirot*, the ten emanations, each with their numerical attributes, through which the infinite Ein Sof is revealed and from which both the heavenly and earthly universes were constituted? At the summit, Keter (the Crown), the ineffable, interminable and unformable presence, beyond conscious apprehension. Then, Hokhma, wisdom; Hesed, loving kindness; Gevurah, forceful power; Tiferet, beauty; Netzah, victory; Hod, splendour; Yesod, foundation; and the two female presences, Binah, the generative womb of understanding, and Shekhina, the divine radiance. When merely enumerated in a history like this they seem no more than the usual mystical vapours which are always the outriders of institutionalised theologies and laws; but that is to sell Kabbalistic cosmology, or at least its perennial appeal, short. It was, after all, wrestling with the same questions that had taxed the perfervid community of the *yachad* at Qumran – how is the origin of the universe and the persistence of disorderly evil explained? The development of a numerology that might be manipulated or endlessly reformulated has not altogether disappeared from modern philosophical and scientific engagement with the origins of the universe.

Isaac Luria, who had been born in Jerusalem and had spent years pondering such matters with the help of the *Bahir* and the *Zohar* on an island in the Nile, ended up in Safed in 1569, sitting at the feet of Moses Cordovero and eventually replacing him as the fount of a new metaphysical knowledge. According to reports by his pupil Hayim Vital (the master himself being averse to setting them down), Luria took the older idea of *tzimtzum*, the post-creation withdrawal of the Ein Sof (the Without End), into a zone of ever more contracting space: an entropic black hole, a primal void, into which all light and matter collapsed. And from that not-space, creative force could be generated. That process itself, however, was not a gradual evolution but a series of explosive eruptions of light and vapour, shafts which could splinter and shatter. Only through a slow process of *tiqqun* or repair (which we might translate as cooling) could earthly matter become constituted.

Does all this make the Kabbalists of Safed Big Bangers, uncanny anticipators of modern astrophysics? No, but it certainly makes them more than simply deluded mystics, hyperventilating beneath the Galilean stars until the heavenly chariot appeared. Though historians debate the impulse given to the new Kabbalism by the traumatic expulsions from Spain and Portgual, and the persecutions of the Inquisition, Luria's genius was to make *tzimtzum* into a godly exile or estrangement; to be repaired by some sort of *tshuva*, a return, a reconstitution of the world. Psychologically the move turned the dispersion of the Jews from a punishment to a wandering that was being experienced sympathetically by God Himself. First the enveloping void; then the burst of radiance.

On a less dizzying level, the thousand or so Kabbalists turned themselves into a true community: exchanging new ways of intensifying meditation so they might catch the celestial chariot, the *merkabah*, into the empyrean realms relating dreams for interpretation.[18] In the spirit of the patriarch Joseph, Cordovero and especially Luria were famous explainers of dreams and visions. Multiple generations seemed to commune together in the thin air of the hilltops. From more than a millennium before, Shimon bar Yochai and his brethren rabbis, Rabbi Hiyya and Rabbi Jose, would materialise, encountering wizened donkey drivers who seemed to be asking gnomic questions – 'Who is a serpent flying in the air with an ant in its teeth?', or 'Who is the ravishing maiden, eyeless, her body concealed and revealed?' Answer: the Torah of course, only to be revealed glimpse by glimpse to her devoted lover. Sacred erotics in the tradition of the Song of Songs and medieval Hebrew poetry appear over and again. The unattainably glorious virgin appears immured in a doorless tower challenging all comers to find a way in. They fail, with the exception of a poor young man who discovers the merest crack or chink, enough at any rate to behold the maiden for forty days and nights. Moved by his devotion, the girl opens everything to him, as would the Torah and the mysteries of the *sefirot* to those most dedicated to unlocking them.

A wall was built to guard the little town against the robber gangs who smelled an opportunity, and watchmen hired to mount patrols. (Occasionally those same watchmen colluded with the thieves to extort or rob the Kabbalists.) Synagogues, no less than thirty-two of them, a Turkish official reported, were built, many painted cerulean blue in the interior – the favoured colour of ascending Kabbalah – and the intensity of meditative prayer became reinforced by the euphoria of sacred song. Cordovero inaugurated the lovely practice of walking in the hilltop meadows before the Friday-evening service to greet the oncoming Sabbath, and it was for that little rustic ceremony that Solomon ben Moses Alkabetz composed 'Lekha Dodi' ('Come my Beloved'), greeting the Sabbath like a lover or bride. It remains one of the very few Jewish hymns in the liturgy to sound the same anywhere in the world.

But Safed was not just a place for idle dreaming. It supported itself from a burgeoning textile industry importing raw Balkan wool and spinning the product on domestic wheels and looms, much of the labour done by the women who were largely locked out from the entirely male-dominated culture of Kabbalism. This was more than a cottage industry. Safed textiles, along with a bigger industry in Salonika, by this time a two-thirds Jewish city, were the mainstay of woollen textiles in the entire Ottoman Empire.[19] It may have been this micro-economy which gave Doña Gracia and Joseph Nasi the idea of a new Jewish town down below by the lake shore at Tiberias. Though they supported Kabbalist publications, neither of them was mystically inclined. What they had in mind was something radically new: an autonomous miniature city state – under Turkish jurisdiction, of course – that would take in those fleeing from persecution, especially in Italy. New Tiberias would be self-governing and self-supporting. It would be the germ of something truly momentous. In 1560 Gracia – in her imperious fashion – petitioned Suleyman's grand vizier Rüstem Pasha for a lease of land and property within the province and this was duly granted. The sultan and his vizier were just the first in a cycle of non-Jewish rulers who came to believe that an intensive resettlement of Jews in the land that had formed their religion and culture could serve both their interests and those of their imperial overlords.

Not for the last time, the indigenous Arab population did not share this enthusiasm. An ancient Jewish wisdom that the messianic age would begin with a return to Tiberias was matched by an equally popular Muslim fear that the return of Jews to the Holy Land, and especially to Galilee, would presage the fall of Islam. Raids, robberies and attacks were met with Ottoman punishments and the building of a protective wall. Masonry blocks lying around by the shoreline were recycled for modest fortifications and for the construction of new houses. Doña Gracia sent encouragement and funds, while Joseph, through an emissary, Joseph ibn Adret, armed with an imperial firman, handled the politics and administration. Wool and indigo were imported for the textile makers and mulberry trees were planted for an embryonic Galilean silk industry. In a politic move of charity, some of the profits were earmarked for the soup kitchen which fed the Damascus poor.

It was the inauguration of the classic vision of a reborn Jewish home in Palestine – simultaneously an asylum for the oppressed, and a place of moral and social transformation. The rhetoric of an unhealthy wasteland turned into a paradisial garden seemed to be about to be realised with figs and date palms growing by the lake shore; fishing boats multiplying on the waters. News of the miracle of a Jewish home in Galilee spread far and wide. In the small town of Cori in the Campania near Naples, the local doctor and rabbi Malachi Gallico, who had received news of Tiberias from his Kabbalist cousin Elisha, summoned the congregation to a meeting in their synagogue.[20] Encouraged by what they heard at that assembly, the community decided to emigrate en masse to Tiberias. To raise the funds needed to get them all to Venice and aboard one of Joseph Nasi's ships, the Jews of Cori produced a pocket history of their plight. The brochure was then to be taken around Italy and beyond by two 'emissaries', Rabbi Michael ben Aaron and Joseph ben Menahem, to make the case for supporting the fund. Poignant and tearful, the letter recited their reduction by the persecuting popes into 'a heap of bones':

it is not enough now to enclose us in every place where we dwell but we have been surrounded with walls ... so no man can any longer go forth among his neighbours ... the regulations are so strict that we cannot engage in any commerce whatsoever whether in food or new clothes nor can we even occupy ourselves with handicrafts. Moreover the Gentiles are changed against us from sweet to bitter saying that it is forbidden to them to give us any assistance or domestic help in any way. From the time these woes are come upon us our eyes have welled up with weeping ... Now when the groans and tribulations of the congregation of Cori became great, there came to us one who announced good tidings ... we speak of the crown and glory and grace of the Nasi, the Lord and Noble one ... the pillar of exile ... Lord Don Joseph to whom God caused to be given the land of Tiberias ... we have learned that many have already set out across the seas ... we have been told that he seeks Jews who are craftsmen so they may settle and establish the land on a sound basis ... On hearing all this we became stirred with one heart and went as one man to the synagogue ... and there we made an agreement to go dwell beneath the pinions of the Almighty in Tiberias ... Wherefore oh you generous merciful sons of merciful sires, help the poor ones to go in Justice from the Exile to our Land and make true the path of the Righteous.[21]

Whether the Jews of Cori reached their cherished destination is not known. Nightingales were succeeded by mourning doves. Though a house had been built in Tiberias in happy expectation of the arrival of Doña Gracia, she never came. The odyssey of altered lives that had begun on Diogo Mendes' chartered caravel in 1537 ended amid the cypresses and silk divans of Galata in 1569 while the Golden Horn was freezing over in the bitterest winter known to Constantinople. Shivering householders were careless with fires and conflagrations swept through the city engulfing the Jewish quarters on the south bank. What persuasion could not accomplish – the gathering of Romaniot and Sephardi Jews in consolidated districts – the urban inferno of 1569 achieved, as fugitives from the flames were taken in and, courtesy of the great patrons of the city, given soup and shelter.

More than ever the Jews of Ottoman Turkey looked to Joseph as a true Nasi: a guardian prince. The long, prodigious reign of Suleyman the Magnificent had come to an end in September 1566 during yet another siege in Transylvania. Moses Almosnino said Kaddish and added the sultan's name to other prayers of mourning, eulogising Suleyman as a 'shepherd', a second Moses: the first time this had been done for a Gentile prince. Selim's only serious rival for the succession for the throne, his brother Bayezid, had already been disposed of years earlier thanks to Joseph's support. When Selim rode out from Constantinople (one of the rare occasions he would be seen with his army) to be acclaimed by the elite Yeniceri soldiers as the new sultan, he had the Jew with him as *muterferik*, a gentleman of the imperial retinue, newly invested with the Duchy of Naxos. This made Joseph Nasi the master monopolist of a mineral mined on eastern Naxos: emery, the abrasive aluminium oxide also known as corundum which was then, as now, the indispensable tool of manicurists. Since Joseph also controlled the trade in volcanic pumice from Santorini, he was (among other things) supplier of cosmetics to an Ottoman world in which they were the necessary commodities of refinement. Needless to say the Jews were known in Constantinople (as they had been in Italy) as purveyors of the rarest and most exotic cosmetics and perfumes.

But Joseph's commercial empire extended far beyond abrasives and unguents. He was the controller of alum production from the mines near Corinth and his commercial reach extended far north to Poland and Lithuania, into which Jews had been moving since the thirteenth century. Sable from the north was the trim of choice for high-end robes and coats, and after the winter of 1569 no one on the Bosphorus questioned the need for it. In that year, Selim's army came to grief in a siege of Astrakhan, which only made Joseph's strategy of outflanking the Kievan state by importing grain and iron from Poland all the more urgent. And Polish bees played their part in this new commercial connection, for wax and honey were both much in demand. It was understood in Cracow that if the Polish king Sigismund wanted to negotiate with the sultan, he had to do it through the agency of Joseph Nasi. Fulsome letters survive from the king in which the Jew is greeted as if he were indeed a brother prince. Joseph might have been forgiven for thinking that way. He stood at the hub of a global network of exchange. Persian silks came to him from Hormuz and spices and dyes from beyond in India; even ceramics from Ming China, where there was yet another far-flung world of Jews.

All this grandeur, his closeness to the sultan (and indeed to the slave concubine who had become Selim's wife, Nurbanu), as well as his commanding position as revenue collector, tempted Joseph's political ambitions. Unlike his rival, the equally intelligent Bosnian vizier Mehmed Sokollu, the span of Joseph's life – from Lisbon to student days fencing with the Habsburg Maximilian, and from the house of Mendes in Antwerp, on to Venice and his Aegean fiefs right at the heart of the great naval struggle for supremacy in the eastern Mediterranean – gave him panoramic strategic vision. He took in the embattled world, as much-travelled Jews do, at a single glance. For all the new aggression of the Catholic world, what he saw with those eagle eyes was an opportunity for counter-attack. The revolt of the Netherlands against Spain, with its most violent events unfolding in Antwerp, was one such opportunity and Joseph used his old connections in Flanders and in England to communicate with the Prince of Orange and give him encouragement. At that same moment the Granada rebellion of the Arabic-speaking Moriscos – the Muslim equivalent of the Marranos, grudging forced converts – gave Joseph further hope that these cracks in the adamant facade of the Church Militant could be opened still wider.

Which left, most crucially, Venice. It had taken until 1567 for the republic to rescind the death sentence against him imposed when he had taken Gracia La Chica off in the night gondola. Joseph was too worldly to take this personally, although when a Turkish raid burned down the Arsenale in 1569, it was widely imputed to his resentment against the republic for the indignity. Personal passions aside there was an obvious choice for Ottoman policy. The grand vizier Sokollu leaned towards an understanding, if not an outright alliance with Venice in the face of Habsburg and French threats in the Mediterranean; Joseph, on the other hand, believing that Venetian maritime power was on the wane, took a more opportunist and confrontational view. The immediate target was Cyprus, held by Venice but, as he believed, ripe for the picking: a source of enormous wealth and obvious strategic importance. In 1570 a battle for control of the island was under way, the advantage swinging back and forth but eventually won by the Turks, a victory which immediately gave rise to the dangerous rumour that the campaign had been launched to make Joseph king of Cyprus, and turn his island kingdom into a commonwealth of Jews.

In tandem with anti-Venetian belligerence, Joseph took the economic war to the French. This too put him in the vulnerable position of being seen to pursue a policy of personal vindication. French ships were stopped in the Bosphorus and other Turkish ports, and cargoes confiscated, a move so provocative that the sultan was forced to repudiate it. But the damage had been done. The muscular confidence of Joseph's policy had only succeeded in putting together what had otherwise been an unthinkable alliance of imperial forces, the Venetians and the papacy. They came together in the immense armada commanded by the Genoese Andrea Doria, which took on an equally imposing Ottoman fleet at Lepanto in 1571. Joseph Nasi welcomed the naval Armageddon and lived to rue it. The Turkish fleet was comprehensively destroyed in the bloodbath, ensuring that its power would not progress any further west in the Mediterranean. Its hold on the Aegean swiftly recovered, but Joseph Nasi's influence did not. Henceforth the sultan, when he could be bothered to rouse himself from his dissipated lethargy (the state which his enemies attributed to Joseph's wine-fuelled power), trusted the Bosnian rather than the Jew.

Joseph moved to Ortaköy further up the Bosphorus, to a new palace from where he continued to issue ducal pronouncements, though he never set foot on his Greek island domain. Further off, Jewish Galilee was giving concern. The textile industry in Safed (as well as in Salonika) had been a victim of its own success. Soaring demand had sent the price of raw wool and dyestuffs up to the point where the finished product was becoming uncompetitive. In both Safed and Tiberias, physical threats to the Jewish towns were becoming more serious. Local watchmen colluded with Beduin and Christian monks who had never been reconciled to a Jewish renascence in Galilee to make the towns unsafe.

But there was not much now that Don Joseph could do about any of this, so he made the best of it. Every so often he would receive tributes of dried fruit and Cretan wine which pleased him in the long summer afternoons. He spent more time in the *studiolo* and the library and became exercised by the spurious spell of astrology on both Jewish and Christian scholars, debating so eloquently with the latter when they visited the Belvedere that Rabbi Isaac Onkeneira, his interpreter, implored him to set down his objections. This he did in a modest polemic, titled with a touch of lordly self-congratulation *Ben Porat Yosef* (*Joseph the Fruitful Bough*). Others came and went: poets, especially; hunters of rare volumes who knew he couldn't resist another;

petitioners seeking funds for the ransom of Jews taken by pirates, or the upkeep of a synagogue or cemetery.

By the end of his life, mortality had reduced the great dynasty of the Marrano epic. His brother Samuel had died in 1574, and in that same year a fire leapt from an oil pan in the Topkapi grilling kitchen, devastating a large part of the Second Court of the palace. No cauldrons had yet been overturned but it was taken as an ill omen nonetheless. A few months later Selim – blind drunk, so the souk talk said – slipped on the floor of a bathhouse, and perished from a fever shortly after. Brianda-Reyna, who stayed in Ferrara to the end of her days, was long since gone. In 1579 Joseph, who had seen and done so much, whose life had been an entire history of the Jews unto itself, joined the list of the dead. There had been rumours from the disaffected that in his last years he had, shockingly, sought a reconciliation with the king of Spain, Philip II, and that he had even raised the possibility of returning as a penitent son of the Church; but his Jewish memorialists dismissed this out of hand as scurrilous myth. Historians in Joseph's debt like Joseph Ha-Cohen eulogised the Nasi as the greatest of the great, wise, powerful and omniscient, and allowing for neo-biblical hyperbole they were not altogether mistaken. He had been, after all, master of the Jewish escape, lord of trade, patriarch of Jewish learning and literature; and without anachronism he might even be called, with Gracia, the first of the Zionists. But where he had blundered he had blundered calamitously, and a counter-biography persisted in the Gentile mind: the presumptuous, hard-hearted, imperiously mercenary Jew. Christopher Marlowe, someone drawn to outlandish daring, would in due course take the history of Don Joseph and turn him into a demonic figure – Barabas, the Jew of Malta. It was Joseph's life as caricature: the jumped-up Hebrew, provoked by scorn into a monstrous conspiracy which destroys him, the customary, banal satisfaction inflicted by a Cambridge wit on the body of the Jew.

Joseph's widow, Reyna (Gracia's daughter who, as the child Brianda, had been on the same Lisbon ship as the twelve-year-old João), survived him by some twenty years and became the final matriarch of this line of formidably intelligent and strong-minded Jewish women. Learned and pious works and commentaries were dedicated to Reyna, and sang her praises as they had those of her extraordinary mother. She was their Sarah, their Rachel, their Miriam. Reyna honoured the memory of her family by continuing to fund hospitals, schools and yeshivot; visiting the sick and poor in her black silks, sipping a little of her late husband's wines now and again, pottering about the garden pavilions and almost certainly spending time in the company of other women who were the last powerful Jews in the palace of Topkapi.

Those Jewesses were the only subjects of the sultan allowed to come and go from the harem as they chose. Indeed their coming and going was the reason for their influence with the *valides* or 'queen mothers', the wives and concubines. They were known as the *kiras* (from the Greek for 'lady'), the Jewish intermediaries between the harem and the Grand Bazaar. A succession of royal women – Suleyman's Hurrem, Selim's Nurbanu and Murad III's Safiye – had all begun as slave concubines taken to provide the sultan with an heir. In due course they had become wife to the ruler, then achieving the status of *valide* on his death. No longer a sexual threat, the matriarchs exerted immense influence both in the palace and sometimes even on policy, especially when the sultans had chosen seclusion within Topkapi over military campaigning or almost any other public activity. (The exceptions to this immured life of pleasure were the hunts, although even these were organised in the palace parks and gardens, boat processions on the Golden Horn and parades on days of circumcision.) The more secluded the sultans became, the more the women of the palace moved into the vacuum. It was a sign that a centre of power had moved to the harem when Selim spent his nights there rather than returning to the sultan's quarters in the male section of the palace. Nurbanu and Safiye became patronesses of building projects, including the expansion of their own quarters so that it came to resemble a miniature cloistered palace within a palace, complete with its own council chamber. They were also patronesses of mosque complexes and royal baths, and benefactresses of public soup kitchens and hospitals (not least in Jerusalem). Towards the end of the century it was they rather than the sultan who answered ambassadors and addressed letters directly to foreign sovereigns. And the *kiras*, along with another marginal group, the black eunuchs of the harem, were at their right hand.

In their concubine years Hurrem, Nurbanu and Safiye had all relied on the *kiras* to supply them with the spectacular costumes, glittering gems and rare perfumes and cosmetics on which their prospects depended, as well as drugs and medicines when they were sick or bafflingly infertile. But with their *passepartout*, the *kiras* did not just traipse in and out of the harem; they spent long hours there as companions and advisers. They taught embroidery (a Jewish speciality) to the concubines and wives, and imparted the secrets of their pharmacopoeia.

When royal women also needed to realise the value of gems and gifts that had been presented to them by the sultan, it was the Jewesses who were their only channel to a good price. Given that Murad III had forty wives and countless concubines, a career spent as their inter-mediary with the outside world was going to be lucrative. Over the generations the *kiras*, taking commissions on all this business, became fabulously rich in their own right, and were granted tax exemptions that would remain in their families. Customs and tax farms fell into their laps, attracting predictable envy and hostility.

The first of the known *kiras* was one Strongilah, who ended her long and prosperous life as the convert Fatma. Her successor Esther Handali, the widow of a jeweller, remained steadfast in her Judaism and, following Selim's unfortunate death, became confidante and coun-sellor to the new *valide*, Nurbanu. After the terrible fire of 1569, Esther took it upon herself to feed and shelter many of its Jewish victims almost as if she were the mother-protector succeeding Doña Gracia, and like her used her money to provide dowries for poor Jewish girls; put clothes on the backs of orphans and indigent children; fund the pieties and scholarships of yeshivot.

After Esther's death, which seems to have been sometime in the 1570s, she in turn was replaced by Esperanza Malchi, who was close enough to the next *valide* to have penned an informal letter to the aged Queen Elizabeth I in 1599. The relationship between England and Turkey had been growing closer, bound by the common threat from Spain. Special terms were granted to their respective merchants, notwithstanding the fact that cheap English broadcloth was actually making serious inroads on the Jewish product manufactured in Salonika and Safed. In 1593 there was an exchange of precious gifts – garments of gold cloth and diamonds (the *valide* and *kira* knew what the old queen liked) along with fine and flowery greetings. Believing the Turks were won over by intricate devices, a spectacularly complicated and

handsome clockwork organ had been shipped out together with its
maker Thomas Dallam, who nonetheless failed to prevent it from
coming unglued on the long journey. Repaired, its performance before
Murad's heir, Mehmed III, beat all expectations, not least with flocks
of mechanical blackbirds and thrushes rising in full warble from a holly
bush at the top of the case.[22]

In November 1599, on the departure of the English ambassador,
Safiye sent further gifts to Elizabeth: a girdle, a robe, kerchiefs of
cloth and gold, and a 'necklace of pearls and rubies'. But then
Esperanza, who calls herself 'Hebrew by law and nation', gets down
to business:

> Your Majesty being a lady full of condescension I venture the following
> request namely that there are to be met with in your Kingdom distilled
> waters of every description for the face as well as odoriferous oils for
> the hands. Your Majesty would favour me by sending through my hand
> for my most Serene 'Queen' (Valide) as being articles for ladies she
> does not wish them to pass through other hands. Likewise if there are
> to be had in your kingdom articles of wool or silk suitable for so high
> a lady as my mistress Your Majesty might be pleased to send them as
> my Mistress will be far more gratified by them than by more valuable
> objects. I have nothing further to add but to pray God he may give
> you victory over your enemies and that Your Majesty may be prosperous
> and happy. From Constantinople 16th November 1599. Your humble
> Esperanza Malchi.[23]

There is something wonderfully breezy about the tone of this: the
ornamental courtesies of diplomacy turned into the mutual shopping
list of two magnificent old trouts: Esperanza and Elizabeth, Jew and
queen. Quite how Gloriana, who could be ticklish on niceties of
protocol, reacted (if ever she was shown the letter) we can only
imagine; but like all the *kiras*, Esperanza was evidently in the habit
of throwing her considerable weight around (she was described by
the English ambassador as a 'short fat trubkin'). And as was so
often the case she paid the price for this when the time came to
overthrow the *valide's* cauldron. One morning in 1600, parts of the
kira's limbs were found nailed to the doors of those to whom she
and Safiye had favoured with influence, office and riches. She had

been stabbed through the heart the day before by disaffected *sipahis*, the sultan's mounted bodyguard who blamed her for the debased coinage that had devalued their pay. On the following day Esperanza's elder son was killed, mutilated like his mother, and the pieces of his body dragged beside her remains. The younger son speedily converted to Islam as the corpses of his mother and brother lay unburied for days. The *kira*'s estate and fortune in property and jewels – 100,000 ducats, it was rumoured – were confiscated for the sultan.

The sway of the *kiras* was over, and the last of the Mendes-Benvenistes, Reyna, an old lady now, was satisfied to be a half-hidden patroness of hospitals, soup kitchens and yeshivot, dutifully preserving the history of the great epic she had herself witnessed. Down below and across the Golden Horn, Jews got on with their lives in Balat and Eminönü, still picking enjoyably meaningless quarrels with each other as to which was the superior liturgy, or Passover food: the Italian, the Greek, Salonikan, Catalan, Portuguese, Cordoban? And still busy always pressing a glass to their eyes to inspect the gems; testing between the balls of a soft thumb and finger the delicacy of silk; coppering their pans and bowls; jabbing a finger at the chests of unreasonable hagglers; discreetly inspecting the young men from the women's gallery for a suitable husband for their Sara or Esther or Miriam. Before the *kiddushin* a hen party would be thrown for young and old. Then would come the wedding, 'a time of gladness, a time to unveil nakedness, and sing and dance before the bride, when crowds and crowds of boys and old men would be as happy and joyous as if they had found a great fortune'. The feasting would go on for days. There would be much Candia honeyed wine. Special songs would have been composed for the bride and groom, and if you were well enough off you might even hire the first Jewish wedding singer we know of, Avraham Shandur, to do popular numbers from the songbook of Shelomo ben Mazaltov: 'Come out of the Cleft of the Rock my Lovey-Dove' or 'Song to a Doe'. Suppose there was a Romaniot–Spanish match (and such things were not unheard of), then there would be music from both traditions: a fiddle, a drum, or the santur – a dulcimer-like instrument – a Turkish harp, an oud. If, God willing, all went well, five months into the pregnancy another party would come along to celebrate the cutting of the first pre-partum nappy. More gifts; more wine; more music; more jokes.

THE TIME OF THE NIGHTINGALE

The wide world turned; the Bosphorus shone in summer; and glowered in winter. The old English queen and the implacable Spanish king died. *Te Deums* were sung at the biers of popes and inquisitors while in Constantinople and Salonika, Cairo and Alexandria, Adrianople, Bursa, Damascus, Baghdad, Aleppo and Jerusalem, Jews got on with their lives, worrying about their workshops and their warehouses, frying fish on Fridays, bobbing in their prayer shawls and putting something aside to dower their daughters and keep a place in the cemetery. This also happened in the bustling port of Smyrna where, at some point in the centuries which followed, the Schamas arrived from God knows where and began to buy and sell flaking scrolls of cinnamon, each one shaped just like the Sefer Torah.

5

MUSIC AND MOURNING

I. Leone

There is nothing worse than watching your child die except seeing it twice, which is what happened to Leone Modena. It made no difference that the angel of death spread his wings wide over Venice in the early years of the seventeenth century; that he sowed his harvest with smallpox, plague, fevers and fluxes too many to name or number and that body after body was ferried over the lagoon to the Jews' burying ground on the Lido. The social historians are wrong. No culture has ever been inured to the death of children, however commonplace the passing. Even the death of infants in his extended family or among friends tore at Leone. When a fourteen-month-old grandson died he mourned that the baby had been 'my daily delight'. And when the time came to write of his son Mordecai's death at twenty-six he could barely manage the words. 'My bowels writhe with pain; the chambers of my heart moan within me.' All he could do was to search his life story for the transgressions which had caused God to take his son.[1] Had it been his gambling habit – a vice he himself had denounced in print at the age of twelve, but which had nonetheless turned into an addiction? Or had it been his permission, even encouragement, of the alchemy which had proved the death of Mordecai?

He ought to have known better after his uncle Shemaia, the Modena pawnbroker, 'attracted by alchemy', had been fatally deceived by wicked men. Promising to multiply Shemaia's gold and silver alchemically, they had persuaded him to bring them his treasure, after which one of them thrust a sword into his belly. Italy was full of such demons disguised as men. But the Philosophy was a deep vein in

Jewish learning and practice. Some believed that Moses himself had been the first, and no less than the great Kabbalist of Safed, Hayim Vital, had written a lexicon of alchemical practice.[2] Leone had been known to 'go after the foolishness', enticed by the physician of Rome, Rabbi Abraham di Cammeo.[3] Along with preaching, teaching, translating and writing, Leone Modena was a seller of amulets, both protective and invigorating, and the science of their power was connected to the greater art. So when Mordecai came back from his studies in Talmud and Torah, 'slender, with a hairy body, and a small rounded beard, neither happy nor sad' and 'always respectful of his parents', and asked if he might learn the craft from the learned priest Giuseppe Grillo, Leone had not forbidden it. Mordecai, his firstborn, his 'Angelo'; he could refuse him nothing. God knows he had nothing material to give the boy as fathers should.

For a time the work went well, if slowly. Mordecai had set up his alchemical chamber in a room in the Ghetto Vecchio and had succeeded in translating nine ounces of lead and one of silver into ten of 'pure' silver, fine enough to fetch a good price. A miracle! How could father and son not have been encouraged? But he must have got careless. The chamber was too narrow, too closed to be safe. 'All persons who engage in alchemical work must beware of the strong kinds of drugs that they use when silver and gold are being melted in the fire and must stay away from their smoke,' Hayim Vital had warned; 'above all beware of the smoke from quicksilver when it is on fire for if it enters your nose it is mortal poison for out of it is made soliman [mercuric chloride].'[4] But Mordecai had needed all manner of perilous materials: cinnabar, antimony and, most lethally, 'realgar': white arsenic. Leone tormented himself by going over all the signs which ought to have cautioned him. In 1605 Mordecai, then still a boy whose lungs were prone to inflammation, had become so ill from the bad air of Ferrara that he had been unable to take part in the Purim play, a matter of great unhappiness for him.[5] Ten years later on the feast of Sukkot (Tabernacles), the sweetest of the harvest festivals, Mordecai began to vomit blood. The craft was abandoned but the harm had been done. Between these profuse bleeds he was capable only of 'light activities', and the onset of the bloody fits became more regular. Their monthly recurrence became a weekly terror, and then by Passover 1617, to the consternation of his family, they happened

each and every day. There seemed to be no remedy. By the autumn
of 1617 eleven different doctors, Christian and Jewish, had been called
upon, to no avail. Mordecai begged Leone to ask Grillo, his old
instructor, for some arcane medicine from the priest's Book of Secrets;
but seeing that the older alchemist had been the source of the evil,
and afraid some strange drug would only make the sickness worse,
Leone refused to administer it until Mordecai was at death's door. By
then it was too late. Leone began to have dreams heavy with personal
guilt. In one of them his son appeared and told him he had taken a
house outside the ghetto. 'Tell me where and I shall come and visit
you,' Leone said, but the dream-Mordecai replied that he would not
tell him as he no longer cared to have paternal visits. At times Mordecai
would rally, enough to go and hear his father preach in the synagogue.
But on 7 November 'he lay dying for three hours and then at the ninth
hour (3 a.m.) his soul returned to the Lord who had given it him'.[6]
'And Mordecai went out abandoning me to the valley of agony and
the depths of despair.'[7]

Leone approached the edge of madness. Everyone knew him in
the ghetto. He was a regular preacher and cantor (*chazzan*) at the
Italian synagogue, and at the others too; taught children, Jewish and
Christian alike, and wrote formal letters in any language for the many
who had not mastered the polite art. The *shiva*, the seven days of
mourning, would have seen an unending stream of consoling visitors.
But the anguish of saying Kaddish for your own child was a thrice-
daily torture. The tradition that a merciful God took the sharpness
of memory away from the heart and mind did not apply to him. 'Not
a day passes when his death is not fresh to me as if his corpse were
lying before me.' It was then, in the abyss of his grief, that Rabbi
Leone Modena began to write his autobiography. There had been
travel memoirs before, of greater and lesser reliability – Eldad Hadani,
Benjamin of Tudela, the picaresque romance of *The Book of Tahkemoni*,
all printed in Renaissance Italy – and Flavius Josephus' brief autobiographical sketch from his childhood to his days in Rome had also been
published; but Leone's was the first true autobiography, and it is still
one of the most vividly affecting. Leone wrote that he had wanted
to write *The Life of Yehudah Aryeh* (Judah Leon, *aryeh* being Hebrew
for both lion and Leon) for his firstborn 'whose bright countenance
resembled mine' and was 'the apple of my eye and the root of my

heart' so that he would learn something of his origins, wanderings, beliefs and character. Now that Mordecai was gone, his purpose was strengthened. The book would now be a fatherly gift of sorts to his other children, the two boys Isaac and Zebulun and the girls Diana and Esther. The translation of recollection into writing itself required a measure of calm, a break from grief, though even so he could only manage it in spurts, at six-month intervals. And alongside the autobiography, and while he was saying Kaddish every day, Leone also wrote a booklet of prayers and comforts for friends to take to the house and the bed of the sick and dying.

The autobiography sometimes reads as a romance of misfortune, beginning with the Ferrara earthquake which struck the city while his mother was carrying him in the womb, so that he was nearly thrown into the world by the convulsions of the earth. Instead 'I Leone, the bitter and impulsive' was born in Venice, emerging into the world arse first and facing frontwards, an inauspicious beginning. But then, Leone the enthusiastic astrologer insisted, the constellations were always warring against his family. Though he descended from a dynasty rich in learning, piety and material substance, his father lost his wealth when a period of blindness made it impossible to work. The family had gone down in the world, so far that it became apparent Leone would have to use all his many talents to help support it. Just as well, then, that the range of those gifts was prodigious. The boy was a precocious Hebrew scholar and preached pipingly in synagogue, but he was also accomplished in music, and given a chance would sing his little heart out. A reciter of poems, a marvel of the mouth was Leone. Early on, too, his chin was chucked by Gentiles and Jews alike, so that he became a jobbing tutor, preacher and translator for anyone who would pay, Jewish to the core but at home in the Gentile world. Yet the stars refused to align in his favour; and in the midst of rejoicing, trouble found its way to his door.

A match was made with a cousin, Esther. Happiness beckoned, not least because the marriage would get Leone out of the small town of Montagnana where the restless young scholar-teacher felt imprisoned. The betrothal took place, the contract was drawn up and the wedding, the *huppah*, set for June 1590 around the time of Shavuot, the Pentecostal festival. Family and friends converged on Venice for the celebrations. The groom was nineteen; the bride a few years younger. But when Leone and his family arrived a little in advance of the joyous day 'we found the bride confined to her bed. Everyone said it was nothing, a little diarrhea and that she would soon recover. But her illness grew worse and worse from day to day until she lay near death. Yet her heart was that of a lion and she was not afraid.'[8] On the day she died, Esther called for her bridegroom, took him in her arms and, to general consternation, kissed him. Wanting to experience the touch of physical love before she died, Esther said, 'I know this is bold behaviour but during the whole year of our betrothal we never touched each other not even with our little fingers. Now at the time of death I have the rights of the dying. I was not allowed to become your wife but what can I do, for it was thus decreed by heaven?'

The 'Sabbath bride' came with the evening and the real bride departed this earth. The bereft bridegroom collapsed in grief and horror, likewise Esther's family; yet before she was cold in the ground they rallied enough to propose her sister as a substitute. 'Just as good a girl.' One must be practical. A match is a match, after all. Notwithstanding his own misery, Leone was pressed so hard that he agreed to the family stand-in from sheer 'embarrassment'. Two weeks later he and his dead bride's sister, Rachel, went under the *huppah*.

The Life of Yehudah Aryeh can feel like one long extended sigh punctuated by the odd howl. No sooner does something good happen (a book is published) than it is punctured by pain – in one case literally, when Leone steps on a piece of pointed metal and has to lie in bed for two weeks. But between the moans there are moments of rejoicing: children are born and live and he becomes a name in Venice and beyond. This is one of the first printed books which lives both inside and outside the Jewish world. Leone acquired such fame as a preacher that Christians would come and hear him from beyond the ghetto, beyond Venice, beyond Italy. It was a conscious aspiration. Leone possessed and studied the collected sermons of one of the most popular Christian preachers of the age, Francesco Panigarola, Bishop of Asti, and he tried to graft some of his style onto the Jewish tradition of the *derush*, a commentary on Bible text and the Talmud.[9] His own book of sermons the *Midbar Yehuda* (*The Desert of Judah*) makes it plain that he also brought a study of classical rhetoric to what he conceived of as a homiletic art.

It was during his lifetime that the ghetto of Venice became a tourist attraction and Leone was the rabbi the visitors were told they must see, hear, meet.[10] Not everyone was won over to the devotion of the Jews by what they saw. Most of the travellers remarked (as Christians going to synagogues always will) on the sheer *noise* of the assembly, from the 'bellowing' of the preaching rabbis, the '*battologia*', to the 'tedious babbling of the repetitions and the incessant chatter of the congregation'.[11] To the travelling clergyman Samuel Purchas, the body language of Jewish worship, the swaying and bobbing, the histrionic hand gestures, was a symptom of everything wrong with Judaism: physical gesticulation masking the emptiness of belief.[12] For many, it was all too much: the incomprehensible gibber, the theatrical din, the ponderous heaviness of everything. But others, especially those who listened to Leone's Christian-friendly, classically organised sermons, kept an open mind. And very few of those who saw the five *scuole* of Venice thought them dwellings of demons and their living confederates, as had been the case in much of medieval Christian Europe.

Jews walked among Venetians. The ghetto bridges and gates were closed only at dusk. During the day Jews exited to work at almost everything, as doctors, dancing teachers, silk vendors, and moneylenders; while Gentiles entered the ghetto as porters, wet nurses, bakers' boys, cloth shearers, cutters, dyers and tanners, working alongside Jewish artisans. Even within the confined space of the ghetto there was a universe of Jews: Ashkenazim from the German-speaking world; 'Ponentines' (Spanish–Portuguese) from Iberia; 'Levantines' (who might be Romaniot Turkish or Sephardi Turkish, also Moroccan); black Jews (the Jewish *moro*, Moor, often an ex-slave, which could easily have made Othello Jewish, thus folding two Shakespeare plays into one). Cases brought before the Inquisition (in its relatively mild Venetian incarnation) confirm that not a few Christian men and women spent more time in the close company of Jewish men and women, even after the hours of gate and bridge closing, than was legally permissible. Indeed, some of them took to living there. In the course of examining Valeria Brugnaleschi, a physician's widow, and her daughter Splandiana on suspicion of witchcraft, it emerged that the two women had stayed in the ghetto for two years teaching seventy to eighty girls, and, as the inquisitors discovered, eating fried fish and matzot, a sure sign of their having gone native. Outrageously, Valeria had the gall to suggest to her examiners that ghetto life had taught her that the Jews followed their laws a good deal more conscientiously than the Christians theirs, an impertinence which did not help matters when it was later discovered that she had invited Jews back to her house in Zanipolo for their 'magic'. Lower down the social scale the sailor Giorgio Maretto had been seen at numerous Jewish weddings and circumcisions; and like the female ghetto-goers, conspicuously enjoyed kosher food, in particular spitted chickens which he gnawed on in the street. Giorgio courted a Jewish girl, Rachel, but only, he claimed, with an eye to her baptism. Some of the evidence, however – as when he was reported to have donned a yellow hat (just 'a good joke', he said) – suggested that the conversion process may have been the other way round.[13]

This gradual – and partial – discovery of the Jews as fellow human beings was made possible in Venice because for a few generations the republic resisted the supreme authority of the Counter-Reformation popes and in particular their institutionalised dehumanisation. Unlike its Roman counterpart the Venice ghetto was not a place of absolute physical segregation, nor were Venetian Jews stripped of all occupations other than the reviled rag trade and moneylending. Much Jewish life was lived, even if contentiously, in the non-Jewish world. On Purim Jew and Gentile laughed together and feasted together. Gentiles listened to Jewish music and poetry (if in Italian), and would come into the ghetto to talk philosophy with the likes of Leone Modena.

It was for those interested parties beyond the ghetto, from Venice and abroad, that Leone wrote the first detailed guide to Jewish beliefs, observances and practices, from circumcisions to burials to days of mourning, explicitly intended for non-Jews. It was, in effect, the Gentiles' *Shulkhan Arukh*. Around 1612, the English ambassador Henry Wotton (who is likely to have seen Marlowe's and Shakespeare's versions of Maltese and Venetian Jews) suggested to Leone that he write such a handbook for King James I, who had commissioned a new Bible and was famously interested in Hebrew. But it was not until the sorrowing days following the death of Mordecai that Leone got down to work in earnest. Though a manuscript version of the book became known, parts of which were used by the antiquarian and jurist John Selden, the work did not see the light of day as a printed book until 1637. Published in France without his prior knowledge, Leone was for a while terrified that allusions to Roman Christianity might get him into trouble. Jews were strictly forbidden from making anything that could be construed as derogatory or even sceptical remarks about the Church and its teachings.

If Christians began to regard Jews in a slightly subtler light, that regard turned into an excited gaze when it was directed at their women brushing past them on the campo or seated in the galleries of the synagogues. In 1608 the indefatigable traveller Thomas Coryate paid the Jewish women of Venice the ultimate compliment by comparing them favourably to the roses of Albion, writing that 'I saw many Jewish women whereof some were as beautiful as ever I saw and so gorgeous their apparel and chains of gold and rings addressed with precious stones that some of our English countesses do scarce exceed them having marvellous long traines like Princesses that are born up by waiting women'.[14] This Christian ogling was greedy. What it wanted from Jewish women was everything: the sexual allure of violent Judith; the unavailable desirability of the exotic; and the virtuous submission of Esther, the queen who, strong-minded as she was, bowed before her un-Jewish king. It was no accident that it was at this time that both heroines became commonplace subjects of Christian art, painted by the likes of Guercino, Artemisia Gentileschi and Domenichino.[15] It was as both seductress and convert that Jewish women caught the eye of Christians.

II. Sarra

It could take a while for this to sink in. When Sarra Copia – eighteen years old, blonde (as many Venetian women were, with or without the help of bleach recipes from the Book of Secrets), clever, married and living in the ghetto – read an epic poem called *Esther the Queen*, she thought it a hymn of praise to Jewish women in their own right. Stranger things had happened. The Purim drama was often the first place where Jews and Christians rubbed shoulders when the latter came to the ghetto to see a performance or had Jews act it in their patrician houses. The Book of Esther had become a shared story.

Recovering from the miscarriage which had nearly killed her, Sarra both identified with the heroine and admired the Christian author for painting, as she supposed, a heroic portrait of the resourcefulness of Jewish women. So smitten was she that in the spring of 1618 Sarra wrote directly to the author of the poem, Ansaldo Cebà, expressing that admiration, comparing him to Homer, and seeking to know him better. She was in the grip of a massive crush. She kept the poem, she told Cebà, on her pillow every night. He was fifty-three, a retired diplomat with a literary sideline. This onrush of teenage adoration caught his attention; made him uneasily happy.

Sarra Copia was, as Cebà would later write, blessed with 'a noble mind, a generous heart, a lively intellect' and 'beyond every other virtue, the grace of the Muses'.[16] All those who went to see her on Cebà's behalf (for he never did himself) confirmed her *bella figura* – beauty of face and form. She evidently had been the particular darling of her father, Simon Copia, and had been educated in all the disciplines – including music – now thought fitting for Jewish women in the more outward-looking sections of the ghetto. She performed improvised arias to heroic poetry and may even have accompanied herself on a stringed instrument.[17] Leone Modena, equally interested in poetry and music, was a family friend. Sarra's husband, Jacob, came from a like-minded family, the Sullams: cultured bankers originally from L'Escalette in south-west France, a place rich in learned piety whose population had suffered the last of the expulsions of the 1490s. Sarra's father-in-law, Moses Sullam, was a great power in Mantua, the patron and protector of its Jewish composer Salomone Rossi. Jacob followed his father into banking, although whether he had come to Venice before or as a result of their marriage is not known.

Sarra had not only been brought up by her doting father to be an independently minded young woman, but to expect the best of her Gentile neighbours. Simon Copia had established an informal 'academy' at his house in the ghetto of the kind that were sprouting like mush-rooms all over the cities of Italy and this one was a mingling place for mutually sympathetic Christians and Jews. Young patricians and aspiring poets, singers and musicians would come to the ghetto from all over the city and there spend time listening, reciting, and chewing over knotty matters of philosophy. After Simon died, Sarra, still very young, expanded the academy and began to write poetry. There were other Jewish women poets in seventeenth-century Italy, but, like the Roman Debora Ascarelli, they confined themselves to translating into verse the *piyyutim* of Hebrew liturgy.[18] Sarra was bolder. When she made her first ardent approach to Ansaldo Cebà she enclosed a poem beginning with the endearingly shameless introduction *'bella Ebrea'*, the beautiful Jewess, alluding to Cebà's Esther, as if both queen and fan in one person were championing his claims to literary immortality.

These kinds of versified eulogies were two a penny, but all the same Cebà was taken aback by the ardour of this one, not to mention the fact that it came from a young Jewish woman, evidently a living Esther. There was something about the overture – simultaneously brazen and modest, forward and chaste – that he found unexpectedly thrilling. It was not what he anticipated at this time of life. Bald on top, his beard was grey, though at the height of their exchange Sarra called those hairs precious silver. She knew what she was doing. As befitted a pious poetaster, Cebà, retired in Genoa, was preparing himself for the end of his days – which would come, as it turned out, rather sooner than he would have ideally liked. It was this stoical retreat which had been besieged and invaded by the onslaught of Sarra's gushing adoration.

Who could resist? Whatever reservations he may have had Cebà responded in kind, using the conventions of Platonic love in such a way as to protect them both from dangerous immodesty, yet in the outpouring of sudden, mutual passion, testing with every letter (and at one point they were coming every week) the boundaries of an intellectual relationship. From the beginning Cebà may have wanted to make some sort of literary event, a publication, out of their correspondence – the first between a Christian man and a Jewess. But only fifty-three of his letters were preserved along with a number of Sarra's poems. However, by way of responding to her, Cebà recapitulated in great detail what she had written to him, making the surviving correspondence less one-way.[19]

Bowled over by a sudden surge of emotion, the grey-haired veteran and the new Esther egged each other on. From the start Cebà told Sarra he would 'make love to your soul'. At other times he called her his mistress and himself her servant, which was either an image of employment or again perhaps not. Early on in their relationship he told her that 'you must be less delighted with my love than I am with yours' since she bombarded him with titles like 'Your Excellency', and 'among lovers as you know, titles are not used'. Throughout, his teasing banter affected a kind of twinkling coyness that ranged from droll to creepy. He understood, he said, the reluctance to be familiar since 'you, as I understand, are young and beautiful and I am neither … Yet if by special grace of your kindliness you should still wish to make love to me … let us both … maintain an amorous decorum and leave the use of "Your Most Excellent" expressions to those miserable persons who evoke the greatness of men by the vanity of words.'[20] Their Christian–Jewish game of love-play was enacted on the brink of peril, no less exciting (and perhaps more) for all the professions that it was their minds and souls that were in a state of such intense arousal. Towards the end, in October 1620, Cebà would become desperate (he would die in 1622). 'Let us seize time as it comes Signora Sarra and make love in earnest.'[21] The image he chose for their being finally united in a single faith was that of sharing the same room.

When it all became too much Cebà told himself that this intense emotion, the grey embers which had suddenly become inflamed, was nothing more than the ardour of a shepherd leading a stray lamb back to the fold. But often this pious self-deception fell away. His experiences with the two women who had mattered most to him, he told Sarra, had both ended badly, one with rejection and the other with premature death. In whatever form it took this was a last burst of love before the end, and even if its consummation would not be sexual but spiritual, it would be an ecstatic conquest nonetheless. No letter to Sarra was without an appeal for her conversion. Eros and salvation became indistinguishable in the heat of his passion for the Jewish blonde on whom he had never set eyes. The to-and-fro of their exchanges, not just of words but gifts, in this case a crystal goblet she had sent him, became the occasion of sensual psychodrama:

> Although I refused
> To touch your crystal with my mouth
> I did not do it, Sarra, to refuse something you mistakenly sent
> My lips were embittered
> By the burning voices
> I have uselessly sent to the winds
> For your salvation[22]

Sarra's worship of the literary Cebà continued, notwithstanding the relentlessness of his appeals for her baptism. When the rhythm of their correspondence was broken she became anxious, petulant, even frantic. She would sublimate her emotion by gift-bombing her lover. Candied and dried fruit would arrive one day; on another, a box of *bottarga*, grey mullet roe (Jews do food first); a portrait of herself; a comb case she had embroidered with pearls and gold and silver threaded flowers, prompting yet another round of poems, some of them without the obligatory genuflection: 'These white and crimson flowers you make from your stitches / These rays with which you make roses and lilies bright / I see so well bring out the beautiful colours in your own face.'[23]

Gradually, though, there was a shift in the erotic potlatch. The pursuing fan took active pleasure in being the pursued object, and started to weary of Cebà constantly raising his eyes to heaven when-ever he felt backed into an amorous corner. When Cebà tried to be witty about their forthcoming union, doubling the 'p' in her name and addressing her as 'Coppia' – a couple – Sarra was quick and severe, removing the unwanted middle letter. And then from either exas-peration or amusement or both, the invincibly Jewish Sarra Copia suddenly turned the tables. You will not stop asking me to become Christian, she said. You accuse me of not wanting to become your equal in matters of faith. But there is another way in which that end could be accomplished. How would it be if you became a Jew? After he got over the shock and his bitter mirth, Cebà wrote back: 'Should I come to Venice to be circumcised or should you come to Genoa to become baptised. Tell me freely your will. Consider however that I have no need to shed blood for what good would that do me? You however have good reason to seek water for you lack it.'[24] To which Sarra said, on the contrary, she had been born and lived her life amid the waters of the canals and lagoon. At some point Cebà resigned himself: 'it is a new way of making love to be sure, this way of ours when each seeks out such different things. I would like you to be a Christian and you would like me to be idolatrous.'[25]

It was hopeless but he would not quite give up. More than any other conquest he wanted this one before he died. The stronger she became the more he fantasised about how she should look if he were to come to see her, rather 'with the locks piled up on your head ... than with them parted and arranged by the artifice of your maidservant'.²⁶

In 1621 things between them went downhill. Sarra became seriously ill, but instead of writing with his usual attentiveness, Cebà went for months without sending a letter. And this was a time when Sarra needed to count on her true friends, for she had become embroiled in a public controversy not of her seeking. One of the regulars at her academy, the scholar-priest Baldassare Bonifaccio, in a New Year's greeting to 'Signora Sabba the Jewess'²⁷ wondered out loud whether or not in Eden both body and soul had originally been immortal. Had the soul remained 'obedient to the Creator' things might have stayed that way. But once man had fallen, and the soul 'wasted through sin', the body perished and only penitence recovered the soul's capacity to be imperishable. What did she think? Sarra replied in the witty locution that was obviously the habitual style of the academy's discussions; it gave pause that the year was new, yet we age, and so on. But then she answered Bonifaccio in a way so modern that it would cause her a world of trouble. It was indeed right to ask how matter (like the body) could be corruptible if forms originally housed with it (the soul) were meant to be imperishable. But the answer did not have to turn, as Bonifaccio – and by extension Christianity – insisted, on fall and redemption through penitence. Neither the body nor the soul suffered total extinction. The gross matter of body dissolves at death but becomes eternal, forming new matter and likewise souls were perpetuated in eternity. But this denied the separability of bodies and souls, matter and form. It was the continuity of matter which required heaven to create forms with perpetual endurance.

Whether from misunderstanding or manipulation Bonifaccio turned Sarra's argument upside down. Instead of the soul's immortality being an answer to matter's endurance, he attributed the opposite, scandalous view to her – that if the matter and form were alike it was as mortal corruptible stuff. And in an incendiary tactic (almost certainly calculated) he published his accusation that Sarra 'alone among Jews' denied the immortality of the soul.

The imputation, based on a wilful misreading of her text, could not have been more explosive. A condition of their toleration had always been that the Jews say nothing to outrage the doctrines of the Christian religion including the immortality of the soul. So the last

thing that Sarra Copia and her mentor Leone would have wanted
would be an accusation of subscribing to that particular heresy. Quite
aside from its jeopardising their position in Venice, the notion that
the soul, created with the body of flesh and blood, also perished with
it, was deeply upsetting to families with histories of martyrdom to the
Inquisition, and indeed those like Leone himself who had suffered
the traumatic loss of a child. Sarra counter-attacked Bonifaccio's libel
with her own *Manifesto* dedicated to the imperishable memory of her
father Simon, who 'though divested of the ephemeral veil [of life]
resides amidst living spirits and will reside there for all eternity'.[28] This
was a practical demonstration of Sarra's faith in the afterlife of the
souls 'continuing that inexpressible love' her father had for her, 'forever
preserved'. Aware that she would be accused of needing help from
men (Leone in particular), Sarra was at pains to insist the counter-
attack was her own work. If she was allowed salvation, she said, 'it
will be in intellectual works for which I have been granted some
fruitfulness'. She then proceeded to launch a fierce polemic against
Bonifaccio: his vaunted knowledge of Judaism belied by his ignorance
of Hebrew, his obtuseness in misunderstanding her. She began with
an unequivocal statement that the 'soul of man, Signor Baldassare, is
incorruptible, immortal and divine ... this truth is certain, infallible
and indisputable to me as it is for every Jew and Christian'.[29]

Sarra now began to realise that what seemed to be intellectual
comradeship almost always collapsed back into a campaign for her
conversion. In Genoa Cebà spoke of his efforts to his friend
Marc'Antonio Doria and the grandees of the local nobility and clergy;
while in Venice Bonifaccio was leading the crusade. It had all become
a kind of conversionary theatre with her as the great prize, and
young as she was she was increasingly repelled by the charade. For
his part Cebà too was close to giving up, his comments taking on
a waspish tone. Her husband Jacob might not look on the 'traffic
of letters with particular enthusiasm', yet 'not because of the word-
assault of your lover but because it came from a Christian'.[30] These
parting shots soured. 'Let me die', he finally wrote, 'without being
vexed any more by your letters.'[31] And so he did, later in 1622, four
years after their first exchange. 'The conversations that pass
between us', he told a third party (for him they were anything but

confidential), 'are enough to make one laugh but the outcome is such as ever to make one cry.'[32]

With his finger on the pulse of both the Jewish and Christian worlds of Venice, Leone Modena appreciated that Sarra, all of twenty-one years old at the time of Bonifaccio's accusation, had been put in a painful position. Her writing, her character, had been made public property by the very people she had welcomed across her threshold. Leone knew many of them personally, including Bonifaccio. And he was especially exercised by the need to vindicate her because just two years before he had had to excommunicate a Portuguese Dutch Jew, Uriel da Costa (of whom much more below), for explicitly denying the immortality of the soul. Though Leone probably made himself available to help with Sarra's rebuttal, should she wish it, he knew that if he did so she would immediately be accused of publishing his words under her own name – which is exactly what happened. He was content to make Sarra, as she wished to be, a latter-day independent Esther. Leone had himself extensively rewritten an older dramatised poem about Esther, originally the work of Salomon Usque, the translator of Petrarch into Spanish. And Leone had dedicated it to 'Signora Sarra Copia, Jewess' – that is to say, someone who would stay that way. To Sarra he apologised, in a prefatory sonnet, for his effort not being 'woven in golden threads' like the work of Cebà she so admired. His version followed the drama 'in an unassuming manner', destined as it was for Purim entertainment. But on the strength of the name alone, he added, he hoped 'you will accept a crow as a dove'.[33]

III. Leone, Salomone, Simone: Facing the World

1622 had looked to be a good year for Leone Modena. He had his hands full with work inside the ghetto and out. There was never any shortage of pupils, Christian as well as Jewish. His sermons were sought out not just in the Great Italian synagogue but also in the Ponentine synagogue of the Sephardim, then being enlarged in the Ghetto Vecchio into a building of surpassing magnificence. The work was being done by builders and masons from the workshop of Venice's greatest architect, Baldassare Longhena, which by itself spoke of mutual confidence Jews and Gentiles had in a shared future. The walls were clad in oak panelling. Inlaid marble floors were so beautiful that, in keeping with a tradition that only the hand of God could produce perfection, a deliberate fault was set into its patterning. You can still find it.

Later that year there would be a grand wedding in Mantua. Sarra Copia's sister Diana, another beauty – albeit one more likely to be found staring at herself in the mirror than pondering philosophy – was to be married to the son of Isaachino Masserano, the master choreographer. To avoid attack on the road (as in fact happened a year later), Leone and his fellow travellers would be protected by an armed escort on horse. While in Mantua Leone would make it his business to speak with Salomone Rossi, whom he had encouraged to compose choral music for the synagogue, a shocking innovation.[34] Rossi's polyphonic *Hashirim Asher Lishlomo* were thirty-three songs set to the words of the most familiar prayers and hymns in the Jewish liturgy – 'Aleinu', 'Shir Hamalot Aleinu', 'Ayn Keiloheinu', 'Adon Olam' among them. He and his sister 'Madama Europa', the diva of the court opera, were living embodiments of the possibility that joyous vocal music (and, Leone dared to hope, instrumental too) was compatible with Orthodox Jewish practice, notwithstanding a long rabbinical consensus forbidding any kind of unseemly rejoicing after the destruction of the Temple. In 1605 there had been a terrible to-do in Ferrara provoked by an attempt to introduce composed song into the synagogues. Leone, who had sung and played instruments himself in his youth, had been asked his opinion and had duly delivered a responsum: a millennium and a half had passed since the Second Temple was destroyed, he said; it was more than time to recover the beauty and joy of the original Solomonic Temple, as the Bible had described it. There was at that time something of a vogue in reimagining the architecture and decoration of that first imagined Temple and Salomone and Leone agreed that music, played by the Levites, from trumpets and harmonious voices, had been heard everywhere in its precincts. Leone was now quite certain – and said so in trenchant language – that God could not possibly *wish* for His worship to be confined to lamentations, bereft of harmonies, which could only concentrate the worshipper on his adoring devotions, rather than distract him from them. The harmony of Jewish voices would echo the harmony of God's creation. How could that not be pleasing to Him?[35]

There was something else to be considered. When the Gentiles wanted to sneer at the inferiority of Jewish culture they often pointed to the poverty of its music, above all the unfitness of Hebrew for the purposes of song, especially sacred song. It was one thing to have them perform, as they regularly did, at Christian weddings, court masques and entertainments; quite another for them to compose any kind of religious music. That prejudice was born of ignorance and the long centuries in which it had been forbidden by the rabbis. Leone could understand how the monotonous chants and shouts which sometimes made him wince would never gain the appreciation of lovers of 'the science of music', as he put it. God deserved better. Perhaps Salomone and Leone knew of the hymns of the twelfth-century proselyte to Judaism, Obadiah Ha-Ger – Obadiah the Apostate – who had, without any disrespect, composed Jewish plainsong, a stirring hymn for Moses Our Teacher?[36] Now the challenge – in the musical world of that other Mantuan court composer Claudio Monteverdi, and in Venice Giovanni Gabrieli – was to take the idiom of madrigals and *canzone*, part songs, and make them sing out the expressive glories of the Hebrew liturgy. Besides, Jewish musicians denied performance opportunities in the Christian courts by the ghetto enclosings might now be available for the new sacred music.[37] If that could be accomplished then Christians would flock to the synagogues of Venice to hear it just as they now did to hear Leone's sermons and laugh at the Purim plays.

This must have passed through his mind as he stood before a standing-room-only congregation in January 1622, much of it comprising members of the Venetian nobility. They had come to hear him preaching, as usual in Italian – itself a sign of Judaism facing out into the world. It was one of the great moments in Leone Modena's life: evidence if ever it was needed for a shared community of understanding. But he also believed that he was now so sought after that he might be able to escape the drudgery of endless teaching, letter writing and selling of amulets, and devote himself to higher things. 'I was extremely happy because the school term had ended and I had emerged into the freedom for which my soul had longed. Even though I was empty-handed and had many debts I praised the living God.'[38]

To add to this pleasure, his youngest son, Zebulun – in a family demonstration of Leone's belief in synagogue music – sang a piece his father had composed especially for the occasion. 'The listeners could not stop praising his sweet voice.' It was the pure delight of that moment which made what followed so unbearably cruel.

Leone and Rachel had been as unlucky in their sons as they seem to have been fortunate in their two daughters. After Mordecai's death, the middle son Isaac had not been much of a consolation. Writing of him, Leone implies dissipation, irresponsibility and arguments so violent that he was not displeased when Isaac went off to Amsterdam and thence to Brazil, where there was a Jewish community living under the protection of the Dutch. Leone's youngest, his Zebulun, he loved, in spite of the fact that he had inherited his father's gambling habit. Zebulun was often getting himself into the bad company that went with that kind of hazardous pursuit, not to mention the debts. All this was a trial to his parents, especially when following one of Venice's more gruesome murders Zebulun was called on to testify in court against the Jewish gangsters Shabbetai and Moses Benincasa (known as 'da Hindelina') who had perpetrated the crime. Oaths of revenge had been sworn against Zebulun and had come to Leone's terrified ears. Perhaps it was just big talk. In public, under the eyes of the authorities, both Jewish and Christian, those who had sworn vengeance now spoke 'peaceably' to Zebulun. But in the summer of 1621, a fight had broken out between Shabbetai and Zebulun which rapidly turned lethal, for Zebulun was not someone to shrink from a challenge. Shabbetai had chased Zebulun through Cannaregio waving a slaughterer's knife. At some point Zebulun saw a peasant with a sword, took it from him, turned and fought back, cutting his assailant deep in the shoulder. Shabbetai saved himself by jumping into a canal.

The affray was serious enough for authorities to step in and demand peace. Once again da Hindelina pretended to be reconciled; but in the spring of 1622, on the night before the first Seder of Passover, as the ghetto was full of the aroma of leaven being burned, a gang of eight followed Zebulun to 'the House of the Levantine'. Catching wind of what was about to happen, Leone ran about the quarter, frantically looking for his son. He found him just as calls were coming from the street asking Zebulun, as a comrade *bravo*, to join the gang in a fight. Leone seems to have been as tricked as his son. As soon as Zebulun emerged from the house he was set on, his head beaten, his throat slashed. Leone stood rooted to the spot helplessly watching his son's murder. Before Zebulun breathed his last came the cry no father ever wants to hear: 'Father, Father, I am dying.'[39]

'Blood spurted out like a spring and as he could not make it home he collapsed in the house of my brother-in-law Johanan, may God protect him ... there he fell on a bed roiling in blood. Before the doctor could arrive he lost his lifeblood. By the time the physician arrived there was no longer enough of it to keep him alive and his entire right side lost all feeling.' Then he slipped into unconsciousness, barely hanging on for four days before leaving the world in the middle of Passover, and was buried out on the Lido beside his brother Mordecai.

> Upon his coffin while it was being carried away was placed his blood-soiled clothing. The sight of it and the sound of my cries and my woebegone wife caused everyone – even Christians and Turks – to shed tears ... There was no one who had ever spoken with my son including many Christian commoners who were friends of his who did not weep ... He was thirteen days short of twenty-one and so handsome. There was no one like him in the community. He sang with a voice as sweet as an angel. He was wise understanding and cheerful and a writer both of prose and poetry; brave in battle ... Alas I always told him 'your big heart will kill you one of these days'. His courage and weapons he used only to hallow God for he could not abide the debasement of any Jew.[40]

The portrait is heartbreakingly vivid: Zebulun the beautiful, dashing, exuberant blade, the singer of poems including his own, the quick-to-the-draw avenger of Jewish wrongs cut down.

It was barely five years since Leone had sat *shiva* for Mordecai. Now his distraction threatened to drive him out of his wits. Only his determination to bring the murderers to justice kept him on the rails since he was a primary witness to the crime. The assailants were all tried, convicted and banished. A thousand ducats would be given to anyone finding them on the territories of the republic, with the licence to cut off heads to claim the reward (customary procedure in baroque Italy). Leone and Rachel praised the firmness of Venetian justice.

Unlike the aftermath of Mordecai's death, Leone did not take his woe to the gaming table. Music saved him. In 1622 Salomone Rossi paid him a visit, and the timing for the composer was not fortuitous. Ten years earlier his own community of Mantuan Jews had been driven into a ghetto, more restrictive than anything operating in Venice. It must have been in the spirit of defiance as well as consolation that together the two men prepared to publish through the great house of the Bragadin Rossi's *Hashirim Asher Lishlomo*.[41] Anticipating (correctly) a furious controversy inside the Jewish community about what was fit and what unfit for the synagogue, Leone would add his responsum of 1605 defending polyphony. The two men then had to decide a tricky matter of the printed page, for Hebrew was read right to left while musical notes ran in the opposite direction. Leone took the decision to print the Hebrew backwards, figuring that would be less confusing, and relying (reasonably) on the singers' familiarity with the Hebrew words. The result may not quite reach the heights gained by Rossi's contemporary and fellow Mantuan Monteverdi, but it is nonetheless extraordinarily beautiful, an exultation of voices. One of the most powerful of the thirty-three is the mourner's Kaddish – also sung, however, by the whole congregation at various points in the service.[42] Rossi did not compose a deep lament; instead, a blaze of harmonised voices. But then the prayer itself never mentions the dead and is instead an invocation to 'exalt and magnify and sanctify' God's holy name. It is not a lying down before the tomb but a transcendence of it, and for that purpose, Rossi's music remains the most sublimely fitting accompaniment any Jewish hand has composed.

Sung to a mixed congregation they would indeed have given the lie – without any defensiveness – that Judaism was incapable of what Leone called *musika* – high music. Just such a congregation assembled in 1629 to hear him preach at the Ponentine synagogue being rebuilt by the workshop of Longhena. It seems to have been in Venice that the custom began of preaching in the vernacular, with the passages from the Torah portion under discussion quoted in Hebrew and then translated, the convention followed to this day in all but the most ultra-Orthodox synagogues. Leone *wanted* the congregation sitting in the beautiful chamber to grasp his discourse, and in all likelihood, as a sweetener, there would have been a choir and the singing of Rossi's versions of the closing hymns, 'Ayn Keiloheinu' and 'Adon Olam',

Lord of the Universe, ringing out over the canals. Listening to it on that day in 1629 was the brother of Louis XIII, Gaston of Orleans, and his grandiose entourage. While elsewhere in Italy, in Rome especially, Jews had been forced to suffer the invasion of their synagogues by friars haranguing them to come to the baptismal font, in Venice (on that day at least) the very cream of French nobility, courtiers of the Most Christian King, sat good as gold to listen to the Jews.

As is the way in this long story, clouds rolled in shortly after. The bride and groom of the 1622 Mantua wedding had come to a terrible end when Isaachino Masserano's son, in a fit of insane jealousy, blinded his wife, Sarra Copia's sister, with a pair of scissors. In 1630, the ghetto into which Mantua's Jews had been herded was wiped out by an Austrian army fighting a war over the duchy's succession, following the extinction of the Gonzaga line. Survivors fled to Venice only to find themselves overtaken by the worst outbreak of bubonic plague in living memory. For some months, Leone wrote, the ghetto seemed miraculously protected from its ravages, while all around the city Venetians were dying in horrible misery; but eventually it caught up with the Jews too. Prayer had not been enough. Other terrors followed. In 1636-7, some of the Jewish criminal gangs were arrested for fencing stolen property; others for bribing authorities; and the entire city and its governing class turned so fiercely on the ghetto that there were demands to expel the Jews altogether from the republic. In response, two books were published by the two pre-eminent rabbis in Venice, Leone Modena and Simone Luzzatto, describing in illuminating detail the traditions, teachings and observances of Judaism. Both moreover paid special attention to the ethics of commercial and economic dealings between Jews and Gentiles, to the obligation laid on all Jews to be especially moral in their dealings with non-Jews.[43] Leone's work for James I had first been written in Latin, then was translated into French, then Italian, and over many generations into almost all the major European languages, including an English edition early in the eighteenth century. Luzzatto's was written in Italian, addressed to the government of Venice, and thus was the first vernacular 'guide' to Judaism and Jewish life expressly meant for non-Jewish readers. Both were meant as antidotes to Shylockian caricatures of the mercenary vengeful Jew; Modena and Luzzatto found a better way to argue for the common humanity of

Jews than 'if you prick us do we not bleed': dispassionate ethnography. This is who we are, the two books said; this is what we do. You have been to our synagogues, listened to our words and our music, and if not, then come, cross the bridges into the ghetto. We are merchants of Venice too.

Luzzatto went so far as to make a personal appeal (armed with his book) to the doge, and it worked. There would be no expulsion. The merchants of Venice would stay where they were until the Nazis took them away, as they did in elegant Ferrara and musical Mantua.

But this is to jump the gun. The twin explanatory works of the two great rabbis of Venice, together with Rossi's *Songs of Solomon*, Sarra Copia's 'Academy' and her brave withstanding of her literary hero's blandishments, and Leone de Sommi's double-handed theatre, played to Jews and to court and city – all of these great overtures Jews made in the world of Renaissance Italy added up to a heroic belief in the possibility of cohabitation without conversion, of a common stock of wisdom, even a mutual nourishment of Jewish and Christian culture. In this sense the history of Jewish modernity began in the world of the dukes and the doges.

Which does not make Leone Modena some sort of avant-garde reform rabbi. In his last years he saw himself as an heir of Moses Maimonides, the great medieval sage who had spent his life attempting to reconcile Torah wisdom with rational humanism. Leone attacked Kabbalah and the excesses of visionary mysticism, attempted to contain his gambling habit with limited success, and fell on penurious times. His remaining son Isaac the wanderer had sent word of his sudden riches but then abruptly cut off communications, so that Leone feared the worst. His wife Rachel suddenly turned on him, so relentlessly that he fled the house. After she recovered from a stroke, Leone (slightly shockingly) reported that much of her remained paralysed but not, alas, the blade of her tongue, which cut him as sharply as ever. He was being looked after by his daughter Diana who had remarried after her first husband's death, and the grandfather took pleasure in his grandson though was frightened when the boy was jailed for some months for an infringement of Venice's censorship laws. In 1640 Leone drew up a will and set down specific instructions for his funeral, telling his executors to heap all his published works (and there were many of them) in a pile on his coffin.

In 1641, a barge lit with forty great candles, as befitted the passing of a sage, ploughed through the black waters of the lagoon to the burial ground on the Lido. Although Jews were required to bury their dead beyond a city's walls, it is obvious that the signory of the republic wanted them as far away as possible. But the cemetery which few visit is a beautiful place, overhung by shade trees, its gravestones crumpled by the passing of the centuries and the beat of the Adriatic winds. Many are profuse; all have Hebrew inscriptions, some with additions in Italian, Ladino or Latin. One of the retaining ashlar walls supports the most grandiose tombs of the mighty of the ghetto Sephardim: their stones ornamented with heraldic devices, plumed helms, the elaborate coats of arms the Jews of Venice loved; and everywhere the Jewish lions, lions for the Leons, none of them the winged cats of St Mark. The lions carry nostalgia for a world most of the dead and buried could never have known – that of Jewish Castile and Aragon – but it was preserved in language, food and music. And the lions are also of course Lions of Judah: the rampant flanking guardians of the Aron Hakodesh, the Ark of the Torah. There are tombs over which doves flutter, deer race, and bears dance; there are garlands and wreaths, olive trees and roses of Sharon and the occasional disconcertingly grinning skull.

The graves of Mordecai, Zebulun and Rachel were waiting for the patriarch and thither his body eventually came. A stone of extreme simplicity marks the spot. Not far away is Sarra Copia's tomb, beside her father Simon. Beyond, under the racing clouds, lies the lagoon, stretching out to the immense horizon where sky and water melt together. Along that thin edge of the world Jews would be shipping their goods and themselves to some distant port. They could live, somehow, on the edge of the world. The question for the rest of modern history was could they live, happily, at its centre?

6

JEWS WITHOUT PAIN?

No fear (except on Yom Kippur when standing accountable before the Maker). No guilt. No murderous mobs gathering around the corner. No luggage standing by. No scanning the timetables. No wailing, gnashing, hand-wringing, rending and roaring. No Jews, then, since there had never been a time when calamity had not fastened itself to them like a shadow. Where could such a place have been? In dreams. You might as well go to China.

How did it feel for the Jesuit to be taken for a Jew? Was Matteo Ricci, Superior of the Jesuit mission in China, amused or aghast? The mistake occurred in the third week of June 1605. In the Beijing of the Ming emperor, scholar trees had leafed out into their full, plumy crowns, and the tea houses were full of chattering patrons. At the mission, Ricci – Li Madou to his Chinese hosts – received a visit from a middle-aged man dressed in the long silk coat and cap of a mandarin. The visitor declared himself to be Ai Tian who had travelled, so he said, from the city of Kaifeng, 470 miles away in Henan province on the Yellow River. Kaifeng had been the capital of the northern Song dynasty, and though the Song had long gone it was still a metropolis of a million people. Somewhere in the middle of the city, Ai Tian said, at the place where Earth Market Character Street met Fire God Shrine Street, stood his Temple of Purity and Truth, two great stone lions at its gate. Lions were not, of course, unusual in China. But these stood in memory of the guardian lions of the Jerusalem Temple, universally present in the iconography of diaspora Judaism. There, the Jews of Kaifeng (some two thousand of them) assembled to read the scriptures and say their devotions. As with all Jews everywhere, the pious came three times a day, for the morning, afternoon and evening services; the not quite so pious on Sabbath, Mondays and Thursdays, when portions of the Law were read, and then there were many who attended just when they could. Ai Tian had been meaning to come to Beijing in search of a different and better post. He was sixty; it was his due after a lifetime's dignified, assiduous service. (He would secure a school superintendency and inspectorate, the kind of position he had in mind.) But recently he had been given to understand that in Beijing there was now a small sect of barbarians who, like his own people, believed in a single, indivisible God, the God of the *shema* who thus followed the Dao, the way. They could only be Jews. If this was so, a blessed reunion was at hand. After innumerable generations of separation, China's Jews were about to be joined by their brethren from beyond the Middle Kingdom. He would be the first to experience the joy.

An irony was in the offing, richly comical-tragical, for Matteo Ricci laboured under a mirror misapprehension. The man who stood before him, he decided, must be a secret Christian or descended from ancestors who had once been of the fellowship of Christ. Countless medieval travellers had confirmed the existence of Christians and Jews in China, and Muslims were known to be there in abundance. To be sure this seemed to be a Christian who had lost touch with the gospel. But God had sent him nonetheless. This was the day of St John the Baptist. Now it was for Ricci to be the Forerunner. He ushered the mandarin into the octagonal chapel of the mission where on the simple altar were set two paintings, one of the Virgin and Child, the other of the Baptist. Father Ricci knelt before them, his eyes closed. Remarking, as he had to, that it was not his custom to prostrate before images, Ai Tian obeyed the courtesies and in some fashion followed the obeisance, adding politely that the paintings were handsome likenesses of Rebecca and Jacob, with the hirsute Esau on one side. Ricci endeavoured to point out the unfortunate error while sensing something was amiss. But it got worse when his visitor assumed that pictures of the apostles and evangelists were representations of the founders of the Twelve Tribes of Israel.

Gradually, disconcertingly, the truth sank in. This was a Chinese Jew, fully of one kind of nation and yet somehow fully of the other. His faith was that of Yiselie, Mandarin for 'Israel'. Learned in everything, Ricci was likely to have heard of the existence of such people.

Marco Polo had commented on their presence in 1286, merchants presumably come from the Silk Road. It was even said that in a spirit of tolerant ecumenism Kublai Khan made a point of observing the festivals of the different God-believers in his lands: Christian, Muslim and Jewish! And there had been several Arab geographers, not least the great Ibn Battuta in the fourteenth century, who had confirmed their existence along with Muslim communities, also during the time of the Yuan Mongol emperors. Perhaps indeed they had come in their train from central Asia? Judaeo-Persian was a common tongue among them, along with Mandarin which suggested a long presence on the Silk Road.

It was a disappointment but not a crushing one. Throughout the whole world the Church was doing everything it could to shepherd the Jews to Christ, for thereby lay the imminence of the Last Days and the Second Coming. Everywhere, too, the hunt for the Lost Tribes, the Israelites uncorrupted by the rabbis and the Talmud, went on ceaselessly. On his third voyage, Columbus imagined he was drawing close to the Edenic terrestrial paradise, encouraging succeeding explorers of Spanish America to think that sooner or later they would encounter the descendants of ancient Israelites and gather them in.

So Ricci was undeterred by the misunderstanding. Ai Tian returned a year later with further information about the Jews of Kaifeng. And in 1607 Ricci dispatched two Chinese converts, one of them a lay brother, north to Kaifeng with a letter for the rabbi, Abishai, telling him that in Beijing he had all the Hebrew sacred texts precious to the Jews and a New Testament which would be seen to be more precious still. When the reply came back from Rabbi Abishai, it was apparent that the misunderstandings persisted. If Ricci thought the Chinese Jews might originally have been backsliding Christians who could be returned to the gospel, the rabbi took the Jesuit for some sort of eccentric, wayward Jew. He was old, he explained; Ricci might come and succeed him in the synagogue, though he would have to give up eating pork. And he had to accept his mistake about the Messiah who, it was well known, would not appear for another ten thousand years. Through all this comedy of mutual errors, there was a thread of persistence. In 1610 Jews came from Kaifeng to the Jesuit mission and were treated to a banquet (without pork).

Even now, Ricci's hopes of a conversion were not altogether dashed. His emissaries to Kaifeng had returned with a copy of the beginning and end portions of the Torah, written in Hebrew. Since their settlement was very ancient, and since they had been isolated for so long from the rest of the Jews, it was possible, he thought, that they had remained uncorrupted by the later perversions of the Talmud.[1] They were, in fact, a living relic of pre-rabbinic Torah religion; purer than the Karaites. It had long been an article of faith among theologians that it was the supercession of the Talmud over the Bible which had prevented Jews from seeing that the prophecies of their Old Testament regarding the Messiah had been fulfilled in the New. Now if indeed the Chinese had been miraculously uncontaminated, they were surely primed for saving illumination. If one of their Torah scrolls could be acquired and compared with those routinely used by other Jews, he felt sure that the disparities would convince them that the rabbis had made falsifying additions. Without those obstructing corruptions, the light would shine through.

Ricci died in 1610. As subsequent missionaries learned more about the Kaifeng Jews, their synagogue and their world, so they became less confident of the likelihood of their imminent conversion. For they were not some anomaly waiting to be brought back to the fold. They were, in fact, perfectly fitted into the cultural universe of Ming China: at once deeply of their host culture and just as deeply Jewish (if not especially Talmudic).

A community of two thousand Jews was a tiny enclave in a city of a million, but it was nonetheless distinctive. While one of the four stone inscriptions in the temple claimed they had been in China since the Han emperors, another stated that the settlement had taken place in the tenth century during the reign of the second emperor of the Northern Song dynasty, Taizong, famed for his interest in foreigners and barbarians, and who had made Kaifeng his capital. A temple had first been built in 1163 but then had been rebuilt after the usual disasters of fires and floods in 1279 and again in 1465 and would be once more in 1642, always on the same site and to the traditional pattern. In 1722 another Jesuit would make drawings of the temple showing it to be superficially indistinguishable from any other pagoda. The free-standing portico, where worshippers removed their shoes, had a triple tier of roofs with curling gables, trees on each side and a double row of columns. As in all such temples, themselves modelled on the layout of an imperial residence, a succession of three further court-yards enclosed the two pavilion halls which made up the heart of the synagogue. The main hall was a spacious eighty feet by sixty feet. But the resemblance to a Buddhist or Confucian temple did not make the building any less Jewish. After the destruction of the Jerusalem Temple, synagogues had invariably conformed to the style of the cultures around them. The synagogues of classical late antiquity had had colonnaded aisles and floor mosaics; the medieval synagogue in Prague was Gothic; one of the two great synagogues in Toledo boasted Moorish horseshoe arches standard in mosques, and the rebuilt Spanish–Portuguese synagogue in Venice would be baroque. Thus it was with the Kaifeng temple's standard Chinese architectural style. What made it nonetheless a house of Judaism was whether it was designed as a place to say daily prayers and have the Torah read.

Three features of the principal hall of worship gave the answer. The first was a 'Chair of Moses' (which, intriguingly, was also present in one of the earliest known synagogues of all, at Dura-Europos in third-century Syria) from which the Torah was read, the scrolls leaned against its back. On days when the rabbi gave formal judgements, he did so seated on the Chair of Moses, a canopy of authority above his head. Then at the end of that same hall was an Aron Hakodesh, the Ark where the sheepskin scrolls of the community were kept. Handsome lacquered wooden scroll cases survive, preserved like other Kaifeng Jewish artefacts in the Royal Museum of Ontario.[2] The Kaifeng Jews read the Torah in a cycle of fifty-four *parshot* sections, another custom they held in common with Persian Jews. Even more dramat-ically, on the wall above the Ark, was written, encircled in gold, the opening lines of the *shema*, the ritual affirmation of God's uniqueness, recited thrice daily, facing west towards Jerusalem, in the morning, afternoon and evening prayers, and tellingly set above stone tablets praising the emperor. The usual Jewish order of priorities, honouring the heavenly king (known as 'August Heaven') above the earthly, was in uncontroversial evidence at Kaifeng.

Kaifeng Jews were self-governing, having at their head both the rabbi and a second 'spiritual leader', the *man-la*. Like Chinese Muslims they abstained from the staple meat of pork, as well as from cats and dogs. Ritual slaughterers, the *shokhetim*, supplied kosher meat, with the sciatic nerve of the thigh muscle extracted (in memory of Jacob's thigh bone dislocated in his wrestling match with the angel), so that in some quarters the Jews were known as the Sect Which Plucks the Sinews. They circumcised their male children eight days after birth, and kept Sabbath, refraining from any kind of labour and preparing the food on Fridays just as in Salonika, Cairo, Cochin or Amsterdam. They prayed with heads covered by blue caps but also in bare feet, and often kneeled during the service, customs which had originally accompanied Jewish prayers and which survived in Kaifeng. There were no *tallit* prayer shawls, nor *tefillin* phylacteries, though 'proper adjustments of dress' were mentioned which suggests some sort of ritual clothing for the devotions. Passages in the inscription of 1512 have been translated, perhaps over-optimistically, by Tiberiu Weisz as the eighteen daily blessings of the Amidah – the standing prayer at the heart of the thrice-daily services. And these were certainly accompanied, as specified in the 1489 inscription, with the rhythmic bowing for the right way, the Dao, practised among Jews generation after generation, worldwide.[3] Before praying, they immersed themselves in the purification bath of the mikvah and observed all the festivals on the correct dates of the Hebrew calendar.[4] On the Feast of Unleavened Bread and Lamb, they ate sweet mutton soup as their 'bitter food' commemorating the travails of Egypt. (A most beautiful seventeenth-century Passover Haggadah written with a classical soft ink brush survives in the library of the Hebrew Union College in Cincinnati.[5]) They built the tabernacle on Sukkot; and even celebrated Purim, the feast of Esther, in the usual riotous fashion, Chinese style. Yom Kippur was their 'Day of Great Abstention and Confession of Faults'. The non-Jewish writer of the third inscription of 1663 described the fast in terms every Jew everywhere instantly understands as authentic:

> At the end of autumn [the Jews] close their doors for a whole day and give themselves up to the cultivation of purity, cutting themselves off entirely from food and drink in order to nourish the higher nature. On that day the scholar interrupts his reading and the farmer suspends his work of ploughing or reaping and the traveller stops on his way. Desires are forgotten, attainments set aside, and all apply themselves to preserving the heart and nourishment of the mind so that through direction there may be a restoration of goodness.[6]

The Jews of Kaifeng (and there were or had been communities in Ningbo, Hangzhou and other towns too) were thoroughly at home on the banks of the Yellow River. Though Christian orthodoxy insisted (most recently in the papal bull of 1555) that the Jews had been condemned to a *worldwide* eternity of servitude, degradation and homelessness as punishment for their crime of killing Jesus, in Kaifeng they appeared to be living a rooted, frictionless life. Instead of being hedged about by confining walls, they were at liberty to live wherever they chose. If they congregated near their synagogue, it was for the usual reason of needing to be within walking distance on Sabbath and holy days. They were also free to pursue whatever occupation they wished – the 1663 inscription presupposes there were Jewish farmers and there had indeed been grants of land made to them by the emperor, another unthinkable concession in the Christian world. While many were merchants and shopkeepers, others like Ai Tian were readily accepted into the class of scholar-mandarins that governed the empire; there were Jewish soldiers, doctors, artisans, perfumers, labourers and porters, and as one might expect, silk merchants. Ai Tian described to Matteo Ricci his typical, somewhat upwardly mobile Jewish family. He was the *chokhem*, the smart one, who had been encouraged to sit for the daunting examinations of the Four Books, Mencius, Confucius and the rest which would open the elite to him. But, he ruefully confessed to the Jesuits who showed him a Bible, his Hebrew had suffered as a consequence of all that study. His two brothers, who had not taken the examination route, had better command of the sacred Jewish language.

In other ways, too, the Kaifeng Jews fitted into the local culture without sacrificing their religious identity. Many were polygamous and kept concubines, but that of course was not a violation of the Torah (though since the thirteenth century it had been frowned on by the European rabbis). Their descent, as among the Jews of south India, was patrilinear, again as it had been in biblical times. In contrast to the ferocious prohibitions operating in Christian and Muslim societies, there were no objections to the cohabitation between Jews and non-Jewish Chinese 'handmaidens', nor to their conversion to Judaism. It was as Ruth had been for Boaz, and the children of such unions were accepted as full Jews.

The affinity between Torah ethics and the Confucian way, expressly celebrated on one of the limestone slabs in the Kaifeng synagogue, did not necessarily dilute their Judaism any more than it had in Hellenistic Alexandria or Umayyad Cordoba. It could be said (and has been) that this Chinese-coloured Judaism was so Confucianised as to make it unrecognisable and that the Dao was the way of nothing except the inevitability of complete Jewish assimilation and inevitable disappearance. But the community of Chinese Jews had already existed for at least seven hundred years (assuming the earlier Han and even earlier Zhou datings were legendary) and would survive for another two centuries. Turning the self-extinction presumption on its head, it could be argued that a convergence with the host culture sustained rather than sapped that endurance. It helped, of course, that Confucianism was more a system of ethics than a theology, and that imperial China – which made room for Buddhism and Daoism – never saw itself as imposing a state religious orthodoxy. The ancestor worship required of all the sects as a condition of their toleration in imperial China took the form of incense burning in chased lotus burner bowls set on the floor and on tables in the temple. But the Kaifeng Jews made a careful distinction between reverence and worship, and the incense-burning obligation was virtually identical with the requirement to light annual memorial candles on the anniversary of a parent's death, and to say the memorial prayer, the *yizkor*, on high holy days and festivals. Likewise the formless, faceless, numinous God of Judaism (known to the Kaifeng Jews as Etonoi or Yotoi, close to the Hebrew 'Adonai' for Lord) was so similar to the non-human creative force in Confucian cosmology as to represent a natural kinship between the two rites. Aware of the popularity of sacred statues, above all in Buddhism, the first inscription goes out of its way to emphasise the aversion to idols as a founding principle of the Jewish Dao. Confucianism, to be sure, had no Yahweh-like 'jealous God' marching through history, bringing about the rise and destruction of kingdoms and empires. But there is a striking affinity between the passive force of Creation and the God of Safed Kabbalah, withdrawn to some indeterminate place leaving a creative void.

There were certainly some hybrid elements in the cosmology and scripture recorded on the four inscriptions which would have struck rabbis as entirely outside scripture and the faith. In one of the inscriptions Adam, the first man, is made contemporary with the primordial cosmic giant Pan Gu, out of whose dissolving remains Nature was formed. But just as often there are striking complements. The five coloured stones from which the vault of heaven was rebuilt after a universal deluge was akin to the rainbow spectrum through which God made His promise to Nuoya (Noah) to refrain from another such act of global annihilation. Creation myths aside, the Kaifeng Jews' understanding of their religion closely followed Hebrew scripture. Yabolahan (Abraham) had meditated beneath the sky and had been the originator of Judaic wisdom, passing the covenant to Yisa (Isaac) and Yage (Jacob). Moses (Moxi) was Shifu, the Master of Laws, the Patriarch of the Correct Way. Since the third great biblical authority is said to be Ezra (Yisila) – who was also Fumin, He Who Makes the Light Shine Brightly Forth, whether from his eponymous Book or from Nehemiah – it can be assumed that the Kaifeng community had the entirety of the Hebrew Bible, and given that Rabbi Abishai had tried to tell Ricci that he knew the writings of Jesus well – that is to say Jesus bar Sirach, the author of Ecclesiasticus – we know they had at least some of the Apocryphal books too.

The compatibility between Jews and imperial Chinese life was carved into those four stone inscriptions. In their respective ways they were all founding (or refounding) charters and histories, even when they disagreed on the dates of the events. The earliest inscription, commemorating rebuilding after a flood, emphasised a Tiandao, a 'Way of Heaven' common to Judaism and Confucianism, and narrated a founding myth of mutual interest and benign curiosity. 'They [the founders] brought western cloth as a tribute to the Song emperor who then said, "Come to our China: honour and preserve the customs of your ancestors, stay here and hand them down through the generations."'[7] According to the same inscription this act of imperial hospitality was sealed by the all-important grant of full Chinese names to the incoming Jews. Thus 'Liewei' (likely to have been originally Levi) became Li, and was joined by other name-clans – the Ai, Jin, Gao, Zhao, Zhang, Shi and more – all of which became the family lineages around which the Kaifeng Jews organised their lives: their marriages and burials, the provision for the sick and the poor. Hebrew names existed alongside Chinese ones, with the rabbis known as Abishai or Pinehas – much as they have in every diaspora culture,

but the bestowal of indigenous names as an honorific gift of acceptance was in glaring contrast to the baptismal renaming done, for the
most part under terrifying coercion, to New Christians. The only
godfather of those Chinese names was the benevolent emperor. When
he presented a gift of incense to An San, a common Jewish soldier
(who may also have been a physician), in gratitude for the part he
played in foiling a palace conspiracy, and formally permitted the
rebuilding of the synagogue, the emperor was doing the opposite of
what came instinctively to Christian princes. Instead of perpetuating
the stereotype of the eternal alien, dangerous and unassimilable, the
Chinese ruler was confirming the naturalness of a fit between a
Chinese and a Jewish life.

That fit was exemplified by the fact that none of those who made
the inscription of 1663, from the scholar-mandarin who composed it
to those who carved it into the stone, were themselves Jewish.[8] The
hero at the centre of it – a Jewish imperial army officer and learned
scholar – commissioned the account in which he figured as a Chinese
Nehemiah, simultaneously restoring the physical fabric of a broken
community, and ensuring its perpetuation in both Jewish and Gentile
memory. The principal author-scholar-scribe Liu Kuang-tso made sure
to mention that he had studied the writings of the Jews with whom
he was evidently close, and had written his account in such a way
that anyone reading of the 'restoration of the Scriptures and the
synagogue would recognise the merit of the religion and its resistance
to obliteration'. More Jewish it does not get.

The central drama of the history was a rebel siege of the city by
a rebel Manchu army in 1642 during the reign of the last Ming
emperor, reducing Kaifeng to such extremities of starvation that
human flesh was sold for consumption. Sources then disagree as to
whether it was an imperial relief force which cut the Yellow River
dykes with the idea of swamping the besiegers, or whether it was
the rebels themselves. A catastrophic flood followed, in which 300,000
lives were said to have been lost and the city (including the synagogue,
sited close to the Yellow River) engulfed. As much as half of the
Jewish community may have lost their lives, but throughout the ordeal
had stayed loyal, and once order had been restored in 1645 one of
their number, a Major Zhao from the defending force, became the
Nehemiah of Kaifeng.

He repaired the roads, built bridges, and summoned the people to return to their occupations. Fearing that the members of his religion, through the ruin of their synagogue, might disperse and never come back together and unable to contemplate the work his ancestors had built and preserved through the centuries destroyed so suddenly, he posted troops to patrol and protect [the ruins] of the synagogue by day and by night.[9]

Still more meaningfully, the history describes two young scholars, Gao Hsien and Li Zheng, looking for the Scrolls of the Law and twenty-six sacred books carried off by the floodwater. Fragments of the scrolls were found in the mud along with ten sacred books, and were carefully dried out by the rabbi and the *man-la*, the spiritual leader. The pieces were then patched together but for the moment only one scroll could be made legible enough for use in the temporary temple. Some surviving fragments of those Hebrew scrolls do indeed show signs of water damage consistent with this history. Eventually thirteen scrolls were reconstructed from fragments and the temple rebuilt on its original site. From a flood, then, rebirth; out of calamity, redemption. When Major Zhao, who had spent a great deal of his own money on the rebuilding, came back to his home after a military campaign in Shaanxi in the north-west, he struck a grandly biblical note: 'The glories which have been established for hundreds of years have returned and we behold their abundance.'[10]

As soon as one thinks about it, the affinity between two cultures, both of which bestowed governing authority on the learned, seems obvious. Yet there was nowhere else in the world where it had been realised in quite the Chinese way. Major Zhao had two cousins, Zhao Yingcheng (also known as Moses ben Abraham) and his brother Zhao Yingdou, both of whom, in the years following the flood, became committed to the work of restoration. The two of them were scholar-mandarin officials, but Zhao Yingcheng had been able enough to attain a top jinshih academic degree. With that achievement came high office as a judicial official (Secretary of the Board of Punishments), then one of the governorships in Fujian province. In that capacity he took charge of quelling a revolt by an army of 'brigands'. Once they were defeated and captured and the province was pacified, Zhao Yingcheng built a special assembly hall for readings and lectures (such a Jewish gesture), the sign of true peace being that for the first time in many years of disorder 'the sound of reading was heard'.[11]

The major and the two scholar-mandarins made it their business to uncover the foundations of the old ruined synagogue. Before he died in his late thirties, Zhao Yingcheng had written what must have been (for it did not alas survive) his Chinese-Jewish history: *A Record of the Vicissitudes of the Scriptures*. His younger brother wrote a different book no less indispensable to the life of a Jewish community, *A Preface to the Clarification of the Way* (a preface which, as is often the case in Jewish religious literature, is ten chapters long). We will never know, but this sounds very much like the Kaifeng version of Maimonides' *Guide for the Perplexed*, or perhaps Joseph Karo's *Shulkhan Arukh*.

To survey the predicament of Jews in much of the rest of the world is to marvel at what the Kaifeng community escaped. In China, Jews were not subjected to violence and persecution, nor demonised as God killers. Their synagogues were not invaded by conversionary harangues. They were not physically segregated from non-Jews nor forced to wear humiliating forms of identification on their dress. They were not forced into the most despised and vulnerable occupations, not stigmatised as grasping and vindictive, and portrayed neither as predatory monsters nor pathetic victims.

Ming China turns up in another community, three thousand miles away, and, like the Kaifeng Jews, living for the most part without terror. The floor of the Paradesi synagogue in Kochi's Old Town (Fort Cochin) on the Keralan coast of south-west India is covered in a carpet of exquisite blue-and-white tiles. (There too, as in China, worshippers evidently said their prayers barefoot, leaving their shoes at the entrance.) The tiles may have been shipped directly from China, whose junks, in the last years of the Ming, were sailing further west; but more likely they were imported by the Dutch who controlled Cochin after 1663. That China–Kerala–Netherlands connection describes a triangle of toleration where Jews could make a home without the cycles of terror that dogged them in Christian Europe.

The Paradesi still stands at the end of the principal street of 'Jew Town' in Fort Cochin, close to the site of the protecting palace of the rajas, the faces of its clock tower inscribed on one face in Hebrew and the other in Judaeo-Malayalam. At the centre of the ceramic floor stands an elliptical *bimah* reading dais, enclosed by a graceful run of brass rails. Teak settees and benches line the perimeter of the walls and the Ark is carved from another tropical timber – sandalwood, I believe. Halfway up the lane Sara Cohen, now in her nineties, who has herself become a tourist attraction as 'the last Jew of Cochin', still presides over her embroidery and linen shop, while the other staple of Jewish craftsmen – ornate metalwork – has been taken over by local townspeople. Conducting any sort of service in the Paradesi depends on recruiting vistors to make up the required *minyan* of ten adult males. There are many Fridays when this does not happen. Sara tells me that nonetheless she goes to the Paradesi on Friday nights to have 'a cry'. Sometimes you can't escape lachrymose history.

But these are the tears of solitude and ghostly absence. In the seventeenth and eighteenth centuries there was less cause for lamentation. Though it was not intended for their community the Paradesi is also the custodian of the Sasanam, a medieval proclamation of hospitality, publicly displayed in much the same way as the stone inscriptions of Kaifeng. The scrolls, written in a vernacular form of Tamil, have been dated to the eleventh century, and proclaim to the leader of the Jews (then most likely in Cranganore, north of Cochin), one Joseph Rabban, the right of Jews to settle within the realm of the local raja. They would be permitted to practise the rituals of their religion undisturbed; build synagogues; make and use palanquins; light day lamps of honour, sound trumpets and enjoy certain tax exemptions. It is likely too that they were granted land for cemeteries. The oldest extant Indo-Jewish tombstone with Hebrew inscriptions dates from the thirteenth century. In token of his authority, Joseph Rabban was given the tax farm of Anjuvannam district on the edge of Cranganore as a source of income for himself and the community, as well as the property of 'seventy-two free houses'. Plainly the raja wanted Jews in his dominions.

The copper founding charter of the Malabari Jews was passed from generation to generation and travelled from place to place, as vicissitudes of habitat and politics moved them along the shore, ending up in Dutch-protected Cochin. Along with it came the usual heavy cargo of arrival myths. Some, like the supply of apes to Solomon's Temple, were endearingly absurd; others, locating the origins of Indian Jews in a wave of emigrants following the destruction of the Second Temple, or the female Jewish flute player who understood St

Thomas's Hebrew when he came to India in search of converts, were only slightly less fanciful. But the Jewish presence in India is richly chronicled in the Middle Ages. The Radanite merchants of the ninth century went as far as the subcontinent, and the Cairo Geniza is full of documents to and from merchants trading across the Indian Ocean to southern Arabia, Hormuz, Aden and the Persian Gulf.[12] Jews are blown off course, captured by pirates, make money fast and lose it even faster, and drown in wrecks (among them, to Moses Maimonides' unquenchable sorrow, his brother David). The regional princes in whose domains these traders planted footholds were predominantly Hindu. But there was always a sizeable, competing Muslim population, along with Parsi and indigenous Christians, so the rajas seldom felt the need to impose the kind of religious monopoly which turned Jews into supplicants at best and vulnerable anomalies at worst.

The Jewish traders of the Malabar coast were thought of as a parallel *nayar* mercantile caste in a culture which increasingly saw its prosperity linked to long-distance maritime trade. Just as with the Kaifeng Jews, they found a fit with their host society. Because Jewish descent (again as in China) was patrilinear, local women were converted, and generations of dark-skinned Malabari Jews came to be physically and in many other ways indistinguishable from the culture around them. Once again a local language – Malayalam – was married to Hebrew and Jewish forms and produced a Judaeo-Malayalam vernacular. Women took a distinctive place in the life of the community that would have disconcerted European Jews: as singers of a gloriously rich Jewish hymnody; going about the streets bareheaded and, like their men, attending synagogue in bare feet and anklets. As in China, the core of Jewish practice – Sabbath, the fasts and festivals – were all observed but with south Indian variants that developed organically. 'The Closing of the Doors' which ends Yom Kippur, the Day of Atonement, was dramatically ceremonious, while on Simchat Torah, the Rejoicing of the Law, the synagogues were covered in jasmine and brocaded satins embroidered by the women of the community. A special portable Ark was made to carry the Scrolls of the Law around the streets to the sound of drums and brass, not unlike the processing of Hindu gods such as Ganpati, and at the end of the day, the Ark was dismantled and its pieces sent into the flowing waters of the rivers or bays, very much like the rituals of Hindu rebirth.

Not all the Malabari Jews were merchants or even shopkeepers. Many, known as the 'Saturday oil pressers' – confusingly, named after the day on which they refrained from that work – were artisans, or even cultivators, carters, porters and boatmen. Mostly they were concentrated in and around Cranganore, and known in the community as 'Shingli'. But after the Periyar River flooded and silted up in 1341, the harbour was no longer viable and many moved south to Cochin, although there was still enough commerce left at Cranganore for a number of new immigrants to make their way there after the expulsions from Spain. Many were Ladino-speaking Sephardim from Iberia; others were from the world of Indian Ocean trade: Yemen, Hormuz and Ottoman Turkey; still others from Safed and Jerusalem, Aleppo and Baghdad. Their connections with the European and Mediterranean world, hungry for pepper and spices, and their ability to deliver the goods to Lisbon and Antwerp (to the house of Mendes in fact), brought them a near monopoly of the supply end of what had become in the early sixteenth century the world's most valuable commerce. The conspicuousness of these new Indian Jews triggered a predictable reaction from mostly Muslim competitors, who in 1523–4, together with the raja of Calicut, mounted a violent assault on the Cranganore communities, both 'Black' and 'White'.

The raja of Cochin saw an opportunity to bring the 'Paradesi', the Foreigner-Jews, to his territory, and the synagogue went up in 1568, close to his palace of Mattancherry. But just as had happened with the arrival of the Sephardim in Ottoman Turkey, the Malabari and Paradesi communities lived in parallel rather than a common world. Reproducing all too faithfully Indian preoccupations with skin colour and caste, they seldom if ever shared synagogues, marriages or food. The Paradesi 'Whites' wouldn't touch meat slaughtered by Malabaris, however strictly they may have followed ritual laws. Though the older community incorporated medieval liturgical poetry (the *piyyutim*) into their services, the incoming Paradesi, whether from Iberia or not, fancied themselves as coming from a richer and more sophisticated culture.

They did, however, have a common threat from the Portuguese Christian empire. Hardly had the Portuguese made landfall on the western coast of India and taken Goa, than complaints were heard about the numbers of Jews and suspicious New Christians who were thronging to the pepper and spice trade. Trust the Jews and crypto-Jews to get in the way of the two great ventures of the Portuguese Indian empire: winning bodies and souls for Christ, and spices for the treasury. The Jewish infestation, as both the friars (and later the Jesuits) and the soldiers saw it, was so serious that the great admiral Afonso de Albuquerque asked permission from the king to 'exterminate the Jews, one by one, as they are encountered'. Nine years after the Inquisition was introduced in Portugal, it arrived in Goa, to the great joy of the Jesuit fathers who had asked for it. The first inquisitors immediately made it clear who was the supreme authority, moving the Holy Office into the palace of the Indian ruler and obliging the Portuguese governor to find a less imposing residence. In its first few years the Goa Inquisition arrested over four thousand and murdered seventy-two in autos-da-fé.

As many Sephardim as could escaped Goa to Cranganore, but the Portuguese military, always with the Jesuits and Dominicans in its train, took that port city as well, triggering another exodus south to Cochin. They were running just ahead of the crushing rock that was Portuguese imperial power. And eventually it reached Cochin too. Only the fact that the Portuguese calculated it was better to come to a modus vivendi with local Indian powers rather than be forever involved in military campaigns, meant that the Inquisition stopped at the walls of the Old Town where the jurisdiction of the raja continued to protect the synagogues and dwellings of Jew Town. Their proximity to his palace at Mattancherry was more important than ever.

Portuguese Christians and the Jews they had expelled or forcibly converted were caught in a cat-and-mouse game. Samuel Usque's *Consolation* had represented the misery of endless uprootings into opportunities to find new places of safety; with the global expansion of Portuguese power, those asylums were coming to be few and far between. But on the run as they were, the Jews did not cut themselves off from their old Iberian culture (any more than the German victims of Nazism would repudiate Goethe and Schiller). On the contrary, they traded (often literally) on their grasp of the Iberian languages as well as Italian, Hebrew and Arabic to make connections between supply and demand, exotic raw materials and European consumer demand. At the same time as the monarchy pressed hard on their heels, it understood the value of that dispersion. Occasionally, in the strategic interests of its trade, the Crown chose to turn a blind eye to the doubtful religious loyalties of New Christians. And even when priests and soldiers decided to hound the Jews wherever they went, they could not always be sure of forcing local powers who had given them protection to stand aside. Sometimes those native rulers valued what the Jews had brought.

In the first two decades of the seventeenth century, a small but thriving colony of openly professing Portuguese Jews and reverting New Christians established itself on the West African coast of Senegal. Though Portuguese power (now part of the Spanish monarchy) established on the island archipelagos of Cape Verde and São Tomé loomed large, it stopped short of outright conquest on the African mainland, not least because the Wolof kings of Senegambia would have made formidable adversaries. The Jews moved into the interstices between these two powers and prospered by selling the sword and dagger blades the Senegambian warrior kingdoms needed to maintain their own dominance, especially in captive raids upriver.[13] In exchange, the Jews took hides, beeswax, ivory and slaves. The ivory and wax went home to Amsterdam; the slaves to the Caribbean and Brazil.

As in India and China, the relationship with the Wolofs was close enough for some of the men to take African concubine-servants and even wives who were then converted, and the mulatto children accepted as full Jews. Patrilineal rules of descent again applied in defining who was Jewish and who was not. A mixed-race generation of Eurafrican Jews, the males all circumcised, then grew up with strong connections to their native origins. The result was that when the Portuguese pressed the kings to get rid of these undesirable competitors they ran into unexpectedly stiff resistance.

In West Africa, knowing the Portuguese would bring them trouble, the Jews went on a pre-emptive counter-attack against the Christians.[14] When the Portuguese targeted a group of Jews based in the town of Joal on the 'Petite Côte', they fought back (in an area where some of the rulers were Muslim) by describing the Catholics as pagans. Ruefully one of the Portuguese reported that the Jews represented them as 'people who worship sticks and stones and who seek to harm them [the Jews] because they followed the way of Musa, Moses in the language of the Blacks and further they presented themselves to the King [of Joal] as initiates circumcised like the King himself and the other Black people'.[15] The Jews on the Petite Côte

also knew how to appeal to the tribal kings' indignation at Portuguese
pretensions to rule inland as well as the island dominions and coastal
forts. When they got another comeuppance, a New Christian (many
of whom reverted to Judaism in Africa and remained Jewish when
they went back to Amsterdam) made no attempt to disguise his
pleasure at the African king's refusal to go along with Portuguese
presumptions.

> To this port [Porto de Ale] came people who profess the Law of Moses
> and here they do maintain their rituals and ceremonies like the ones
> of Judea, and the Portuguese seeking to kill them and expel them from
> that place ran a serious risk. Because the King took the side of the Jews
> and told the Portuguese that his land was a market where all kinds of
> people had a right to live. And no one could cause disorder in his lands
> otherwise he would order their heads cut off. If they wanted to make
> war they should do it by sea and not on [his] land.[16]

Even if the Portuguese succeeded in making life difficult for the
Senegambian Jews, in the spirit of Usque's infinitely self-adjusting map
of refuges, there was somewhere else for them to go: the Dutch
republic. Unable to repress the revolt against them in the northern
Netherlands, and haemorrhaging treasure, the Spanish monarchy
entered into a truce with the Dutch in 1609 which lasted for twelve
crucial years. The breathing space allowed Portuguese Jews and New
Christians to exploit their connections between old and new homes to
commercial advantage right across the Atlantic and Indian oceans.
A community rooted; synagogues opened, and some of the Senegambian Jews and their mixed-blood children moved to the next Jerusalem,
Amsterdam. One of these Jewish mulattos, Moses de Mesquita, became
a pillar of the Portuguese community in Amsterdam, marrying himself
and his relatives into the cream of Dutch Sephardi society.

When hostilities between the Dutch and the Hispano-Portuguese
monarchy resumed in 1621, the armed trading fleets of the West and
East India companies became the principal (and, except in Brazil,
ultimately victorious) threat to the short-lived empire of Lusitania.
On the Malabar coast, the Portuguese dug in at heavily fortified Goa
and at Cochin. Goa withstood Dutch attacks, but in 1662 the East
India Company launched an onslaught on Portuguese-dominated

Cochin, where the raja made the mistake of allying himself with the Dutch. Anticipating a Dutch victory and looking forward to making another Jerusalem on the Indian coast, the Jews – both Paradesi and Malabari, 'White' and 'Black' – put their knowledge of the defences and their money behind the besiegers. The immediate result was a calamity. While the Portuguese held off the Dutch, they slaughtered as many of the Indian Jews as they could get their hands on, and burned the Paradesi synagogue. A year later, in January 1663, the fortunes of war went the other way, and the leader of the Jewish community of Cochin was present with the Dutch admiral when he took the formal surrender of the Portuguese governor.

Jewish Cochin and the rest of its little communities in Kerala would flourish under the Dutch. Twenty years after the siege, Mosseh Pereyra de Paiva – from a family of Sephardi diamond and gem traders based both in Amsterdam and Surat in the Mughal dominions – came to Cochin and was royally and relentlessly entertained by the local Jews, including concerts on land and water, of brass, strings and drums, and generously lengthy banquets on the Sabbath day.[17] 'We got down', he wrote, 'among a big concourse of people who had come to welcome us. They led us in procession along a long street with songs and I shed tears of joy.'[18] When the time came for him to depart on Dutch ships (presumably back to Surat, since he seems never to have left India), he was treated to another farewell throng gathered on the jetty and packed into innumerable small boats from which psalms and Indo-Jewish songs were sung by both men and women. Blossoms were thrown on the water. The community had put on its finest Indian apparel and treated him to yet another round of feasting, despite the fact that, as Paiva noted, some of them were still in mourning for the loss of their loved ones. Choice gifts had been brought for the departing Sephardim, and so endearingly that Paiva was at a loss how to express his gratitude for them and for the flow of tears. The leader of the community, the *haham*, made a short, emotional speech of farewell, and recited the priestly blessing over his co-religionists 'with such affection that the Captain [of the ship] and I wept. We then took our leave of them and they went home, very sad.'[19]

There is no shortage of weeping in the pages of Jewish history, so it is good to mark the moments when the sorrow was, at least, bitter-sweet.

7

COHABITATION

I. The Queen at the Temple

Off to see the Jews! A Thursday in May 1642. Three Highnesses plus one Majesty are rowed on the Amstel in a canopied barge. Spring sunlight dances on the river scum. The blades dip, avoiding the flotsam of drowned dogs. Beneath the velvet canopy, heavily attended, seated on a grandly fashioned chair of state is the Prince of Orange, Frederik Hendrik, stadholder of the seven United Provinces of the Dutch republic: courtly, trim and, for an old commander, relatively good-humoured. Facing him are the children, a recently wedded couple. The son, William, stern for his sixteen years, shows the wispy beginnings of a princely moustache feathering his upper lip. But this sign of manhood is lost on his bride as she is ten years old. The princess, Mary, is a doll edition of her mother, Henrietta Maria, queen consort of England and Scotland, on whose many portraits the obliging chevalier Van Dyck had worked miracles of painterly cosmetic. Mother and daughter wear *coiffures frisées*, dark curls clinging to their pale brows. Strings of creamy pearls lie at both their throats.

Gems have brought mother and daughter to Amsterdam, and to the gem-people: the Jews. The queen has come to pawn the Crown jewels, even the ones she is wearing, should it come to that. Her husband Charles I's attempt to rule without Parliament had failed. Ruling with Parliament, so the king and queen believed, had come to mean rule *by* Parliament, so now they saw no other way to restore the fullness of majesty except to bring these contentions to a trial of strength – which meant a trial of arms. The disputatious Presbyterian Scots were resisting the royally authorised Prayer Book, and Charles needed to raise a force without recourse to the extortioners of Westminster who would demand yet another piece of his sovereignty as their price. In his own mind he was already their prisoner, and the queen needed to be free if a restoration of rightful powers were ever to be effected. Princess Mary's marriage to the young Prince of Orange was part of this strategy of royalist independence. Its solemnisation a year before in Whitehall had been auspicious, glittering. The sometime Royal Jeweller in Ordinary, Diego Duarte, had provided the four-diamond cluster brooch that sat atop the bride's stomacher, the jewels faithfully rendered in Van Dyck's double portrait of the young couple. During the 1630s when Charles had governed without Parliament, Diego Duarte had been granted residence in London. It suited everyone to pretend he was a Portuguese Christian, but behind the lightly worn mask of church piety was, of course, the Jew Abolias. In Antwerp, his father Gaspar Duarte, the master of the diamond business, also kept up spurious appearances in the Church of Our Lady, the better to protect his handsome household, its walls crowded with fine Flemish pictures.

The brilliance of the Duarte clan was to be measured in more than a carat-count. They served the cultivated of the Netherlands, north and south, Protestant and Catholic (notwithstanding the slogging war). The Low Countries were still torn in two, but diamond-loaded you crossed frontiers. Gaspar numbered among his friends the leading lights of Dutch letters who were also wielders of power, none more elegantly learned than Constantijn Huygens, private secretary to Frederik Hendrik, and in his own right poet, philosopher and patron of the up-and-coming, one of whom was Rembrandt van Rijn. Huygens had been Duarte's guest in Antwerp; and had been so enthralled by the sweetness of his daughter's voice that he had made arrangements for Francisca Duarte to travel to Holland where she had been acclaimed as the 'French Nightingale' (though there was nothing French about her) in the circle of the poet P. C. Hooft at his toy castle at Muiden.

The Duartes were Huygens's kind of Jews: polished, courtly and multilingual, who could be safely brought into the world of the Stuarts and the Prince of Orange, and be relied on to act as if it were but an inconsequential afterthought to furnish them with gems. Now, in the spring of 1642, with her husband's predicament weighing on her, a

transaction in the opposite direction was needed and she supposed
that Duarte must have co-religionists who would supply funds against
the security of her jewels.

The queen and the princess bride lodged in The Hague with the
queen's sister-in-law, Elizabeth, yet another inconvenienced monarch-
in-exile. How the Dutch collected them! Henrietta Maria wasted no
time seeking out jewellers who might oblige her with the needful.
Charles's pearl buttons went first. 'You cannot imagine', she wrote
her 'Dear Heart' the king, 'how handsome the buttons were when
they were out of the gold and strung into a chain, many as large as
my great chain. I assure you that I gave them up with no small regret.'[1]
That 'great chain' and a golden cross given to Henrietta Maria by her
mother were the next to go, and she was preparing to send a ruby
collar to the Duartes in Antwerp; still another piece shipped to
Denmark. But after the first successes the queen found the jewellers
in The Hague disappointingly unreceptive. The coolness may have
had something to do with the disputed status of the Crown jewels,
which Parliament adamantly insisted belonged to the nation, not the
private persons of the king and queen. And Parliament had its own
representatives in The Hague, some of whom came to inspect the
gems while they were on pre-sale display.[2] Hence the need to go to
Amsterdam where the Jews imported rough stones from India, cut,
polished and sold them. Surely they would be forthcoming.

Henrietta Maria had nothing against the Jews; quite the contrary,
the court in France where she had grown up had been accustomed
to rabbi-physicians, famous for remedies that worked when conventional pharmacopeia failed the mighty. The most unapologetically
Jewish was Filoteo Eliyahu Montalto. Like so many of his generation,
the ostensible Portuguese New Christian, born in Castelo Branco and
educated in medicine at the University of Salamanca, had long been
secretly attached to Judaism. When, in Livorno, he had advised another
young New Christian to 'follow the good road' it was quite clear what
he meant. By 1611 Montalto was in Venice, where he could openly
profess his Judaism, listen to the sermons of Leone Modena and the
anthems of Salomone Rossi, and rock and bob in the panelled
synagogue of the Ponentines. Leone assigned one of his star pupils,
Saul Morteira, to give Montalto Hebrew lessons, and then, once
mastered, plunge into the limitless ocean of Talmudic commentary.

Professionally, Montalto became renowned as the author of a treatise on the delicate anatomy of optics. Grand offers came his way: chairs at Pisa, Messina, Bologna; all declined, for he was unsure whether there would be liberty to observe his religion in those places. At some point Concino Concini, the favourite of the French Queen Mother, Marie de' Medici, invited him to become her personal physician, and while he was at it, perhaps treat Concini's wife Leonora Dori Galigaï for her spasms and seizures, rumoured, in this ensorcellated time, to be symptoms of demonic possession. Montalto was confident enough to insist on his own terms. An account of this unusual negotiation was published six years after Montalto's death, recalling that 'he promised to come but only on the condition that he would not be expected to hide or disguise his profession of religion but to exercise the Jewish religion', and he made it clear he could not accept payment for any treatment given on the Sabbath.[3] Lest he feel isolated in Paris, his young teacher Morteira was to go with him as secretary and adviser in all things Jewish. Morteira also kept any eye on any difficulties and threats encountered by New Christians in Rouen, Bordeaux and Paris, and when necessary tugged the sleeve of Montalto, who brought such matters to the attention of the royal council of which he eventually became a member! (It helped that he had diagnosed the convulsions of Galigaï as epileptic fits and provided symptomatic palliatives and sedatives.) It may have been this personal engagement with the forces of persecution which gave Montalto the boldness to write a fierce tract, pointedly in Spanish, against the errors of Christianity (especially the notion of Jesus as the divinely born Messiah) and this at exactly the time when Counter-Reformation tracts thundered against the miserable blindness of the Jews. Echoing what had been said by generations of medieval defenders of Talmud and Torah in public disputations, Montalto asked whether the age ushered in by Jesus could possibly be the promised messianic time, since any reasoning soul could see that the world had got worse, not better. The reign of a true Messiah would bring about an end to persecutions for both Jews and Gentiles in an ecumenical wave of charity. 'And the reformation shall not be limited to the people of Israel but will be universal for all peoples though Israel will be its leader.'[4]

At court as a girl Henrietta Maria saw the Jews, hatted and long-gowned, moving through the chambers of Fontainebleau and the

Louvre. When Montalto was struck dead in 1616 by a seizure during one of Louis XIII's royal progresses, the Queen Mother ordered the body embalmed pending Morteira's arrival from Amsterdam, where he had moved to become teacher and mentor to New Christians returning to Judaism in the freer air of Holland. Though Jewish law requires speedy burial, there was nowhere proper for the interment of Montalto so, with Talmudic dispensations for just such difficulties in his mind, Morteira took the body back to Holland where it could be laid to rest in the recently opened Sephardi cemetery at Ouderkerk, known poetically as Beit Hayim, the House of Life, three miles up the Amstel from Amsterdam. An austerely beautiful tombstone, reminiscent of the elaborate tombs of Venice, was raised. 'He was to Israel like the mountains of God,' reads the inscription. 'May the light of his star live on.' It was this unearthly light that Jacob van Ruisdael makes shine over the sepulchral darkness in his two paintings of the Ouderkerk cemetery, the great Montalto tomb at their centre. Henrietta Maria's memory of the rabbi-doctors was keen enough that when she became queen of England she sought out similarly recommended Jewish Italian physicians like Antonio de Verona, and made sure they received polite if not hospitable treatment in Oxford and Cambridge.

There was something else about the Jews which had long intrigued Henrietta Maria – as it did many of the princes of Christian Europe inclined to mystical illuminations. This was the Kabbalistic tradition which held God to have been the true architect of Solomon's Temple, with the king merely executing instructions.[5] She had married into a family of Solomonic obsessives. Her father-in-law, King James I, had had his image as the Wise King painted by Rubens on the ceiling of his Banqueting House in Whitehall, the throne supplied with the twisted order of columns known as Solomonic. *Solomon's Temple and the Coming of the Queen of Sheba* had been a favourite masque played before visiting royalty (notwithstanding an unfortunate performance in 1606 when the queen of Sheba had got so drunk that she vomited into the lap of the king of Denmark). Charles I had inherited this Solomon fixation. Scotland and England were often compared to Israel and Judah, north and south, with the implied warning that should they divide Britain, each, like the biblical kingdoms, would fall in its own time and way. Kabbalistic devices associated with the first master mason of the Jerusalem Temple were inserted into the court masques. For all their misfortunes, degradations and their wilful blindness before the gospel light, the queen held Jews like Filoteo Montalto to be the custodians of profound revelations.

Mirabile dictu! The queen had been informed that a scale model of the Temple, precisely following the details given by Ezekiel and in Flavius Josephus' *Antiquities of the Jews*, had been constructed in Amsterdam in the middle of the Jewish quarter. Not only that, but the very rabbi responsible had been Hebrew teacher to Constantijn Huygens, who would vouch for his learned worth. Henrietta Maria expressed a wish to see this wonder.

The party was, in any case, making its way to the place where the Jews lived and prayed: the four-block-square urban island of Vlooienburg. The district had been hastily added to the industrial edge of the city south-east of the Zuiderkerk in the 1590s to house the influx of immigrants, many from the theatre of war in Flanders. Amsterdam grew this way, piles driven deep into the mud, platforming a new living space here and there. The wood was to hand for the great lumberyards were all around, making rough music and doing strong business. Vlooienburg was a harbour of noise: sawing, sanding and sizing timber for the hulls of vessels, large and small, assembled so cheaply, thanks to economies of scale, that they made the merchant marines of other countries uncompetitive. Rafts of logs, whole Scandinavian forests translated to Holland, bobbed from canal landings held loosely in place by floating rope fences. The new addictions – sugar and tobacco – were processed in small shops and open courts, treacly aromas scenting the morning mist. Vlooienburg was workaday Amsterdam; distant, in every sense, from the graceful concentric rings of canals built in the previous decades for the merchant princes of the city. Vlooienburg houses were made of wood, not brick. Open to the winter winds, the streets and back alleys, the *steegen en slopen*, filled with dirty water, brimming over from the canals and the river. Yet it was also the place where after a ten-minute walk beyond the walls and bridges the city turned sweetly rustic. When he needed respite from the heroically reckless thing he had embarked on – ostensibly a painting of the militia company of Captain Frans Banning Cocq, but actually the envisioning of an idea, the idea of a rumbustiously free city – Rembrandt van Rijn, who had lived in the neighbourhood, would sometimes take himself up the Amstel path with a sketchpad, shake off the expectations of patrons and throw down some lines on Japanese paper, which would miraculously resolve into the rods of anglers or the faces of lovers cuddling in the bushes.

It was to the streets of Vlooienburg, cleared of the cigar hawkers and the Ashkenazi *schnorrers*, present in Amsterdam in increasing numbers and who, the Portuguese Nation complained, lowered the tone, that the royal party now made its way. A fateful moment in the history of the Jews was about to unfold at the Portuguese synagogue on the Houtgracht.

Through the medieval centuries, preaching friars, the prelates of the Church and their royal patrons had been free to invade synagogues on Sabbaths and fasts, forcing the congregation to attend to their conversionary harangues. In some places, where the Inquisition had no serious reach, the presence of Christians in the synagogues had ceased to be a day of terror. In Constantinople and Venice, the synagogues had become tourist attractions for visiting princes and their retinue. Almost invariably they admired the women in the gallery and deplored the shocking unseemliness of the murmured chatter which proceeded unstoppably throughout services. William Brereton, who came to Amsterdam in the 1630s, was entirely typical, complaining that there was scarcely any sign of devotion in the synagogue (equated with silence) but rather a mere hubbub of singing and talking. The royal party was going nonetheless, the first such princely company to be formally received in a synagogue. So on this particular Thursday, 22 May, the 'Kahal Kados Talmud Torah' (as the Portuguese Jews now called their congregation) welcomed not just Henrietta Maria but the Prince of Orange himself and the (very) young married couple. There was a ceremonious greeting, a poem written expressly for the occasion by Jonah Abravanel of the famous Sephardi dynasty. Then Jonah's brother-in-law, Rabbi Menasseh ben Israel, born and baptised in Portuguese Madeira as Manoel Dias Soeiro, stepped forward to read the welcoming address he had written for the stadholder.

Despite all they and their ancestors had suffered at the hands of the Iberian Church and monarchies – so many stories of Inquisition torture and live burnings, years lived in fugitive terror – the Sephardim of Amsterdam clung, almost perversely, to their old culture.[6] The speaker, who among other things was the first publisher-printer of

Hebrew literature in Amsterdam (as well as vernacular works in other languages), had already established a reputation in Christian circles as the exemplary Jew: learned, humane and sociable. This even extended to Catholics who knew him. Pierre Huet, later Bishop of Avranches who was in Amsterdam as a young man, called him 'a gentle spirit, easy-going, reasonable' (though he also wrongly supposed Menasseh to be unpersuaded by Kabbalah).[7] The great humanist thinkers and writers of the time Caspar van Baerle, professor and rhetorician at the Amsterdam Athenaeum and unofficial city orator, and Gerardus Vossius of Leiden University were both Menasseh's friends and correspondents, so much so that the rabbi had serious hopes of an appointment at the Athenaeum to add to his meagre salary as rabbi and teacher. The title of the work that had made his name in 1632 was the *Conciliador*, drawn from his sermon notes reconciling the many contradictions and inconsistencies found in the Bible, and the common interest that Jews and Christians shared in such reconciliations.[8] His standing in Amsterdam was such that Salom Italia, a young Jewish artist who had arrived there from Mantua, engraved Menasseh's portrait in 1642, grandly posed in the conventional style celebrating luminaries contained in a cartouche, the inscription describing him as '*philosophicus et theologus*'. Possibly for this very reason Menasseh was not treated with commensurate respect inside his own community, where he eked out a living by teaching at the Etz Hayim (Tree of Life) school, ministering as *haham*, telling who would open the Ark and who read from the Torah on Sabbath, both reverend figure and poorly paid menial. Despite his prolific Hebrew publishing (or possibly because of it) Menasseh was so reduced to scraping along that in 1639–40 he had considered emigration to the Dutch-held territories in Brazil where Jews were thriving.

But now Menasseh ben Israel, a short, plump man with a rosy complexion and controversially trimmed spade-end beard, streaked already with a little grey, was in his element. That the speech – the *gratulação* – was written in the old formal language of Portuguese only made the change of allegiance it celebrated all the more dramatic. 'We no longer look upon Castile and Portugal but upon Holland as our Fatherland,' Menasseh declared. 'We no longer wait upon the Spanish or the Portuguese king but upon their High Mightinesses the States-General and upon Your Highness as our Sovereigns, by whose blessed arms we are protected and by whose swords we are defended. No one need wonder, then, why we say daily prayers for Their Excellencies the States-General and for Your Highness, and also for the noble governors of this world-renowned city.'

It is hard to recapture the intensity of emotion that must have passed through the congregation of the synagogue on the Houtgracht at that moment.[9] Writing this from the security of New York, it is easy to take for granted that, sooner or later, a western society would provide some sort of haven where Jews could worship freely without being looked at as suspicious, comical or dangerous. Even in the Dutch republic the liberal space for Jews to be themselves, and yet also local patriots, did not open up easily or swiftly. But it did happen. Unless the Sephardi Jews chose (as some did) to venture back, whether for business or family, to the 'lands of idolatry' as the rabbis called Iberia, they were now beyond the reach of the perennially busy Inquisition. Menasseh would have felt the blessing with personal acuteness as his own father had been racked by the inquisitors. Eighty years of war between Spain and the Dutch had not yet run its course, but the threat of violent intolerance had moved further and further away from the heartland of the republic. *Hollands vryheid*, Dutch liberty, not least of conscience, would establish itself for another three hundred years. In Holland there were no ghettos, no invidious marks of dress (still very much in force in both Muslim and Christian lands). Jews with their prayer shawls over their heads could shout *omeyn* as loud as they wanted as the pearly Dutch light washed over them. Inevitably some called Amsterdam a new Jerusalem.

With a temple to boot, albeit a 1:300 scale model. Following the solemnities at the synagogue, Henrietta Maria and the children (and perhaps the stadholder himself) walked a few hundred yards round the corner to the Korte Houtgracht, where they stopped before a modest house bearing a plaque set into its wall indicating they were 'At King Solomon's Temple'. There they were greeted by another acquaintance of Huygens, a man dressed indistinguishably from any good Christian of the city – the same skullcap worn by Calvinist preachers; the same modest black coat over which lay the usual softly fallen lace and linen collar; the same neatly trimmed whiskers and beard: bright as a button, Jacob Judah Leon, whom everyone called 'Templo', who ushered the court and courtiers into the exhibition.

Templo was the first showman of the Bible. Here he is amid the tents of Israel – how goodly they are – the staff of Moses (or possibly Aaron) itself the ancestor of Templo's own trusty pointing stick. In his own way Templo is also a miracle worker, his inspiration powered by the breath of God. The genius of the Jewish story, he has realised, is its portability. The first tabernacle (which he will also reconstruct) was made to be on the move; the first Ark a cupboard on a litter, capable of being borne into battle like the fetishes of the idol-worshipping pagans. So he makes his model temple collapsible and modular, each part numbered and designed for swift reassembly. In The Hague and Haarlem, at the site of the Sint-Jan Kermis midsummer fair, he would establish himself on a display site big enough to take the model. Payment of a modest entrance fee gave access to the marvel (for even a godly temple builder needed bread, soup and herring). Then – *a bonus attraction!* – he would set out the accompanying fixtures and fittings: the seven-branch menorah made from copper and painted as best as possible to resemble gold; the shewbread table (ditto); the vestments of the high priest with its pectoral, studded with four rows of three gemstones, each representing one of the Tribes of Israel; the *urim* and the *thummim*, which on the Day of Atonement God would make shine according to the fortunes decreed for the coming year; the tall, multi-tiered turban-tiara and the tinkling *rimmonim* pomegranate bells which dangled from the robe's hem. Lining the walls of Templo's exhibit were hand-coloured pictures of the Jerusalem crowds swarming by the courtyard gates. Another showed the Twelve Tribes of Israel marshalled, each in correct rank and order in the wilderness: Gad and Issachar, Reuben and Naftali, Zebulun and Benjamin. Out would come the flourishing pointer. Visitors would gape at the majesty of the Temple, above all the tapered leaning buttresses supporting the main structure, continuing the upward rake of the mountain; and Templo, with a silence-prompting little cough, would begin.[10]

There was not much in his early life to suggest that he would become the great impresario of scripture, the minister of storytelling. His family had followed the course of so many others determined to emerge from the shadows of Iberia and into the daylight of Judaism that that they were prepared to run the terrifying risks of emigration. Untold numbers of the courageous were caught in the snares of the interrogators. But Jacob Judah's family were fortunate. They left their

small town near Coimbra and reached the safe haven of Amsterdam
sometime around 1605. The boy was thought, at least by his parents,
to be (of course) a precocious genius in Hebrew, destined to be a
famous rabbi. But Sephardi Amsterdam seemed to produce a glut of
such boy wonders, too many even for their three synagogues. The
family moved on, first to Hamburg, an alternative destination for the
re-Judaising New Christians. There Jacob Judah became a Hebrew
teacher, and on returning to Amsterdam around 1628, when he was
in his mid-twenties, was charged with the thankless assignment of
keeping good discipline in the Talmud Torah: one hand on the switch,
the other keeping place in the *Shulkhan Arukh*. Ten years later the
amalgamation of the synagogues made him surplus to requirements,
but Jacob Judah's name was known enough for him to be offered a
position in a private synagogue in the Zeeland town of Middelburg,
where both the East India and West India companies had admiralties.
It may have been there that he encountered and began a working
partnership with Adam Boreel.

Boreel was one of those advanced Protestants, rapidly multiplying
in the seventeenth century, who believed that all Churches were impure
representations of the perfect creed of Christ's gospel. That impurity
disqualified them from being a governing institution of any kind
whatsoever. Pretensions at worldly authority were sinful, a betrayal
of the original Christian aversion to power. All that was sovereign was
the word of scripture. Accordingly Boreel's 'College', as he preferred
to call it rather than 'Church', was open to all and sundry: the shouting
and the silent; the demonstrative and the ruminative. No doctrine was
deemed too dangerous or improbable to be heard; no opinion was to
be abridged. Likewise the Hebrew Bible, the Old Testament, was not
read (as the Catholics did) for evidence of its own supercession by the
New. No, it was history in its own right and the Jews were to be
considered children of God in their own particular way.

It had become a commonplace for the Protestant Dutch to see
themselves as the New Chosen People, saved by miracles from the
idolatrous image-besotted Catholics; so many Davids against so many
Goliaths; led from bondage to freedom by a divinely appointed leader.
Moses had stammered; the sixteenth-century William of Orange was
known as William the Silent. The fascination with all things Hebraic
(Johannes Leusden, the professor of Hebrew at Utrecht, said there

were more Hebrew grammars in the republic than there were weeks of the year) also produced, in 1621, the first modern map of the Holy Land meant equally for Jews and Hebrew-reading Christians. It was the product of another cross-religious collaboration between the mapmaker Abraham Goos and his Jewish counterpart Jacob ben Abraham Zaddik, who provided the textual descriptions along with a self-portrait, dressed to the nines as a prosperous Dutch burgher, along with one of the earliest six-pointed Stars of David known in print or painting.[11]

His wish to be close to Jews like Templo did not mean that Boreel, any more than any other Christians of his time, had abandoned the mission of Jewish conversion. But he believed that this was more likely to be realised through immersion in Hebrew texts, including the Talmud. The Jews would respond better to those who had troubled to read and understand their own sacred works than to those who merely dismissed them out of hand. That principle had been estab-lished as far back as the thirteenth century when the Dominicans and the Franciscans – often guided by Jewish converts – took to Hebrew with much the same end in mind. But their tone had been militantly confrontational. They hectored and admonished the Jews, but the likes of Adam Boreel and John Dury, who had been educated in Holland and wanted to establish a College of Jewish Studies in London, were committed to sympathetic, learned engagement in Judaism as an indispensable tool of their mission. The instrument of persuasion was friendship, and from working comradeship sprang mutual respect, sometimes more than the Christian side had bargained for. This alter-ation of tone was not a small thing, for it took as a truism the approachable humanity of the Jews. In some of the most ardent evangelical American churches today (the linear theological descend-ants of conversionary Anglo-Dutch Protestantism) this is still the case.

The road from Zeeland led to the Temple Mount. The paths that Jacob Judah and Adam Boreel took towards their Jerusalem epiphanies were distinctly different, but they converged. Boreel the millenarian believed that the Second Coming of the Saviour and the Christian thousand years of peace was imminent – dates in the 1650s were ventured – and would be inaugurated with the building of the Third Temple thereby removing the last obstacle to the conversion of the Jews. For Jacob Judah, the Messiah would be human not divine but

he would liberate Jerusalem, lead the Jews to their redeemed Zion
and rebuild that Temple. Both therefore needed to have an exact sense
of the dimensions, structure and decoration of the Solomonic prototype. They consulted the best-known works (of which there was no
shortage in this Temple-obsessed time): the book of the Jesuit Juan
Bautista Villalpando, published at the beginning of the century, which
in turn was a springboard for the work of the Leiden Hebraist professor
Constantijn L'Empereur, whose chair was expressly designated for the
'Refutation of the Jews'. Both had used the Bible, especially the cubit-
by-cubit guide described in Ezekiel 40–8. But scripture was supplemented by the richly detailed account of Flavius Josephus in his
Antiquities of the Jews. L'Empereur, who was friends with many Jews
including Menasseh ben Israel, had published a Latin translation of
the particular tractate of the Mishnah, the second-century compilation
of laws and observances, which (with the destruction of the Second
Temple still relatively recently in mind) went into yet more detail
about the Temple. So at the same time as they were working on their
book, Boreel and Templo created a vocalised version of the Mishnah
(the vowels identified and indicated), so that both Hebrew-learned
Christians as well as Jews could speak it out loud. It is often assumed
that the Jewish side of such collaborations was naively innocent of
the conversionist goals of their Christian colleagues and that they
were walking into a cunningly sprung trap; but that was seldom the
case, and certainly not with Templo and Boreel. It was just as likely
that the Christian party, while leery of going native, warmed to the
dignity of their Jewish collaborators and by extension to the people
they exemplified.

Ice was being broken. Scholarly contact could sometimes turn into
social proximity. The Calvinist theologian and professor of Hebrew
at Basel University, Johannes Buxtorf, got himself into trouble with
the city authorities by hobnobbing with Jews whenever possible,
bringing rabbis to his house to consult with them while he was
preparing his *Synagoga Judaica*, and entering into a heady dialogue on
abstruse matters of the Mishnah, Talmud, and even the Aramaic
spoken paraphrases and interpretations of scripture known as Targum.
The result was a work of ethnographic description in which Buxtorf's
admiration for Jewish customs and his delight in rabbinic explanations
shine from almost every page, notwithstanding his official mission to

expose the contemptible blindness of the Hebrews. On nursing infants
and feeding children he can hardly contain himself reporting the views
of the sages. Nursing mothers have to eat well so their milk is abundant and nourishing: 'the *chachamim* hold it of great importance to
give your children enough to eat so that they grow up fast and strong
to serve God. God gives with a full hand to all creatures what they
need. This is also true of a woman. If she gives her children enough
food that they suffer no shortage she walks in God's ways and thus
she may reach eternal life. For this purpose he gave her two breasts
not one ... Rabbi Abha says that the breasts are positioned near the
heart so that the child should nurse and receive understanding.'[12]
Buxtorf's inheritance from Luther's malevolent hatred of the Jews
fought with his discovery of their humanity. Often this is just a matter
of looking at their ordinary routine. The spectacle of Rabbi Chasdai
doing his part preparing for the Sabbath by chopping cabbage while
Rabbi Nahman cleans the house (based on the principle 'that no one
should think himself too elegant, rich or clever to help') was obviously
born of familiarity. Against all his higher principles – and indeed the
whole polemical point of his work – Buxtorf was touched by the
poetry of Jewish ritual custom, noting that the thumb of a dead man
was bent and secured with the *tzitzit* fringes of the prayer shawl in
which he would be buried in such a way that the whole hand makes
the letter *shin*, short for Shaddai, one of the names of the Almighty.
Thus God would protect him from the wiles of Satan on his way to
the afterlife. Better yet for Buxtorf is the rabbinical observation that
men die with their hands open to show they are done with life, while
babies are born with clenched fists clasping with them the essence of
life's fullness which they do not yet want to release.

If Buxtorf the fierce antagonist could, here and there, melt into
humanity, the 'philo-Judaism' of this time, principally in Protestant
countries, was a real phenomenon, despite Luther's vicious demonising. The goal certainly remained mass conversion, but the means
– friendly familiarity – put that mission on hold, and for some relationships, including that between Boreel and Templo, the working
friendship softened the theological obligation.

Their great book, ceremoniously presented by Templo to his grand
visitors, had one advantage (at least for the stadholder and Prince
William) over earlier treatises. It had originally been written in Spanish

but a Dutch translation had been made and printed expressly in time for the great occasion.[13] Soon there would be editions in five other languages including Latin and English. If anyone wanted the last word on both Solomon's Temple and the Second Temple which was resurrected in the fifth century BCE and famously completed by Herod the Great, they were going to get it from Templo. Already impressed (probably by Templo's oral performance, along with his pointing rod), Henrietta Maria herself conceded that the Jew was correct in interpretations and learning. At some point, so Templo later claimed, the eager young Prince William suggested he add a model of the wilderness sanctuary to his show, and – more to the point – offered to finance its construction. (The model duly came about, though not, it seems, the promised subsidy.) But even for those unable to make a personal visit, the handbook itself was a popular acquisition. The Dutch edition was in the library of even so great a Bible sceptic as the sometime Orthodox Jew, Baruch Spinoza.

Even so, the book was not the main thing. The great model was. The grandees of the richest city in the world came to admire the Temple, including the patrician burgomaster Gerard Andriesz Bicker and Frans Banning Cocq, the captain of the Arquebusier company whose explosive group portrait Rembrandt was completing in 1642. Intricately crafted architectural models had been made in Venice by and for the great architects of the city like Andrea Palladio and Sebastiano Serlio, and were treated as works of art – masterpieces – in their own right; but they were made primarily for connoisseurs or for the builders themselves.[14] Templo's model was meant for the public as well, and he advertised it on hand-coloured posters. Shoehorned into the modest space of his house, the model – twenty feet by ten – was a wonder, painted and set on a high platform, as if atop the Temple Mount. Admiring visitors could picture themselves walking through one of the great gates, towards the outer wall (the surviving western section of which had already been known for centuries as the place where Jews went to pray their lamentations on the 9th of Ab); into the Court of Women; the Court of the Priests; and finally, since Templo and Boreel had designed a removable roof, into the Holy of Holies itself, penetrated only by the *hacohen hagadol*, the high priest, on the Day of Atonement.

This was not all. Following the tour of inspection, shortly to be augmented with a model of the sanctuary, paying visitors would be directed towards the reconstructions of the ritual objects, including a mock-up of the four-horned sacrificial altar and the engravings of the Israelites, encamped in the wilderness. This last was also of topical importance (everything was) for it was known that a sign that the millennial reign of peace was at hand would be the emergence of the Lost Tribes from their fastness beyond the Sambatyon River. So the Reubenites on the wall were given special scrutiny. Though no record survives of what the royal party thought of Templo's exhibit, others who came not long after, especially the biblically minded, voiced their admiration. John Dury returned to Amsterdam at least twice, once while he was still a Royalist and again in the 1650s on a mission from Oliver Cromwell's Protectorate. 'This peece I have seen,' he wrote to his polymath friend Samuel Hartlib, 'amongst the rarities and antiquities which are to bee taken notice of, there is none therein to bee compared.'[15]

A generation or two on from their arrival in the Dutch republic, when the newcomers felt secure and for the most part prosperous, they allowed themselves to believe that a Prince of Orange visiting their synagogue and being received by the elders of the congregation, a queen and a young prince being shown Solomon's Temple by a Sephardi rabbi-teacher, were the most natural things in the world. It had been decreed in the heavens that there should be a fit between the Jews and the Dutch. They both had founding epics of liberation from idolatrous tyrants; they were both peoples who believed themselves to be God's chosen, whose miraculous history of freedom and redemption must have been the special project of the Almighty. In this chronicle of covenant and consolation, the Dutch republic had always been the saving ark in an ocean of persecution. Amsterdam was just 'Ha-Makom', 'The Place', to which the Jews had been guided by a providential hand, as surely as if it had been a pillar of cloud or fire, somewhere they could, at last, feel safe. So an anecdotal scripture of arrival made up of picturesque moments and exemplary characters (a shepherding rabbi; a head-turning Jewish beauty; a conventicle of secret Jews stumbling into the open) was handed down through the generations and given canonical form by the prolific poet-historian Daniel Levi de Barrios in the late seventeenth century.[16] Each of the three founding stories had some basis in fact, but what was treasured was the poetic embroidery.

Obviously the original rabbi had to be a Moses: Moses Uriel Halevi, living in the port of Emden, just the German side of the northern border of the Dutch province of Groningen. Along with Saint-Jean-de-Luz in France, Rouen and Hamburg, Emden was one of the places where crypto-Jews found homes on escaping Portugal and Spain. When a ship blown off course landed its New Christians near Emden, and Halevi had discerned their wish to live openly as Jews, he told them of a community in Amsterdam secretly practising the rites of the faith and told them to go there to be reunited with their brethren. A seed of settlement was sown and Moses followed his disciples to the Amstel. But the documentary record tells a more grubbily prosaic story than the lore. Moses Uriel Halevi shows up in Amsterdam court reports not as a prophetic liberator but as a common fence, arrested for receiving stolen goods as well as performing illegal circumcisions and working under the assumed name of Phillips Joosten. Under interrogation in prison, Moses/Phillips admitted observing Jewish rituals in private, slaughtering and supplying kosher meat. But the confession did not, as he must have feared, earn him a more severe punishment, much less banishment from the city. This bewilderingly easy-going approach to the letter of the law was a promising sign for the small community of New Christians who were secretly practising Judaism in the 1590s and the first decade of the seventeenth century. Reprieved, Moses Uriel Halevi did end up being the patriarch of the budding community. When the first synagogue was opened in 1612, it was his personal Sefer Torah which was used for Sabbath readings.

The second hero of the founding myth was Maria Nunes, who had been sent from Portugal to Amsterdam along with her brother. En route, so the story went, her ship was captured by English privateers. Brought to London, the dark-eyed beauty turned all heads. None was more smitten than a great (unnamed) noble who fell hard and begged her hand in marriage. But Maria Nunes was not made for farthingales. She resisted the perfectly turned sonnet and the imploring madrigal. The *belle dame* was supposed to be *sans merci* of course, but not when she was exotic. Queen Elizabeth was asked to help the suit along. Equally taken with Maria, the queen drove her in the royal coach and asked her to remain in England. But all the appeals, no matter how commanding, fell on deaf ears. More important than elevation to the duchy of Some-Shire was the irresistible pull of ancestral religion. Turning her back on England's blandishments, Maria took ship again for Holland, and married her Sephardi intended. This tale, too – royal excursions and noble swains aside – was not entirely mythical, and the queen had a Marrano physician who might have effected an introduction, but as is so often the case in Jewish history, the truth is a lot more compelling than the fable.

Maria's parents had been imprisoned by the Inquisition. To escape a similar fate, Maria had disguised herself in male dress and had been taken off the ship, captured by the English while still looking like a beardless youth. Maria Nunes was real; her covert marriage to fellow Marrano Manuel Lopes Homem in Amsterdam in 1598 was equally authentic and documented. But what was inconvenient for the fable was the fact that by 1612 the husband was back in Lisbon, received at the court of King Philip III who had turned into an enthusiastic patron of the Inquisition, and he may never have returned to Holland and his beautiful wife at all.[17]

And then there was the moment of accidental exposure. On patrol to winkle out secret Catholic conventicles in Amsterdam, one of the city sheriffs, the *schout*, discovered a room full of praying men. But the day was the Day of Atonement and these were not Romanists but Jews; such a relief for all concerned! By all means continue to pray, the sheriff is said to have told the Jews, but make sure you pray to the God of Israel for the well-being of the most noble city of Amsterdam and its great and good governors. In response one of the first immigrants – Manuel Rodriguez Vega, now known as Jacob Tirado – stepped forward to argue both the justice and the economic benefits of their toleration. Whatever the truth of the story, Tirado was also a real figure.

Through all these romances of arrival ran a strain of pluralism: an encounter of two peoples open to the traffic and the tongues of the world. What was a truism in the Netherlands, but nowhere else, was spelled out by the merchant Cornelis Pieterszoon Hooft: 'The nature of these lands and especially this city existing by God's grace mostly of trade and shipping urgently demands amiability among men.'[18] This congruence between profit and hospitality could extend, at last, to the globe-sailing Jews.

Then there was the shared experience of suffering at the hands of fanatical coercion. Inquisition memories, common to the Jews and Dutch Protestants, were not a myth. Autos-da-fé were engraved (literally) in historical memory in the prints accompanying contemporary histories of the Dutch revolt against Spain, just as they featured in the written histories of the New Christians who had become Jews again. Both peoples had their cults of martyrs, victims of cruelty: each of them casts of characters made familiar in the retelling to generations of children. The Dordrecht *Martyrs' Book* published in 1612 is strikingly similar – not least in its close-up narrative of physical atrocity visited on innocent women and children – to the martyr narratives of Jewish history which had begun with the Books of Maccabees and the tales of self-immolation in the First Crusade. A prayer book printed in Spanish and Hebrew in Amsterdam adapted the solemn memorial prayer of *yizkor* to embrace the memory of specific family members burned alive in the Iberian autos-da-fé, much as the same prayer now often includes mourning for the victims of the Holocaust. But the Amsterdam prayer had an edge of passionate revenge. 'May He avenge his/her blood from His Enemies with His Mighty arm and repay the foes as they deserve.'[19] This too the Dutch would have easily understood. The author P. C. Hooft's wife's grandmother featured as one of the victims in his bloodied account of the 'Spanish Fury at Antwerp'; his pages and those of others who shaped the mentality of the first generation of the free Dutch are full of violated weddings and impaled infants.

So it was not a trivial aside when, in 1598, the great jurist Hugo Grotius (whose own *De Rebus Belgicus* was a contribution to these histories of ordeal and liberation) had expressly referred to those 'Portuguese' who had come to Amsterdam to escape inquisition into their religion, 'preferring it to all other cities'. In these narratives of collective self-description, cruelty was always thought to be the offspring of idol-worship: enslavement to images rather than obedience to the pure word of God. For Protestant Netherlanders, whose rebellion had begun in 1566 with the destruction of painted images in Flanders and who had whitewashed their churches clean of them in the republic, Catholicism was a form of thinly Christianised paganism. And 'the land of idolatry' was the standard term used by the Sephardi Jews of Amsterdam when they warned against returning or even travelling on business to Spain.

None of this guaranteed full, principled toleration.[20] Article XIII of the Union of Utrecht, which in 1578 had bound seven provinces of the Netherlands together in allied resistance to Spain, committed the republic to protect 'freedom of conscience' but this was understood as intended for dissenting Christians. And it was as ostensible (New) Christians that the first few families arrived in Amsterdam in the 1590s; hence their furtive existence there in the early years, worshipping in private houses on the Vlooienburg, adopting Dutch cover names like 'Phillips Joosten' or keeping their baptismal ones from Portugal. Amsterdam's caginess in accepting Jewish immigrants prompted other towns in Holland to try and pre-empt them by advertising a welcome: Alkmaar in 1604, Haarlem in 1605 and Rotterdam in 1610. The reasoning of their city fathers was usually naked economic pragmatism. The Rotterdam city fathers made no bones about 'finding it useful to invite merchants of the Portuguese Nation to come and reside in this city with some privileges and freedoms in order to improve trade and commerce'.[21] Jews exiting Spain and Portugal brought with them unparalleled familiarity with the very commercial empires into which the Dutch wished to intrude as competitors, from West Africa to India and Brazil. They spoke the languages; they still had the connections back in Iberia. When Manuel Rodriguez Vega came to Holland he brought with him experience of silk making and sugar importing, a network of brothers based in Antwerp, Rouen, Amsterdam, Brazil and Guinea, and further business contacts in Emden, Venice, Morocco and Danzig.[22]

The death of the implacable Philip II helped relax the pressure a little. In 1601 Philip III's chief minister, the Duke of Lerma, offered the possibility of emigration for New Christians able to pay the enormous sum of 170,000 cruzados for the privilege. A more influential turning point was the truce signed in 1609 between the Dutch republic and Spain which would last twelve years. The hiatus was the formative period for the creation of the Sephardi community in Holland. Since it was now safe for the 'Portuguese naçāo' as it called itself to travel back and forth, hundreds of New Christian families seized the precious opportunity to go to Amsterdam and, once there, come into the open as practising Jews. By 1620 there were probably a thousand of them living on Vlooienburg and the street to the north, the Sint Anthonisbreestraat which would eventually end up being known as the street of the Jews, the Jodenbreestraat. By 1640 there were two thousand Sephardim and at least a thousand poorer Ashkenazi immigrants from German- and Polish-speaking lands.

However, like citizens of other Dutch towns, Amsterdammers were clearer about what they did not want – Spanish Catholic coercion – than what they did want from their war-born republic. The freedom of new republics often becomes a theatre for contention as citizens attempt to answer the question: 'What was that battle truly for?' In the Netherlands a long, bitter and inconclusive argument divided liberal humanists who believed the state (whether Catholic or Calvinist) had no business prescribing or proscribing religion, and those who wanted to see the Reformed Church established as the state confession. Though the uncompromisingly Calvinist party won a victory in 1618 removing 'Remonstrants' from power and executing their leader Oldenbarneveld, it was never so decisive as to give them a religious monopoly, much less institutionalised domination. The stumbling block was the passionate attachment to the sovereignty of the local which had been the great engine of the rebellion against Spanish centralising autocracy. But the rhetorical force of Calvinism still rained down from the pulpit every Sunday, and books like Abraham Coster's *History of the Jews* rehearsed yet again a long inventory of Jewish errors and insults against the gospel as a way of precluding the toleration of synagogues. Were that infamous eventuality to come to pass, the more adamant preachers argued, such impious places should be limited to the reading of the Bible.

The hostility of the Reformed Church meant that the most that the incoming Jews could expect was de facto toleration rather than some official declaration which might have served as a charter of their protection. Jewish life in the Dutch commonwealth of Christians evolved piecemeal and with many retractions and reservations on the part of the hosts. But if that was all that was on offer, considering the European alternatives, the Jews would take it. The benevolence of the blind eye was still benevolence. In Amsterdam in 1614 Jews were openly praying in their first synagogue on Vlooienburg. In Frankfurt in 1614, on the other hand, the gingerbread baker Vincent Fettmilch, calling himself the 'new Haman', led a mob of guildsmen against the Judengasse and its synagogue, killing some of the worshippers and precipitating a mass flight. In many parts of the German world,

German Protestants shared Martin Luther's violent contempt for the Jews, whom he characterised as walking demons. In Amsterdam, by contrast, the exterminating enemies of the Jews became the stock villains of theatre. Haman could be seen on stage in any number of dramas by Jacob Revius and Johannes Serwouter, in which he always featured as the murderous villain, a thinly disguised version of the arch-villain of the Dutch revolt, the Duke of Alva. Affinity and curiosity, however loosely imagined, had replaced enmity and alienation.

And despite the stand-off between the tolerant and the godly, things concerning the Jews came to be said by men in the Dutch governing class which had seldom, if ever, been said by Christian magistrates. Hugo Grotius declared that since the Jews had chosen Amsterdam as a place of refuge from which to flee the Inquisition, they might as well be permitted to reside there openly. Grotius had been taught by the Calvinist theologian François du Jon, known as Franciscus Junius, whose family had directly felt the blows of fanaticism. His father had been murdered by a Catholic militant, and scarcely had Junius himself been appointed chaplain to William the Silent than his hero was fatally shot on the staircase of the Prinsenhof in Delft by another Catholic assassin. No wonder, then, that Junius declared that 'no man should be extirpated on account of his religion for faith is a gift from God and all men by nature are brethren'. After a nomadic life, much of it in flight from arrest, he ended up a professor at Leiden University as the great light of tolerant humanism. His most famous pupil, Grotius, composed a 'Remonstrance' between 1615 and 1619 which, although not formally adopted by the government, spoke the language of humanist toleration. There was, he wrote, a 'natural community' of all men, Jews included not least because their forefathers were those 'from whom Christ descended in the flesh'. More radically Grotius confronted the historical truth of the mistreatment of the Jews. 'It is known how in many places they were ill treated. They are derided, taunted, pushed, beaten, thrown at, not only with the connivance but even with the approval of the authorities.' Grotius himself was not altogether free from ancient prejudices. He was capable of pleading for empathy while regretting the Jews had been admitted to the republic in the first place, and repeating, as if a truism, that the Jews had been known to do Christians harm. (The assumption that the Jews had only become malign through generations of mistreatment would become a standard text in the modern canon of those who regarded themselves as qualified philo-Semites.) Grotius himself graciously explained that the cause of their antisocial behaviour was to be found in the conditions to which they had been reduced, forced into usury. Thus the cure also had to be social and political. They should be 'allowed to live freely in the towns of their residence and be at liberty to trade, do business and manufacture, enjoying freedoms, exemptions and privileges in the same way as other burghers and citizens without being burdened with any special taxes and tributes'. Then followed, of course, all the morning-after qualifications. There must be some limit to numbers lest Holland be swamped with Jews: two hundred families in most towns, perhaps three hundred in Amsterdam. But he was unequivocal about granting the open practice of their religion. To forbid that, or to confine worship to readings from the Bible as suggested by the more zealous Reformed, was to condemn the Jews, either to the dishonest double life of New Christians, or else to be satisfied with a Judaism so watered down it was no Judaism at all.

Some went much further. Caspar van Baerle, a professor at the Amsterdam Athenaeum, wrote a preface to Menasseh ben Israel's book *On the Problem of Creation* in which he took the principle of cross-confessional amity, especially within the republic of scholars, to a stirring conclusion. It is as close to a statement of religious pluralism as could be imagined in an age of unrelenting, murderous, religious wars. 'It is for everyone to worship God. It is not, we believe, for one age or one people to be pious. Albeit we may have different under-standings of such things let us live as friends before God. May a learned mind be esteemed everywhere according to its own lights. That is the sum total of my faith. Believe this, Menasseh! As I am a son of Christ so be you a Son of Abraham.'[23]

Van Baerle's hospitality, with its implication of the fraternal equality of faiths, triggered an instantaneous storm of denunciation. To the hard-bitten money men who governed Amsterdam, professions of warm-hearted brotherhood were all very well, but, if pushed too hard, risked blowing up the unspoken modus vivendi which was better for business than some sort of war of principles. Much better to allow the preachers to let off steam, nod in agreement and then for the most part ignore what had been said. Measures could be taken to restrict Jewish rights knowing that none of them would be rigorously enforced. No one was about to institute a Dutch snooping-inquisition.

This benign hypocrisy allowed the first synagogue to appear in Amsterdam. In 1612 the congregation of Beit Jacob asked permission to build a large house on the Houtgracht, making it clear that it would be used as a synagogue. This turned out to be a mistake. Expressions of horrified outrage at once rained down from the Sunday pulpits. To calm matters the city fathers struck the pose of good Christians, at the same time offering ways by which their own show of umbrage could be circumvented. Jews could not buy such property? The answer was to lease it from a show buyer. Fury at the presumption of the Jews continued, so the city council did another round of ostentatious foot-stamping, declaring categorically that the building could be used for no ceremonies other than those of presently accepted churches. The penalty for any violations would be the demolition of the building.

Tipped off that it was all hot air, the elders of Beit Jacob were undeterred. Building went ahead, it being glaringly obvious that it would indeed be a synagogue since the carpenter hired for the job, one Hans Gerritszoon, was instructed that he would not be required from Friday to Saturday evening. As a sop to Christian sensibilities he was also told not to show up on Sundays. Hans Gerritszoon had a cushy job and the first synagogue in Amsterdam opened as planned and would hold services for the next twenty-seven years. At no time was there a serious threat of paying the penalty for infringing the rules. In an age when much of Christian Europe was torn apart by doctrines of mutual extermination, the governance of the wink may not have been such a bad thing.

Two years passed and objections to Jewish property purchases relaxed still further. The acquisition of land for a burial ground was uncontroversial. Judaism prescribed cemeteries beyond city walls and the Dutch certainly didn't want them within town limits. The earliest cemetery was a good thirty miles outside Amsterdam. A parcel of land at Ouderkerk, just three miles from Vlooienburg, was bought, authorised, and opened its gates in 1614. Little by little, the Jews were finding a living space in Amsterdam without unduly affronting their hosts. Later on, in deference to the understood rules of leading a (relatively) quiet existence on the Amstel, the Jewish governing boards warned against noisy street processions at weddings, the carnival

merriment of Purim, and the street dancing with the Sefer Torah that
was a tradition on the feast of Simchat Torah, the Rejoicing of the
Law. Being Jewish, Dutch style, called for at least an effort at sobriety.

The period of probation was a success, so that during the truce-
driven immigration the arrival of shiploads of Marranos aroused no
new hostility. In 1619 the States of Holland (the provincial authority)
and the States General (the legislature of the republic) did what they
did best: devolving responsibility for matters concerning the Jews to
the many local city councils. Three years earlier, Amsterdam had
allowed Jews to apply for, and be granted, *poorterschap*: the status of
citizenship, a first in the whole history of Jews in Christian Europe.

Yet that momentous concession did not make Amsterdam Jews the
equal of Christian burghers, since, unlike the rest of the Dutch, they
were not allowed to pass citizenship automatically to their descendants
but were made to reapply, generation after generation. It was still
equality on condition of best behaviour. All the same, the regulation
of 1616 transformed the lives of Jews fortunate enough to live in
Amsterdam (or indeed anywhere in the Dutch republic) largely by what
it refrained from doing. There would be no confinement of the Jews
to a specified district of the city. In fact the only issues on which the
government of the States of Holland intruded on the right of each and
every town to make their own arrangements were its stipulations against
establishing such ghettos, and a ban on any invidious distinctions in
dress. These matters – where Jews lived; how they appeared in public
– were not trivial. Odious discriminations and urban imprisonments
had done much to perpetuate the sense of Jews as somehow incapable
of, and undeserving of, civility. The document was not entirely free
from the traditional medieval threats and warnings, included at the
behest of the offended Calvinist clergy. The Jews had to forbear from
defaming or insulting the Christian religion in writing or utterance.
(This was less a matter of form than one might imagine, since a ripe
kind of anti-Christian polemic had indeed developed in response to the
bitter experience of the Inquisition.) They were never to attempt conversion and were to refrain from sexual relations with Christians. Both
these prescriptions were ignored. Cases are known of Christian maid-
servants converting to Judaism as a preliminary to marriage with their
employer. More extraordinary was the conversion of the Dominican
confessor to the Spanish infanta Maria, Vicente Rocamora turning into

Ishack Ysrael Rocamora, marrying into the Sephardi family of the Toura, making a living as a doctor and producing two sons who inevitably followed him in the same profession.[24] The ban on sexual dalliance with Christians was even more optimistic. Jewish men, young and old, were constantly being reported to the *ma'amad*, or governing board, in Amsterdam for fornicating with their servants, for which they received not much more than the rhetorical equivalent of a rap over the knuckles. But city magistrates also heard from pregnant servants claiming maintenance from the Jews whom they accused of being responsible for their condition. Brothel visits, like the one in which Abraham Pessoa, aged fifteen, and Gabriel Henriques were caught in their underwear with two working girls, were so common as to incur not much more than a roll of the eyes and a fine from the *ma'amad*.

Did Jews and Christians share a common life on the streets of Amsterdam? It is easy enough to find zones of separation, above all in their livelihoods. In 1632, in response to protests about low-wage, low-price competition, and bearing in mind that similar protests had turned violently ugly in Germany, Dutch Jews were removed from any trade or craft organised in guilds. This meant they were kept out from most of the occupations of the Dutch working population. Until the Batavian republic in the 1790s abolished the guilds, there would be no Jewish bakers, tailors or – surprisingly – dressmakers. Exceptions could be made. Such was the demand in the Christian population for Hebrew literature, and Bibles of all sorts, and so well did Jewish printer-publishers meet it (the great Joseph Athias claimed he could produce a Bible in four hours), Jews were allowed into this trade, beginning with the Gentiles' favourite Jew: Menasseh ben Israel. And, naturally, the Dutch republic, like Christian societies everywhere, broke the rules for Jewish doctors. A Jewish physician, Joseph Bueno, originally a New Christian, was at the deathbed of the stadholder Maurits in 1625, notwithstanding the prince's flinty Calvinism. Bueno's son Ephraim, educated in Bordeaux, became a cross-religious eminence in Amsterdam: poet, philosopher-philanthropist and patron of Menasseh's publications, portrayed by both Rembrandt and his old Leiden rival, Jan Lievens. Lievens's etching of Ephraim Bueno, with the luminary's conventional Dutch hat removed to expose the skullcap beneath, used the millinery to exemplify all the happy ambiguities of the man and the culture he embodied.

Bueno was a special case. The occupational restrictions affecting
the rest of the Jews moved them into businesses like tobacco processing,
too new to have been organised as a craft confraternity, and where
they had well-established access to raw materials: Keralan rough
diamonds and Brazilian tobacco and sugar. None of this worked out
unprofitably for anyone. Jews also moved swiftly and in dispropor-
tionate numbers into the most novel and unregulated (except by its
own internal conventions) zone of profit and peril: the stock exchange.[25]
The Jewish weakness for gambling was notorious. There were those
who thought that their reputed access to cryptic numerologies and
signs may have predisposed them to the cards (which in Italy they
also printed). If it was odd that rabbinical figures who laid down the
religious law as authoritatively as Leone Modena could also have been
helplessly addicted gamblers, this combination of traits – the *chokhem*
and the chancer, the sage and the fool – was not uncommon in their
world. When the skill of the applied hunch was allied to the versatility
they had shown over the centuries in raising capital, Jews were bound
to become stockbrokers in considerable numbers, constituting 10 per
cent of the business on the Amsterdam Bourse by 1700. The first
extraordinary account – albeit a wild picaresque semi-comic quasi-
poetic romp in the style of the old medieval Jewish romances like
Judah Alharizi's *The Book of Tahkemoni*[26] – was written by the Marrano
José Penso de la Vega. While the *Confusion de Confusiones* is not to be
confused with a documentary account, neither is it completely far off
the mark.

In all these places – the diamond-polishing shop, the stock exchange,
the tobacco-drying yard, the apothecary and the print shop – Jews
would have worked alongside Christians and would have come into
daily contact with them. But a great deal of their lives, whether Sephardi
or Ashkenazi, was spent on the inside of their communities. The
Sephardi grandees met regularly on the self-perpetuating governing
board of the *ma'amad*. Hats and pipes would gather about the carpeted
table and the usual business would begin: scandals, both domestic and
doctrinal; rows over wills, marriages, property. After chewing them
over, delivering their arbitrations, they would step into the wet streets
satisfied they had the governance of the *kahal* congregation decently
in hand. Around their inner circle revolved the doings of the busy
wider community, always moving to the rhythm of the Jewish calendar,

Mid-sixteenth-century pen and ink copy of illustration from Moses of Castellazzo, *The Building of the Tower of Babel*, Picture Bible, 1521.

The banner of Solomon Molkho.

Interior of Balat synagogue in Istanbul. The sixteenth-century building was damaged by fire but the eighteenth-century rebuild seen here stayed close to the original, including the ship-shaped teva reading dais.

The Ten Sefirot of the Kabbalah, from *Portae Lucis* (Augsburg, 1516) by the Jewish convert to Christianity, Paolo Riccio, a good example of a work designed to cater to Christian fascination with the Kabbalah.

Frontispiece portrait from Leone
Modena's *Historia de'riti hebraici*,
1638.

Tombstones in the Jewish cemetery on the Lido,
Venice.

Spanish-Portugese ('Ponentine') synagogue, Ghetto Vecchio, Venice,
enlarged by the workshop of Baldassare Longhena, ca. 1635.

Poster promoting Templo's reconstruction of Solomon's Temple.

Engraved portrait of Menasseh ben Israel by Salom Italia, 1642.

Yakov ben Abraham Zaddik, colophon self-portrait etching, from Abraham Goos, *Map of the Holy Land*, Amsterdam 1620–1.

The seventeenth-century interior of Paradesi Synagogue, Cochin, India.

Portrait of Dr Ephraim Bueno,
Rembrandt van Rijn, etching, 1647.

Moses with the Tablets of the Law,
Rembrandt van Rijn, 1659.

Detail of map of Amsterdam by Balthasar Florisz van Berckenrode, 1625, showing
the district of Vlooienberg, home to many of the earliest arriving Jews.

The Inauguration of the Esnoga in 1675 by Romeyn de Hooghe.

Romeyn de Hooghe's *Sephardi Family Circumcision scene* (1668) is thought to be the family of Moses Curiel d'Acosta.

Portrait of a Young Jew, Rembrandt van Rijn, 1648.

the Sabbath and the festivals, the high holy days and the fasts: the cantors and the Talmud Torah teachers; the *shokhetim*, the kosher slaughterers, and the *mohels*, the circumcisers. This last group, sometimes but not always rabbis, were kept especially busy in the centre of Sephardi life in the first generations because so many uncircumcised erstwhile New Christians were being re-Judaised in Amsterdam. And, certainly because of the pain and physical drama involved in this bloodletting, circumcision was treated as *the* major sign of conclusive return. Whole families of males from boys to grandpas were circumcised in ceremonial batches and received their Hebrew names in great celebrations, one of which was famously and spectacularly drawn by Romeyn de Hooghe in 1668. Even as they were decisively throwing off the last vestiges of Catholicism, Jews inadvertently retained something of its mindset by seeing circumcision as a sacrament without which they would be excluded from their share in the Life to Come. This was taken so literally that at least one case is known – the grandfather of Baruch Spinoza – who was circumcised after his death as the condition of his interment at the Beit Hayim cemetery.

This interior world of the Dutch Jews was organised and governed for itself, but the imposition of decorum meant it could also turn confidently outward, when occasion demanded, as on the day in May 1642 when it welcomed a prince and a queen. The community was somehow simultaneously autonomous and yet integrated into the life of the Dutch republic. That was because the republic was itself a multi-celled social and political organism. For the first time in a Christian world the Jews were not a glaringly alien presence, but just another micro-universe amid so many others: Mennonites, Lutherans, Catholics. Because there was no institutionally supreme Church in the Dutch republic, nor an autocratic monarchy imposing allegiance around its dynasty, there was also no monolithic sense of 'Dutchness' against which Jews could be judged to be unassimilably alien. There was just a constellation of interests. So the Jews came out and – a turn-up for the books this – could actually lead a more openly religious life than Catholics whose prayer houses had to be secret. For the Jews such dispensation, however indirect, was the quietest kind of revolution; the only kind they could handle, but a revolution nonetheless.

In Holland, to a degree unthinkable in the rest of Europe, Jews and Christians shared the same city. If most Jews resided in one part of it, that was by choice, so as to be within walking distance of their synagogues. They also shared the same law as other Amsterdammers. (Jews had to adjust to the legal requirement of registering their marriages with the civil magistrates.) This little historical miracle of equal legal rights was brought home in 1628 to David Curiel – whose extended family included members who had been imprisoned and tortured by the Inquisition. In that year Curiel was struck down in the streets of Amsterdam by a German robber. A hue and cry went up and Curiel's Christian neighbours joined him in pursuing the criminal through the streets, finally hunting him down. Justice took its course. The thief was hanged and his body, as was the custom, was sent for public anatomy to the guild of surgeons in Leiden. What was certainly not customary, not for Jews, was the invitation sent to the victim to attend the anatomy. That story became yet another exemplary scripture in the memory chronicle of the Dutch Jews. But while that canon mostly comprised atrocities and martyrdoms, this modern addition (surviving in five manuscripts) became a celebratory *megillah* for the Jews of Amsterdam, added to the synagogue reading of the Book of Esther every Purim.

The Esther cult – almost as much of a fixation as Solomon's Temple – tipped the Jews off to something which was a genuine bond between their history and that of the nation they now found themselves among. The Hebrew Bible, the Old Testament, was fundamental to both their sense of identities. In countless histories and printed sermons the Dutch described themselves as the new Children of Israel, or even *'het uytvekorene volk'* – the chosen people. The great, formal portrait engraving of William the Silent by Hendrick Goltzius expressly represents him as a latter-day Moses, with scenes from the Book of Exodus filling the marginal cartouches. At other times he was represented as David; Maurits the successor stadholder as Joshua. The great poet-playwright Joost van den Vondel (who as a regular at Muiden Castle would have met Francisca Duarte) wrote his drama *Passcha* (*Passover*) to drive this lesson of a new exodus, from bondage, through ordeals, to godly freedom.

The affinities were charted positively as well as negatively. A whole body of political theory, initiated in Modena by Carlo Sigonio but catching fire in Venice and the Protestant world, took what Segonio called the 'Hebrew Republic' as their model of a commonwealth of laws.[27] In this view – embodied, for instance, in *De Republica Hebraeorum*, published by the Dutch humanist Petrus Cunaeus in 1617 – Moses was the original civil lawgiver; but the true legislator was God Himself. Grotius had even held up the 'Hebrew Republic' as God's evident preference among all possible systems of government. Absent from that perfect commonwealth were princes or ruling priests. In this view ancient Israel drifted from the straight and narrow of God's law when they were tempted into kingship (notwithstanding the builder of the Temple). And whatever the virtues of David's reign, his transgressions, above all the royal freedom he had given himself to take Bathsheba while sending her husband to a certain death, was symptomatic of the abuses of monarchy. According to the Hebrew republicans, the Sanhedrin assembly had been a 'magistracy' or senate, and the Twelve Tribes of Israel (who never seemed to go away) imagined as the model for a confederated political society akin to the Dutch republic. Cunaeus even managed to interpret Josephus' *Antiquities* in such a way as to argue that Hebrew government had refrained from elevating one doctrine and its followers over another – thus the Sadducees, Pharisees and Essenes, all of whom, in their different ways, stood in as the ancestors of the different and contending varieties of Protestantism in the Dutch republic![28]

This is why Moses was bound to feature in the decorative programme of paintings ordered by the Amsterdam council for their palatially scaled new town hall.[29] Ferdinand Bol's picture of him holding the two tablets of the Ten Commandments as he glares down at the golden-calf idolatry of the Israelites below (represented on a sculpture frieze) can still be seen in the chamber of the *wethouders*, the aldermen. And it is possible that the full-length painting made around 1659 by Bol's original master, Rembrandt (one of the most beautiful of the many Old Testament scenes he created), was meant for the same civic installation.[30] As usual, Rembrandt departs from the stock expressions assigned to biblical characters, preferring instead the complexities of interior psychological conflict. Moses' countenance registers sorrow as well as dismay. And since it is a product of human observation, not the old, mad demonologies, the horns on Moses' head (made literal in Michelangelo's tomb sculpture for the Pope) have become euphemised into fluffy tufts of rabbinical hair. Rembrandt has been talking to someone who knew their Hebrew. The lettering of the Ten

Commandments (the latter ones made more visible than the former, for perhaps it would have been too paradoxical to show the prohibition on graven images) is accurate. And someone has put the artist right on the meaning of the *kareyn* mentioned in Exodus 34:29: the radiance shining on Moses' face as he descended the mountain after being in the presence of God.

This was not the only time Rembrandt took the transcription of Hebrew seriously, as the moving force of the story rather than a pedantic footnote to the Bible episode he was painting. More than any other artist of his time, Rembrandt was the great dramatist of apparition, of sudden revelations divinely delivered: Lazarus raised from the dead; the talking donkey hee-hawing Balaam to think again before cursing the Israelites; Abraham's hand stayed from slaughtering his son by the iron grip of the angel's intervention. But in *Belshazzar's Feast* painted in 1635, the agent of the drama which interrupts the Babylonian king's banquet – profaned by using the Temple vessels, shaking his table, his company of courtiers and courtesans, and his empire – are Hebrew letters written on the wall by a mysteriously disembodied hand. They form an undecipherably cryptic Aramaic message – '*Mene, mene tekel upharsin*' – and Rembrandt paints the words to be read vertically rather than right to left in the customary Hebrew manner. Even though he gets the last of them wrong, turning the long-tailed final *nun* into a *zayin*, it is possible (though not certain) that he got his calligraphic instruction from Menasseh ben Israel who, after all, was a Hebrew teacher as well as printer-publisher, *haham* of the nearby Neve Shalom synagogue. Two decades later the artist would illustrate a Kabbalistic book of the rabbi's, the *Piedra gloriosa de la estatua de Nebuchadnesar* (*The Glorious Stone of the Statue of Nebuchadnezzar*), in which Menasseh reiterated that 'the non-Jew who is virtuous and has the law fresh in his mind will not fail to gain his reward in the afterlife'.[31] But even in the 1630s Menasseh had been drawn to the combination of deep learning and prophetic intuitions, the eye-popping illuminations which Rembrandt also loved to dramatise.

Proximity is no guarantee of mutual sympathy. Neighbours can fall out, and Rembrandt certainly did with the tobacco merchant Daniel Pinto, over the noise and expense of building along their shared property line. (It was Pinto who did the complaining.) Rembrandt's neighbour on the other side of his house was also Sephardi, Salvator Rodrigues, with whom relations seem to have been more peaceful. But the only time a patron rejected a commissioned portrait on the grounds that it bore no resemblance to the sitter, the disputing party was a wealthy Jewish merchant, Diego d'Andrade, who infuriated Rembrandt by withholding money due on completion. (The sitter, a girl, may have been d'Andrade's daughter, hence the umbrage taken.) You have to hope that the artist didn't mutter about The Jews, Their Money and Their Taste while the row was going on.[32] It certainly didn't stop his collaboration with Menasseh.

In the 1640s Rembrandt had catered to the growing wish among the Sephardim, themselves fast becoming collectors and connoisseurs, to have their own portraits painted and etched. Ephraim Bueno, funder of both the rabbi and Templo, was depicted in rather the same way as Rembrandt's patron, the merchant-poet Jan Six, as a citizen animated by both thought and action. Rembrandt had made a little oil sketch of Bueno's head so beautiful that, three centuries later, Hitler took it for his intended Führer Museum at Linz, where the catalogue lists it, correctly, as 'Jewish doctor'. Which is all the odder since both portrait and etching testify to the possibility of visualising Jews shorn of any signs of apartness at all. Rembrandt's finished etching catches Bueno coming down a staircase. Thoughtfulness shadows his brow. He is lost in some sort of reflection even as he descends into the world of the street. The ring signifying both profession and obligation is sharply lit on his finger. Bueno is the citizen-physician, poised between the chamber of a patient and the pressing demands of the world, Maimonides on the canals.

Rembrandt was not a principled 'philo-Semite' in the way Templo's friend and collaborator Adam Boreel was, seeing the Jews as agents of a Divine Alteration. Some of Rembrandt's most memorable paintings – Jacob reversing the birth order of his grandsons by blessing Ephraim (the blond harbinger of the reign of Christ) rather than the darkly Jewish Menasseh – dramatise the ultimate victory of the New Testament over the Old. But it is not as if the Old Testament in its own right did not generate many of Rembrandt's most spectacularly powerful history paintings: Jeremiah grieving while the Temple burned; the naked Bathsheba at her ablutions spied on by David and thus by us; Jacob wrestling with the angel. When the artist looked at the Jews he did so less as a lay theologian than as a casting director. Rubbing shoulders with them every day, he made mental and actual sketches, and saw beneath the ordinary Dutch high hats and capes of the Sephardim – and the less ordinary soft Polish *kolpak* hats, long coats and beards of the Ashkenazim – the walking descendants of the Bible whose stories he compulsively translated into painted dramas.

There was, too, another aspect of the Amsterdam Jews which held Rembrandt's attention: their double identity as both civic-minded burghers of the city and yet also as world-wanderers. From the inventory of his possessions drawn up at the time of his bankruptcy, which included Japanese armour, exotic musical instruments and costumes, it is obvious that Rembrandt was himself an armchair world-wanderer. He drew his own copies of Mughal miniatures on Japanese paper, made sketches of lions and elephants, and painted many figures (including himself) in turbans and silk robes. This home-and-abroad aspect of his personality, perfectly Dutch, inevitably included the Jews within his cosmopolitan company of the human comedy. Though he never travelled anywhere beyond the republic, Rembrandt van Rijn may have been the least parochial artist Christian Europe ever produced.

And living where he did, working as he did, he could hardly have been unaware of the latest chapter in the nomadism of Jewish suffering: Ashkenazi Jews fleeing the murderous onslaught of the Chmielnicki Cossacks in Poland in 1648. Survivors made their torturous way to one of the few places in Europe where they had a chance of being humanely treated. Yet the Ashkenazim had been coming in numbers to Amsterdam for years and, unlike the Sephardim who adopted the Dutch style of dress, they wore their own Polish style of dress: broad-brimmed flat hats or tall soft ones. Although the 'synagogue' in which a *minyan* of ten adult males are gathered is stonily fanciful, more like a corner of Templo's Temple than the wooden buildings of Vlooienburg, Rembrandt's etching of the Ashkenazim owes something to direct observation. Even so, the elderly, stooped, shuffling and gossiping Jews of the etching are Types, whether sympathetically or unsympathetically rendered. Rembrandt's *Young Jew*, painted in 1648, the year of the Cossack massacres, is something else again, a visual reinstatement of the Jews into the common family of humanity. It is all the more affecting for not being a commissioned portrait but a *tronie*, a character study. But unlike Rembrandt's

guffawing ruffians or withered ancients, there is no trace of theatri-
cality in the beautiful head. This is not a stage Jew. He is, instead, an
actual Jew. Indeed it is possible he might be one of the mixed-race
Jews who had returned from the Guinea coast or Brazil. And although
Calvinist preachers were painted and etched with skullcaps, none of
them have the open-neck collar, the mud-brown woollen coat and
vest, nor the curly locks. This is the habit of the wanderer fetched up
on the Vlooienburg.

You can see how this kind of head prompted all the later romantic
fairy tales, especially in Germany, about Rembrandt's empathy for the
Jews, although usually they were based on workshop studies of bearded
old men who were added to an expanding inventory labelled 'rabbis'.
You would have to be a sceptic to the point of blind irrationality,
however, to suppose the face we have before us in *here* is, say, a
Mennonite. We will never know which way round it was. Did
Rembrandt project onto the heavy lids, the shallow sacks beneath the
eyes, the furrowed brow, the fleshy lips, everything he imagined about
the perennial melancholy of the Jews? Or did he himself create that
image through the power of the painting; its background and costume
roughly brushed in the better to make the unconventional beauty of
the face more hypnotic?

It hardly matters. Coming from the usual mysteriously hidden
source, the light strikes the young Jew's rumpled white collar and
illuminates one side of his face. His gaze does not directly meet ours
but is a little lowered, distant from ingratiation, as if lost in some
altogether more important matter: the meaning of this week's Torah
reading; the price of candles; his wife's cough; God's perplexing deafness to his prayers. No painter does pensive better than Rembrandt.
No European artist for a very long time could find a way to represent
the heaviness of Jewish history, alleviated by the light of thought.

II. Going Astray?

So much could go wrong if you wanted to shoot someone in
Amsterdam in 1640, even if you were sound of mind, which Uriel da

Costa was not.[33] The April rain might have dampened the black powder; the barrel of the pistol may have been left fouled from the last discharge, however clean it seemed when you peered down the muzzle; the flint might strike the frizzen off-kilter so it would fail to spring open the pan; the sparks might fly off sideways instead of making firing contact with the powder in the muzzle. Or the doglock pistol might work as it should but your shaking hand would make the ball miss its target. Whatever the particular matter, Uriel's shot failed to kill his cousin, or, as some said, his brother, whomever it was he blamed for thwarting his marriage prospects, betraying him to the *ma'amad*, subjecting him to the ordeal of excommunication, his body thrown on the floor so the congregation might step over him as they exited.

He missed his target. The hated relative, the imagined author of his misfortunes, fled. But Uriel had prepared for such an eventuality. Vengeance was only half of it. Before any sort of hue and cry could go up, he was already back inside his house, the door slammed and locked. A second gun, primed, was waiting for him on a table. This time the doglock barked at his temple and he was gone.

But not his story. When his body was found, so was his autobiography, sitting on a table, waiting for vindicating readers. Just four years later, in 1644 it was published by a Lutheran clergyman, Johann Muller, into whose hands a copy of the manuscript had fallen. Another forty-three years elapsed before a more widely read version was given by the Remonstrant cleric Philip van Limborch. He did not do this out of tragic fellow feeling but something like the opposite. Reciting the usual slanders and paranoias, he accused the Jews, collectively, of being a 'worldly and carnal people', 'bent on dominating others'. So the drama of Uriel da Costa, martyred for speaking his mind to the congregation, exposing the hypocrisy of the rabbis, their unfaithfulness to the laws of Moses, was just Limborch's cup of tea. But from being Limborch's useful polemicist against the wilful stubbornness of the rabbis, Uriel became, especially for reform-minded Jews of later generations, something more transcendent: the tragic hero of Jewish freethinking. The nineteenth-century non-Jewish German writer Karl Gutzkow turned Uriel's life and death into a melodrama, which once translated became a staple of the Yiddish theatre companies of central and eastern Europe. Sholem Aleichem made the play the favourite staple of his touring company in his beautiful lime-lit novel *Wandering Stars*. The legend stuck. Uriel had perished so that Jews could think freely and still consider themselves Jews, however deep the scowls and violent the imprecations of the crabbed and narrow-minded rabbis. Without Uriel da Costa's vanguard temerity, the genealogy of secular Jews goes, Baruch Spinoza would not have dared to think and write as he did and the world would have been a different and more oppressively orthodox place. The truth was different, of course: more complicated, less heroic, more richly neurotic. And yet the legend and the history were not entirely disconnected.

Uriel began life as Gabriel; one of those names that meant something whether you were Christian or Jewish. He was, as was the way with so many *conversos* in Portugal (his town was Oporto), of both religions. In his autobiography, he characterised his father as a sincere convert, an ennobled New Christian and a tax farmer for the Portuguese Crown. He himself studied canon law at Coimbra University, and was secretary to the archbishopric before returning to the university, where he was taught by its most eminent authority, the preacher and confessor Antonio Homem. But there may have been two kinds of teaching. For in 1619, five years after Uriel had secretly left Portugal, Homem was arrested by the Inquisition, accused of presiding over a secret conventicle of Judaisers who met to observe fasts and feasts. Also condemned for acts of sodomy, Homem was garroted and burned five years later in 1624. In his autobiography Uriel claimed to have had no experience of Judaism in Portugal, yet there was undoubtedly Judaising in the family. In 1621 his sister Maria and her husband were arrested for Judaising and in depositions to the Inquisition testified that their mother Branca gave instructions to wear clean shirts for the Sabbath, light candles, abstain from forbidden foods – the usual habits which made the Marranos feel they were still Jews and one day would be so openly. On the face of it, incriminating one's mother seems callous, but it was common practice for accused *conversos* when those they fingered were well beyond the physical reach of the Inquisition, as was the case with Branca and most of the family. So notwithstanding his professions, it seems likely that Gabriel/Uriel grew up secretly attached to his people's history and religion.

The quest for the real Gabriel did not lead straight to the heart of Judaism. In 1614 Branca, like so many others, used the breathing space of the truce between the Dutch and Spanish to take her family to Amsterdam, though leaving Portugal without permission had been strictly outlawed in 1610. Two of her sons remained in the city, and immediately reverted and were circumcised, Miguel becoming Mordecai, and João, Joseph. Branca, Gabriel/Uriel and his brother Jacomo, now Abraham, travelled on to Hamburg. No sooner had Uriel (as he now was) encountered the reality of living Judaism in the port than he took against it for failing to live up to the high ideals he had nursed during his years of secret devotion. Instead of lofty ethics and spiritual realisation, all he could see were trivial, mechanical rituals, mindless hair-splitting and irrational injunctions. Having little or no knowledge of Hebrew did not deter him from launching, in 1616, barely a year after arriving in Hamburg, a ferocious broadside against rabbinical Judaism and the entire oral law tradition. Though he represented his disenchantment as a result of his encounters with the daily routines of Judaism in Amsterdam and Hamburg, Uriel's attack on rabbinical legalism could just as easily have been drawn from sources in both Christian and Jewish traditions. The notion that a purer Judaism had been corrupted and usurped by the Talmudists had been a commonplace of Christian (and especially New Christian) polemics, but it was also the defining criterion of the Karaites.

Alarm bells rang, not least in Venice where Uriel sent his inflammatory letter. The most alarmed of all was Leone Modena, who had become responsible for long-distance monitoring of the re-education of *converso* Sephardi returnees. Most had grown up with no more than the casual customs of the secret life; no knowledge of Hebrew, still less of the Talmud. Re-education was crucial if the Judaism of their religious rebirth was to be the real thing and not some specious form of immigrant convenience. Acts of mischief of the kind committed by Uriel da Costa had to be nipped in the bud before they set scepticism running among the Marranos. But there was another, more devious reason why Leone took such umbrage. For while Uriel's most shocking claims – that rabbinical Judaism had nothing to do with the Torah and that in all likelihood it had not been the work of one hand – were furthest from Leone's thoughts, he too was pondering what was extraneous and what was essential to the practice of Judaism. But he disguised this reform as the work of someone else, a manuscript written a century before that had been placed in his hands, and called it *Kol Sakhal* (*The Voice of a Fool*). Though much of what the Fool proposed was anything but folly – the shortening of services since 'not everyone is a Talmudic scholar' – the last thing Leone wanted was to be exposed as someone opening the doors to heresy. So when faced with Uriel's diatribe against rabbinical Judaism he became the arm of orthodoxy. *In absentia* in Venice, Uriel was subjected to the *herem* ban, and the Ponentine congregation in Hamburg was required to follow suit.[34]

On the face of it, the *herem* was a merciless separation, an un-Jewing. The banned party was disqualified from counting as one of the *minyan* needed to conduct prayers. His sons could not be circumcised; other Jews could not share his table no matter how ostensibly kosher. The ostracism made it impossible for any business dealings to be conducted with the punished. But in practice it was often used to encourage the contrite return of the guilty party back into the fold of the congregation. When Menasseh ben Israel made a scene in the synagogue at people who refused to call his brother-in-law *senhor* (how more Jewish can one get?), he was sentenced to a ban of a single day. On the other hand this flexibility encouraged some ruling bodies – especially the *ma'amad* of Amsterdam, who were given the exclusive right to impose and withdraw the *herem* – to use the ban as a deterrent against every conceivable kind of transgression, from adultery to bringing weapons into the synagogue.

The dissuasion did not work as planned with Uriel da Costa. In 1623 he returned to Amsterdam with his mother and swiftly published an even more incendiary tract, *Exame das tradicoes phariseas* (*Examination of the Pharisaic Traditions*).[35] This too had a faintly Catholic whiff about it since it had long been a staple of Church arguments that the Pharisees had reinvented and distorted the original teachings of the Hebrew prophets. Eccentrically, Uriel projected his own views onto the Sadducees – the priestly establishment of the Temple – the defenders of the older rites and faith, though the passion for all things Temple may have led him to believe this a good tactic. Once again Uriel poured scorn on customs and rituals he said were rabbinical inventions: the two-day celebration of festivals in the diaspora (justified by calendrical uncertainties of distance) rather than the single day specified in the Torah. More combatively he criticised the external signs and habits which nourished Jewish solidarity and tied the Jew to daily communion with God: the *tallit* prayer shawl and the daily binding of the *tefillin* phylacteries. None of these, he claimed (incorrectly), had any scriptural prescription. Uriel's critics attacked him for a kind of intellectual snobbery, too eager to chuckle at inherited custom, and they were not entirely wrong about that. He certainly felt himself to be the inheritor of Renaissance learning, struggling with the upholders of mindless superstition.

Much more subversive than sarcastic attacks on tradition was his insistence, in an unpublished work, that there was nothing in the Bible to support the belief in the immortality of the soul. The soul was made of the same material substance as the body, and thus perished at the same time. Prior knowledge that Uriel was likely to sound off in Amsterdam, possibly in print, triggered consternation in the community where Leone's star pupil, Saul Morteira, had brought the body of Elijah Montalto for burial in 1616 and had stayed to become *haham* of one of the three synagogues, Beit Jacob. For Morteira and the *ma'amad*, Uriel's bombshell threatened to blow up the essential condition of Jewish toleration in Amsterdam and indeed the whole Dutch republic since the regulation of 1616: that the Jews would neither speak nor publish anything offensive to Christian tradition. The first generations of Dutch Jews had been scrupulous in observing that propriety.

Now they had to deal with the scandal of Uriel da Costa, still officially under the ban of 1618. As usual, the first effort was friendly dissuasion. But it rapidly became obvious that far from Uriel rethinking the offensiveness of his earlier views, including his outright rejection of the immortality of the soul and the promise of resurrection, he had codified them into the *Examination of the Pharisaic Traditions*, written, moreover, in Portuguese for the easier understanding of his fellow Marranos. In other audacious ways, too, the book struck at the foundations of Judaism. It was absurd, Uriel argued, to suppose the Torah had been written entirely by Moses, or under divine inspiration. All those laws were a kind of political coup designed to bolster Moses' magistracy and the supreme authority of his brother Aaron. What Moses had done was to commit 'a fabrication'.

Not surprisingly, then, as soon as it was published in 1624, and undoubtedly at the urging of the Amsterdam community, Uriel was arrested, imprisoned for ten days and fined three hundred guilders. He was released when his brothers put up bail and security of twelve hundred guilders (a huge sum) for his good behaviour in the future. All copies of the book were ordered to be seized and publicly burned. But two of them somehow escaped the pyre; and one of the pair of survivors, auctioned in The Hague in the eighteenth century, is probably the copy rediscovered in the Danish Royal Library in Copenhagen by the brilliant scholarly sleuth H. P. Salomon.

To correct his mischievous diffusion of 'erroneous, false and heretical opinions', the Hamburg *herem* was now put in force in Amsterdam. This had the immediate effect of severing Uriel from his brothers and sister, who were now obliged to cut off all contacts with him. No more family meals or meetings; no more letters. There was one exception to his ostracism. In a touching show of maternal tenderness and loyalty, Branca, now called Sara, defied the ban, going to live with him in Utrecht in 1627. In violation of one of the express prohibitions of the excommunication, she cooked and ate the meat which her son had butchered, and loyally followed his rather than the official Jewish calendar of feasts and fasts. This meant that on the day all other Jews abstained from food, Uriel and Sara were eating, and the week everyone else accepted as Passover, they were consuming leaven. These outrages put the now elderly Sara in jeopardy of being denied burial in the Ouderkerk cemetery of Beit Hayim. But in Sara's case the normally flinty Morteira was prepared to relax the rules.

Sara died in 1628 and was indeed interred in Beit Hayim. It seems inconceivable that Uriel was not at the funeral with his siblings, and also that it was the emotional force of the moment which led him to attempt a reconciliation with the community. All he had to do was to retract his errors, and his efforts at this were enough to let him return to the city, though he seems sometimes to have assumed the alias of 'Adam Romez'. But the *Exemplar*, his memoir, paints a picture of gathering misery, Uriel accused of eating non-kosher food and, more dangerously, dissuading incoming *conversos* from returning to rabbinical Judaism. Some sort of crisis was at hand. In 1639, he is recorded living in the Vloonburgsteeg, a stone's throw from the newly unified synagogue on the Houtgracht, and transferring his

worldly goods to his common-law wife Digna, the act witnessed by
a Gentile tobacconist and a Jewish maker of automata with swivelling
eyes, necks and heads, designed for the amusement of fairground
crowds.

By the late spring of that same year Uriel had had enough and
undertook a formal ritual of atonement in the synagogue. The procedure was a traumatic public humiliation. The atoning man was
dressed in mourning black and held a black wax taper as if suspended
between life and death as his transgressions were read aloud. Though
the prescribed thirty-nine lashes, once physically carried out, had been
virtualised into the touch of a whip or strap on his bare shoulders,
the supplicant was actually required to lie prostrate while the congregation stepped over his body.

It is not known whether it was after or before the congregation
had stepped over him that he began to write the story of his life; but
the actual writing deepened his despair, and with the last page Uriel
lost himself in thoughts of self-immolation. Powder and pistols came
to his distracted mind. In the midst of his attack on Jewish tradition,
Uriel had ridiculed the generations who had committed *kiddush
hashem*, the sacrifice of themselves and their children, rather than be
coerced into conversion. Those suicides, he said, were the product of
pointless delusion, for there would be no heavenly welcome for their
martyred souls; only darkness and dust. But the masquerade of a third
recantation was insupportable. All the signs are that when he ended
it all it was without hope of an afterlife.

Uriel da Costa was not a profound man, but the moment he
embodied in the Jewish story was: the painful birth and premature
demise of the secular, obsessively polemical, rationally driven Jew who
for all his scepticism wished to remain a Jew. Even his relationship
with his mother spoke of this pathetic ambivalence. For the renegade
who poured scorn on the notion of the soul's immortality, of the
afterlife itself, nonetheless did not want to obstruct his mother's burial
in a cemetery where she would lie among Sephardim who all expired
assuming their souls were headed straight to the paradise garden.
What the *herem* did, when laid on hard, was to strip a Jew of the
ultimate sense of connection, not with the Law of Moses, but with
the blessed nourishment of family. Uriel lost his brethren and failed
to find kinship elsewhere. That the *herem* thwarted his attempts to

become engaged, as he complained in his autobiography, may have been the final straw.

As clumsy, childish, confused and obstinate as he was, Uriel da Costa, thrashing this way and that, began something that would not end with his suicide. In other ages – our own – he would have found a synagogue that would have accommodated all his doubts, questions, even his fits of piqued rage. A rabbi, not necessarily a man with a beard, would have sat him down, calmed him, and tried to find a way to keep him Jewish (knowing that this is what the anguished man wanted).

But in Amsterdam in the seventeenth century men like Uriel da Costa must have seemed all too much like the Wicked Son at the Passover Seder: a callow sophist whose only pleasure was to bring down what countless generations of sages had built; to make light of Jewish sacrifices; and with no knowledge of the language in which it was written (especially perhaps the fine-wrought classical Hebrew of the Mishnah), to use his self-congratulatory cleverness to set traditional Judaism at naught. Uriel was intolerable many times over. To Leone Modena – who had himself in matters of liturgical music been charged with outraging tradition – he threatened to replace the figure of the Good Jew (lauded by the Gentiles, much visited in synagogue and salon) with the Bad Jew (who would not hesitate to subvert revealed authority). The more the guardians of the communities thought about it, the reasons for outrage multiplied. What was he, this novice, this sometime Christian who on one day professed his Judaism, the next attacked it with all the ancient stratagems of the persecutors, charging the Talmud with usurpation and even Moses with fraud? Who was he to spit on the graves of the martyrs who had gone to their end steadfast, reciting the *shema* as they burned into charred bone and ash? Who was he to put in jeopardy the little breathing space the Gentiles had given them in Amsterdam? This was the historical meaning of Uriel da Costa. His was the earliest test of the challenges of freedom: how to keep the outliers from going rogue. Other such tests would follow. For Amsterdam was first the nursery and then the laboratory of the secular Jew.

There was nothing about the long-nosed dark-eyed boy sitting on a bench in Talmud Torah class that would have tipped off his teachers

that Baruch Espinosa would turn out to be even bigger trouble for
the *kahal* than Uriel da Costa. His father, Michael d'Espinosa, was a
businessman, an importer of dried fruit and nuts from Spain and
Portugal: Malaga raisins, figs, Algarve almonds and olive oil from
further afield. A member of the Beit Jacob synagogue, Michael was
well enough respected in the community to serve as a *parnas*, a
representative of the fifteen-strong board (comprising deputies from
the three synagogues before their union in 1639) responsible for
governing the affairs of the community and representing them before
the Amsterdam regents. Michael was also one of those in charge of
the community's pawn shop, and a *parnas* of the Talmud Torah, the
body governing all the community's schools including the ones which
his clever son Baruch attended from seven to fourteen. There Baruch
would have acquired a good reading knowledge of Hebrew, studied
the Torah and learned, in Spanish, to explain the significance of the
weekly reading. Whether he then went on to the more senior classes
is unknown, but, tantalisingly, if he had been in the fifth form – to
learn the *Shulkhan Arukh* – his teachers would have been first
Menasseh ben Israel and then Templo. Even if Baruch did not become
one of the learned *bokhurim*, most of whom were training to be
rabbis, there is no doubt that he was steeped in the Jewish literature
on which he would later train his critical sights.[36] Although he left
the Etz Hayim school probably at fourteen to help with his father's
troubled business, Baruch seems to have attended one of the weekly
study groups meant for adult laymen, Saul Morteira's Keter Torah,
the Crown of the Law. It may have been when, a few years later,
Morteira learned that his ex-student Spinoza was letting it be known
that the Torah was not of divine origin, that Moses should command
no more respect than Muhammad or Jesus, and that the entirety of
rabbinical Judaism was a spurious road to salvation – indeed that
there *was* no salvation, nor an afterlife of the soul – that his rage
prompted him to issue an excommunication as ferocious as that laid
on Uriel da Costa.[37]

On 27 July 1656, the *ma'amad* pronounced that *herem*. It was just as
well, perhaps, that Baruch's father Michael, as a member, was no
longer alive to wring his hands over the fate of his son, now chillingly
severed from his family as well as the congregation of Israel. Just a
year before, Baruch would still have been saying Kaddish for his father

and paying communal and charity taxes – though on a sliding scale meant to help the financially distressed, meaning that the import business had all but collapsed. To escape his liabilities in the event of a liquidation, Spinoza actually had himself made an orphaned ward of the Board of Guardians, while his age (twenty-three) still allowed. Majority was reached at twenty-five, so that Spinoza's transparent tactic of avoiding liability was strictly legal, but is certain nonetheless to have caused a good deal of ill will.[38]

In its *herem*, the *ma'amad* said it had 'for some time ... known of the evil opinions and acts of Baruch Spinoza' and had tried to dissuade him from uttering reprehensible opinions and infamous deeds (probably showy violations of the Sabbath and the dietary laws of kashrut). Baruch's family had shrunk. His mother, Debora Hanna, had died in 1638 when he had only been six years old and it had evidently been a bone of contention that Baruch had been deprived, as a minor, of what he felt was his inheritance from her. His father, his stepmother (Michael's third wife) and his sister Miriam had all died in the space of a year. A maritime war with England had made things even more difficult than usual for an import business. English privateers and Barbary corsairs were taking ships loaded with wine, olive oil and dried fruit, which were the staples of the Spinoza import business. Though Baruch had been attempting to maintain the firm for nearly two years after his father's death, it was sinking under an untenable weight of debt.[39] The surrender to Portugal of Recife, the last Dutch redoubt in Brazil, dried up the supply of another Spinoza commodity: sugar. Brazilian Marranos had arrived back in Amsterdam, many of them destitute, and the fearfulness spreading in the community gave the *ma'amad* the sense that it needed to keep an even more vigilant eye on heterodoxy. Marrano loyalties could be hard to pin down and, as the Uriel disaster suggested, they could easily be led astray by impulsive heresies. This was no time to give the community a bad name in the eyes of Christians. This young Spinoza was just such a threat.

Apparently the crisis had not come on suddenly. The *herem* stated that 'the lords of the *ma'amad* had endeavoured by various means and promises to turn him from his evil ways. But having failed to make him mend his wicked ways and on the contrary receiving daily more and more serious information about the horrendous heresies which he practiced and taught and about his monstrous deeds and having for this numerous trustworthy witnesses ... they became convinced of the truth of this matter ... they have decided that the said Espinoza should be excommunicated and expelled from the people of Israel.'[40] The language which then followed was more extreme than bans used on any of the thirty-eight previous cases, including Uriel da Costa's. Baruch, whose name meant the blessed one, now became the cursed one.[41]

By the decree of the angels and by the command of the holy men, we excommunicate, expel, curse and damn Baruch de Espinoza with the consent of God ... Cursed be he by day and cursed be he by night; cursed be he when he lies down and cursed be he when he rises up; cursed be he when he goes out and cursed be he when he comes in. The Lord shall not spare him but the anger of the Lord and his jealousy shall smoke against that man and all the curses that are written in this book shall be upon him and the Lord shall blot out his name from under heaven. And the Lord shall separate him unto evil out of all the tribes of Israel according to all the curses that are written in this book of the Law ... no one should communicate with him in speech or writing nor accord him any favour nor stay under the same roof as him nor be within four cubits of his vicinity nor shall read any treatise composed or written by him.

How had it come to this? When he was cast out in the summer of 1656 Spinoza had not yet published anything (unlike Uriel); but when he did begin to explain his views around 1660, he admitted that they had been the product of 'long reflection'. Just how long is hard to say, but in 1655 a Jew harbouring the same doubts had arrived in Amsterdam. Daniel (or Juan) de Prado was twenty years older than Spinoza, a physician and poet, tall, swarthy, bearded and 'big-nosed' according to a witness. He met Spinoza when they both attended Saul Morteira's Keter Torah yeshiva, the rabbi's expositions of the Talmud only adding to their secretly shared impulse to repudiate it. While egging each other on, a third rebel, also an immigrant Marrano, joined their company: Daniel Ribera, who had only recently abandoned the Catholic Church full of heretical doubts, and was now ready to bring them to bear on his rediscovered Judaism.

It is a commonplace of Spinoza literature that it was the Latin School of Franciscus van den Enden in his house on the Singel which tipped Spinoza into his 'heretical' rejections of the Torah and Talmud. Van den Enden was notorious both as a libertine and a dangerous freethinker, and it is known that Spinoza associated with him in 1657–8. It is possible that Spinoza went to live in his house, and it is certain that he acted in van den Enden's productions of plays by the Roman writer Terence. There is no reliable documentary evidence, however, that Spinoza was anywhere near van den Enden in the years preceding his ban, much less that he was already a disciple of René Descartes' mind–body dualism. The mentors of Spinoza's disbelief at this period were all Jewish ex-*conversos* with strong ties to Spain and Portugal. Prado, who had inherited many of Uriel da Costa's heresies, may well have become informal tutor to the more profound younger man. In August 1659, two (friendly) witnesses before the Madrid Inquisition – Friar Tomas Solana y Robles and Captain Miguel Perez de Maltranilla – testified to having met both Prado and Spinoza the previous year.[42] They were described indivisibly as having the same opinions and having suffered the same fate of being expelled from the Jewish community for deciding that the Law of Moses was false. What was meant by 'false' seems very likely to have been the explosive argument Spinoza would later articulate in the *Tractatus Theologicus-Politicus*, that the Torah should be understood essentially as an act of political constitution rather than a revelation.[43] Just as confrontational was the insistence, shared by Prado and Spinoza and inherited from Uriel da Costa, 'that souls died in the body and that there was no God except philosophically'. The previous year, 1658, Prado and Ribera had been accused by ten teenage boys (among them one Jacob Pina, who described himself as a 'poet') of pushing scandalous views on them, including Moses being 'a sorcerer'; his laws drafted to benefit himself and Aaron; the myth of a divine providence intervening in the human world; the antiquity of the world being much older than the Bible asserted; and the pointlessness of rabbinically prescribed ritual and its meaninglessness as a route to assure an afterlife. The teenagers even accused Prado and Ribera of egging them on to take swords into the synagogue hidden beneath their capes, and to make 'a revolt' there against more ridiculous laws, to the point of threatening the rabbis with death. This last may, or may not, have been a joke.

Daniel de Prado, then, was the ringleader of a rowdy group of aggressively posturing unbelievers who cast themselves to a following of impressionable young boys as Jewish Lords of Misrule. The antics of the unbelievers were predictably juvenile: ostentatious smoking in the streets on the Sabbath; tucking into a menu of forbidden foods; kicking up a row in the forecourt of the synagogue – or even inside. The crudeness of Prado's rebellion is not to be confused with Spinoza's meticulous philosophical reflections, but equally there is no doubt that for a while, both before and after the *herem*, Spinoza ran with the pack of the nose-thumbers. It was perhaps predictable that when it came down to an excommunication, Prado was the ringleader by virtue of his years and an air of dangerous charisma. Equally predictably, he was also the first to fold. Threatened with excommunication in July 1656 he became distraught and pleaded with the *ma'amad* to revoke the ban. There was no shortage of Jewish doctors in Amsterdam so that being cut off from his modest pool of patients was tantamount to ruin. So at some point he mounted the *tevah*, beat his breast and recanted, 'rescinding his evil opinions'. It was, however, a very temporary atonement. In February 1657 he was put under a ban, and this time was asked whether he might not prefer to leave Amsterdam altogether, in which case the *ma'amad* might help financially to expedite his departure.

Getting the troublemakers out of Amsterdam before jeopardising the standing of the community with the city regents was the immediate priority. Removing Daniel Ribera, the ex-priest, may have been even more pressing as he was also a teacher, and of poor students at that, whom the *ma'amad* might have thought the most impressionable. Yet Ribera seems not to have waited to be banned or asked but left of his own accord, travelling to Brussels to live with his brother, a cavalry officer, and quite probably returning to the Church.

Spinoza was made of different mettle. One of his earliest biographers, Jean-Maximilien Lucas, claimed that following the formal ban, the *ma'amad* petitioned Amsterdam's regents to have the renegade banished from the city forthwith. And of course they could have claimed that Spinoza's irreverence, particularly his denial of the immortality of the soul, was a menace to the church as well as the synagogue. But this approach to the city councillors never happened. No one from the Jewish community made any such representations to have him

gone. On the contrary, the community seems to have gone out of its
way, notwithstanding the violence of the curses, to offer him money
to behave and to put in the occasional appearance in synagogue.
Anything to keep the peace. But Spinoza, as he later wrote, was not
interested in living the life of a hypocrite.

Cut off from his brother Gabriel (who nonetheless continued to
call their import firm, such as it was, Bento y Gabriel Spinoza) he left
Vlooienburg, but remained very visibly in Amsterdam. Spinoza did
not move into the darkness of solitary philosophising – just the opposite. Whether or not he stayed with van den Enden in the Latin School
on the Singel, he certainly took up with him and a lively company of
sceptical scholars, thinkers and talkers. He may also have gone to
meetings of those from Adam Boreel's Amsterdam 'College' too, in
which case it is not beyond the bounds of possibility that he encountered Rembrandt, who like him was going through the collapse of
his economic fortunes. It was the beginning of a lifelong engagement
with the like-minded and the speculative. When he eventually took
himself off, first to Rijnsburg and then some years later to Voorburg,
and began his work as a lens grinder and polisher, Spinoza was seeking
the quiet he needed to concentrate on his philosophy, but just as telling
was the fact that both locations were very close to major centres of
learning, religion and politics, since all three were at the heart of his
preoccupations. Rijnsburg was a few miles from Leiden, and its university's libraries and lectures; and Voorburg was similarly close to The
Hague, where Spinoza would seek out the Huygens family. Christian
Huygens, Constantijn's son, whose own work on optics must have
encouraged Spinoza to make an approach, tolerated his attention yet
referred to him, tellingly and invariably, not by name but as 'the Jew
from Voorburg'. Christian's brother, Constantijn Junior, seems to have
been more welcoming. But Benedict (as Spinoza now styled his
Latinised forename) was a tireless correspondent, pursuer of philosophical helpmates, and encourager of disciples, hungry for mutual
engagement in knotty conundrums of perception.

Spinoza may have stayed in Amsterdam for as long as five years
after the *herem*, though, and it was there, not in brooding self-imposed
isolation, that he began to set down the reasons for his repudiation
of the entire religious culture in which he had been brought up, thus
drastically altering his life. In this first work, *The Treatise on the*

Emendation of the Intellect (written when he was still in his twenties), he witheringly dismisses the revelatory scripture of any religion as 'fiction'. But he begins the *Treatise* with a general consideration of the worthwhile life, or rather the pointless death:

> After experience had taught me that all the usual surroundings of social life are vain and futile, seeing that none of the objects of my fears contained in themselves anything either good or bad, except so far as the mind was affected by them, I finally resolved to enquire whether there might not be some powerful idea ... which would affect the mind singly to the exclusion of all else, whether in fact there might be anything the discovery and attainment of which would enable me to enjoy continuous and supreme happiness.

There then follows the familiar humanist catalogue of false trails to that happiness – fame, riches, sensual love, honour – famously scorned in Moses Maimonides' *The Guide for the Perplexed* (which Spinoza would certainly have known and digested in his school years): 'What men esteem the highest good – riches, fame and pleasure – so distract the mind that it cannot consider any other good.' Fame makes the seeker live his life according to the lights of his fellow men; the pursuit of riches is destructively addictive and sensual pleasure is just a prologue to morning-after repentance. He had come to see, he writes, that all the good deemed desirable by the multitude actually leads to death, and that he himself was in mortal peril, 'like a sick man struggling with a deadly disease' unless he abandoned 'certain evils for a certain good'. The great mistake was to love what was perishable, for that was a guarantee of perpetual, self-destructive restlessness. 'But love towards a thing eternal and infinite feeds the mind wholly with joy and is itself unmingled with any sadness wherefore it is greatly to be desired and sought after with all our strength.'

That great object – the infinite, immutable, majestically impassive order of nature – was already in Spinoza's sights, even as early as 1660 or 1661, though it was as yet not much more than an instinctive notion glimpsed on the horizon of his searching intellect. If those initial exercises in self-clarification – the polishing of the lens of his own lucidity – sound vaguely familiar, it is because they owe something not just to the long classical tradition (from Plato and Aristotle) of devotion to illumination rather than the shadow world of common gratifications, but also to a parallel Jewish tradition which defined the worthy life in much the same way. As early as the ninth century, Saadia the Gaon in Mesopotamia had insisted on the indispensability of reason for the resolution of inconsistencies in the Torah. In the eleventh century, the poet-philosopher and rabbi Abraham ibn Ezra had already noticed additions, repetitions and interpolations in the Torah which precluded the possibility that Moses had written all of it, and questioned the literal truth of the more improbably sensational miracles, the favourite being the same one used by Spinoza as evidence of the fictitious nature of the Bible: the stopping of the sun over the Battle of Ai until Joshua could win the day. But Spinoza's narrative of an intellectual pilgrimage of illumination, progressively shedding inferior forms of gratification and culminating in the mind's perception of its own union with the immutable universe, might almost have come straight from the numinous, climactic pages of Maimonides' *Guide for the Perplexed* (with its own strong debt to the Greek philosophers). Almost. Maimonides' course of reasoning stopped before the gates of pure faith; the ultimate unknowability of God.[44] As with most Aristotelian visions of the universe, the world was divided into intangible, abstract essence and materially created existence, and it was in the latter lower realm that nature was to be discovered, its sublime patternings and orders dimly reflecting the majesty of an organising idea. Transferred to the Torah and Hebrew scripture, Moses, his face radiant with burning light, had been allowed only the sight of God's back, the divinely written laws being the residue of that illumination, prescribed for the world of men and to be carried through the generations by the Children of Israel.

But for Spinoza there was to be no division between godly and earthly understanding; no reason (except unexamined timorous reverence) to make such a distinction. Nor, although he would teach the philosophy and epistemology of Descartes to students, did he subscribe to the French philosopher's mind–body dualism. He was all monism. Once the clutter of inherited fictions and superstitions had been cleared away, and once prophetic visions could be seen as products of the inspired imagination, yielding an inferior kind of knowledge to that of natural, scientific enquiry, then the uncaused God could be seen as simply identical with the totality of created nature. The strenuously

persevering mind was capable of apprehending the perfectly interlocking qualities and actions of that nature – the revolutions of its
planets or the symmetries of its crystals – without having to postulate
a tirelessly interventionist deity. The true God was nothing more, but
also nothing less, than this natural universe in motion, a system which
proceeded impervious to the doings of men; oblivious to the concept
of 'sin' (evidently a human creation), much less any prescribed way
to salvation. This *Deus sive Natura*, as Spinoza later put it, was morally
indifferent, organically self-sufficient and without history or moral
instruction. He, and it, just was.

It followed, then, that this God-or-Nature had to be universal and
not the property of any one religion's claim to exclusive revelation.
Did this mean that his immense shift in understanding had removed
him altogether (and more decisively than any excommunication) from
anything that could be described as Jewish; that Spinoza's importance
for the world was conditional on his ceasing, in any meaningful sense,
to be a Jew? As Jewish identity was formally understood in the seventeenth century, the answer has to be yes. For the premise of sharing
Spinoza's one-size-fits-all God-or-Nature was to discard all the fantasies
(as he saw them) of an anthropomorphic God who spoke directly to
the patriarchs and prophets; who made a special covenant with the
Children of Israel, and delivered the laws which established their way
of living Jewishly. Whatever was good about those laws had to be
good for everyone. Moses and whoever else it was who had subsequently written the Torah had only claimed them as the special,
peculiar possession of the Jews, in the sense of promising them that
if they observed them, the political society they had created would
endure. Their directly divine origin was a fable of convenience, tailored
to the 'childish' level of understanding of the Hebrews and necessary
to ensure their cohesion.

Once the divine authority of revealed scripture was disposed of, or
at least relegated to an inferior kind of knowledge, the whole massive
superstructure of explanatory commentary provided by generations
of sages and rabbis (and, for that matter, Christian divines and theologians) became redundant. Just what kind of actions qualified a Jew
for the afterlife and what transgressions put it at jeopardy was entirely
beside the point, and the image of a judging God, inscribing some
but not others in the Book of Life on Rosh Hashanah, the New Year,

was in the Spinozist mind a crudely anthropomorphised, cartoon adulteration of the essentially formless entity which had set nature in motion and then abstracted itself from its worldly operations.

On the other hand, setting aside for the moment the ways in which Spinoza's account of the universe was not entirely unlike elements of Kabbalist cosmology (which also presupposed an abstracted and indifferent deity, removed in *tzimtzum* to a creative void), it would be more accurate to say that what Spinoza had abandoned was Judaism, the Jewish religion. For millennia, this was all the Jewishness there was, the abandonment of which presupposed conversion to one of the alternative systems of monotheistic belief. Until Spinoza, there was nowhere else to go for a thinking Jew who wished nonetheless to uncouple himself from the literal prescriptions of religious literature or a literal reading of the Bible. Now Spinoza had created just such an oasis of understanding. 'Secular Jew', the casual term of choice for multitudes of Jews, is perhaps too much of an oxymoron for this as it seems closer to the atheism which Spinoza repeatedly and vehemently rejected. Spinoza did not regard the universe as a self-created piece of material machinery; on the contrary, the essence of its operational genius was identical with the uncaused God. But the difficulty of grasping this understanding as somewhere a Jew could go and still be a Jew, meant he would have no following until generations, centuries, later. Until, in fact, there were scientists like Albert Einstein, who regarded himself unequivocally as a Jew, who was never separate from Jewish history, and who also pitied the aridity of atheism, deaf, as he scornfully put it, 'to the music of the spheres'; but when pressed on his belief in God in 1929, Einstein explained that 'I believe in Spinoza's god who reveals himself in the lawful harmony of the world, not in a God who concerns himself with the fate and doings of mankind'.

For the vast majority of Jews in Spinoza's world, however, this was not enough. The philosopher was asking them to abandon exactly what had kept them together over the millennia in the face of relentless persecution, massacre and oppression: their sense of divine historical appointment; their self-invention through a body of literature at once poetic and ethical; their conviction, annually reiterated in the sacred calendar, of liberation into law; the consolation amid inconceivable suffering that in the end God's master plan for themselves and the world would be realised – the Messiah would come. And for what, precisely, were they supposed to leave all this behind? For a faceless truth that told them all this history was a chimera, a phantom, and that they were in fact dissolved into the general body of mankind, no better and no worse, subject to the same laws of nature that governed everyone else; indeed without any semblance of free will to choose between a life of righteousness and a life of iniquity?

It would be nice, of course, if others had come to the conclusion that, scientifically and philosophically speaking, the Jews were just as other people dwelling beneath the sun and moon. But beyond Holland, and even within it, there was precious little evidence of that. So it was not enough.

A passage from the *Tractatus Theologicus-Politicus* reveals, inadvertently, the psychological dryness of Spinoza's appeal to his fellow Jews and to the Christians who shared with them the imaginative abundance of the Bible. To demonstrate the inferior and unreliable order of knowledge yielded by scripture, Spinoza pointed out that the measurement of the dimensions of the First Temple, provided ostensibly by Solomon in the Book of Kings (and subsequently much embellished in Ezekiel, a favourite object of commentary), could not be taken seriously since the king did not have the mathematical learning to make those dimensions credible, but merely a rudimentary grasp of the relationship between the diameter and the circumference of a circle. Spinoza was thus striking out against two forms of credulousness: the rapidly accumulating proto-Masonic lore of divinely and cultically derived architecture and engineering, and of course the crowds flocking to Templo's model round the corner from his old home on Vlooienburg. But they continued to go there all the same.

III. Jewes in America!

A storm was boiling up on the Cordillera. Columns of black cloud, baggy with rain, hung over a train of mules creeping along a mountain pass. Antonio de Montezinos, of Vila Flor in Portugal, was taking his goods from the north-west of New Granada into the volcanic upland country of Quito province. A spiteful gust, heralding the

downpour, caught the train sideways, knocking bags, chests and
animals clear down the slope. The Indian porters scrambled to recover
what they could as the elements unloosed their violence. Later, in
the night camp, Montezinos heard the porters cursing their luck
and the Spanish who used them so badly. The mule-owner, Francisco
de Castillo, known as 'Cazicus' – the *cacique* or captain – did what
he could to raise their spirits, reminding them that a day of rest was
coming. But the men replied they scarcely deserved it, for their
miseries at the hands of the Spanish was God's punishment for
their having mistreated another people, and those folk 'the most
innocent of all'. Montezinos brought cheese and bread and bowls of
curds to Francisco while berating him for speaking ill of the Spanish,
to which Francisco flashed back that he had not spoken of half of
the countless evils they had inflicted on the backs of the helpless,
but their victims would not go unavenged. Assisted by an 'unknown
people' the Indians would repay the Spanish in kind.[45]

Who were those 'most innocent of all' peoples? The question
nagged at Montezinos as he lay in his cell in Cartagena, imprisoned
by the Inquisition de las Indias. Scarcely had he returned from his
mountain journey than he had been seized for secret 'Judaising', which
was no less than the truth since, notwithstanding the great care he
had taken to appear an impeccable New Christian, he was also Aharon
Levi. Ever since Columbus' voyages, the third in particular (on the
lookout for the terrestrial paradise), the perennial search for the Lost
Tribes had acquired an American geography.[46] The apocryphal second
Book of Esdras was plumbed for cryptic statements that the deported
Israelites had been sent to the most remote regions of the world,
including 'distant islands' which immediately suggested the Caribbean.
One of those who speculated in this way was *another* Antonio
Montesinos, a Dominican friar of Lima, who in 1511 had flatly stated
that 'the Indians of the islands and mainlands of the Indies ... are
Hebrews, descended from the Ten Lost Tribes'.[47] He was one of many
Spanish writers and travellers in the conquered Americas who had
come to the same conclusion, often for not very compelling reasons.
In his *History of the Indies*, Francisco López de Gómara said that the
size of Indian noses made it obvious they had to be descended from
the Israelites. As sophisticated a commentator as Bartolomé de las
Casas thought the word 'Cuba' came from the Hebrew *kova* for a

helmet or hat. And Diego de Landa, the Bishop of Meridor, in the 1560s swore that the elderly Indians in his Yucatán diocese had 'heard from their ancestors that this land was occupied by a race of people who came from the east'. Many of the theorists of the Jewish Americans argued they had migrated there from north-east Asia, in the land which since medieval times had been called 'Arzereth'. Either they had crossed on a land bridge which had since been flooded (not altogether far from the prehistoric truth), or else, as the Bishop of Yucatán believed, 'God had delivered them by making twelve roads through the sea'. If that were true, he said, 'then it must follow that all the inhabitants of the Indies are descendants of the Jews'.[48] It was as though, deprived by the expulsion of 1492, the Spanish had robbed themselves of Jews intrinsic to the grand historical plan the Almighty had determined for their Christian empire. Discovering Original Israelites in the Americas brought the Jews back again into that providential planning, without the inconvenience of actually having to live with them.

It's not that hard, then, to see why Aharon Levi, racked and wretched, would want to take the Indian–Israelite story away from his torturers and develop a fantastic tale in which the Indians cursed Spanish barbarity, and in which he, from the oppressed nation of Judah, should come face-to-face with the Lost Tribes. He went over and over the tantalising details. The grumbling porters had spoken of the put-upon people as 'unknown', concealed perhaps not just by the density of the forest but by an unfordable river, a Sambatyon of the tropics? For eighteen months of his incarceration, fruit bats hanging in the trees behind the house of examination, he worried away at this like a man scratching a grub which had burrowed into his skin. Were he to come out of the ordeal alive, he would return to the mountain country and look for the hidden people. Otherwise there could be no peace for him.

Montezinos was released in September 1641 and almost immediately set out for the interior. At the river port of Honda, where a bridge crossed the Magdalena River, amid Ondaima Indians chewing coca, he found his old guide Francisco, 'Cazicus', who agreed for the usual price of three pieces of eight to return upcountry with Montezinos. The journey would change Montezinos' life, and his report of it would electrify the Jewish and Christian world.

At some point along the way, the *converso* revealed himself as Aharon
Levi of the tribe of Levi, and announced dramatically, 'My God is
Adonai and everything else is a lie.' Francisco did not seem surprised,
but asked the Jew whether he was prepared to penetrate further inland
towards the heart of the mystery. The roles of master and follower
reversed. 'If you have a mind to follow your leader,' Francisco told
him, 'you shall know whatever you desire to know,' but Montezinos
was warned that he would eat only roasted maize and would have to
obey his guide's instructions without cavil. Before they set off again
Montezinos was ordered to remove and abandon the visible signs of
gentility – his sword and cape – and to replace his boots with linen
pack-thread sandals. There would be no mules, no porters, just the
two of them carrying the knotted ropes, staffs and iron grappling
hooks they needed to help them up the slopes and across marshes
and rivers.

The two men walked west into the clouds for over a week, resting
on the Sabbath, the arboreal silence broken by the gibbering of unseen
creatures. On the bank of an unnamed river 'as broad as the Douro'
(and possibly a tributary of the Amazon, or even the great river itself),
they halted. 'Here you shall see your brethren,' Francisco announced.
At once there was a great smoke on the opposite bank, and as it
drifted up and away, Montezinos saw a canoe paddled by three men
and a woman coming towards them. These people were 'somewhat
scorched by the sun; some of them wearing their hair long down to
the knee, others much as we commonly cut it. They were comely of
body and well-accoutred.' They wore white shirts and stockings, and
a headdress like a turban, also white, was wound round their head.[49]
The woman left the boat, spoke to Francisco in a language Montezinos
could not make out, but whatever had been spoken between them
was reassuring enough for the men, who emerged and took the startled Montezinos into their embrace. The woman then did the same,
after which Montezinos watched while Francisco stooped in a low
bow to the people. As if in a ceremony, two of the men stood either
side of Montezinos and recited (he swore this was true) the first lines
of the Hebrew *shema,* the daily prayer of affirmation: 'Hear O Israel,
the Lord our God the Lord is One', words which come instinctively
to any Jew on beholding a marvel or a terror. Speaking through
Francisco and with finger-counting on held-up hands they told

Montezinos that they were the Children of Abraham, Isaac, Israel (Jacob) and Reuben. A strange formal recitation of utterances followed which to Montezinos had a cryptic-oracular tone as if from the mouth of one of the minor prophets. 'We will bestow several places on them who have a mind to live with us.' 'Joseph dwells in the midst of the sea.' 'One day we shall all speak together saying Ba-ba-ba and we shall come forth as if issuing out of our mother earth.' They then asked to be sent twelve men 'bearded and skilful in writing'.

Elated by the certainty that he had found the Lost Israelites, Montezinos wanted to know more but all that he could get from the Hebrew Indians was the repetition of these same formulaic utterances. After three days of this, his impatience got the better of him and he made a clumsy attempt to take their boat with a mind to paddle it to the shore from which they had come. There was a struggle. Montezinos fell into the river and, being unable to swim, would have drowned had he not been rescued by the 'brethren'. Affronted by the impulsiveness, Francisco told Montezinos that he must allow the tribe to tell him their story in their own way and in their own time, warning that if he pressed or threatened them they would respond merely with ingratiating lies. So Montezinos contained his impatience, and when it was time to leave, the Hebrew Indians brought him all that he might need for the return journey: meat, clothing, animals.

'Thy Brethren are the Sons of Israel,' Francisco told him as they made their long way back, 'brought hither by the providence of God who for their sake wrought many miracles you will not believe.' According to the traditions he had inherited from his fathers and they from theirs, these Reubenite people had been settled in the country long before his own, who had made war on them and chased them into the forests and mountains. After many vain pursuits, their magicians, the *mohanes*, admitted they had been in error, and that the God of those people was, despite appearances to the contrary, omnipotent. One day they would emerge, rid the country of the Spanish and their enormities, and take possession of it as of old. At the same time their brethren would likewise appear in arms from one end of the world to the other and establish a reign of the just. At that moment they would be 'Lords of the World'. Therefore, one of the Indian magicians had said, it would be best to attach yourself to them and await the day of deliverance. Hence everyone's expectation of the message and the messenger.

At Honda, Francisco brought another three Hebrew Indians to see Montezinos, and once he had told them he was Levi from the tribe of Levi they replied in biblical oracles: 'Upon a time you shall see us and not know us. We are all brethren though by God's singular favour. As for the country be secure for we rule the Indians. After we have finished our business with the wicked Spaniards we will bring you out of your bondage with God's help not doubting but he who cannot lie will help us according to his word.'

Such was the fantastic story Montezinos recounted to Menasseh ben Israel in an Amsterdam room in the spring of 1644, a notary taking everything down. In the course of his six-month stay in the city, Montezinos told the tale again to members of the *ma'amad*. And in a letter to an Italian correspondent, Elias Péreire, he wove further details into the already colourful embroidery of the story: he had stayed with the Reubenite Indians in their village of grass huts, noticing that the distance between the huts was according to social rank; he had 'slept in their arms, ate and drank with them', and they had told him they had been settled there for 250 years.

Understandably his listeners were torn between suspicion and excitement. It was impossible to have come from the world of Portuguese *conversos* and not recall the cautionary history of David the Reubenite, a century and more earlier. While he found details of the tale hard to credit, there was nothing about Montezinos' demeanour or his pedigree which suggested a fraud or an adventurer. He was not asking for money, just for belief. 'Before me', Menasseh wrote, 'and in the presence of several people of quality he took a solemn oath that all he had said was true.' That oath was repeated on Montezinos' Brazilian deathbed three years later, 'at a time', Menasseh added in his book presenting the story, 'when it is better not to commit perjury'.[50] Besides, Menasseh had drawn up a messianic calendar. It all added up to 1648, or possibly 1656 or thereabouts. Before the Messiah could appear and set to his work of redemption, the dispersion of the Jews throughout the earth, prophesied in Deuteronomy 28:64 and Daniel 12:7, had to be fulfilled. Now that it was known that there were Jews in China, in India, in burning Ethiopia, it had only remained for the Americas to reveal an ancient exile for the prophecy to be fulfilled to its utmost. Menasseh ben Israel wanted Montezinos' story to be true.

The more he thought about it, however, the more doubts crept in.
But the tale was so sensational and became so widely known in
Amsterdam that it got away from Menasseh and rushed into the
transatlantic obsessions of Protestant millenarians. Mass Jewish conversion was conditional on global Jewish dispersion, so American Jews
were good news. A former governor of Plymouth Colony in
Massachusetts, Edward Winslow, published letters from two Puritan
missionaries to the Indians, presuming that their 'Jewish' antecedents
would predispose them to receive the gospel. In short order the Anglo-
Dutch pastor John Dury, sometime chaplain to Princess Mary at The
Hague but now (and for the time being) a Commonwealthman, whose
projected 'College' of Jewish Studies in London was to have had
Menasseh ben Israel as one of its professors, was enquiring about his
views on the American branch of the Lost Tribes. Menasseh was at
pains to insist that though the Jews may have been 'the first finders
out' of America, and had left a settlement there, the Indians were not
to be confused with the Israelites, and that at most a portion only of
the Lost Tribes might be discovered there.[51] None of this stopped one
of Dury's friends, the Norfolk preacher Thomas Thorowgoode, from
bursting excitedly into print in 1648 with *Jewes in America! Or Probabilities
that Americans Are of that Race*. Before everything got out of hand and
became the property of the conversionists, Menasseh published what
was intended as a corrective geography and history of the Lost Tribes
of Israel: *Mikve Israel* (*The Hope of Israel*), first in Judaeo-Spanish, then
in Hebrew, and then, successively, in Latin, Dutch and English.[52] It
was a gazetteer of the Israelite dispersion which, Menasseh explained,
had not happened all at once but in successive stages until at last it
extended throughout the earth from the 'Isles of the Sea', which he
interpreted as the West Indies and America, to Persia, India, Ethiopia,
'Tartary' and China. It was as if Menasseh had taken off on angels'
wings ascending to see the entirety of the diaspora from on high,
summoning all the generations of travellers, from Eldad the Danite
to Garcilaso Vega de la Inca, as his reporters on the dispersion. Of
the existence of the Sambatyon he had no doubt, nor of the glasses
in which the sand itself shook and ran for six days but on the seventh
refused to tell the hour. His own father had heard it tell of a man
who ran through the streets of Lisbon showing his Sambatyon hour-
glass to the furtive *conversos* so they would know when to shut their

shops for the Sabbath. On he went, to the very recent past and the moment when Father Ricci set eyes on Ai Tian and realised he was in the company of a Chinese Jew. At some point Israelite exiles in northern Tartary had crossed over a land bridge connecting Asia with the American continent and which had since been providentially flooded to make the 'Straits of Anian'. (His geology, unlike his anthropology, was not so fantastical after all.)

Samuel Usque and his *Consolation* had been right. The dispersion was not just punishment; it had enabled Israel as well as Judah to survive to the moment when they would be reunited. 'If the Lord fulfilled his word in calamities, he will fulfill it also in sollicities' is the lovely way Menasseh and Moses Wall, his English translator, put it. And that collaboration was itself significant, for Wall was an ardent Christian millenarian, and Menasseh knew that his news of the near universal scattering would be, for the Gentiles, the announcement of an imminent conversion. He on the other hand was in no doubt that it foretold the appearance at last of the redeeming Messiah. All that remained to be accomplished was the colouring Jewish of the last two empty places on the map.

There were two such countries: the Scandinavian lands of the north, and the country from which the Jews had been expelled 350 years earlier in 1290: England.[53] In the *Vindiciae Judaeorum*, which Menasseh wrote in 1656 as a fierce corrective to Judaeophobic slanders circulating in print in England, he explained how he had made up his mind to go to England.

> Our universal dispersion being a necessary circumstance to be fulfilled before all that shall be accomplished which the Lord hath promised to the people of the Jewes concerning their restauration and their returning again into their own land ... I conceived that by the 'end of the earth' [in Deuteronomy and Daniel] might be understood this Island ... I knew not but the Lord who often works by naturall meanes might have designed me for the bringing about of this work. With these proposals therefore I applyed myself in all zealous affection to the English nation, congratulating them on their glorious Liberty which at this day they enjoy.[54]

In 1650 Menasseh had dedicated the English edition of *The Hope of Israel* to 'the English Parliament and the Council of State', believing that England's transformation into a godly republic would make it more receptive to his mission. 'The Kingly government being now changed into that of a Common-Wealth, the antient hatred ... would also be changed into good will; that those rigorous Laws ... against so innocent a people would happily be repealed.'[55] 1650 was also the year in which the stadholder William II (the same prince who had visited the synagogue in 1642 and married Charles I's daughter) had died of smallpox after an attempt to exert his will over Amsterdam by military force. This radical alteration, on both sides of the North Sea, must have persuaded Menasseh that the parliamentary Commonwealth would replace the arbitrariness by which the Jews had been expelled by the high-handed, cruel Plantagenet Edward I with the 'tender-hearted' (as he put it) and tolerant People. Ardent Christians in the new Commonwealth were saying as much themselves. Hugh Peter, the most eloquent and prominent chaplain of the New Model Army, was known to be a friend and distributed through the ranks a tract written by Edward Nicholas, called *An Apology for the Honourable Nation of the Jews and all the Sons of Israel*. The parliamentary army command seemed benevolently receptive. A 1648 petition of Johanna Cartwright and her son Ebenezer, living in Amsterdam and calling for readmission, was addressed to the Council of Officers of the New Model Army which ordered it printed as a statement of their position on the matter. Menasseh's translator Moses Wall was close to the parliamentary and military elite: Sir Henry Vane, the Earl of Warwick, Oliver St John and Cromwell himself, who had married St John's cousin.[56] Menasseh could hardly be deaf to this chorus of friendly voices. The clearest and warmest belonged to Henry Jessey, the ubiquitous Baptist preacher who never went anywhere without a Hebrew Bible, was an exorcist of demons, an enthusiastic anointer of women with oil, kept Sabbath on Saturday, and had published a book called *The Glory of the Salvation of Jehudah and Israel*.[57] Menasseh knew very well that much of the sudden enthusiasm for a reborn Anglo-Jewish community was driven by millenarian and conversionist motives, including John Sadler, Cromwell's private secretary, who had written: 'The more I think upon the great change now comming on them and with the world [he is having a millennial moment here], the more I would be just and mercifull to them all, Nay universal sweetnesse if I could, a Christian overcoming all with love.'[58] Menasseh had heard much the same in Amsterdam and perhaps this familiarity made him take the occasional warning signs more lightly than he should have done. Initially the Council of Mechanics resolved that all religions would be tolerated in the Commonwealth, 'not excepting Turkes, Papistes nor Jewes', but then had second thoughts, issuing a clarification restricting the licence to Christian sects only.[59] Godly England, Menasseh would discover, was not of one mind on the matter of the Jews and divided into those who wanted the Jews back for reasons entirely to do with their imminent conversion or those who would not have them at any price.

If Christians were not at all sure they wanted the Jews back, the handful of Jewish families already living in London under New Christian cover, trading in diamonds and pearls or putting out shoots through their Iberian connections into the scattering of English possessions in the Caribbean, were also anxious about being revealed. The blind eye turned to them by the Stuart government had allowed them to worship discreetly in private houses. For many this was quite enough. They imagined that having their legal status made a matter of high politics might jeopardise this quiet accommodation, with the risk of incarceration for illegal presence followed by a second expulsion from the English empire where (as in Guyana) they had a stake and had been given rights of residence.

But the fate of the Jews had become state business. In 1651, Cromwell's cousin by marriage Oliver St John and other 'divers eminent persons', as Menasseh put it, were welcomed 'with great pomp and applause' in the same synagogue visited nine years earlier by the now deposed Queen Henrietta Maria. (Doubtless they were also taken round Templo's exhibition, as were all the High Tourists.) Cromwell had sent St John to Holland as the head of a negotiating team that was supposed to bring about the union of the two republics in one invincible pan-Protestant empire. In Cromwell's vaulting politico-religious imagination, the Dutch half of the Union of Republics was supposed to get Africa and Asia while the English took the New World, north as well as south, from the Iberian papists. This was the kind of boundless vision circulating in the early years of the kingless Commonwealth which makes the new fascination with the Jews explicable: pragmatism and prophecy folding together. The Dutch, on the other hand, had their feet more firmly planted on the reclaimed soil of their freedom, and were not about to surrender any portion of it to Cromwellian dreaming. Typically, and a little disingenuously, the Dutch proposed instead a free-trade union across the North Sea, precisely the kind of arrangement they were economically equipped to dominate at a time when the English were battling to take a bigger share of shipping to the British Isles. The government of the Commonwealth may have been steamed up with godliness, but it was not stupid. Resentment at being blindsided by the canny Netherlanders led to hostility. A two-year calamitous maritime war ensued until the English and Dutch had barraged each other into exhaustion and economic disaster, while giving their common foe, the Spanish, breathing space.

Following the St John mission, Menasseh had been issued with a safe conduct, a sure sign that the possibility of readmission had been positively considered by the English visitors. But the Anglo-Dutch war put any practical action on hold, not least because the Sephardim who had contacts on both sides of the North Sea were suspected of being double agents. The great project of Jews in England seemed frustrated, as was its principal author. Smarting from the discrepancy between his reputation among the Gentiles and the pittance he earned from his fellow Jews, Menasseh looked elsewhere for support. No Jews in Sweden either! And the lesbian cross-dressing, hard-riding, deep-reading, intellectually omnivorous, sensationally mercurial Queen Christina of Sweden had shown interest.[60] Menasseh had already supplied her with Hebrew books for her library; and by the astonishing improbability which only happens in history rather than fiction, came to be living next door to Christina in Antwerp when she lodged there for a few months after her abdication in 1654. Her residence belonged to a Sephardi dynasty, the Texeiras, known to both of them. So the queen was on one side of Menasseh, and Isaac La Peyrère, the theorist of a 'pre-Adamite' world in which mankind had existed long before Adam and Eve, on the other. The conversations between the rabbi, the queen and the biblical archaeologist have, alas, to be imagined. The sweetly voluble, courteous Menasseh talked up his acquaintance with Christina, notwithstanding her removal from power, into an ambitious project in which he would become her archlibrarian (for needless to say she was a millenarian too), creating an empire of polyglot rabbinics to fill the void left by her vacated throne.

There was no dream so fanciful it could not take flight in these years of expectant wonder.

But the Signs were not always auspicious. On 12 August 1654, two months after the regalia was removed from Christina, leaving her standing in a white shift, a total solar eclipse shrouded Europe. Portent-mongers were in full cry on the streets of Amsterdam and London, allowed a second opportunity of prophecy after a similar Black Monday in 1652 had failed to bring about the apocalypse. This time they had a sheaf of disasters to cry up. In Brazil the last redoubt of the Dutch, Recife, had fallen to the Portuguese, which meant the return of the inexhaustible monster, the Inquisition, with its talons if anything sharpened since the Jews of Brazil had been such enthusiastic benefi-ciaries of Dutch power. A tide of dispossessed (but well-connected) Sephardim washed into Amsterdam and Middelburg, adding to the impoverished refugees from Germany, and Poland–Lithuania, who were still arriving after the Cossack pogroms of 1648. So many packed into the cramped little district of Vlooienburg that the elders of the Jews actively considered resettling the refugees elsewhere: in the Caribbean, where there were already early plantings in Curaçao and Surinam. But the Sephardim were also looking to the modest scat-tering of English settlements in the Atlantic: to slave-ready Barbados; and to the mainland. Almost unregarded, the true history of Jews in North America had begun with landings in New Amsterdam on Manhattan island, and two further ships bearing Sephardi emigrants from Brazil docking in the roadsteads of Providence Plantation at Newport. That second landfall was more auspicious because Roger Williams, the founding father of that colony, insisted that since all earthly churches were impure incarnations of the one and only heav-enly church, none ever had the authority to govern according to their own imagined lights, or in fact govern at all. Williams, another Hebraist (unlike Pieter Stuyvesant, his opposite number in New Amsterdam), was especially well disposed towards the people of the scripture, regarding himself as something of a Moses.[61]

The currents of history bore these frail vessels of hope along. Once the Anglo-Dutch war ended, the two Protestant republics could turn their attention to the Catholic empires. Sephardi traders who had lost possessions in Brazil and elsewhere could appeal to both the Dutch and the English for their recovery. One of those merchants,

Menasseh's brother-in-law Manuel Martinez Dormido (otherwise known as David Abravanel), came to London in the autumn of 1654 in the company of Menasseh's son Samuel. In February of the following year the impoverished but ambitious Dormido petitioned Lord Protector Cromwell for the right of residence and trade in England and for help with the restitution of his lost Brazilian estate. Astonishingly, although Dormido was a member of a community whose presence was still officially illegal (if an open secret) and not then an English subject, Cromwell did in fact write directly to the king of Portugal on his behalf![62] This could not possibly have been a cold overture. Dormido's approach presupposes that the water was being tested for something much bigger, and that Cromwell himself may have been encouraging it.

By the summer of 1655, on the strength of reports received from his son, Menasseh decided to use the safe conduct which had been issued to him annually since 1651. The information Samuel conveyed to his father, however, was not always reliable. In the spring of that year he claimed to have been awarded a doctorate at Oxford University, which might, so far as he knew, have even been true, though the diploma was a fake. Such things gladden and then sadden a father's heart, especially when the father is himself a doctor, as was Menasseh. But when Menasseh set off from Middelburg, bid farewell by a throng of hopeful Jews, many of whom had lost property and homes in Brazil, it was with a strong sense of the gravitational pull of history. He even printed an address to his own people reinforcing that sense of a providential turning of the page. The terrible expulsion of 1290 would be erased. What had been done by a king would be annulled by the executioner of another king.

He arrived in London in September, just before the Jewish New Year, with a retinue of three other rabbis: Isaac Aboab da Fonseca, deputy to the fierce Morteira and a Brazilian refugee; Raphael Supino; and an Ashkenazi rabbi. Since there were as yet no synagogues, the group would have prayed in one of the houses rented by the likes of Dormido. Sephardi merchants in hope of great things and their own resettlement – Antonio Robles, Antonio Fernandes Carvajal, Menasseh's son Samuel and others who had hitherto led a secret life – would have made up the *minyan*, the ten men needed for a service. Their prayers must have mixed the grave solemnities of the high holy days with a modicum of optimism. May this be the year we are inscribed, in England, in the Book of Life? Menasseh knew that for his hosts the Jews were necessary instruments in the realisation of the greater Christian drama. But he would allow them their benign delusions if it offered a resting place for the dispossessed of Brazil. His messianic calendar had recalibrated to 1656. Why should he not be the one to hasten the fulfilment of Daniel's prophecy?

'Humble addresses' were sent to His Highness the Lord Protector and then published so as to win favour with both government and people. With that wary audience in mind, Menasseh dropped the exalted messianic tone of *The Hope of Israel* for a more carefully reasoned approach, although he made sure to include the verses from Daniel 12, and included a statement that 'only this considerable and mighty Island' remained 'before the Messiah come and restore our Nation'. There was also an odd addition to the usual arguments made for 'a strange Nation wel-beloved among the Natives of a land where they dwell' (profit and loyalty to the ruler) and that was 'nobility of blood'; a bizarre importation from the very Iberian obsessions which had ultimately produced the expulsion.[63] Menasseh's principal task was to persuade the rulers of the Commonwealth that Judaism posed no threat to the republic; that his people could be loyal citizens while being good Jews. Menasseh was assuming that the success of Jewish citizenship in the Protestant Dutch republic could be unproblematically reproduced in the Protestant English republic. Just as he had offered the bouquet of his rhetoric to Queen Henrietta Maria in the synagogue on the Houtgracht (an awkward memory, perhaps), so he hoped to be able to greet the Lord Protector in the same manner and with the same patriotic pride and gratitude. Hence the judicious posture of the *Humble Addresses*. It was not much, he thought, to ask for: 'the Liberty of a free and publick Synagogue wherein we may daily call upon the Lord our God'.

Then, with shrewd courage, Menasseh addressed himself directly to the baneful Shylock legacy: the unfounded but deep-rooted social prejudices which for centuries had portrayed Jews as unscrupulous moneylenders and petty criminals, parasitic excrescences on the Christian economy. 'How Profitable the Nation of the Jewes Are', included in the *Humble Addresses*, was a *tour d'horizon* of all the blessings the presence of the Jews had conferred on their host societies,

from Italy and Turkey to Hamburg and the Barbary states of North
Africa. But Menasseh opened his potted sociology of the Jews (the first
of its kind) with the declaration that 'it is a thing confirmed that
merchandising is as it were the proper profession of the Jews'. Far from
being defensively apologetic, Menasseh wrote that the prospering of
the Jews was a mercy from God, showing that while he had 'banished
them from their own country' yet they were not exiled from his
'Protection'; 'Necessity stirs up a man's ability and industry'. Menasseh
continued by arguing that since their removal from 'their own country'
(a phrase he tellingly repeats), barred from the possibility of tilling land
or 'like employments', they had no choice but to give themselves
entirely to 'merchandising and for contriving new Invention, no Nation
almost going beyond them. And so 'tis observed that wherever they
go to dwell there presently the Trafiq begins to flourish.' Livorno was
cited as a prime case, well known to the mercantile community of the
City of London, but he could as easily have invoked Ferrara, Mantua,
Salonika, Smyrna and Constantinople. Perhaps mindful of the reputation of the impoverished Ashkenazim, refugees from the Cossack
pogroms, Menasseh was at pains to emphasise that the Sephardim were
a great asset to any nation with commercial-imperial ambitions: 'having
perfect knowledge of all the kinds of Moneys, Diamants, Cochenil,
Indigo, Wine Oyl and other commodities that serve from place to
place; especially holding correspondence with their friends and kinds-
folk whose language they understand, they do abundantly enrich the
Lands and Countreys of strangers where they live not onely with what
is requisite and necessary for the life of man but also what may serve
as ornament for his civill condition'.[64] The implication was that as a
people of international trade, the Jews would bring England into the
new global economy, whether in Asia and the Levant or the Atlantic.
But the knock-on effect on employment would also be domestically
benevolent: 'the affording of materials in great plenty for all Mechanics
[such as] wooll, leather, wines, Jeweles as Diamants Perrles and such
like' in the increase of 'venting and exportation of many kinds of
manufactures' means that the presence of the Jews would be an
economic plus not minus. And in a shameless evocation of the contemporary truism that true commerce led to peace (the evidence of recent
history being the opposite), the *Humble Addresses* claimed that this too
would be an effect of Jewish residence and business.

Finally, Menasseh tackled head-on the most perennially emotive accusation against the Jews: their loyalty to each other rather than their adopted country. On the contrary, in place after place, from Mantua to Brazil, they have proved with their blood and treasure their undying allegiance to the sovereign. Every Sabbath day in synagogue they pray 'for the safety of all Kings, Princes and Common-wealths under whose jurisdiction they live ... unto which duty they are bound by the Prophets and the Talmudists', with Jeremiah 29:7 commanding them to 'seek the peace of the City unto which I have made you to wander and pray for her unto the Lord for in her Peace you shall enjoy peace'. No man, Menasseh insisted, should imagine that it was because of any true disloyalty that the Jews were expelled from Spain and Portugal but from malign and unfounded libels. Then, with a trace of the pure Sephardi snobbery from which even as gentle a soul as Menasseh ben Israel was not free, he insisted again on the 'nobility' of the Jews, though on that subject he tactfully recommended doubters to read the works of Henry Jessey, and Edward Nicholas's *An Apology for the Honourable Nation of the Jews and all the Sons of Israel.*

As a pre-emptive offensive against all the usual libels, prejudices and phobias left over from medieval England (including rapacious usury and infanticide), the *Humble Addresses* was a masterful perform-ance, an attempt once more to have Christians look at Jews rationally and historically. Many more such efforts would have to follow down the centuries (and still do) and they too often enough met (meet) with the same result: deafness, blindness and renewed hatred. The reason-able tone adopted by Menasseh (in contrast to the blazing opening of his *Vindiciae Judaeorum* a year later) was the effect of his being received inside a charmed circle of Commonwealth Hebraists, and those who believed conversion would come as the fruit of mutual understanding. Such men as Jessey and Sadler and the sympathetic members of the Council of State – Cromwell himself, Secretary of State Thurloe, Major Generals Lambert and Whalley – were fine friends but few. However, the procession of eminent men who lined up to visit Menasseh in his lodgings opposite the New Exchange in the Strand strengthened his optimism. The scientist Robert Boyle came with his sister, the Countess of Ranelagh. Henry Oldenburg, who would be the first secretary of the Royal Society and the origin-ator of peer review for scientific publications, knocked on the door

of his rooms; so did the madder sort like Arise Evans, the Welsh
millenarian who, throwing political caution to the winds, tried to
persuade Menasseh that the Messiah was indeed at hand and that his
name was Charles Stuart II, the son of the beheaded king. Adam
Boreel, Templo's collaborator and founder of the Amsterdam 'College',
paid his respects, as did Ralph Cudworth, the professor of Hebrew at
Cambridge who was as interested in Kabbalah as he was in
Neoplatonism. Plans were discussed for the creation of a new polyglot
Bible. It was all very encouraging.

But the words of sweet reason and mutual sympathy deceived.
Menasseh and the three rabbis were living under a bell jar of optimism.
Outside, beyond the Strand, beyond Whitehall, the words were manic.
The Jews, the Jews, the Jews had offered their filthy lucre to buy St Paul's
Cathedral; ditto the Bodleian Library (all those Hebrew manuscripts);
they would acquire the entire village of Brentford for their London
ghetto; they were enquiring into the Davidic descent of Oliver Cromwell
to assure themselves that he was their redeeming Messiah, or perhaps
they thought he was the Messiah from 'the line of Joseph'; they had
come to circumcise England, to bewitch it with their notorious, potent
magic, deliver Christian children into the devouring jaws of Moloch as
they had in the reign of their evil king Manasseh. Most feverish of all
was the *Short Demurrer* written and published by William Prynne, sometime lawyer, the veteran polemicist who had had the initials 'S' and 'L'
branded on each cheek for the seditious libels he had been accused of
serving up in the reign of Charles I. From being a hero of English liberties, Prynne had become a perennial thorn in the side of those who
thought themselves its guardians, Cromwell in particular, whom Prynne
correctly suspected of coveting a crown. Who better to fund a
Cromwellian throne than those ubiquitous and obliging moneybags,
those lickspittles of the overmighty, the Jews? Brushing aside the politely
documented history of Menasseh's *Humble Addresses*, Prynne rehearsed
all the ancient accusations levelled against the Jews in the English Middle
Ages from child murder to extortionate avarice, and concluded that the
expulsion had been one of the few good things that might be laid at the
charge of the old monarchy, and moreover that it might not be rescinded,
not at any rate without an additional Act of Parliament.

That was not what the Lord Protector had in mind. From his quasi-
regal fastness in Whitehall, Oliver Cromwell, while contemptuous of

the small-minded captiousness of the tribunes, was equally mindful never to appear the tyrant. So when the asses began to bray he knew it impolitic to stop up his ears. Matters, as usual, would have to be managed. Early in November 1655 he put the business to the Council of State: whether it was lawful to admit the Jews, and were it to be so, under what conditions might they be permitted to reside and trade in the Commonwealth. A subcommittee of seven (from the full membership of eleven) was appointed to deliberate, packed with as many known sympathisers as Cromwell could contrive, among the clergy, the law and the major generals. But such was the gathering din out of doors that the councillors, sensing they had been given a charge of inflammable powder, passed it off as quickly as they could to a more general deliberative body in Whitehall, a conference of twenty-eight selected from all the constituencies of England, to debate the matter the following month. Neither the council nor the conference would hear directly from Menasseh ben Israel, though by one account at least he was 'civilly entertained' by the Lord Protector himself. The details are not known (especially of the catering arrangements, since Menasseh was strictly kosher); but no historian has supposed that between the two men – come to this providential moment from such different worlds, Marrano Portugal and Puritan East Anglia, bridged by Hebraic passions – there could not be a meeting of minds.

Which was of little help, however, in forwarding the matter in hand. Henry Jessey's narrative account of the Whitehall conference confirms the probability that the twenty-eight divided into three groups: those (evidently a minority) who wished to see the Jews admitted forthwith; those who brought themselves to accept it but only under the strictest conditions; and an evidently loud and forceful group who would not entertain the possibility for theological, commercial or national reasons. Churchmen – of many stripes – believed the presence of the Jews would be insidious and dangerously seductive to good Christians; the City merchants shouted with rising hysteria that the Jews would purloin their trade. There was some cheer for Menasseh. The representatives of the judiciary had declared there were no legal grounds preventing a rescinding of the royal expulsion of 1290; the issue then became a matter of the restrictions to be imposed on such as might be admitted. But those conditions looked as though they would be suffocatingly narrow and, worse, they were supported by those whom Menasseh had supposed his champions. John Dury, of all people, now let it be known that the Jews, poor people they could not but help themselves, were incorrigible in their 'designs' on nations and perhaps it were best to keep them at a distance. Henry Jessey, allegedly in an attempt to accommodate the objectors, proposed restricting the Jews to 'decayed ports and towns', thus testing Menasseh's assertion that they would be an elixir of commercial regeneration wherever they settled.

Cromwell demurred. Under such conditions, London would forfeit the chance to become a true rival to Amsterdam; the rich assets of capital, intelligence and enterprise vested in the Portuguese Jews, not to mention funds for the expansion of his godly empire, would be wasted. The Sephardim would move on. At the last and only public session of the conference on 18 December, a week before the Christmas which his major generals were trying to abolish, he erupted from his scowling silence. The conference, he said, was 'a babel of discordances'. He had hoped to achieve clarity from the advice of the churchmen but this had not been forthcoming. If, as they claimed they wished and hoped for, the conversion of the Jews was a furtherance of the designs of the Almighty, how could this be accomplished without their actual presence in the land where the gospel was properly preached? How indeed? As for the delegates of the City, 'you say they are the meanest and most despised of all people. So be it. But in that case what becomes of your fears? Can you really be afraid that this contemptible and despised people should be able to prevail in trade and credit over the merchants of England, the noblest and most esteemed merchants of the whole world?'[65] Since the conference had failed to resolve the matter, Cromwell added, it would have to be settled by his Council of State after all.

Any hopes Menasseh might have had, as the calendar turned to 1656, were confounded by the council's own report on the Whitehall debates. Though it made no attempt to reverse the decision that readmission would be lawful, it surrounded it with statements of the forbidding hostility. 'The motives and groundes upon which Menasseh ben Israel in behalf of the rest of his nation ... desireth their admission in this commonwealth are such as we conceave very sinfull for this or any Christian nation to receave them upon.' A litany of the old paranoias and unreconstructed prejudices followed. 'The danger of their seducing the people of this nation in matters of religion is very great ... their having synagogues or any publicke meetings for the exercise of their religion is not only evile in itself but likewise very scandalous to other Christian churches.' Their customs of marriage and divorce were unlawful and a wicked example. An old misunderstanding of the Kol Nidrei opening of the eve of the Day of Atonement service, which cancels vows made between men and God, was turned into an accusation that Jews set all contracts at nought. And their very presence would damage the trade of the City. This would have been a devastating blow but for the fact that someone in Cromwell's government, probably John Thurloe, doctored the report, adding restrictive conditions to apply to the Jews – no holding public office, no employment of Christian servants, no work on Sundays and the like – which presupposed the *legal* issue of admission had been settled in their favour. It also said nothing about where they might live or the professions they might adopt.

Months passed without any further action. Cromwell returned to the dark tent of his taciturnity. Menasseh gave up on the kind of grand declaration he hoped would be the legal charter for a reborn Jewish community. But a new war with Spain indirectly offered a different kind of overture. When a ship and its cargo belonging to the Sephardi merchant Antonio Robles was impounded on the grounds of ostensible Spanish nationality, the seizure gave Robles (in conjunction with other merchants including Dormido) cause to petition the government for its release on the grounds that they were not Spanish at all but of 'the Hebrew Nation'. Menasseh's name was on the petition. It was in effect a coming out of the secret community of forty or so families that until that moment had presented themselves as New Christians. Material aggravation produced an effect which all of Menasseh's appeals to principle could not. The short petition asked for safety of residence, permission to acquire land for a cemetery, and for the practice of trade and business.

To ensure this would not happen, new phobic tracts were published, in particular Alexander Ross's *View of the Jewish Religion*. William Prynne's *Short Demurrer* became less short when he expanded his inventory of Jewish crimes and antisocial habits in a second edition, repeating his earlier vindication of the original thirteenth-century expulsion. This fresh tide of poison, along with the stinging memory of the prejudices rehearsed in the earlier sections of the Council of State report, persuaded Menasseh to break his habit of restraint and publish as a counter-attack the *Vindiciae Judaeorum* in April 1656, a work meant to refute once and for all the most vicious libels directed against his people. Explanations of Jewish ritual, tradition, customs and principles of faith had been published in Italy by Leone Modena whose *De Riti Ebraica*, originally commissioned for King James I, had just been provided with an English translation, and by his near contemporary, Rabbi Simone Luzzatto. Both were invoked in Menasseh's text, but he evidently saw as his true forebear the first of the Great Explainers, Flavius Josephus, whose work *Against Apion* had attempted to dispel the libels and legends circulating in the Roman world about Jewish avarice and abduction plots. Thus Menasseh begins with cold rage directed against those who perpetuated the abhorrent medieval lie of the blood libel:

> I cannot weep but bitterly and with much anguish of souls lament that strange and horrid speculation of some Christians against the dispersed and afflicted Jewes that dwell among them when they say (what I tremble to write) that the Jewes are wont to celebrate the feast of unleavened bread, fermenting it with the bloud of some Christians whom they have for that purpose killed; when the calumniators themselves have most barbarously and cruelly butchered some of them. Or to speak more mildly have found one dead and cast the corpse as if it had been murdered by the Jewes into their houses or yards as lamentable experience hath proved in sundry places and then with unbridled rage and tumult they accuse the innocent Jewes as the committers of this most execrable fact. Which destestable wickednesse hath been sometimes perpetrated that they might thereby take advantage to exercise their cruelty upon them.[66]

He then proceeds with what patience he can muster to remind Christian readers of the biblical injunction that 'it is utterly forbid the Jewes to eat any manner of blood whatsoever ... if they find one drop of blood in an egg they cast it away as prohibited. And if eating a piece of bread it happens to touch any blood from the teeth or gummes it must be pared and cleansed from the said blood.' Since that is the case, commanded by the Torah and reinforced by the guide to obser-vance, the *Shulkhan Arukh*, 'how can it enter into any man's heart to believe that they should eat human blood which is yet more detest-able?' Furthermore the commandment against killing in the Decalogue 'is a morall command. So that the Jewes are bound not onely not to kill one of those nations where they live but they are bound by the laws of gratitude to love them.' In Amsterdam where he resides, he goes on, 'I have continually seen ... abundance of good correspond-ency, many interchanges of brotherly affection and sundry things of reciprocall love. I have thrice seen when some Fleming Christians have fallen into the river in our ward called Flemburgh [Vlooienburg] our nation cast themselves into the river to help them and to deliver their lives from death.'

In the same vein, Menasseh then invokes Jeremiah's counsel to the captive Israelites to pray for the welfare of the city to which they had been taken as the example for Jews in all countries and generations to include in their prayers blessings for the 'Prince or Magistrate under whose protection they lived'. He narrates a detailed history of the origins and spread of the blood libel and the iniquitous persecutions to which Jews remained vulnerable. In Lisbon in 1631, when a silver box with the host in it went missing from a church, fingers pointed quite arbitrarily to 'a young youth of our nation (hence a converso) whose name was Simao Pires Solis' who, passing not far from there to visit a lady,

> was apprehended, imprisoned and terribly tortured. They cut off his hands and after they had dragged him along the streets burnt him, one year passed over and a thief at the foot of the gallows confessed how he himself had rifled and plundered the shrine of the host and not that poor innocent whom they had burnt. This young man's brother was a Friar, a great Theologist and a preacher; he lives now a Jew in Amsterdam and calls himself Eliezer de Solis.

Menasseh moves from denunciation to explanation, concentrating on those constitutive principles of Judaism which were likely to strike a sympathetic chord with Protestant England. The Jews were the first to abandon the worship of images, and they avoid it so rigorously that if one were to pass by a church which has images on the exterior and a thorn happened to pierce the sole of their foot, they would not stoop to extract it lest they be thought of bowing to an image. Whereas in Asia the decrees of kings have been traditionally received by his subjects kissing the image of their benefactor,

> we owe much more to words and to his divine commandments ... the Israelites hold for the Articles of their Faith that there is a God, who is one in most simple unity; eternal, incorporeal, who gave the written Law unto his people Israel, by the hand of Moses the Prince and Chief of all the Prophets, whose Providence takes care of the world he created; who takes notice of all men's work and rewardeth or punishes them. Lastly that one day Messiah shall come to gather together the scattered Israelites and shortly after shall be the resurrection of the dead.

The prayers of Jews were for all men, Menasseh asserted, and despite the burdens the Egyptians inflicted on the Israelites they should not be hated, for as the Torah said, 'once thou wast a stranger in his land'. In their commercial dealings they were required to deal justly with Gentiles, bound by commandment never to defraud or abuse anyone with whom they had business. Likewise they were not to offend the religion of their host people, nor seek proselytes among them.

Menasseh ends with the hope shared by all those attempting to overthrow slanders committed against his people, which were transmitted from generation to generation of the credulous: that if examined by reason, those hatreds would disappear and the Jews be seen as men and women akin to any other, save in the antiquity and endurance of their faith, the steadfastness of their belief and the unique brutality of their sufferings. If truth was upheld against calumny, then surely benevolent justice would be done and give pause to those Jews who, despairing of action on the part of the government, were now taking themselves off to Italy and Geneva. 'To the highly honoured nation of England I make my most humble request, that they would read over my arguments impartially without prejudice and devoid of all passion, effectually recommending me to their grace and favour.'

It is not impossible that this last great cry of Menasseh's, and the first of the noble attempts to overcome anti-Semitism with reason and true history, made some difference. The following month, the justices returned a favorable verdict on the Robles petition to have his property and ship restored to him. And still without any decisive utterance from Cromwell, much else followed. In 1657 land was bought in Mile End in the East End of London for the first cemetery plot, and it too remains, now within the grounds of Queen Mary College on the Mile End Road. But the cemetery was not opened quickly enough to accommodate Menasseh's son Samuel who died that year, a crushing catastrophe for his father. Samuel had in any event wished to be interred in his Dutch homeland. His grief-stricken father – who had won some sort of victory but not the great one of principle he had so ardently desired – travelled back with the body of his boy to Middelburg in Zeeland, whence he had departed two years before with such high hopes. There he laid Samuel to rest and two months later with nothing else to live for and the Messiah unconscionably tardy in making his appearance in the allotted year, he too passed to the paradise garden. His mortal remains were taken to the House of Life at Ouderkerk and set beside those of his father.

In due course England, too, became a garden where the Jews could do a little planting. And this became possible despite renewed efforts by the relentless Judaeophobes to reverse the de facto decision to allow them residence. No sooner had Cromwell died than petitions to that effect were sent to his son and successor, Richard. When the protectorate was replaced by the restored monarchy, and much else was reversed, representations were made to Charles II to rescind what the usurper-regicide had done. But the king was unmoved. For a while there had been Commonwealth Jews, and Charles had also had support from royalist Jews in The Hague. Those supporters maintained all along (and with some truth) that they had never approved of Menasseh's approach to Cromwell. Far from responding to the Judaeophobe petitions, Charles II upheld the earlier decision, and even extended it to include formal protections for the security of Jewish lives and property. Before long the City community, which had been so vocal in their hostility, decided that the Jews were an asset rather than a liability, as Menasseh had predicted. Solomon Dormido, Menasseh's nephew, was the first broker admitted to the Royal Exchange, the customary oath sworn on the New Testament being expressly waived for him. Antonio Carvajal's leased house in Creechurch

Lane, where the Sephardim had met in private worship, now became a synagogue; and when a much grander one opened in 1701 at Bevis Marks, its narrow oak benches were taken there in pious memory of how a community returned to London. Whenever I sit on them I think of Menasseh, the poignant generosity of his optimism, and the cleansing fire of his rage.

8

THE CROWN

I. Apparitions

How lost could the Israelites get? According to the intelligencer-printer Robert Boulter, whose antennae were fine-tuned to the faintest millenarian signals, they had fetched up in Aberdeen.[1]

In the third week of October 1665, a ship bound for Amsterdam had been blown off course by dirty weather and had put into the Scottish harbour. It was odd to discover that its provisions consisted only of rice and honey, but not as odd as the sheets and shrouds which seemed to be made of twisted white satin. On the mainsail a legend in red announced: 'THESE ARE THE TRIBES OF ISRAEL'. A Scottish 'Professor of the Tongues' had gone to speak with the crew, whose blue coats were striped with black; but he could barely make out anything from their speech which seemed to be a mysteriously fractured Hebrew.

That autumn, while Benedict Spinoza was applying the blade of his reason to 'childish superstition', the community he had left behind in Amsterdam was alive with wonders, not all of them brewed up by the delirium of the plague. Letters were received from Morocco and Livorno testifying to marvellous things concerning the Jews. Reports from merchants, rabbis and doctors had been exchanged between Cairo and Salonika, Prague and Venice, Lublin and Mantua, all reporting JOYFUL TIDINGS (albeit in slightly varying details). The Israelite tribes were on the march! They were coming from beyond the peaks of the Caucasus, from Anatolia and Persia, from the desert wastes of Arabia and/or Africa. A vast Jewish horde, more than a million, sometimes said to be led by a general called Jereboam, sometimes not, equipped only with bows, arrows, lances and psalms, had already defeated the regiments of the sultan Mehmed. The Turks had shot cannon and muskets at the Israelites but the fusillades had rebounded on their hapless artillerymen. The Janissaries were perplexed, terrified. Mecca was under siege. The haj had been called off. The panic-stricken lord of the Ottoman Empire had offered the Israelites Alexandria or Tunis if only they would preserve Mecca for the Faithful. Across the Atlantic in Boston, Increase Mather preached sermons to his flock based on the certain information that the Israelites were returning to their ancestral land. In Fez, it was said that a host of Israelites was marching inland towards a lofty mountain of sand, preparing to tunnel its way into a secret vault wherein lay a brass trumpet which, once blown, would resound about the world. When its blast was heard, the earth would shake and all the disputing religions of the world along with their contending houses of worship would crumble into dust. Mutually hostile believers would stand forth as one body of people under the Almighty God and His Commandments. 'There will take place a general gathering and assembly of all the nations of the world in one pasture which shall be Zion and there all contentions shall cease.'[2]

It was not just the credulous and the ignorant who were stirred by this news. After the disappointments of 1648 and 1656, learned men had stayed up late recalculating the millenarian calendar by candlelight. The signs and portents were all there. The comet of 1664 had been followed by plague in London and a mysterious mass death of trees lining the Amsterdam canals. War had broken out again between the English and Dutch. 1666, with its notoriously devilish implications, would be the year in which the Last Days would be heralded. Or 1667. Peter Serrarius – a Walloon minister of a millenarian cast of mind, Hebraist and friend of Menasseh ben Israel – on the strength of information received from a Jew of Livorno (who had had it passed to him from an acquaintance in Alexandria) was convinced he would shortly see the Last Days and confirmed to his many correspondents the Jewish siege of Mecca and the miraculous invulnerability of the Israelite army.[3] In the last months of 1665 and through the winter, the madness built. A fleet of eighty ships packed with Jews was apparently on its way from India to Palestine to prepare the way for a mass exodus to Israel. Another fleet of 125 ships was being fitted out at

Amsterdam for a great convoy of redemption. The enemies of the Jews were quaking in their boots. The persecuting Germans and Cossacks were to be bloodily vanquished for all the tens of thousands of rapes and murders they had inflicted on innocent, defenceless Jews. The heavens shook with anticipation. Bolts of lightning revealed monsters in the sky. As had been prophesied, the Sons of Moses had crossed the Sambatyon: Reubenites, Gadites, Zebulnians and the rest arrayed in force, singing psalms as they marched along.

All this could only mean one thing: that the Messiah was at last about to appear, and the King of the Jews born of the line of David would lead them back in triumph to Jerusalem. (The identity of the second Messiah, of the line of Joseph, He Who Had Fallen in Battle, was to stir disagreement among the hopeful.) The Temple would rise again, exactly as Templo of Amsterdam had drawn it. In Prague, the robe of Solomon Molkho, mystic letters dangerously embroidered on its fading silk, was taken from its resting place in the Pinkas synagogue and paraded about the streets of the Jewish district. Solomon had been the forerunner. God had waited for more than a century. But now he had sent the king.

Nathan Eliyahu Ashkenazi knew the identity of this Messiah-King even before he had crossed his threshold. In 1665 Nathan was twenty-two, another studious yeshiva *bokhur*, gaunt from self-imposed fasts. Born in Jerusalem, he had moved to Gaza, a city of great Jewish piety, scholarship and the Hebrew poetry of the Najar dynasty. Nathan was also a Kabbalist in the style of the Safed field walkers and stargazers of the previous century, a tradition which had grown in influence (though perhaps not as universally as its great historian Gershom Scholem argues).[4] Like so many of his generation Nathan was restive under Talmudic legalism. Gemara and commentaries on the *Shulkhan Arukh* were not enough to nourish his whirling imagination. His extended fasts, followed by days of complete isolation, brought on deep trances. In one such state of heightened vision, described later in his *Book of Creation*, Nathan ascended high enough and far enough so that during the seven days of his cosmic suspension, he beheld the entirety of creation. As he rose still further into the sea of stars, the heavenly chariot – the *merkabah* of which the Kabbalah text *Zohar* spoke – came into view and on it was figured the beautiful, soft face of a man. Without willing them, words came out of his mouth:

'Sabbatai Zevi is his name and he shall cry, roar against his enemies.'[5]
On returning to earth Nathan felt he had been visited by a *maggid*: a
benevolent sacred persona who had used his lips and tongue to
pronounce an oracular truth.

Within the Jewish community of Gaza, Nathan was already known
as a healer of souls. His gift was to identify the particular transgressions and doubts of individuals, the interior blemishes which caused
their carriers sickness and distress. Nathan would diagnose the trouble
and prescribe the remedy, usually a regime of penitential prayers he
himself had written for such cases along with the severe, extended
fasts of the kind he inflicted on himself. Penitential mortification
would bring healing illumination. This was *tiqqun*, the principle drawn
from Kabbalist cosmology by which the vital sparks trapped in particles of gross matter could be liberated from material imprisonment.

As with the cosmos, so with people. The penances and purges
prescribed for their spiritual maladies would allow that vital energy
to float free and make body and soul whole again. The tall, plump,
ruddy-faced man with the round beard who came to see Nathan in
the early spring of 1665 was, Nathan surmised, just such a sufferer.
His violent mood swings (the classic bipolar pendulum between manic
elation and abysmal melancholy) were a symptom of some terrible
dislocation within his sense of self. The patient expected a cure. Instead
he received a revelation from the younger man that he, Shabbetai
Zevi, son of a Romaniot agent for English merchants in the port city
of Smyrna, was, in fact, the expected Messiah. At this news, Shabbetai
is said to have laughed, conceding that he himself had once thought
so too, but this conviction had gone away. But since the learned young
Kabbalist was so sure, all of the visions and voices which had haunted
Shabbetai since his youth resolved themselves into a moment of self-
recognition. In Hebron, where the rich Amsterdam merchant Abraham
Pereyra had established a yeshiva, all doubts fell away and the head
of the academy, Rabbi ben Meir Hiyya Rofe, became an early enthusiast of the cause. On their return to Gaza around the feast of Shavuot,
Shabbetai's condition threw him from manic euphoria into a catatonic
abyss. While he was thus incapacitated, Nathan, in the company of
the 'scholars of Gaza', became possessed, pacing back and forth,
reciting by heart an entire tractate of the Talmud, and ordering various

of the number to sing particular anthems. As this was going on, it was said that the room filled with a fragrance so unusual and so wonderful that some of the company exited the house to discover its source, unaware it was issuing from Nathan, who now began to dance, tearing off his clothes until he was dressed only in his underthings. Jumping high in the air he then collapsed on the floor and lay there stock-still.[6] To those who felt for it, Nathan seemed to have no pulse. He was declared dead. A cloth was set over his face. After a little while, though, from beneath the cloth a low sound could be heard, and when it was removed, another *maggidic* transmission was heard: 'Have a care of my beloved so, my Messiah, Shabbetai Zevi,' the voice said. Not long after, Nathan anointed Shabbetai and declared him 'worthy to be King over Israel'.

Truth be told, the Messiah was a bit of a *nebbish*. As a boy in Smyrna, the hustling port of the Ottoman Empire, Shabbetai had been a loner. His mother Clara had died when he was six. At the height of his fame he would order pilgrims to visit her tomb, so her loss was felt keenly throughout his life. Around the same time as her death (as his admiring biographers later claimed), the small boy had been visited by the female radiance of the Shekhina, in the form of a fire which had scorched his penis. Neither of his first two marriages would be consummated. His birthday was Tisha B'Ab, the 9th of Ab, the day on which the Second Temple was destroyed, commemorated in a solemn fast of grieving, but also according to the sages the day on which the Messiah would be born. This may have given him early intimations of his destiny, for Shabbetai regularly violated the ban on uttering the name of God, pronouncing the Tetragrammaton, 'YHWH' as it was spelled, loudly in public. Between these exhibitions, Shabbetai would take ritual immersions in the sea, the podgy boy bobbing in the salty waves muttering his purifications. For years he was just an eccentric teenage nuisance, following the mystical three-step: fast, trance, seclude. But his outbursts became tiresome to the rabbis and perhaps too dangerous for Shabbetai to be allowed to stay in Smyrna. Wandering suited him. Off he went to Salonika and then on to Jerusalem where he lodged in a single cell-like room. Walking into the Judaean desert he sought the shade of ancient caves where he communed with the angels of the covenant.

Exasperated by his provocations, the Jerusalem rabbis sent Shabbetai to Egypt to raise money for their yeshivot. In Cairo he hit a mood upswing. The *nebbish* became a charmer, attracting the attention of Raphael Joseph, tax farmer and man of substance who had just become *chelebi*, the head of the community. A Kabbalist himself, Raphael Joseph was more attracted than repelled by Shabbetai's sacred stunts. To dare to do such things, to say God's name and not be struck down, there had to be something there! In Cairo Shabbetai married for the third time. His previous two marriages, one swiftly following the other, and to women whose names are still unknown, ended in divorce for failure to provide marital satisfaction.[7] The latest bride, however, proved more durable. An orphan of the atrocious massacres of 1648, Sarah had been taken in by a Polish Catholic family (some accounts said a noble household) and brought up in the Church. Said to have been exceptionally beautiful, she was to have been married off to the son of her benefactors but on the eve of the wedding she was visited by her dead father who revealed her true religion to her and (by one account) instructed her to go to the cemetery of the Jews where a body was to be interred the following day. Sarah found herself there, wearing almost nothing (or nothing at all, depending on the source), covered only by the animal skin her father had given her and on which appeared in mystic letters the message that she would be the bride of the Messiah. This she took seriously, turning prophetess, and in Livorno repeatedly announced her destiny in public. Anti-Shabbeteans added to this biography her habit of sleeping with anyone and everyone, some said for the pleasure of it and some said for profit too. Hearing of this woman's resolution to become his bride, Shabbetai saw no reason why this should not come to pass. In all likelihood her violation of the proprieties only made the possibility more intriguing. Had not the prophet Hosea counselled 'taking a bride from whoredom'? They were duly married in Cairo. Commentators disagreed on whether or not a consummation of some sort finally did take place, although the son born later to Sarah suggested it had. But it was at least a change from the ceremonies Shabbetai orchestrated in which, beneath a decorated *huppah*, he married the Torah.

It was Nathan who turned the man into the Messiah; Nathan who had the gift of ecstatic promotion and mythic invention. Before Shabbetai was properly launched on the world, Nathan claimed to have 'discovered' an ancient apocalypse text which, centuries earlier, had prophesied the coming of Shabbetai Zevi the redeemer. Needless to say he had written this himself with considerable help from the delirious verses of Solomon Molkho and had gone so far as to distress its surface to give the appearance of antiquity. (There was good precedent for this. The Books of Kings and Chronicles have the high priest during the reign of King Josiah of Judah 'discovering' an ancient text of the Torah in the decayed fabric of the Temple while it was being renovated.) In Nathan's apocalypse, one 'Rabbi Abraham' living in thirteenth-century Germany has a dream in which a voice proclaims the future birth of Shabbetai, who as the true Messiah would 'subdue the great dragon living between the rivers' (the standard poetic allusion to the pharaohs of Egypt). The victory would be achieved without 'hands' (notwithstanding those armed Israelites) but rather with chant and song, and it would establish a kingdom which would endure to the end of time. A man 'like polished brass' appears, followed by a ferret and a chameleon and a second bearded man, this time the Messiah himself boasting a cubit-and-a-half penis (that'll show the *goyim*). The prodigy smashes up a mountain with a hammer into which he then falls and disappears. Be not afraid, says the brass man, 'you shall see his power'.

The phantasmagorical visions were not, in fact, that much more extreme than some of the wilder prophetic books of the Bible – Ezekiel, for instance – or pseudepigrapha like the Book of Enoch. In an age of extreme visions they cast a spell, but it was a long letter sent by Nathan to the *chelebi* Raphael Joseph in Egypt which became, as Gershom Scholem says, 'the order of the day' for Believers, printed, translated and read from the pulpits of synagogues throughout Europe where Shabbeteans had the majority, which was between November 1665 and the autumn of 1666. The letter consisted of yet more elaborate Kabbalah, followed by an almanac of the coming messianic years. Victory through psalms would be achieved so conclusively that the sultan would become Shabbetai's lieutenant and viceroy. The building of the Third Temple would get under way once the Messiah had identified its precise site in Jerusalem and recovered the ashes of the sacred red heifer, the great purifier. Leaving his loyal servant to govern his domains, Shabbetai would retire behind the Sambatyon River for some years, returning with his true bride, Rebecca, the daughter of the resurrected Moses. He would come riding a celestial lion, the beast bridled by a serpent with seven heads, and when the 'nations see him they would all bow to the ground'.

Much of this might have been brushed off as madness, but the illumination had come from the Promised Land: from Gaza, Aleppo, Hebron and (intermittently) Jerusalem, and not, as had been the case with Asher Laemmlein Reutlingen and David Ha-Reuveni, from Germany and north Italy, or from the mythic geography of Afro-Arabia. As a pair of enchanters, Nathan and Shabbetai, the word and the deed, were a potent combination. Both of them (but particularly Nathan) were sufficiently immersed in the traditional texts and the Kabbalistic canon to bring the signs, portents and symbols into prophetic alignment, especially in the 1660s when expectations in the Christian as well as Jewish world were feverish. All this was enough to make impressive converts among the senior rabbinate, along with laymen of power and substance in Jewish communities from Podolia to Egypt. If men like Raphael Joseph in Cairo and Abraham Pereyra (the founder of a yeshiva in Amsterdam as well as one in Hebron) had become passionate disciples, the latter to the point of selling up his enormous estate and commercial fortune to join the messianic mission, who were lesser Jews to disagree?

Gershom Scholem argues that because Kabbalah had become the normative Judaism of its day, the Jewish world was ripe for a phenomenon like Shabbetai. But from Leone Modena on, through to the rabbi Jacob Sasportas in Hamburg, some of the most articulate voices were also the most vigilantly guarded, if not actually antagonistic to the wizardry of Kabbalah, which they believed flirted with heresy. Leone Modena's appeal had been to a rational engagement with the Torah rather than the uncertainties of the trance. God was to be worshipped as the source of reasoning intelligence, as had been taught by Maimonides, and by Saadia before him in ninth-century Mesopotamia in his great work *Beliefs and Opinions*.[8] His laws were the way to a concretely realised earthly life rather than an illumination of primordial cosmology. But Nathan was himself steeped in Maimonides and knew that in the *Guide for the Perplexed*, metaphysical meditation kept company with reasoning. In any case, there was no putting the Kabbalistic genie back into the bottle. After all, the Talmud was an empire of inference, and the authority of an oral law received at the same time as the written one had to be taken on trust. So why *not* make the assumption that the apparent meaning of the Bible was just a membrane covering a body of far deeper knowledge which could be apprehended through the intense, disciplined contemplation of the hierarchy of signs? Words, and the letters which made them, conveyed the lighter meaning and the deeper truth. Christian, Muslim and classical scholars, deep readers of Plato, all believed they could be led, step by step, towards unearthly wisdom; so why not the Jews?

Doubtless many initiates and practitioners of Kabbalism were predisposed to invest Shabbetai with the messianic aura, the embodiment of mystical truth floating free of the formal laws of Torah and Talmud. But Jacob Sasportas – who had gone from Hamburg to London as the embryonic community's rabbi, only to return to the German city as the plague engulfed England – was a Kabbalist who saw in Shabbetai not the incarnation but the vulgar perversion of the Mystery. It was exactly the vulgarisation which worked the spell. Shabbetai appealed to immense multitudes of Jews on whom the higher cosmology and complicated symbolism of Kabbalah was completely lost. In large part his adherents were still synagogue Jews for whom *halakhic* legalism was all very well day by day, Sabbath by Sabbath, but which somehow failed their sense of the fatefulness of Jewish life and memory.[9] The Messiah filled the psychic vacuum. Shabbetean Jews were not, after all, the only ones with such visions. Even in their day, the resemblance between Jewish and Quaker visions was noted. It had not been long since the prophet James Nayler had imitated Christ, riding on a donkey into Bristol and declaring himself King of the Jews. Looming over everything was the atrocious experience of the mass slaughters of 1648 in Poland and Ukraine. It is true that some of the most intense centres of Shabbetean hysteria were also some of the safest cities in Europe for Jews – Amsterdam, Hamburg, Venice and Salonika – but those were the places to which traumatised and destitute survivors had come with nothing but a pack of nightmares. (It is estimated that almost 90 per cent of Poland's and Ukraine's Jews were either killed or forced into flight in these years.) Shabbetai's Sarah was one of these walking wounded, badly in need of an avenging Messiah. For both the immediate casualties and the communities of their host cities, the prospect of a magically victorious return to Jerusalem

– and retribution visited on their persecutors – was itself enough for them to sign on to the legions of the Messiah.

Moving among ululating, prostrating, chanting and dancing throngs in Aleppo, Nathan and Shabbetai understood how they complemented each other. Nathan was the carrier of words, meanings and predictions. Shabbetai, not so good with words, specialised in sacred theatre, and was the virtuoso of transgression, appreciating the thrill of rebellious violation (because he had experienced it himself), and passing it on as not just a blessing but a duty to his bellowing flock. At Jerusalem, in defiance of the Muslim prohibition against equestrian Jews, he declared his elevation beyond conventions by mounting a horse and riding it, Joshua-like, seven times around the city as if willing Suleyman's great walls to fall before the force of his charisma. But his anti-commandments were directed at the entire structure of rabbinic and Talmudic authority based on the perverse paradox, *bittulah shel torah zehu kiyumah*: 'in the violation of the Torah lies its fulfilment'. His acts of juvenile daring in Smyrna – the out-loud pronunciation of the Tetragrammaton without being struck down for the blasphemy – now became a sign of his exalted status. When Shabbetai proclaimed the redundancy of the Law of Moses, his followers shared in a holy communion of New Revelation. Fasts (except for the Day of Atonement) became feasts celebrating the imminent rebuilding of the Temple. Some of the dietary laws (another favourite target of the rationalist sceptics) could be set aside, Shabbetai making a performance of eating *heleb*, the forbidden kidney fat. He was swathed in the costume of his kingship – green silk which his acolytes emulated by pinning green ribbons to their coats – or he rode showily (this too must have been tricky) with the *tallit* prayer shawl draped over his head. I may do with Israel what seems right to me, he had told Nathan after accepting the messianic mantle. The more he dared, the more credible he became.

At Hanukkah in Smyrna, Shabbetai's self-belief turned into megalomania. There was another formal marriage to the Torah beneath a wedding canopy. Entries into the synagogue took the form of processions, preceded by bearers of vases of flowers and sweets. Both sexes made up his train and were called to readings. Chosen rabbis held the hem of his robe. His bipolarity perfectly served the impression of arbitrariness assumed to be part of the messianic temperament. There was Shabbetai the singer of sweet anthems; Shabbetai the frightening monster of petulant revenge. A secretary of his, Samuel Primo, had written that there was no greater sanctification of the Sabbath than to assault, physically, within the precincts of the synagogue itself, anyone daring to express disbelief. Many of the most fanatical of his followers did just that in Italy and in Holland.

The king with his warbling melodies and portly body could turn into a thug. During the Smyrna Hanukkah, Shabbetai learned that the Portuguese synagogue was a nest of unbelievers. In all likelihood, its most eminent figure, the merchant Hayyim Peña, would refuse him entry. To test the resistance, the big man led a retinue of rowdy, indignant followers to its doors and smashed his way in with an axe. Peña, who had already once narrowly avoided being killed by a Shabbetean mob, beat a retreat through a window. When he got home he discovered to his deep dismay that his two daughters had become believing prophetesses, given to visionary convulsions and shouting 'Crown, crown' at their father. 'When the news got out everyone was anxious to hear the prophecies of the daughters, despite the fact that there were many prophets aside from them. For everyone wanted to determine if it was true that the daughters of Hayyim Peña were prophesying about Shabbetai Zevi.'[10]

Inside the Portuguese synagogue, the Sabbath service turned into a shock spectacle, the Messiah acting out his indifference to all conventional proprieties, daring the congregation to oppose his liberty to revise its laws and customs as he saw fit. He declared the Amidah of eighteen blessings, the meditative spine of every service – morning, afternoon and evening – redundant. The *shema* would suffice. Then Shabbetai marched to the Ark and rapped on its doors a number of times with his staff as if commanding its obedience. The Torah, the bride, was his now, not vice versa. Instead of reading the weekly portion from the scrolls, he took out a worn *chumash* (the book version of the Pentateuch) and read snippets from it, breaking into choruses of his favourite Ladino romantic song 'Meliselda', and then distributing 'kingdoms' of the Ottoman Empire to his followers, beginning with his two brothers Elijah and Joseph.

During the winter of 1665–6, news of Shabbetai's exploits circulated rapidly through the diaspora, throwing communities into contentious upheaval. Ferocious denunciations were issued in almost every major centre, but in none did the sceptics have the upper hand. The best that the beleaguered *parnassim* and community elders could do was to manage some semblance of nervous neutrality. But in the meantime, most of their congregants threw themselves into paroxysms of repentance, as ordered by Nathan's instructions. In Italy, where since the days of Leone de Sommi theatre was a legitimate Jewish pleasure, audiences agreed to forgo the shows, along with the masquerades and dancing of Purim. Dice and cards, the Jewish craze par excellence, were abandoned from Rome to Amsterdam. So many people, rich and poor, studious and ignorant, crowded into the yeshivot that benches had to be added to accommodate them. In many places, the penitent and the ecstatic vied to outdo each other. Fasts became dangerously prolonged and repeated each week for two or three days at a time. In Ferrara even this was not enough for three Jews who died after a fast of six consecutive days and nights.[11] The winter itself became an arena of self-mortification. Leyb ben Ozer, the notary of the Ashkenazi community in Amsterdam, wrote of men and women immersing themselves beneath the ice in Poland; others rolling naked in the snow for half an hour at a time. The ordeals would often take place in the long nights, since Nathan's devotions were expressly intended to be recited and sung at midnight. Repentance demanded pain. Some devotees poured molten wax down their bodies; others thrashed themselves with thorn branches until they were a mess of shredded skin and blood. But the prized instrument of penitence was nettles. Those who were most serious about their repentance tied cords of stinging nettles about their body, front and back, and then dressed in tight woollen clothes to aggravate the pain. The result of this enthusiasm was a nettle shortage, forcing the penitents to seek supplies from distant fields and woods or paying premium prices to have them shipped in.

Amsterdam: the prosperous, secure Kahal Kados Talmud Torah Portuguese community was turned upside down by the mania. Its rabbinate was split down the middle. Isaac Aboab da Fonseca became an enthusiastic Shabbetean, along with Aaron Sarphati who had come to Holland from Morocco, as did both cantors of the Sephardi community and some of its cleverest scholars like Isaac Nahar who had studied in the same Talmud Torah as Spinoza. Jacob Sasportas – the arch-antagonist, deeply conscious of his having been a descendant of

Nahmanides, the great Catalan defender of the Talmud in the Barcelona disputation of 1263 – was appalled by all the singing and dancing in the streets as well as within the synagogue. 'The Scrolls of the Law were taken out of the Ark with all their beautiful ornaments without considering the possible danger from the jealousy and hatred of the Gentiles. On the contrary they publicly proclaimed [the news] and informed the Gentiles of the reports.'[12] From Hamburg, he hurled denunciations at the wicked and the credulous, but until Shabbetai's apostasy to Islam in September 1666 he had little success, for most important Jews in Amsterdam like the sugar magnate Abraham Pereyra were passionate Shabbeteans. A low point for Sasportas came on the 9th of Ab, when the fast-become-feast was celebrated by congregants guzzling on food and wine. So many people wanted to dance that even the Shabbeteans had to restrict the numbers thrashing about the *tevah* to twelve at a time. The most the opponents could do was to exit the synagogue ostentatiously when prayers for the Messiah Shabbetai Zevi were read out not just on the Sabbath but on Mondays and Thursdays too. Doubters were intimidated into silence for fear of the consequences. When a famous unbeliever, the merchant Alatino – who had upbraided the believers, shouting 'You are mad! Where are the signs? Where are the tidings the prophet Elijah is to bring?' – dropped dead suddenly after a morning at the Bourse, between washing his hands and partaking of bread, the timid took the lesson to heart.[13]

In this most businesslike city, Jewish property and capital began to be liquidated, knocked down at rock-bottom prices. Jews were forbidden to profit from the messianic discount by buying from other Jews. In the German lands, townsmen and peasants eager to scoop up bargains took it on themselves to hasten mass departure by the usual acts of violence. No matter: to all would be given in the Land of Israel. In the meantime, social rank and custom dissolved. Bachelors married brides without dowries; the well-off took the studious and impoverished into their houses. On the other hand, the challenges of conveyance continued to sort out the well-to-do from those who stood in line. Pereyra, who had sold off his estate for 50,000 guilders, had no difficulty in getting himself and his family to Venice where, for whatever reason, he stayed put until the messianic debacle shattered his dreams. Less wealthy Jews scrambled to find passage. In eastern Europe, especially in Lithuania, an ancient *midrash* tradition that, come the messianic time, God would transport His people on clouds to Israel, found ready believers. Chuckling Christians and Jewish anti-Shabbeteans reported much cloud-gazing among the gullible Jews. A pregnant wife, worried that her condition would make the long journey to Jerusalem impossible, was comforted by her husband's reassurance that cloud transport would ease her passage. At Arta in Greece another Jew broke his neck and died falling from his roof while attempting to jump over a cloud.

It was absurd but not incomprehensible. For there was, during this brief period, a social communion of enthusiasts, a camp of ecstatic hope amid a people for whom even the most secure asylum must always have seemed provisional. Shabbeteanism was the opposite of resigned fatalism, the endless scuttling from calamity. This was a running to redemption; the call to Zion. And its improvisatory nature, the shocking, thrilling violation of commandments, coupled with relentless self-purification, created what cultural anthropologists call a liminal space: a transitional zone in which everything could be refashioned. Many Jews – not just Uriel da Costa, Daniel de Prado and Baruch Spinoza – evidently felt that Jewish refashioning was in order. It is not that hard to understand how the cult of anguish and elation, a collective bipolar condition, could get the upper hand.

It had to end, and it did in the land of Sultan Mehmed IV whose soldiers, according to the fantastic reports, had fallen to Israelite lances and their massed choirs. After the triumph in Aleppo, Nathan and Shabbetai had gone their separate ways to spread the word. Leaving his home town in the grip of his followers, and entirely captive to his own mythology, Shabbetai sailed to Constantinople in March 1666. According to his acolytes, his ship was saved from being wrecked in a great tempest only by the mysterious pillar of fire which appeared at various moments to preserve him from peril. But the fire failed to spare him from being arrested, taken to the grand vizier, Ahmed Köprülü, interrogated and thrown into prison. Manic elation turned into depression. Though dumbfounded by the Messiah's impotence in the face of his captors, the Jews of Constantinople, Adrianople and Salonika (and Smyrna, once the news was known) reasoned that this was all part of the messianic plan. Perhaps captivity and suffering was merely the preliminary to redemption and resurrection.

Concerned as much about a Muslim attack on the deluded Jews as any attempt on their own part to liberate the Messiah, Köprülü ferried the woebegone Shabbetai across the Sea of Marmara to the impregnable fortress of Gallipoli on the Dardanelles. His strategy was to deflate the danger through anticlimax (rather than the execution of a martyr). Instead of the grim dungeon into which Shabbetai had been locked in Constantinople, he was given everything he needed at Gallipoli fort save his liberty. Lavish food, drink, rugs and hanging curtains were his to command. Pilgrims who came to visit – like Rabbi Mordecai the Mediator and Master Isaiah the Reprover from Poland – marvelled at the opulent vessels of gold and silver from which the Messiah ate, and were entertained by Turkish musicians and singers with whom Shabbetai sang his favourite melodies. Shabbetean believers convinced themselves that either it was a miracle that their king had not been executed in Constantinople, or, more likely, that the sultan and his minions, knowing with whom they dealt, were frightened of dispatching him for he would arise from any grave to vanquish them. Far from the incarceration in Gallipoli ending the messianic excitement throughout Europe and North Africa, if anything it rose to new heights throughout the spring and summer of 1666, especially after Shabbetai himself rallied from his low moods to resume an ebullient high. Demonstrations of Shabbetean enthusiasm took place among the Jews of Kurdistan and in Yemen, where they nearly brought down on themselves another of the periodic massacres which took place in southern Arabia. In Poland, so many carried images of Shabbetai Zevi through the streets that they threatened to provoke a Catholic attack, and the king, John Casimir, had to ban the public display of such pictures while issuing stern warnings against attacking his Jews.

No place was too far, no journey too long for the pilgrims to Gallipoli. For them he was now the Amirah, the acronym made from the Hebrew for 'Our Lord and King, may His Majesty be Exalted'. Sometimes hundreds, even thousands, stood before the fortress gates, renamed 'The Tower of Strength', high above the Aegean in the hope of setting eyes on their Lord. Those who could come up with the ready, did. They were rewarded not just with the spectacle of the Shabbetean court, but with a man who had somehow slipped more easily into the grace of his role as captive than when he had been free and raving. A delegation from Ukraine, led by its rabbi, asked if it might relate to him the horrors of the massacres of 1648–9 and the blessed martyrs who had perished. But Shabbetai responded merely by pointing to the book recording that history which he kept open on his table. Then he enquired after the well-being of the rabbi's father. As well as could be expected, came the reply, for someone eighty years old; he was frail. Might the Amirah help to make him more robust, and live a little longer? Shabbetai took a piece of sugar, gave it to the rabbi and told him it would make his father better, and then took a scarf woven with gold and a coat to give to both father and son. For all his preposterous vainglory, there were moments when Shabbetai did indeed conduct himself as though he were the healer-sovereign. No wonder that many came back from an audience at Gallipoli claiming that the face of the Lord shone with an unearthly radiance, so intense that no mere mortal Jew could look directly at him and not be burned. It was at this time that poems were written in his honour from one end of the Jewish world to the other, in Yiddish and Judaeo-Spanish, in Portuguese and Italian and Hebrew. Even Sufi dervishes, intrigued by tales of his mystical majesty, came to pay homage.

From his courtly confinement at Gallipoli, Shabbetai decreed, well in advance, that not only the 17th of Tammuz but also his birthday on the 9th of Ab should be altered from fasts to feasts, and prescribed the anthems and feasting with which it should be celebrated. And it may have been the eruption of disorderly rejoicing that broke out throughout Europe, and more particularly in Turkey itself, that changed Köprülü's mind. In mid-September Shabbetai was brought to Adrianople, the favourite summer resort of the sultan. Now that it was imminent, the encounter which Shabbetai had long desired disturbed him and changed everything. From a latticed alcove window Mehmed IV watched as Shabbetai was confronted by the *kaimakam* governor of Adrianople, the sheikh al-Islam and the famous court preacher Mehmed Vani Efendi. Shabbetai was told that he was to be made the target of the sultan's archers. If, as he claimed, he was indeed the Messiah, the arrows would bounce harmlessly off him and all would acknowledge the truth. If he declined the test, however, he would be taken to the impaling stake set up at the Seraglio Gate. (An alternative account has the threatened execution take the form of a march through the streets of the city, with flaming torches pinned to him burning away his flesh.)

There was, of course, a third alternative and Shabbetai immediately took it, throwing off his hat and (some said) trampling it underfoot while donning the white turban of a *kapici bashi*, a gatekeeper of the palace – no small honour. The Messiah from the line of David was now translated into Mehmed Efendi Pasha. A purse of silver was his, and costume befitting his new faith and rank. Ahmed Köprülü and the sultan knew they had ended the threat.

Astonishingly, though, as the confounding news reached his legions of followers it was greeted by many with stubborn disbelief. Shabbetai had not apostasised, it was said, but had ascended to heaven leaving only the shell of his body to be capped by the white turban. Or he had (temporarily) descended into the dark realm of the *qelippot* husks, the better to defeat it and conserve the last sacred sparks. Or he was merely assuming the guise of a loyal Muslim subject of the sultan by way of preparation for taking over his government. Or he had done this otherwise inexplicable thing, as a King-Messiah would, to spare the Jewish people from a general massacre. Or he had simply disappeared behind the Sambatyon River; there was always and forever that. The astute Ahmed Köprülü decided against any sort of collective punishment for the mass of believers, though some of the leading rabbis who had encouraged the movement were rounded up. The grand vizier and the sultan simply let disillusionment do its own work. And so, for the most part, it did, both in the Ottoman lands and in Europe, where the anticlimax was a bitter blow. The remarkable thing about the aftermath of the apostasy is not the falling away of belief but how many persisted in their devotions. Returned to Amsterdam, unapologetic, Abraham Pereyra continued to meet with other impenitent Shabbeteans, including one of the cantors, in a private house and say prayers for his welfare. Even more astonishing was the tenacity of *Christian* belief. One Christian woman became a Shabbetean prophetess, and refused to recant. And in his last years the Walloon minister Peter Serrarius, who had known and was friends with just about everyone in this great drama – Menasseh ben Israel, John Dury, Baruch Spinoza – committed himself to a translation of Nathan's devotions, and travelled, in his late eighties, to meet Shabbetai in person in Adrianople, dying en route (which may have spared him some disappointment).

Shabbetai knew this and encouraged it by leading a double life in Adrianople. He became something of a Muslim Marrano – faithfully attending mosque, Friday prayers and listening to the sermons of the imams – but also continuing, as many reported, to have candles lit on Friday night and observe the Sabbath as best he could. Eventually he became too reckless, and in 1673 was denounced for either insulting Islam or relapsing. The accusation could have brought about a summary execution, which would have pleased the rabbis who had excommunicated him and anyone professing belief in him. But Köprülü again decided on the softer way, banishing Mehmed/ Shabbetai to a remote part of Albania where, after yet another marriage with a young woman, he died in 1676.

However, the notion that Shabbetai had, in secret, continued to be Shabbetai meant that despite the denunciations and excommunications raining down from Jewish pulpits, there were many who, well into the 1670s, continued to believe. Nathan of Gaza was one of them, even when he was reduced to a vagabond life traipsing from one Jewish community to another in search of the furtive faithful. He made two visits to Adrianople where he reunited with his Messiah turned royal gatekeeper, who may well have persuaded Nathan that beneath the mask of Mehmed Efendi Pasha was still Shabbetai Zevi. In Venice Nathan allowed a 'confession' to be concocted purporting to admit that he had been deceived into error and folly, but it was so lame as to be incredible. The ferocity with which he was pursued testified to the anxiety that he might still be dangerous. Joseph Halevi, one of the fiercest of the critics, described Nathan as a 'brainless adolescent who, not satisfied with proclaiming himself prophet, went on to anoint as King of Israel the coarse malignant lunatic who used to be Shabbetai Zevi'.[14]

Worse things were said about the fallen Messiah himself, partly to deter the seeding of further prophets, for there were many candidates, especially Abraham Miguel Cardoso, a *converso* doctor living in Livorno at the time of Shabbetai's appearance, whose sister-in-law was capable of both visions and miracles, curing him of cataracts and herself of deformed limbs. Cardoso's narrative – including the account of his

three-year-old daughter reciting messianic visions and telling her father
that she heard it all 'from that man who is in your head' – is inspired
storytelling, and there were others like it (though not of the same
narrative quality), notwithstanding the apostasy. The urge for redemption and restoration, concentrated in the person of a Messiah, would
not die in the centuries that followed, and for all the vituperation of
the guardians of orthodoxy like Jacob Emden – who called Shabbetai
'a slick-tongued rascal ... who caught his prey in his paws ... like a
slut spreading her legs for every passer-by and copulating with
a donkey' – the mystical impulse in Judaism never went away.

There were, though, scenes of pathetic dismay. The diarist Gluckel
of Hameln's father-in-law, a great believer, had sent barrels of linen
and dried food off to Hamburg, in preparation for the voyage to the
Holy Land. For three years after the apostasy he refused to have
the casks opened. 'For three years the casks stood ready ... while my
father-in-law awaited the signal to depart. But the Most High pleased
otherwise.' Even prunes, dried peas and sausage don't last forever.
Only when the decomposing food threatened to spoil perfectly good
linen could the old man consent to have the barrels prised open,
wherein lay the maggoty mess of the messianic dream.[15]

II. The Triumph of Routine

Somewhere, between the obligations of rigour and the delirium of
dreams, the pulse of life beat on in Vlooienburg, the Jodenbuurt:
bonnets and baskets, the glitter of the Vismarkt and the shouts on
the Bourse; high hats and rustling satin; hoops and tops, the stubs of
cheroots and the nails of cloves; the two-tone honk of the shofar on
Rosh Hashanah mornings interrupting the chimes of the Zuiderkerk;
the shuffle of boots on the sanded floor of the synagogue, a barge
loaded with a shrouded body sailing up the Amstel to its resting place
in the House of Life. Here, too, is life enacted in the ceremonial
theatre of a Jewish family: a *brit milah*, a circumcision; only the oldest
in the picture remembering how it was when grown men from Spain
and Portugal decided to be cut for the covenant. It is two years after

the apostasy in Adrianople and already this seems much more important: the *mohel* taking centre stage, much like Captain Frans Banning
Cocq; the proud father and the nursing mother still in her natal four-
poster; the older child fidgety and playful; the white-bearded rabbi in
patriarchal pose; perhaps the *haham*, old Isaac Aboab da Fonseca
himself, nearly blind, the embarrassment of his Shabbeteanism gone
like a bad dream. And at the back of this drawing another story of
unknown details but spectacular essentials: a collaboration between
Gentile and Jew. The Jew (whom some have thought to be Mozes
Curiel, one of the richest and grandest of the community) would
have commissioned the drawing as a family memento; the Gentile
was Romeyn de Hooghe, the most gifted graphic artist of his generation, still an up-and-comer but heading for fame and fortune as the
satirist-polemicist of the stadholder William III, and when the prince
became King William III of England, royal eulogist on paper, too.[16]

It is the ordinariness of all this which, in the annals of Jewish history,
is such a wonder: the natural fit between patron and artist; between
a Jewish ceremony and the uniformly Dutch dress, the Jews indistinguishable from any other Amsterdammers but for the triumphant
gesture towards the tray of the circumciser's knife. There had been
two kinds of spectacle in the Amsterdam Sephardi synagogue within
ten years: the *herem* laid on Baruch Spinoza, and the dancing on the
9th of Ab with rabbis Aboab and Sarphati clapping their hands. Each
of those scenes led forward towards the future of Jews in the modern
world. Those highways out of Amsterdam diverged about as widely
as they could: one leading to the rejection of legalistic observance,
the historicisation of Bible and Talmud, a synagogue car-park kind of
Judaism, an ecumenical *tiqqun* of interfaith bonding; the other leading
deep into the heart of the mystery, an eyes-shut, back-swaying, self-
liquidating absorption, *kavanah*, devotion to the utmost, to the exclusion of anything but the chanted words, or the silently mouthed
blessings or the ecstasies between the words.

But in Amsterdam there was also a third way: the way of routine,
a settling back into the rhythms of the week, the month, the year;
the Sabbath; the counting of the Omer; the shaking of the palm frond
on Sukkot; the children singing at Purim. Something which had eluded
Jews since Christianity had begun, and had somehow been accomplished in the Dutch republic: a semblance of a normal life. By 1670

there was more of it, too: more money, more begging, more stone fronting the houses of the rich, some of whom had moved out of the Breestraat and onto the Binnen Amstel, or in the case of 'Baron' Belmonte, even to number 586 Herengracht. There was more music in the *saal*, the parlour, more paintings on the walls; more food, more wine, more wigs, more poems, more plays, more Italian dancing masters and French song recitals; more books in more languages, and a lot more Jews: 2,500 Sephardim and 1,800 Ashkenazim.

Which made it time for temples. So at exactly the same time that Spinoza was finally, but anonymously, publishing his *Tractatus Theologicus-Politicus* – in which God, in so far as there was one, was no more but no less than the predetermined operation of Nature, indifferent to sin and virtue, punishment and reward, the laws and the massacres of the Jews, indeed to the Jews at all – the Ashkenazim and the Sephardim both felt they must have houses of worship grand enough and beautiful enough to mark their irreversible establishment in Amsterdam. The Ashkenazim, with a sense of making a statement that would refute, architecturally, the condescension they got from the Sephardim, hired Elias Bouwman (whose last name means 'builder') from a family of master masons who had worked on the Oosterkerk and other monuments of the most handsome city in the world. But Bouwman worked under the supervision of an even more formidable figure: Daniel Stalpaert, builder of churches and the massive East India Company's warehouse. Needless to say, this only spurred the Sephardim to outdo them. On 23 November 1670, Isaac Aboab da Fonseca delivered a sermon in the synagogue on the Houtgracht appealing for funds for a new house of worship. He raised 40,000 guilders – nearly half the full cost – after that one speech. Those were the days. Not to be outdone, another grandee from the de Sotto family offered to advance a cool 100,000 on condition of setting his schedule of repayment. He was declined by the *ma'amad*, which was now full of magnifico millionaires with houses in the country and bulging bank accounts. Affronted by the presumption of the Ashkenazim, the *ma'amad* selected the same team of Bouwman working under Stalpaert to outdo the rival community. There was some discussion about whether the new synagogue should be on the same site as the old, but a substantial tract of land was acquired on the Muidergracht, opposite the 'Leper House' and a hundred yards

or so from the Ashkenazi 'Grote Sjoel' (Great Synagogue). The competition was a little crass but together the two synagogues would be the
twin temples of Amsterdam's Jews.

Work began in 1671, but was quickly interrupted by catastrophe in
the form of a surprise double attack on the republic in 1672 – the
rampjaar, the year of calamity – from English ships and the armies of
Louis XIV. The French invasion was so sudden and so terrifying that
only the opening of the dykes and a defensive inundation stopped the
country from being overwhelmed. A mob in The Hague murdered
the scapegoated Grand Pensionary Johan de Witt and his brother
Cornelis, displaying the mutilated cadavers and hawking choice parts
about town. William III, the grandson of the stadholder who had
visited the old synagogue in 1642, was the beneficiary of the chaos;
he took command of the republic as its captain and admiral general,
and, with the help of loans and war materiel supplied by Jewish
bankers, among others, fought the invaders to a standstill. Romeyn
de Hooghe celebrated the victory in eulogising prints of battles on
sea and land along with propaganda prints of inquisitorial fanaticism
enthroned in occupied Utrecht, the Sint Jans Kerk turned into a
Catholic cathedral. One of the poems de Hooghe wrote on the inauguration of the 'Esnoga' (the Portuguese Synagogue) drove home the
point that Jews would seek in vain for shelter 'on the banks of the
Seine or the Tagus . . . wiser is the city on the Amstel' which recognises
the religion of the Jews.

Freedom from religious persecution – the bane of Europe for
centuries – was, by then, a Dutch commonplace. But all the same, it
was truly astounding, once building had resumed after a further
setback – a raging hurricane which descended on the city on 1 August
1674 – to see rise from the mass of city buildings the *two* synagogues,
at a time when Roman Catholics and Mennonites still had to disguise
the street fronts of their churches, effectively worshipping in secret
(if an open one). The Jews, by contrast, were confident enough not
just to build on the grandest imaginable scale but actually boast about
it, quoting texts instructing them to create houses of prayer taller and
greater than anything surrounding them. The grandeur of the central
block (like the Temple itself) was accentuated by its free-standing
within a courtyard enclosed by a lower range of buildings. Together
they made up a whole community: lodgings for the two *samasim*, the

sextons, and the two *chazzanim*, cantors (the pride and joy of the services), the schoolrooms of the Etz Hayim, a capacious and beautiful library, meeting rooms for the *ma'amad* and a washing place for incoming congregants.

To go into the Esnoga itself was to be bathed in light, and this too was a telling difference from the little Gothic spaces of the medieval synagogues built above all for shelter and safety (often in vain). Its roof was a hundred feet high, allowing for three rows of windows, square on the ground floor and the top floor lighting the women's gallery. Between them were stupendously tall arched windows, five on the front and rear walls and seven along its side, allowing light to flood the interior space, very much along the lines of the grandest Calvinist churches. The dimensions of the synagogue were also unprecedented: 130 feet long and 100 feet wide, space for 1,200 men down below and 400 women in the galleries. One of the inaugural sermons claimed that the Esnoga was only a mite smaller than Solomon's Temple, as described by Villalpando and modelled by Templo.[17] Both the *tevah* and the *heichal* – Ark – containing the Torah scrolls were made of oak, covered with a veneer of pernambuco rosewood, known as palisander or *sakkerdan* to the Dutch, the most exquisite and expensive of all timbers provided and paid for by Mozes Curiel. Carved elements were made of solid rosewood, and at the *heichal* they rose as Corinthian columns towards the inscription of the commandments. A forest of brass chandeliers held 800 candles.

They were all lit on Friday evening, 2 August 1675, for the inauguration of the Esnoga. To the spectacular building on the Muidergracht came le tout Amsterdam: not just its Jews but the luminaries and eminences of the city: burgomasters, aldermen and the city sheriff, the *schout*. It was the eve of Shabbat Nachamu, the beginning of a week of 'consolation' following the fast of the 9th of Ab, and when the verses from Isaiah 40 – 'Comfort ye, comfort ye my people' – were chanted. The inauguration was to run for eight days, the same number as the Maccabean purification of the temple after its liberation from Hellenistic paganism. No one could miss the calendrical and historical symbolism. For such moments of local redemption, a Messiah was not obligatory.

The eminences of the community gathered in the new *ma'amad* room where they took up the Torah scrolls, gloriously arrayed in

mantles embroidered in silver and gold and topped with crowns and
finials. Old Aboab had the honour of leading the procession with the
first scroll, and the others followed in strict order: the officers of
the school and the governors of the *bikur holim*, the fund for the sick,
then the *velhos*, the elders of the community, and before each one
marched a selected member of the congregation with a lighted torch
in his hand. Through the courtyard they went and into the Esnoga
and around it three times, the candlelight reflecting off the brass
chandeliers. When the doors of the Ark were opened the congregra-
tion could see another splendour: gilt-stamped leather covering its
interior walls, patterns of flowers impressed over its surface in crimson,
said to be a Sephardi tradition brought with their memories from
Lusitania. The *haham* preached the first *derasha*; seven more would
follow on subsequent days, including disquisitions on the power of
prayer, the harmonisation of religion and *Hollands vryheid*, and an
ambitious comparison between God's work as builder of heaven and
earth and the community's construction of the Esnoga. At the inaugural service a *shahachiyanu*, the blessing for a new house, a new season,
a new wonder was said. To music composed by Salomo van Raphael
Coronel, the *yimlokh* was sung and then the psalm of David, the
mizmor le David.

At Curiel's request, de Hooghe made a print of the great scene,
incorporating the procession, and carefully faithful to every architectural detail. But above the *heichal* he inserted an allegorical composition testifying to the natural place which this community now had
within the wider city and the republic which was, after all, still very
much a Christian commonwealth. On one side are the personifications
of the republic and the Maid of Amsterdam with their respective
coats of arms, and on the other the personification of the synagogue
itself, until this moment a standard element of Christian iconography
signifying obstinate blindness. This time, it was accompanied by the
figure of Aaron holding an open Torah scroll. The Latin inscription
reads *Libertas Conscientientiae Incrementum Republicae*, 'Freedom of
Conscience is the Mainspring of the Republic'. It was beyond astonishing that the living proof of this was the house of the Jews.

In subsequent years, whole series of prints were made demystifying
Jews and Judaism for anyone who wanted to learn the truth, as well
as for Jews who revelled in the depictions of their ceremonies and

customs. The Passover Seder was celebrated rather than made the scene of sinister conspiracy (for the blood libel was alive and well in many other parts of Europe). Weddings and burials at Ouderkerk, complete with weeping mourners, were depicted without the defensiveness Menasseh ben Israel could not avoid when trying to disabuse the English of their worst fantasies. At some point too the artist Emanuel de Witte, whose stock-in-trade was church interiors, painted three copies of the inside of the Esnoga, at least one of them for a Jewish patron.[18] As with his church interiors, de Witte took a little licence. Fashionably dressed women stroll and socialise downstairs; the odd dog, standard staffage, does, even in the precincts of the Esnoga, what dogs will do. It is perhaps one of the many scenes of tourist visits since the Esnoga had now become even more of an obligatory stop for visitors than its predecessors had been. Complaints were constantly being made to the *ma'amad* of congregants jumping up from their seats to welcome Gentile visitors into the beautiful space. The mutual affinity would stay this way in the Netherlands for generation after generation. The Esnoga and the Ashkenazi *shul* were an integral part of the neighbourhood, part of the city; which was why, when the Nazis began their round-ups in 1940, Gentile neighbours, dockers and other workers put themselves in mortal peril by going on strike.

Only one fixture of the Amsterdam Sephardim was missing from all this, though in a sense he was there by architectural proxy: Jacob Judah Leon Templo. Beautiful hand-coloured prints, newly made by Jacob de Geurs for Templo, had been consulted, and the curved buttresses dominating the exterior walls of Solomon's house of God were repeated, albeit in a minor key and mostly ornamentally, on the exterior walls of the Esnoga where they met the ground.[19] Templo must have been satisfied to see the stones fashioned this way since his fortune if not his fame had waned somewhat. He had been making ends meet by teaching at the Etz Hayim school as the successor to Menasseh ben Israel, but from the fact that many pupils opted for private lessons from someone else, his heart could hardly have been in it. In 1661 he was forbidden, understandably, from opening his Temple model to paying visitors on a Saturday![20] Increasingly he was looking beyond Amsterdam, beyond the republic for attention – and remuneration. His last published work was a Spanish-language edition of the Psalms: suitable for the international Sephardi community. And he may have sensed that interest in his Temple model was keener on the other side of the North Sea, especially among fellows of the Royal Society in London. In 1674, his old Hebrew pupil Constantijn Huygens, now in his seventies, but still a force, sent a letter of introduction to Christopher Wren, himself very much in the temple business, and a prolific modeller. Wren was asked to arrange for the model and its maker to be shown around to members of the Royal Society, the Archbishop of Canterbury and the court of Charles II.[21] Together with his family, Templo made the trip to England to be present at the exhibition of his model, which is said to have caused a great stir among savants, scientists and the public. It may, in fact, have been the spur for Isaac Newton to have embarked on a weighty, multi-year project about the Solomonic Temple which resulted in learned publications on the measurement of the biblical cubit, a commentary on Ezekiel's description, and much else amounting to an obsession which endured right through to the 1720s when another model, that of Gerhard Schott, was exhibited in London.[22] In the summer of 1675, Templo returned, alone, to Amsterdam for reasons unknown, but perhaps feeling mortal and wanting to end up in the House of Life at Ouderkerk, where indeed he did, in July, just a few weeks before the Esnoga owing much to his model was formally opened.

The model itself remained in England where it was reported to be still on show in 1680. The scientist Robert Hooke recorded having long discussions with Isaac Newton about it.[23] In the middle of the following century it was much admired by British Freemasons whose whole cult was based on temple mysteries. In 1771 a newspaper in The Hague reported it was being shown there, evidently with an eye to a sale as the notice ended 'This Temple can be purchased by anybody interested'. Apparently there were no takers, as in 1778 it was back in England owned by one M. P. Decastro, accompanied by a new English edition of Templo's book, titled *An accurate description of the grand and glorious Temple of Solomon*. There are speculative notes locating it, from time to time, both in Holland and England, but it has been lost from view. It would be good if someone found it under some dust sheet and brought it back to the city which, for its maker at any rate, was his own Jerusalem: Amsterdam, Ha-Makom, The Place.

MEETINGS OF MINDS

I. Ruins

It was when the rabbi carried the Torah scrolls into the women's section of the Frankfurt *shul* that the congregation knew something dramatic was in the offing. Such a shock – but he was Judah Ha-Hasid, revered and righteous, so no one thought to stop him. It was 1700 and Shabbes Hagadol, the Great Sabbath, the last before Passover, a day reserved for the most momentous utterances. Standing on the reading dais, the *bimah*, the folds of his prayer shawl wrapped about him, Judah Ha-Hasid did not disappoint. Prepare yourselves, he said, the end of days is coming; and with it the Moshiakh, the Messiah. Shabbetai, may his name be blotted out, had been a curse and a trial. This time was different. He had consulted the calendar with the utmost scrupulousness and there was no mistake. They should make atonement and come with him to the Land of Israel where the Almighty's promises would at last be fulfilled. It would be this year, not the next in Jerusalem. A house had been bought that would be their synagogue in Zion; lodgings would be ready to receive them. Come.

There was some shoulder-shrugging, eye-rolling. But others let the excitement take them. Suppose the *rebbe* really was the prophet, the herald. What was so wonderful about Frankfurt that they should stay? True, Jews had lived there continuously for centuries but what did one see now? An antheap, a dunghill, five hundred families, the most the regulation of 1616 would allow, crammed into the Judengasse; two thousand, three thousand souls. They had implored the elders of the imperial city to allow a little more breathing space but all in vain. A ghetto was a ghetto. The Jews were forbidden to leave on Sundays,

were kept off the highways, penned inside their warren-world of dirt
and pickles. As their numbers grew, the houses on each side of the
Judengasse were sliced down the middle, making four rows of lodgings on the street. The only direction for building was up, so up the
houses went, pushing out a bit, the timbered overhangs reaching so
far into the street that they all but touched. Year by year, the lit space
on the street below shrank before the shadows. Closeness should have
bred caution. Anyone in the top storeys getting up to no good and
pretty soon the whole Judengasse knew about it. Closed shutters
turned loose talk into certainty and an outbreak of Yiddish nodding
when the women took the stew to the bakers' ovens on Friday afternoon. Closeness bred scandal but also disease. The music of the
Judengasse was coughing. Rooms on the inside now had little or no
air. But still the births came with a faster tempo than the deaths. God
must have wanted it thus.

More mouths to feed in the Judengasse, then. The regulation
allowing for the five hundred families also precluded their working in
any of the occupations controlled by the guilds. So there were no
artisans or even retail shops outside the ghetto. It was wholesale as
usual, but a living could be made from cloth, grain, wax, and then,
as everywhere, old clothes, moneylending, pawnbroking. There were
also the butchers and slaughterers, the *mohels*, the matchmakers, the
teachers at the *beit midrash*, and always on the corners like a rash that
never went away the *schnorrers*, the beggars, *pfuey*. But even they were
a notch above *Beteljuden* out in the country; armies of them, no better
than gypsies, but more pitiful and more dangerous: houseless, lawless,
filthy, stinking, lousy, covered in sores, rags falling off them, the blind
stumbling with their sticks, the rest shuffling from place to place, a
step ahead of the watch who made sure they were kept from their
town. Dogs barked and snapped at their footfall until they melted into
the forest or the swamps. Pushed to the last extremity, beggar-parents
would sell their children to whoever would take them for servants,
scrub them down and set them to work. But then you never knew
what you were getting. In 1773, the lawyer for a fifteen-year-old girl,
who had murdered the master to whom she'd been sold, defended
her by painting a picture of her destitute plight. She was just one of
those *Beteljuden*, trudging the highways, packs on their humps, indistinguishable from cattle.[1]

So, please, again, what was so wonderful about the Judengasse that it should keep them from Zion? There was another reason, too, for the Frankfurt Jews to assume their lot might not improve any time soon – not in the Ashkenazi world anyway. At the same time that Judah Ha-Hasid was delivering his message, the first copies of Johann Eisenmenger's two-volume treatise *Entdecktes Judenthum* (*Judaism Unmasked*), published in their own city, were appearing. The book was all the more poisonous for appearing under the guise of erudition. Eisenmenger was an authentic Hebraist, a professor at Heidelberg, and had assiduously carved his way through Talmud and *midrash* hunting for evidence out of the mouths of the Jews themselves that they were the spawn of Satan, incorrigibly devoted to the destruction of Christians and Christianity. Should Christ come again, they would be eager to crucify him a second time. Though the rabbis professed not to proselytise, it had been the case of three Christians converted to Judaism in Amsterdam which had triggered Eisenmenger's fury in the first place, and the upshot of his work, which recycled all the most grotesque libels about Jewish infanticide, was that there was no living with those people. They were human contaminants, walking infec-tions, vermin on two legs. This was why the Egyptians had rid them-selves of their presence and why they needed to be cast out from Christian communities, reduced to only the most beggarly and degrading occupations, and the synagogues closed down. It was the old argument of Paul IV's 1555 bull *Cum nimis absurdum* restated for the baroque age. And in the face of all the efforts by Jews and their Christian illustrators in Holland to humanise their rituals and religion, Eisenmenger had demonised them more exhaustively than anyone since Martin Luther.

Why not go, then? Some of Frankfurt's Jews began to prepare for departure. Property and possessions were sold off. A room or two became available and the rush created the usual buyer's market. Judah Ha-Hasid, who had come from Poland, now went on his way, spreading the word through Brandenburg, Saxony, Bohemia, Moravia.[2] A small army of followers devoted themselves to the rituals of penance, even more extreme than in the days of Shabbetai Zevi. They looked for ponds still as cold as if spring had never come, and plunged deep until they went blue and shivered with contrition. They obeyed the Hasid's command to forgo their beds. Why sleep, when they could pray and

study? If they must slumber then it should be on the bare floorboards
or the stony ground. The truly repentant would not need more than
two days of sleep a week, nor for that matter would they need food,
certainly nothing that had come from animals, neither meat nor milk.
Never mind if it was Passover, there could be no butter with their dry
matzo. Hunger was the handmaid of vision.

A *chevrah*, an association of friends committed to the great journey
to Zion, was formed across the German-speaking lands and further
east. Some of those in the more populous towns appointed emissaries
to the Ashkenazi world. Organised and scripted by the Hasid's deputy,
Hayim Melech, they appeared before their fellow Jews in white satin
robes raising hopes and money. By the time they were ready to depart,
half of them from Venice, half from Constantinople, the *chevrah*
numbered seventeen hundred souls. Their numbers dwindled from
sickness, and disenchantment on the way to Zion: but even the thousand who arrived in October 1700 suddenly doubled the size of the
indigenous Jewish population of Jerusalem. Studious, chronically
impoverished, and suspicious of yet another caravan of messianic
pilgrims, the locals sighed at the incoming enthusiasts with familiar
resignation. They knew trouble when they saw it.

Six days after the arrival in Jerusalem, Judah Ha-Hasid dropped
dead. He had not been sick. He was not improbably old. Now he
joined the list of the pious sages who had barely survived the realisation of their dream, above all the rabbi said to be his ancestor, Moshe
ben Nahman, 'Nahmanides', the champion of Judaism in the
Barcelona disputation of 1263. The new *shul* was close to the medieval
'Ramban' where the memory of Nahmanides was perpetuated. Now
patriarch and prophet were reunited in the afterlife while the Hasid's
little flock swayed in baffled despair at the latest caprice of the incomprehensible Almighty.

The rest of the story was predictable. Anguish turned to anxiety;
destitution gnawed at their empty bellies. They grew hollow-eyed and
frightened. The children cried without cease. Hayim Melech turned
out to be king in name only. Debts were incurred; taxes imposed by
the Turkish authorities fell due and could not be paid. Neither shouting
nor prison could shake the money out of them for there was nothing
to be shaken out. Many tried to find a way back to Frankfurt and
Prague and Posen and Breslau. Others stayed put, turning to Islam

or the Church, whichever could best save them. The *shul* fell into disrepair and was left to its own ruin for another 140 years when a new cohort of pious Zionists rebuilt and revived it in the middle of the nineteenth century. That synagogue, known as the 'Hurva', or ruin, was comprehensively ruined again by the Jordanian army during the war of 1948. Its latest edition has only recently been opened, amid bitter controversy between the ultra-ultra Orthodox who have taken possession of it and the 'modern' (not quite so ultra-ultra) Orthodox who resent their exclusion, and of course between all of the above and the Jerusalem Palestinians resentful at seeing a new synagogue rising in the heart of the Old City and who believe it to be another act in the plot to build a Third Temple on the Haram al-Sharif.

There were other princes in Israel but in 1700 they too were beset by ruin. Around the time Judah Ha-Hasid was leading his thousand to Zion, the handsome *Residenz* of Samuel Oppenheimer on the Bauernmarkt in Vienna was being torn to pieces. A mob of enraged artisans, led by a sword cutler and a chimney sweep, shouted that the Jews were driving the Viennese to the wall. Oppenheimer – the *Hoffude*, the 'court Jew' – had taken over the empire and the emperor. He drove around in a coach and four, his coat of arms painted on its panels, while honest Christians starved. Even worse, it was rumoured that the Jew was in league with the Turk. So the Oppenheimer mansion, rising above the stalls of the vegetable sellers, was ransacked, picked clean of its offending gold plate and silver candlesticks. Tapestries and drapes too bulky even for the waiting carts were slashed, shredded, danced on with muddy boots; broken china landed among the turnips. Oppenheimer wines flowed down the gullets of the rioters who pulled faces at themselves in ormolu-framed mirrors, their surfaces webbed with cudgel-cracks.

The object of the violence escaped down a tunnel expressly built for such contingencies. When the furore had died down Oppenheimer's patron and erstwhile protector, the Holy Roman Emperor Leopold I, saw to it that the sword cutler and the chimney sweep were hanged. Not that he cared so terribly much about the Jew, but disorder had a way of spreading. Just a year earlier there had been serious peasant unrest. They had taken it out on the Jews of rural Franconia but you never knew where it would end. Oberkriegsfaktor Oppenheimer was no fool. He knew the cutler and the sweep were culprits of

convenience and that those who now affected to execute justice had
had a hand in the crime. The timing of the riot had not been a coincidence. He was owed a lot of money, 200,000 florins, by way of
reimbursement for sums already paid to his subcontractors. Did the
gentlemen of the council think horses and wagons, rye, wheat and
milled flour, cannon and powder, muskets and carbines, grenades and
balls, coats, hats and boots grew on trees? If the emperor wanted to
do battle with Louis XIV, year after year, someone had to provide,
and he had done so. Now he applied to the Hofkammer for repayment as contractually promised. But the *Finanzminister* shrugged,
raised his empty palms and said *entschuldigen Sie mich*, but there were
still troops in the field and he had not a groschen to spare. Ah, a
default then, a repudiation. Such nice consciences they had while they
accused the Jews of double-dealing. He had seen this before. Ten years
earlier he had been owed a cool 5 million and they had palmed him
off. As then, word would spread, subcontractors would be left high
and dry and there would be a pretty panic on the Bourse. As he had
done once before, Oppenheimer wrote directly to the emperor but
was informed by return that he was labouring under a misapprehension. Jews owed the realm, not the other way round. Samuel's enemies
were everywhere. Cardinal Kollonitsch, a Jew-hater, had not forgiven
the collapse of his own consortium of Catholic bankers. The attack
on Oppenheimer's house was meant as an instructive reminder that
should the presumptuous Jew persist, life could get worse. He already
knew what it was like to be in an Austrian prison, for just three years
earlier he and his son Emanuel had been arrested on a trumped-up
charge of plotting to murder his rival Samson Wertheimer.

Like the repeated messianic disappointments, the ruin of
Oppenheimer was an old Jewish story. The court Jews of the baroque
were merely the latest edition of what had begun in the medieval
centuries. Through long-distance, extended-family trade connections,
Jews had been able to secure small-bulk, high-value merchandise like
gems and spices and bring them to market at large profit, amassing
capital. The high rates charged by Christian moneylenders and the
official Church disapproval of interest had helped give them an advantage over the loan competition and they could offer upfront revenue
in return for profitable tax farms and customs. There were incalculable
risks, however. They knew from repeated experience that at any

moment their debts might be repudiated, their property confiscated, they or their heirs dispossessed or imprisoned, whenever it happened to suit the indebted ruler. Yet they continued to offer their services, since for every Jew Suess Oppenheimer, hanged to general public rejoicing in Württemberg when his ducal patron died (fine coins and medals were struck with the noose around the Jew's neck), there were many success stories of bankers and mint masters who survived the perils to become stupendously rich. And even the lesser among them enjoyed special privileges of residence and travel, and might be granted exemption from the taxes which weighed on lower-ranked Jews.

The needs of princes – armies, citadels and palaces – had not changed from the Gothic to the baroque centuries. But the scale of those demands had. By the middle of the seventeenth century the Habsburgs, both in Austria and Spain, had finally abandoned the campaign launched by Charles V a century earlier to crush the Protestant heresy and reunite Christendom in a crusade against the Turks. By 1700 no one imagined a confessional reunification. But intra-Christian war had barely ended before it was replaced by armed mercantilism. Its working premise was zero-sum-game macroeconomics; the last stage of competitive asset-counting before the gods of infinitely elastic growth came to rule the world. In the view that held sway for a century or so between 1650 and 1780, there was a fixed amount of treasure to be had in the world, and woe betide the realm that failed to use pre-emptive force if necessary to maximise or increase its share. Wealth might be aggregated in population, land, slaves, capital, gold, ships, merchandise, mines, manufactures. Predator dynasties – the Swedes, the Prussian Hohenzollerns, the Bourbons – eyed their competitors, ready to pounce on the weak, or the easily surprised. Barren queens heralded a war of dynastic succession, each of the big players putting up proxies. Action was power. To sit still was to die slowly.

Thus was the baroque arms race launched and the bills were steep. Vauban, Louis XIV's great military engineer, had transformed defensive architecture, but arrowhead bastions, their walls thicker and more impenetrable than anything yet seen, came with an extravagant price tag. In turn they brought on the design of monstrous siege artillery. Armies tripled, quadrupled in size; warships and their armaments competed to outdo each other in broadside power. All this happened at exactly the same time that the economic destruction inflicted by decades of war, the reduction of territories to burnt waste and half-demolished cities, meant that the conventionally liable – bonded peasantries and their landlords – were unequal to the needed revenues. Aggravating the logistical squeeze was the irritating habit of noble 'estates' denying a king or a margrave the resources he needed to pull his weight amid the contending warrior states. The notion that were the prince so minded he might use his firepower to reduce them to political impotence was on the mind of those gatherings of aristocrats who could dig in their heels and starve the princes of funds. There was only so much a ruler, desperate for his own knock-off of Versailles, plus a train of heavy artillery, could do. Yet without the gilt and the grenadiers he would be unable to look his rivals in the eye.

Enter the Jew. Enter Oppenheimer, or 'Samuel O' as they addressed him in the chancelleries, *Hofoberfaktor* and then *Oberkriegsfaktor* to the Holy Roman Emperor Leopold I. Enter, also, the Amsterdam firm of Machado and Pereyra which provided the same services for William III's invasion of England in 1688, followed by his campaign on the Boyne against the Irish–French Catholic army of his father-in-law, James II. Then enter, right on cue: Solomon Medina who subsidised the campaigns of the Duke of Marlborough in the War of the Spanish Succession against Louis XIV; the Gumpertz family of Cleves, court Jews and mint masters to the Hohenzollern Great Elector of Brandenburg-Prussia; the two successive husbands of Esther (née Schulhof) of Prague, Israel Aaron and Jost Liebmann, who fed King Frederick of Prussia's jewellery habit and his insatiable craving for palatial luxuries of every kind; also Berend Lehmann who paid for Augustus the Strong's eye-popping palace the Zwinger in Dresden, complete with grottos, bathing pools, a mass of pompous statuary; and many more.[3] The princes to whom the Jews delivered the funds with which to make war over so long a period included the Lutheran Prussians, Calvinist William and Holy Roman Leopold. There were all sorts of reasons for the hard-pressed finance ministers of the German states to prefer Jews over the Swiss or Huguenots. Their rates of interest could be pegged at no more than 6 per cent, and could be forced down further. Repayment of principal could be extended from generously long terms to never. They had a convenient habit of feuding with each other, so that one factor's rejection would be another's opportunity. And through their long-distance networks, sometimes of families, sometimes just through counterparts in remote Ashkenazi communities and ports from Ukraine to Denmark, they could, at relatively short notice, supply military quantities of Dutch cloth, Bohemian saltpetre and Polish grain.

Until his fortune ran out in 1700, Samuel O had repeatedly come to the aid of the Habsburg emperor. In 1683, with the Ottoman troops of Kara Mustafa at the gates of Vienna, his services made the difference between resistance and catastrophe. Oppenheimer, who had been publicly reviled and displaced in favour of a syndicate of Catholic bankers, delivered when clerically anointed funds failed. His bravura portrait is a breathtaking study in self-advertisement, unprecedented in Jewish iconography. There stands the great siege-breaker, a cross between a rabbi and a field marshal, pointing to all he commands: powder and mortars, muskets and, most brazenly of all, the helmet usually associated with sovereignty and a paper bearing the double-headed eagle of the Habsburgs.

But the boast was made good by the deed. Samuel O mobilised fleets of river rafts and barges to transport troops, draught animals and artillery down the Danube to beleaguered fortresses in Hungary. Floating pens of cattle, sheep and poultry honked, bleated and squawked their way along the river en route to their appointment with the regimental spits and pots. Cantonments and barracks were supplied with bread, ammunition and bandages. Sabres, muskets, cannon and pistols, powder and shot, slow fuses and short, even matches and tinder, all materialised as if by magic. In one week in February 1683, Oppenheimer's son managed to raise one hundred and fifty horses, and five hundred more by March. Twenty-six thousand grenades alone were delivered to the great encampment at Linz. The Oppenheimer fleet with crews of fifty and more sailed the northern and southern seas until it found what was needed. Above all, he was able to get his hands on the most precious commodity of all, the one which really determined the outcome of war: oats. No oats, no cavalry. No oats, no artillery wagons. No oats, and the army might as well surrender and go home. Indeed when Oppenheimer's oat supply faltered from a subcontractor's delay and he was forced to look beyond his usual suppliers in a hurry, the advance of a whole imperial army division stalled. Fifteen thousand

pecks were eventually produced. The most exquisitely plotted stratagems would all collapse for want of oats.

By the time the king of France replaced the Ottoman sultan as the
primary enemy, Jewish money was routinely factored into strategic
calculations. Whatever the misgivings of the Church, and indeed the
emperor himself, his great marshal, Prince Eugene of Savoy, knew
that when the niggardly English Parliament refused him subsidies he
could always count on the Jew. When the War of the Spanish
Succession began in 1701, the Austrian government turned to
Oppenheimer yet again and once more he obliged them. On his death
in 1703, his former erstwhile employee and junior partner Samson
Wertheimer, who had become a deadly rival, stepped forward in
Oppenheimer's stead. Oppenheimer's son Emanuel staggered on with
the family business, until the systematic bad faith perpetrated by
governments broke him. When he died in 1721, his widow, denied the
automatic inheritance of his right of residence, was ordered to leave
Vienna forthwith.

Sobered by the vicissitudes of his old patron, Wertheimer was
nervous about military contracts. But if he was to retain imperial
favour, they were unavoidable. The letter of appointment described
him as 'industrious, indefatigable, efficient, loyal and selfless', which
really meant he could be depended on to advance a million florins
up front as long as the empire was at war, which seemed likely to
be forever.[4] As the personal banker of the Hungarian Esterhazy
dynasty at Eisenstadt, forty miles south of Vienna, Wertheimer had
developed a reputation for managerial probity and, more important,
an unfailing ability to come up with the cash. The fact that he was
also acknowledged as chief rabbi (*Grandrabbiner*) of Hungary, Moravia
and Bohemia, a deliverer of trenchant sermons, somehow translated
into a reputation for managerial integrity. His businesses were legion.
He exploited the salt mines at Siebenburg and the tobacco monopoly
in the Balkans, becoming in effect a one-man department of state
for the Habsburg emperors. Wertheimer could be depended on to
pay the cost of foreign embassies abroad, but also he would lean on
the right people when an expensive dowry was required to cement
a diplomatic marriage alliance, extricate the empress from the usual
web of debt, or pay for the fireworks, the music and the processions
of an imperial coronation. When Charles VI succeeded his brother

Joseph I as emperor in 1711, Wertheimer and his son were invited to
the festivities. They had, after all, paid for them. All the same, it was
something: the two Jews in their rabbinical black silks and skullcaps,
amid the ocean of jewellery, the cascades of lace, the swords, canes
and plumed hats of four thousand aristocrats.

In Vienna, Prague, Frankfurt and Eisenstadt, Wertheimer came to
be regarded as a treasury of wisdom as well as hard cash. So much
so that Leopold presented the Jew with his portrait in imperial robes
as a condescending gesture of appreciation. This may have given
Samson Wertheimer the idea of following suit, making sure to pose
in the robes and beard of a rabbi, holding a letter. He had become,
in effect, the heir to the long tradition of the *resh galuta* (leader of the
exile), the *nasi* and the *shtadlan* – protector of the Jews in times of
difficulty, which were never far away. While Oppenheimer had tried
to use his financial leverage to have Eisenmenger's *Judaism Unmasked*
suppressed, it was the more diplomatic Wertheimer who initially
succeeded in the campaign. But the book's appeal to German readers
had become so widespread that it was republished in Berlin in 1711.[5]

For all the periodic expulsions, abuse and assaults, Wertheimer
continued to believe in a Jewish future in the Habsburg Empire. After
the Jews had been evicted from Eisenstadt, during the insurrection of
the Hungarian gentry in 1708, Wertheimer persuaded them to return
to the town, and built a private synagogue at his house accessible for
their use. Damaged by a fire in 1795, it was rebuilt in the 1830s in the
restrained classical style that is still visible. In November 1938, when
the incinerations of Kristallnacht, abetted by the many Austrian enthusiasts of the recent *Anschluss* union with the Third Reich, destroyed
the principal synagogue of the town, the Wertheimer *shul* somehow
escaped, possibly because it was on the first floor of the old house.
Its congregation did not have such a lucky reprieve from the flames.
Now it functions as a place of ghostly piety: the Jewish Historical
Museum of Austria.[6]

Both inside the Jewish world and without, Wertheimer came to be
known as the Kaiser der Juden, the Emperor of the Jews. It was not
invariably a compliment. There were those at court and in the high
reaches of the Church who sneered at his pretensions, and resented
his power. Though they knew they could bring him down with a
stroke of their pen, they also knew that this would be imprudent. His

treasure chest paid for topiary avenues, hunting lodges and enfiladed state rooms down which awed ambassadors trod before reaching their audience with the enthroned.

In the limited number of imperial cities open to them, Jews had a more complicated feeling about Samson Wertheimer. They deferred to the rabbi-banker, and yet envied and often resented the exclusiveness of his privileges. But they knew they couldn't do without the *Hofjude*. Once the Protected Jew had the goodwill of a ruler, it was extended to the handful of useful Jews permitted to reside in Berlin or Budapest, Vienna or Prague, albeit usually subject to punishing special taxes and the exclusion from most occupations. So the court Jews, urban feudalists, lorded it over their co-religionists as benevolent despots and sometimes overplayed their hand. In 1684 Jost Liebmann was given licence to build Berlin's first synagogue inside his palatial house. Jews had been allowed to reside in the city since 1671, though without permission to build any places of public worship. But the expulsion from Vienna a year earlier prompted the Elector to think he might attract Jews to his city by offering them the right to open a private synagogue in one of their houses. No sooner had Liebmann taken advantage of this permission than a rival faction wondered out loud why it too should not have the same privilege. Theirs? I wouldn't be seen dead in it. Feuding between the competitors became so bitter that the authorities had to step in and pacify the disputants. After Liebmann died in 1702, the management of the family firm fell to his widow Esther, like so many women of the period a formidable and active manager of the family firm, accustomed to accompanying her husband to the Leipzig Fair and doubtless driving a hard bargain. Esther was not happy to learn of yet a third project, organised by Markus Magnus, to construct a *public* synagogue meant for the whole community. She did her best to try and have the new king of Prussia, Frederick William, scotch the project, but because it was a Hohenzollern tradition to detest your father and because Frederick William particularly despised his paternal predecessor, the first King Frederick – a prime customer for the Liebmann gem business – the new monarch declined to ban the public synagogue. On the contrary, he looked forward to becoming its royal patron.

Esther died in 1714 in a state of chagrin, insolvency and the usual bone-picking squabbles of the heirs. The public synagogue went up

on the Heidereutergasse, close to the Spandauerstrasse where many
of the wealthy Berlin Jews lived but also very close to a church. When
foundation stones were laid, a special prayer for the king was inserted
into one of the masonry blocks. Two years later on New Year's Day
1714, the synagogue opened with the notoriously irritable monarch in
good-humoured and gracious attendance. While the exterior was
severely classical, the interior – designed by the Christian master
carpenter Michael Kemmeter, who had also decorated Berlin's
Lutheran Neue Kirche – was conceived and executed on a handsome
scale. Not surprisingly, then, the synagogue resembled a German
Protestant chapel, just as Elias Bouwman's Esnoga had drawn on the
lofty, light-filled churches of Amsterdam.[7] The Berlin place of worship
was long, tall and washed by light; the very opposite of the vaulted
cave-like prayer rooms of the German and Bohemian Middle Ages,
concerned most of all with shelter, modesty and a prudent low profile
amid a hostile and suspicious town.[8] The Heidereutergasse synagogue
was meant to make an impression. Ten gilded bronze chandeliers
hung from a ceiling forty feet above its floor. The windows were, in
the manner of the Protestant baroque, slender and arched. The
women's gallery had an elaborately carved balustrade screen from
which they could look down on the services and their fashionably
periwigged husbands. On entering from the street the eye was led
through the processional space where the Torah would be walked
towards the Ark, soaring two storeys and sprouting columns, cornices
and broken pediments. A steeply raked double flight of steps gave
those ascending for an *aliyah* the honours of the service: the opening
of the Ark doors, or the lifting of the Sefer Torah, a theatrical sense
of their own importance. It also conferred on those who assigned the
honours of the ascent a strong sense of their own standing in the
pecking order of the community.

No expense was spared for *hiddur mitzvah*, the 'glorification'
expanded by the Talmud from a mere exclamation in Exodus 15:2,
'this is my God and I will glorify Him', to mean beautification of holy
objects: the handsomest prayer shawl, the most finely wrought reading-
dais railings. For as long as there had been synagogues, stretching back
to late classical antiquity, the names of donors had appeared on the
floors and walls. Now they were woven into heavily brocaded Ark
curtains of silk damask, or into the Torah mantles. Though there was

a venerable goldsmithing tradition in Jewish culture, the demand for precious ritual object was so strong that Christian master craftsmen like Jeremiah Zobel in Frankfurt, Matthias Wolff in Augsburg and Johann Konrad Weiss in Nuremberg were given early commissions for parcel-gilt Torah breastplates, crowns and finials. Eventually, in northern Italy and Germany, Jewish craftsmen came to specialise in exuberant silverwork, fashioning the spectacular Torah crowns and *rimmonim* pomegranate finials, the cylindrical cases for Purim scrolls of Esther – often engraved with scenes from her scripture – Sabbath *kiddush* wine cups and the spice boxes used for the Havdalah ceremony that ended the Sabbath, all of which came to embody the shared glory of the community. The more scrolls you had in your Ark the better, every one of them preciously ornamented.[9]

The elders of these reborn communities in Germany, Bohemia and Hungary must have felt a natural fit between their own ceremonious-ness and that of their Christian neighbours. While absolutely faithful to Jewish traditions, their communal fellowships often imitated or echoed the guildsmen of the German towns.[10] So that the burial soci-eties, the *chevrah kadisha*, for example, organised elaborate processions bearing the dead to their resting place in the cemetery just beyond the city limits as prescribed by the Torah and Talmud, and then commemorated their communal fellowship in ornate silver goblets or loving cups, engraved with their names, or scenes from a burial, from which each officer would drink in an annual feast.[11]

All this showy ceremony – the stage-setting of the Torah readings, the happy self-importance of the *groyse makher*, the Big Shot – will be immediately familiar to modern Jews, other than those in the ultra-Orthodox communities where the more ascetic traditions of the eastern Hasidic shtetl still hold sway. But the grandeur of Ashkenazi Germany commenced with this trumpet flourish of the Jewish baroque. Exhilarated by the stupendous architecture, the sumptuous textiles, the flashing silver, the Ashkenazim of Prussia, Bohemia and Moravia allowed themselves to believe they had come into their own.

Until, that is, in December 1744, when the Habsburg empress Maria Theresa summarily ordered every last Jew to be out of Bohemia and Moravia by the end of the following January.

The edict fell like a hammer blow on the 30,000 Jews of Prague. They were the heirs of their great sixteenth-century forebears:

Mordecai Maisel, who had built two synagogues and a town hall; of Rabbi Judah ben Loew, the mystical 'Maharal', from whose wheeling mind the Golem had been created, and who could exchange Kabbalistic speculations with the emperor Rudolf. Their presses had produced the first engraved Passover Haggadah. They made books, silver, music, philosophy, money. Somehow they had survived the ferocious wars between Christians during the seventeenth century. In 1689 an uncontrollable fire had burned down most of the old Jewish town. Slowly they had rebuilt, stone replacing the older timber firetraps. In keeping with municipal edicts the streets of the quarter were wider, straighter. It no longer felt like a ghetto.

Then the order to go; a reminder in the midst of their prosperity and confidence that, at any moment, they could be the victims of royal caprice. It made no difference at all that the empress's new palace of Schönbrunn had been financed by the Sephardi Baron d'Aguilar, whom she had ennobled and admitted, for the usual reasons of convenience, to her Council of Finance. What counted was that during wartime the Jews had done business with Prussian troops who had briefly occupied Prague in 1744.[12]

In fact, everyone else in Prague and through the towns and country of Bohemia and Moravia during that campaign had done the same, but it was only the Jews who were singled out for brutal punishment. Maria Theresa's own Judaeophobia was of ancient vintage and very deep. 'Her aversion at the sight of Jews', the British ambassador to Vienna Sir Thomas Robinson reported, 'is too great to be concealed.' Visiting Pressburg (now Bratislava) she was horrified at having to drive her coach through streets filled with Jews. The first order she gave on arriving in Prague was that no Jews were ever to be admitted anywhere within the palace precincts. The empress was so enthusiastic in Jew-hounding that she even offered uninvited help to the rulers of Italy to rid their domains of Jews.

The act was pitiless. By the terms of the decree of 18 December 1744, the Jews of Bohemia had six weeks to liquidate their livelihoods, sell or just abandon their homes and remove themselves from the kingdom. By 31 January 1745, it was emphasised, not a single Jew was to be present in Bohemia. All were to be thrown into the freezing winter of central Europe. 'What shall we poor souls do?' the elders of the community wrote, in a heart-rending appeal to their co-religionists throughout Europe. 'The children, women, infirm and aged are in no condition to walk especially now in the cold and frosty weather and besides ... many have been stripped to their shirts.'[13] The Prague elders asked for intercession with governments where Jews might have influence. 'Do it for the sake of the nine splendid synagogues; do it for the sake of our cemeteries with tombs of our saints who rest there, do it for our thirty or forty thousand souls who because of our sins are now in peril.'

Remarkably, at least some of those governments, particularly the Dutch and British, did express dismay to the imperial government through their embassies in Vienna. King George II was said to have been much moved by the plight of the expelled Jews recounted to him by Moses Hart and the eminences of the Duke's Place synagogue. The king directed Sir Thomas Robinson to request that, at the very least, the execution of the edict be delayed until the weather improved. The protests worked to the extent that the January deadline was relaxed, but by the time spring buds appeared, the machinery of expulsion was revived. Through late spring and summer, the Jews of Prague traipsed miserably out from their city home, leaving behind them all those fine buildings, the empty synagogues. An unsympathetic canard had them taking windows and doors with them in hopes of a return. If only that were true. Another letter from the evicted wrote poignantly of their 'wandering from town to town ... the sick sent over the whole countryside, till they reached a lazaretto since the Jews have no permission to bring their sick into any towns ... many die in carriages and on the roads and those who survive, on arrival at that place (the leper house) have scarcely a breath in their bodies and are glad to find a grave'.[14]

By 1747, what had been one of the most flourishing Jewish communities in Europe was in a state of physical as well as social ruin: houses pillaged of anything that could be taken; others simply stove in and destroyed; the synagogues looted. For all their representations, foreign governments had been able to do little to change the empress's mind about the Jews or the decree, though when the British ambassador threatened to end all financial assistance to the Habsburg armies, she did pay attention. But it was rather complaints of their collapsing economy from the non-Jewish townspeople in Prague and the other cities which moved Maria Theresa to allow a select number of Jews back (at the usual steep price) in 1748. As the War of the Austrian Succession ended others followed and gradually, as was their wont, the Jews found a way to repair their fortunes, their culture and their lives. A second great fire, in 1754, set everything back but in the next decade the synagogues were restored and redecorated in Judaeo-rococo. Maisel's town hall, standing next to the Altneuschul, was one of those buildings and it was now given a fine gabled baroque clock tower, the first thing visiting tourists notice about Jewish Prague. Famously it bears two faces, one with Roman numerals, the hands sweeping in the usual direction, the other bearing Hebrew numbers, running anticlock-wise, back to the future. Whatever else they had learned, the Jews of Prague knew it was a good idea to hedge your bets.

II. Walks in the Garden

Can the reappearance of a book trigger a cultural revolution? It could when it was the *Guide for the Perplexed* of Moses Maimonides, the medieval physician-philosopher. Originally written in Arabic, then translated into Hebrew by Samuel ibn Tibbon, it had been immediately denounced by the severest rabbis for applying Greek logic to the immaculately revealed Torah. The critics had it banned, and in some places, burned. The *Guide for the Perplexed* had survived in Tibbon's version and in an early-sixteenth-century Latin translation.[15] For centuries Hebrew publishers shunned the *Guide* yet it remained the lodestar for Jews struggling to convince themselves of the compatibility of faith and reason. Such Maimonideans thought it possible to doubt whether the sun had really stood still at Joshua's command until he had polished off the Amorites, while remaining faithful to Torah Judaism. In fact, along with Maimonides they were certain that the reasoning faculty exalted, rather than betrayed, their religion. Everything that mattered could be rationally justified. Rightly or wrongly the *Guide* was the work which in the minds of its devotees separated the mechanically obedient from the thoughtful Jew. For those who had not read it, however, it was a wicked sower of doubt, the first step on the road to assimilation. It was too dangerous to be

at large. The twenty-five-year-old Lithuanian Jew Shlomo Yehoshua
found this out the hard way. In 1778 he came to Berlin where he hoped
to become yet another philosophically minded physician. When interrogated about his intentions at a poorhouse on Rosenthaler Gate
which acted as a holding pen for the scrutinised, 'filled with the sick
and a lewd rabble', Shlomo made the mistake of telling the examining
rabbi that he was working on a new edition, with commentary, of
the *Guide for the Perplexed*. He could scarcely contain his enthusiasm
for encountering true, Jewish, philosophy. The discovery, he wrote,
could only 'be compared to a man who, having been long famished
suddenly comes upon a well-stocked table and attacks the food with
violent greed, even to the point of surfeit'.[16]

But instead of the expected commendation, the young man received
a flea in his ear and a boot out of the door. No heretics were wanted
in Jewish Berlin. Thunderstruck at the rejection, Shlomo's distress was
aggravated by an overseer of the almshouse who ushered him out of
the city gate.

> There I threw myself on the ground and began to weep bitterly. It was
> Sunday and many people went as usual to walk just outside the city.
> Most of them paid no attention to a whining worm like me but some
> compassionate souls were struck by the spectacle and asked the cause
> of my wailing. I answered them, but partly because of my unintelligible
> accent, partly because my speech was broken by sobbing, they could
> not understand what I was saying.

These hysterics disarmed the overseer, who brought the lachrymose
young man back for a brief reprieve, where despair brought on a raging
fever. Shlomo shivered and shook. But as soon as the symptoms subsided,
the wandering pedlar of dangerous notions was thrown on the road
again together with his subversive manuscript. When he returned many
years later, he had become convinced that an obtuse despotism was
ruling the lives of religious Jews and that he would never grovel to the
ignorant and the fearful. As the declared enemy of 'superstition', he
now added the name of his hero to his own, and lived out the remainder
of his dramatic, tortured life as Solomon Maimon.[17]

The copy of the *Guide* which got him into trouble at the Rosenthaler
Gate must have been the two-volume quarto version of Tibbon's

translation published in 1742 in Jessnitz, the first modern edition to break the centuries-long stretch of non-appearance. It was printed at the Hebrew press founded by Moses Benjamin Wulff, banker to the court of Saxony-Anhalt. Jessnitz was close to the neighbouring town of Dessau where there was a lively and growing Ashkenazi community.[18] The local rabbi there was David Fraenkel, who preached in Wulff's house synagogue and whom no one could accuse of fashionable scepticism. Fraenkel's chosen field of commentary was the Jerusalem Talmud, second fiddle in the lexicon of rabbinic commentary to the more widely followed Babylonian Talmud. When it came to matters concerning Temple sacrifice, Fraenkel thought, the Jerusalem corpus must have been closer to memories of the original rituals. This conviction launched him on a discussion of the minute prescriptions surrounding the animal sacrifice, the *korban*, and which blemishes might rule a beast out and which not. Such compulsive fastidiousness was deemed the mark of a serious Talmudist. Yet at the same time Fraenkel was also a staunch Maimonidean. Three years before the reappearance of the *Guide*, he had supervised a new edition of the philosopher's *Mishneh Torah*, his digest of Jewish law, through the Jessnitz press. It was a kite flown for the more daring project of the *Guide*.

As it happened, the rabbi of Dessau had a young pupil on fire with curiosity: Moses Mendelssohn, a small, intense, eager boy, the son of Mendel Heimann, Torah scribe and *shammes* in the local synagogue. Recognising the boy's gift for learning, Fraenkel had sped him through the early stages of religious instruction and had introduced him to the works of Maimonides. As the lad grew more avid for learning, his poor father, finding himself with more mouths to feed than money to support them, grew ever poorer. So when David Fraenkel received a call to Berlin, to occupy the grandest post imaginable – the rabbinate of the synagogue in the Heidereutergasse, together with a commission to create a yeshiva for the rapidly expanding community – it seemed a fine idea to ask Mendel's son to follow him. The rabbi would further the boy's studies, fulfil his promise; why would the father stand in the son's way? Berlin meant not just another chapter of religious education but something even more tantalising: advancement through social connections. Moses' mother, Bela Rachel, would have been particularly conscious of this, since on one side she was a descendant of the great

sixteenth-century religious scholar Moses Isserles, and on the other
had family connections to Moses Benjamin Wulff. She may have called
her son Moses after Wulff, as the great man had died just days before
the boy's birth. A family tale had it that Wulff had been exiled from
Berlin by being on the loser's end of a feud between himself and the
competition: Jost and Esther Liebmann. On one occasion, comically
disastrous, the bad feeling had deteriorated into a full-on beard-pulling
fight between the two *Hofjuden*, and even this might have been a
forgettable and forgivable lapse had the fisticuffs not taken place in
the house of the Prussian director of finances. Judged the guiltier
party and banished from the city and the kingdom of Prussia, Moses
Wulff had made repeated applications to return to Berlin, for Dessau
was too small a pond for so big a fish, but was thwarted on every
attempt. If the great man himself could not get back to the city, then
at least protégés like Fraenkel might establish a presence there.

After the doughty Esther Liebmann passed away, Wulff connections
remaining in the city made it easier for Rabbi Fraenkel to return to
Berlin. It helped that David Fraenkel's brother-in-law was Veitel
Ephraim, a formidable money-lord, one of the grandest of the *Hofjuden*
in all the German lands. It was through him that Fraenkel got his own
appointment. Like his predecessors, Veitel Ephraim had begun as
jeweller to the Hohenzollerns, continued as mint master to the
Prussian Crown, and financier of Frederick the Great's undeclared but
mischievously effective attack on the Habsburg province of Silesia in
1740. Frederick did not much care for Jews, however rich or however
learned. He and Voltaire, for a while his house intellectual, may have
enjoyed a shared snigger at their expense, since the philosopher, ostensibly the apostle of toleration, was virulently allergic to Hebrews. But
given the scope of his vaulting ambitions, Frederick was resigned to
the fact that the Jews were disagreeably indispensable. Veitel Ephraim
and his partner Daniel Itzig profited from the military urgencies of
the Prussian state, and especially following the Seven Years War (1756–63)
rose to extraordinary power and status. Veitel Ephraim lived in princely
style in his house on the Spandauerstrasse, and before long would
build himself a summer house at the Schiffbauerdamm by the Spree
(not far from the present theatre of the Berliner Ensemble). There he
grew hothouse oranges and peaches and gazed at the gliding swans.
Itzig was even more grandiose, knocking down a row of houses

on the Kopernikusstrasse to make a single grand residence, impru-
dently described as 'royal' and which boasted a private synagogue,
plumbed bathrooms and a music chamber. Outdoing his partner he
had the landscape architect Heydert lay out gardens where an orchard
of a thousand fruit trees rioted in blossom come the Berlin Maytime,
while mourning doves moaned Jewishly on the branches. In due course
Itzig would build a dairy farm next door with a pavilion for his son
Isaac Daniel who, in the pastoral manner recommended by Rousseau,
was a periodic rusticator. So convenient, a downtown farm, delivering
daily butter and cream to the Itzig kosher kitchens! But the urban
cowherds were outnumbered by a whole army of perruquier-barbers,
tailors, coachmen, grooms, footmen, postilions, musicians, tutors and
secretaries. Unlike the older generation of Oppenheimers and the
Wertheimers who made sure to present a rabbinical appearance for
the portrait painters, Daniel Itzig and Veitel Ephraim shaved and wore
perfectly powdered and curled bag wigs or tie wigs, a little gold thread
sewn to the velvet: the very picture of modern Jews.[19]

This did not make them irreligious, much less vainly philistine.
Some of the *Hofjuden*, especially Samson Wertheimer and Samuel O's
nephew David Oppenheimer, were stupendous book and manuscript
collectors, the latter boasting a library of 4,500 books and 780 Hebrew
manuscripts. But even Veitel Ephraim and Daniel Itzig were determined to be seen as more than walking moneybags. Their libraries
were stacked not just with the treasures of the Jewish tradition
(including the two Talmuds, the canonical commentaries, Maimonides,
Abraham ibn Ezra, Samuel Usque, Elia Delmedigo and Menasseh ben
Israel) but also with the bottomless wisdom of pagan antiquity and
the new vision of the moderns: Leon Battista Alberti on painting and
architecture; Newton's *Principia*, Leibniz's moral philosophy, Locke
on understanding. Their furniture was elegantly inlaid, but Veitel
Ephraim wanted cabinetmakers of the mind as part of his social
fixtures and fittings and, quite as much as any enlightened despot
scouting for big-name philosophers they could attach to team Frederick
or Catherine, the court Jews were on the lookout for precocious talent.

Could any Jewish boy be better suited for this happy prospect than
Mendel of Dessau's young prodigy? Even his round shoulders and
scoliotic backbone could be thought the mark of the true scholar,
stooped over his books. Fame beckoned in Berlin! *Zay gezunt en zol*

zayn mit mazel (Stay well and go with luck). Reality set in as soon as the boy left his house and Dessau behind. Rabbi Fraenkel would have departed in a coach; Moses Mendelssohn walked the eighty miles, trying not to be mistaken for a *Beteljud* sleeping in the lowest taverns and lodgings, turning his face from the drunks and the girls. But eventually, there he stood at the gates of the city, the one patrolled by the Jews themselves who might or might not let you in depending on whether they liked the look of you, the boy Moses, barely beyond his bar mitzvah, not just unprepossessing but the very picture of what the Gentiles sneeringly imagined when they conjured up Jews: short, swarthy, hook-nosed and crook-backed. If you had to prophesy who would become the most famous Jew in Europe, the first intellectual darling of the Gentiles, the fourteen-year-old Moses Mendelssohn would not have come to mind. But although there was no question of his entering the privileged ranks of the 'Protected Jews', the recommendation from the new rabbi was enough to get him through the gate. He would join all the other hangers-on in the religious service industry who stayed only at the pleasure of the Protected Jews as well as the city authorities.

Once in Berlin, Moses would have been lodged in a small dark, bare room smelling of onions and cabbage, supporting himself by teaching the *chumash* to younger children. This was the textual initiation into Hebrew for those who heard only Yiddish at home and in the street. The reassertion of Hebrew, a disciplined grasp of its grammar and an immersion in its poetic richness, paradoxically would become one of the pillars of modern Jewish learning. But a choice would have immediately presented itself to the young Mendelssohn: would he lead the rest of his life circumscribed by the known ways and endlessly rehearsed texts, adding his quibble to the mountain range of Talmud nitpicks, or would he step out beyond it into intellectual terra incognita? For such a leap of daring he would need non-Jewish languages: Latin, Greek, German, French, the lingua franca of the new thought, and possibly English to read Hobbes, Locke, Leibniz, Newton, Montesquieu and Shaftesbury.

Moses Mendelssohn taught himself all those tongues mostly with the help of dictionaries and the side-by-side comparison of words. His physical world was narrow while his mental world expanded beyond anything he could have imagined in Dessau. But he was not a solitary explorer. The romance of the Haskalah – the Jewish Enlightenment as I was taught it in Hebrew school in the 1950s – depicted the young Moses, conscious of carrying the name of both the biblical lawgiver and the medieval philosopher on his curved back, as the sole creator of a new Jewish mindset, a heroic loner. The reality, as Shmuel Feiner, David Ruderman, David Sorkin and the cohort of modern historians of the Jewish Enlightenment have shown, is that he was joining a generation thirsty for what both its champions and its antagonists sarcastically called the *chokhmot*: the modern wisdoms. Some of the new *chokhems* were already making themselves felt in the small world of Jewish Berlin (around 2,000 people in a city of 100,000) and acted as Moses Mendelssohn's reassuring mentors.[20]

Two of the *chokhems*, one older, one a little younger, could not have been more different from each other.[21] Israel ben Moses Halevi Zamosc had come to Berlin from deepest Galicia in southern Ukraine, the cradle of Hasidism: the cult of emotive communion. Israel Zamosc's enthusiasms, though, were classically Maimonidean – mathematics and philosophy – and he needed to escape to Berlin to immerse himself in them. Veitel Ephraim had taken him in as teacher in the *beit midrash*, the school he had created. The hospitality bore fruit. Two years before Mendelssohn's arrival Zamosc had published a work on the astronomy and geometry of the Talmud, yet another strenuous attempt to wrestle the rabbinical tradition into scientific reasonableness.

The links in the chain were already joining up. The rich patron hired the rabbi, the rabbi encouraged the scientifically inclined teacher and scholar of Maimonides, and into their charmed circle came the bright young prospect.

The second tutor of Moses Mendelssohn's engagement with the *chokhmot* hailed from an altogether different social world. Aaron Gumpertz was independently wealthy, born into a dynasty of court Jews who had started out in Cleves, a western outlier of the Prussian domains, close, both geographically and culturally, to the Dutch republic. As Hohenzollern power expanded under the Great Elector, an unjustly imprisoned member of the Gumpertz family was compensated by the ruler with the position of Berlin mint master. But there was another string to the Gumpertz bow, and that was, inevitably, medicine. The collegia medico-chirurgica, notably the one in Berlin, were open to Jews who then went on to graduate from either the

University of Halle or Frankfurt an der Oder. One of Aaron's uncles, Moses Salomon Gumpertz, had graduated from the latter institution in 1721 before becoming doctor to the Jewish community in Prague.[22]

For centuries medicine had been the enlarger of the Jewish mind beyond the enclosure of the Torah and Talmud.[23] Ironically, the high reputation enjoyed by Jewish doctors at the courts of caliphs and kings rested on the assumption that somehow they had access to arcane knowledge unavailable to others, whereas the truth was that they were acute observers, diagnosticians, mappers of the anatomy, almost always following in the footsteps of Greek and Arab predecessors. But those Jewish doctors (like Ephraim Bueno in Amsterdam) were very often also learned in Judaic tradition, along with mathematics, philosophy, astronomy and medicine. From Renaissance Padua, where they had come into contact with non-Jewish scholars and professors, they took what they had learned back into their own communities and began to impart it to their own culture through Hebrew translations of medical classics or through original contributions of their own, often specialisations like optics or the digestive tract (two topics of perennial Jewish concern). Many of them were especially zealous in combating folk medicine: potions and amulets said to cure ringworm (a scourge) or soothe a bad case of piles. The most eccentrically beautiful of the books of new instruction was the *Ma'aseh Tuviyah*, the *Work of Tobias*, published by Tobias Cohen in Venice in 1708.

The Cohen family were Polish and Tobias's grandfather and father had both been doctors before him. Tobias began his medical education in 1679 at Frankfurt an der Oder, but on encountering Jew-hatred, moved to the more sympathetic climate of Padua University. He then led a peripatetic life, an Ashkenazi Jew in the largely Sephardi world of the Mediterranean communities of the Ottoman Empire, first in Adrianople and then Constantinople where, in the tradition of the Hamon dynasty, he became court physician to five successive sultans before moving to Jerusalem at the end of his life, thus reversing the migrations of his forebears who had migrated from Palestine to Poland. Tobias's *Work* was an attempt to anatomise the Jewish mind in the setting of the world, proceeding through the structure of knowledge from the cosmic elementals to the biological fundamentals. Accordingly he began with 'theology', moved on to astronomy (he was an ardent Copernican addressing a largely pre-Copernican rabbinic orthodoxy). Then followed mathematics, anatomy, hygiene, the sexual diseases (syphilis especially), medical botany and finally a study of the temperaments, the same subject that would form the basis of young Aaron Gumpertz's dissertation.

For Tobias Cohen (and it was obviously important that he *was* a Cohen from the priestly line), medicine and natural sciences were not alternatives to Judaism but organic extensions of its core belief in the uniqueness of the Creator, and the incomparable ingenuity of his creation. He was, therefore, halfway towards the idea of a 'natural religion' before Gottfried Leibniz and Christian Wolff had defined it as such. The axiom that the genius of the Almighty was revealed as much in the discoverable phenomena of the natural world, discerned and analysed through rational enquiry, as in the letter of the written and the oral law, became the great truism of the Jewish as well as the Christian Enlightenment. Spinoza had famously equated divinity with nature, but that *Deus sive Natura* absented him from its subsequent operations and was indifferent to its doings, especially those of humanity. For the likes of Christian Wolff and Tobias Cohen, and their readers Aaron Gumpertz and Moses Mendelssohn, the ingenuity of creation, and the possibility of remedying its ills, was evidence of the presence, not the absence, of God (notwithstanding all the evils and calamities which might periodically mar His work). Raphael Levi, a disciple of Leibniz who lived in the philosopher's house in Hanover for six years, declared that he had studied and written about astronomy in order to better comprehend 'the grandeur of the Creator and the master of the heavens'.[24] A lovely portrait of Levi, preserved in the Leibnizhaus, posed amiably with compass, telescope and globe but with the dress of a cleric-scholar, makes the same point about the unforced compatibility of faith and science.

By these lights, to be properly religious in the modern world meant to be scientific, in every sense, a doctor of philosophy as well as a healer of the sick. The acquisition of secular knowledge did not necessarily involve a loss of faith, though it did presuppose scepticism about some of the more irrational 'superstitions' still lodging in the credulous mind. The Jewish seekers often presented themselves as restorers of an ancient, omnivorous, open-minded Judaic learning which had been desiccated into aridity by the casuistry of the Talmudists. Moses Steinhardt, the son of the rabbi of Fuerth, said of this decline 'that

we have plummeted from the highest peak [of learning] to the deepest
abyss, we have become objects of shame, mocked by all the nations'.
His antidote was to 'fill many notebooks with all of human wisdom,
all sciences philosophical and divine'. And Steinhardt signed himself
as 'engineer, astronomer, philospher, rabbi of Hanover'.[25]

Sometimes, this rekindled lust for learning made itself felt literally.
While still a student, Asher Anshel Worms, who would become
physician at the Jewish hospital in his native town of Frankfurt,
dreamed of constructing an entire Hebrew lexicon of the natural
and moral sciences. His first passion was algebra (closely followed
by chess), on which he published the first modern Hebrew text as
early as 1722, before he had even graduated as a doctor. In Worms's
overheated imagination algebra was a 'fair virgin' discovered by the
narrator, 'face pressed to the ground', on the desert island to which
he had been washed ashore after a shipwreck.[26] Had she been wrecked
as well? Anshel is in love. Anshel is very, very excited and proceeds
to apply his lifesaving techniques to the conveniently prone Miss
Algebra. 'I emptied her of the water she had swallowed, and anointed
her body with oils and perfumes until the breath of life was in her.'
Properly grateful for the resuscitation, Algebra offers to reveal her
hidden depths to her blissed-out rescuer for 'now I shall walk in the
land of the living'.

Often, as Shmuel Feiner has brilliantly documented, the lure of
wordly knowledge was resisted as if it were sexual temptation. Rabbi
Shlomo of Chelm wrote of his heart craving 'the delights of wisdom',
his 'little finger lightly touching the science of nature and what lay
beyond it', before pulling himself together and returning to the Torah,
demoting the pleasure of familiarising himself with forbidden illuminations to 'secondary importance'.[27] Sometimes, however, the recourse
to medicine almost inadvertently opened the doors to dangerous
knowledge. The great rabbinical authority of the Ashkenazi world,
Rabbi Jacob Emden, depressed by business losses in Amsterdam, took
to drinking tea – pot after pot of it – in order to bring himself a
modicum of cheer. Flooded by a perpetual torrent of tannin and
caffeine, his urinary tract rebelled. 'My blood turned to water so that
my urine spouted forth like a fountain and I had to urinate virtually
every minute causing me severe pains in my private parts ... I could
hardly take a step without needing to relieve myself.'[28] This is not

good for a rabbi whose response to questions demanded patiently sustained reflection. Having tried everything else, including prayer, and found no relief, poor Rabbi Jacob turned to 'a foreign medical book written by one Dr Buntekel'. Or so he says, for the famous treatise of the Dutch physician Cornelis Bontekoe actually recommended drinking tea for a whole variety of maladies. At any rate, once he had stepped into the fields of alien wisdom something deep stirred in Emden and he went from anxious self-protection to a ravenous hunger for all kinds of modern and ancient knowledge. 'I was completely ignorant of non-Jewish literature though I was always interested in studying worldly matters about other nations, their religious beliefs, ethics, character and history, all facts on which our religious Literature provided no information.' At the very least Emden thought he would be better equipped to refute the sceptics if he shared the common ground of their understanding. Unable to afford a private tutor, he asked a Christian servant to help him through the German alphabet and from there went on to words, sentences and whole books. He followed this with Dutch and Latin, and came to understand (since by this time Genesis was evidently insufficient)

how our earth came into existence which according to their literature was caused by the motions of the planets. For those some mention of this is made in our texts the description is very brief. Again I was keen to learn about the world of Nature: the character of minerals and the specific qualities of plants and herbs. And above all I was eager to learn something about Medicine [but also] the problems of monarchs and their wars, apart from other historical events. I wanted to know something about the new geographical discoveries, the oceans, rivers, deserts, also the craftsmanship and arts of other nations.[29]

Emden's encyclopedic craving for worldly knowledge was tactical, the better to strengthen the fences around the Torah. After the description, in his autobiography, of his appetite for modern knowledge he made sure to add 'that I took care not to study any of these topics in any depth'. But even though his object was broad, shallow, selectively deployable learning, he could not help confessing, in an allusion to Samson's riddle, that 'still, on several occasions I extracted sweetness from the strong and the honey I found in them I scraped into my hand'.

For other, less conflicted souls, the pursuit of new learning became an end in itself. Mastery of its wisdoms offered the possibility of a double reconciliation: between science and Judaism but also between Jews and Gentiles who might now speak to each other, scholar to scholar, on the basis of common knowledge. This is what happened to Moses Mendelssohn's mentor Aaron Gumpertz.[30] He began, of course, by trying to please the parents. His mother had rabbinical ambitions for Aaron so he put in the time at Israel Zamosc and David Fraenkel's yeshiva. His father, on the other hand, wanted him to be a doctor so he entered the university at Frankfurt an der Oder, graduating when he was twenty-eight in 1751. This made him the first qualified Jewish doctor in Prussia. But what Gumpertz wanted more intensely was to be the first Jew since Spinoza to be taken seriously by the non-Jewish intellectual world. He had read deeply, both in the rational theology of natural religion – the work of Leibniz and his disciple Christian Wolff – and, just to make sure, in the polemics of their adversaries who presented themselves as devotees of Isaac Newton. His German and French (which was the lingua franca of the minds being collected by Frederick the Great at Potsdam) were fluent. And he was confident enough of his persuasiveness to knock on important doors. In 1745 he approached the royal librarian, the Marquis d'Argens, one of the king's hired talents, a prolific and (incomprehensibly) popular writer of philosophical novels, the most famous of which was *Lettres Juives* (*The Jewish Letters*).

It was the ostensible subject matter of d'Argens' book that must have given Gumpertz the confidence to propose himself as a secretary, amanuensis, anything useful to the marquis. The Jews of its title are spurious products of d'Argens' imagination – the rabbi on the brink of straying into Karaite heresy, the Livorno merchant, the traveller – all given vaguely exotic names and none of whom ever rise above the level of literary contrivance. The reverse-colonial trick of using the astonishment or disgust of wide-eyed exotics to make Europeans think again about the oddities and iniquities of their own culture had been pioneered by Montesquieu's *Persian Letters*, in which a pseudo-Jew also featured. D'Argens knew that presenting a Jewish literary exchange would sell precisely because it ran against type. So it probably amused him to have an actual specimen showing up in his apartment, minus turban or kaftan but clad in correctly powdered wig; to all intents and purposes a civilised fellow which just showed you never could tell. Gumpertz was a delightful curiosity. He could be shown off like a parrot reciting the catechism.

And yet Gumpertz was serious enough, or useful enough, that two years later, d'Argens recommended him to the *Präsident-Direktor* of the Royal Academy of Sciences, another Frenchman, Pierre-Louis Maupertuis, mathematician, *homme de lettres*, adamant partisan of Newton's physics. The reigning orthodoxy, established by Leibniz, with its reassurance that this must be the best of all possible worlds (for how could a benevolently inventive God of nature have chosen otherwise?), made Maupertuis feel ill with rage, and he devoted much of his life to growling and storming against its shallowly imagined complacency; a heroic irritability that undoubtedly rubbed off on Voltaire, who arrived at the king's behest in Berlin in 1750. Maupertuis was an action scientist. To prove that Newton had been right in his assertion, based on the laws of physics, that the earth was not in fact a perfect sphere but flattened at its polar extremities, he went to Lapland, taking his measuring rods out amid the indifferent reindeer until all was proven to his satisfaction. Like the mercurial king, Maupertuis was not easily palmed off with literary ingratiations. And yet, unlike the king, he discovered there were clever, attentive Jews who could hold their own in witty conversation and Aaron Gumpertz was one of them.

First-hand experience of these tournaments of the Gentile mind served Aaron well. By 1752, still only in his late twenties, he was the Jewish doctor, lecturing from anatomical dissections, revealing the chambers of the body that Tobias Cohen had mapped so exhaustively. He had become a fixture of the gatherings of the learned in Berlin. There he was at meetings of the Monday Club on the Mohrenstrasse (which, naturally, initially convened on Thursdays), which he had helped found. There he sipped his coffee (the new addiction) with the likes of Carl Philipp Emanuel Bach, the philosopher Johann Georg Sulzer (who almost inadvertently invented the battery by putting two slips of metal on his tongue, activating a charge through his saliva), the statistician Johann Peter Süssmilch, and the playwright and critic Gotthold Ephraim Lessing.[31] The company exchanged thoughts across the confessional boundaries: Lessing was the son of a Lutheran pastor, Sulzer a Catholic; but no cross-confessional salon would be complete without a personable, articulate Jew. It was, in fact, this particular Jew whom Lessing had had in mind when he began writing his play *Die Juden* in 1749, published four years later; the one that launched his literary career. The play also inaugurated a phenomenon it is all too easy to forget yet vital to remember: German philo-Semitism.

Lessing was known for literary charm housed in the sharpest of minds. There were elements of comic ingratiation in *Die Juden* (false beards, bumbling drunken servants) but its aim was missionary. It was, he wrote, 'the result of serious reflection on the shameful oppression suffered by a nation which, as I see it, a Christian cannot contemplate without a kind of reverence. In former times it produced so many heroes and prophets but nowadays people doubt it contains a single honest man.' Lessing observed the madness with sardonic calm. He knew Jews. He lived close to the Spandauerstrasse, a stone's throw from the synagogue in the Heidereutergasse. Gumpertz went there; so did his protégé Mendelssohn.

Die Juden was the first fruit of the affinity between Lessing and Gumpertz. The dramatist's principal aim was to make his audience, and by extension the wider audience who would hear about the play and read it, ashamed of their own prejudices and of the poisonous libels perpetuated by Eisenmenger's overwhelmingly influential *Judaism Unmasked*. That it was a one-act play with a knockout twist at the end only helped the delivery of the polemical punch.

A baron, travelling with his daughter, is assaulted and robbed by a gang of bearded lowlifes who, from their appearance and gross accents, were meant to be instantly recognised as Jews, who had an unearned reputation in Germany (as well as in England) for thieving and every kind of unscrupulous dishonesty. In fact the thieves are the baron's own servants, including the manager of his estate. An anonymous traveller comes to their aid, pitching into the thugs, and in the chaotic brawl the robbers lose their beards and are revealed. An outpouring of gratitude prompts the baron to offer his daughter's hand in marriage to the handsome rescuer since she seems so smitten herself. The paragon-hero of the piece, so noble, so handsome, so altruistic, cour-teously expresses his deep appreciation for the gesture but declines since he declares himself – a gasp from the audience – a Jew! Stereotypes are reversed. The Gentiles are shown to have the lowlife vices habitually attributed to the Jews while the real Semite is indistinguishable from the most magnanimous Christian. The Jewish 'Traveller' even defies stereotypes by being indifferent to money. Disappointed that there will not be a wedding, the baron asks the stranger to help himself to his riches since 'I would rather be poor and grateful than rich and ungrateful'. The Jew turns him down again, since 'happily the God of my fathers has provided me with more than I need'. 'How respectable the Jews would be,' the baron exclaims, 'if they were all like you.' The Jew shoots back: 'And how worthy of love the Christians would be if they all looked like you'!

The compliment paid by the baron is also the problem, for it unwittingly reinforces the very stereotype Lessing aimed to correct. The pearl amid the dirt only makes the dirt seem dirtier. What was needed was not the astonished discovery of exceptions but the recognition that the common run of Jews were fellow men and women. Even so, there were those who found the notion of a brave, altruistic, eloquently intelligent Jew strictly inconceivable. The critic Johann David Michaelis witheringly dismissed the hero as a figment of Lessing's sentimental imagination. It was not utterly impossible, he conceded, but extremely improbable. The playwright responded with a trump card – not one but *two* such Jews. One of them wrote of his pain and outrage to the other, his friend Gumpertz, and Lessing published the letter along with his own rebuttal. The magnificently infuriated author was the twenty-four-year-old Moses Mendelssohn. 'What an exaggerated contempt!' he wrote to Gumpertz; 'the rabble of Christians has always seen us as scum of nature, the sore of humanity. But from a learned man I would have expected something fairer ... how can an honest man have the impudence to deny a whole nation the possibility of a single honest man.' The final stroke of passion, touching the thing that mattered most to the thinkers of his generation, Mendelssohn saved for the rousing end: 'Do not deny us virtue, the only virtue of hard-pressed souls, the only refuge of the forsaken.'[32]

It was the recipient of the poignant letter, Gumpertz, rather than its author who decided to take up the challenge of expanding an exceptional dispensation into a general change of heart and mind, though he may have found a willing collaborator in Lessing. Between writing *Die Juden* and publishing it, Lessing had travelled in Holland and England where he had observed two very different attitudes to their respective communities of Jews. In Amsterdam he saw a place where, in so far as was possible in the eighteenth century, the Jews seemed at peace with their Christian hosts (even if there was grumbling about the poverty, begging and superstitions of the Polish immigrants). But Lessing happened to arrive in London in 1753 during the hysteria greeting the passage of the 'Jew Bill', a public madness so intense it forced the Pelham government to repeal it, even though it had been of modest scope, restricted to waiving the Test Act – the formal profession of allegiance to Anglican Christianity – for private parties petitioning Parliament. Lessing heard the absurd paranoia about Jews buying St Paul's to turn it into a synagogue, and saw the grotesque caricatures, depicting England under the circumciser's knife.

In 1753 Lessing and Gumpertz (with the doctor taking the lead) drafted a proposal for granting full civic rights, not just to Jews singled out here and there as 'deserving', whether on account of their wealth (like the court Jews) or their learned distinction, but to the generality of the people.[33] It was published anonymously and was the first sustained argument that the degradation of Jews was the product of the social conditioning imposed on them by their persecutors, not some sort of innate characteristic. Even though Voltaire (present in Berlin from 1750 in his brief assignment as Frederick the Great's intellectual talent signing) included Jews on his list of those to be tolerated, he believed that deep down there was something unreformably obnoxious about them. But there were others among eighteenth-century social thinkers – Montesquieu and Scottish writers like Adam Ferguson and Lord Kames – who insisted that cultures were the products of their environments; not just geography and history, but the long impact of institutional conditioning. If impoverished Jews were reduced to begging, thieving, disreputable trades like dealing in old clothes, a passive-aggressive conduct at once ingratiating and defensive, it was because centuries of being herded into ghettos, the rigid exclusion from all 'honest' trades and crafts, from schools and universities, from the professions and owning of property and land, the insane lies about child murder reiterated in Eisenmenger's volumes – all had naturally deformed their social conduct and had necessarily restricted what instruction they could get to what the rabbis alone could provide. As Mendelssohn would succinctly put it, 'you tie our hands and then accuse us of not using them'. Liberate the Jews from prejudices (both their own and those of the anti-Semites), release them from social and economic restrictions, broaden their education and they would conduct themselves like any other citizens. Though this proposal would become the commonplace of Jewish emancipation towards the end of the century, it was first plainly set out, albeit in cautious anonymity, a generation earlier.

Never Mendelssohn's intellectual equal nor as prolific, Aaron Gumpertz was the adventurous forereunner of the Jewish Enlightenment and the one who persuaded sympathetic Gentiles to pay attention to the cause. It is likely that Gumpertz introduced Mendelssohn to the Monday Club, for he was known to C. P. E. Bach, and to the Learned Coffee House – two rooms rented once a week by the group in an establishment where members read newspapers and periodicals, including the ones they wrote for, and played taroc, the ancient card game featuring a pack of seventy-eight with tarot pieces as the court cards. This did not preclude arguments. 'How wonderful,' Gumpertz drolly exclaimed at one card game, 'three mathematicians who can't count to twenty-one.' That other staple of cafe culture, chess, was already popular, some of the masters using the first modern manual to the game written by the polymath medic Asher Anshel Worms. A billiard table was set up and the modest fees charged for games helped pay the rent of the rooms. There was a constant supply of coffee, and once a month there was a lecture; serious content dressed up in the light clothes of intellectual entertainment. In May 1755, the publisher Friedrich Nicolai reported listening to the great Swiss mathematician Leonard Euler reading a paper on billiards entitled 'On the motion of two balls on a horizontal plane'. Snuff was sniffed, pipes smoked, huge amounts of coffee drunk which since the rabbis (many of themselves severely addicted) had pronounced perfectly kosher, and indeed even consumable on the Sabbath when warmed by a Gentile, the Jews drank deepest of all.[34]

Into this heady company came little Moses Mendelssohn of Dessau. His fellow imbibers were invariably struck by his urbane charm (so unlike a Jew, they muttered behind their hands); his disarming honesty always merrily articulated; his gentle self-mockery (more like a Jew); the staggering breadth of his reading; his self-taught mastery of many tongues; the clarity of his thinking; and something no one could quite put their finger on but which the wits and the minds of the age were constantly seeking like some human holy grail: his unmistakable decency. He was, as he would say of himself, just *'ein Mensch'*. But what *ein Mensch*! Together with Lessing, Friedrich Nicolai and Gumpertz, he made up a quartet of like minds, conscious that they were embarked less on a campaign for toleration, notwithstanding the Gumpertz–Lessing pamphlet, than the direct experience of it. Unlike the French *philosophes* who steered clear of Jews and never in their lives encountered one, the world of *Kaffee, Kuchen und Kant* (who in Königsberg took on Jewish students, despite suffering the indignity of being runner-up in an essay competition won by Mendelssohn) was always a mixed society.

As his writings began to appear in German in the 1750s, all this brought Moses Mendelssohn the attention of the curious, and a helping of literary fame. But, belles-lettres and the *Philosophical Reflections* he published did not a living make. In his second decade in Berlin he was working as a bookkeeper for the Jewish silk manufacturer Isaac Bernhard, one of the industrial entrepreneurs Frederick the Great was eager to add to his inventory of Prussian assets. Mendelssohn also acted as tutor to Bernhard's children, and fretted and fumed, in a style exactly recalling the grousing of his namesake Moses Maimonides, that he was forever short of time to pursue the work God had intended him for: the happiness of perfecting his mind. Nonetheless his progress with languages – especially Latin and French – was astonishing, and the three other members of the quartet encouraged Mendelssohn to translate works from French into German for publication as a way of improving both. Jean-Jacques Rousseau's *Discours sur l'inégalité* (*Discourse on Inequality*) was a telling choice for an early trial in the genre, not least because there was something so obviously *'honnête homme'* about Mendelssohn himself. When his portrait was painted in the 1770s, he adopted, whether consciously or not, the plain, vaguely fustian, generally brown costume of the Man of Simple Virtue, and was almost as well known in this guise as its other two virtuosi: Benjamin Franklin and Rousseau. Thus he became not just the Clever Jew but the Good Jew. Like those others, Mendelssohn was cast as the antidote to vain fashion, not least because he genuinely reconciled religious conviction with philosophical sophistication to a degree the scoffers had deemed impossible or hypocritical.

This, paradoxically, brought him back, time and again, to that other Jew whom he thought had been mistakenly charged with severing belief from reason: Baruch Spinoza. It was obvious, especially to his friends, that Moses identified with the 'fallen' Jew who had both anticipated his own vocation of Jewish philosopher but in the end had concluded the vocation was an oxymoron. Characteristically, Gotthold Lessing meant to flatter Mendelssohn's own interior thoughts when he called his friend 'a second Spinoza, identical in every way except his [Spinoza's] errors'.[35] The more he knew about Spinoza, the brutal vehemence of the ancient terms of excommunication with its monstrous reiteration of curses, the more he imagined him alone in his garret near The Hague, the more deeply he read him, the more Moses longed to bring him back, posthumously, into the fold: to reclaim him fully as a Jew. On some important matters, he could never concur. Moses stuck by his original namesake, unshakeably believing the laws had indeed been given on the mountain and he never supposed the Exodus was anything but historical fact. But he found nothing shocking or un-Jewish about Spinoza's assertion that the lawgiving had to be understood in the context of its time and place and was intended for the governance of an uprooted unruly people. Unlike Spinoza, however, he believed that the historicity of that legislation did not make it redundant when circumstances changed. Mendelssohn also demoted the drama of revelation on Mount Sinai to secondary significance, for he agreed with the author of the *Tractatus* that it was absurd to suppose that the laws – or rather the social ethics which underlay their detail – could have been given for the benefit of one people alone. In this respect the origin of the lawgiving was to be distinguished from its destiny; one was particular, the other universal. Mendelssohn believed that Israel had been made the custodian, not the sole proprietor, of a system of ethics which was intended for the common practice of mankind. Revelations divided; reason reconciled. That was the heart of the matter.

The re-Judaised Spinoza became the touchstone of much that Mendelssohn wished to accomplish. He wanted a Judaism liberated from defensiveness – there had been too much talk of Talmudic 'fences' about the Torah. While certainly not rejecting the Talmud, Mendelssohn believed that, properly understood, the ethical core of the law needed no fences, indeed it should be something which might bring Jews and Christians together. (He would not have minded the modern cliché of the 'Judaeo-Christian tradition'.) Mendelssohn also saw no reason why the idea of God as the uncaused originator of the universe should necessarily be inconsistent with the biblical account of creation, once that was read with allegorical discernment. But unlike Spinoza and the deists, Mendelssohn did not think that was the end of the divine presence in the world; on the contrary, following Leibniz and Wolff he assumed that divinity could be read in the everyday phenomena of nature, from the opening of a bud to the setting of the sun. In contrast to the usual tenor of Jewish preaching, and much of the synagogue liturgy, Mendelssohn's Jewish God was not a hanging judge, ever on the lookout to punish backsliders, either singly or in entire cities and empires. Mendelssohn's Jehovah wore an eighteenth-century smile. How could He not, since His earthly creation was intended for pleasure and happiness, and His corrections were more akin to that of a celestial gardener, periodically pruning and weeding, the better to ensure a new blossoming.

The weekly (and short-lived) Hebrew periodical Mendelssohn founded and edited in 1758, the *Kohelet Musar* (*Moral Preacher*), self-consciously belied its name, except in the way it echoed the quizzical tone of the original *kohelet*, the Teacher of Ecclesiastes. But while the prevailing tone of that wisdom book was gnomic gloom towards the human condition, Mendelssohn's teaching was one of relish for earthly life, a pleasure he assumed God had wanted man to enjoy.[36] In particular Mendelssohn celebrated the beauty of the natural world with an exuberance not much seen in the Jewish tradition since the poets of medieval Spain. Judah Halevi's philosophical *Kuzari* and some of his poetry had returned as a subject of learned reading, and Mendelssohn believed, rightly, that that medieval generation had made use of a richly vital and elastic Hebrew which had also been the instrument of the writers of the Bible but had become dried out in the centuries of endless exegetic commentary. Mendelssohn's reawakening of Jewish pleasure was matched, then, by his conviction that Hebrew could return to its bardic splendour and be made, once again, the vehicle of both metaphysical illuminations and earthy verse.

The Hebrew God was often said to be a sublime architect, and occasionally characterised as the original artist, but if that was true then His genre was landscape and His masterpiece was the teeming glory of the natural world. God was, in fact, a gardener and when Mendelssohn strolled in the actual garden of his friend the publisher

Nicolai, or enjoyed a walk along the sanded avenues of Itzig and Ephraim, he was confirmed in his belief that the relish of natural beauty was not only *not* a distraction from the imperishable teachings of the Torah, it was actually a way to come close to the sublime mystery of creation.

Mendelssohn gave Jews permission to be happy. His reply as editor of *Kohelet Musar* to a fictitious letter-writer to his magazine declared, 'I have taken joy into my heart since I became a man. I abide in joy at eventide and song at daybreak ... I call to my comrades and cause them to drink of spiced wine and pomegranate juice ... we awake in the vineyards and lodge in the villages. Joy flows like water in our bowels, like oil in our bones.'[37] In one issue of *Kohelet Musar*, commenting on the obligation to recite a blessing on seeing the first blossoms of spring, Mendelssohn rhapsodised: 'the buds and flowers of the field give joy and innocent pleasure to all who see them. The eye cannot receive its fill for seeing of their beauty. For as long as a person gazes on them his soul will add satisfaction in their goodness and will never regret this joy in his heart. His face will glow as if with oil. He will go back and forth between the rows of fragrant flowers with strength of spirit and his eyes will see the goodness and blessing which God has blessed him with.'[38]

In the spring of 1761 he experienced a personal blossoming. Writing to Lessing from Hamburg, Mendelssohn reported going to the theatre and meeting scholars, and then coyly confessed 'this is bound to seem strange to you, I have committed the folly of falling in love in my thirtieth year. You laugh? By all means go ahead, it may happen to you when you reach thirty.'[39] The love object, he wrote with a clumsy mixture of facetiousness and patronising grandeur, 'is by no means beautiful and by no means learned, nonetheless her gallant lover was so impressed by her that he believes he can live happily with her'. What he did not say was that Fromet Guggenheim was the great-granddaughter of the fabled lord of the Bauernmarket, the first and greatest court Jew, Samuel Oppenheimer. But what was left of the Oppenheimer fortune, after his fall and death, had gone elsewhere, so Fromet was only modestly dowered. It was a love match all the same. After leaving Hamburg he wrote her a love letter declaring 'even the kisses I stole from you were mixed with bitterness for the approach of our separation made me heavy of heart and unable to enjoy anything'.[40]

While away, Moses wrote to Fromet twice a week, and even before their marriage, which took place the following year in Hamburg, he told Lessing that he thought of his spirited bride as a partner rather than a passively dutiful wife. 'I would like her to share not only my happiness and my life but also my ideas.' He appointed himself her tutor in matters philosophical, and when travelling for the silk firm made sure '*Herr Doktor*' (Gumpertz), 'who never says no to teaching as I know from my own experience', continued the instruction. Shaftesbury, Locke, the usual suspects were sent her way. Mendelssohn adored the role of husband and father, grieved bitterly over the death of their eleven-month-old Sarah, and never forgot her *Jahrzeit* memorial or the pain of the loss. Becoming the good burgher he smartened up just a little, stopping short of modish vanity, but, in defiance of rabbinical denunciations, wearing a contemporary wig – the *Stutzperrucke* – and trimming his beard back to a mere goatee.

Later (possibly in 1774), Fromet and Moses presented the synagogue with a *parokhet*, an Ark curtain, made, as was sometimes the custom, from her wedding dress, its white silk embroidered with the blooms of spring: gillyflowers and jonquils, tulips, blue scabious and crimson peonies, carnations, daisies, roses of Sharon and lilies of the valley. Their names were also embroidered in gold thread in equal size and prominence, side by side. Every time the doors of the Ark opened for the reading of the Law, Hamburg's Jews could feast their eyes on that abundantly stocked herbaceous border.

By the end of the Seven Years War in 1763 Mendelssohn had become famous in Hohenzollern Berlin, among both Jews and Christians, and was confident (or reckless) enough to have reviewed a slim volume of poems written by the king, when that assignment would seem to have been the ultimate poisoned chalice. He delivered faint praise without a hint of damnation, but nimbly sidestepped the issue of quality by pretending to complain that by choosing French for his poetry he had deprived his native German of a royal gift! The Jews of Berlin stayed passionately patriotic through the vicissitudes of the war, and Mendelssohn and others composed prayers to be read in synagogue for the health and triumph of the king. He in turn was finally awarded the status of a Protected Jew, with permanent rights of residence, rights which were not, however, extended to his wife and children. But when he was elected a member of the Royal

Academy, proposed by d'Argens and heavily voted for by the fellows, the king stepped in to veto the appointment of 'the Jew Moses'.

In 1767, *Phaedon*, Mendelssohn's treatise on the immortality of the soul – written in the form of a Platonic dialogue, but with a self-consciously updated eighteenth-century Socrates – became an unlikely publishing triumph, selling three thousand copies in its first weeks, going quickly into four German editions and into translation in many other languages. Gracefully written, it demonstrated Mendelssohn's astonishing capacity to inhabit almost every literary and philosophical genre with which he engaged. By the end of the decade he had achieved the impossible: remaining constant to Judaism and practising as a learned scholar of the Bible, while fully participating in the universal debates of the day on the most strenuous matters: the 'Great Chain of Being' from simple to complex natural forms ending in man; the relationship between moral and mathematical science; the indispensability of aesthetics while still managing new German translations and commentaries on the Psalms and Ecclesiastes.

All of this celebrity made him a target for conversionary opportunists, the most determined of whom was Johann Caspar Lavater, a Swiss theologian, who in 1769 prepared an intellectual ambush. As the inventor of 'scientific' physiognomy, by which character could be deduced from facial characteristics, Lavater was also much taken with the Genevan scientist-philosopher Charles Bonnet's bizarre work. Bonnet claimed to have discovered the anatomical existence of two brains (one governing the soul, the other the body). But he also argued that since true immortality, residing in the perpetuation of memory, could not be apprehended by reason alone, the Creator had commissioned the Saviour to proclaim it through revelation. Excitedly, Lavater translated what he thought was an irrefutable 'scientific' truth of Christianity into German and dedicated the publication to Mendelssohn, asking him to confound its arguments. The dedication then became the most backhanded of compliments, since Lavater insisted that should Mendelssohn find himself unable to refute Bonnet, he must do 'what prudence, love of truth and honesty bid you – what Socrates would have done had he read this treatise and found it irrefutable': namely, convert to the true Church.[41]

Much was riding on this abstruse little mind game and Moses Mendelssohn knew it, and all his friends from Lessing to Gumpertz

knew it, annoyed as they were by Lavater's stratagem. At the heart
of it were the terms on which their modern experiment in a
company of shared but not identical beliefs was based. For centuries
the sympathy shown by Christian Hebrew scholars, Catholic and
Protestant alike, towards the Jews had been predicated on their
conversion, sooner or later, to the Gospel of Christ. But even if
such an outcome might have made Lessing happy, it was a point
of pride with him to have Mendelssohn and Gumpertz as *friends*,
without requiring any abandonment of their convictions. The entire
trajectory of human progress, as he and enlightened Jews and
Christians both saw it, was towards a harmonisation of differing
beliefs, coexisting in a shared society. It was not about contrived
affinities based on the presumption of absorbing Jews into the body
of Christianity. Discarding the principle that full citizenship for the
Jews was conditional on their becoming Christians inaugurated
modern western pluralism.

Deeply affronted – not least by the presumption that he would be
weak-minded enough to be flattered by Lavater's 'dedication' –
Mendelssohn refrained from rising to the bait. He would neither read
Bonnet nor demean himself by mounting a full-on defence of Judaism
as if he were some medieval rabbi caught in the trap of a rigged
disputation. He would not, he said, stoop to polemical exchanges with
people half learned in rabbinics who produced 'trashy' digests. Instead
he contented himself with pointing out the difference between the
conversionist ardour of Christians and Jewish aversion to proselytism.
'We do not send missions out to the Indies or Greenland to preach
our religion to these distant peoples ... the divine religion in which
I was brought up teaches me that all the nations of the earth may
attain eternal happiness if they live by the laws of reason, that is
practise virtue and that God, for special reasons imposed certain
particular duties ... on my nation exclusively.'[42] Three years later he
set out the principle of friendly coexistence still more generously. 'I
have the good fortune of having for a friend many an excellent man
who is not of my faith. We sincerely love each other, though we
suspect that in matters of religion we hold totally different opinions.
I enjoy the pleasure of their company which benefits and delights me.
Never did my heart secretly whisper to me: what a pity that such a
lovely soul is lost!'[43]

Predictably Mendelssohn's fierce push back against Lavater triggered an eruption of anti-Semitic abuse in Berlin among those convinced that the Jews spent most of their time in synagogue cursing Christ and defaming the Church. For some reason the prayer *Aleinu* which comes close to the conclusion of services and which involves a brief bowing and bending of the knee was thought, on the rumour of those who had seen it, to be a parody of Christian genuflection. So in his ecumenical fashion Mendelssohn went out of his way to summarise the good that Jews had to say about the founder of Christianity. Once again he was deliberately making the best of it. In his coffee-house circle where Jews and Christians met as friends, doubtless the former had no trouble in praising the goodness of Jesus as moral teacher. Opinions on that subject might have been ruder had he listened in the Frankfurt ghetto or the backstreets of Brody. Jews, Mendelssohn insisted, accepted the ethical core of Jesus' teachings and the inspiring innocence of his life and preaching. But by that very token, they denied the attributes which had been projected retrospectively on that innocent after his death. Jesus had never claimed co-equal divinity with God; never asked to be worshipped, nor during his entire lifetime showed the least sign of overthrowing the religion of his ancestors which, after all, he himself practised. Such observations did little to calm the bad feeling in Berlin. As it became more bitter, Mendelssohn was asked by Elkan Herz, one of his admirers, whether he regretted getting embroiled in the whole Lavater business. On the contrary, Mendelssohn retorted: 'I wish I had got *more* involved. Thank God I have no regrets about this and pay no attention to the rubbish written against me.'[44]

The controversy may nonetheless have taken a toll. One morning in March 1771 Mendelssohn awoke to find he could neither open his eyes nor speak a word. His limbs refused to move at his command and before long he experienced a violent burning pain in his back as if 'fiery rods' were puncturing his spine. His doctor, Marcus Herz, was summoned by Fromet, and pronounced the problem to be 'congestion of blood in the brain'. Much merriment has been made of this admittedly rough-and-ready diagnosis but Herz, along with the Gentile Dr Zimmerman who supplied a similar verdict, may have been describing a small stroke or 'apoplexy'. A bigger one would eventually kill Mendelssohn nearly fifteen years later. Though this was no doubt out of the question, Herz forbade the least mental exertion: no reading or writing, which for Mendelssohn was tantamount to a slow death sentence. The patient was to eat no meat, and drink no wine or coffee, though lemonade was permitted. Footbaths with mustard seeds and mustard plasters applied to the soles plus leeches at the ears were prescribed. If this was the best that Jewish medicine could do, it still had some way to go. In a year or so the condition abated somewhat but Mendelssohn was terrified it might return. Yet he would not cease his life as a creature of deep thought, notwithstanding that afternoons spent in a little light philosophy, translating parts of the Bible into German, or even writing letters, were deemed a gamble with death. The intervals between attacks grew mercifully longer. But they never quite went away.

When he was well enough to consider his present and future, Mendelssohn did the opposite of retreat. Whatever years were left to him, he wrote, he wished to devote to the future welfare of his six children and by extension to his nation. Thus it was that he went from philosopher-critic (and by the 1770s he was being lionised in the Gentile world) to public campaigner; the protector and mediator of his people. Up until Mendelssohn embraced this role, the qualification to be such a *shtadlan*, like the Jewish exilarchs of the Middle Ages, was big money, if possible allied to religious learning, the profile of Samson Wertheimer. Mendelssohn had little money, but much religious learning, and in addition he had the language and the intellectual wherewithal to talk to the courts of the enlightened despots.

It was in that capacity that he received an appeal from the Jews of Mecklenburg-Schwerin to intercede with the local duke who, following contemporary alarm over cases of live burials, had banned the Jewish practice of interment on the day of death. Originally in 1772 the appeal from Schwerin had gone to the pillar of orthodoxy Jacob Emden who, confessing he hadn't the German to negotiate such matters with the Gentiles, passed it on to Mendelssohn, assuming he would defend at all costs the traditional practice set down in the Talmud. To Emden's horror Mendelssohn did no such thing. The Schwerin Jews, he said, were making too much fuss. Same-day burial dated from antiquity when the Jewish dead were interred in funerary caves and had watchers posted for three days. Matters were different now. Live burials might actually happen. The ducal ban was not unreasonable and Judaism was, above all things, rational. Using his clout Mendelssohn concocted a compromise with the ducal government by which the Jewish practice could be continued on condition that a valid death certificate was first supplied. This did not prevent Emden, who had been an admirer, from writing to Mendelssohn upbraiding him for daring to set aside a traditional obligation for the sake of appeasing Gentile fashion. Before long the Talmud would be dragged along behind the chariot of 'rationality'; Mendelssohn should be ashamed. But Moses was not ashamed. He was angry and a fierce exchange of views followed with neither side backing down.

Never an egotist, the small man with the curved back was nonetheless accepting grandeur. Jews were already speaking of him as the successor to the other two Moseses: the Prince of Egypt and Maimonides, physician to caliphs and viziers. When nearly half the Jewish population of Dresden was threatened with summary expulsion for failure to pay the crushing poll tax imposed on them, their Moses was the one they turned to for intercession. Mendelssohn felt their humiliations personally in 1776 when on a visit he had been obliged to pay the *Liebzoll* due on the transit of cattle and Jews within Saxony. And he had met one of the elector's ministers, Fritsch, six years earlier when he had been summoned to Frederick the Great's immense baroque pile of a palace, Sans Souci. It was the Prussian king's way of complimenting and simultaneously insulting the Jew, a classic Frederician tactic. Fritsch had been paying a visit to the palace in Potsdam and had mentioned to the king that he would go from there to Berlin to see the famous Mendelssohn about whom everyone was talking. Frederick proposed rather that the Jew be asked to the palace, and so he was.

The summons arrived during Sukkot, the feast of Tabernacles, and the appointed time fell on the holy day of Shemini Atzeret when carriage travel was forbidden. But the moment was so auspicious that Talmudic minds bent the rules, not for the first time. So long as Mendelssohn descended from the carriage before the gate and walked the rest of the distance to the palace entry, it was all kosher. He was of course stopped by the guard, and in response to the enquiry about who he was, someone mentioned his fame. Famous at what? the guard asked. '*Ich spiele aus der Tasche!*' ('As a *conjurer!*'), Mendelssohn bellowed back. The episode became an immediately popular story, the

Polish-German artist Daniel Chodowiecki producing a little print of
the encounter between grenadier and Jew.

On he went up the *grande allée* and the vast stone staircase, walking
beneath the cupola with its Three Graces, into the grand gallery
floored with acres of white marble and red jasper, floor-to-ceiling
mirrors catching the reflection of the small man in his best black silk
coat and stockings; through to the king's apartments where, of course,
there was no Frederick, the monarch having absented himself, leaving
the Saxon minister to receive Mendelssohn as politely as possible in
the circumstances.

Years later, through Fritzsche, Mendelssohn found someone sympathetic to the plight of the Dresden Jews: a Baron von Farber, to whom
he explained what the brutal shock of an expulsion meant:

> Good and beneficent God! Where are these wretched ones to go with
> their innocent wives and children? Where are they to find shelter and
> protection after having been thrown out by the country in which they
> lost their possessions? For a Jew expulsion is the hardest punishment.
> It is more than mere banishment, it is, as it were, an extirpation, a
> removal from the face of God's earth, turned away by force of arms
> at every frontier. Must human beings suffer this hardest of all punish-
> ments even though they are guiltless, merely because they are
> committed to a different belief and through misfortune have become
> reduced to poverty?[45]

His personal fate was now inescapably tied to that of his people. More
than any of the *gvirim*, the gentlemen bankers and merchants with
their *Residenzen* and teams of carriage horses, Mendelssohn was looked
to for wisdom and succour, precisely because he was made of mind,
not money. To those who believed religious intolerance had poisoned
the world, the expansive generosity with which he conversed with
those not of his faith exemplified the way reason could prevail over
prejudice. In 1779 Lessing, who had only two more years to live,
published *Nathan the Wise* featuring a thinly disguised version of
Mendelssohn transplanted into Crusader Jerusalem, and mediating
between Christians, Muslims (including Saladin) and Jews, all of them
tangled together in family histories. Its first performance took place
only after Lessing's death and the play was accused by Christian critics

of belittling the Church. At such moments, Mendelssohn was depressed by the distance between the prejudiced and the enlightened. But within the confined circles of the educated – whether writers, government reformers or clergymen – he had shrunk the space between Jews and non-Jews. Much of the credit should go to the eagerness with which unusually sympathetic figures like Lessing were prepared to respond. But they did, and those friendships across the religious divide were unprecedented in mutual warmth and intimacy. This mattered because the *idea* of friendship was fetishised in the eighteenth century as the most authentic and honest of all human bonds; beyond love with its carnal complications, beyond even the affection tying parents to children for they were subject to estrangement and mortality. For Jews and Christians to make friends and stay friends was itself a revolutionary act.

By the 1780s, in his fifties, Mendelssohn was campaigning not only on behalf of the Jews but through them for the cause of humanity. So many evils at large in the world were the result of mindlessly inherited hatreds; of bloodstained fairy tales. Just as it had once fallen to the Jews to be the first custodians of a code of ethics destined for universal practice, so now the treatment of Jews would be the touchstone of civilisation's capacity for humane toleration. To see his people as fellow humans first and Jews next, and to grasp that they were fully capable of anything undertaken by Christians, was to end not just the oppression of the Hebrews but the blindness of everyone else.

He was not short of occasions to take up that cause. In 1779 in Alsace, a vitriolic Judaeophobe lawyer, aptly named François Hell, published a pamphlet recycling Eisenmenger's accusations of crime and murder and the biological impossibility of Jews being anything other than fanatical criminals. For the first time but not the last, they were accused of constituting 'a state within a state'. Hell's solution was simple – physical extermination, or if governments were too squeamish, then mass permanent banishment. Mendelssohn received a plea for help from the Strasbourg army contractor Herz Cerf Berr, sufficiently eminent to have received the full privileges of a subject from the government of Louis XVI. Busy with translations and editions, Mendelssohn recruited a thirty-year-old Prussian state official, Christian Wilhelm Dohm, whom he knew to be sympathetic to the Jews, to prepare a memorandum, explaining that it was centuries of persecution that had been responsible for Jewish degradation. If they were reduced to peddling, dealing in old clothes and moneylending, it was because all other avenues of making a living had been closed to them.

Dohm obliged, although the memorandum duly sent to the French Council of State did little to change the condition of the Jews of Alsace and Lorraine. At least their enemy Hell was arrested, albeit for crimes other than wishing mass death on the Jews. But the Prussian, encouraged by Mendelssohn, was moved to write a longer, more sustained memorandum, setting out the persecutions of the Jews and insisting on their common humanity. They were no more morally corrupt and incapable of modern citizenship than anyone else. They were what their tragic history had made them. Take away the crushing disabilities and exclusions imposed on them and the Christian world would see immediately they could be artisans, agriculturalists, people who produced things, rather than just money men, great and small.

Prussia was not ready to hear this, much less act on Dohm's social optimism. For all the fuss made of Mendelssohn (or possibly because of it) the old king showed no sign of abandoning his distaste for the Jews whether they wore a beard or a powdered perruque. But as it turned out there were princes who did share many of Dohm's assumptions: the radical King Gustav III in Sweden, and the Habsburg Austrian emperor Joseph II, the son of the empress Maria Theresa who had expelled the Jews from Prague in 1744. In the same spring that saw the appearance of Dohm's treatise, Joseph published a *Toleranzpatent*, the Edict on Toleration, setting out measures by which a wholesale transformation could be realised. Most likely the document was drafted by Joseph's visionary minister Joseph von Sonnenfels, the grandson of a rabbi but a convert to the Catholic Church. The Edict on Toleration was a radical exercise in Enlightenment social engineering. All impediments to Jewish participation in trades, industry and even agriculture were to be abolished along with the onerous taxes levied only on them. The edict stopped well short of granting full legal equality and civil rights to the Jews of the empire, and in fact reaffirmed restrictions on residence in some parts of the empire, but it raised them from a defenceless population, always vulnerable to the whims of rulers, to quasi-citizenship.

In keeping with the wisdom of the day, the great engine of change was to be education. Jews were already admitted to high schools in the empire but Joseph made elementary education compulsory for all his subjects, Jews included. A choice was offered. Should the Jews opt for Christian schools, they would be protected from conversionary efforts, and 'modern subjects' – languages and mathematics – would turn them into 'useful' subjects of the empire. But if those schools were objectionable the state would supply Jewish schools with teachers of modern subjects.

Some of those in Mendelssohn's circle shared that view of education as liberation. Daniel Itzig's son-in-law David Friedländer had opened the first Jewish 'Free School' in Germany in 1778, where both religious and secular subjects were taught. But none felt more passionately about educational reform than Naphtali Hartwig Wessely, who in the same year of momentous publications, 1779, produced *Divrei shalom ve'emet* (*Words of Peace and Truth*), a wholesale programme for the reform of Jewish instruction. Wessely was not proposing to do away with traditional religious instruction, only to introduce alongside it modern secular disciplines of mathematics, science, history and geography. But it was the way he framed the justification for having the two kinds of learning coexist within the same school which brought down on his head a storm of abuse from the rabbinical guardians of orthodoxy (especially the vigilant Ezekiel Landau, the chief rabbi of Prague). In Wessely's view there were two kinds of Torah: the Torah Hashem, which was the traditional body of commandments and teaching, and also the Torah Adam, the Torah of Man, and to the horror of the rabbis, he proposed that the latter should be at least as important as the former. This would have been music to the ears of Sonnenfels and the reformers in Vienna who said much the same. For the most severely Orthodox rabbis, Wessely was now demonised as an 'evil man' and an 'enemy of Judaism', someone who had tied the Torah and the Talmud to the vainglorious chariot of Gentile learning, who preferred 'etiquette' to the sacred texts, and who would, if ever his ideas were put into action, put future generations on the path to cultural self-destruction. Rabbi David ben Nathan of Lissa wrote that his only consolation for all the harm Wessely had done was the news that in Vilna (Vilnius) his book had first been hung by an iron chain in the synagogue courtyard before being burned.[46]

Mendelssohn was spared the full force of rabbinical denunciation because it was known that he was an irreproachably observant Jew;

indeed he argued that observance of the Torah was the defining essence of Jewish identity. Not a morsel of forbidden *trayf* passed his lips when he spent time with Nicolai and Lessing. He and Fromet kept the Sabbath to the letter and rejoiced in his family gathered around the table: candles, salt, bread, wine, blessings, rosy cheeks and full-hearted voices in the *birkhat hamozen*, the grace after the meal; the entire domestic scene orchestrated by the tireless Fromet. Sabbath with the Mendelssohns became known far and wide as a Jewish idyll. Their doors were thrown open to visitors who were treated as extended family, and on Friday night or Saturday afternoon would join in the running colloquium Mendelssohn gave on the Torah portion of the week. When Solomon Maimon returned to Berlin he wanted to seek Mendelssohn's opinion on his own criticism of Immanuel Kant's philosophy. But when he arrived on the threshold of Mendelssohn's house and peeked in, Maimon froze. A bourgeois home, *Kultur*, *Kuchen*, *Kaffee*, drapes and rugs, armchairs covered in damask; laughter, banter, high-spirited conversation. What was he? A perpetual student. A nobody with a head full of opinions. This visit was a mistake. Time to go before it got worse. But then the little man with the crooked nose appeared, gently steered him inside, introduced him, treated him with kindness. The welcome warmed Maimon; he began to glow with happy confidence. Next to being congratulated by Immanuel Kant for having discerned the nub of his philosophy (even when he presumed to criticise it), this was the best moment of Solomon Maimon's mercurial life.

But Mendelssohn was not always radiant with optimism. Lessing's death in 1781 had left him bereft. When his dead friend was accused of being more or less a follower of Spinoza, a pantheist – an atheist by a fancy name – for whom God was merely nature, Mendelssohn became embroiled in a long, bitter controversy to vindicate Lessing. Two of Mendelssohn's children died cruelly early: Mendel when he was a boy of six, and a daughter, Sarah, after eleven months. The worst thing was to have to say Kaddish for your children. His health was unpredictable. He went to bed putting himself in the hands of the Almighty, not knowing if in the morning he might wake to paralysis and pain. And for all the momentous changes embodied by Joseph's edict and Dohm's treatise for emancipation, Mendelssohn felt uneasy about both templates for the Jewish future. In the emperor's obsession with uniformity, he smelled a conversionary project in disguise. For all the carrying on about Usefulness and his well-publicised aversion to monks and Jesuits, Joseph II was still the Holy Roman Emperor, and those Christian schools with their lessons in German and algebra might not be entirely innocent of the old campaign for baptism.

Well intentioned (who could doubt it?) as Dohm was, there were things he said which were clumsy if not offensive. It was all very well wanting to make Jews more 'productive', but why should he assume that a life in business was somehow less 'useful' than one spent as an artisan, farmer or manufacturer? Had it not occurred to him that Mendelssohn was himself just such a merchant, in charge of Bernhard's silk business after his employer's death together with his widow? What was the good, after all, of producing commodities without a merchant to transport them to markets at home and abroad? Jews, with their incomparable network of extended families and firms, their mastery of countless tongues, their instinctive map of the connections between exotic supply and metropolitan markets, were the conduits through which international trade flowed. There they were in the ports and marts of the world: Bordeaux, Livorno, Trieste, Salonika, Tunis, Alexandria, Madras. There they were every year at the Leipzig Fair buying Polish rye and Russian fur and selling porcelain and wine; there they were in India buying rough diamonds and selling Mediterranean coral. In a liberal economic system they would be seen as 'productive' as anyone working the land or a loom.

Still more troubling was Dohm's provision that even when integrated into the institutions of the realm, the Jews would be permitted to retain their own courts, authorised to excommunicate members of the community judged to have violated their norms. Whether he liked it or not Mendelssohn was never far away from the ghost of Baruch Spinoza. True toleration, he said, must extend to those deemed heretics, outsiders, even atheists; anyone of any opinion. Since those of differing religions could never agree, none had the right to criminalise what they deemed to be sinful or ostracise those whom they judged transgressors. Jewish courts might judge matters of property between members of the community if they preferred such adjudications to those of the civil authority. But they had no right whatsoever to decree someone a pariah, with all the social and economic isolation that invoked. 'Reason's house of prayer requires no closed doors. It is not meant to guard anything inside or oppose entry to anyone from the outside.'

This was written in Mendelssohn's preface to a German translation of Menasseh ben Israel's profoundly moving *Vindiciae Judaeorum* of 1656, the same year in which Spinoza was cast out from the Sephardi community of Amsterdam, and buried alive beneath an avalanche of curses. Menasseh's pamphlet, a defiant counter-attack against English prejudice, had been a report from the long, irrational, violent history of Jew-hatred. Now, all too conscious, not least from cases of the blood libel in Posen and Warsaw, that the ugliest slanders had not been laid to rest, Mendelssohn brought the dismal history up to date. Once upon a time, he wrote, Jews were said to have 'desecrated communion wafers, pierced crucifixes, made them bleed, secretly circumcised children, dismembered them since we required blood for Passover ... now times have changed. Those defamations no longer have the same effect. Now it is "superstition" and stupidity, of all things, with which we are charged, and lack of moral feeling, good manners; an incapacity for art, science and useful occupations ... and irrepressible inclination to fraud, usury and crime.'[47]

As the possibility of Jews being fully integrated into civil society approached, so the fierceness of the attacks on them intensified – not with the perennial abuse of the streets, but from the barbed quills of the enlightened. Johann David Michaelis, the same reviewer whose scepticism about the likelihood of Lessing's Good Jew in *Die Juden* had begun Mendelssohn's career, now asserted that the Mosaic laws were themselves an insuperable barrier to the Jews ever being integrated into a truly united commonwealth. Their Sabbath meant they could not answer the country's call to arms; their obsession with a return to Zion meant that would always be their primary loyalty. The line of attack then became personalised. Another polemic asked, in terms reminiscent of Lavater, how Mendelssohn could possibly square his ostensible liberalism with the irrational obscurantism of his religion. If he truly believed in natural religion, in a creed of reason, the only reasonable thing to do was to accept the inevitable at the font.

With a heavy sigh Mendelssohn accepted the responsibility of an answer since the broadside was only incidentally about him and for the most part about Judaism and the Jews. His reply, *Jerusalem, or On Religious Power and Judaism*, appeared in 1783, three years before his death. What choice did he have? If not him then who else? The treatise, one of the great achievements of eighteenth-century liberalism, was in two parts. The first hit the sustaining pedal that had initially been depressed in his preface to Menasseh's *Vindiciae Judaeorum*, by denying to religions any of the powers possessed by the state to ensure the general good. Mendelssohn tracked through Hobbes and Locke, pondered from them the implications when men passed from a state of nature to a contract of sovereignty. But he ended insisting that the use of state power for religious coercion was not just a usurpation but also an offence against God. 'Reward and punish no doctrine ... let no one usurp a right that the Omniscient has reserved to himself.'[48] In a fair and rational society, nothing short of the absolute separation of church and state could protect the indispensable good of freedom of conscience.

Then Mendelssohn had to make a sudden swerve to defend his own adherence to Judaism and the religion itself from charges of it being irreconcilable with the general good of state and society. Hence yet another rudimentary tutorial on the true character of Judaism, in the spirit of Josephus, Leone Modena, Simone Luzzatto and Menasseh ben Israel. How many times did this have to be spelled out? Judaism, said Mendelssohn, was not based on revelation but laws: precepts, 'rules for life'. The epiphany on Sinai had given them a sacred aura, but they were above all a set of instructions for living, not a theology of salvation, neither did they carry with them any kind of dogma. None of the commandments in the Torah actually required a particular kind of statement of belief. For a brief period historically it was true that the Judaean state had allied itself to the Mosaic religion but that had ended with the destruction of the Temple and now those rules and moral guidance were the essence of what made a Jew Jewish. And there was nothing in them which made it impossible for such an observant Jew to be also a conscientious citizen of wherever he or she lived. The experience of life in a tolerant society like the Dutch republic proved as much. Military service was entirely possible for a good Jew if the defence of the land required it.

Those particular laws were made for Jews alone, thus relieving them of the obligation to force them on anyone else. Hence Judaism was, in fact, the least coercive religion imaginable. But its practices rested on more general principles – to be discovered and mulled over in endless oral conversations with the text: a common core of ethics, available to all. Free men might subscribe to those ethics if they were so persuaded, but there was nothing dogmatic about Judaism. While Christianity *demanded* unconditional submission to a belief in Christ the Saviour, the salvific meaning of his sacrifice, as the only way to save mankind from original sin, the Torah at no point expressly asked anyone to believe in any theology. Ultimately, Mendelssohn argued, it was indifferent to revelation except as the backstory of the founding of a moral code. Judaism even entertained the expansive notion of a set of ethics known to have existed *before* the giving of the Mosaic laws. Those who abided by the ethical instructions supposedly given to Noah, the 'Noahide laws' comprising the essence of ethical conduct – the aversion to pagan idolatry, the belief in a single God, the horror of murder and so on – would *not* be turned away from the gates of heaven but would have a share of 'the life to come'. For how, he asked rhetorically, could a loving God possibly deliver a set of laws dooming most of mankind to perdition?

This ethical cohabitation was vital to Mendelssohn because his personal experience of the Enlightenment was so gregariously social. Its bedrock, friendship – or as the legislators of the French Revolution would have it, *fraternité* – brought people together in mutual under-standing even when they differed on important things. The Monday Club or the Learned Coffee House was his template for an entire political society. There, between the card players and the billiard tables, the music and the periodicals, he could have a good argy-bargy with whomever over whatever came to mind without the obligation to blow each other's brains out should they end the discussion with no agreement. Such a place of diverse utterance was the only one Mendelssohn thought where Jews could truly thrive, for it meant they could sustain their observances unintimidated by a religious or polit-ical majority and without drawing the accusation of disloyalty. Liberal pluralism was the only system that could be truly good for the Jews. But they would give back, for this new blessing cut both ways; it was the only system which would also be good for mankind.

So if there was nothing in the laws of Judaism pulling its practi-tioners away from the fabric of civil society, why should Jews be required to abandon their precepts as the price of admission? Because, it was repeated, the retention of those rites and customs offended civil union. Really? Circumcision for their sons? Kosher meat? Dancing with the scrolls inside their synagogue on Simchat Torah? If, against all reason, others insisted on this irreconcilability, Mendelssohn wrote, better the Jews should renounce civil union rather than abandon the ways of their fathers.[49]

In a virtuoso coda, Mendelssohn made a brilliant polemical swerve back to his original conviction, the one that mattered most for Jews and thus for the world at large. What, he wondered, was so precious about 'union' anyway that it must always override the claims of diversity? Different beliefs, especially where they were grounded in mutually exclusive revelations, would never be capable of dissolving themselves into some fictitious or temporarily expedient comity. 'If you care about true piety, let us not feign agreement when diversity is evidently the plan and purpose of providence.'[50] Why not accept that, and restrict the role of the state to ensuring that irresolvable conflicts were not taken to the point of physical harm? The alternative to tolerating diversity was coercion for the sake of unity which was bound to be an admission of failure, the persuasiveness of a doctrine being the only sure way to make an enduring community of faith.

If all this sounds a commonplace piety now, it was not so then. Treading in the footsteps of Locke and the deist John Toland – and very much in tune with what Jefferson had to say just a few years earlier in the draft statute of toleration for the Commonwealth of Virginia, a document Mendelssohn is unlikely to have known – *Jerusalem* is the classic statement of western liberalism's commitment to the protection of free conscience. Its title is significant. Like Blake's, Mendelssohn's was a Jerusalem of the un-manacled mind. His reply to Michaelis's accusation that the longing for Zion made Jews a permanently disloyal population was that a physical return to Palestine was not on the cards. The greater urgency was to build a Jerusalem in the here and now and in a fashion that had eluded the actual thing: an encampment of unlike beliefs agreed on the necessity of coexistence. That was the true site of the temple of peace, the only one that mattered. Where Jews flourished beneath the canopy of toleration, humanity at large likewise prospered.

Mendelssohn's arguments remain shockingly relevant to our contemporary world where, in so many places, intolerance is once more murderously in arms. They remain a guiding light because, unlike Voltaire's strictures on the same subject, they were born from a love of religion, not a contempt for it, and thus take full measure of human psychological needs. 'Let everyone be permitted to speak as he thinks, to invoke God after his own manner or that of his fathers and seek salvation where he thinks he may find it as long as he does not disturb the public peace and acts honestly according to the civil laws. Let no one be a searcher of hearts and judge of thought. Let no one assume a right the Omniscient has reserved to Himself alone.'

Like all the greatest writing of his generation, from Scotland to Naples to Weimar, from Adam Ferguson to Giambattista Vico to Johann Gottfried Herder, *Jerusalem* also has a strain of social anthropology in its arguments, especially its discussion of the origins of language and the nature of signs. That it should find a place for free expression beside other similarly impassioned creeds, rather than reimagine the world as a happy playground of sceptics, was the measure of Mendelssohn's challenge, one that has not diminished with the centuries. Only in classes of political theory might its arguments seem a truism. To much of the rest of the world, from that day to this, they remain a utopian pipe dream or an obnoxious, threatening heresy. Just ask a Christian Copt in Cairo or a Muslim in Mandalay. Of all the many advances the *philosophes* supposed would become irreversible as humanity progressed towards the light – the eradication of illiteracy, ignorance, superstition, poverty and disease – the inability in much of the world to create tolerant societies would have confounded them the most.

As he got older Mendelssohn became oppressed by the insuperable difficulties in the way of building his Jerusalem of peaceful differences. The pains of his body seemed to ebb and flow with the torments of the world. When he could, he took himself off to parks and gardens to smell the fragrant blooms that had been sown on Fromet's bridal dress and which now adorned the Torah Ark. There he wandered the paths with Fromet or sat in an arbour with a book. The long road out of Dessau had brought him back, and always to language, which is why he had tried to puzzle through its origins and implications in *Jerusalem*. To be able to move between different tongues with equal or approximate ease was the key to the resolution of difference. The opposite of war was conversation. The mediator of misunderstandings was translation. The linguistic way ahead for the Jews, then, was obvious. To remain steadfast in the Torah they needed to experience all over again the strength and poetic beauty of Hebrew. But to act in the world of their neighbours they needed German. Yiddish, neither one thing nor the other, would leave them in no man's land, forever separate, forever exposed, forever strange to those who overheard the argot. Thus convinced, he had embarked on the enterprise which he hoped would build a bridge from the language of their religion to the language of their social emancipation.

The 'Bi'ur', as it became known, was a translation into High German of the Pentateuch, the Torah. But to make the transition easier, it was written in Hebrew characters, rather in the manner that some Arabic was written by Jews in Hebrew characters during the medieval centuries of Islam. Meant in the first place as a teaching tool for the Mendelssohn children, it was intended to take back from Christian Hebraists the scriptures they had rendered into their German. Re-enacting the way in which Mendelssohn himself had mastered German it was, and is, a beautiful but fantastical thing. In the Monday Club of Mendelssohn's mind as he quietly read to himself what he (and his family's tutors Dubno and Herz Homberg) had written it seemed unproblematically euphonious, a true meeting of minds and tongues. There had after all to be a beginning if a German-Jewish culture was to be properly made. *Bereshit, bara Elohim et hashamayim ve'et ha'aretz. Im Anfang schuf Gott die Himmel und die Erde.* In the beginning God created the heavens and the earth.

But while read silently the characters sound one song, the words they form make quite another.

And sometimes words misbehave. There was a summer evening in 1780 when Mendelssohn had been out strolling with his family in the Berlin gloaming. It was what Jewish families in Europe did and would do in Vienna, Prague, Paris, Budapest. But on this particular evening the serene satisfaction of being at home in the city was shattered like a pane of glass. Mendelssohn's family were set on by a crowd of youths hurling stones and abuse. The street rang with *'Juden, Juden, Juden'*.[51] Frightened, the children turned to their father and asked what they had done to deserve the terror. 'Yes dear Papa ... they are always chasing after us in the streets, cursing us, *Juden! Juden!* Is just being a Jew enough of a reason for them to curse us?' In the letter relating the encounter to a Catholic correspondent, Mendelssohn confessed that at that particular moment he was at a loss for words. He could say nothing by way of comfort to his scared and perplexed children, all of whom would grow up to grapple, in their own ways, with the problem. He could only say under his breath: 'People, people, when will you stop doing this?'

Unhappily we know the answer. And so, in his bleaker moments, did Mendelssohn. In a letter to the Swiss physician Johann Georg Zimmerman, who had tried to treat Mendelssohn's periodic onsets of paralysing pain, he reflected that 'we dreamt of nothing but Enlightenment and believed that the light of reason would illuminate the world so brightly that delusion and fanaticism could no longer be seen. But as we now see from the other side of the horizon the night with all its ghosts and demons is already falling. More frightening than anything is that evil is so alive and potent. Delusion and fanaticism act while all reason does is talk.'[52]

JEWS WITHOUT BEARDS

I. The Fighter and the Fancy

Even when he was beating the living daylights out of an opponent, delivering a *facer* to that particular spot between the brows which would bring on temporary blindness, or a *sickener* to the *mark*, the pit of the stomach, there was something oddly cherubic about Dan Mendoza: the long lashes fringing wide brown eyes; the Cupid's bow lips; the mass of dark, curly hair, grown long and artfully cut, tied at his neck with a black silk ribbon. One day that lovelock would be his undoing. He was too pretty to be taken seriously. And too short and too light into the bargain: five foot seven and barely 160 pounds, the weight of an apprentice. But when he stripped before the *set-to*, the *Fancy* saw that the handsome head was planted atop a bull neck and a barrel chest, and this should have warned anyone taking him on that they might not escape without a good deal of hurt. But one after the other, cocky bruisers looked at Dan and saw nothing but a dirty little Jewish tough from Mile End chancing his arm. Go on, how much damage could an Ebrew do? Quite a lot, as it turned out. Mendoza had *bottom*, as Pierce Egan, the writer of *Boxiana, Or Sketches of Ancient and Modern Pugilism*, recalled years afterwards, 'a bottom never impeached; and possessing wind that was seldom disordered'.[1] Without *bottom* (the fortitude to take punishment and come back smack-sharp from it) and without *wind* (staying power) you could have all the skill in the world and you would still go down. But Dan had both, and more too, for he was reckoned the neatest stopper and the quickest hitter in the game.[2] Others could deliver a more violent blow but Dan would stop them with his hard arm as if they had hit a rock, and then would counterpunch so quickly that the barrage of hits turned into a single rhythmic fusillade.[3] If you were unguarded, the punishing counterblow, the one you would still be feeling days later, would be the *Mendoza*, otherwise known as the *chop* or *chopper*: a sudden upward (or, more rarely, downward) diagonal swipe with the knuckled back of the hand. To land those you not only needed great rigidity between wrist and elbow but phenomenal flexibility at the shoulder. Try a mock Mendoza, preferably in the air, and you'll see what I mean. Those who got chopped usually assumed a look of surprise. There were those of course who judged the Mendoza a typically Jewish trick: low-down and dirty; but then they would, wouldn't they?

A good part of the Fancy who pursued his set-tos up and down England, once converted to the skills of the Jew, gave him the confidence of their bets. Then, they did handsomely out of the fortunes of Dan and joined in the lusty choruses of 'Mendoza forever!' For the Jews, to have one of their own cheered rather than pelted with abuse or stones was a giddy novelty. So, not quite believing their luck, they too sang the praises of their hero. There were eight thousand Jews living in England by the late eighteenth century and a thousand of them were said to have shown up at Doncaster for the third and last of his great grudge matches with Richard Humphreys. 'Daniel, Daniel, *vekhayam!*' they chanted after the victory; 'Daniel, Daniel, live forever!'

Mendoza lived long enough, at any rate, to publish his memoirs when he was fifty-two, the first of any professional sportsman, but then he was the first in many things. No Jew before him had been taken to Windsor in the royal carriage to converse with King George, and easily too, as if they were old companions strolling the castle terrace.[4] Before Mendoza, with the notable exception of Gluckel of Hameln's memoir, Jewish autobiographies had been the exclusive province of rabbis, philosophers, men of mind and faith like Leone Modena and Solomon Maimon.[5] But not all Jews, then and now, however regrettably, see their fate governed by the exertions of philosophy, and this was especially so in worldly, violent, business-crazy Hanoverian England. Not that Mendoza was mindless; quite the opposite. He was, conceded Pierce Egan, 'intelligent and communicative', singular qualities in a Broughton's Rules fighter.[6] Mendoza liked to think of himself as a 'professor of pugilism' and he created an 'academy' of self-defence while he was still in his twenties. His first book, *The Art of Boxing*, was dedicated to 'his Scholars'. Bare-fist pugilism, though often accused of 'blackguardism', he believed to be a science which, properly analysed, comprehended and learned, would always prevail over brute disadvantages of height and weight.[7] His teaching was in the first place for all those who wanted to follow his example, and many, especially among the Jews of London, did. A succession of Jewish pugilists – 'Dutch' Sam Elias, Elisha Crabbe, Aby Velasco and many more – were his disciples. But his memoir is full of instances of his being picked on, insulted and assaulted as a Jew, and this was the strongest motive in Mendoza's choice of vocation. He was certainly not the first Jew to have fought back against intimidation with something more physical than reasoned indignation, but he was the first to write about it. Jews who mastered a Mendoza would no longer be taken as easy quarry; there had been centuries of stooping and shuffling. 'Spit in a Jew's face, give him a box on the ear with one hand and a farthing with the other,' a character in a popular novel said, reflecting what had been commonly assumed, 'and he will pocket the affront and thank you.'[8] After Dan you might, instead, expect a Jew to take a fighting stance.

When Mendoza was born in 1764, no one among England's Jews had forgotten the paranoid hatred which had greeted mild attempts to pass a Jewish naturalisation bill eleven years earlier. It had been met with a barrage of vicious absurdities. Squibs and broadsides claimed the Jews, those inveterate accomplices of 'Old Corruption', had bribed the Pelham government. Members of the Commons and Lords had apparently agreed to be circumcised in return for election funds. One caricature had a prominent supporter of the bill, Sir William Calvert, being circumcised on the very steps of St Paul's! But the Ancient Constitution would not 'give an inch'. Ha ha ha. The Jews were notorious clippers, whether of foreskins or coin. Everyone knew Jewish brokers controlled the stock market, never mind that the number of brokers was limited to twelve. Now they would buy up the shires! Locusts is what they were, a horrid creeping swarm, stripping anything on which they alighted. And like vermin they carried contagion on their foul-smelling bodies. 'I verily believe,' wrote one typical pamphleteer, 'that if the naturalisation bill should occasion a second swarm of this kind of locusts to come and settle in the town we should have a kind of plague or sickness as often they have in

Constantinople.'⁹ The lord mayor of London, Sir Crisp Gascoigne, warned that the measure would 'tend greatly to the dishonour of the Christian religion'. Before you knew it the cathedrals would be turned into synagogues and the tombs at St Paul's and Westminster would contain the remains of 'Sir Nadab Issachar' and 'The Rt Hon. the Earl of Balaam'. On Guy Fawkes Night 1753, the effigy of the gunpowder plotter was replaced by a mannikin Jew, with hooked nose and beard, burned to black ash on the bonfire in imitation of a Spanish auto-da-fé. 'That I hate every Jew / Believe I speak true' ran the popular refrain. A fantasy of the anti-Semites was that Jews secretly craved and gobbled the very pork they pretended to abhor. Caricatures featured buxom Jewesses, their breasts spilling from the neckline, leaning greasily forward to kiss a piglet, an anglicised version of the old German *Judensau* in which Jews sucked at the teats of porkers or greedily swallowed their shit. 1753 and the years following saw random pork forcings. Jews on the road or in taverns were jumped on, roped to a pillar, their mouths pulled open and crammed with scalding gammon and bacon. 'Get a bit of pork / Stick it on a fork / And give it to a Jew boy, a Jew.'¹⁰ (Some tavern keepers served only pork items, as a display of anti-Jewish patriotism.) In mid-Wales on the road between Abergavenny and Crickhowell, the body of the pedlar Jonas Levi was found. His box of wares had been plundered and his skull smashed in; fragments of bone were scattered beside the rest of him.¹¹ There were other murders, some in the navy seaports where Jews bought and sold from sailors. Strains of this frantic hatred, often taking the form of spitting randomly into the face of a passing Jew or pulling his beard, persisted well into Mendoza's time. Francis Place, the radical tailor, remembered that 'when a Jew was seen on the streets it was a signal for assault. I have seen many Jews hounded and hunted, kicked, cuffed, pulled by the beard and spat upon and so barbarously assaulted in the streets without any protection from passers-by or police ... Dogs could not be worse used.'¹²

If you went to the Jewish districts of London, one author wrote, you will find that 'the followers of Moses are the most nasty, filthy people under the canopy of heaven'.¹³ On Easter Sunday, in some school playing grounds, Robert Southey recalled, you could hear the merry chant of the boys: 'Christ is risen / Christ is risen / All the Jews must go to prison.' Some of the abuse recycled medieval persecution, proposing punitive taxes to be imposed on Jews for their presumptuous temerity. In 1775 one such petitioner to the prime minister, Lord North, was considerate enough to make it clear that he was 'not for exterminating them [the Jews], but surely My Lord it will be equitable and just to make them pay something for such extraordinary favours' as they presently enjoyed.[14] Most of the English looked on Jewish religious rituals with supercilious bafflement, but others were capable of going much further. 'There is something hateful in the very nature of those ceremonies which they have the infamy to call religious,' wrote the radical William Cobbett in one of his many anti-Semitic outbursts.[15] Others wanted to impose the yellow badge or the old twin-tablet white badge ordered by Edward I, since the most dangerous Jews were those who didn't look Hebrew enough – not the bedraggled hairy hawkers, but the unbearded, the smooth-jawed who might pass for Christian. On the other hand, for all their spurious airs of civility, if you looked hard enough you could always tell. There were certain giveaways. 'You know a Jew at first sight,' wrote William Romaine, a famous evangelical preacher at St George's Hanover Square, 'look at his eyes. Don't you see a malignant blackness underneath them which gives them such a cast as bespeaks guilt and murder. You can always tell a Jew by this mask it throws such a dead livid aspect over all his features that he carries enough evidence in his face to convict him of being a crucifier.'

No one said that of Daniel Mendoza's face, or to it, especially not after it had become one of the most famous phizzes in England. In the late 1780s and 90s it was everywhere: on tankards and teapots; snuffboxes and rummers; posters and songsheets. And it was a departure from the usual Jewish grotesque beloved by the caricaturists: lank-haired, bearded, greasy-chopped, hook-nosed.[16] Though it was beyond even his power to succeed entirely, for a while at least, Mendoza elbowed Shylock aside as the archetype of a Jew. No squalid usurer he, hunched over his counting table, 'my dearing' you to death while he cracked his knuckles and took your measure and your money. All Mendoza had in common with Shylock was his mercilessness to those who had impugned him, betrayed him, not lived up to their word. He was a great one for keeping one's word was Daniel Mendoza.

No sportsman before him had taken control of his own persona, promoted it so creatively, and turned 'Mendoza the Jew' from an expression of surprised contempt to one of star-struck admiration; created, in fact, the first thoroughly marketed sports celebrity cult. The astral metaphor was used on a sportsman for the first time when it was written he was 'a star of the first brilliancy'.[17] Though he was not especially observant, so far from running away from his Jewishness, Mendoza turned it into a promotional asset, especially when matched against paragons of English manhood like Richard Humphreys, 'Butcher Martin' or Tom Tyne. And his strength came almost as much from his words as from his bare knuckles. He played the press like a fortepiano, turning his bouts into theatrical feuds into which the opposition walked: inadvertent extras in a stage melodrama. Exchanges of letters were published in the papers. The public took sides and then bought tickets. Seconds and 'bottle holders' were hired from the growing circle of Mendoza's defeated opponents who turned into his devotees, so that the personnel around the stage resembled platoons of rivals. When their hero was impugned or, as they saw it, robbed of a decision, they were ready to get stuck in themselves and, much to the joy of the spectators, a by-fight ensued. No one understood better than Mendoza how that newborn but ravenous monster, the English Public, needed feeding not just with gory spectacle but with a gripping Story. In the very improbability of a Fighting Jew he knew he had a thriller. In his raw-boned, chop-fisted way, Dan Mendoza was yet another consummate narrator of the story of the Jews. But he was also aware that he had begun an entirely new chapter: the Jew who fights back.

The Jewish London in which Mendoza grew up was a culture of social extremes, even by the standards of Hanoverian England. At the bottom end were the trudging legions of street hawkers and pedlars; at the other end, the Monied. Grandees like Samson Gideon and the brothers Goldsmid made fortunes as financiers of government debt at a time when to fight far-flung imperial and European contests, administrations were chronically short of funds. But they also worked on the capital market as stock jobbers, licensed brokers on the Exchange, denizens of Jonathan's Coffee House where they traded gossip and stock predictions, even sometimes, to the outrage of the rabbis, on the Sabbath itself following morning services at the Ashkenazi 'Great Synagogue' in Duke's Place, or the Portuguese synagogue of Bevis Marks.[18] Alongside them were merchants of diamonds and coral like the Francos, de Castros, the Franks and the Pragers, importing rough stones from Madras where they stationed buying agents, often family members. As with almost all Asian trade, it was difficult to find a commodity the Indians wanted in return for their merchandise. Usually this meant shipping out bullion. But the diamond traders had managed to acquire one item southern India could not get enough of: *Corallium rubrum*, red coral, branch or staghorn. High-caste Hindus roped chains of it about their throats, arms and ankles and laid it on the funeral pyres of departed kin to ensure a safe passage to the future life.[19] Every spring, hundreds of boats sailed from Marseilles, Livorno, Naples and Corsica, towards the North African coast. They dropped anchor at a safe distance from the reefs while diving boys working from skiffs harvested the precious underwater tongues and branches. Six thousand to eight thousand pounds of coral was considered a decent harvest, brought to market at Livorno where a thriving Jewish community shipped much of the merchandise on to London for the outward-bound diamond trade. Most of the rough diamonds coming into London from India (and later Brazil) were first sent to Amsterdam and Antwerp for polishing and cutting into rose facets, table stones or Peruzzi brilliants, before being returned to the city for retail. But there were some polishers and cutters in east London like Abraham Levy, and Levy Norden, 'an opulent and very considerable jeweller ... having diamond mills in Wheeler Street, White Chapple', who imported, cut and sold all within the same firm.[20]

Some of the old-fashioned among the monied continued to live above their business chambers and warehouses in Bishopsgate and Broad Street. They put in regular appearances at one of the big synagogues, the Ashkenazi Great Synagogue on Duke's Place near Aldgate, enlarged to magnificence in the 1760s by George Dance the Elder, or the Sephardi Bevis Marks, opened in 1701, its exterior hidden away but the interior modelled on the grand Portuguese wonder in Amsterdam: dark panels and branching brass candelabra. They came to the services, tricorn-hatted and wigged, the young men grudgingly forgoing dress swords replaced by wooden substitutes, which, after some debate, the rabbis had allowed were permissible according to *halakha*. Without those sham hilts showing, they ran the risk of being set on while they walked to *shul*. The communities adopted the same kind of genteel obligations as elsewhere in the European diaspora:

a modest, six-bed hospital for the poor; funds for burials; Hebrew schools with a smattering of modern instruction. When George III succeeded to the throne in 1760, the two communities combined to form a 'Board of Deputies' to make representations to the government and inaugurated its duties by presenting ceremonial congratulations to the new monarch.

A number of the bigwigs sought more fashionable, leafy addresses. Daniel Defoe reported in his *Tour* in 1722 that 'the Jews have fixd upon Highgate and Hampstead for country houses', while some bought houses in the newly constructed squares of the West End and Marylebone. By the 1760s, those at the top of the tree ventured south to the riverside hamlets of Richmond, Teddington, Isleworth, Mortlake and Twickenham. When Yosef Hayim Azulai, an emissary from the Palestine communities, seeking financial support, came to London and tried to do the rounds of prospective benefactors, he was told, with the usual shoulder shrug and outspread hands that signified Jewish regret, that alas they had all 'gone to the country ... to tend their gardens'. Modish architects were lined up to build Anglo-Palladian or Adam villas, complete with little rotundas, and libraries stocked with Sir William Chambers's *Designs of Chinese Buildings* or Colen Campbell's *Vitruvius Brittanicus*, Pope and Dryden as well as Maimonides and Mendelssohn. On a fine summer evening the Jewish gentry would stroll out to the sandy riverside path, a pair of small dogs gambolling at their heels, drop a pinch of snuff into their anatomical snuffbox between thumb and index finger, take a deep, nostril-sucking sniff, and as the tingling pleasure set in, survey the winding river; their delightful Thames. It was all very *comme il faut*. When the son-in-law of the diamond merchant Jacob Prager, who himself lived comfortably in Amsterdam, went to stay with Jacob's brother Yehiel at his house in Clapton, he found himself in an idyll of gentility surrounded by footmen, valets, gardeners. Jacob wrote to his brother that though the boy had returned home it was with 'English air in his head – all he talks about is the richness, the influence, the pleasant life you lead ... unlike anyone in the world'.[21] Back in town the rabbis vented their displeasure at the disgraceful immodesty of fashionable Jewish women 'naked to the cleavage ... two full spans back and front'. 'The whole aim' of such get-ups, wrote Hart Lyon, the long-serving, long-suffering chief rabbi of the Duke's Place synagogue, was 'not to appear like daughters of Israel'.[22]

For the grandees themselves, though, going riverside was not to be taken as abandoning the ancestral faith. Indeed there were some ceremonies – *taschlikh*, the casting of bread on the waters on Rosh Hashanah afternoon, to carry off sinful impurities – for which the proximity of the Thames came in handy. And although the new suburban addresses put them well beyond walking distance of the city synagogues, many of them built private prayer rooms inside their houses from which on the New Year, a *shofar* could be blown to the surprise of passing bargemen. They made the most of their milieu. Benjamin Goldsmid's house boasted thirty bedrooms, all with laid-on water, and a substantial art collection which included work by Rubens and Van Dyck on New, as well as Old, Testament subjects, but it also had a fine private synagogue. Their tables were abundantly supplied (mostly but not invariably kosher); their writing desks and armoires handsomely inlaid; their hounds glossy-coated, their manners irreproachable, their cellars enviably stocked. Baronial-scale portraits of Goldsmids done by the masters of the Academy stared from the walls. It was all damn'd magnificent. When Benjamin threw an enormous party to celebrate his friend Nelson's victory on the Nile, the whole of society clamoured for invitations. When his brother Abraham moved into his own grand villa, Morden Lodge, he threw a feast for three hundred. Naturally, the Prince Regent was among the guests, trailing the usual entourage of fops, blades and macaronis.

Whether they formally stayed Jews or abandoned rigorous observance, the patriciate socialised with Gentile friends and neighbours. The repartee of the Thames Jews and the chatty informality of their women were diverting enough for them to be asked to dinner by the nabob of Strawberry Hill, Horace Walpole, who thought the odd Jew added to his dinner company brought social colour and intellectual liveliness. How amusing these Jews could be when they put their minds to it! Why, a man might almost forgive them the barbarousness of their superstitions; and if they insisted on taking the knife to their infants' foreskins in the name of some strangely invented covenant it was, one supposed, entirely their own affair.

One of those riverside Jews whose company Walpole enjoyed was the diamond merchant Aaron Franks, member of a dynasty that stretched across the Atlantic. His New York nephew Moses had come to London in the early 1760s, swiftly becoming a Figure in the

Ashkenazi trading community and a major donor to the rebuilding of Duke's Place in 1766. Before long Moses Franks was himself the owner of a fine villa, with large stables, at Teddington known as 'The Grove' into which he moved with his wife, Aaron's daughter Phila, whom Joshua Reynolds did his best to flatter. In November 1774 they would have encountered Horace Walpole at Aaron's house in Isleworth when he arranged a chamber recital by the *chazzan* of the Great Synagogue at Duke's Place, Myer Lyon. As 'Michael Leoni' the opera singer, Lyon was much in demand by society, and that November evening he delighted the mixed gathering. 'I heard Leoni,' wrote Walpole (usually hard to impress), 'who pleased me more than anything I have heard these hundred years.' Lyon/Leoni's performance of Handel songs and arias was 'full of melancholy' – a quality predictably associated with Jewish performers. Though full of vocal feeling, Walpole added that he sang 'in a genuine simple style and did not put one in pain like the rope dancers'.

Myer Lyon had come from Frankfurt in 1767 to be cantor at Duke's Place and held the post for decades while also making a brilliant career in opera and theatre. He was typical of a whole subculture of London performers who managed to stay unapologetically Jewish and yet find a place in the public world of the theatre. His post at the Great Synagogue was conditional on being a *yehudi kasher*, an observant Jew, so no Saturday performances (until Sabbath was over in the evening) and no celebratory pork pies. Like Mendoza, he knew very well how to turn his Jewishness into a cultural asset, so that he became admired for elaborate melismas, assumed by both fans and critics to be an extension of his cantorial flourishes. (They were probably right.) Scaling the octaves and hitting the falsettos when called for, he developed a following which crossed over from the Jewish to the non-Jewish public and which would come in throngs to Duke's Place on the Sabbath and high holidays to hear him perform. One of them, the hymn composer Thomas Oliver, was so taken by the *chazzan*'s 'Yigdal Elohim Chai' that he turned it into 'The God of Abraham Praise' for church use. In *Hymns Ancient and Modern* the composer is still listed as 'M. Leoni'.[23]

Lyon also took on pupils, coaching them both for *shul* and, if they showed enough promise, for the stage. His star protégé was the orphan John Braham, whom he said he found on the street selling pencils and

trained as a *meshorrer*: a descant chorister for the synagogue. When
Braham was just thirteen, Lyon gave him his debut at Covent Garden
on the evening of his own benefit recital in 1787 where the youth gave
his all to Thomas Arne's 'The Soldier, Tir'd of War's Alarms'. After
Lyon emigrated to Jamaica to be cantor in the synagogue at Kingston
(his opera voice declining), Braham was taken in charge by Abraham
Goldsmid, who paid for lessons by the castrato Venanzio Rauzzini.
By the time his voice broke, he had developed into a tenor good
enough to sing with and for the best: royalty, quality and *both* Napoleon
Bonaparte and Horatio Nelson. In his prime he could command the
immense sum of £2,000 for fifteen performances in Dublin, and his
singing in *The Death of Nelson* in 1811 was so affecting that Emma
Hamilton collapsed in an emotional swoon and had to be carried from
the house. Or so it was said. Though Braham took up with the very
un-Jewish Nancy Storace, he does not seem to have converted and
may even have sung at his old place of worship on special occasions:
weddings, Kol Nidrei. Like Mendoza and the Jewish prizefighters after
him, Braham was conscious of being seen and heard as a Jew and
never hid from it. How could he, when sneeringly anti-Semitic verses
were published about him? 'His voice and his judgement completely
atone / for that heap of repulsion he cannot disown,' a typical product
rhymed. Even a tepid admirer like Leigh Hunt thought the 'nasal'
quality of his singing could be attributed to 'moral, even monied
causes'.[24]

Stage Jews – caricatural knuckle-cracking wheedling figures – were
a standard feature of a lower type of comedy; but Jews on stage made
themselves strongly felt across a whole range of Georgian entertainment. As would forever be the case, Jewish talent welcomed the chance
to play to the gallery of expectations while taking back the stereotypes
from the Gentiles and stopping short of gross self-mockery. Hannah
Norsa knew lowlife London better than most, and became the first
and most famous Polly Peachum in John Gay's *The Beggar's Opera*,
getting the authentic colour of her acting from her father's Covent
Garden tavern, the Punch Bowl. Being the mistress of the supreme
master of patronage, the prime minister Robert Walpole (often taken
as the butt of Macheath jokes), did nothing to harm her career. Jewish
conjurers and magicians were in demand, none more so than Jacob
Philadelphia who hailed from that city, many of them hired by the

circus impresario Philip Astley.[25] But Jacob 'Jemmy' Decastro was the
first great Jewish comic actor of the English theatre, prepared, if needs
and the purse must, to do a bit of clowning on the side for Mr Astley's
Amphitheatre or his kowtowing hanky-panky *Ombres Chinoises* show.
Decastro's Jewish progress through show business would become very
familiar in the generations which followed, all the way through to the
era of music hall, radio and cinema.[26] He was an East End Sephardi
boy from Houndsditch (like Mendoza), with an uncle who was a
warden at Bevis Marks and a severely rabbinically minded father who
made sure Jacob was schooled in Gemara and who raised eyebrows
at his stage work. But the adolescent Jacob fell hard for the beauties
of English literature, oratory and theatre, saving up to see David
Garrick, who seemed to him to combine all three arts, whenever he
could. At fifteen he formed a Purim theatricals company and was so
fine in the comic parts that he was in demand at all the great Jewish
houses, and some non-Jewish ones too. Despite all this rumbustiously
precocious talent, what young Jacob really wanted was a nice position
with one of the Madras diamond-trading houses and was bitterly
disappointed when that prospect failed to materialise. So he fell back
on the talent which had everyone chuckling and applauding. Jemmy
Decastro was a born mimic: an impressionist. He could do everyone,
but his speciality was the comedian Tom Weston. When Jemmy started
off in the Weston voice 'LAWD he was frumpt', polite company fell
apart with laughing, so much so that if Weston was unavailable or
too expensive, Jemmy would be hired to play him in his place. For a
while it seemed that the Decastro Weston, much to the comedian's
annoyance, was funnier than the original. And Jemmy had other strings
to his bow, none of them especially subtle but all of them entertainment gold. He could warble Jewishly and in the Italian style with a
falsetto that couldn't quite make it but the audience knew was Leoni
or Braham. He became a fixture at Astley's Amphitheatre and on tour
with both father and son, and, needless to say, was recruited as an
after-dinner act by the talent collector Abraham Goldsmid who just
had to have the best musicians, singers, comics and tragedians on tap
at Morden Lodge whenever he needed tip-top entertainment for his
friend Nelson, or the Prince of Wales.

There were other ways to service Gentile delight. Virtuoso silversmiths like Abraham Lopes de Oliveira, just two generations out from

a New Christian grandfather banker in Madrid, were excluded from the regular profession by the Guild of Goldsmiths and worked most of the time for synagogues providing exquisite crowns and finials for the Sefer Torah. But Oliveira's moment came when he was commissioned to make the elaborately wrought and chased plate which served as the annual gift for incoming lord mayors of London. On Lord Mayor's Day, Oliveira's dishes would be piled high with pyramids of toothsome Sephardi confectionery – *bolos de amor*, the little love cakes flavoured with just a drop of orange-flower water; sugar-ring *rosquilhas*, sometimes with anisette, sometimes not; *quejados*, and melting *masapoin* – all coming from the sumptuous kitchen of the Sephardi queen of confectionery: Leonor Marais.[27]

Inevitably, there were some, especially among the 'Deer Park' Jews, who were tempted by the pragmatic font. After all, they could not help noticing that the landed but embarrassingly mortgaged classes were open to the possibility of assistance from Jewish money through intermarriage. The pattern is familiar: the first generation retained its accent, its knowledge of Hebrew (sometimes even publishing learned commentaries in the ancestral tongue), keeping accounts and business correspondence in Yiddish or Ladino, and even sometimes keeping its beards. Their lives were coloured by the habits of the last family address: Hamburg, Altona, Amsterdam or Frankfurt. But in the next generation, beards, accents and any vestiges of distinguishing dress had all gone, the patriarchs and matriarchs accepting the assimilation, if not always happily. Samson Gideon supposed that in exchange for ponying up a cool million at the time of the Jacobite rebellion and invasion, and another timely £300,000 so that Britain could enter the War of the Austrian Succession, allowing George II to pose as the Victor of Dettingen, it was the decent thing to do to make him a baronet. But notwithstanding its obligations, the quality looked at Gideon and saw the coarsely pretentious stockjobber of the Exchange and passed him over. For all Gideon's airs and his insistence that he was *not* in fact a supporter of the naturalisation bill, he still found himself grotesquely caricatured. An anti-government print called 'The Good Conference with the Jew Predominant' has Gideon speaking in fractured, thick-tongued English: 'Dare [*sic*] Gentlemens, my very good friends, dere be de puss [purse] collected by my tribe for de great favour.'[28] But Gideon's honour was merely postponed a generation. The father knew

what had to be done, and the baptism of his son allowed his heir to
be raised, in due course, to a baronetcy. Transformed into Lord Eardley,
the younger Samson Gideon married a girl of impeccable country
pedigree and without more fuss or ado the erstwhile Jew vanished into
the velvet-coated ranks of the landed aristocracy.

Hanoverian England was a monied oligarchy, and despite nose-
holding in the shires at the disagreeable prospect of riding to hounds
with ambitious Hebrews, there were few sections of Georgian society
that would not, ultimately, open their doors to persons of Jewish
origin, assuming that their 'better sort' would do the decent thing at
the font and add a little sweetener at the bank. One by one institutions
opened up even to the nominally converted. By the last quarter of
the eighteenth century, men who had been born Jews, and in many
cases whose parents remained so, could be found in the fellowships
of the Society of Antiquaries, the Royal Society, the Royal College of
Physicians, Oxford colleges, Masonic lodges (a crucial site of social
connection), as privy councillors to the government of Ireland, barris-
ters in the Inns of Court and as senior officers in the Royal Navy.
They were on friendly terms with the leading lights of Hanoverian
culture, with David Garrick and William Hogarth, and their portraits
were painted by the best, including two successive presidents of the
Royal Academy, Joshua Reynolds and Benjamin West.

As elsewhere, in other times and places, Jewish medicine made
more friends than Jewish money. Isaac Schomberg – son, grandson
and brother to physicians – was Garrick's doctor, and was, therefore,
the last person Garrick saw alive in 1779. The great thesp is reputed
to have looked at his Jewish doctor and friend and said 'Though last
not least in love', which sounds suspiciously epigrammatic for a
dying man. It is thought that Thomas Hudson, who painted a sweetly
sympathetic portrait of Isaac, did so as repayment for services
rendered. Isaac was known for his 'warm benignity of soul'. Yet the
path to acceptance was never uncomplicated. Isaac's father had been
born Meyer Löw in Vetzburg, Württemberg. That Meyer's father
was also a doctor doubtless encouraged the son who, like other
Jewish students in Germany, was able to study medicine at university,
in this case the Ludoviciana at Giessen. Dr Meyer then moved around
the Ashkenazi world, practising in Schweinsberg and Metz before
settling in London in 1721. If his English was weak (as it almost

certainly was), he could get by on Judaeo-German Yiddish spoken by most of the congregation at Duke's Place. And the language would have been an asset in his first post as doctor to the Ashkenazi poor who made up the largest part of the population of the City and east London. This, however, was not the kind of job Meyer Schomberg (as he now called himself) was likely to settle for. The better-off and well-connected Jews of Duke's Place, much taken with the learned doctor, whose English improved by leaps and bounds, helped with introductions to the City's merchants, and Schomberg had his own strategies for enlarging his practice. A grudgingly admiring observer described him as 'a fluent talker and a man of insinuating address' who had the nerve to do something which had never occurred to anyone in the English profession: rent a large property and, on certain days, keep open house and a generous table. 'All the young surgeons were invited and were treated with indiscriminate civility that had much the appearance of friendship but in reality meant nothing more than that they should recommend him to practices.'[29] Such cordial hospitality without regard to rank was thought shockingly improper, but it had exactly the hoped-for effect. Schomberg's practice grew until he was earning four thousand guineas a year by 1740. He was made a fellow of the Royal Society in 1726, a brother of the Regular Order of Swan and Rummer Lodge of Masons in 1730 and their Grand Steward four years later, thus guaranteeing an even wider circle of patients. It helped of course that the Masonic cult was based on their ritualised obsession with the architecture of Solomon's Temple. Meyer and his wife Rachel had seven sons and a daughter Rebecca. Their life as middle-class professional London Jews should have been full of satisfaction.

Which, somehow, it was not. Meyer feuded with a fellow doctor, the Sephardi Jacob de Castro Sarmiento who, for some reason, he could not abide and whose career he actively tried to thwart, publicly accusing his rival of misprescribing opiates and other sundry malpractices. This argumentative side he passed on to his son Isaac, who embarked on a two-decade bitter dispute with the Royal College of Physicians. Most of Isaac's famous patients came to him notwithstanding his lack of the college's certification.

Another son, Ralph, became a thorn buried deep in his father's side. Educated at Merchant Taylors' School, one of the few places

that briefly admitted Jewish boys in the eighteenth century, Ralph
turned into a dissolute spendthrift and was packed off by his father
to European academies where he proceeded to waste Meyer's
generous allowance of £100 per annum.[30] Not satisfied with stiffing
his papa, Ralph actually tried to sue him when the allowance was
stopped. Summarily ordered home from Europe Ralph took himself
off to Scarborough, where there were no Jews at all but where a
family acquaintance, Dr Shaw, offered to keep an eye on the wastrel.
As soon as he got wind of this supervision Ralph moved further
off to Malton until once again he had exhausted all means of
support.

    In a show of contrition, Ralph attempted a reconciliation with
Meyer, asking him whether he might, perhaps, return to London
and set up (like one of his brothers) as a notary public. At this point,
the father could deny the son nothing. He not only agreed but
established Ralph in an office by the Royal Exchange with a partner
who in no time at all was complaining that Ralph had neglected
business quite disgracefully. Rather after the fact, Ralph then
announced that notarising suited him not at all. Before Meyer could
bear down on him with the full force of fatherly fury, Ralph shipped
off to Barbados where he became tutor to a planter family, still
somehow managing to draw heavy bills on the long-suffering Meyer's
account. When that line of credit ran dry, back he came to London,
and despite an ongoing career which made the lives of Fielding's
heroes seem constant by comparison, managed to win the affection
and hand of Elizabeth Crowcher, the daughter of a prosperous
London merchant. This was the moment (as for so many others in
the second Jewish generation) when a quick trip to the font might
have been in order to seal the match and plan the church wedding.
But it is not at all clear that Ralph was ever baptised. If he were not
still a Jew, why would he pursue his latest career project – that of
becoming a physician like his brother Isaac and his father – at
Marischal College in Aberdeen? For in the spirit of the Scottish
Enlightenment, indeed the embodiment of its liberalism, Marischal
College had become the first and only institution in Britain to accept
Jews as medical students. Undertaking a correspondence course,
Ralph qualified as a doctor in 1744. The newly reminted Dr Ralph
Schomberg went off again to establish himself in a practice at Great

Yarmouth. Over the uncharacteristically quiet years which followed he and Elizabeth produced a brood of ten children. Like his baptised brother Alexander, educated at St Paul's before embarking on a brilliant naval career which saw him serve with James Wolfe in the St Lawrence campaign, Ralph underwent this passage into Englishness without ever thinking of changing his name. He was just Dr Schomberg the provincial physician. Occasionally of course the respectable ordinariness of it all made him restive and he would go off to Bath where on the pretext of taking the waters, or ministering them, he managed to enjoy its society to the full. Apparently he was not the only Jew there, either. 'Bath is at present very full and brilliant,' Ralph wrote merrily to his good friend Emanuel Mendes da Costa, known to him as 'Manny', 'to which the presence of HRH the Duke of York does not a little contribute. I am not idle. We have a good many Bnei Israel here.'[31] But the occasional outing in society seems not to have been quite enough to satisfy Ralph's itch for petty devilry. The image he liked to project in his retirement at Pangbourne was that of the valetudinarian country gentleman, part-time doctor, a mild and upright soul which is how Gainsborough portrayed him, full-length, leaning on his cane in some oaken glade of Albion. But according to sources possibly not altogether cordial towards rusticating Jews, or at any rate this one, he had been caught with his hand in the Sunday church collection.

Emanuel Mendes da Costa would have his own serious difficulties with the law, but not before he had made a name for himself as a serious, estimable, natural scientist.[32] Like the Schombergs, da Costa was a second-generation Jew, conscious of the journey his family had made (Portugal and Holland) and of the lustre of the extended da Costa clan. But unlike Meyer Schomberg, Emanuel's father would come to grief in a rash commercial venture. Misfortune prompted the sons to cast around for some sort of anchorage in British society, though they went about it in very different ways. Emanuel's brother Jacob, who came to call himself Philip, attempted to elope with a wealthy heiress-cousin, Catherine da Costa Villalene. When she dismissed the idea, Jacob was caddish enough to sue her for breach of contract![33] Emanuel, on the other hand, became passionate about fossils, accumulating a large collection of specimens and contributing to the debate on the formation of the earth's crust – the arguments

between Vulcanists and Neptunists as to whether geological fire or
flood had been primordially decisive. Emanuel, who also dabbled in
ancient Hebrew history, produced enough respectable notices on this
and that subject for him to be elected both to the Royal Society and
the Society of Antiquaries, both palladiums of the learned in Georgian
London. To the scientific gentry, the Jewish fossilist – and author of
A Natural History of Fossils – became in his own right a charming
human curiosity: the Jew who remained faithful to his religion and
yet had plunged scientifically into the history of creation. Any teasing
about his Jewishness was generally of the most genial kind. Invited
to help create a fossil grotto for the Duke of Richmond's garden, his
host enquired about the dining arrangements during his stay, 'unless
the lobsters of Chichester should be a temptation by which a weaker
man might be seduced'. There could be other foods too 'which would
be an abomination to your nation'. Then came the genuinely touching
expression of enlightened fellowship: 'we are all citizens of the world
and see different customs and tastes without dislike or prejudice as
we do different names and colours'.[34]

Emanuel seemed content enough to be established among this
company of science and learning. But he was always a little hard up
or, by his own judgement, hard done by. His wife was a Pardo but
from the less propertied end of the family, and his impoverished father
upbraided Emanuel and his brother David for not doing better, so
that they might give some assistance to their old pa in his declining
years. 'I have not one son,' the old boy bitterly grumbled, 'to give a
helping hand.' Emanuel and David had not 'followed his advice and
found wives with fortunes [and] it shocked him to think they were
bringing so many beggars into the world'. At the time they made
their matches 'you were all young and healthy and no father or mother
or sister to maintain but only your sweet selves'.

Emanuel was not listening. He was caught in the fossil trap. The
bigger his collection, the more he could publish learned Notes, and
the more admiring interest he attracted from natural scientists at
home and abroad, his network of learned correspondents stretching
from Sweden to France. The great naturalist the Comte de Buffon
knew all about him; so did Linnaeus. He was on personal terms
with the archaeologist of Avebury and Stonehenge, Sir William
Stukeley, and with the great octogenarian physician-scientist Sir

Hans Sloane. It was with the good wishes and support of these patriarchs of British science that Emanuel campaigned for the clerkship of the Royal Society which, if secured, came with rent-free lodging in Crane Court off Fleet Street and a £50 stipend. In the spring of 1763, the new clerk-librarian moved into Crane Court. Four years later, Emanuel Mendes da Costa was revealed to have systematically embezzled funds from the Society by misrepresenting full members (who paid the entirety of their subscription) as partial members (who paid in yearly instalments), either pocketing the difference or more likely treating it as an interest-free loan. When a fellow complained that his name had been published under the wrong category, the fraud was exposed, and after the usual expressions of incredulous indignation, Emanuel was bundled off to the King's Bench Prison. The ugly stereotypes of the double-dealers seemed to have been vindicated by the kind of person who ought to have served as a counter-example of the disinterested pursuit of knowledge. This was definitely Not Good for the Jews.

Astoundingly, it was not all *that* bad for Emanuel Mendes da Costa! He had lost his great collection, most of his library and all of his patrons and colleagues, but such was the unstoppable, ingenuous sense of self-belief, and what must have been a gift for instruction, that a whole new avenue opened up for him: shells. He became the first great British conchologist; indeed the coiner of the term itself. Inside King's Bench were other gentlemen and ladies who had unaccountably fallen from grace and fortune but were enthusiastic about taking courses of lectures on both fossils and shells from da Costa, who supplied them for a fee. His classes in the prison were between fifteen and twenty, and were in such continuous demand that after four years he was able to buy his way out of confinement. By this time he had enough material to write and publish his *Elements of Conchology* in 1776 and, two years later, on a note of scientific patriotism, his *British Conchology*. Neither made him much money, but somehow he recovered, especially abroad, from his disgrace and became something of a figure once more in the natural sciences, adding credentials from foreign academies from Sweden to Austria; the further away from his embarrassment the better. Once a month on the Monday before the new moon, he would join the discussions of the Society for the Promotion of Natural History. He was even capable of some moral righteousness at the liberties taken by Linnaeus in his anatomical description of the *Venus dione* shell, a lavender-pinkish furled beauty of a bivalve whose parts Linnaeus had evidently enjoyed labelling 'anus', 'vulva', 'labia' and so on. Mustering shock at the 'obscenity', da Costa suggested instead 'slopes' and 'declivities'. The rabbis would have approved.

Were Ralph and Manny, and for that matter the rest of the better-off, better-educated London Jews, with their fashionable pretensions, their modish dress and bag wigs, not to mention their periodically shifty relationship with English society, Jews at all? Or were they just in the waiting room for complete assimilation? For all their straying from the strict and narrow, there is no doubt that the two old rogues thought of themselves as Jewish. Manny would periodically order pots of 'sour crout' from Ralph's wife Elizabeth, to whom he had presumably taught the art of ethnic pickling. With the autumn high holy days coming on, Manny would make sure to wish Ralph, up in un-Hebraic Great Yarmouth, 'a good Rasasana [Rosh Hashanah]', though it seems unlikely that either of them would be going to *shul* to hear the shofar. But in his habitually warm-hearted way, and even from the King's Bench Prison, Manny made sure to wish Elizabeth 'a merry Christmas and a happy New Year'. They were, to be sure, the kind of Jews of whom the rabbis complained they seemed to prefer Christmas puddings to matzot. So by the rigorous standards prevailing in Lithuania or Poland, where there was strict observance to the letter of the law (setting aside, as Jews usually could not, just who was qualified to adjudicate what that letter was), Manny as well as Ralph had definitely left the fold.

For some of the guardians of Judaism the business of the whiskers was not trivial. To take the hirsute or the smooth-chinned path was to tell the world if one wished first and foremost to join with its ways or whether Jews had been commanded to keep themselves distinctively separate. Rabbi Hirsch Lewin, who was scandalised by the casualness of English Jews, especially the demands of those who had married Christian wives, to be called up for the Reading of the Torah (as many were), proclaimed that shaving itself violated a fundamental principle of the Torah and told you all you needed to know about the pseudo-quasi-Jews of England. Naphtali Franks, one of a transatlantic dynasty whose mother Isabel had warned about the loose ways of his London cousins, thrived there, stayed Jewish, married a cousin and became a great dignitary of Duke's Place, but he shaved, wore a bag wig, and looked in all visible respects just like anyone else in the world of society and business. When asked why he was leaving Duke's Place, Rabbi Hart Lyon replied that it was because *that* was the first religious question he'd ever been asked during all his years at the synagogue. It is certainly true that, however it had come about, the community of English Jews was seldom riven by intense philosophical debates between both Jews and Jews, and their Gentile counterparts. Maimonides did not haunt the coffee-house chatter, and the mighty tides of Hasidic and messianic Judaism storming through the east European diaspora turned to dribbling shallows when they washed onto British shores. Which does not mean there were no arguments within the synagogues. But they were most often arguments of the shouted kind that happen in families and between neighbours rather than reasoned debate. A typical incident was when the din (usually made by *gregger* wooden rattles) racketing away at the mention of the villain Haman on Purim during the reading of the Esther scroll turned so tumultuous that the officers of Bevis Marks called in the watch to arrest the worst offenders. Among them was a young man belonging to the Furtado family, and although he may have been part of a group who later apologised for the near riot, his father Isaac took the opportunity of publicly denouncing the synagogue as a nest of hypocrites. 'I do renounce your Judaism ... the inherent sentiments and principles of your World to Come, and have sent you the key of my drawer [beneath his synagogue pew] to dismember myself from so irreligious a society ... you are dropsical with pride.' It was an outrage, he went on, that the hospital for the Jewish Poor on which they took such pride had a mere six beds; that for the most part the patients were treated by an apothecary rather than a physician; and that at Passover all they got to eat were matzot. At the end of his magnificently abusive notice of quit (a kind of reverse excommunication), Furtado made sure to add that his wife Sarah 'also wishes to dismember herself from your society'. Nonetheless the choleric Isaac Furtado remained at least a social Jew, building tenements for some of the poor of the East End and making sure he was buried in the Jewish cemetery. Those last rites were often telling. Joshua Montefiore, the uncle of the much more famous statesman Moses Montefiore – who had led a life of astounding colonial adventure, attempting to colonise Bulama Island off the West African coast for the Crown, and taking part in the campaign to conquer Martinique and Guadeloupe from the French – ended up on a farm in Vermont. But knowing his end was approaching he wrote out the Kaddish in transliterated English so that his second non-Jewish wife could read it at his funeral.

Some of the outbursts against rabbinical conservatism were more than the usual. In 1746 Meyer Schomberg published his Hebrew *Emunat Omen* (*A Physician's Faith*). It was a withering critique of the pettiness of rabbinical and institutional hair-splitting in Orthodox Judaism, the endless scholastical picayunery as well as the hypocrisy of the pillars of the community. He and his sons had been criticised for sporting those wooden sword hilts, a necessary measure of prudence rather than a trifling vanity, by bigwigs of the synagogue who habitually kept Gentile mistresses 'as if they were fulfilling a commandment without shame ... and they also live and lodge with them in intimate embrace while they reject the kosher daughters of Israel who are our own flesh and blood'.[35] He was almost certainly thinking of Joseph Salvador, one of the leaders of the Sephardi community but notorious for patronising infamous courtesans like Kitty Fisher and Mrs Caroline Rudd. Schomberg moved from the polemical to the theological, invoked Maimonides' principles of the faith in his *Mishneh Torah*, while claiming that King David had already reduced the 613 commandments of the Torah to an indispensable eleven. Most of Schomberg's principles amounted to a kind of thinly Judaised deism which he himself (along with like-minded Jews) believed brought them closer to some sort of commonly held enlightened faith. 'The absolute first duty of a Jew is to believe in a God, an existing Being who brought into existence everything before our eyes.'[36] What sounds like an early version of reformist Judaism was a farewell gesture, since although he and two of his sons stayed loyal to Judaism, Meyer actually encouraged his boys to walk to the font if it would further their prospects. Only the naval officer Alexander (later Sir Alexander) and Isaac – one baptised, one not – had fulfilled his expectations. And as hard-hearted parents do, he expressed his disappointment by dividing the vast part of his legacy between those two, the remainder of the Schombergs getting just a shilling each. No wonder old Ralph was reduced to filching from the Sunday collection.

II. Oranges and Lemons

Oranges and lemons
Say the bells of St Clement's
You owe me five farthings
Say the bells of St Martin's
When will you pay me?
Say the bells of Old Bailey
When I grow rich
Say the bells of Shoreditch[37]
When will that be?
Say the bells of Stepney
I'm sure I don't know
Says the great bell of Bow[38]

Poor Jews sold those oranges and lemons. The chimes of the nursery rhyme in *Tommy Thumb's Pretty Song Book* plot the map of their day. St Clement's was not St Clement Danes at the end of the Strand, but St Clement Eastcheap, down by the Thames wharves where citrus boxes shipped in from Jewish traders in Livorno were unloaded. Close by St Martin's – not St Martin-in-the-Fields but St Martin Outwich – was the moneylender who had stood them the necessary to buy their fruit. They had better sell enough to repay him or he would have his claws deep in and no mistake and end up in Newgate, where they would hear the leaden chimes of St Sepulchre, right opposite the Old Bailey. Their lodgings – rookeries and tenements – were in the narrow streets and alleys named for the old ditches: Houndsditch, Shoreditch, Fleetditch, some of the most crowded and impoverished places in London. Whitechapel and Stepney – the parish of St Dunstan's – were already as they were to be for another two centuries, packed with Ashkenazi Jews, around five thousand of them, from Poland and Germany, sometimes by way of Holland. But the records of the *ma'amad* at Bevis Marks synagogue in the City show there were poor Sephardim too – perhaps fifteen hundred or so – from Italy, Morocco and Tunis, who had come to London via Livorno or Amsterdam and who specialised in dried fruit, citrus and tobacco. From St Mary-le-Bow and Cheapside the orange sellers would claim a selling turf in the

heart of the City, around Leadenhall or Threadneedle Streets, or north
in fancy Finsbury Circus, or else down along Cannon Street, past St
Paul's and Fleet Street all the way to the Strand and Leicester Fields,
crying and plying their wares, hoping to sell all they had by nightfall.
Many didn't. Court records are full of orange sellers who had another
string to their bow, not always legal.

The lives of the street vendors never went near the gardens of
Teddington, Isleworth and Roehampton. But some, even many,
of them might have crowded into Duke's Place and Bevis Marks on
the eve of the Day of Atonement or the New Year. We know of at
least one poor but religious Sephardi Jew who prayed with the propertied in Bevis Marks because while he was doing this on Rosh
Hashanah his son Abraham was out stealing silk handkerchiefs and
yards of fine cloth, clearly untroubled by the prospect of being struck
off the Book of Life in the year to come.[39] It might have caused the
pious father more grief to hear the name of his errant son called out
for excommunication, as happened to all Jewish criminals under the
jurisdiction of Bevis Marks. Other than when the synagogues filled
for the festivals and high holidays, most of the contact between the
shaven and the unshaven poor Jews would have been through charity:
visits from the doctors or apothecaries at the Jews' Hospital on the
Mile End Road, the first of the old-age homes in Stepney, and on
inspection days at the Jews' Free School for orphaned boys, founded
in 1732 by the patriarch of Duke's Place, Moses Hart, and then, as
numbers expanded, moving to Houndsditch in 1788.

The speech of the vast majority was Yiddish and a modicum of
fractured English, though never as broken as the grossest caricatures
in print and on stage liked to make out. Jack Bannister, the great low
comedian of Drury Lane who certainly knew thespian Jews like Jemmy
Decastro, had a speciality of nasal Jewspeak which could never be
exaggerated enough for the hooting gallery. Occasionally Christians
would be confounded to hear humbly dressed, bearded or bonneted
Jews and Jewesses speak the King's English without all the usual
gargling and honking. When Samuel Taylor Coleridge, downwind of
an old-clothes hawker, asked why he couldn't say 'OLD CLOTHES'
rather than the habitual guttural cry of 'Ol clo, ol clo' or 'O cloash',
he was startled to receive the reply in perfect English that 'Sir, I can
say "old clothes" as well as you can but if you had to say so ten times

a minute for an hour together you would say "ogh clo" as I do now'.[40] Coleridge confessed to being so stunned that he ran after the old-clothes man and gave him a shilling by way of condescending apology.

The masses of poor London Jews were hawkers of second-hand merchandise of one kind or another. Traditionally – as in Venice during the foundation years of the ghetto – this is all they had been legally permitted to do. Even after some of the restrictions had been lifted (and in many places they had not), the daily trade in used clothes and haberdashery was the staple of the Jewish poor. They were the Jews with the sacks slung over their shoulder, empty in the morning; with any luck bulging with items ready to be sold by mid-afternoon. But there were also countless box Jews: often the latest newcomers who had been set up by Duke's Place or Bevis Marks with an initial pedlars' pack; the money to be repaid in weekly or monthly instalments as they became established in their street trade. Inside the boxes, slung from straps around their necks (much as in street trading to this day in much of the world), were pencils, sealing wax, fancy cane-heads, crystal buttons, needles, pins and thimbles, fans, crude portrait prints of the king and queen, badly painted plaster figurines, cheap trinkets and jewellery, watches, the occasional cuckoo clock and dried rhubarb – the precious cure-all, especially for constipation or other growls of the bowel. After they were set up, the families were on their own, though since both peddling and old-clothes selling were so territorial, there would generally be kindly councillors in the Houndsditch coffee or grog shops who would give them a sense of where not to go; or where, after the passing of a fellow hawker, a patch had opened up.

The old-clothes day started before the light.[41] Out from the rookeries of Houndsditch, Whitechapel and Mile End would emerge the bearded Jews, on their heads the flat, broad-brimmed slouch hats their fathers and grandfathers had worn in Brody or Posen. By the end of the day they would be covered with other hats for sale at Rag Fair, so they would go through the streets with a multi-tiered tower of the hats wobbling on their crowns. The men would likewise be covered by the long kaftan-like coats, heavy in all weathers, some of them embroidered with black thread and slightly waisted in the old Polish way. On their feet were buckled shoes rather than boots. If they wore out beyond what the 'clobberer' repair men could save, well, there were always more old shoes waiting for them. Sometimes they walked alone; sometimes with their wives, layers of aprons and woollen skirts about them, with a bag hanging from the belt for the goods; and sometimes, too, young children, for eight or nine was the age at which the boys at any rate were to be initiated into the trade.

First off, the needs of the stomach: a 'wishy-washy' coffee from one of the local hole-in-the-wall establishments; a 'tuppeny buster' heel of bread, dipped in milk if they were lucky; and if they were feeling rich, a piece of fried fish – an unheard-of novelty until the Sephardi Jews brought it to England – eaten cold, the common delicacy of the merchant tables of the Thames-side villas and the West End and the low haunts of the East.[42] For most of the used-clothes *shleppers*, that would be the only meal of the day, not least because the majority kept kosher and if their walks took them into the West End or north-east London, there would be no providers of Jewish food. Meyer Levy claimed to be able to last the day with 'only the smell of an oily rag', though others took a little box of tea leaves in the hope of finding some hot water to make a midday cup.

The business was intensely territorial, everyone abiding by their own walks – unless they didn't, in which case matters would come to abuse and blows. Occasionally two old-clothes buyers might agree to share a route and its proceeds, known as a 'rybeck'. Dawn hours would see a procession of men with sacks walking towards the markets – Billingsgate, all slithery brightness, pails full of fish guts; Smithfield, the kingdom of bloody aprons; Leadenhall's avenues of hanging hides; and Newgate, where the stinking Fleetditch had been recently covered as a closed sewer and paved over to make an arcaded market. On warm days the better sort of people covered their faces with perfumed handkerchiefs and sniffed at a cloved orange sold by the Jewish citrus men. In all of the markets, porters, haulers and packers had aprons, leggings, shoes to sell. But some of the walkers emerging from Whitechapel, after a morning nip of brandy and water, would go east to the dockyard districts – Shadwell, Wapping and Limehouse – where sailors, nursing sore heads, their money gone while they slept on tavern floors or in the laps of whores, would sell items from their bags and bundles to the Jews.[43] If the old-clothes men were lucky and savvy they knew which of the tars might have got their hands on a little braid and frogging, surreptitiously cut from some officer's coat or hat. You could go on prospecting all morning for this kind of gold: further east to the barracks at Woolwich, more soldiers, more finery – some of it saved from the dead and stowed away by mates. Downstream on the eastern walks lay mournful treasure: the hulks, prison ships moored in the Thames Estuary where the obliging captains made the clothes of convicts available. The prisoners would get some of the money but at a price specified by the buyer, and only after the captain and crew had taken a cut for their services.

Western walkers, descending from Tower Hill down Cannon Street into the City, would make for livery and hackney stables where the coachmen and their families lodged above the horses. These were the places to get their hands on old saddles, harnesses, reins, whips, boots and carriage lanterns, as well as the prized 'glasses' that had been coach windows and could be cut down if needed using rough cutting diamonds to be had in Whitechapel. Enterprising buyers would then make for middling-sort districts in the West End: a long trudge to Fitzroy Square and Bloomsbury but with the sure prospect of tempting a tradesman's wife with china, glass or trinkets, in return for long-cast-off clothes that she knew her husband would never miss. The inevitable haggling would take place between the ladies' maids and the Jews, for even if they were the wife of a grocer or a master dyer, it was unthinkable to be dealing directly with the ignoble Jew. Finally there would be the back mews and servants' doorways to the houses of the great and the rich in the new West End: Hanover Square in the shadow of St George's; Mayfair, Cavendish and Devonshire Squares. It was said that the Jews encouraged the footmen and the ladies' maids to filch from their masters and mistresses, but the fact was that the discarded wardrobes of the fashionable had to go somewhere, and servants knew very well what need never be seen again. There was seldom a handkerchief count in the great houses. Into the sacks went hose and breeches, out-of-style bag and tie wigs; gloves and stockings; even silk and satin gowns not worn for many a year.

Past noon, past one, it was time to be walking back, west from the hulks or east from the Strand, many of the hawkers crowned now with two or three hats, their sacks heavy; but never so full that they wouldn't opportunistically stop a likely cove in a coffee house or even on the street if they thought they might be willing to part with an item or two. From all over town, from Limehouse and Leicester Fields, from Tottenham Court Road and Gray's Inn, the army of the multi-hatted

Jews converged single-mindedly on one place as if bent on pilgrimage: Rag Fair. It was nothing more than a yard at the end of Rosemary Lane (now Royal Mint Street, the continuation of Cable Street) on the Whitechapel side of the Tower. But it had become one of the sights of the city. Tourists came to marvel and be elbowed, ignored or robbed of their handkerchiefs by small boys trained to spot the bright 'Kingsmen' insufficiently tucked away in a coat pocket. Fagin's little crew was not, in fact, a fiction. At 'full business' times, between three and five in the winter, four and six in the summer, Rag Fair was jammed with more than a thousand old-clothes people who had emptied their sacks, usually in piles on a patch of the ground covered with a piece of linen or blanket. On the perimeter were the specialists, operating from fixed stalls or shops, dealing in wigs or glasses, watches or hats. But most of the cramped space was a rowdy bazaar, a theatre of shouted cries, jabbing fingers, exchanges of odd bits and pieces; of insults and accusations which often enough turned riotous, prompting yet another petition from the neighbours to the magistrates to have Rag Fair closed down. Quiet came to Rag Fair only on Friday nights and Saturdays, for unlike the better-off Jews who couldn't quite keep away from Exchange Alley even after Sabbath services, the rag-trade men loved and respected their Shabbes: its loaves and its fish; its candles and watery wine; its songs and the children who had a week's grime washed off them.

It was only in the first decade of the nineteenth century that the carnival of schmatters was superseded by an Old Clothes Exchange, created by the enterprising Lewis Isaacs, one of London's first true Jewish businessmen beyond the City money folk. With a shrewd eye Isaacs bought the entirety of Phillips Buildings in Houndsditch, between Cutler Street and White Street, enclosed it on four sides with a hoarding and a little awning to protect against bad weather. He charged a halfpenny as entrance fee which ensured that only the serious 'forestallers' – the middle men – would get admitted, and rows of chairs and benches were set in the middle of the enclosure for their convenience. Around the perimeter, sellers of pies, fried fish and ale did good business (for those not fussy about keeping kosher) while the trades were going on.

One thing did not much change with the mutation of Rag Fair into the Old Clothes Exchange: the difficulty of distinguishing what was lawfully come by from what was not. Few of the buyers bothered to ask, though the Old Bailey Sessions papers involve buyers coming to forestallers as if they thought they were fences, looking expressly for items they knew to have been illicitly acquired, and being sent on their way with expressions of shocked distaste. Such upstanding characters were probably not the majority. Most of London knew Rag Fair was a place where Monday's buyer would be Tuesday's receiver. And there were brazenly famous receivers like Mrs Sherwood of Bowl Yard or Isaiah Judah, on whom hands could never be laid for lack of proof of the origins of Kingsmen or an array of rings and watches. In the days of both Rag Fair and the Old Clothes Exchange, there was a thriving export trade on to Europe and even further afield to North Africa, America and the Caribbean (one almost certainly tainted by the slave trade). Linens, shawls, scarves could be in and out before anything much could be done about them. Another woman forestaller admitted that the time between the rag men buying and selling on again was around five minutes.[44]

Where there were receivers there would always be more sinister and violent takers to supply them. And they were not above preying on their own people. Sometimes they snatched the boxes from high-end hawkers, who had themselves been supplied from shifty sources. Abraham Davis, whose box was stolen in 1778, listed a movable treasure trove as its contents, including sixty-eight watches, thirty gold rings, another thirty gold buckles (for shirt and shoe and coat), and silver items galore.[45] Many of the accusations levelled at Jews as a whole, especially that of silver coin-clipping, were recycled stereotypes from medieval anti-Semitism. It was a common charge, for instance, that unwitting customers buying in Rag Fair would get short-changed in clipped coin. But there was undoubtedly a subculture of Jewish criminals at work in the City and East End (alongside and often in competition with an Irish one). Every so often a spectacular crime would rebound badly on the whole community, and the guardians were sufficiently nervous about this for Moses Hart and Naphtali Franks to pass on information about suspected Jewish criminals to Sir John Fielding, the ubiquitous magistrate of Bow Street. It was to Fielding in 1771 that Daniel Isaacs, one of a gang of Jewish robbers (most of them hailing from Holland), confessed his bad conscience about a burglary in Chelsea that had gone wrong. Isaacs turned King's evidence in the hope that once he had admitted his part and helped catch the criminals, the

Duke's Place charitable overseers would see their way to offering him some monetary assistance. Not surprisingly he was disappointed.

The case gripped London, not least because the gang leader was a wicked Jewish doctor, Levi Weil, who had qualified in medicine at Leiden University but had found his true vocation robbing houses in England along with his brother Asher. In the late spring of 1771, one of the Weil gang cased the house of a widow, Mrs Hutchins, on the King's Road, getting inside on the spurious pretext of seeking someone supposedly known by the householder. It was a warm June night. The gang lurked for a bit around the Chelsea gardens before making their way to the Hutchins house, forcing a way in, tying up the servants, throwing petticoats over a maid's face so she would not see theirs, then demanding valuables. One of the manservants got free, at which point a panicky melee broke out during which the bold servant was fatally shot along with one of the maids, while the brothers Weil took sixty-four guineas and a watch from the terrified widow who watched her house servants die. After Isaacs spilled the beans to Fielding the malefactors were arrested and, following a sensational trial in December 1771, catnip for the crime-hungry press, the brothers Weil and two others were hanged. A huge crowd showed up, including a number of Jews. Unlike the practices of the Newgate chaplains, the rabbis who had attended on the prisoners during confinement (and who had excommunicated them in *shul*) were not present at the end. This was all good criminal theatre but at the conclusion of the trial there had already been an astonishing moment when, after pronouncing the sentences, the presiding recorder went out of his way to congratulate all the Jews (even the criminal informer Isaacs) for their public-spirited collaboration with the authorities, and expressed the hope 'that no person would stigmatise a whole nation on account of a few villains'.[46] Best of British to that.

III. The Prophet Daniel

It wouldn't have taken much for Dan Mendoza to have ended up swinging from a Tyburn rope. As a young man out of work he was asked to transport 'different sorts of merchandise from the coast and that I was to be furnished with an excellent horse for that purpose ... Immediately upon my engaging on it I was informed I was lured for the purpose of escorting smuggled property and was likewise told that I should be expected to guard and protect (even at the hazard of my life) whatever might happen to be entrusted to my care.'[47] But he wasn't going to touch that sort of thing, not with a bargepole, not least because he knew he was not always in complete control of his alarming strength, although he swore he was never merciless. And indeed when he saw Humphreys, beaten to a bloody mess in their third and last bout, he made sure, as was noticed, of letting the vanquished foe keep a little of his dignity, rather than, as was often his habit, treating him to a display of visible scorn. It was hard to say which Mendoza would show up on any given day: the ferocious bruiser or the Jewish paladin. His boiling point was low, the force of his hammering hands overwhelming, and his aim selected with deadly calculation. Mendoza's extraordinary *The Art of Boxing*, first published at the height of his spectacular career when he was just twenty-four, explained to the novice with clinical precision (he was as much doctor as professor) the effects that different blows would work on the adversary's anatomy. A punch between the brows would bring on temporary blindness; one beneath the left ear would flood the brain with blood, causing a kind of seizure; a hard knock at the temples, the 'stunner', could be literally lethal; one on 'the short ribs' or kidneys would 'put him into the greatest torture and for a time a cripple' along with an 'instant discharge of urine' soaking the breeches, always a useful psychological blow against the opponent. A punch landing hard in the pit of the stomach, the solar plexus, would trigger an explosion of bloody vomiting, but should one be unlucky enough to receive one of those (and they were a Humphreys speciality) it had been shown that the severity could be avoided by bending the thorax down over the stomach while inhaling deeply.[48]

At the very beginning of *The Art of Boxing*, Mendoza made it clear that all this practical advice was not just meant for professional or even amateur pugilists, but for the citizenry at large in a dangerous urban world. He specifically referred to his work as the 'art of self-defence', and other than the late-seventeenth-century Dutch manual of the wrestler Nicolas Petter, illustrated by Romeyn de Hooghe,

Mendoza's is the first such book to present itself in this way. The practice of 'pitched battles', he writes – that is, organised bouts of bare-knuckle – has been accused of 'bordering on brutality and black-guardism', but this is to misunderstand its true aim which is the safety and self-respect of all citizens.

> It must be confessed ... that knowledge of the science is both useful and necessary to every man of spirit for no other reason [than] to protect himself when insulted ... to a man even of the most harmless disposition an acquaintance with the art cannot fail to be serviceable as it enables him to walk the streets with an idea of security and if he does not choose to resent an insult he has the satisfaction of reflecting that it is in his power.[49]

It was, of course, a particular population of London that Mendoza had in mind as being especially vulnerable to verbal and physical abuse: his own. Though nowhere in his boxing manual does he specifically single out the Jews as most in need of both the resolution and the 'art' of fighting back against the verbal and physical assault to which they were daily subjected, it is plain from the stories of his young life related in the memoirs that this was the formative experience that made Mendoza not just a fighter but an instructor of the defenceless and the vulnerable. No Jew before him anywhere since the writers of the Books of the Maccabees had done this. From his father, he says, he learned the difference between 'true and false courage', and the difference between mere bullying and proper self-defence. No one held 'the character of a bravado or quarrelsome man in greater abhorrence'; but

> whenever I returned home with a black eye or any external mark of violence my father never failed to enquire strictly into the cause and would reprove me severely when it appeared I had involved myself wantonly in a quarrel, but on the other hand if he found I had acted only in self-defence or any justifiable motive he would freely forgive me and declare he would never exert his parental authority to prevent me from standing in my own self-defence when unjustly assailed.[50]

As a young lad he was already getting into trouble early and often, but equally no one felt more keenly the need for Jews to stand up against intimidation. In one respect Mendoza was not so different from the philosophical counter-punchers Menasseh ben Israel and Moses Mendelssohn in understanding the experience of Jews to have application beyond themselves to the rest of humanity. When Mendoza claimed that the qualities he was championing (in his case 'spirited' self-defence and the capacity to counter-attack), while essential for his own kind, were by extension essential for the practice of citizenship, it was akin to Mendelssohn's belief that tolerant diversity, while Good for Jews, was also best for the world at large.

Mendoza may not have been a weekly regular at Bevis Marks, although as a matter of fact we don't know that he wasn't. His father and mother, from a modest but not impoverished Sephardi family, were in all likelihood observant since they made sure to send Daniel to a Jewish school, almost certainly the Free School founded by Moses Hart, where he learned Hebrew and studied the religious texts. But his memoirs make clear that he also learned good English along with other 'modern' subjects like mathematics. This mixed education was crucial to his rise to fame since it enabled Mendoza to enter the world of non-Jews on his own terms and with great confidence; in fact, with the shrewd mastery of expression that is apparent on every page of his books. Whether he stayed within the fold or not there was no time in his life when Mendoza was not acutely conscious of his Jewishness; indeed his entire public and professional identity, his deter- mination to school other young Jews in his art, was built round it, and in this respect he was the very model and forerunner of the unapologetic, non-rabbinical Jew, more usually located in the writing of deists. No one beyond a small circle of the learned would have paid much attention to their utterances. But everyone in Britain from the king at Windsor to the bruisers of Bermondsey knew about Mendoza the Jew.

Right from the start there was something about Daniel that made the unsuspecting have a go at him – perhaps the broad-shouldered cockiness on the little boy – and his apprenticeship was a procession of lessons dished out to overgrown bullies: first the son of a master glazier to whom he had been apprenticed after his bar mitzvah; then, when he was working for a local greengrocer, the neighbourhood toughs who made a habit of insulting the woman of the family shop 'on account of her Jewish religion'.[51] Having a go at the Jews was not

a good idea when the Jew in question was little Mendoza. On one
occasion between his many jobs (tea merchant, confectioner, tobacconist), Daniel went with a cousin to Northampton where he'd been
told the job prospects might be brighter. Walking from a pub towards
the town they ran into the local bully who announced that he 'hated
to see such fellows strolling about the place' and that 'It was a pity we
were not sent to Jerusalem'.[52] After the inevitable 'set-to' in which the
loudmouth came off worst despite being Northampton's best knuckle
fighter, the adversary's father actually sought Daniel out (or so Mendoza
tells us) to congratulate him for administering the discipline to his
unruly boy that he himself had failed to deliver. The two lads were
ordered to make it up and did so with a shake of their hands. Now
that everyone was such good mates, the Northampton father offered
his house for free board and lodging to the two Jewish cousins for as
long as they wanted to stay. Too good to be true? Probably.

One of these early brawls changed Mendoza's life. He was working
for a tea merchant in Whitechapel and when a porter delivered a
consignment from the docks, Daniel offered him the usual pint of ale
and a tip for his labours. Normally that's how it went. But for whatever reasons this particular porter took offence, spurned the beer,
demanded more money and carried on so threateningly that the
sixteen-year-old Dan decided to take him on. They stripped off and
set to it outside where a ring was chalked on the street, and though
as usual the lad was overmatched in size, years and bulk, he delivered
a thrashing to the rash offender. A crowd had gathered. Among them,
by chance it seems, was the handsome, powerfully built Richard
Humphreys, at that time England's paragon of pugilistic grace, force
and elegance, billed as THE GENTLEMAN BOXER, a cut above the
raw-knuckled run of ex-soldiers, sailors, stevedores and labourers who
made up much of the fighting fraternity.[53] But Humphreys was also
a shrewd manager of his own career and he recognised star quality
when he saw it; the potential for theatre; for box office. So even before
he had seen Mendoza box he offered himself as his impromptu second
for the fight. The sixteen-year-old battered the bigger lug into submission; dancing about, his body low to the ground; making himself an
elusive target; catching every blow of his opponent with his arm and
dishing it back with a pell-mell rain of punches. With every minute
of the street fight that passed, Humphreys was more and more

convinced that he was looking at the future; that there was something prodigious in the offing. He smelled spectacle; he smelled money.

It was not yet time to move in on the boy, who carved his way through a procession of slow heavies, often sailors and dockyard men looking for a brawl. It didn't always work out as Mendoza expected. There was the time near St Katharine Docks when he and his friends came on a fight between two women, shrieking and spitting while they clawed at each other's eyes, a crowd of men jeering and cheering. 'I was never fond of seeing contests of this sort and therefore endeavoured ineffectually to reconcile them.'[54] The intervention failed so Mendoza put money on one of the Amazons and won. The loser's boyfriend, a sailor, was unhappy about this so a second fight ensued. Days later Mendoza was waylaid by a gang, seeking to avenge the losing girl and her companion, and doing it with cudgels. Beaten unconscious, Mendoza was left for dead. The battering only quickened his appetite and his fearlessness was becoming talked about from the Kent Road to Shepherd's Bush and among the Fancy from Brighton to Bristol. Humphreys sought him out again. Flattered – and how could he not be? – Mendoza let himself be adopted; instructed, trained, patronised. There was still some uncertainty in Mendoza's mind whether this was a choice profession. There had been Jewish fighters, especially among the London Sephardim, known to the public in years gone by. *Boxiana* described 'Isaac Mousha' (whose real name I suspect must have been Smouha) and Abraham da Costa taking on the formidable Jack 'the Plasterer' Lamb in the 1750s but both coming off worse. Inevitably there were sniggers at the defeat of the 'Tribe of Israel'. 'They were most terribly disappointed in not finding the LAMB quite so tender as they imagin'd, by his proving what they did not like – a prime piece of pork!'[55]

Mendoza would not be such a convenient amusement: the comically adventurous Jew laid low. Humphreys would be his promoter and teacher. They sparred. Bouts that would draw the public and money were arranged, the biggest with the famously brutal Tom Tyne. Mendoza lost but thereafter would have no trouble in arranging contests for twenty, thirty guineas, the beginning of serious prize money.

It was during the preparations for another fight that things went awry between mentor and protégé. Humphreys had arranged for

Mendoza to train at a house in Epping Forest belonging to a friend of his. But it quickly became apparent to Mendoza that the house was a brothel and the streak of bourgeois self-righteousness that was never far from the surface was outraged at the insult, however inadvertent. Mendoza exited in a fit of mortification and it was now Humphreys' turn to take offence, not least because, separated from his star protégé, he forfeited money due to him as Mendoza's promoter. So the little Jew Boy thought he could go it on his own, did he? A good thrashing would teach him otherwise. If need be he would administer it himself. It is the oldest story in sport and this time it was true.

They ran into each other, whether by chance or calculation, at the Roebuck in Aldgate. In front of the drinkers, many of whom were also his followers and fans, Humphreys called Mendoza out. 'After using very scurrilous and abusive language he seized me by the collar and tore my shirt with great violence.' The Roebuck was a Humphreys pub and Mendoza knew better than to try and settle things on the spot. He told his sometime friend and new enemy that 'though I did not choose to resent the insult just then' – 'resent' being the boxers' code word for turning offence into a physical encounter – 'he might be assured that I should not readily forget it and that I doubted not that the time would come when I would be requited'.[56]

Humphreys waited for Mendoza to bite off more than he could chew; assuming surrogates would administer the chastening on his behalf. It never happened. A fight was arranged at Barnet racecourse against the second most famous and formidable boxer in England after Humphreys himself: 'Butcher' Martin of Bath. It took Mendoza twenty-six minutes to finish the Butcher off. Not long before, Humphreys had needed an hour and three-quarters to do the same job. Worse still, as a result of the famous victory over the Butcher of Bath, Mendoza was a *thousand pounds* to the good and the lord of the latest entourage following their dark-horse hero in a long line of horses and carriage, the hoi polloi bringing up the rear, roaring 'Mendoza, Mendoza, Mendoza forever!' The cult of the fighting Jew had started, the most unlikely enthusiasm of Regency England.

For Dick Humphreys, this was embarrassing, intolerable. The only thing which could stop Mendoza in his tracks would be a defeat at his own hands; more than a conquest, a lesson, to the presumptuous little Jew. Overtures between the two sides took the form of bloody skirmishes between the rival camps of supporters. War broke out in the London streets, fairs and pleasure gardens. Bludgeons and whip handles were in action; broken heads and bloody noses, stompings by the docks. His public visibility had made Mendoza a little heady with fame but it also exposed him to real danger. Strolling with his heavily pregnant wife in Vauxhall Gardens one evening, he was surrounded by twenty of Tom Tyne's men (working for Humphreys), carried off and locked in a room. He escaped by dropping through a window to find his wife sitting on a bench, unmolested but terrified and tearful. She begged Dan to stop fighting and, moved by her entreaties, he promised to make an end of pugilism – once, that is, the business with Humphreys was settled. There was no retreating from the challenge. The two men traded insults, aired to keep the public interest stirred up. Why, sir, you have been taking liberties with my name, Humphreys said to Mendoza in one such encounter at another inn. (Mendoza was sure Humphreys was deliberately dogging his footsteps to provoke public arguments.) Why, sir, the same might be said of you, and if you should wish to settle matters between us here and now I am at your disposal. A ring was drawn in the innyard; the two stripped, set to it, and in a few minutes Mendoza had closed one of Humphreys' eyes. But this was knockabout, a warm-up for the hacks. The real pitched battle was yet to come.

Whether he sought the attention or not (and most likely he did), Mendoza remained on view, day and night. His boxing academy at Capel Court, the first of its kind, became famous. Merchants, the gentry and nobility, even men from the legal profession lined up to be instructed in the manly art of self-defence which for the first time became a popular obsession; violence made civic. Mendoza sparred for money in theatres (until he was stopped as being in infringement of regulations governing the stage), and gave exhibitions and lectures, featuring the assumed boxing styles of different champions of past and present (including Humphreys). But then he went into serious training along the lines recommended in his manual. The Mendoza diet was precise and rigorous: daily workouts but never to the point of exhaustion. Regularity rather than intensity was the goal; the augmentation of strength and stamina but never at the expense of quickness, so walks rather than runs; cold baths and dry rub-downs.

Breakfasts were to be light: rennet whey not tea; a glass of wine diluted with water. For supper, stewed veal and rice or 'well-fed fowls' boiled to a jelly in the evening; a glass of hock afterwards; nothing that would lie too heavily on the stomach; no spiritous liquors; chocolate rather than coffee; no salt; rusks rather than bread; a dab of hard white butter with a toasted biscuit. Think tactics; practise them. Always look the opposition full in the eye; judge his reach and his body language so that it would tell you the direction of his blows and his choice of targets. Only take your eyes off his when you made a feint and wanted to deceive *him* as to the choice of hits.[57] Keep moving. Keep him off balance. Walk don't run. Keep moving.

Odiham in Hampshire was the venue in January 1788. All England knew about it and all the enthusiasts of the Fancy made sure to be there: dukes, knights of the shire, City aldermen, monied merchants. It had been raining hard the previous day and the stage was still perilously wet. But the downpour had given over as if providence was watching too. The drama of the moment was irresistible. Humphreys was fair flower of English manhood; the living embodiment that gentility was not to be confused with social rank; that it was a matter of character, the testimonials of which were written in the form of a fine body. Matched against the gallant was the swarthy Jew whose victories drew on the better qualities of his people: ingenuity, artfulness, lively energy. Perhaps even his famous 'bottom' – the resilience and fortitude to come back from a severe blow and return it with interest – might be said to be a quality of the race in general, for how else had they managed to survive the poundings of the centuries? Mendoza gloried in all this. His second, his bottle holder and his chosen umpire were all Jews: Mr Jacobs, Mr Isaacs and a Mr Moravia. To immense cheering, Humphreys climbed onto the raised stage, a literally glittering figure since his stockings were spangled with gold thread. There never was such a beautiful pugilist. Mendoza, *Boxiana* recalled, opted for understatement, merely showing a 'neat appearance'. The heavy money was all on Humphreys, but as the rounds went past and none of the champion's famous blows seemed to be doing much damage to the Jew, the odds began to shift and with them the bets. The slippery surface of the stage made each of them occasionally unsteady, Humphreys being the wobblier. At the twenty-minute mark (each round was a minute), Humphreys complained about the tightness of his glamorous hose, especially where they packed into his slippers, and stopped to change them 'into plain worsted hose'. According to Mendoza this was a ruse for him to catch his wind, the change taking a full forty seconds longer than the rules permitted. A 'levelling' blow by Mendoza was then caught by one of Humphreys' seconds right at the edge of the ring. Two fouls then, which by Mendoza's lights should have given him the verdict. Instead he did what he would have counselled his pupils never to do: allowed his passions to sway his strategy. Impatiently he attempted to throw Humphreys, perhaps with a lethal cross-buttock move. Sensing he could catch Mendoza off balance, Humphreys held on to the stage rails with an iron grip, and threw the thrower. Mendoza landed on his head. Worse, a violent pain shot through his 'loins'. An ankle was sprained or worse. Standing up was beyond him. This one was over. Humphreys lost no time writing to one of his patrons who had been unable to be there in person: 'I have done the Jew and am in good health.'

Mendoza had lost the battle but not the war, especially not the publicity battle. Knowing that there would be at least one return match (Humphreys seemed eager for it), a Mendoza industry got to work. An image of the two men fists up – the Gent and the Jew – was everywhere in the England of 1788. Dan-like characters showed up on stage at Covent Garden and Drury Lane; Dicky-Dan ballads were the rage, especially those crowing over the fall of the presumptuous Hebrew. The Hebrews themselves were all on fire for their new Maccabee.

But he was hurt and in low spirits after the death of his only child. His groin injury was slow in mending and training for the rematch had to go easy. He was also prudent enough not to force it. His sensible reticence gave Humphreys – who understood that their contests had now gone beyond the confines of the usual crowd of sportsmen and following to become something of a national obsession – the chance to stir the publicity pot with a little public baiting. Immediately after the fight, still incensed at the disallowed fouls, Mendoza had taken to the press, in particular *The World*, to restate his version of the fight.[58] Humphreys instantly responded, taunting Mendoza with sour grapes, sore loser and the rest, and implying that the injuries he used to postpone the rematch were the pathetic whining of a cowardly malingerer. Mendoza's publication of a letter from his surgeon – a doctor's note – opened him to further ribaldry. Of Mendoza's injury, Humphreys teased, 'why there were people who swore they saw three bones come out ... the disorder moved gradually to his hips from whence lest it should be mistaken for a rheumatic complaint, it settled with most excruciating pain in the loins where I am aware it may abide for as long as he finds convenient'.[59]

Six months after the first fight, in July 1788 Humphreys made an unannounced appearance at Mendoza's gym during a sparring session, parking himself prominently at a seat by the ring along with his usual entourage of supporters. Mendoza, who was dressed in mourning black for the recent death of his only child, played the gentlemanly part, courteously thanking Humphreys for honouring his establishment with his presence. But then Humphreys climbed into the ring and mocked Mendoza in front of his own people for running or limping away from the rematch. Mendoza joined him. Now they were sparring but with their mouths.

MENDOZA: You cannot suppose Mr Humphreys that I am afraid of you.

HUMPHREYS: You seem to feel some palpitation.

MENDOZA: YOU, sir, seem unwilling to engage with several persons who wished to fight you.

HUMPHREYS: That is not the question. I wish to fight no one but yourself.[60]

Despite his reputation for impetuousness, Mendoza refused to be goaded into a premature bout. He took his time. Gradually his fitness came back. A recuperative diet – rusks and rennet and stewed veal – helped. The quality was now paying attention. A patron emerged: Sir Thomas Apreece, himself a bit of a boxer, and there was solicitous interest from a trio of royal dukes, Cambridge, Cumberland and York, all of whom had been to the synagogue, appropriately in Duke's Place.

On 6 May 1789, while the Estates General at Versailles were beginning the end of the Ancien Régime, a revolution of the ring unfolded in England. The place was Stilton in Huntingdonshire, in the park of one of Mendoza's new and passionate supporters among the quality: Henry Thornton. Interest in the grudge return was so immense that a custom-built arena had been constructed to take the audience of thousands, all of whom had paid the princely sum of half a guinea to be present at the fight of the century. Rows of terraced bleachers had been raised to accommodate the throng. Given how the previous fight had gone, the odds and the big bets were all on Humphreys to repeat his victory, but this time they shifted more quickly and more decisively to the Jew. For after a few rounds it was shockingly apparent that he was giving the Gentleman a lesson in pugilism; especially in that 'neat stopping' for which boxing history would remember him: the Jew who caught the blows. The harder Humphreys punched with round and straight blows, the more exactly Mendoza took them on his arm, striking back with a punishing volley of counter-blows everywhere but especially to that handsome face of his opponent which was turning into a bloody mess. Everyone watching knew they were witnessing the end of one reign and the beginning of another.

In the twenty-second round Humphreys 'dropped'. The rules were that if a boxer did so *without* a blow touching him, the fight was judged to be lost. Mendoza's corner cried as much. But raising himself again, Humphreys insisted he had received a blow and that the fight must go on. Humphreys' corner taunted their opponents with claiming a hitless foul in order to avoid fighting on. Furious, Mendoza's corner insisted their man should not resume fighting; that he had already won the day. The altercation of the corners became so fierce that it threatened to turn into a by-fight. But Dan himself wanted no shadow of dispute to hang over this bout as it had over the last, and declared himself ready to set to. They went at it for another thirty minutes before Humphreys dropped again without being touched, and this time his corner did not contest the verdict. Victory belonged to the Jew. Later, in his memoirs, Mendoza remembered the wild carousing long into the night at the Bull Inn, then on to a second party, and finally, and with a note of self-mockery, the whole gang, looking for the house of a Mr Newbury, their host, got lost, stumbled into a farmyard and fell into a pit 'filled with dung', the kind of comedy most sporting heroes would generally omit. But then Mendoza was, as England came to acknowledge, generally a good sport.

Now that Humphreys and Mendoza had each won a fight, a third was to settle things once and for all. It was arranged for 29 September 1790, at Doncaster. A great and menacing upheaval had broken out on the other side of the Channel, but it became a commonplace of the writing of that time to insist that no British eyes or ears paid the revolution in France much heed for they were all on Humphreys and Mendoza. The location was the yard of an inn beside the Don, bordered on one side by the buildings and on the other by the river. The bankside was railed off by palings but hundreds had been ferried over by local boatmen and in no time at all the palings had been made short work of. Other locals had moored their vessels on the river, and for a price made the spars available for punters to sit aloft in prime viewing positions like so many perching crows.

By this time Humphreys knew that his only chance of winning was by landing one of his incomparably punishing blows in the early going, followed by a hit to the mark of the stomach. But Mendoza's famous bottom was on display, taking what was given and returning with savage force. As early as the third round he knocked Humphreys clean down. In the fifth, Humphreys got in one of the shattering stomachers for which he was famous, but Mendoza took it and returned a blinding facer. Round after round they went at it, ever more brutally, Humphreys almost blind with injuries around his eyes, his nose broken, lacerations over his face, upper lip split in two, still slugging on. Mendoza just waited for the draining fatigue to do his work for him, and as Humphreys stumbled and dropped and dropped and staggered, would gently hold him up like a wounded comrade on the battlefield; a gesture everyone noticed had something of generosity and something of contempt mixed in. At length Mendoza laid Dick Humphreys on the floor of the ring as though he were putting a child to sleep.

This of course did not stop some of the writing about the fight turning from scorn at the feebleness of Jews to distaste for the 'hardness of the Jew's heart'. Others said and wrote that while the plan had gone to science over grace, it was the latter which transfigured the true hero, vanquished though he was. For his own part, in the memoirs at least, Mendoza paid tribute, as he now could, to his archrival and erstwhile teacher, that throughout their contentions he had acted honourably (which was not always how he had felt at the time).

As is so often the case, the repeated trials of strength exhausted both parties. Humphreys never thought to face Mendoza again. And though he seemed in the prime of his powers, and went on to defeat the new up-and-comer William Warr twice in a row, it was evident that the prolonged epic of the Humphreys battles had taken a toll on the victor. In 1795 he was matched with John Jackson for two hundred guineas apiece. Notoriously, when they were closing, Jackson seized Mendoza by his pride and joy, the long locks of his curly mane, and held them fast while smashing facer after facer at him 'till he fell to the ground'.[61] By this time he was doing his best to fulfil his promise to his wife by finding other less directly bruising ways to exploit his prowess. There were more theatrical exhibitions in which Mendoza illustrated the techniques and styles of champions past and present along with a hired sparring partner, engaging in sham bouts and concluding with a drum roll by assuming his own famous posture. His self-defence academy moved into its own theatre, the Lyceum on the Strand. His boxing pupils – a number of them Jewish, like 'Dutch' Sam Elias, and 'Ikey' who bore his nickname of 'Ikey the Pig' in relatively good humour – got their initial instructions. Another, who was not a pupil but very much a disciple of the Mendoza style, Elisha Crabbe, became known in his turn as 'The Jew', got as far as a big prize match at Horton Moor with his mentor's old adversary and enemy Tom Tyne, but lost. Typically it was said that 'the Jew proved the most showy fighter but Tyne did the most execution'.[62]

Mendoza himself was now part of show business, going on tour with the Astley circus, almost certainly in the company of Jemmy Decastro and even taking up acting with a professional stage company for a while. There were exhibition tours to Dublin and Edinburgh, Manchester, East Anglia and the West Country, Exeter, Plymouth, Bristol. The whole of Britain wanted to see the wonder who was 'not the Jew that Shakespeare drew'. For despite allusions to his exoticism and his exercises in cunning like the Mendoza chop (stopping this side of unsporting), none of the accounts of Mendoza made him appear some sort of shifty alien on the edge of proper British society. The king himself and the whole royal family believed him the personification of exactly the kind of patriotic manliness much in demand as Britain girded itself, uncertainly, to a trial of arms with revolutionary France. According to Mendoza, on a visit to Windsor, before the informal conversation with the royal party ended, George III making many 'ingenious observations' about pugilism, the Princess Royal asked the famous fighter whether he might let her little boy strike him so that he might always be able to say he had landed a punch on the great Mendoza, a request Daniel smilingly granted. History does not record whether he got a stomacher to the mark or not, but if he did, he is likely to have doubled up in mock agony to make the little prince laugh.

Into his thirties the myth began to leave the man behind. Mendoza was as bad at business as he had been formidable in the ring. He accumulated debts and, his championship star fading, found it impossible to meet the creditors, and so, with ten children to support, he landed three times in the King's Bench Prison, sometimes at his own request to avoid the loss of his property. He tried the life of a publican, owning and running the Admiral Nelson in Whitechapel; then when that failed as warrant server for the sheriff; and enforcer of the 'New Price' tickets at Drury Lane, which had triggered riots of indignation among the supporters of the cheaper 'Old Price'. Recognising Mendoza, the Old Price rioters started to sound off again about The Jews.

Every so often he came out of retirement for the odd fight. There was a relentless, slogging encounter at Grinstead Green in Kent in 1806 with Harry Lee, a veteran like himself. They had a full fifty rounds, the valiant, half-dead Lee refusing to give up and drop. Assuming this was a farewell fight for both pugilists, a number of the new champions like Henry 'Hen' Pearce (known as the Game Chicken) and John Gulley attended thinking it was the last chance they would have to appreciate the great man's style. In a sense they were right for when, shockingly, Mendoza at the age of fifty-six had one last slog in 1820 with an old foe, Tom Owen, the grudge match was barely more than a curiosity.

This was enough. Writing his memoirs, Mendoza had a chance to relive the thrilling epic of his rise from obscurity to the days of the great gladiatorial matches with Humphreys. Gentleman Dick went into the coaling business and settled down to a peaceful and relatively prosperous middle age. Daniel ended his days in his seventies in the same place he had begun – the stretch of Jewish London from Whitechapel to Bethnal Green – and was buried in the Portuguese cemetery on the Mile End Road. At some point the remains of a number of bodies were reinterred on a site in Essex, but the Sephardi burial ground, now in the front courtyard of Queen Mary's College, bears a plaque with his name.

He had changed, though not completely and not forever (no mortal could do that), the ingrained prejudices the British had about Jews, even if many who previously had sneered at the cowardice and feebleness of commercial and learned Jews now began to dislike them for their brute force in what they claimed to be 'self-defence'. Pierce Egan was more perceptively generous when he stressed that what was so striking about Daniel Mendoza was not just the string of victories but 'the manner' in which they were obtained. 'Prejudice frequently distorts the mind, that, unfortunately, good actions are passed over without even common respect; more especially when they appear in any person who may chance to be of a different persuasion or colour.' (Black boxers like Tom Molineaux were about to follow the Jews into the ring.) 'Mendoza in being a Jew, did not stand in so favourable a point of view respecting the wishes of the multitude towards his success, as his brave opponent ... but truth riseth superior to all things and the humanity of Mendoza was conspicuous throughout the fight.'[63]

Mendoza was pleased to have himself described as an honourable man since a strong element in his entire adventure was to show his countrymen that a Jew could be a 'manly' Briton too; that the image many had of the craven, feeble, untrustworthy Jew was wide of the mark. Britain was the only country where the sport had become a professional pursuit and a mass audience pleaser, and Mendoza saw himself as a specimen of pure patriotic virility: one of the few heroes for whom the king and the Prince of Wales could share an admiration. 'I trust it will not be imputed to vanity,' he wrote in the preface to his memoirs, 'but I cannot refrain from asking, was curiosity ever more ardently excited, or the general feeling of the nation ever more interested by any public exhibition than by the contests between Mr Humphreys and myself?'[64] Let the French have their doubtful slaughters. He was the best of the British, and still every bit Mendoza the *Jew*.

In Britain, institutions moved slower than attitudes. The next attempt to emancipate the Jews, following the success of the Catholic bill in 1829, would fail. Another two decades would remain before they could stand and be admitted to Parliament. While Mendoza still lived, the opportunities were narrower. The articulate, hotly anti-rabbinical Isaac D'Israeli thought it best for his bright son Benjamin to be baptised if he wanted to get ahead, though making it clear the boy should never forget his origins – and nor did he. Meyer Cohen came to the same conclusion and renamed himself after his Christian wife's maiden name and so became Francis Palgrave, the great founder-custodian of the Public Record Office and thus the keeper of the memory of British history (his son anthologised the *Golden Treasury* which defined the English poetic tradition for millions of readers). The two Goldsmids, Benjamin and Abraham, in separate moments of financial disaster, exited that world by hanging themselves in their fine houses by the Thames, while another name altogether, Rothschild from the Frankfurt Judengasse, rose to take their place by the Exchange.

But something had happened between Christian Britain and the Jews; something unlike a connection made anywhere else, even in liberally tolerant America. What that something eventually turned out to be would change the history of the world.

II

CITIZEN-JEWS

I. Hear O Israel

7 January 1750, Choisy-le-Roi. Louis XV has moved the court from glacial, echoing Versailles to his more intimate chateau by the Seine. The palace is not much more than two wings connected by a pavilion projecting out towards the riverbank. But it is charming enough. Even in winter the prospect soothes. Barges sail past on their way to Paris, decks top-heavy with logs or limestone slabs. Behind the upper-storey windows, the king, guided by his *maitresse en titre*, Mme de Pompadour, has furnished the rooms with blue and white porcelain and bow-legged, lightly gilded secretaires; nothing to weigh the spirits down. Chinese cranes glide across the wallpaper, bony legs extended. Following the Feast of Epiphany, the king will return to the court, informally assembled though still properly attentive to protocol. While he is aware of his reputation for lassitude, the days of Louis, *le bien-aimé*, are not entirely monopolised by billiards, stag hunts and the luxurious couch. When the mood takes him, which is more often than commonly supposed, the monarch is a dynamo of scientific curiosity. The latest advance in mechanics will bring a smile to his fleshy face every bit as broad as the prospect of a hothouse peach or Mlle O'Murphy. The colonel of the light cavalry of the Maison du Roi, Michel d'Ailly, Duc de Chaulnes, is happy to cater to this commendable appetite for learning, for the officer is also president of the Académie Royale des Sciences. He has a reputation as an astron-omer and physicist but in the Age of Enlightenment, the Duc de Chaulnes is mostly renowned for his mastery of optics. He has designed compound microscopes, one of which he presented to the

king, and he has built, at considerable expense, the largest glass globe electrostatic generator yet known. Impervious to sneering in envious quarters that he has accomplished this precisely at the moment when such contrivances have become obsolete, the *duc* takes pleasure in the pulses of radiance emitted by his globe.

But in keeping with Condillac's insistence that we are little more than the sum of our sensory impressions, the Duc de Chaulnes has lately become interested in sound as well as light. On this particular winter's day, the diversion he has arranged for the king involves a deaf mute to whom a Jew has restored hearing and, still more miraculously, the capacity for speech. This Jew – you would almost not know it to look at him – is the Marrano Jacob Rodrigues Péreire, born and baptised in 1715 as Francisco Antonio Rodrigues near Peniche in Portugal. At some point the merchant and his wife, anxious about the especially aggressive Portuguese Inquisition, had moved east across the border to Spain. But after the death of the merchant whose name at home was Abramão, the Spanish Holy Office came sniffing after the widow Abigaile despite her care to appear regularly at church. Before the Holy Office could pounce she made her escape along with her four children.

In 1734 the wandering family came to rest in the relatively free air of Bordeaux where some three thousand Sephardim lived as 'tolerated' subjects of the king of France. For generations under the reign of the old Sun King they had had to pretend to be New Christians, and were unmolested by eccelesiastical scrutiny. But since letters patent had been granted by Louis XV, the *'nation Portugais'*, as it inevitably called itself, was allowed to worship openly in synagogues and bury its dead in its own cemetery rather than occupy an outer edge of the Franciscan plot.[1] As in Amsterdam the Sephardim added Jewish names to their baptismal ones without, however, replacing the latter. Thus the merchant's family became Rodrigues Péreire and the two sons were circumcised in their twenties. The community they joined in Bordeaux was what historians now classify as 'port' (as distinct from the contrastingly rhymed 'court') Jews.[2] As in Livorno, Trieste and London their sensibilities were turned outwards to the ocean which brought them merchandise they could profitably market in Europe: indigo, rice, sugar, all supplied by the sweat of atrociously enslaved Africans. That is, *some* of the Bordelais Sephardim made their money from Atlantic trade: the big names, Gradis, Furtado, Peixotto. Others, as in London, were brokers, small or big time: speculating on market-price fluctuations and the commercial paper that supported them. Many more were plain poor, subsisting on badly paid communal jobs. They koshered Bordeaux wine, cut foreskins, buried the dead, browbeat the boys through the Mishnah's contentions. Not many could get through the winters without some help from the community elders. In bad years Abraham Gradis, the *syndic des pauvres*, was doling out funds to almost every other Jewish family in the city.[3]

The Rodrigues Péreires were not among the impoverished. They had managed to bring a decent sum with them out of Spain, but they were not in the top tier of fortunes. His mother dead, Jacob was prepared to do what it took by way of business to support the family, but only for so long as he could also feed his hungry mind. It was the mind of a scientist: a mathematician above all, but one which ranged adventurously through the astral cosmos and the earthly globe. Like so many clever Jewish youths before him, Péreire acquired a medical degree while he was doing business. But while he was counting crates in the warehouse or blistering a patient, something, or rather someone, else was on his mind, commanding more and more of his attentive intellect: the sister who was stone deaf.

There was already a considerable literature on deafness, much of it originating in the Hispanic and Netherlandish worlds and thus familiar to a young Marrano. In 1620 Juan Pablo Bonet had published the first book codifying a system of manual signs, each representing a letter by which the deaf could spell out whole words and sentences. He in turn was thought to have developed a basic manual lexicon originally created by the Benedictine monk Pablo Ponce de León for the pupils at his own school for the deaf, the first of its kind. It has been suggested, plausibly, that a monastery, with strict limitations on spoken speech, was the logical place for a language of gesture to have been invented.

It was because that approach seemed resigned to the loss of sound that Johann Conrad Amann, a Swiss doctor living in the Dutch republic, published his *Surdus loquans* (*The Talking Deaf*) at the end of the seventeenth century. In England, John Wallis had had a famous success producing utterances out of the deaf mute Alexander Popham. But it may have been a more eccentric contribution to the anatomical and remedial literature of the deaf which caught Péreire's attention. Franciscus Mercurius van Helmont, a Fleming, and thus from a culture which still had a strong Marrano element in its midst, was a Hebraist and, more significantly, a Kabbalist. The *Sefer Yetzirah*, the *Book of Creation*, would have introduced van Helmont to the mystical fancy that the world had been created in some metaphysically essential way from the articulation of Hebrew letters. But van Helmont's *Alphabet of Nature* published in 1667 went much further. Psalm 103's verses 'by the word of the Lord the heavens were made and all the host of them by the breath of his mouth' he took literally to mean that not only was Hebrew the original tongue in which God had communicated with Adam, but that God had specifically designed the anatomy of speech expressly for the communication of Hebrew. Hence the Jewish tongue was the fundamental 'natural' language because its original expressions – the formation of names of things – had summoned natural beings into existence (rather than the other way round, as we all idly suppose). Before he died in 1698 van Helmont published a work on Genesis arguing that 'Elohim', one of the names of God, if pronounced correctly would actually sound out the essential attributes of the Deity: the first letter *aleph* through both its shape and sound embodying infinity, and so on. The palate, uvula, tongue, larynx and glottis, he believed, were designed to sound out Hebrew, the language which then must be considered innate and universal, whatever corruptions and variations had evolved from it. By way of demonstration van Helmont claimed that he had been able to get a deaf mute to speak in three weeks by instructing the patient on how to articulate Hebrew letters and then Hebrew words. This miracle, of course, could only work in the Jewish tongue.

Returning as an adult to the Judaism of his ancestors, Jacob Rodrigues Péreire was himself learning Hebrew. As he sounded out his *aleph-bet* (his a-b-c), however fantastical van Helmont's speculations may have seemed, the sense of Hebrew as the Fundamental Alphabet, and the indispensability of vocalising, both to Judaism and to humanity, stuck with him. The most severely rabbinical view had held that since the deaf were locked off by their infirmity from the reading of the Law, they could not be considered true Jews, a view Péreire is likely to have found abhorrent given his sister's impairment. But although he valued the system of physical communication invented by Bonet,

Péreire came to believe that any language for the deaf consisting exclusively of manual signs without any attempt at coaxing utterance from the tongue-tied was no true cure at all. Unlike the monks, no Jew had ever taken a vow of silence. The sacred obligation was voice. Being alive, being human, meant hearing from your fellows. *Shema Yisroel!* Hear O Israel! Read the Torah out loud. It had been that way since the days of Ezra the prophet. Vocalise; make a joyful noise unto the Lord. Talk till you drop. Ignore the futile *shaaaah*, the pointless *shush*. It's only the Christians who bow their heads and shut their mouths in their houses of prayer. Us, we chant, we gabble, we cantillate, we shout. The prophets themselves get into arguments with the Almighty and even if we're no prophets God needs to hear from us on a regular basis too.

Turning from studying to teaching, Péreire resolved to restore the deaf (including his sister) to humanity, by allowing us to hear them. His first great success was a thirteen-year-old tailor's apprentice, Aaron Beaumarin, encountered on a business trip to La Rochelle in 1745. Initially, Péreire used a lightning version of signage, his *'dactylologie'*, the fingers of one hand quickly forming letters to spell out words. (It was suggested that he took his cue from the Kabbalistic manual of the Tzeruf, where the Hebrew alphabet was also expressed in motions of the fingers.) But at the same time Péreire insisted on raising from their long sleep the physical instruments of voice production. It was he, in fact, who first coined the anatomical term *cordes vocales*. It may be that following van Helmont, and his reading of the Tzeruf, Péreire used Hebrew, as the awakeners of the vocal organs, but gently moved into French. It was in French that the boy made such swift progress that Péreire moved to La Rochelle to give Beaumarin an intensive course of lessons. As his articulation improved in quality and quantity, Péreire confined finger signing to the bare minimum, to encourage vocalisation. After a hundred lessons, Aaron commanded a vocabulary of thirteen hundred sounded and understood words. He would appear in public demonstrations with his teacher to say, slowly but distinctly, *'Madame'*, *'Ch-a-peau'*, *'Que voulez-vous?'*[4]

Among those watching the boy and his tutor was Azy d'Etavigny, the director of the Cinques Grosses Fermes, the tax and customs administration at the busy port and naval base. His own son, then sixteen, had been born deaf mute, and all the physicians to whom his

father had dragged him in Italy and Germany, as well as France, had
failed to bring him out of the silence. The boy had been sent to an
institution in Normandy run by an old, deaf cleric where the only
language was signs. In 1743 he had been transferred to a new college
at Beaumont-en-Auge, established by the Duke of Orleans, said to use
more advanced methods, but to little avail. Would Péreire consider
taking him as a pupil? For three thousand livres, he said he would.
D'Etavigny thought again and took him back to Normandy where
the lad languished in the Benedictine abbey. A second meeting between
father and prospective teacher was arranged which this time reached
agreement. Péreire moved to Normandy and began his course of
instruction in the summer of 1746. After just a few days the young
man was, to his father's astonishment, capable of saying *Papa, Maman*,
and many more such words, not parroted either but with evident
understanding of what it was he was saying. The transformation was
so sudden that the case became locally famous. The boy and the Jew
appeared before the sceptical Bishop of Bayeux and a committee of
doctors. There he recited whole sentences, pronouncing each syllable,
loudly and distinctly as if a separate word – *'CHAP-EAU'*, *'VAISS-EAU'*
– yet all understood and understandable. When introduced to the
bishop the boy barked out *'MONSEIGNEUR, JE VOUS SOUHAITE LE
BONJOUR'* ('Your Grace, I wish you good morning'). Suspicious this
was a drill, the boy was asked questions to test his comprehension.
The bishop, was he *'mauvais'* (asked the sly bishop himself)? *'NON!'*
Now, the young d'Etavigny, was he *'mauvais'*? *'NON!'* replied the boy,
visibly angry and distressed, no longer deaf, much less dumb.

Péreire's fame spread swiftly in a France avid for novelty. First the
local Academy of Belles-Lettres at Caen examined his work and
pronounced its approval. Then in 1749, the leading lights, the *lumières*
of the Royal Academy of Sciences in Paris, including the Comte de
Buffon, became interested, as did the Academy's president the Duc
de Chaulnes, whose own godson Saboureux de Fontenay was a congen-
ital deaf mute. When he met Péreire – who by this time had set
himself up on the Quai des Augustins on the left bank in Paris, assisted
by his brother and sister – the *duc* thought he had discovered a Jewish
wonder-worker, the man who opened the padlocked voice.

Hence the audience – never had the word seemed more apt – with
the king in January 1750. The *duc* had brought Péreire and the boy

d'Etavigny in the morning, hoping for a private reception, but had been kept waiting. Minutes stretched into hours. Punctuality was not the courtesy of this particular monarch. In the afternoon, around half past four, the light over the Seine already pinking up, a crowd, canes and glittering rings, gathered in the *salle* where the Duc de Chaulnes was still waiting with his protégés, both dressed in sober black, a contrast with the heavily plumed Chevaliers de Saint-Esprit. Louis entered along with the Pompadour, and a platoon of her deadliest enemies, seven of the eight *mesdames*, the princess-daughters. Everyone smiled, especially the king who enjoyed this rigmarole. After a few minutes of empty politeness, a space was cleared in the room by the chamberlains and the gentlemen ushers and an introduction was, at last, effected. The teacher prodded. The boy spoke, trying his best not to let his trembling go to his lips. 'Sire, I appreciate the honour of being permitted to speak to Your Majesty.' The king nodded, smiled again and turned to walk about the room. This was to be expected; but what was not to be expected was that every so often he interrupted his perambulation to return to the speaking deaf boy, on each occasion asking him something or other and getting a distinct response. Eventually the lad recited the paternoster for Louis, who turned to Péreire and congratulated him: '*C'est merveilleux; le roi est plein d'admiration.*' The compliment was genuine. The king liked the odd Jew, here and there. Where would his army be without Liefmann Calmer, the dependable supplier of animals, fodder and munitions? After the next war was over he would naturalise Calmer and in 1774 even give his assent to his becoming a *vicomte*! The first and only Jewish noble. This Péreire was, in his way, also a noble type. The day after the audience, the king awarded the Jew eight hundred livres to continue his work, which then turned into an annual grant.[5]

Thus officially anointed, Jacob Rodrigues Péreire became the man to bring back the deaf and dumb into the company of humanity. In September 1750, the Duc de Chaulnes finally hired Péreire to be teacher to his godson. Fifteen years later Saboureux de Fontenay, who had appeared before the Academy in January 1751, his godfather happily presiding, published a eulogistic memoir in the *Journal de Verdun* (partly in response to the criticisms of Péreire's rival, the Abbé de l'Épée, who insisted on the primacy of signing over utterance). Saboureux de Fontenay wrote that until he was twelve and had been brought to Péreire, words had been entirely beyond him. It was not just that he had been unable to hear or speak; it was that he could not comprehend. Péreire had changed this, first with the dactylogy which had turned fingers into pens, and which included not just letters and words but punctuation, accents, pauses; marks of syntax and grammar.[6] After the Royal Academy of Sciences in Paris had formally examined Péreire and his pupils, who now included two girls, Marie Le Rat and Marie Marois, it too endorsed the view that his work had been wonderfully effective: 'It is as if by happy metamorphosis [the deaf] had been translated from the condition of mere animals to that of men.'[7]

Jacob Rodrigues Péreire was now a fixture of the garrulous, gossipy milieu of Saint-Germain, and beyond it, in the wider republic of sciences of the academies and clubs of provincial France. He was the Jewish miracle-worker. Denis Diderot, hitherto no friend of the Jews, was so struck by Péreire that after a demonstration with Saboureux de Fontenay he went off to pen his own *Letter on the Deaf*. Jean-Jacques Rousseau, Charles de la Condamine, fellow mathematician as well as explorer, and Buffon all became ardent admirers. In addition to his remedial powers, Péreire seemed to be their *beau idéal* of the benevolent doctor and *honnête homme*. Latterly he declined to charge the families of the deaf anything until there was substantial proof of progress. Who would believe such a thing possible of a Jew? It was true that he kept the secrecy of his methods very much to himself but those were evidently gentle towards the deaf, for his charges all retained a strong personal devotion to their teacher and became his champions in the teeth of the envious competition.

Thus Jacob Rodrigues Péreire became spoken of in the same breath as Moses Mendelssohn, not just as the paragon of the Useful Jew but the maker of Useful fellow citizens out of damaged men and women. For citizenship too depended on listening and comprehending and in turn making utterance. To be such a citizen presupposed something more than a dumb and passive material on which authority would imprint itself. To hear, to speak, was to be free. Happy to be so regarded Péreire then turned his attention to matters of practical importance to his adopted fatherland. There was nothing he wouldn't tackle: the language of the Tahitians encountered by Bougainville; counting machines, initially for the deaf and then for general use in schools;

how to give sailing ships some forward movement in near-dead calm; solving the perennial government deficits through a variety of lotteries. He was becoming the Indispensable Jew: a fellow of the Royal Society in England in 1759; translator and interpreter to the king and his successor grandson.

Péreire's many admirers among the *philosophes* all assumed that, becoming a celebrated projector, one of the officially Ingenious, meant that he must be progressively abandoning what much of enlightened France regarded as a primitive and unreasoning religion. But this is exactly what did not happen. Instead, Péreire attempted to channel the public admiration he was receiving from the Gentiles into something that might assist his own people. No Jew of this evidently superior kind was more respected by the Gentiles, so Péreire became formally acknowledged in the long tradition of the *nasi* or the medieval *resh galuta* as the 'agent' of the 'nation' of the Sephardim before the royal government. Doubtless the relevant powers supposed (and he did not altogether disappoint them) that in times of fiscal and military crisis Péreire might work another kind of wonder, expediting the necessary funds to service the urgent needs of state especially in the Atlantic dockyards. Repeating the commonplace optimistic piety enjoined by that other Bordelais, Montesquieu, that there was nothing to which the Jews would not turn their hand once they were liberated from the fetters of guild restrictions and prohibitions, Péreire argued forcefully before the courts for their loosening – an uphill struggle as it turned out. On the accession of Louis XVI in 1775, though, he was able to secure letters patent a year later which permitted the 'Portuguese' Jews of Bordeaux to travel and reside anywhere in the kingdom, a huge change.

But there was a dark side to all this advocacy of Péreire's, for it was used exclusively on behalf of his own kind of Jews, and if necessary at the expense of not just the poorer Yiddish-speaking Ashkenazim of eastern France but even the Jews living in the papal enclave of Avignon, a number of whom, to his displeasure, had migrated to Bordeaux and become dependent on its Jewish charity. In an ugly exercise of this assumed superiority, Péreire actually petitioned the royal intendant in the 1760s on behalf of the elders of the community to have the Avignonnais expelled from the port!

Bordeaux and, still more, the district of Saint-Esprit by Bayonne on the right bank of the River Dour (to which they had been confined in a kind of Sephardi ghetto) were border towns, and the world they bordered was the one that the Sephardim had left but whose languages they still spoke, albeit in their Judaised version – the musical tongue of Ladino. Travel through France to the border furthest away would bring one to the frontier lands of the east, the provinces of Alsace and Lorraine which had been conquered by Louis XIV and annexed as a result of peace treaties. Along with the rolling hills, the wine, the pastured cows and the manufactures came the Jews, who had been there far longer than the French. By the middle of the eighteenth century there were around 28,000 of them, the largest number in Metz (one of the 'Three Bishopric' cities that made up its own province within the kingdom); others scattered over eighty small towns and villages of Alsace and the duchy of Lorraine (between 1737 and 1766 ruled, grandly, by Louis XV's father-in-law Stanislas Leszczynski). Too much can be made of the contrast with the Jews of the southwest. Though most of the Bordeaux Jews were shaved and wigged, many, if not most of them, including some of the wealthiest of their elders, were, like the Ashkenazim, fiercely religious. Conversely there were *les grands* among the Ashkenazim of the east. None was more formidable in Alsace than Cerf Berr, the leaser of ironworks who resided in a house of *Hofjude* splendour in Strasbourg (where thousands of Jews had been massacred at the height of the well-poisoning paranoia in 1349), a special privilege granted to someone deemed indispensable to the state.

In the small towns of Alsace the Jews lived by horse trading, literally, along with cattle and mules, another occupation which made them logistically important, a fact that was brought to the attention of the authorities when they were the target of abuse, verbal and physical. Even more vitally, some had connections with the Ashkenazim of Mainz and the towns of the Rhineland from whom they would be able to import grain in the years of harvest shortfalls, which seemed to come ever more frequently. Then there were, as usual, the legions of rag dealers, hawkers, and, of necessity, pawnbrokers and moneylenders, the source of much *tsuris*, misery, for all concerned. To non-Jewish contemporaries, what distinguished the Péreire kind of Jew from the Metz kind of Jew, even from the likes of opulent Cerf Berr, was the difference between Ladino and Yiddish, despite being the ancient and rich 'Yiddish-Daytsh', not far at all from medieval German.

But somehow it became a snobbish truism that Judaeo-Spanish speakers were more likely to become fluent francophones than the guttural throat-clearers of the east. In fact, both sorts of Jew shared many of the same burdens and disadvantages. Aside from having almost all trades and occupations locked off by the prohibitions of the guilds, both were required to pay special taxes. Every time an Alsatian Jew wanted to go to Strasbourg on business for the day, he was required to pay a 'body tax' for the privilege, made insultingly the same as the duty levied for conveying a pig to town. Ho-ho-ho, *drôle, n'est-ce pas*? Other feudal debasements lingered on into the Age of Enlightenment. Both sets of Jews were obliged to ask the king's permission to marry. This degrading requirement was meant as a measure of population control. For in the minds of the Gentiles, the Yiddishites bred like rabbits, and if allowed to couple unchecked, would soon swamp the native population.

Whatever the Sephardi view of them, the Ashkenazim of the east – and especially of Metz – believed themselves to be no less ceremonious, no less dignified, no less worthy of being thought civilised than the Gradises and the Péreires; and in matters of Judaism, more so. They, after all, had an unbroken tradition of Talmudic learning dating from the medieval centuries while the Iberian Jews had been lost to the faith for generations and had had to be re-educated. There were occasions, too, when although condescended to as 'foreign', the eastern Ashkenazim could show themselves every bit as *French* as the next community. On special occasions, mostly joyous (the recovery of the king from an assassination attempt, the birth of the dauphin, a royal wedding), the Ashkenazim not only offered special prayers for the royal family in their synagogue services but put on such a public display of loyalty as to silence any doubts about allegiance. Cerf Berr threw banquets and balls both for public entertainment and the notables of the region at his opulent house, entertainments so lavish the Gentiles could hardly refuse, even if they made churlish noises about those ostentatious Jews the next morning. But for the communities themselves, these celebrations were moments when they could advertise their wholehearted sense of being unproblematically French.[8]

So out came the triumphal car, carefully copied from Roman proto-types, festooned with the royal colours of blue and white and adorned with the fleur-de-lys. Out trotted companies of Jewish horsemen, the mounts – not any old nags but the handsomest in the stables – caparisoned in silks of scarlet and gold. In the middle of the troop, sitting high in the saddle, was Samuel Levy, master horse trader, the man without whom whole regiments of the royal army would be left to plod behind the cannon. Summon the trumpeters and the drummers and the piping fifes! Let the flourishes sound far and wide. Strew the synagogue with lilies – the fleur-de-lys! Unfurl the tapestries; bring out the Torah topped with the most elaborate *rimmonim* finials. Raise the silverware, shake the little bells. Drape the banners of '*Vive le roi; vive la reine*' on the triumphal arches (for on two occasions Louis and Queen Marie Leszczynska graced the Jews of Metz with a public audience; and for the little dauphin a marvellous contraption was built, a colossal mechanical dolphin which, as it rolled through the streets, rising and falling along the cobbles, snapped at the presumptuous small fry swimming by its side). Down the rue des Juifs the parade went, the street where in the evening casks of wine would be tapped for the people to fill cups to the brim; then out from the quarter into the town itself: stopping at all the sites of local power and authority. First, there was a halt at the citadel and a greeting from the military governor; then on to the Parlement to stand with the president of the court, and finally and most remarkably to the bishop's palace where a select group of Jews including the rabbi would stand on the terrace with the Prince of the Church himself. Hurrah! Who could possibly say, now, that the Jews did not belong in Metz, or imply their loyalty might ever be divided?

Some, apparently. For in 1729, on that same day of the dauphin, when the procession returned to the Jewish quarter, eagerly anticipating the illuminations, the fireworks and the wine, they found the gates of the rue des Juifs had been closed, locking them out. Frantic and indignant messages were delivered post-haste to the governor, and they were unlocked again. But the squibs had been dampened. Was this someone's idea of a mockery? Was it a gesture meant to puncture the delusions of the Jews of Metz; to remind them, in the end, that they were still penned animals, unloosed or confined at the grace of the king and good Christians? Or was it a reproof of their presumptuous display? In any event, as Jews are wont to say, it could have been worse. It was reported that gunpowder charges had been discovered in several places along the rue des Juifs. An innocent firework display, with crowds watching, would have been interrupted by another kind of explosion. That would teach the Jews their place.

Both communities, east and west, wanted to demonstrate whenever possible the truth of Montesquieu's contention that, with their imprisoning shackles removed, the Jews would be seen to be like all other men. Far from being traduced as a barbarous and antisocial cult, Judaism would be recognised as the original fountainhead of all civic morality. But it was also true that the elders of the Bordeaux Sephardim, including Péreire, continued to feel undermined in this argument by what they thought of as the 'backward' manners and mores of the Ashkenazim. Péreire, who was now among the company of the *philosophes*, squirmed at the malicious vehemence of Voltaire's attacks on Judaism. His Gentile friends pointed out then (as many still argue) that Voltaire had attacked the Old Testament the better to bring down the New. But no honest reader of his polemics could fail to notice that his assault was on Jews as much as Judaism. However many Péreires the Jews might fortuitously manage to produce, Voltaire believed that, as a group, the Jews were inescapably the product of their savagely fantastical books and the bizarre rituals which separated them off not just from Christians but from the rest of mankind. Unless they ditched Judaism en masse they would always remain unfortunate curiosities at best, and at worst, something alien and sinister.

Unquestionably, Voltaire had a thing about the Jews. Though the champion of toleration deplored their centuries-long persecution he had also drunk deep from classical Judaeophobic slanders, first set down in Alexandria by the grammarian Apion and then rehashed by the likes of Tacitus, Seneca and Juvenal: their alleged enmity to the rest of mankind; their propensity to kidnapping and infanticide. Voltaire evidently found one commonplace of ancient Jew-hatred especially satisfying, because it punctured the pretensions of the biblical exodus and thus the foundation myth of Jewish superiority – instead of a divinely engineered liberation from bondage, Apion recycled the version of their departure narrated by the Egyptian priest Manetho: that the Israelites had been expelled from the Nile Valley because of their uncleanness, an infection which in all likelihood was tribally transmitted leprosy. This allowed Voltaire to sneer that throughout the ages, the Jews had been distinguished for three things above all: fanaticism, usury and leprosy. They were, in fact, walking diseases, set loose on the world. To Terence's famous epigram *Homo sum, humani nihil a me alienum puto* (I am a man, nothing human is alien to me), Voltaire was prepared to make an exception for the Jews.

This unreason on the subject of his people pained Péreire so acutely that he commissioned Isaac de Pinto, born in Bordeaux but resident in Amsterdam, to write a public reply to Voltaire's censures. Before it was published in 1762, Pinto sent Voltaire, then living in Ferney in the Genevan republic, the manuscript of his *Apologie des Juifs*. To the chagrin of Moses Mendelssohn in particular, this was indeed an apologia, at least to the point of Pinto urging Voltaire not to confuse the regrettable social mores and hoary superstitions of the Ashkenazim with the superior talents of the enlightened Sephardim of Bordeaux and Paris. Encounter us and you will see we are just like everyone else, indeed just like you, was the special pleading. 'We wear no beards and our clothes are no different from anyone else's!' The two kinds of Jews led such different lives as to be considered two entirely different 'nations'. And this was not surprising since they descended from wholly different ancestors. The Sephardim traced their lineage from the exiles of the house of Judah transplanted in antiquity to Spain. God only knows where the Ashkenazim came from. Were one of his 'nation' to marry an Ashkenazi, it would be regarded as a calamity, scarcely better than marrying a Gentile. Nor could a member of either community allow themselves to be buried in the same cemetery or buy from the same butcher.

Much has been made of this dismal strategy of inter-communal invidiousness. Péreire, as we have seen, was not immune from it himself. Three years before his death in 1780 he was made a registrar of the Jews of Bordeaux and Bayonne with power to determine who should stay and who must go: an ominous moment of social arbitration. But it was also true that Pinto (and by extension Péreire himself) wished to hold up the Sephardi world of the port city, sophisticated and modernising (this was not exactly true), as an example of what Jews, even the most unfortunate of the eastern Ashkenazim, might achieve were they given the opportunity. Just look at Amsterdam or London, they said. There, the Jews were in the van of commercial empire building; the multipliers of wealth, not just for themselves but for their respective states; harbingers of modernity. That it is a common

Portrait engraving of Shabbetai Zevi.

The human body as a house, from Tobias Cohen's medical encyclopedia, *Ma'aseh Tuviyah*, Venice, 1708.

A New Year's postcard from the late nineteenth century showing the Hurva Synagogue in Jerusalem.

Portrait of Samuel Oppenheimer
by Johann Andreas Pfeffel.

Moses Mendelssohn at the door of Berlin
in Potsdam, waiting for an audience with
King Frederick II.

Portrait of Moses
Mendelssohn by
Anton Graff, 1773.

Dr Ralph Schomberg by Thomas Gainsborough, ca. 1770.

Moses Mendelssohn's eyeglasses.

Portrait of Daniel Itzig.

Daniel Isaac Itzig
(son of Daniel Itzig)
by Johann Christoph
Frisch, 1777.

Ark curtain made from Fromet Mendelssohn's bridal dress. Unusually Moses and Fromet's names are embroidered side by side.

John Braham as Prince Orlando by Thomas Woolnoth, 1828.

The Game of the Jew, eighteenth-century French board game.

Rag Fair by Thomas Rowlandson, London, ca. 1800.

The English boxing champion Daniel Mendoza, by James Gillray.

Rabbi Israel ben Eliezer, the founder of Hasidism, often called Baal Shem Tov (BESHT).

The decorated Ark of Satanow Great Synagogue before restoration.

'Chasing hares' tombstone from the cemetery at Satanow.

characteristic of emancipatory movements to present themselves as a vanguard elite seeking recognition from a hostile wider community, and to cast themselves as missionaries of the backward of their own people, does not of course make this stratagem any more palatable.

In any case, Voltaire paid only the scantest lip service to Pinto's point. He responded by showering the author with compliments, amazed that any sort of Jew could muster reasonable arguments, and apologising for having stigmatised an entire people when apparently there were Pintos and Péreires among them. But if Pinto wished to be taken seriously as a civilised man he must act on his pretensions. '*Soyez philosophe,*' he wrote back; take the plunge. Leave the mental ghetto. Or, in other words, do what Péreire had not done: abandon your comically detestable religion. For the rest of the Sephardim, Voltaire cared little how many ships they chartered or whether they could quote Plutarch. He still held them contemptible; all the more so for their commercial acumen; a euphemism for the sharp practice of which he had direct experience in London and Amsterdam. Beneath the tie wigs, really, they were all the same. It was actually of Sephardim like Pinto, Péreire and Gradis that Voltaire wrote 'these marranos will go anywhere there is money to be made ... nonetheless they [all Jews] are the greatest scoundrels who have ever sullied the face of the earth'. As he got older, Voltaire became still more unhinged on the subject of the Jews, convinced that so deeply encrusted were this people in the barbarousness of their culture, they were ineligible of being classified as human. In 1771, he had a 'Syrian' in his *Letters from Memmius to Cicero* speak for him when he declared that 'they are the most insolent of all men, detested by all their neighbours, always robbers or the robbed, brigands or slaves, murderers or the murdered'. 'Every nation commits crimes,' he added, getting into his stride, 'only the Jews boast about them.' The trouble was not so much social as biological. 'They are all of them born with raging fanaticism in their hearts just as Bretons and Germans are born with blonde hair. I would not be in the least surprised if this people would not some day become deadly to the whole human race.'[9] 'You have surpassed ALL nations', he would rage, 'in impertinent fables, wicked practices and barbarism. You deserve to be punished for this is your destiny.' In the centuries which followed there would be no shortage of people, including many of the high-minded, eager to take up Voltaire's challenge.

II. Êtes-vous de la Nation?[10]

Never mind. Here's a turn-up for the books: ornamental Jews, a whole roomful of them, decoratively depicted at the centre of the Nouvelle Combinaison du Jeu du Juif, a brand-new, 1783 edition of the ever-popular Game of the Jew.[11] Not so charming perhaps in the older versions of the board game, first produced in Augsburg, where the Eternal Jew is more usually represented fist-deep in the cash, wearing the same expression of crazed elation that would overcome a dice thrower landing on the space that delivers the whole pot. But these are enlightened times so the game has changed its face and the Jews in its central panel, the one from which all players must begin, wear a variety of charming costumes, from old-fashioned fur-trimmed Polish soft hats to broad-brimmed flat ones and even (assuming this is still a Jew) a tricorn like everyone else on the street. Their long coats are of different colours and some of the Jews appear positively *aimable*: conversational, gregarious, chatty. Nor are the Jews counting their loot. No, here they are playing – well, of course – The Game of the Jew, and looking happy into the bargain, so no offence taken, surely. Never mind that until you throw a double six, the directions tell you, you remain 'in the hands of the Jew' and there you sit trapped between his palms until you throw the liberating combination which lets you set off around the board.

This is also an improvement on earlier versions of the game, each space now decorated not with images of deplorable Jewish habits, but with diversions that have nothing to do with Jews at all (except for the common truism that rich Jews kept Christian mistresses). Now, the panels feature games and pastimes, mostly saucy, and certainly saucily drawn. Land on *la balançoire*, the see-saw on which the see-sawing décolleté girls have allowed themselves to be swung right off into the arms of their gallants, and you lose one token. Number 6? *Cache-cache* (lose four tokens), hide-and-seek where the sought is tightly hugged in the undergrowth away from the seeker. Throw 7 and you land on *l'escarpolette*, the swing where you win one token, while a high-flying beauty receives the admiration of low-down, ogling, pigtailed Chinamen. Likewise the Jews have become picturesque *staffage*, *vaudeville* walk-ons, wallpaper and drapery prints like Hindoos

or Tahitians or Esquimaux, the hatred drained away into mere ethnographic curiosity of the kind inspected by lorgnettes. Just what kind
of diversion they provide, however, is made clear in the verses inscribed
on the banner hanging over the Jews gathered at the gaming table of
The Game of the Jew:

> Qu'il est doux de subtiliser[12]
> Une Israelite jolie
> Comme on aime à Judaiser
> Quand c'est pur la tendre folie.

> How sweet it is to seduce
> A pretty Jewess
> Oh how one would love to make a convert
> When it's for the sake of tender passion.

But, as it turned out, on the eve of the revolution, the more serious
unpleasantness had not gone away. In 1786 a different kind of folly
did the rounds: *Le Cri d'Un Citoyen Contre les Juifs de Metz* (*The Cry of
a Citizen against the Jews of Metz*). Its author went by the pseudonym
'Foissac-Latour' but was in all likelihood Jean-Baptiste Aubert-Dubayet,
a cavalry officer stationed in the garrison town. His toxic little production, at once sanctimonious and vivid, portrayed platoons of innocent
young soldiers in the garrison town pounced on by mobs of Jews
eager to lend them what was needed to support the dashing life
expected of a cavalry lieutenant. Enticed into the spider's web of
usury, they would abandon themselves over to a carnival of luxurious
debauchery, and become the helpless quarry of the merciless Jew.
Thus the flower of France's manhood, stationed on the very borders
of the realm, would be milked dry for sordid gain and the kingdom
was robbed of its defenders.[13] But then what did the Jews care for the
honour of France and its army? Their allegiance, it was well known,
was to no one other than themselves.

The genre of *The Cry* was *sensibilité*: the romance of innocence
seduced by the wickedly selfish. In the 1780s it was everywhere: on
stage, in the sentimental genre paintings of the biennial Salons, and
after the publication of Rousseau's wet-eyed *Confessions* in 1782 it
became the script of political rhetoric as well, the battle between

mercenary guile and pastoral simplicity. The Jews weren't the only
social types to be cast as villains in this social romance, but in eastern
France they became the choice target of demonisation. 1778, the year
of Voltaire's death, saw the outbreak of violent riots in Upper Alsace.
Terrifying reports circulated amid the Jews of the province that a
general slaughter was being organised for 30 September, Kol Nidrei,
the eve of the Day of Atonement, when they would all be assembled
defenceless in their synagogues. With measures of deterrence in place
by the government, this never happened, but the social war remained
an open wound. For years the peasants indebted to Jewish moneylenders claimed they were being hounded, notwithstanding having
already paid off their debts. (The lenders were scarcely better off than
their debtors, but they were the only sources of credit in the region
for the purchase of seed, draught animals and the like.) Receipts were
flourished to prove the peasants were being pursued by the merciless,
lying Jews. Except, as a royal investigator sent to examine the records
discovered, the receipts – two thousand of them – were all forgeries.
There was, in fact, a minor industry in falsifying loan receipts, perpetrated by a ring of thirty-odd forgers (including two Jews!). For their
crimes, three of the malefactors were hanged, fifteen sentenced to
the galleys for life, another ten for lengthy stretches, and the remainder
sent to prison.

It was at this point, in 1779, that the Alsatian lawyer François Hell
published his *Observations d'un Alsacien sur l'Affaire présent des Juifs
d'Alsace*.[14] A batch of false receipts had been discovered at Hell's own
house, making it more than likely that he had had a hand in orchestrating the ring as a way of launching a career as the chastiser of the
Jews. Operating on the principle that the best line of defence is attack,
Hell conceded that while technically the forgeries had indeed been a
crime, that was nothing beside the paramount need to draw attention
to the evils of Jewish usury. The tradition by which piffling facts were
not allowed to complicate hearty bursts of Judaeophobia was already
long established in France. Earlier in the century Hirschel Levy had
been executed in Colmar for a robbery in the face of overwhelming
evidence that he had had nothing to do with it; a cause his widow
and family spent twenty years vainly trying to vindicate.

Like 'Foissac-Latour', Hell knew well how to tug the heartstrings
of the Romantic generation while accusing the Jews of maliciously

preying on the vulnerable. His sentimental narrative featured honest households ruined by Jewish entrapment into debt: the knuckle-crackers versus the sons of toil; mothers driven to beggary, babies dead in the cot. The Jews now murdered and sucked blood, not literally as in the medieval tales of child abduction, but indirectly through economic vampirism. This updating did not mean François Hell had abandoned the ancient recriminations, which still found a place in modern Judaeophobia. Hell repeated the Christian commonplace that the Jewish killing of the Saviour condemned them for all eternity to the wandering life of unabsolved criminals; the blood was indeed on them and their posterity. The eighteenth century may have been the age of accelerated travel, but there was good travel and bad travel. Jewish wandering was in the latter category because they called no place truly home other than the company of their own tribe: their only deep loyalty. In 1769, Abbé Charles-Louis Richer had reminded his readers that 'a Jew is a born and sworn enemy of all Christians. It is a principle of his faith to regard them as blasphemers and idolaters who should be put to death and to whom as much harm as possible should be done.'[15] Hence the Jews were incapable of fraternal sentiment towards the peoples amid whom they dwelled. Wherever they went, they constituted 'a nation within a nation'. Hell himself would become one of the tribunes of the true nation, for after serving a brief banishment for his part in the forgeries (exile with his in-laws in the Dauphiné), Hell returned to Alsace in 1782 as the champion of the oppressed. He took part in the reforming Assembly of the Notables in 1787, and was elected to the Estates General which became the National Assembly.

This was all very ominous. The fate of France was about to turn on the question of what precisely *was* the nation and how might it be reconstituted. In the first instance this new 'nation' was to be built politically and legally. Out of the archaic incoherence of multiple corporations, legal orders and jurisdictions, a coherent, homogeneous nation state would be hammered with whatever force was needed to complete it. So the traditional communal autonomy of the Jews, should they obstinately cling to it, was always going to be an obstacle to their incorporation within the newly united *patrie*. Language was another crucial element in the fashioning of a new France. In 1789 a large majority of ordinary people living within the 'hexagon' did not speak French, but Breton, Provençal Langue d'Oc, or one of the countless local patois from Flanders to the Pyrenees. In this respect, then, the Yiddish speakers of the east were not exceptional, but the obstinate oddity of their language and their appearance made those Jews a test case, both of the revolutionary nation's promised homogeneity, and its capacity to 'regenerate' even those it judged unpromising human specimens.

The question had been broached some years before, in 1774, when a young Metz lawyer, Pierre-Louis Lacretelle (who would go on to be a deputy in the revolutionary Legislative Assembly), accepted a brief from Jews wanting to open shops in the towns of Lorraine. They insisted that a royal edict of 1767 encouraging 'foreigners' to establish profitable enterprises overrode the ancient ban imposed by the guilds on any retail and wholesale businesses. The Jews went ahead and opened for trading. Local police landed heavily on them, but they refused to desist. Instead they went to Lacretelle and asked him to represent them before the Parlement of Nancy. Taking the suit, Lacretelle smelled publicity. Those kinds of cases were golden opportunities for the hordes of young lawyers falling over each other to make a reputation, and they were a hothouse school for political oratory. Accordingly Lacretelle, the up-and-comer, played shamelessly to the gallery. The Jews, he argued, must indeed be *français* since their enterprises had long been established in the kingdom. Thus they fell within the purview of the law designed to encourage 'zeal and talent'. No one contested the Jewish reputation for industriousness, intelligence and 'resourcefulness'; but Lacretelle was also cannily aware of how far he could push the argument without running into incredulous hostility. Like so many others casting themselves as Friends of the Jews, he conceded that they seemed to suffer from an addiction to money, however gained, but this was to be understood as the inevitable result of historical oppression. The remedy was to remove all the restrictions of their residence and to institute a reverse ghettoisation. In place of a confinement the Jews should be scattered about the towns and rural provinces of France. Once they were in contact with the 'honour' of the French, they themselves would become honourable. But *truly* French? Up to a point, *messieurs les juges*. 'If we cannot receive them as compatriots,' Lacretelle declared, 'then let us at least receive them as men.' The glaring reservation expressed by the Jews' own advocate did not go unnoticed by the judges of the Parlement who had little hesitation in denying the Jews' case.

Lacretelle, on the other hand, published his plea in the popular publication *Causes Célèbres*. He had become a figure. The Jews could always be depended on for coverage.

Ten years later, entries to the competition organised by the Royal Academy of Arts and Sciences in Metz on what might be done to make the Jews 'more useful and happier' produced their own list of challenges for Jewish compatibility with citizenship. The most critical harped on the Jews' irredeemable dishonesty and usury, while the friendlier contributions – those of the lawyer Claude-Antoine Thiéry and the priest Henri Grégoire – even as they described the Jews as wretched scum assumed this would all change with their 'regeneration', especially if they were obliged to attend non-Jewish schools. But there were also those who believed there was something intrinsic to Judaism itself – not, to be sure, the 'pure' Judaism of the Old Testament, but the Talmudic version which had supplanted it – which ensured that the Jews would stay forever foreign. Many of the harshest assailants took care to exempt Karaites from their criticism, since they alone were Jews who obeyed only the laws of the Torah, refusing to accept rabbinical authority. This was a safe bet since there were no Karaites to be seen in France. The charge of Talmudic usurpation was an old song, dating back to the medieval disputations, the result of profound ignorance of the books themselves or dishonest selectivity by those, as Hebrew readers, who were familiar with the rabbinic canon. Jewish responses to the accusations that rabbinical Judaism encouraged antisocial and unethical behaviour (not to mention hatred towards Christians) – especially the eloquent case written by the Hebrew specialist at the royal library, Israel Bernard Valabrègue – patiently attempted to disabuse the enlightened. Valabrègue, writing as 'Un Milord', pointed out that far from the Talmud encouraging dishonest practice and usury, it went to inordinate lengths to spell out ethical conduct in matters of business, above all when parties to any contract were non-Jews. And he took pains to let his readers know that since Judaism assumed a place in the world to come for non-Jews subscribing to the 'Noahide' laws, the core of the Ten Commandments, it was actually a more inclusive religion than Christianity, which held that the only way to salvation lay through Christ. To those who wished to make the Jews 'moral', Valabrègue insisted that any honest and clear-eyed account of the Jews would acknowledge that it was *already* the perfectly moral religion and society the *philosophes* wanted to establish. Jewish families, however poor, were chaste and loyal, upright, charitable and sober. What more could be asked of an honest citizen?

The possibility that Jews, as citizens, might fit unproblematically into the dawning political nation was complicated by the fact that the French themselves were sharply divided on what kind of society that would be. A minority of modernisers put their faith in trade and commerce, and therefore might not have been put off by Isaac de Pinto's unfortunate analogy of Jews as chameleonic: taking on the colour of wherever they were. Melting into the background helped deliver the goods for trade. Commerce needed chameleons. On the other hand they hopped around a bit. So perhaps their professed loyalty to wherever they happened to be was merely opportunist. The iron laws of profit to which the Jews were said to be committed even more than the Law of Moses would, in that view, always supersede attachment to homeland. Their real homeland was each other.

For a more numerous and influential group of economic writers, commercial shape-shifting did not recommend the Jews as prospective Frenchmen. For they held that true economic value lay above all in the land, and there were no Jews, whither west or east, who were tillers of the soil. So those among the physiocrats – the agricultural champions – who nonetheless wanted to promote the cause of the Jews, argued that this severance from the land only dated from the destruction of the Temple. Before that there had been farmers in Judaea, not to mention soldiers and craftsmen, all honourable occupations. It had only been the dispersion and Christian oppression which had forced them into moneylending. There were *still* Jews they knew of – in Ethiopia, Persia, India and Palestine – who were potters, leather-workers, weavers and goldsmiths, and, so they had been told, in Poland and Lithuania, husbandmen and herders. A century later, the revival of lost Jewish pastoral life would actually become something of a French obsession, both in Palestine and elsewhere around the world, and would become realised, too. But in the 1780s, it needed a lot of imagination to see them as improvement-conscious farmers, investing in intensive manuring and seed drills. When Jews who had enough money and the ear of the right people attempted to buy land, they ran into a firestorm of adamant opposition. The military purveyor Liefmann Calmer (né Moses Eliezer Lipmann ben Kalonymus), naturalised by the king in 1767, attempted to spend 1.5 million livres on a Norman barony in 1774 via a frontman buyer; but when the true purchaser was revealed the barriers went up. For the local church it was outrageous that a Jew could have the right to appoint priests to the livings that went with the estate. Nonetheless, Liefmann Calmer became Viscount of Amiens and Baron of Picquigny just in time for his heirs to be deprived of the title by the revolution which emancipated his co-religionists. The Jewish *vicomte* died in 1784, and instead of his three sons inheriting the estate, two of them perished under the blade of the guillotine.[16]

So when, following the successful emancipation of Protestants in 1787, the more liberal of *les grands* adopted the Jews as the next great project for humanising citizenship, they often wondered out loud if it was folly to try. A commission presided over by the great jurist and liberal philosopher Lamoignon de Malesherbes was established in 1788 and consulted with delegates from Bordeaux, Abraham Furtado and Salomon Lopes-Dubec, about what might be done; but Malesherbes, normally the soul of enlightenment, was himself another high mind who nonetheless assumed the incorrigible separateness of the Jews ('they have become a power independent of all others on earth and perhaps dangerous'). It was not surprising, then, that the deliberations of his commissions were inconclusive.

But in the elections to the Estates General in the winter of 1788–9, the first since 1614, anything seemed possible; even, conceivably, the transformation of a perennially oppressed and degraded people into voters. The Friends of the Jews believed the historic moment was at hand. Henri Grégoire, one of three who had been singled out for distinction by the judges of the Metz essay competition, wrote excitedly to Cerf Berr in February 1789 not to shilly-shally. 'Should you not be consulting with others of your people so that your nation can claim the rights and benefits of citizens?'[17] This was not entirely a pipe dream. In Bordeaux, propertied Jews were allowed to vote for electors who in turn went on to elect deputies for the Third Estate of the city. David Gradis was himself voted in as one such elector. In the east, hope contended with nervousness about the possibility that losing their communal autonomy would be the price for joining the nation. In both areas, Jews hoped Christian deputies might be elected expressly to represent their interests and concerns.

But the *cahiers des doléances* – the statement of grievances drawn up in every village, town and canton – told a different story in the east where the aim was not to liberate the Jews but to be liberated from them. Some wanted the establishment of closed ghettos; others wanted expulsion; nearly all demanded restrictions on marriages and numbers. This too was the French Revolution. And in February 1789 the complaints were registered, as so often before, in physical attacks on Jewish communities. This only made the need to defend themselves, both physically and politically, more urgent. Cerf Berr wrote in April 1789 to Jacques Necker, the controller general who had proposed the Estates General as a way of legitimising national credit, that his people ought somehow to be represented: 'Justice, humanity and the national interest all militate in favour of the Jews. Can they be condemned without a hearing?'[18]

When excited expectations met paranoid anxiety, the result was *la Grande Peur*, the Great Fear. The excitement had been generated by the meeting of the elected Estates General and its conversion into a National Assembly, when clergy and nobility, deserting their separate Orders, joined with the deputies of the Third Estate to form a new, sovereign legislature. But through the late spring and early summer of 1789, rumours spread throughout France of an armed counter-revolution being hatched at court and led by Marie Antoinette and the brothers of the king. In Paris the result was the call to arms that ended on 14 July with the fall of the Bastille. Out in the countryside, though, the rumours mutated into conspiracy theories that aristocrats, determined to resist the end of the seigneurial regime, had mobilised whole armies of 'brigands' to massacre good patriots. Despite many claiming to have seen these regiments of brigands they were entirely phantoms of the popular imagination. But the spectres were thought to ride by night along with sundry other agents of the reaction, among whom, needless to say, in eastern France at least, were the Jews. While they were about burning manorial rolls, armed bands also delivered to the flames records of debts owed to the Jews. From torching chateaux, the brands were taken to Jewish districts of the Sundgau and Lorraine. Houses and synagogues were ransacked. The terror was so widespread that around a thousand Jews in the affected areas fled over the border to Basel.[19]

Throughout the tumult, from Bordeaux, Bayonne and Avignon to Nancy, Bischheim and Metz, the leaders of Jewish communities fell over themselves to demonstrate that they were good patriots, loyal to the *patrie*. Many volunteered for the citizen militia – the National Guard – which both in Paris and town after town, village after village, had become the armed protector and enforcer of the new regime. But because the status of the Jews was still undetermined, and also because the 'nation within a nation' suspicion had become so ingrained, especially towards those who spoke a different language, many if not most companies of the National Guard flinched from accepting Jews in their ranks. It did not help that the foreign states bordering each of their communities – Spain and the Prussian Rhineland – were both countries which declared themselves early enemies of the revolutionary regime they believed had illegitimately overturned the Bourbon monarchy. Now who would make perfect spies of the fifth column if not these border-country Jews, with known relatives and extended families across the frontiers? To arm even those professing ardent loyalty to the nation would be folly. Nonetheless there were some muncipalities where Jews were allowed to join the Guard and responded enthusiastically. Rabbi Aaron Worms went so far as to shave his beard so that he might enlist, and in keeping with the new spirit took his son Abraham out of yeshiva and apprenticed him to one of the 'useful trades' the emancipators of the Jews were constantly urging on them. Those who were barred compensated for their exclusion from the Guard by contributing *dons patriotiques*, patriotic donations to the cause, urgently needed if France should have to fight a war of revolutionary defence against enemies internal and external. Cartloads of silver shoe buckles from the Jews were delivered to local treasuries and the Jews were commended for their patriotic zeal.

Borne along on the fast-flowing tide of rhetoric, deputies in the National Assembly competed in expressions of devotion to the newly discovered unity of the *patrie*. Catholic priests (some of them) ostentatiously embraced Protestants; disinterested *ci-devant* aristos pompously celebrated the end of their seigneurial rights. Address me as plain *citoyen* if you please! And as August progressed the Assembly proceeded to debate the document which more than any other would define the character, not just of the new France, but the new age; of humanity reborn, the fetters of inherited, unwarranted tradition struck off by the hammers of the people's will. A Declaration of the Rights of Man and Citizen was in the offing. Boniface Louis André de

Castellane (one of the sometime nobles) had said, plainly, that 'no man should be harassed for his religious opinions'. Bravo. So, no more degrading discriminatory taxes, no occupations off limits, no city barred to them maybe? But still, in Bayonne and Peyrehorade, Avignon and Saint-Jean-de-Luz, Carpentras and Cavaillon, Sarrelouis, Bischheim, Wolfsheim, Nancy and Metz, Jews of different stripes and tongues and fashions and styles of singing *adon olam* were all wondering just what it would mean to be a citizen. How much of a new world would it be and could they still be Jews within it?

Representations were sent to Versailles where the National Assembly was still meeting. On 26 August, the last day of debate, a deputation from the 500-odd Jews living in Paris – some of whom were personally known to the Assembly – set out with forthright clarity exactly what it was they expected and hoped for: 'We ask that we be subject like all Frenchmen to the same laws; the same police; the same courts; we therefore renounce for the public good and in our own interests, and always subject to the general good, the rights we have always been given to choose our own leaders.'[20] It was a moment of breathtaking optimism and courage. The Paris Jews were declaring that they were prepared to leave behind all the familiar protections and restrictions of their ancient self-governance for the new abstract world of citizenship. Henceforth they would do without those courts which had forever ruled on whether a brother of the deceased was obliged to marry his widowed sister-in-law; which had arbitrated the endless bickering over wills and dowries; collected communal taxes; the disciplinary boards that handed down punishments to the wayward; made sure that boys were drilled in *chumash* and Gemara. Was all this now to be jettisoned for the as yet unformed national community of citizens with its own version of schooling, law and what was owed, financially, to the state? The Parisians and the Bordelais had an easier time answering yes, because for generations the Sephardim had looked to royal, not rabbinical, courts for adjudication on civil issues, especially when the judgement of the Jewish courts went against them. This was also true, to a lesser extent, of the Jews of Lorraine and to a lesser extent still in Alsace. But for the Ashkenazim, happy expectations were shadowed with apprehensiveness. Now, they could live wherever they wanted? Very nice, but where should they want to live except among other Jews? You needed a *minyan*, didn't you? You

needed a cemetery, a *mohel*, a *shokhet*? You needed each other. Would
the nation really take care of *tante Sara* left alone in her old age and
sickness? Would the Gentile schoolmasters drum into the heads of
the boys disrespect for their religion; to make, God forbid, little
Spinozas out of them? But matters were moving so quickly the
moment of justice and freedom might not come again. Some sort of
forthright statement was called for lest the revolution roll right over
them. The Ashkenazi Jews of Paris decided to assume they had been
included in the declaration. 'We are henceforth certain that in this
empire, our *patrie*, the title of Man offers us the title of citizen, and
the title of citizen gives us our rights along with all other members
of society of whom we form part.' Likewise Berr Isaac Berr, a tobacco
merchant from Nancy, understood out loud that the declaration had
made all those living in France 'free and equal, far beyond anything
expressed in the *cahiers*', and that therefore 'by general request we
have decided to obtain the rights and title of citizen'. To Rabbi David
Sintzheim, Cerf Berr's brother-in-law, liberty meant the liberty to
move to Strasbourg or for his relatives to be shopkeepers, but it also
meant liberty to keep rabbinical courts, officers of the community,
and collect monies for the upkeep of schools, cemeteries and places
for the indigent and the sick. When he said so, five days after the
promulgation of the Rights of Man, there was an uneasy stir even
among his own people in Alsace. Perhaps this was not the right time
for special pleading. Leading Jews in Lunéville and Sarreguemines
dissociated themselves from the rabbi's views, and aligned themselves
with the Parisians who were bolder in leaving the old institutions
behind them. The Sephardi leaders were appalled, anxious that the
Ashkenazi conservatism would compromise their own prospects for
equal citizenship. The Jews were not marching with linked arms
towards the light of liberty; as usual they were elbowing, shouting
and jabbing fingers of indignant dissent at each other.

Their self-appointed benefactors in the National Assembly ascended
serenely above the contentious clamour. For them it was a matter of
principle rather than people. Regardless of the Jews' mixed feelings
on the matter, their eligibility for citzenship was the acid test of the
revolution's democratic inclusiveness; its indifference to old, pernicious religious distinctions. The revolution, it repeatedly told itself,
was an exercise in *régénération*, a sloughing off of the dead skin of

inherited traditions and conventions. Henceforth nothing could claim legitimacy merely from the bald statement that it *had always been so. Always been so* was a prison. Its confining walls had been smashed with the Bastille. And who needed a liberation from that prison of habit and prejudice more urgently and more justly than the Jews? They had been the perennial victims of Christian superstition, deemed to be punished *forever* for their crime; to wander hounded and home-less, separated by the atrocious bulls of popes and the edicts of tyrants, from the rest of mankind. If ever there was a moment to erase such prejudices, to reunite the Jews with the family of humanity, that moment had come. The Friends of the Jews were aware that the deputies from the eastern provinces were adamantly hostile to emancipation and that in August they had succeeded in tabling – forever, they hoped – the question of whether the Jews could be included in the Rights of Man. The issue was no longer academic though. Jewish houses were being ransacked; men and women assaulted on the streets. Immediate measures were needed to extend to the Jews the protection of the new government.

But the shofar was calling. The objects of all this solicitousness had returned to their synagogues, back to Lunéville, back to Cavaillon, back to Bordeaux, back to Sarrelouis for the high holy days. But once the Rejoicing of the Law had been celebrated in October, the campaign restarted. Their leaders took their speeches and pamphlets to the Salle du Manège, the old riding school of the Tuileries where the National Assembly had installed itself. On 14 October Berr Isaac Berr addressed them in person. All his people asked, he said, was 'that men look upon us as brothers and that the ignominious institutions which have enslaved us be reformed'. The hall fell silent with shamefaced respect. A little wave of fellow feeling washed through the chamber. This was a *Jew*? What, no beard, no jabbering? Berr Isaac Berr resembled neither the parvenu Sephardi silk merchants parading around Saint-André des Arts with their glossily dressed families, nor the Ashkenazi old-clothes and rag traders living in squalid garrets near the canal Saint-Martin and Saint-Denis. Berr Isaac Berr was merely eloquent, modest, simple, like the very best of their own number. The deputies were so moved by his words as to ask the Ashkenazi delegation to remain for some time further in their presence. Fraternity broke out. Jean-Paul Rabaut Saint-Étienne, the Protestant pastor, outdid everyone by repudiating the idea of 'toleration' as shamefully condescending. 'I demand the word be proscribed,' he roared, as 'meaning something worthy of pity.'

None of this guaranteed that the matter of Jewish citizenship would be resolved or even be brought back to the Assembly while the majority of Alsatians and Lorrainers were so opposed. So the great voices of the Assembly chimed in on the matter of the Jews: the former bishop, Talleyrand, and the philosophical lawyer, Maximilien Robespierre – the latter more warmly than the former. The most influential of them all was Mirabeau, also *ci-devant*, the noble who had led the exodus of his aristocratic order from the Estates General to join with the Third Estate, and thus create the new sovereign nation. Mirabeau the thunderous orator, Mirabeau the charismatic rake, Mirabeau the Voice of the People (so he believed) was also one of the few deputies who actually knew Jews personally. As self-cast renegade outsider, he thought he understood a whole people of outsiders. And besides, Mirabeau's perennial need for warm-hearted company and bags of cash was bound to send him their way in London and Amsterdam. But Mirabeau, who was a walking encyclopedia of ideas and learning, also knew when he ran into a fellow *philosophe*. So in Berlin he was *bouleversé* by the generous intellect and friendly openness of Moses Mendelssohn. He published a fulsome *éloge* to Mendelssohn, adding to the growing pile of encomia. And it was Mendelssohn's example which opened Mirabeau to the possibility that there was no reason, actually, why Jews should not retain the essential characteristics of their religion, culture and communal identity, and still be fully citizens of the new Nation. This was the exact opposite of Voltaire's insistence that the condition of acceptance was the abandonment of distinctive Jewish life.

Mirabeau took this conviction to the National Assembly, maintaining with the lawyer Adrien Duport that retaining Jewish religious courts and other communal institutions should be no bar to exercising full citizenship. Philosophically this was a difficult position, given that the revolution was at that very moment liquidating all the Christian institutions said to stand in the way of true popular sovereignty embodied in the nation. But then there was a singular breadth of social imagination in much of Mirabeau's thought. In the teeth of the ruling orthodoxy which decreed an indivisible, monolithic definition of nationhood, he argued that the happiest societies were those constituted from a myriad of little communities and self-cohering associations – clubs, Masons, academies, debating circles – which, so long as they recognised the bounds of their authority, posed no threat to the common good. He was, in fact, a rather Anglo kind of liberal. And his persuasiveness was, as always, compromised by his appetites, both fleshly and political, which fatally got in the way of strategic discipline. Mirabeau, the tribune of a new world, was also Mirabeau the inveterate intriguer. This made him bad as well as good for the Jews.

Finally, in the last week of December, the cohort of sympathisers, who had steadily gained support, yet never sure of a majority, managed to bring the matter of the Jews to debate. Even then the motion arrived by the back door. The claims of the Jews to equal rights and obligations were bundled together with sundry other groups who, by virtue of the socially and morally dubious character of their occupations, had been deemed ineligible for civil and military office. So on 21 December 1789, the Jews joined actors and public executioners in the queue of claimants. Two days later, Mirabeau declared that 'in church men are Catholics, and in synagogue, Jews, but in all civil matters they are patriots of the same religion'.

But Mirabeau was not the star performer on behalf of the Jews. He was followed by yet another ex-aristo, Stanislas de Clermont-Tonnerre, who introduced a draft motion to remove all the disabling measures preventing 'non-Catholics' from exercising full rights of citizenship, including the right to vote and hold public office. Since these rights had already been acquired by Protestants two years before and there were precious few Muslims in France, no one was fooled by the portmanteau wording. Jean-François Reubell, the deputy from Colmar in Alsace, and an adamant foe of Jewish emancipation, interrupted Clermont-Tonnerre in mid-flow, to make the issue crystal clear. 'Do you mean Jews?' he barked. 'Yes,' was the equally forthright answer. Clermont-Tonnerre's unequivocal stance on the matter was all the more striking since, during debates earlier in the year over whether the Jews should be protected by the National Guard from rioters, he had said that although the causes were to be found in Christian oppression, the Jews 'deserved' the hatred. Now, by contrast, he announced his complete identification with the persecuted. 'I think as the Jews do,' said Clermont-Tonnerre. '*They* don't believe they are

citizens.' Reubell shot back once more, setting the tone for the bitter
debate which ensued over the next days. The usual objections were
raised. Abbé Maury said that Jews could no more be citizens than
Danes or Englishmen who had not renounced their loyalties. The
Bishop of Nancy, de la Fare, offered 'protection' and 'toleration', but
under no circumstances would he countenance equal citizenship.

In some ways Clermont-Tonnerre was an unlikely champion; in
others not. His father had been chamberlain to the king of Poland,
hence his own Slavic first name, perfectly respectable since Louis
XVI's grandmother, the late queen, had after all herself been Marie
Leszczynska. The Polish connection meant that the family certainly
had known the better-off Jews within the old kingdom before it had
disappeared into the realms of the Prussian, Austrian and Russian
monarchies. And for the present and future of the Jews it was also
significant that Clermont-Tonnerre came from an old military family.
This gave him first-hand knowledge of just how much the royal army
owed to Jewish contractors and purveyors for their effectiveness in
the field. Stanislas's grandfather had been a Maréchal de France, and
he himself had served as a colonel of the Cuirassiers in the regiment
of the Royal-Navarre. The admissibility of Jews to the National Guard
had become a contentious issue throughout France precisely in this
period, partisans on both sides dividing on whether they could be
trusted, or whether they would be in league with foreigners whose
German language they spoke. Were they not also profiteers
whose sordid speculations were sabotaging the revolution by keep
ing food prices artificially high? But Clermont-Tonnerre brushed all
this aside. He could see nothing in the way of Jews serving the new
France in uniform should it be asked of them. Indeed he made a
point of saying that he had received a letter from a Jew who was
already a soldier in the National Guard. The Guard was constituted
both from citizen militia and units of the former royal army, and
together in July they had conquered Paris for the revolution.

Clermont-Tonnerre put the onus on the foes of emancipation. Since
the declaration had been intended universally, 'it would seem that
there is nothing left to debate and that prejudices should be silent in
the face of the language of the law'. Yet there had been harassment,
exclusion, resistance directed at a particular group of citizens being
admitted to their rights, entirely on grounds of their religion.

Clermont-Tonnerre then turned to the Enlightenment canon – Milton, Spinoza, Locke, Voltaire – in the matter of conscience, articulating as clearly as anyone before him the moral birth certificate of the new Europe. For centuries, Christendom had been disfigured by persecutions committed in the name of religious dogma. Catholics and Protestants had slaughtered each other in barbaric attempts to impose their confessions. Worse, Christians had subjected Jews, generation after generation, to torment and degradation, dooming them to perpetual punishment for the sin of the crucifixion. Beneath the dawning sunlight of liberty and humanity this would now cease. The hand of state power would henceforth be forever withdrawn from the speculations of the soul.

> No one shall be persecuted for their religious belief. The law cannot affect the religion of a man. It can take no hold over his soul. It can only affect his actions. It must protect those actions when they do no harm to society. God has permitted us to make moral laws but he has given no one but himself the right to legislate dogma and to rule over conscience ... leave man's conscience free that sentiments and thoughts leading one way or another towards the heavens will not be crimes that society punishes by the loss of social rights.[21]

All the ancient dogmatic reasons to punish, confine and oppress the Jews for their obstinate refusal to accept Christ's gospel were discredited remnants of a redundant theological regime. Now, there were but two choices for an equitably constituted state: either replace the old Christian polity with some sort of imposed 'natural religion' (this would indeed happen in the form of Robespierre's deist dictatorship), or else 'everyone must be permitted to have their own religion'. Moreover, no one could be excluded from any kind of public office for exercising that freedom. Under this new dispensation, 'Every religion must prove but one thing: that it is moral. If there is a religion which commands theft and arson it is necessary not merely to refuse eligibility to those who profess it but also to outlaw them. This consideration cannot be applied to the Jews.'

Clermont-Tonnerre then addressed himself directly to those who argued that Judaism was inherently antisocial and immoral. All this, he insisted, was a puerile lie since anyone who knew anything about

Judaism understood that it was a religion which was nothing *but* social morality. 'The reproaches one makes of them are many. The gravest are unjust, the others are merely specious.' To those, especially in Alsace and Lorraine, who equated Jews with predatory usury, Clermont-Tonnerre retorted that 'usury is not commanded by their laws, loans at interest are forbidden between them' and what could be charged to others was strictly subjected to ethics laid down in the Talmud. More 'useful' ways of earning a livelihood had long been put off limits to the Jews so that 'men who live on nothing but money cannot live but by making that money valuable ... it is *you* who have always prevented them from possessing anything else!' Let them have land 'and a country and they will lend no longer. That is the remedy. As for their "unsociability", it is exaggerated. Does it even exist? And anyway what do you conclude from it?' They don't want to marry us. Very well, what of it? 'Is there a law which obliges me to marry your daughter? Is there a law which obliges me to eat hare with you? Doubtless these religious oddities will disappear but if they do survive the impact of philosophy and the pleasure of being citizens and sociable men, none of them are infractions of the law.'

The moment seems so slight; the man so grandly sententious; the opinion so obvious, even banal. To be peculiar, to dress this way or that way, to eat at a different table, was not to live outside the law. And yet no non-Jew had ever, anywhere, thought to put it quite like this. (The American dispensation was comparable but the Jewish population in the United States was tiny compared to that of the Ashkenazim of Alsace and Lorraine.) The Jews of the newborn France could be modern and as indistinguishable in their speech and appearance from the rest of Frenchmen as Berr Isaac Berr, or they could be as 'odd' and singular in whatever their religious customs they wanted to observe and *still* there was *nothing whatsoever* in the way of their citizenship. All that was asked of them was that they abandon the binding jurisdiction of their courts in civil matters. That was the price of admission to the nation of free and equal citizens. But there was nothing to fear from this inclusion. A glorious destiny awaited them: that of Frenchmen and Frenchwomen professing Judaism. They had to embrace it, though, accepting that their nation was now the France of free men and women. Then came Clermont-Tonnerre's famous formulation: 'Jews should be denied everything as a nation; granted everything as individuals; it is claimed that they do not want to be citizens ... [but] every individual wants to become a citizen. If they do not want this then they must inform us and we shall be compelled to expel them ... [for] the existence of a nation within a nation is unacceptable to our patrie.'

For a moment, at the word 'expel', the cordial handshake of fraternity remade itself into a fist. But it relaxed once more, as Clermont-Tonnerre dismissed his own rhetorical reservation. There was, he said, no sign whatsoever of the civic churlishness their critics attributed to them or any shrinking back from the extended hand of fraternity. In the absence of any such signs to the contrary, he went on, 'the Jews must be assumed to be citizens ... as long as they do not actively refuse to be so, the law must recognise what mere prejudice rejects'.

The Assembly was already accustomed to Clermont-Tonnerre's lengthy disquisitions on all manner of things: the rights of veteran soldiers, the state of the nation's finances, and so on. For a soldier he was notoriously wordy. That last epigrammatic flourish was surely his cue to sit down? Apparently not. One imagines him sitting and then to muffled groans rising again as if something of additional importance had suddenly occurred to him. He went on. Faced with what seemed like insuperable opposition from the deputies of the east, pressure had been growing to table this business of the Jews: to let it die from calculated inattention. Clermont-Tonnerre was furious at the very thought. The question must not be brushed aside on the pretext that there were weightier and more urgent matters at hand. Nothing was more important. This, he insisted, was the great test of the revolution's capacity to make a true nation of citizens. There could be no procrastination. 'It is necessary to explain yourself on the condition of the Jews. For you all to keep silent would be the worst of evils. It would be to have seen the good and not wanted to do it; to have known the truth and not dared speak it; finally it would be to set prejudice on the same throne as law, error on the same throne as reason.'

His eloquence was initially in vain. The Bishop of Nancy made sure to chime in with stories of how things *really* were in his diocese: when, in the summer, the people wanted to sack the houses of the Jews he had gone along to remonstrate with them, fearing the worst, and they all told him that the Jews had cornered the grain markets;

they always kept themselves to themselves; their houses were too big and too grand; they just about owned the whole city and if you, Monsieur the Bishop, were to die, heaven forfend, they'd have a Jew in your place, since they end up taking possession of everything else, it was bound to happen. So, continued the bishop, he had only the Jews' best interests at heart when he said that emancipating them would spark a terrible conflagration in which the Jews would be consumed. He could not have that on his conscience, yet if they presumptuously insisted on their 'rights' he, for one, would not answer for the consequences; too dreadful to contemplate . . .[22]

The motion was put and lost, but by the slimmest of majorities: 408 to 403. The Jews were nonetheless deeply downcast, and the disappointment did not bring out the best in them. A week later, Berr Isaac Berr from Nancy engaged a young deputy, also from Lorraine, Jacques Godard, to keep pressing their case before the National Assembly. But the leaders of the Sephardi community in Bordeaux had drawn a different conclusion from the bitter defeat. It had been the equivocations of the Ashkenazim on the issue of communal autonomy, they believed – with some reason – which had cost them a good result. They, who were perfectly happy to trade in their old communal status for full citizenship, had been handicapped by the Ashkenazi determination to cling to the old regime. Now they were left with no choice but to part company with the people who made themselves liabilities in the campaign for emancipation. Once representatives from Bordeaux had arrived in Paris there was a final attempt to mount a united front in a meeting at Cerf Berr's grand home in Paris. Some differences were patched up but the two groups now went their own ways.[23] The Bordeaux Jews made lightning house calls on influential sympathisers including the Marquis de Lafayette, Abbé Sieyès and Dominique-Joseph Garat, the editor of the *Journal de Paris*. The ubiquitous Talleyrand, who was to report to the Assembly on the matter, could not be persuaded by the Ashkenazim to make it clear that any change should be for all Jews. The young Godard had written a hundred-page 'Petition of the Jews Established in France' but it did not appear until 28 January 1790, the same day that Talleyrand brought the issue forward. In a strange throwback to old regime law, he claimed merely that the letters patent granted to Bordeaux Jews by the kings were already enough for them to be considered full citizens. Grégoire then intervened to ask that this recognition be extended to the Jews of the east as well, and was met by a barrage of hooted dissension. The vote was taken to declare full citizens the Sephardim of Bordeaux and other towns in the south-west (Peyrehorade, Saint-Esprit near Bayonne) and the south-east (Avignon, Carpentras, Cavaillon), while the case of the Ashkenazim was referred to committee. The Sephardim had succeeded in their long campaign to be recognised as citizen-Jews, but they had done so by uncoupling their Ashkenazi brethren from the train of progress. In so doing they reinforced all the stereotypes about new Jews and old Jews, good Jews and not so good Jews, Jews who were with others and Jews who were with only their own kind. It was, then, a tainted victory that the Sephardim had won.

The vote also excluded Paris Jews – the button-makers, tailors, butchers and bakers of Saint-Martin – from civic status, even though many of them were precisely the 'people' whom the revolution claimed to liberate. With this in mind, Godard, Zalkind Hourwitz, a librarian at the Bibliothèque du Roi, and the diamond merchant Jacob Lazard mounted a campaign with the Commune – the city government of Paris – on their behalf which could then be extended to the rest of the Jews of France. Claiming that there were a hundred Jews in the ranks of the National Guard, Godard told a meeting, including the mayor Sylvain Bailly, 'These men are our brothers, these men are our companions in arms.' His eloquence was infectious. The president of the Commune, Abbé Mulot, burst into a rapture of fraternity. 'The distance of your religious opinions from the truths we hold as Christians cannot prevent us as men from bringing ourselves nearer to you and if mutually we believe each other to be in error ... we are nevertheless able to love each other.'[24] Over the weeks of intensive campaigning that followed a majority of the district representatives were swayed, but not all; inevitably there were some who still thought the Jews 'foreigners' in their midst. And whatever the sentiments of the Commune or Parisians, they were never strong enough to overcome the obstacles the opponents of Ashkenazi emancipation put in the way of debate every time the issue arose – which it did on a monthly basis – before the National Assembly.

It was not until 28 September 1791 that citizenship was finally extended to all French Jews. In the year and a half leading up to that day, the Ashkenazim were themselves increasingly divided between moderns and traditionalists. Once they could live in Strasbourg, a number of the young moderns enlisted in the National Guard and were accepted by the mayor Dietrich. In February 1790 the Amis de la Constitution – otherwise known as the Jacobins, from the club in Paris, and as yet still a forum for moderate revolutionism – voted to accept Jews as members. Now, in contrast to everything said about them, they could be clubbable. Jews in Nancy, Strasbourg and Metz began to try and live their daily lives in French not Yiddish. They memorised all the right slogans. Liberty trees were planted in their villages. Jews went about sporting tricolour cockades on their hats and sashes about their shortened coats. In Paris, their patriotism was conspicuous enough for the Commune to endorse their claims to the rights of citizens.

Months passed. Desultory efforts were made to raise the matter of the Jews. When Henri Grégoire became president of the Constituent Assembly in January 1791, he asked merely that a member of the Ecclesiastical Committee bring the matter before the Assembly. But the most famous and eloquent promoter of their emancipation himself fell silent on the matter, concerned that his own efforts to create a constitutional church that would allow the French to be, simultaneously, Christian and patriot, would be compromised by his association with the endlessly thorny case of the Jews. The fact that it was not until the last month of the Constituent's life – September 1791 – that the Ecclesiastical Committee concluded its report suggests that a majority were still determined to run out the clock. A new constitution was about to take effect, and with it a new Legislative Assembly. Let them grasp the nettle. That this is not what happened was due largely to another declared sympathiser, Adrien Duport, insisting as late as 27 September, three days before the arrival of the Legislative, that the Constituent *not* dissolve itself with this unfinished business on the table.

He would be brief, Duport said, confining himself to pointing out an anomaly. The constitution had already insisted that positions of employment were to be granted solely on grounds of 'talent and virtue' and that, conversely, none were to be denied it for their beliefs. Then came the four words that changed history. *'Je parle des Juifs'*, I speak of the Jews. Since the constitution had already promised them free exercise of their religion, there was no reason to deny them the status of 'active citizens' endowed with the vote and eligible for office. Jews could not be the only exception to these political rights when they had already been granted to 'pagans, Turks, Muslims [*sic*], even Chinese'. But whenever this inconsistency was raised, the matter was perpetually adjourned. No longer. For not to correct the glaring anomaly would, in effect, be to act against the constitution.

Duport had put the onus on those hostile to Jewish rights to show they were not acting unconstitutionally, and the shrewdness of the tactic triggered an immediate uproar. Nonetheless his motion was carried by a large majority. The next day, the former Duc de Broglie proposed an amendment that the swearing of the civic path required to exercise the rights of an active citizen be taken to mean the full renunciation of any previous communal autonomy and jurisdiction. Doubtless he expected Jewish voices attached to that autonomy to reject the condition as too steep a price to pay. But no such voices were heard, at least not in the political arena.

Just the opposite, in fact. From Nancy, Berr Isaac Berr, who had spoken to the National Assembly two years before, now published and circulated throughout the east a letter greeting the measure of the 28th as a redemption sent by Almighty God, who had chosen to work through the representatives of the French people. It was, he implied, the messianic conclusion of the tragedy which had begun with the destruction of the Temple. The tone of the circular was that of a *derasha*, a sermon or a shared prayer, designed so that it could be read out in synagogue services to reassure the most orthodox of the Ashkenazi communities that by swearing the oath of allegiance and bidding farewell to their old self-governance they were not betraying their laws and traditions. It was, after all, possible to be a good Jew and good citizen.

The day has finally come when the veil by which we were kept in a state of humiliation, is rent; finally we have recovered those rights which have been taken from us more than eighteen centuries ago. How much, at this moment, are we indebted to the mercy of the God of our forefathers.

Now, thanks to the Supreme Being and to the sovereignty of the nation we are not only Men and Citizens but we are Frenchmen! What a happy change thou has worked in us O merciful God. As recently as

September 27th we were the only inhabitants of this vast empire who seemed doomed to remain forever in bondage and abasement, and on the following day, the 28th, a day forever sacred to us, you inspired the immortal legislators of France. [God] has chosen the generous French nation to reinstate us in our rights and effect our regeneration just as in other times he chose Antiochus and Pompey to humiliate and enslave us ... from being vile slaves, mere serfs, a species tolerated and suffered in the empire, liable to arbitrary and heavy taxes, we are of a sudden become *enfants de la patrie*, children of the nation, bearing its common charges and sharing in its common rights.[25]

Anticipating the nervousness with which his fellow Ashkenazim might take the leap into full and equal citizenship, Berr Isaac Berr urged them to let go of their attachment to 'the narrow spirit of Corporation and Congregation in all civil and political matters not connected with our spiritual laws; in these things we must appear simply as individuals, as Frenchmen guided only by true patriotism and by the general good of the nation; to know how to risk our lives and fortunes for the defence of our country'. But at the same time as he was urging fellow Jews to step forward as citizens, Berr Isaac Berr was actually anxious about the effect they would have on the rest of the French if they did so in large numbers and with more enthusiasm than understanding. Always the embarrassment about how the Rest of the Jews would behave! So he counselled them to be happy that they had won the right to attend civic and political assemblies, but wait before doing so until their French was improved and modern education had prepared them for the duties of citizenship. He even published a French edition of Herz Wessely's book proposing educational reforms. 'French ought to be our mother tongue' (not Yiddish) and the Jews must master it and not just the 'inarticulate' stuff they were forced to use in most intercourse with their Gentile neighbours. They must also embark on social self-transformation. Let there be Jewish blacksmiths, carpenters, bootmakers! 'If we can succeed in having a man in each and every profession, able to work as a master he will then take and form apprentices and gradually we shall see Jewish workers striving to deserve esteem by honourably earning their livelihood.'

It's not hard to see into Berr Isaac Berr's mind at the very moment of emancipation. Be careful of getting what you want. Suppose the clubs, the voting places, the National Guards were swamped with a horde of his co-religionists, yelling and barging. All the good work would be undone! First make the right impression. This takes time. He need not, in fact, have been so worried, for the provisions of the new constitution required a certain property and tax eligibility for the exercise of active citizenship and the vast majority of the eastern Ashkenazim were too poor to qualify.

But with all the provisos and apologetic nervousness, it was still a great moment and Berr Isaac Berr was right to speak of it in the same breath as the Exodus and the Maccabees. Ahead of the Jews, now, not just in France, but as the *'grande nation'* moved over its frontiers into Italy and Germany and the Netherlands and then beyond, lay a possible future in which being Jewish and being fully part of their homeland was unproblematic. Praise be to the Almighty and praise be to France indeed!

III. The Democracy of Death

The revolution gave and the revolution took away. Total immersion in the new world of citizens and unprotected exposure to its politics carried risks as well as opportunities. It was not a good sign when, in the midst of disestablishing the old Catholic Church in 1791, the revolutionary council in Bordeaux decided to close all churchyards. Henceforth there would be no separate burial places for Protestants, Catholics or Jews. All would share a common resting place. There would be a democracy of death. So the cemetery which Jacob Rodrigues Péreire had succeeded in acquiring for the Jews of his community just outside the city was shut down.

Nor did it help that the most prominent champions of the Jewish cause themselves came to grief as the revolution, under pressure from the threat and then the reality of foreign invasion, became swiftly more radical. Mirabeau, Duport and Clermont-Tonnerre were all compromised by their support for the monarchy, especially after Louis XVI and Marie Antoinette had tried to flee France and put themselves under the protection of the queen's brother, the Austrian emperor Leopold. Suspected of having a hand in the attempted flight or other plots to restore royal powers, many of their circle were arrested or themselves took flight. The fact that most of them had been aristocrats now cast an extra shadow of suspicion over their political transparency and integrity. Duport found himself in prison and would have faced the guillotine but for personal connections among the Jacobins which got him out long enough for an escape over the Swiss border. Mirabeau died before facing the consequences of his double-dealing with the court. On 10 August 1792 a violent insurrection in Paris, reinforced by armed National Guards from the provinces, singing the new anthem of inspirational fury, the 'Marseillaise' (actually composed in Cerf Berr's Strasbourg), invaded the Tuileries where the 'constitutional monarch' was housed, killed his Swiss Guards and declared the monarchy at an end. Anyone associated with the politics of the monarchy was now fair game. The orator of emancipation, the *ci-devant comte*, now citizen, Clermont-Tonnerre, was one of them. Recognised, he was pursued by a howling crowd all the way to his house. The doors were smashed in. Up the grand staircase they clambered and into the first-floor library where they took him amid his books, pulled open one of the elegant windows and heaved Stanislas Clermont-Tonnerre out, where he died after smashing his head on the cobblestones below.

French Jews, except those who lived in or who had removed themselves to Paris, were borderland people which meant, as war broke out on the eastern and (from January 1793) the Spanish frontiers, they could be both useful to the embattled *patrie* and suspected by it. Horses, animal fodder like hay and oats, and the shipment of grain were the stock-in-trade of many Jews in Alsace and Lorraine, so it was often to the Jews that the armies turned for these vital supplies. Sons of Cerf Berr were themselves members of the buying agency, the Directoire des Achats, for both the military and the civilians of towns which now found themselves on the front line facing the Prussians and the Austrians. But, habitually, at the same time, the sources that Jewish horse dealers and especially grain-buyers used were on the other side of the frontier and often across the Rhine. When they made the necessary buying trips, they could be (and frequently were) accused of emigration, which had become capital treason. At one point or another almost all the family of Cerf

Berr were put in this position, other than the radical son Max or
Marx, who himself had become a militant as happens in such families. Cerf Berr died in 1793, but because the Rosenwiller cemetery
had been closed and vandalised, the headstones smashed and replaced
by the gormless Rousseauite cliché 'Death is but an Eternal Sleep',
his body had to be smuggled in and buried amid the debris, until in
1795 it became once again legal to observe religious practices in public.
In the meantime his spirited daughter Eve had to defend herself
against charges of treasonable emigration by pointing out that she
had followed her German-Jewish husband to Frankfurt long before
the revolution had commenced and that there was not a day when
her heart did not care with the utmost acuteness for the welfare,
safety and happiness of her true homeland.

Almost all the assets which the citizen-Jews could bring to the
defence of the *patrie* – mindful that their inability or unwillingness
to do this in a crisis (including performing military duties on the
Sabbath) had been a staple of the objections to their emancipation
– could now be seen as the proverbial double-edged sword. Their
Judaeo-German tongue and close familiarity with the geography of
the eastern borderland was, depending on how it was regarded, either
a vital assistance to the French forces or a way for the Jews to help
the enemy. Their command of grain supplies at a time of chronic,
even desperate shortages was either a godsend or a perfect opportunity for speculation and price-gouging, and there were no shortage
of people in Alsace and Lorraine saying once a Jew always a Jew. Of
the 5 million livres imposed as a special tax on Strasbourg, 3 million
was to be paid by the Jews alone. Though they needed to travel to
secure the supplies the armies needed, in November 1793 a visiting
representative of the revolutionary government proposed denying
passports to Jews and assuming that any of them who could not show
he had married a non-Jewish woman be automatically treated as
suspect. Coughing up huge sums at the point of a bayonet still did
not guarantee safety. Before he died at the age of sixty-seven, Cerf
Berr had been packed off to prison, probably in the disused Jesuit
seminary at Strasbourg, along with other leaders of the Alsace community: Salomon Levy, Abraham Cahn, Meyer Veitel, Isaac Leyser and
one Meyer Dreyfus. The entire Polak family, who had lived in Paris
since 1772 but who had business contacts in Holland, Frankfurt and

Switzerland, were subjected to imprisonment and terrifying interrogation, coming within an inch of conviction and execution before being finally released after a barrage of testimonies of their patriotic conduct.

'*Êtes-vous de la nation?*' became a matter not of legal nicety but life or death. Invasion and defeat would mean mass retribution. Get them before they get us became the order of the day; whether 'they' lay in the Paris prisons waiting for foreigners to release them so they could set about the people, or whether they were Prussian grenadiers. Fifth columns seemed to be everywhere. After French generals – Dumouriez, Lafayette – defected, anyone might be a traitor disguised with a cockade. There were, in fact, some Jews who were in contact with the enemy. One of the sons of Liefmann Calmer (who had died in 1784 still as Viscount of Amiens), Louis-Benjamin, confessed – unapologetically – to having passed letters from the queen to Dumouriez after he defected, and was guillotined in April 1794. His brother and co-heir to the noble estate that no longer existed, Antoine Louis-Isaac, took the opposite path of an impassioned revolutionary, but after an accusation of 'terrorising' also died on the scaffold. Any borderline Jews making money out of war materiels became suspect. Denunciations and counter-denunciations broke out, especially when generals who were former aristos seemed to be fighting with one hand tied behind their back and were in correspondence with the enemy. Jewish contractors accused General Custine and General de Wimpffen, and were in turn accused by them. In the circumstances it was surprising more did not lose their lives.

The Sephardim of the south-west did not escape peril either, though it came in a different guise. At first, emancipation seemed to have been happily realised. They had voted in 1789, and had participated in the electoral colleges the same year, joined the National Guard in some numbers, and the better off were enfranchised by the constitution. In one sense they were indeed truly emancipated, since the dangers facing them were the same as those facing non-Jews: the hazard of political choice in a revolution where today's patriotism could suddenly turn into tomorrow's treason. In Bordeaux, just because the better-off, better-educated Sephardim, the Jews of the concerts, libraries and academies, were already part of the city establishment, and could now hold local office, they lined up with the interests of the port city, which, as the Paris revolution became more militant and more centralist, turned into an opposition. When that opposition took the form of denouncing the summary powers of the Paris Revolutionary Government as 'worse than the Inquisition', they were arrested as 'Girondins', tried by the tribunals whose jursidiction they had rejected, and went to the guillotine in October 1793, singing the 'Marseillaise'. In Bordeaux (as well as Lyons and Marseilles) in the summer and autumn of 1793 the Jacobin government appeared as tyrants, the enemies not the guardians of freedom. An armed federalist movement stirred to defy Paris.

At the height of the federalist revolt, a 'Popular Commission', in effect the procurement and security agency of Bordeaux, was established. Among its members were famous Jews, none more prominent than Abraham Furtado, 'Furtado of the Gironde' in the guise he was briefly and dashingly known, as booted, spurred and sashed as the rest of his comrades. He was a one-man history of the Sephardi emigration and enlightenment. The secretly Jewish family had survived the Lisbon earthquake of 1755, Hannah Furtado being pulled from the rubble with both herself and the son in her womb miraculously intact. The Furtado's moved first to London where Abraham was born and then to Bayonne where Abraham grew up, re-settling in Bordeaux where he became wealthy enough to become the usual well-intentioned philosophising merchants, in his case with a fashionable though untypically Jewish interest in agricultural improvement. After Péreire's death Furtado had been one of the leaders of the community advising Malesherbes in his commission on the Jews in 1788, and had become a local revolutionary notable with the emancipation of 1790, a pillar of the new civically patriotic Bordeaux. In 1793 he had a place, along with Salomon Lopes-Dubec, on the 'Popular Commission' of Bordeaux, in effect an institution of mobilisation and resistance, and was a key figure in the capacity of the city to defend itself against the oncoming army from Paris.

There is evidence that Furtado had seen bad things coming; and that he had warned that armed rebellion risked catastrophe. In his defence he would later claim that he had sat on the commission as a loyal official of the city, not as a rebel. But he was fatally compromised nonetheless, should Bordeaux lose its battle with Paris, which it did. When that army stormed in, led by an energetically vengeful 'Representative on Mission' – the civilian commissar, Ysabeau – both Furtado and Lopes-Dubec were on the blacklist of treasonable federalists. Lopes-Dubec went on the run at which point his son Samuel, known as Tridli, was taken hostage until his father gave himself up. Furtado's first instinct – to surrender – was courageously naive, and he was only deterred from this by a friend who told him he would be putting his life in the hands of men 'for whom justice is nothing'.[26] He too went on the run, moving between friends and poor relatives, often locked into tiny spaces behind walls with a peephole from which he saw comrades led to the guillotine. Camped out in the country suburbs, getting news of the witch hunt of federalists, arrests, summary trials before the revolutionary tribunals and collective executions, Furtado tried to put his mind back in the world of Enlightenment optimism, translating the work of Appian on the civil wars of the Romans until the analogies with France became intolerable, then steeping himself in Rousseau, Buffon, and the local hero Montesquieu, who had promised a sunnier future – for the Jews in particular – than anything that had come about. The terrors of Dante and the dark mirth of Don Quixote were next, as he related in his underground diary. 'I built an intellectual world according to my fantasy and peopled it according to my will.' In that world everyone was a civilised comrade and the Jews were its happy beneficiaries. When the borrowed books ran out he began to live entirely in his mind, composing a love story about Jacob and Rachel. The more cramped his hiding spaces the more sweeping his restless mind. The Girondists were decent but impulsive; the sans-culotte rank and file of the incoming army were animal louts; Robespierre was a monster; the agent of occupation Lacombe was even worse, planning to massacre all merchants in the city because anyone with money, tainted with trade, was assumed to be a traitor. The revolution was a foundering shipwreck and all the passengers one way or another were lost; a democratic republic (this was Rousseau's assumption too) was viable only in a small community; perhaps his own? For some time he considered suicide – almost an epidemic among embattled opposition revolutionaries – but somehow managed to wait out the end of the Terror, after which he became a very different kind of political actor.

The furious political energy liberated by the revolution turned into a struggle between centralising power (the old regime wearing a cockade) and the centrifugal passions of the local. Much of modern French history unfolded from that contest. To make matters still more confusing, the ultra-local could paradoxically be the ally of the centre. So what Paris was for Bordeaux, Bordeaux became for other local communities, including the Bayonne district Saint-Esprit (renamed 'Jean-Jacques Rousseau'). Because Bayonne sat on the Spanish border, a front line in 1793, and was a gathering place for émigrés trying to cross the mountain border and for spies and double agents, many of them unrepentant sons of the disestablished Church, the Jews of 'Jean-Jacques Rousseau' were recruited and volunteered to be the eyes and ears of republican zeal. Many of them – like the swaggering Joseph Bernal, known from his last domicile as 'The American' – did indeed become ardent militants, manning the commissions of surveillance and revolutionary tribunals. The zealots changed their names from Isaac, Moïse and Sarah to Brutus, Virgil and Élodie.[27]

Just two years after Berr Isaac Berr had welcomed the emancipation law for making it possible, for the first time, to be at the same time a Jew 'who observes the religion of his ancestors *and* a French citizen', the Terror turned that assumption into a cruel joke. In the late autumn of 1793, a rolling campaign of 'dechristianisation' closed the churches of France and outlawed public profession of the 'superstitions'. This meant an exhaustive de-Judaisation as well. Synagogue after synagogue was closed down. Hebrew speech was strictly banned. In the larger towns like Strasbourg there was even book burning; not the dawn of a new age but a throwback to the persecutions of medieval France. Ritual vessels, especially made of silver – candlesticks, Torah finials and *yodim*, the Torah pointers – were seized to be melted down, though many, at mortal risk, were hidden. In Metz, the Torah scrolls were ceremonially and publicly destroyed. 'The laws of the clever imposter [Moses] will serve to make drums which will throw down the walls of a new Jericho,' the presiding officer of the desecration grandly proclaimed.[28] At Ribeauville in the Upper Rhine wine country, Jessel Lehman kept a secret Yiddish diary relating some of the elaborate humiliations visited on Jews who had imagined that they would enjoy security under the revolution. Any sign of clinging to the old 'superstitions' was declared counter-revolutionary. The bearded were taken out for public shavings; some were dragged from their beds at night and subjected to the patriotic razor. Women were arrested for wearing the *sheytl* wig. Circumcision was declared a crime against nature and strictly outlawed. Since the republican day of rest had been declared to be the tenth day, 'decadi', the Saturday Sabbath was outlawed along with the Christian Sunday. Any Jew seen to be wearing good clothes, much less gathering for worship, could be arrested on the spot. In Paris, there were secret prayer cellars, while one of the company was assigned the job of dressing in working clothes and ostentatiously performing some job in the courtyard to keep the suspicious away. In Nancy the Jacobin enforcer declared that Jews ought to be forced to marry non-Jews as a demonstration of their patriotism. And there were desperately sad episodes of children born after betrothal but before civil marriage, like the infant of Judel and Elias Salomon who was taken from his parents, given a revolutionary baptism and never restored to them.

The nightmare lasted almost two years. When the brutal and chaotic 'dechristianisation' campaign was replaced by Robespierre's Cult of the Supreme Being, the bans on Jewish practices stayed in place. In Metz, the grandest of the synagogues was used to stable animals: horses for the army and cows for milk and meat.[29] After the overthrow of the Jacobins, traumatised Jewish communities began the long, painful process of getting their synagogue buildings back, and in the few places where ritual objects had not been melted down or elaborately destroyed, getting them returned. On 30 May 1795, a law was passed making the free practice of religion and acts of conscience legal once more. But it was many months before there was proper restitution of half-destroyed edifices. The cows and horses stayed amid the smashed pews and benches, manuring the floor of the synagogue until the last days of December 1795. But there was a second synagogue which had been used by the Jewish women of Metz that had not been so comprehensively ruined. And there on 7 September, before Jewish men and women, a little gathering of the Metz rabbis and cantors – allowed once again to declare themselves as such, their names known to us: Olry Lazard-Cahen, Salomon Raicher, Nathan Jacob Emmeric, Samuel Lerouffe, Joseph Bing, Lazard Nathan-Cahen and Moyse Picard – declared Judaism reborn in Ashkenazi Metz.[30]

IV. Chelek Tov

After the second or third town – Ancona, Reggio, Modena – the
flattery got tedious. The general the Jews called Chelek Tov was
twenty-six and beautiful on his little grey mount. In barely a month
he had destroyed the power of an empire, his soldiers feeding themselves as they went, assaulted by rowdy adoration, helping themselves
to the gifts he had promised them before they crossed the Alps. The
men took silver plate and paintings, bales of silk, girls, whatever
caught their fancy. Then the general delivered a bill of indemnity to
the civilians: the price for pay-as-you-go liberation. Chests were
brought to his adjutant-clerks sitting at trestle tables on the galleried
sides of the piazza by sweating, smiling notables in tricorn hats. But
the same worthies brought out the bands, the flags, ancient bottles
still dusty from long repose in a monastery cellar; and the mayors,
the tricolour sash pinned to their coats, made flowery speeches hailing
the liberator and the incoming reign of liberty and equality; eyes
rheumy with happy tears, hands clasped together pumping up and
down, they had not thought they would live to see the day, gasping
and crying like the bad actors they were. Whooping young 'Giacobini'
saluted the general presumptuously as if he were their brother;
children ran alongside the marching men and the horses, shouting
with glee as if they would never again feel a schoolmaster's stick on
their fidgeting rumps. In the evening everyone danced about the
Liberty Tree, beneath the arcing fireworks, all the noise and the light
without the screams of the wounded. The general let the men carouse
for a night, knowing there was always another battle the next week;
that the Austrians would not yield without some shred of dignity,
however many times their white-coated infantry were torn to fragments, however often it dawned on their exhausted, perplexed,
humiliated commanders that they were dealing with something new
in the world: a brilliant monster. So on it went. Dead horses lay on
the buttercups picked over by stabbing crows. Peasants came out
before dawn to rummage in the coats of the fallen, blood still sticky
on their upturned faces. Sacking covered the field guns from the
spring rain while yet another victory celebration could be heard
tuning up in the piazza.

The Jews in their ghettos would be waiting for Chelek Tov, the 'Buona Parte', the Goodly Portion; their David, their Maccabee, perhaps even their Redeemer. He did not care much for Jews, which is to say he neither especially despised nor especially warmed to them; just that he was indifferent to their relentless enthusiasms, and when they raised their voices, a little put off. (In later years he would move from indifference to raw hostility.) But those who had warned of the guiles of rabbis and the squalor of the hawkers, who had seen long-coated Jews running out from the Judengasses of Mainz and Coblenz, recoiled when their sleeves had been insistently tugged, had evidently not known the Jews of the Italian cities. Here they were passably civilised. In Modena, Chelek Tov was treated to a long speech by Moisè Formiggini, silversmith to the duke, and many other things beside – bookseller, merchant; well turned out, with impeccable, if stilted, French – whose father Benedetto and grandfather Laudadio had been substantial figures before him.[31] Men like the Formiggini needed no tutorials on the modern world; they were the vanguard of its arrival in city states still locked in provincial drowsiness. Where encouraged, or at least not prosecuted, by the local prince, they had founded public libraries and reading clubs, bringing La Mettrie and Rousseau and, despite their attachment to the Moses religion, the atheist d'Holbach to the attention of the mercenary *borghese* and the sybaritic little courts. Similar welcomes were accorded by equally liberal Jews as the French took Bologna, Piacenza, Mantua and the Tuscan boom port of Livorno, though in Ferrara, the elders actually declined their liberty and equality since it also meant abandoning their old autonomy.

In Ancona, both the religious and the modern joined in jubilation. The rabbis had cut loose, dancing and jumping, and the rest of the Jews, men and women, had sung their 'Song of the Sea', full-throated as if it had been the hosts of Pharaoh, not the Austrians, who had been wiped out; as if the general was their Moses. But this was the city where two and a half centuries before, Jews had been burned alive at the behest of Pope and Inquisition. They had long memories, the Jews of Ancona; they knew that nothing much had changed, not in a territory belonging to the papacy. Just when they had permitted themselves a moment of gratitude to a pope, Clement XIV, who seemed disposed to ease the burden of their many confinements along came Pius VI in 1775, as harshly bigoted as any of his Jew-hating predecessors. Pius VI looked back warmly to the ferocities of the past, impatient for a mass conversion. Throughout the Papal States, a vast territory that extended all the way from Ancona down through the Marche and Umbria, in the last third of the eighteenth century it was as though the Enlightenment had never happened. A forty-four-clause edict on the Jews brought back all the old miseries and humiliations. The yellow badge was strictly enforced; Jews were once more uprooted from any trades and professions other than clothes dealing. Ancona banned them from teaching music and dancing, one of their specialities. It was forbidden to possess, much less publish and buy, Hebrew books, and police raids by the *sbirri* carried the volumes off in cartloads, a kind of cultural death sentence. Leaving the ghetto at night became a capital crime. No Jew was allowed to own a coach, which meant of course that Jewish pedestrians, with their yellow badges, were an easy mark for robbery, assault and spat abuse. Orphans were abducted from their guardians to be raised as Christians. If those children were hidden, hostages were taken by the police, Jewish babies tugged from their screaming parents until the community delivered the hidden orphans once more to the Church. Any attempt to thwart the enforcement of the papal edicts was met with threats to burn the ghetto down.[32] It was hell.

So when General Berthier's army took Rome in February 1798 and made a prisoner of Pius VI, there was ample reason for its five thousand Jews to rejoice with a sincere heart. A Liberty Tree was set up in the ghetto. Yellow badges were torn from their coats and replaced with tricolour cockades. The National Guard of the newly founded (and short-lived) Roman republic was opened to them. Chelek Tov's name was sanctified in the synagogues. His soldiers were cheered while they munched on *carciofi giudea* in the Campo de' Fiori. Windows on the houses facing outwards beyond the ghetto – which the papal government had ordered sealed with brick or with wooden panels – were broken open. At last, and for a while, the Jews of Rome could see the light.

If the army of Italy wanted to feel they had some historical purpose, other than simply the aggrandisement of the 'Grande Nation', as it had become, it surely found it in Venice on 10 July 1797. For what could proclaim the end of one era and the beginning of the reign of liberty more eloquently than the abolition of the ghetto? In fact, throughout the lightning Italian campaign as Austrian possessions dropped into his waiting hands, Bonaparte was playing the power game at which he would be the consummate master, alternately teasing and threatening. In talks with Austrian emissaries after the fall of Lombardy and Milan, he made it clear that he would be satisfied with removing the terra firma dominions from Venice, while allowing the city itself to remain its own mistress albeit under the shadow of Austrian and French dominions. But the appetite grew with the eating. When Venetian envoys came to see him at Graz, within Austrian land, he demanded the end to the Senate, the Council of Ten, all the old institutions. Panicky, one of their few remaining warships fired on a French vessel at the mouth of the lagoon. A notional war was declared, though it took the French another two months to occupy the city. A provisional 'representative government' was proclaimed in the Consiglio Maggiore on 7 July, and the new authority announced that three days later the ghetto would cease to exist.[33]

On 10 July, the curtain rose on the theatre of Jewish freedom in the one place that for centuries had signified its opposite. An officer in the newly formed Venetian National Guard, Pier Gian Maria de Ferrari, as patrician as his name, and with the usual revolutionary politics to go with it, was the impresario. Three citizen-Jews from the Patriotic Society and ancient ghetto families – Daniel Levi Polacco, Vidal d'Angeli and Moisè di David Sullam – sat with Ferrari to go over the ceremonies which needed to go off like clockwork but allow freedom for popular rejoicing. They also had to involve the rest of Venice, or that part of it which could be relied on to be sympathetic, or at least not hostile to the Jews. There would be a dependable priest and selected members of his flock; there would be shipyard workers from the Arsenale; dignitaries from the new provisional government.

At five on a summer afternoon, the perfect moment when the heat of the day relaxed its damp grip, uniformed guards, fronted by the best of Venice's military bands, extra drums and tambourines, marched to the ghetto, Gian Maria commanding. Heads popped out from shutters on the way. Street boys followed on the end. The column halted before one of the four massive gates to the Gheto Novo, the last part of the route lined with both Italian and French soldiers; a fraternity of tricolours. The column marched into the centre of the campo which was lined with more guardsmen, 'numerous assembled members of the Patriotic Society and a large number of people of both genders who emerged out of every doorway'.[34] Out from the throng stepped Sullam, d'Angeli and Polacco, facing the officer who read the order ending the ghetto. Then came the moment that more than any other signified what this meant. The keys of the gates were given to Ferrari who in turn handed them to the detachment of Arsenale workers assigned the destruction of the gates. 'One cannot express the satisfaction and happiness of all the people present who, with jubilant cries of "freedom" never tired of dragging those keys along the ground, blessing the hour and moment of regeneration.' Then the axe-work began, as each of the gates was split open. 'In the moment the gates were knocked down, joyous dances by people of both sexes without any distinction wove around the Campo ... the rabbis too, dressed in Mosaic garb, danced, stirring up even greater liveliness.'

This was the signal for the priests of the two neighbouring churches to appear, to more rounds of applause; then came the speeches, of course, drowned out in the end by the uproar which greeted the Arsenale men carrying what was left of the old gates, big enough to be thrown onto the flagstones of the campo and smashed and splintered further into fragments. A pyre had been started; a torch was produced, and into the fire went the confinement of the Venetian Jews. Someone had taken another axe to a tree in a Cannaregio garden and brought it as a Liberty Tree to the centre of the square. The band struck up, the dancing resumed round and round the decorated tree, crowned with a cap of liberty that a woman had taken from her head and planted on its top, shaking out her hair. As the twilight moved in, down the street of the Ghetto Vecchio, the most beautiful of all the ghetto's buildings – the Scuola Ponentina, the synagogue of the Spanish and Portuguese – blazed with light. The joy of Venice's Jews was, at last, literally unconfined. They were free to go anywhere, do anything.

Until they weren't. In October 1797, at the villa of the last doge of the republic, Villa Manin in Passariano, Bonaparte signed the Treaty of Campo Formio confirming French power throughout northern Italy, covered only by the fig leaf of the new 'Jacobin' Cisalpine and Ligurian republics. But under the terms of the treaty, Venice was returned to the Austrian Habsburg Empire. Some of the old restrictions, particularly economic and commercial, were reimposed. The demoralisation must have been profound. But the gates were never rebuilt; the ghetto curfew had gone forever. And when a Napoleonic 'Kingdom of Italy' was created in the wake of Austerlitz, with Venice as part of it, all the civil rights of the Jews were honoured again.

For the rest of the Jews of Italy, especially in Rome and the papal territories, the back and forth swings of military power made their lives frighteningly insecure. There was a price to be paid for their open embrace of French liberation, and during the 'Viva Maria' peasant riots, mobilised by the Church against godless Jacobins and their French protectors, the Jews suffered brutally for their presumption. Partisans of the new liberty – writers, actors, members of the governing councils – were summarily tried and executed, but there were violent assaults on Jewish districts; ancient hatreds rekindled; Jews accused yet again of child murder. Thirteen died in the attacks on Jews in Siena alone; though there were also places like Pitigliano, sitting on its tufa outcrop above the Tuscan maremma, where the citizenry actually defied the peasant bands and protected the long-settled Jews and their beautiful synagogue from destruction.[35]

Was Chelek Tov, then, the liberator of the Jews or just a beguiling opportunist, leading them astray and into the hands of their tormentors? For a decade rabbis all through Germany and eastern Europe in particular debated the meaning of Napoleon Bonaparte for the Jews. But as soon as they became disillusioned he provided them with new reason for hope. In 1798, in the most spectacular gamble of his life to date, Bonaparte took an army to Egypt, his head full of histories of Alexander and Caesar, and a ship loaded with oriental savants, geographers and engineers. In front of the pyramids, he destroyed a Mamluk force, took pains to cultivate the imams, and in September even met with two Cairene rabbis who were grandly characterised in the official reports as 'high priests'. To already excited Jewish imaginations, this seemed to suggest that Jerusalem might be next; that the restoration of the holy Temple might even be part of the plan; that the Almighty had chosen a Corsican general as the Redeemer. Never mind, as the sceptical pointed out, this particular redeemer was partial to lard and *boudin* sausage; what else but the Providential hand could explain such military miracles?

As the campaign turned north-east from Egypt into Palestine, rumours and stories took flight. A report, written from Constantinople, appeared in the *Moniteur Universel* that General Bonaparte had 'invited the Jews of Asia and Africa to gather under his banner to re-establish the ancient Jerusalem'.[36] Apparently he had already distributed arms to his Jewish battalions which even now were threatening Aleppo. Around the same time, in February 1799, Thomas Corbet, an Irish officer serving in the French army – one of those who escaped the debacle of the revolt of the United Irishmen and the failed French invasion of 1795 – had much the same idea. Writing to Paul Barras, Bonaparte's patron in the governing Directory, Corbet proposed that the directors should summon some 'Jews of the highest consequence' and propose the mass mobilisation of men and money in the cause of liberating their ancestral land, thus attaching more than a million Jews throughout the world to the cause of the Grande Nation of liberty. The Irish at the western end, the Jews at the eastern, what could possibly go wrong?

It was all fantasy. If Barras ever read Corbet's enthusiastic scheme he did nothing about it, and it is unlikely that the general himself ever heard of it. In the spring of 1799 he had other things on his mind. Many of his men, it is true, who had got as far as Ramallah, were desperate to march on Jerusalem – more as a kind of legendary pilgrimage in arms than anything else – but strategy pointed otherwise. Horatio Nelson had blown the French fleet to smithereens at Aboukir Bay, precluding reinforcements from Egypt. Taking and holding Gaza, Jaffa and Acre as an alternative door through an English blockade was more important, but the French army was wasting away with yellow fever and plague. With the casually brutal cynicism which would take him far, the general left his men to perish or get themselves back as best they could while he departed to pursue his political fortunes.

And yet, the Jews within the rapidly expanding domains of greater France continued to hail him as a figure of messianic hope. In 1800, Issachar Carpi of Revere in Lombardy was still living off the wonder of the Egyptian campaign. Waxing biblical he described Napoleon as a latter-day Moses who had 'stretched out his hand over the sea to quieten the waves' and had 'flown like an eagle' to the land of the pharaohs.[37] Elsewhere in Hebrew odes, Bonaparte mutated into David as well as Moses. And sometimes the eulogies and prayers went all the way.[38] Diogène Tama, who edited the official proceedings of the Jewish gatherings Napoleon would summon, warbled that the decree calling together an Assembly of Notables in 1806 'will carry unto every generation the sweet conviction which we already saw in our august Emperor, the living image of the Divinity'.

If so, God and His latest servant could not have been that happy with the Jews of the French Empire. For it was as a result of a visit to Strasbourg on the way home after Austerlitz that the emperor, as he now was, decided something had to be done about the Jews. In that city he had been besieged by bitter complaints about Jewish usury and he believed them all. In fact the more involved Napoleon got, the more obvious it became that he bought into almost all the traditional pre-revolutionary canards which had clung to the Ashkenazim and which had had countless airings in the speeches and writings of those who had always opposed their emancipation. They were a 'nation within a nation' and always would be; they were incapable of anything but grossly extortionate moneylending; they were bleeding honest citizens white; and their peculiar habits – especially of marrying only with each other – were evidence that they never really thought of themselves as true Frenchmen. To those who wanted to hear – and even to some in his Council of State who were astonished at the vehemence and crudeness of his prejudices – he referred to the Jews in ripely Voltairean terms as 'the most despicable people on earth'. Evidently he shared the views of the most reactionary members of his governing circle that it had been a mistake to emancipate them and make them citizens since a whole swarm were inundating eastern France. 'The evil done by Jews,' he shouted to a shocked Council, 'does not come from individuals but from the temperament of this people.'[39] Napoleon did not propose entirely undoing the emancipation of 1791 but rather a kind of probation for the Jews, a concentrated campaign to make them change their ways; together with acts of population and marriage control, a prohibition on them engaging in any trade or commerce; a moratorium (imposed in May 1806) on most of the debts owed to them; and a state control over their rabbis to make sure that loyalty to the empire was inculcated among their children: in other words a regression back to some of the most restrictive aspects of the old regime.

To this end, the 'Assembly of Notables' – a gathering of about a hundred prominent Jews, rabbinical and lay, all appointed by the departmental prefects – was summoned to Paris in the autumn of 1806. The form of the summons purported to encourage rather than dismay. 'Exposed to the contempt of nations and not infrequently to the avarice of princes,' it declared, 'they have never as yet been treated with justice. Their customs and practices kept them far from society by which they were rejected in turn.' Though the 'Instruction' to the Notables promised the gathering could have the freest discussion, nothing of the sort was the case. Its members were to answer a specific set of questions posed by the emperor, reflecting his pet obsessions, all issues where what he supposed to be true of Jewish religion and practice conflicted with the Napoleonic law. At all times, members of the Council of State and the Ministry of Religion were to be in attendance, cramping the style of the assembled luminaries.

Well then, were the Jews really French? Did they consider Frenchmen as their brethren? What about marriages? Did they sanction polygamy? (The fact that this question could be put at all was an indication of the crudeness of the inquiry.) Did Jews divorce? (The revolution had legalised it; Napoleon had put it into reverse.) And what about usury? Was it true that they forbade it to each other but permitted or even encouraged it where Gentiles were concerned?

It was a classic exercise in Napoleonic state bullying. And there were additional acts of tactlessness. The inaugural meeting of the Assembly, in a disused chapel behind the Hotel de Ville, was arranged for the Sabbath Saturday. When this was pointed out to the conveners of the Assembly, it was met with the shrug of indifferent bureaucracy strongly suggesting the offence had been intentional. In fact there was nothing to stop the Notables from going to the meeting and listening to the speeches after early-morning services, assuming they could walk there. Some went by coach, probably including Abraham Furtado, who by now was getting on, notwithstanding the fact that he was often the subject of muttered criticism that the only Bible he had ever learned came courtesy of Voltaire. Even before the first sententious words had been uttered, the moment divided the Jews of France; and appeared to exact a price for their civic good behaviour. But no one spoke Napoleonese like Furtado, dependably elected president of the Assembly partly for understanding that whatever hyperbole could be showered on the Great Benefactor, it could never be enough. But by God Almighty he would try. Thus 'it was impossible that his exalted mind could, even for an instant, entertain a thought on our situation without it being materially improved ... this protecting genius who has saved this empire from the rage of factional spirit, the horrors of bloody anarchy ... the enterprise His Majesty undertakes is such as might have been expected from the most astonishing man whose deeds were ever recorded by history.' And on and on and on.

Tensions immediately divided the less from the more orthodox among them, who included all the veterans of the revolutionary struggle for emancipation: Furtado, who had become an eager, not to say obsequious Bonapartist; Berr Isaac Berr; and Rabbi David Sintzheim, who was responsible for editing the replies. He and his colleagues did what they could to respond to the questions while defending the integrity of rabbinical Judaism and the Talmud, all the while prefacing the replies with extravagant bouquets of praise to the benevolence, magnanimity and wisdom of the new Moses/David/Solomon.

The questions had already been relentlessly thrashed over during the original revolutionary debates about emancipation and indeed had involved many of the same Jewish protagonists who could be forgiven of becoming weary at having to repeat the answers. But in the post-Austerlitz world (one in which the French were about to deliver another crushing defeat to the Prussians at Jena), nothing seemed able to stop Napoleon or the extent of his empire, which at its height would stretch from Hamburg to the Pyrenees and, when the satellite kingdoms were included, from Poland to Naples. Why should it not last at least as long as the Imperium Romanum whose modern counterpart it claimed to be? So the Notables, thinking they were establishing the legal grounds for their place as 'Frenchmen professing the Mosaic religion', took their work seriously, however conscious they were of the innumerable state officials over their shoulders as they deliberated. In justice they defended the core of Judaism to the best of their ability, translating it into the kind of anodyne loyalty they knew would give satisfaction to those in power. Polygamy was a thing of the past; divorce was possible but only after civil adjudication had accepted it. On intermarriage, an enormous buzzing bee in the Napoleonic bonnet, they stretched things a little by insisting that it had only been forbidden with 'the seven Canaanite nations, with Amnon and Moab and the Egyptians', though 'we cannot deny that the opinion of the rabbis is against these [mixed] marriages'. The reason was that they would only be considered valid when the rites of *kiddushin* for betrothal had taken place and 'this could not be done for people both of whom would not consider them sacred'. In other words conversion was required of the non-Jewish partner, but the Notables could not quite bring themselves to say so.

On usury, the laws of Israel made a distinction between what was required (no interest) for charitable loans and commerce which was freer, not a distinction between loans made to Jews and those made to non-Jews. So the old canard that Jews only charged interest to the Gentiles was entirely without foundation. Most important of all, 'In the eyes of Jews, Frenchmen are brethren and not strangers. When the Israelites formed a settled and independent nation the law made it a rule for them to consider strangers as brothers ... "Love ye therefore the strangers ... for ye were strangers in the land of Egypt" ... how could they consider them otherwise when they inhabit the same land, when they are ruled and protected by the same government, and by the same laws? When they enjoy the same rights, and have the same duties to fulfil?'[40]

But even before the Notables had completed their work, Napoleon decided he wanted the gloss of piety rather than any sort of political utterance to bind the Jews to their state contract. Ever since his coronation at Notre-Dame, presided over by the same Pope Pius VII whom he periodically made his prisoner, the Napoleonic nose could not get enough of the odour of sanctity. Hence his wording: 'His Majesty's intention is that no plea shall be left to those who may refuse to become citizens; the full enjoyment of your religious worship and the full enjoyment of your political rights shall be accorded to you. But in return HM requires a religious pledge for the strict adherence to the principles established in your answers.'[41] Never mind philosophy, the realm of the vainly cerebral. The awesome spectacles of religion, on the other hand, drew ordinary and exceptional men alike to the source of its authority, or so he had come to believe. (Robespierre had ended his days convinced of much the same thing.) And Napoleon was right of course to sense that only if the document of allegiance came with the imprimatur of the rabbis would it make any impact on the synagogue-going Ashkenazim. Thus a new august body would have to be convened whose binding utterances would have the same authority as the ancient Law of Moses and would indeed complement them.

Hence the 'Grand Sanhedrin' which met in the Hotel de Ville in February 1807, the same year that a treaty would be made on the Niemen with Tsar Alexander, confirming Napoleon as master of at least half the world. Just as his coronation had been mantled in elaborate allusions to the epochal crowning of Charlemagne, and to his vaunted status as Oriens Augustus, the remaker of history, so the new Sanhedrin was to appear as if a true reincarnation of the original, which had met in the century following the destruction of the Temple to reorder the practice of Judaism. Napoleon, the pedantic antiquarian, was blissfully in his element overseeing the details. There would be seventy-one of them as heretofore. They would be seated in a semi-circle, according to age, all repeating the original format. And most important of all, they would establish the quid pro quo governing modern Jewish life: unmolested freedom to practise; equal enjoyment of the rights and laws, on condition of accepting that their rabbis were now a fully functioning department of state, and their congregations unconditionally loyal Frenchmen and women. To this, the seventy-one, dressed in custom-designed robes of black silk and tricorn hats (for elaborate fancy dress was a speciality of the Napoleonic regime), readily assented. 'By virtue of the right vested in us by our ancient usage and by our sacred laws ... we hereby religiously enjoin on all obedience to the State in all matters civil and political.'[42]

What followed was another speciality of the empire: tearing up the treaties, bargains and contracts to which it had just been a party. So in 1808, a set of decrees were enacted, the last of which became known as 'infamous' in the Jewish communities, since it made nonsense of any pretence to afford Jews equal treatment alongside other Frenchmen. Suddenly, and notwithstanding all the folderol of Notables and Sanhedrin, the Jews – or rather the Ashkenazim, since the Sephardim were commended for their acceptable degree of assimilation into Frenchness – were to be subjected to a social and economic parole reminiscent of the most odious discriminations of the old regimes of Europe, but with an additional twist of modernising social engineering. To avoid urban concentrations of Jews, no further settlement was to be allowed in Alsace and Lorraine and certainly not in major cities like Strasbourg and Metz. In the interest of 'encouraging' their economic diversification and the practice of farming and artisanal crafts, the Jews would need a licence from the departmental prefect before they could practise any trade or business whatsoever. Should the slightest suspicion of 'usury' fall on them, that licence would be null and void. Notaries would have to monitor and certify all loans. And there was one further distinction made, immediately noticed by those who had signed up to the solemnities in Paris, especially brutal in a state whose energies were overwhelmingly determined by the perpetuation of war: unlike everyone else in the empire, the Jewish conscript soldiers would not be allowed to pay for substitutes. This was yet another prejudice the emperor of the French shared with the tsar of Russia: that the army, ultimately, was more to be depended on as the school of nationality than anything the rabbis in their consistories could dream up.

V. Cholent

But then history laughs at grand designs.

In the spring of 1813 as ice on the Beresina melted and the human remains of the Grande Armée, bits and pieces of them, floated to the surface, Gabriel Schrameck was taken prisoner by the Cossacks. He had been one of the Jewish conscripts and had joined the section of the army which let him do what he did best: tailoring. After all, there was so much frogging and handsome coats and trousers to be made, repaired and renewed. Nothing compared with the Grande Armée when it came to a beautiful parade. They killed with military glamour. But as the tide of war turned, patching up became the order of the day. Everything that could be reused was: hats from the fallen resewn where shrapnel had shot through them; intact boots pulled from the feet of the dead. So much work to be done, then, though Gabriel Schrameck, like so many other Jews in the army, was always trying to find ways (as the emperor suspected Jews

would) of avoiding profaning the Sabbath while still fulfilling his
military obligations.

But by the early autumn of 1813 those anxieties – how to be a good
Jew and a good soldier of the emperor – seemed to belong to a distant
epoch, to a dream. Now Gabriel Schrameck the military tailor was
himself in irreparable tatters, his Slavic captors the most famous
Jew-haters in the world. He was ragged, his body eaten away with
suffering and the frostbite of the hellish retreat through the Russian
snows. Now he was in Poland, what had once been Napoleon's ally,
the 'Grand Duchy of Warsaw'. Many Jews had served as its officers.
Now they and it had disappeared.

All Gabriel Schrameck could think about was his growling, howling
belly. He had been offered fat and lard on mouldy bread by the Cossacks
but even in his extremity he could not and would not gobble *trayf*.
Better to die right there amid the geese and the fields of standing rye.
If he stayed true to the Torah, he wrote in his diary, 'God will have
the heart to save you.' But harvest time meant, he knew, that it was the
month of Elul. The Yomim Naroim, the high holy days, Rosh
Hashanah and Yom Kippur were coming up. How could he observe
them?[43]

Then, one morning, in some village, some shtetl, not so very
different from his own little hamlet in Alsace, Gabriel Schrameck was
given, if not an answer to his agonised prayers and mutterings, if not
a ram caught in the thicket, then at least, something.

The people of this village, with many young girls and boys among
them, came to look at us. They had heard that there were French
prisoners and were curious to see them. Among those people were
Jews. They looked at us in their Shabbat best clothes. I was wretched
with my swollen and frostbitten shoe-less feet, and crawling with lice.
But I spoke to a young woman because I saw that she had *rachmones*,
compassion, for us. I told her we were Jews too, asking if there was
any way she could let us have a little food, and that I could even pay
her something for it. She said yes, went back to her house and returned
with a casserole full of semolina and meats, still hot. She fed me this
food with two spoons. But I could not, in truth, eat very much because
my stomach had shrunk so badly with the starvation. I left some of
the food for the other prisoners and went off to vomit. Then I asked

the woman how much I owed her but she refused saying, 'This cost me nothing and besides it is the Shabbes, when one is forbidden to take money for anything.'

This is what it had all come to: the epic of emancipation reduced to a tatterdemalion starveling, desperate for a little *rachmones* from Jews whose habitual lives were untouched by the lofty rhetoric of philosophers. What was left of Gabriel Schrameck, tailor, soldier of the empire, citizen-Jew, fully vested in his rights, had, in a way even he did not fully comprehend, somehow come home to a pot of piping-hot *cholent*, the Sabbath stew he had wolfed down as a child, the morsel of pity which in his distress of body and soul, he could not keep down.

12

POH-LIN

I. The Stones of Podolia

The dumbfounding thing is how present they still seem: the countless generations of Jewish eastern Europe. Even the Nazis couldn't kill the dead, so hundreds of thousands of Jewish tombstones, many of them carved with birds and beasts, hands and crowns, have defied obliteration. So many books lamenting the end of the shtetl mourn a vanishing: millions turned to ash and smoke. How could they not? And yet there is new life amid the stones; modest, precious, resurrections. Ukrainian towns whose names ring with the cries heard on nights of pogrom and *aktion* – Berdichev, Zhitomir, Tarnopol, Kishinev – have Jews in them again, praying, singing, eating, gossiping, studying, arguing. In Odessa, where wrought-iron balconies overhang the street as they did in the days of flamboyant Yiddish writers and the first Zionists, there are 30,000 Jews. On Friday nights, braided challah loaves, shiny with a brush of egg yolk, sit beside bowls of hummus and chopped liver. An accordion starts up woozily; an old party starts to bang happily on the table, and survivors of the extermination of the gulag and the battles of the Red Army sing numbers from *Fiddler on the Roof* while big-boned teenagers dance the thumping circles of the Israeli *hora*. In Berdichev, a young Hasidic rabbi, his Judaism recovered from Soviet assimilation and family indifference, toys with the curls of his beard and insists, with an unworldly smile the founders of Hasidism 250 years ago would have recognised, that 'there is holiness in everything, everything'.

There is, at any rate, something stirring in the memory bank of the Ashkenazim other than museums, memorials, Holocaust Days, documentaries, musical laments. It should not be exaggerated. *Ruakh* – the breath of life, which along with *neshama* and *nefesh* make up the anatomy of the soul in the Jewish tradition – was smothered in blood. For every bright-lit synagogue in Odessa there is still the memory of Nemyrov, where, on 26 and 27 June 1941, German soldiers, assisted by Ukrainian fascist militia, herded fifteen hundred Jews into the Great Synagogue and shot them against the walls. Two years earlier, one of the first acts committed by German troops invading Poland in September 1939 was to burn down its wooden synagogues, forcing the local Jews, who had already suffered beard-shearings and murderous beatings, to watch and sing and dance – HOP-HOP *SCHNELL* – as the glorious buildings disintegrated in the flames. Sometimes, to general merriment of the armed bystanders, the Jews were made to light the fire themselves. In Białystok, they were themselves consumed in the fire. In this way some of the most beautiful structures made in eighteenth-century Europe perished along with those who had sung in them: four-roofed Narowla, one tier stacked upon the other went; Przedborz with its bright wall paintings by Yehuda Leib, the lyre-carved ceiling and stained glass all reduced to ashen dirt; Pohrebyszcze and its elaborate candelabra which had taken Baruch of Pohrebyszcze six years to make from collected scraps of discarded copper; Kornik with its Ruthenian onion domes built by Hillel Benjamin of Lasko.[1] The few that survived did so because of the fun the Germans had turning them into public latrines, stables and brothels. In the synagogue of Czestochowa, young Jewish girls were violated and sexually tortured day after day after day.

But a surprising number endure. Synagogues built of brick and stone, common in south-west Ukraine (the first solidly defensive architecture built by Jews since the destruction of the Temple), lived up to their classification as 'fortress synagogues'. It took the Germans two attempts, in 1939 and 1941, to demolish most of the interior of the great synagogue of Przemysl, but until the Communist regime ordered its demolition in 1956, its shell remained defiantly standing. Other fortress *shuls*, built between the sixteenth and the late eighteenth centuries, are still there in varying degrees of dereliction or restoration: in Sokal, Dubno and Bolechow, in pink-gabled Zhovkva, red-brick Uhniv, turreted Sadagora and, most spectacularly, in the imposing cubic citadel sitting on the brow of its hill in the ancient Podolian border town of Satanow (called Sataniv in Ukrainian).

The first stone synagogue in Satanow was built in 1565, a defence against Tatar and Muscovite raids. A century later the Cossack rebel Danko Nechay torched the town, including the interior of the synagogue, while he was busy slaughtering Jews and Catholics. When the uprising against the Polish Crown had ebbed, a citadel was constructed at the north end of the town. At the same time, the original stone house of prayer was massively enlarged and fortified, after which it was known, with good reason, as the Great Synagogue. Like its sister synagogues in Podolia, Satanow's has two storeys rising from basement half-lights. But periodic assaults, especially by the mounted irregulars, brigand soldiers known as the *haidamaks*, persuaded the Jews that they needed to defend their prayers with something more than maximum devotion. *Haidamak* raids could be horrific in their cruelty. At Satanow, as elsewhere, the roof terrace was pierced with embrasures from which muskets or even light cannon could direct fire at attackers. Debris from shell casings and cartridges found on the roof by its restorers make it clear that the sounds of arms as well as prayer could be heard at the Satanow synagogue all the way through the First World War.

Within, the fortress synagogue was a far cry from the rudimentary hut-like spaces imagined to be typical of a shtetl *shul*. In Satanow, the interior space is vast. Four great columns, typical of synagogues in Podolia and Volhynia, rise to a lofty vaulted ceiling. Around the time of its final expansion in the mid-eighteenth century, women had abandoned separate, free-standing prayer rooms of their own and had re-entered the synagogue, worshipping most often in half-screened galleries. To accommodate them, ceilings were raised, and scooped out for an interior dome or stepped lantern skylight, often painted on the inside. Light would fall on an elaborate central *bimah*, itself canopied like a tabernacle, bower or crown, formed by ribbed, arched, copper-gilt branches and hung with chandeliers. As elsewhere in Jewish eastern Europe, from Lithuania to Galicia, there would have been smaller private-house synagogues dotted about the town. In the early days of Hasidism, its adepts, frowned on by the elders for their shouts, cries and ecstatic somersaults, would have gathered in such rooms. But for the most important occasions in the Jewish calendar – Pesach, Sukkot, Rosh

Hashanah and Yom Kippur – the Jews of Satanow walked to their Great
Synagogue on the hill where the Torah Ark was elaborately embellished
with the best that Jewish rococo could provide. Painted gryphons
stretched their leathery wings against an azure ground, the intense blue
still visible even in the days of deepest ruin. Above the gryphons,
surmounting the tablet of the Decalogue, a complicated, elegant decoration of swag and scroll rises to a pair of lions, holding between them
the Keter Torah, the only crown that mattered to these Jews.

All this splendour might have fallen before the People's Bulldozers
in the 1970s, had not a Christian neighbour, Boris Slobodnyuk, begun
a long, indomitable, one-man campaign to stop them in their tracks.
The war over, his service in the Soviet army done, Boris came back
to the low hill of Satanow, and to his house opposite the synagogue.
'I had always thought it was for me as well as the Jews,' he says. After
its congregation had been turned into smoke blown from the chimneys
of Belzec killing camp, Boris felt himself duty-bound to be the *shul's*
custodian. A Hasidic tradition held that if the need was consumingly
urgent, one should stand on a particular flagstone inside the synagogue,
and strive for *devekut*: communion with the Almighty. When Boris's
wife was dying of cancer, he entered the ruin, picking his way through
the thorns and brambles, and stood upon the stone, trying his best
to summon interceding magic. The cancer marched inexorably on
but Boris felt he must save the synagogue of Satanow, even if its spell
had not managed to save his wife. It had given him hope amid his
despair, and, to some degree, peace afterwards. He felt as if the
building, even reduced to a broken shell, was still, as he said, 'a neighbour'. So Boris Slobodnyuk obstructed the bulldozers and pestered
the bureaucrats, working the documentation until the conservators,
the historians and finally the rabbis came back to Satanow. Boris
watched as students uprooted the thorn bushes, closed off the holes
in the roof and walls, repaired and regrouted the brick, pasted back
the plasterwork, carefully restored the mutilated stucco. The gryphons,
lions and unicorns reappeared. With Satanow in the public eye and a
policy of sensitivity to Jewish memory instituted in Ukraine, Boris
became a local hero. Swallowing their irritation, regional dignitaries
sang his praises and handed him official certificates of cultural merit
in self-congratulatory ceremonies. Boris enjoys pondering all these
wonders, his gold teeth glowing in the sunset as he talks about it.

On the other side of the River Zbruch and up a facing hill is the cemetery where thousands of Satanow's Jews lie buried.[2] Climb the slope from the road and a multitude stands or rather leans in lopsided greeting, wave after wave. On the grassy slope a stone menagerie riots in the pale mist. Travellers to these kinds of towns report that following the cultural conquest of Hasidism, some Podolian tombstones were brightly painted; but if this was the case at Satanow, the Ukrainian weather has long since eaten the colour away. But there is still exhilarating animation. Bears clamber for grapes; three-point bucks paw the earth glaring at intruders; a coiled leviathan eats its own tail; a unicorn rams its horn down the gullet of a surprised lion. Nailed to the wheel of time three hares chase each other's tails. The cemetery hubbub roars on; an entire commonwealth of the Jews: *groyse makhers*, big shots, in pride of place; *pishers* tucked in the back rows. In the Levite section on the brow of the slope, jugs of water pour themselves out. Scattered amidst the common Israelites doing them a favour, the hands of *cohanim*, the priests, open their palms, thumbs touching forming the butterfly benediction. In Hebrew, such places are commonly designated Beit Hayim, the House of Life, and Jewish Satanow is all around you. Voices mutter and chuckle from beneath beds of limestone, furry with mustard-hued lichen. Upheavals, meteorological, geological and political, have made the stones tilt this way and that, like Jews in an argument, pressing into each other's space. You tread gingerly between them and eavesdrop. So the *rebbe* thinks he's getting an *ohel*, a canopy, over his grave? What is this, some *zaddik*, and who says so, if you don't mind me asking? Farbish? He ran away to Warsaw, mister high and mighty. Someone saw him mooching around the cafes; him and his big ideas, much good they did him; came back tail between his legs. Plotnik, guess what, he died of drink; some innkeeper he was, his own poison got him, may he rest in peace; and that Gittele of his, eyes like daggers, she'd skin you soon as look at you, you should forgive the disrespect.

You find your way back to the rotating hares. There's something odd about them but you can't put your finger on it until you do. Three hares, three ears between them. The tomb sculptor has positioned them in profile so artfully that each seems to have its full complement.

The hares appear more than once in the Satanow graveyard, but unlike the lions, the bears and the deer, they are not a standard feature of Jewish tombstone iconography. Many of the animals embody first names. If the dead man is a Hirsch, carve him a hind; if he is an Aryeh or a Yehudah, give him a lion. Others have biblical or *midrashic* allusions. Sometimes they stand in for the representation of humans, still forbidden in funerary art, though pretty much everything else was allowed.[3] In place of the spies sent by Joshua to check out the Promised Land and who returned bearing its fruit, two bears tramp along, carrying a horizontal pole from which drooping bunches of grapes are suspended. Doves with sprigs of myrtle speak of redemption as the waters of Noah's flood recede. But the spinning hares are more likely to be found in the churches of medieval France and western England where they were called 'tinners rabbits' by the Cornish miners. The hares have even been found on Buddhist temple walls along the Silk Road, and their motion resembles nothing so much as the limbs of Shiva circling in his wheel of fire.

So the hares bounded into Satanow from somewhere else, perhaps somewhere a long way away. The town was, after all, a crossroads of trade and ideas, sitting as it did between the forested country of the Dniester, the rise of the Carpathian Mountains, the dark-earth, fertile plain of Red Ruthenia and the basin of the Dnieper to the east. When the Galician territory to the west was taken by Habsburg Austria in the Polish partitions at the end of the eighteenth century, Satanow became one of the westernmost border towns of tsarist Russia. It was also not far from the border of Turkish Moldavia–Wallachia to the south-east: a world of July peaches, Romany *musika*, and dry-spiced meats, their *bastourma*, our pastrami. Unsurprisingly Satanow immediately turned into a smuggler's paradise which the tsarist government tried to keep off limits to the Jews. If one puts together the extravagant cemetery, with its festival of carved stone, and the grandiose fortress synagogue on the hill, as well as records of a lively market (thirteen Jewish store-holders shared a building covered by a shingled roof), it becomes obvious that Satanow, like countless comparable towns in Jewish eastern Europe, scarcely resembled the one-cow mudhole conjured by Anatevka, the Fiddler's shtetl. But then Tevye the milkman and Anatevka with its 'small mud huts', 'low and rickety', their 'roofs half buried in the ground', a pathetic swarm of destitute Jews dwelling in dirt-poor streets, 'packed together like herring in a barrel', shut off from the Gentile world, except when visited by pogroms, was the picturesque fiction of Sholem Aleichem, composed at the end of the nineteenth century.[4] Both he and the other great Yiddish bard of the imaginary shtetl, Mendele Moykher Sforim, wrote at a physical and temporal distance (usually urban) from historical reality and at a moment when Jewish towns in the Russian Pale of Settlement were becoming vulnerable to depopulation, a narrowing of economic opportunity and repeated physical attack. Dilapidated ruin as the most obvious characteristic of the shtetl was projected back onto Jewish towns by writers who saw themselves as liberated from its stifling narrowness. They sat before the rattling tramcars of Odessa or Delancey Street in New York smoking their Russian cigarettes, while the bleating of faraway goats and the penitential laments of Yom Kippur filled their heads. Before they knew it they had made an Anatevka as fantastic as anything Marc Chagall of big-city Vitebsk would conjure from his dreams.

The reality of the eighteenth- and early-ninteenth-century shtetl was different, though in its way at least as rich in human colour and social poetry.[5] To begin with, as Israel Bartal and Gershon Hundert have noted, the shtetl of the storytellers was miniaturised, scaled down to a folk hamlet that could house a manageable (and predictable) cast of characters: the rabbi, the matchmaker, the slaughterer, the self-mortifying mystic; the usual. A few hundred souls, perhaps, all of them Jewish, davening, kvetching, scandal-mongering, plotting, chanting. There were such places. But the vast majority of Jews in Poland–Lithuania in the eighteenth century, and afterwards in Austrian Galicia and the Russian Pale of Settlement, lived in urban crowds in true towns like Satanow, of at least three thousand and often many more.[6]

By 1800, Brody in Austrian Galicia had 8,600 Jews – nearly 70 per cent of the townsfolk. In the towns of 3,000–5,000, hundreds of them across the old Polish–Lithuanian commonwealth, Jews made up at least half of the population; often a bigger group than the Poles themselves. It was their world. By 1764, there were 750,000 Jews in Poland alone; by 1800, 1.25 million in Poland–Lithuania; by the Russian Revolution, 5 million in the Pale of Settlement alone.

And unlike so many other places in the Christian world, they did not live a hole-in-the-corner existence. They were conspicuously visible, even – as travellers often complained – ubiquitous, inescapable.

In Vienna, the major synagogues in Leopoldstadt needed to be flush to the street facade, entrances discreet if not hidden. In Satanow and the other towns of Podolia, Volhynia and Kiev province, the grandiose structures stood unapologetically beside or facing churches and some-times overlooking the marketplace where the Jews also dominated the scene. Towards the end of the eighteenth century they made up 70 per cent of Poland's urban population.

Since they had first been allowed into Poland in the thirteenth century, and certainly since their first charters were drawn up, the Jews (with a few exceptions in royal towns like Warsaw) had been able to live where they wanted and work as they wished. The first Polish ghetto was the one the Nazis introduced in 1940. In the bigger towns like Mezhybozhe, at least a third of the two thousand Jews would have had Christian neighbours. There were Jewish craft speci-alities – hatmaking, for instance – but not only were Jews not restricted to traditional work, uniquely in Europe they could and did form trade guilds with all their own rites and ceremonies. In Lwów the Jewish goldsmiths were famous for making – and showing off – their plate.[7] The central position of Jews in the Polish commercial economy made them unavoidable for the rest of the Poles, however mixed their feelings. Whether as market retailers or middle- and long-distance merchants along routes running from the Black Sea through Moldavia–Wallachia north into Ukraine, Lithuania and the Baltic, Jews engaged in transactions with non-Jews every day. From the smaller towns they (both men and women) drove into the countryside to buy farm produce, and to sell the peasants cloth or mirrors, needles, pins, candles or knives. In the bigger ones they would set up shop beneath shingled roofs covering stone-structured market arcades, or in wooden booths or mobile stalls. They would be brought fish, cheese, flax, skins by peasant farmers to whom in return they would sell glasswares, earth-enwares, gloves, hats, silver buckles, fur-trimmed coats, candles, mirrors. At Vinnytsia there were twenty-four such fixed shops run by Jews and thirty-nine wheeled stalls. At Tulchin, not such a big place, there were sixteen stone stores and eighty-five wooden shops.[8]

The Jews of Poland–Lithuania were not, in any sense, stuck in the mud. Countless numbers were ceaselessly on the move: on wagons, in post coaches and on horseback. Jews were horse people, even if they rode on non-Jewish-made saddles. My mother spoke fondly of a

Lithuanian great-uncle who, she claimed, rode bareback in travelling circuses. Jews were water rats too, sailing shallow-draught boats and rafts along the great river basins of the Dniester and Vistula. One in four barge and raft skippers was Jewish, and their crews likewise.[9] If Yiddish was the lingua franca of the trading Jews, for many of the more ambitious and far-roving it was not their only tongue. They were so interknit with the society they inhabited that there was no choice but to know some Polish, German, Russian, Ukrainian. The more adventurous like the Tokaj trader Dov Ber Birkenthal of Bolechow, who left a priceless memoir, may have been halting in Magyar but he had Latin, German, French and Italian, all of which he used for his business. Eighteenth-century travellers regularly mention hiring Jews as interpreters for no one else could function amid the carnival of tongues.

There was nothing they would not buy and sell, far and near: salt and saltpetre; fine calicos, muslins and batistes, taffeta and linens, dyed cashmere and rich brocade; grain and timber, wax and hides; iron and copper; dried Turkish peaches, figs, oranges and almonds, chocolate and cheese; opals and furs; sugar, ginger and spices, caviar and cognac; ink, parchment and paper; perfumes and potions; buckles and belts; cutlery and haberdashery; Chinese tea and Turkish coffee; amber and ironwares; tar and coal; boots and ribbons, kid gloves and black foetal lambskins; Balkan tobacco and wine from all over (both specialities); absinthe and brandy, fruit vodka and mead; amulets and elixirs; books and portrait prints of rabbis and Cossacks, friend or foe they weren't fussy; micrographic etchings (which had become all the rage); pottery and pewter; lowing herds of horned cattle, flocks of sheep and goats, and in more places than you would suppose – Dubno and Rovno, for example – Jews sold fattened hogs and sows.[10] They didn't have to eat them, after all. Add Jewish pig traders to *Fiddler on the Roof* stereotypes and an adjustment to the conventional picture of shtetl Jews seems to be in order.

There were of course the upholders of tradition (though you could be that, a Talmud *chokhem*, and still run a pub, just not on the Sabbath): the slaughterers and circumcisers and cantors and Hebrew-school teachers and those who wanted nothing more than to be left alone to study the imperishable, unfathomable riches of the Talmud every single day of their remaining lives. But then there were the rest of the Jews. They were furriers and stonemasons; carters and ostlers; opticians and barber surgeons; bankers and minters of coin; printers and booksellers; soldiers and musicians; hatmakers and goldsmiths; weavers, embroiderers and dyers; jewellers, watchmakers and glaziers; lumber merchants, sawyers and painters; smugglers and rustlers, con men and counterfeiters; and, one need hardly add, physicians and pharmacists, the *aptekarz* who would sell wormwood for your queasy stomach, a cocktail of warm beer and bullshit for colic, dried and crumbled otter if you were unfortunate enough to suffer from *Plica polonica*, the horrible disease which turned your scalp into a densely matted clot of greasy hair.[11] Jews were industrialists too, leasing and working the deep salt mines of Bochnia and the vast timber reserves of Lithuania. And they were shepherds and farmers. Unlike anywhere else in Europe, Jews in Poland were, under the terms of the 1592 charter of Sigismund III, allowed to lease and sometimes even own landed property which they might then let out to peasant tenants or farm directly themselves with Jewish as well as non-Jewish labour. Travelling through Lithuania, the clergyman William Coxe was surprised to see them in the fields 'sowing, reaping and mowing' and engaged in 'other works of husbandry'.[12] Pushed there by the tsars of the early nineteenth century, there were 15,000 Jewish farmers working the land in Kherson province by 1850. A century earlier Solomon Maimon's grandfather Heiman Joseph leased a number of farms near the Niemen River along with a watermill, river jetties, bridges (not always in good state of repair), docks and a warehouse to store goods on the river route from Königsberg.[13] His brothers were established as his tenant farmers; he kept beehives as well as cattle.

The honey was used for mead, since in addition to being a pious farmer, Heiman Joseph (like so many Jews in country towns) was also an innkeeper, brewer and distiller. From the time that the Polish magnates – Heiman Joseph's Radziwill landlord, and elsewhere the Branickis, Potockis, Zamoyskis, Dembinskis, Lubomirskis, Poniatowskis, Czartoryskis and (at Satanow) the Sieniawskis and the rest – leased to them exclusive rights to make and sell alcohol, the Jews monopolised the industry. In a medium-sized town of perhaps 2,000–3,000 Jews, it was not uncommon for there to be fifty taverns, all kept by Jews, which acted as hostelries as well as breweries and distilleries. The Zamoyski estates had thirty-eight distilleries, 101

inns and 140 taverns.¹⁴ In many of those towns it was rare to find a
Jew of any means at all who was *not* in some form or other involved
in the liquor business, even if only to add to the meagre household
income by keeping a roadside inn serving drinks and perhaps sausage.
In such places the benches were rough, the windows papered rather
than glazed; but the customers weren't there for the decor.

This was not a closed-doors culture. Jews thronged the marketplace,
smoking, gossiping and dispatching lads and girls out to sleeve-tug
passing custom. Nor did they all dress like crows. Poland was one of
the few places where there was no Jewish clothing code imposed or
enforced by church or state, and nor were there humiliating badges
of identification. Those who could afford it showed off in fur and
silks. The market women of Galicia, wives and grandmothers, presided
over their shops and stalls in black velvet 'coronets' coiled at the brim
with ropes of glittering crystals and faux pearls. Better-off Jews like
Michael Kolmanovich of Kamenietz were not alone in wearing
costume *à la polonaise*, a long *kantusz* robe with baggy sleeves covering
a violet or blue shirt, his ritual *tzitzit* elegantly sewn to the lower
corner of the coat. His wife, as Orthodox as himself, wore red skirts
and a short jacket of dark blue velvet. Even the grandmother bright-
ened her gown and coat with fur trim and coloured lace.¹⁵ These
well-off Polish Jews could not get enough of pearls. When the wine
trader Dov Ber Birkenthal's house at Bolechow was raided by brigands
in the summer of 1759 (with him absent on business), they took from
his wife Leah two pearl necklaces, one of four ropes, the other of
five, as well as 'a headdress of great value and beauty; and ten gold
rings set with magnificent and rare diamonds', in addition to jewels
belonging to his sister-in-law Rachel.¹⁶ And while Ber's family was
certainly well off, they were not in the top drawer of Polish Jews. One
who might have been was Abramek of Lwów, whose daughter Chajke
was painted in 1781 by the court artist Krzysztof Radziwillowski as a
royal commission.¹⁷ Chajke is monstrously, blingingly bejewelled. Four
double-ropes of pearls extend from throat to bosom, two of them
with large gold pendant portrait medallions. Yet more pearls edge a
spectacular headdress not in black but delicately striped with white
silk. Her gown is heavy rose-coloured brocaded silk and her dark eyes
look out at the artist, the king and us with a confidence so direct that
it verges on amusement.

For once in their history, and notwithstanding the periodic blood-libel case and Catholic-conversion campaign, Jews lived as if they were not an oppressed minority – nor in fact a minority at all, which in many towns was in fact the case. 'They are everywhere' was the comment of travellers (especially the Scots) who came to Tarnopol or the booming Galician town of Brody and discovered what to all intents and purposes looked like purely Jewish cities. Andrew Alexander Bonar and Robert Murray M'Cheyne were astonished to discover 150 synagogues (some certainly very small) but just two Catholic churches in Brody.

> It seemed a wholly Jewish city and the few Gentiles who appeared here and there were quite lost in the crowd of Jews. Jewish boys and girls were playing in the street, Jewish menservants carried messages, Jewish women were the only females seen at doors and windows and Jewish merchants filled the marketplace; the high fur caps of men, rich headdresses of women and small round velvet caps for the boys, met the eye as we wandered from street to street. Jewish ladies were leaning over the balconies, poor old Jewesses were sitting at stalls selling fruit ... in the 'bazaar' they sold hides, handmade shoes, earthenwares.

Women of all ages sat in their shops or walked about the streets in their creamy pearls 'as if they were queens even in their captivity'.[18]

When the Scottish army doctor Adam Neale, assigned to the British embassy in Constantinople, passed through Galicia and Podolia he observed that 'it has often been remarked by travellers that Poland now seems to be the only country in Europe where the persecuted Jews have gained any great and permanent settlement'.[19] Neale was no philo-Semite. He blamed the un-Scottish sluggishness of Polish provincial life on what he thought was the sinister Jewish monopoly of the liquor business: luring the Polish peasantry into drowsy addiction through flavourings like fennel and caraway, added to make gullet-scalding raw spirit palatable. But if to the Scottish doctor they were devils, they were handsome ones. Neale conceded that

> the enjoyment of liberty and civil rights [in Poland–Lithuania by the Jews] seems to have produced a strong effect on the physical constitution and physiognomy of this singular race, bestowing a dignity and

energy upon them which we may look for in vain in other countries. The men, clothed in long black robes, reaching to their ankles and sometimes adorned with silver agraffes [ornamental hook-and-loop clasps], their heads covered with fur caps, their chestnut or auburn locks parted in front and falling gracefully on their shoulders in spiral curls, display much manly beauty.

Neale was so struck that he even compared those Jews to drawings by Leonardo or Carlo Dolci. 'More than once an involuntary awe seized me contemplating on the shoulders of a Hebrew villager a head presenting those traits of physiognomy ... I had long associated with the abstract ideal countenance of the Saviour of the world ... In feminine beauty the women are likewise distinguished but beauty is not uncommon among Jewesses of other countries.'[20] Thus, improbably, it was among the Ashkenazi shtetls of Poland and Ukraine that the Christian romance of the beautiful Jew was first dreamed up.

Nothing about the Jews of eastern Europe, not even their Talmud studies, was ever static or parochial. They were the human moving parts in a non-stop chain of goods and ideas rolling towards the next horizon and moving to the calendrical rhythm of fairs, both great and small. Long-distance Jewish merchants were standard fixtures at the great international fairs of Kiev, Dresden and above all Leipzig. Not atypical was Natan Nota ben Hayyim, who expected to be able to deliver forty wagonloads of Russian sable and fox every year to the Michaelmas fair at Leipzig. The Brody merchants were so thick on the ground at Leipzig that they built a synagogue there just for their periodic use.[21] A seasonal culture grew up fast around these fairs in the heyday of coaches and barges but before the oncoming of the railways, and the Jews, trying to avoid the pickpockets but not quite steering clear of the pop-up taverns run by co-religionists, *landsmen* or even relatives, flung themselves into it as much as anyone else. At Berdichev they oohed at the circus trapeze artistes, lost bags of zloty at the gimcrack casino, sobbed and guffawed in the Polish theatre, goggled at the Cosmorama or gasped as live doves and rabbits were fed to the coils of an anaconda.[22] But if a trader was loath to absent himself from family or synagogue for too long, he could work a much smaller radius and still move with his goods from fair to fair, for no shtetl was without one or more, usually many. The Boguslawl district alone had 116 such small fairs in the course of a single year; Satanow had one for every month.

Families like that of Dov Ber of Bolechow divided road trips between brothers, though from his memoirs one has the impression that, on the model of his father Judah, who had taken him on buying trips, Dov Ber trusted no other nose than his own to sniff out the wines he knew his lordly clients would be unable to resist. He himself made regular expeditions west into the Hegyalja region of Hungary where he bought precious 'Maslas' vintages from Greek-Transylvanian merchants (reluctantly taking on the lesser 'Ausbruch' wines for ballast), getting to know the grassy plains of Hungary, the dangerous brigand-infested roads over the Carpathians, and the river basins of Ukraine like the back of his hand. If he delegated, there was often a problem. On one buying trip his brother Arieh Leib grumbled that he was getting wines excessively clouded by sediment. Use a flax sack as a filter, Dov Ber told him, and the wine will be restored to its amber clarity. Though wine was the basis of their fortune, the family firm diversified. They drove horned cattle and hides to the Frankfurt Fair in exchange for German fancy goods to sell back home. On other expeditions they shipped potash and lumber down the Vistula to exporters waiting at Danzig.

In this long-distance world of hauling, carting and rafting, it was the Jews who supplied the infrastructure. When timbered towns, the private property of the *szlachta* nobility, burned down (as they often did, whether by accident or the devastations inflicted by mounted irregulars), Jews funded and carried out rebuilding, often replacing wooden structures with much more costly stone ones. They made good the most miserably potholed roads and perilously rotting bridges. When a small town braced for an attack by the *haidamaks*, Jews provided weapons and actively joined in the defence. This meant of course that if those towns fell to the bandit gangs they were the first to pay with their lives for the temerity of resistance, especially when Polish soldiery had disappeared in a cloud of dust or joined the Cossack irregulars. Their taverns often served as service stations: repairers of bent axles, twisted wheels and broken springs. Some even built and furnished coaches as well as more rustic carts and wagons. As those who journeyed east through the hornbeam and birch woods and over the loamy upland plains discovered, if you wanted a berline and a strong team of horses, you went to a Jew to get them. If you needed a driver, he too would be a Jew. The Jew would plan the route from, say, Breslau to Jassy, and could be relied on to know which were the better taverns and hostelries (Jewish naturally) – and given the squalor of the worse ones, this was important intelligence to have in advance. A Jew would tell you where horses could be changed, stabled, fed and watered – invariably at an establishment owned by another Jew. A cousin; an in-law? What a coincidence!

The dust-covered, road-weary traveller would drive through the iron-coated gates of the better class of tavern into a courtyard where the team would be uncoupled from the coach, and taken to the stable for water and oats. A fresh team was waiting for the onward journey. If the traveller had taken advantage of the chain of paid advice, his mail, parcels, and even bills of exchange would have been waiting, as the tavern also served as post office and a small bank. Couriers would have brought gazettes, commercial and political, so that he would have the latest information on the movements of armies, the state of shipping on the seas and great rivers, outbreaks of smallpox. Tavern fare left something to be desired, especially if our traveller had begun his journey in France or Italy. With luck he might be served perch from the river or pike from the lake, the muddiness of the latter made a little more palatable by side dishes of pickled cabbage or cucumber, spiced with fennel or caraway. In game country there might be wood pigeon (kosher) and everywhere there was salted beef and sausage. Be careful with the fruit vodka and steer clear of the brandies altogether, unless you wished to be both ill and robbed. If you were staying overnight you would be lodged in one of the large ground-floor rooms positioned each side of the entrance portico, big enough to hold at least one Dutch stove, a bed and a mirror. In these lodgings the ceiling would be plastered; the floor was stone, possibly covered with a rug or two or at least straw, and a decent number of windows for light and air. The landlord and his family – most often very extended, and including the husbands of his daughters along with their children, and less commonly the wives of his sons and their children – would be living on the first floor divided into ten rooms or more, lit by many smaller windows looking onto the street. The Jews married young (sixteen for a girl was common, betrothal as early as eleven or twelve), so that by the custom of *kest* they moved in with the in-laws for many years. Another storey up would be the servants' quarters, many sharing still smaller rooms. The cold cellars stored winter foods, those ubiquitous pickles but also the staples of the Ashkenazi kitchen: smoked and dried fish, sausages, meat preserved in goose fat, sour cream, hard and soft cheeses, casks of wine, chests of black Turkish tobacco and barrels of rye vodka.[23] The bigger, better places would be surrounded by thatched outbuildings, added on as need arose – stables, warehouses and carriage-repair shops (and on Polish roads, small shops and stalls, breweries and distilleries, and custom-built *sukkahs*, booths with a detachable roof for the autumn festival of Sukkot).

For the Jews, even if it was just to brew stomach-scouring scummy ale and mead or distil rotgut brandy, the tavern was the un-synagogue, but no less central to the life of the community for that. And they were places where Jews and Christians were constantly in each other's company. It was once assumed, not least by Gentiles, who supposed that there was something suspicious about the reputed sobriety of Jewish innkeepers, that their abstemiousness was all part of a plot to incapacitate Christian drinkers who thus became the slaves of the Jews. This was an ancient paranoia going all the way back to medieval fantasies of Jewish doctors and bankers holding Gentile rulers in their thrall through the copious administration of drugs and drink. The Ottoman emperor Selim the Sot was supposed to have become the creature of Joseph Nasi in just this way. But there is plenty of anecdotal evidence to suggest that the Jews of Poland–Lithuania were not invariably models of temperance. Hasidic rabbis were known to wink at or even encourage festive imbibing. Followers of the 'founder' of Hasidism, Israel ben Eliezer, thought it an attribute of his holiness that he was able to consume imposing amounts of alcohol en route to celestial ascents without ever getting drunk or at least feeling the worse for wear. Another famous Hasidic rabbi, Schneur Zalman of Lyady, described hard liquor (usually vodka) as 'the wine of the land', as if it were something over which a blessing was to be recited like the Sabbath cup.[24] Predictably the adversaries of the ecstatic Hasidim, both the austerely Talmudist *mitnagdim* ('opponents') and the modern-minded *maskilim* ('the enlightened'), parodied Hasidic mystical epiphanies as drunken vapours. Levi Isaac of Berdichev was said by his critics to 'drink up a river'. The story of the 'Seer of Lublin', attempting to urinate from an open window, falling from it 'before he finished relieving himself, flesh still in his hand', and dropping into a pile of excrement, turned into a favourite satire of Hasidic bibulousness, though the Hasidim themselves reworked the episode as an elaborate parable of visionary fall.[25]

If the tavern keeper should happen to be partial to a drop of his own hard stuff, his wife and daughters who bartended and often kept the accounts were obliged to make sure they had their wits about them at all times. (Women were an integral, indispensable part of Jewish business, some mothers even going on the road to markets and fairs and taking their daughters with them.) But the bigger taverns like Beirish Kova's at Poritzk in Volhynia, a grand establishment with an iron-gated seventy-foot front on the street, was such a bustling multi-purpose institution, packed with travelling merchants, clerks, soldiers and petty officials, that it needed full-time management.[26] At such houses, many of them given names like 'Little Dove', marriages were hatched and matched; cards and billiards played; bets laid and settled (a huge part of their business); medicines supplied for those who were worse for wear; loans and business contracts signed, sealed and witnessed; wedding entertainments catered for Jews and non-Jews alike, since there were no musicians as good as the cimbalon and fiddle virtuosi (later called klezmorim), especially those who had come north-west from the heartland of the genre: Wallachia and Moldavia. The stand-up *badkhan* could try out his jokes, singers and fiddlers could audition, and it was not completely unknown for women to be made available to the soldiers, smugglers and counterfeiters who would mingle in the warming fug along with more respectable types.[27]

Into these taverns, every so often, would come a lordly invasion, booted and spurred, on the way to or from a hunt. Solomon Maimon saw this with his own eyes not once but twice. While he was still a child, a Radziwill princess, on a noontime break from the hunt, came to his grandfather's tavern along with her ladies-in-waiting. The lad 'gazed with rapture at the beauty of the persons and at the dresses trimmed with gold and silver lace; I could not satisfy myself with the sight'. 'Little fool,' said his father, 'in the next world the *duksel* [princess] will kindle the *peezsure* [stove] for us.' Little Solomon immediately felt sorry for the beautiful princess forced to light fires for the likes of himself.[28] Years later, when he was living with his wife in his tough mother-in-law's tavern, there was a more dramatic incursion. The Radziwill hetman himself, Karol II Stanislaw, master of a private army of 10,000 men, a byword for drunken extravagance, en route from his yellow baroque palace in nearby Nesvizh to Milhany – accompanied by the usual mobile entourage of sixty coaches, companies of wigged and powdered toy soldiers, infantry, cavalry, artillery, *streltsi* body-guards, drummers, trumpeters, Negro pages, valets, cooks and kitchen wagons – had become so much the worse for wear from Hungarian tippling that he needed a bed right away, even if it fell short of princely standards, the linen unchanged and the mattress 'crawling with bugs'.[29] Come the brutal dawn the hetman had no idea how he happened to be in the tavern, but rather than take out his hangover on the Jews (and this was an aristocrat whose favourite pastime, after hunting, was smashing up synagogues), he decided to make the most of the place. An impromptu banquet was ordered in situ. 'In a miserable pub whose walls were black as coal with smoke and soot, whose rafters were supported by undressed log ends, whose windows consisted of broken panes of bad glass and small strips of pine covered with paper – in this house princes sat on dirty benches at a still dirtier table and had the choiciest dishes and finest wines served to them on gold plate.'

This was a Lithuanian whim, but for an aristocrat like Karol Radziwill, sentimental in his velvet and fur about the Old Ways and Days, the bison hunt and the battles with the Tatars, the Jews were part of the centuries-old scenery. In a peculiar way, they belonged. So even when the nobles in their cups bellowed that they were being sucked dry by the parasite Jews, they freely acknowledged that they couldn't do without them. This recognition often (though not always) led them to resist the demands of the more anti-Semitic clergy and urban burghers, throughout the eighteenth century, for their mass conversion or expulsion.[30] When the Bishop of Lwów, Jan Skarbak, dismayed by the sheer growth of numbers of Jews, sent a pastoral letter in 1717 complaining that their numbers 'uprooted Christians but [they] are protected by our nobles', the protest fell on deaf ears. Other matters of scandal to the Church – Jewish celebrations, sometimes public, during Lent; the participation of Christian musicians in Jewish processions; the employment of Christian servants by Jews – were all similarly ignored. When a bishop presumed to seal up a synagogue for some imagined offence, the magnate ordered its reopening or else. The magnates did business with the Jewish Council of the Four Lands (and the regional councils and their representatives or *shtadlans*) until it was abolished in 1764; they recognised that legal disputes between Jews and non-Jews could not be settled without consulting rabbinical courts, and that the killing of a Jew in one of their towns was to be treated as a capital crime. In 1746 in Zolkiew, a Potocki town, a miller convicted for murdering a Jew was hanged for the crime, and his decapitated head stuck on the wall as a warning to malefactors.

This relationship was born from pragmatic need rather than mutual sympathy, although it didn't preclude moments of genuine cordiality. Jews had first come in numbers to Poland and Lithuania in the thirteenth century, fleeing from violent persecutions in the German lands. Others were descendants of Jews anciently settled in countries west of the Caucasus and along the Black Sea, who found themselves in lands of Slavic conquest as the frontiers of the Tatar empires retreated eastwards.[31] Jews had been invited to settle in these conquered lands for the same reasons that motivated all late-medieval and Renaissance princes on the make: the provision of capital to fund a warrior kingdom as it colonised lands vacated by the defeated; and the common truism that whatever disagreeable characteristics they might bring with them, the Jews could be depended on to implant a commercial culture in territories as yet untouched by long-distance trade; or to put it another way, Jews made towns. But Poland was distinctive in being a Catholic country in which the objections of the Church were seldom allowed to override economic opportunism. From the beginnings of intensive Jewish settlement in the thirteenth century the Polish Crown went out of its way to offer incentives. Bolesław the Pious, from whom the first invitation came in 1264, made it clear the Jews might live a life of open worship unmolested while maintaining their own communal self-government. Following the 1569 Union of Lublin, when the Grand Duchy of Lithuania was joined to the Kingdom of Poland, the contrast with the oppression of the western Counter-Reformation was glaring. A fable of origins had the rabbis realising that the words 'Poh-Lin' ('Settle Here') meant the country was uniquely auspicious. This was not quite the case, but the optimism was understandable. In a striking divergence from anywhere else in either the Christian or Muslim world they were allowed to carry arms. They were exempt from many taxes, but in return were required to produce an annual sum for the royal treasury, the amount negotiated by delegates from their Council of the Four Lands. The council then met to distribute the assessment between its regions, and devolve the responsibility for collection to local councils.

Decentralised power was benign for the Jews. In the Dutch republic it enabled them to take advantage of opportunities offered by particular cities and provinces. A bidding war – like the one waged between Rotterdam and Amsterdam – could only help them. Poland–Lithuania was a kingdom in name only. Its real rulers were the twenty-odd dynasties of landowning magnates. They elected the monarch in the *sejm* assembly, where a veto by just one of the deputies could thwart any kind of Crown action. Hence the indifference of many of the sovereigns to their own kingdom. Augustus III, also Elector of Saxony, who came to the throne in 1733 after a bitter war of succession, spent just three of the thirty years of his reign actually in Poland–Lithuania. In contrast, the nobles were sovereigns in their own lands, the owners of immense, widely dispersed feudal estates, but more significantly for the Jews, over half the towns in the commonwealth were also their private property. This extreme devolution, running against all the norms of state-building in the baroque age, had come about as Polish kings attempted to hold together military coalitions capable of fending off the powers who kept coming at the overextended realm to bite off slices of territory: Turks, Tatars, Muscovites, Swedes. The only defence was to keep the great nobles happy, and that meant living with their inordinate power. In the end the policy of dispersed sovereignty would be as self-defeating for the nobles as for the monarchy they were notionally meant to uphold. In an age when armies were growing exponentially, and the finances to fund them had to be raised by centralised bureaucracies, the Polish anomaly was doomed to become a creature of its more powerful neighbour states. When belatedly the Polish ruling class including the monarchy woke up to this fatal weakness and attempted to reform its constitution and assert its independence, it was subjected to military bullying by its predatory neighbours, calculated to maintain Polish weakness. Efforts to assert a stronger sovereignty triggered cynically coordinated partition in 1772 and 1793 which swallowed up Poland between Prussia, Habsburg Austria and tsarist Russia. A final burst of romantic rebellion in 1794 finished free Poland off.

For the million and a quarter Jews of Poland–Lithuania, the post-partition future would be uncertain. But Poland–Lithuania in its earlier heyday presented them with opportunities on which they made good. For generations the Jews became the enablers of magnate grandeur. Some of them like Szmuijlo Ickowitz actually held office as the 'cashier' of Anna Radziwill. Ultimately the extravagance of the lives led by the Potockis, the Branickis, the Zamoyskis, the Czartoryskis and the rest was unsustainable, but for a century or so, thanks to the Jews it took on a spectacular style. When Elzbieta Sieniawska felt short of diamonds she went to Mojzesz Fortis for a top-up. The great dynasts all maintained private armies officered by foreign mercenaries. Their mounts were known to be among the most magnificent hunters in Europe. They built or rebuilt palaces of shocking opulence. Along one wall of their interminable galleries, pop-eyed stags fell to ravening lions; whiskery ancestors seated on crop-tailed stallions glared at intruders. On the other wall, high windows looked onto avenues of elm; rush-fringed ponds choked with thrashing carp. House orchestras played in their salons; their buffoons brought the house down in the theatres while princesses fanned their décolletage. On their banqueting tables were centrepieces created by master confectioners, usually French. A wolf baring its teeth or a displaying peacock dominated the table while goblets filled with Dov Ber Birkenthal's best Tokaj glowed with reflected candlelight.

The bills were steep. The Polish palatial life could be supported, just about, by proceeds from the grain harvested on their many estates, as long as the rest of Europe was in short supply. The Jews would bring the rye and wheat to market and the Dutch would ship the substantial surplus to the hungry west. But in the eighteenth century those terms of trade reversed themselves despite increasing population throughout Europe. Improvements in productivity in England and some of the German lands meant shrinking demand and falling prices. The monetisation of estates had to be urgently recalculated. As the international market for grain shrank, surplus rye, in particular, was taken up by the domestic production and sale of grain alcohol, for the age of potato-based vodka had not yet dawned (though it was not far off). Once again the Jews were on hand to transform the liability of a monoculture into a stupendous marketing opportunity. Not only would they pay for the lease of monopoly rights to manufacture and sell alcohol on Sieniawski or Branicki lands and in Zamoyski or Potocki towns, but they would actually bid against each other for the privilege. The new system of monetising grain, based on universal sozzlement, proved a spectacular success. Characteristically over half the revenue of the magnate estates came from the proceeds of the alcohol leases alone, and the bands played on. The toy armies continued to parade; the great hunts of bison and stag cantered through the woodlands; the candelabra were snuffed at dawn and curtains carefully parted as footmen crept about the slumped bodies of their betters. All was as it should be in Polonia Magna.

The marriage of convenience between the magnates and the Jews produced a great flowering, at least demographically. From around 50,000 in the early sixteenth century, the Jewish population multiplied exponentially on a scale unparalleled in documented Jewish history.[32] There were between 80,000 and 100,000 in 1600, double that by the last third of the seventeenth century, and the numbers nearly quadrupled yet again in the century that followed to 750,000 in Poland alone by 1800 (another 250,000 in Lithuania). Despite the ravages of smallpox the population of almost every region of Europe was expanding fast in the eighteenth century, but the Jewish rate of natural increase far outstripped that of non-Jewish Poles. While population historians are hesitant to identify one overriding cause of this spectacular explosion of numbers, most of them attribute the growth to early marriage, customary among the Ashkenazim, presumably together with a lowering of the age of sexual maturity, usually associated with better nutrition (though a diet of poached carp, pickled herring and egg challah as the root cause of a demographic revolution gives one pause). It is clear that a significant drop in infant mortality occurred among the Ashkenazim of Poland–Lithuania during the eighteenth century. Social historians speculate that the *kest*, together with the attendant care that extended families provided, might have something to do with it. Though the charity records of the communities from one end of Poland–Lithuania to the other make it clear that there were multitudes of Jews living in severe poverty, it is still extraordinary that the vast rise in their numbers did not lead to the kind of mass impoverishment which would in fact develop in Ukraine a century later.

The time-tested social institutions of the *kehillah* (congregation)
must have helped. Though the governing *kahal* was a local oligarchy,
almost always consisting of the better-off members of a community,
this did not preclude it taking its responsibilities seriously. It made
sure that the infirm and the indigent would be cared for, the ritual
slaughterers, the beadles, the circumcisers and the cantors would all
do their work as expected. People driven from one town to another
by misfortune of one kind or another would expect to find in their
new place of abode or asylum the usual: synagogues big and small;
Hebrew schools and houses of study; a rabbinical court which could
adjudicate grievances and disputes.

This does not mean that shtetls were immune to contention and
shock. And the greatest of all such shocks arrived in Podolia in the
middle of the eighteenth century and very nearly broke Polish Jewry
altogether.

II. A Wild Night in Lanckoronie

A traveller arriving in Satanow in the late spring of 1756 would have
found himself in the middle of a hair-raising scandal. The Beit Din
– the rabbinical court of the district – was sitting in the Great
Synagogue, investigating reports that Podolia, their corner of it in
particular, was thick with secret Shabbeteans: unrepentant disciples
of the false Messiah Shabbetai Zevi. The cult had not died with its
embodiment. On his death in 1676, his fourth and last wife, Jochabed,
had declared his spirit – which is to say the essential Shabbetai – had
been translated into the person of her brother, Jacob Querido. Taking
the name Jacob Zevi, Querido founded the sect of the Donmeh,
ostensibly Muslim but continuing to perpetuate the principles and
practices of the cult: the supercession of Moses' Torah by Shabbetai's
law, the conscious violation of the old commandments as a way of
proclaiming their redundancy. The Donmeh numbered some hundreds
in Salonika, some of them, like Hayim Melech, recruited from the
dispirited ranks of those who had gone to Jerusalem in 1700 with
Judah Ha-Hasid. After Querido died during the haj to Mecca, his son

Berachiah claimed to be the latest reincarnation, and presided over the Donmeh in Salonika.

It was there, around 1750, that Jacob Leibovich, who would otherwise have been an inconsequential Podolian caravaneer, came into contact with the Donmeh Shabbeteans. His father Leib, who seems to have been one of the keepers of the flame, had his own unorthodox views of sin. On being told that little Jacob had gone swimming on the Sabbath he asked the boy if this was true. Just floated, came the reply; well, *nu*, said the indulgent father, no sin at all. Leib took his family across the border into Ottoman Moldavia–Wallachia when Jacob was still a child so that the boy grew up along a route map of surviving Shabbeteanism: Smyrna, Sofia, Salonika. Entering adulthood, Jacob became intrigued enough to visit the tomb of Nathan of Gaza in Skopje, Macedonia; became known to the Turks as 'Jacob Frank' (Jacob the Westerner); and after marrying in 1752, became convinced that he was without question the latest incarnation of Shabbetai. In 1755 Jacob Frank crossed the border into Podolia to make contact with followers.

He arrived at a time of great crisis and consternation when one of the most respected rabbinical authorities, Jacob Emden, was publicly accusing another of the same eminence, Jonathan Eybeschutz, of being a secret Shabbetean himself, on the strength of reports that the latter had been distributing dubious amulets, a sure sign of the heresy. Though Eybeschutz denied this at the time, it was probably true but not of itself damning. Amulets were a regular feature of the 'practical Kabbalah' that could cure impotence, barrenness and most of what might ail you. Yet until Frank's arrival upset the apple cart, the Council of the Four Lands had declined to take up Jacob Emden's demand that they launch a campaign to root out Shabbeteans from the house of Judaism. Instead, the council was prepared to let underground Shabbeteanism stay that way rather than risk fracturing the community.

But at the end of January 1756, something happened in the small town of Lanckoronie on the Moldavian border which ruled out an expedient solution. On the night of 27–28 January, someone had peered through the gaps in drapes covering the windows of a certain house and spied a group of twelve to fifteen men, including Jacob Frank himself, singing and dancing in a Shabbetean ritual. Many of the accounts, written up much later, reported that song and dance was the least of it. Jacob Emden, writing just four years on, and in a prosecutorial vein, had a more colourful story to tell. But his account was supported by that of a local Christian canon dating from only a year after the scandalous event. They described the local rabbi's wife, seated as if on a throne, either half or fully naked (depending on the account) wearing a Torah crown on her head. Every so often the men dancing in a circle about her would stop and kiss her breasts, calling her their *mezuzah* – the miniature tablet fixed to Jewish doorposts containing verses from the Torah. The ritual was obviously based on Shabbetai's own notorious 'wedding' to the Torah, enacted under a canopy in the Smyrna synagogue during Hanukkah in which he took the mystic marriage of Jews with the Torah literally. During the processing of the Sefer Torah in synagogue before and after readings, it is customary to touch the covered scrolls with the fringe of a worshipper's prayer shawl and kiss it. At Lanckoronie, the 'Torah bride' had been replaced by an actual bride, notwithstanding her marriage to the rabbi. Jacob Frank's style was to turn matters from the poetic to the physical. Some reports also claimed that the orgiasts had worn the cross around their necks.

The scandal immediately spread beyond the Jewish community. This was partly Jacob Emden's doing since, exasperated by the complacency of the Council of the Four Lands, he had begun to make the case to the Church that both religions faced a common threat of immoral violations of 'natural law'. This opening to the Church was to have terrible consequences. For the moment, local authorities were called in, and arrested the Shabbeteans, who were thrown into prison. As an Ottoman subject, Frank himself was allowed to return over the border. The chief rabbi of Satanow, in whose jurisdiction the outrage had taken place, was asked to go to Lanckoronie to investigate, but pleaded illness and sent one of the elders instead. After inquiries began to reveal a whole network of Shabbeteans throughout Podolia, the Satanow Beit Din was convened to judge the seriousness and extent of the heresy.

It heard from twenty-seven persons, most of them witnesses rather than accused Shabbeteans, but there were some among the latter who confessed to startling transgressions. Samuel of Busk owned up to eating pork and cheese on bread during Passover, thus contriving a compound violation of kashrut and the feast of unleavened bread. Others were said to have consumed tallow and forbidden sinew fat – a sign to some of their allegiance. That was not the worst of it. The most characteristic crimes of the cult were sexual. There had been cases of public masturbation in religious study halls. (The deliberate spilling of semen was regarded in Jewish law as a more serious transgression than adultery. Rabbis agonised over whether nocturnal emissions – *keri* – were innocent or culpable.) Followers of Frank had sought out menstruating women, preferably married to someone else, with whom to have intercourse. Incest was said to have been declared permissible, with daughters, daughters-in-law, and even mothers. Most common were cases of husbands offering their wives to strangers as 'hospitality'. One of the women who had taken it on herself to sleep with a stranger reported her husband's fury that she had done so without his specific permission. At the conclusion of the proceedings in the middle of June 1756, a *herem* excommunication was passed on the miscreants, most dramatically on Joseph of Rohatyn who was given the same punishment as Uriel da Costa – the thirty-nine lashes and laid at the threshold of the synagogue so that members of the congregation could tread on him as they exited. He was ordered to divorce the wife who had slept with strangers on his instructions, his children were declared bastards, and he was banished, to be sent as a criminal wanderer out into the wilderness.

Everything escalated fast. Embittered by their harassment, the Frankists took a leaf out of Jacob Emden's book, calling on the intervention of the Church. Rehearsing the accusation of the medieval friars (many of them converted Jews) that rabbinical Judaism had usurped the true authority of the Torah with the Talmud, they appealed to one of the most Judaeophobic of the Catholic clergy, Mikulaj Dembowski, Bishop of Kamieniec, for a disputation between themselves and the 'Talmudists'. In a document eagerly endorsed by conversionist clergy, the Frankists suggested a convergence between their own version of Judaism and Christianity. God, they stated, could be understood as having three indivisible essences; and could take human form. Since the Messiah had already come, the Jews waited for him in vain and Jerusalem would not be rebuilt until the end of history. Delighted to take advantage of the Frankist overture, Dembowski agreed to a disputation which took place at Kamieniec in September 1756. Forty rabbis were summoned to attend to debate nineteen Frankists, some of whom came from Satanow. The old accusations were recycled: that the rabbis had fabricated a spurious 'oral law' and that they, the 'anti-Talmudists', were the true heirs of Moses even as they insisted the Torah had actually been made redundant by the coming of the Messiah. Dembowski unsurprisingly proclaimed the Frankists the winners, and declared the revelations coming out of Lanckoronie and Satanow to be vicious slanders concocted by the rabbis and elders. This time it was the rabbis who were whipped. Jews were ordered to hand over any copies of the offending Talmud or associated works they had in their possession, and just as occurred four centuries earlier, those books were burned by the public executioner.

Dembowski died in November 1757 and the Frankists were suddenly without their protector. Many of them hastily disappeared over the border and it looked as though the traditional rabbinic institutions and authorities would be fully restored. The reprieve proved to be premature. Another Jew-hating cleric, Bishop Kajetan Soltyk, issued a document arguing that not only were the accusations of ritual murder committed by the Jews true, but that for the first time *Jews*, which was to say the anti-Talmudists, had unequivocally confirmed this. Appallingly, the Frankists had done just that. Four years before, Soltyk had become an important force in the Church hierarchy by orchestrating a blood-libel trial in Zhitomir, as a result of which eleven Jews were executed and thirteen subject to forced conversion. Subsequently, questions had been raised concerning Soltyk's personal honesty, but the Frankists' attack on the Talmudist rabbis shifted attention away from those suspicions. The king, Augustus III, became involved, issuing a three-month safe conduct for an elated Jacob Frank, who returned to Poland together with a troop of followers.

The stakes were raised still higher. For while at Kamieniec the Frankists had presented themselves as a third way – a version of Jews who accepted some doctrines they argued were common to the real Judaism and Christianity – and now they stood forth unambiguously as prospective converts. They only asked that as Christians they might continue to wear Jewish dress, beards and sidelocks, and observe Saturday as the Sabbath, all requests which might have raised eyebrows in the diocese and probably did. A second supplication from the

Frankists even included, at its end, one of the most malignant of Christian accusations: that the Talmud actually required observant Jews to use Christian blood for its rituals. The unspeakable document was immediately translated into Polish and distributed in an edition of two thousand. A second show disputation was to be convened at Lwów Cathedral in the summer of 1759.

Into this lurid nightmare rode Dov Ber Birkenthal, the wine trader of Bolechow. It had been a dreadful time for him and his family. While he had been in Warsaw on business, one of the most ferocious gangs of *opryzniki* – mounted outlaws – had ridden into Bolechow bent on plundering and sacking the town, meaning the Jews. As was often the case the Jews had put up a valiant fight, and Rebbe Nahman, a gun in either hand, killed one of the bandits and wounded another in the foot, before being axed to death. This was the raid in which both Dov Ber's wife Leah and his sister-in-law Rachel were stripped of their jewels. After murdering those who resisted or refused to take them to the treasures, the gang set fire to Bolechow and rode out of town skirts flying, for they had dressed themselves in the fanciest items they could find in the women's wardrobes. The bandit with the wounded foot added insult to injury by wearing the long prayer garment, embroidered with silver thread, that had belonged to Dov Ber's brother. Other ritual garments were used to make the banners which fluttered behind their horses' manes as they galloped off.

This was bad enough, but now Dov Ber found himself at the centre of a nerve-racking scene of public theatre. The chief rabbi of the region, Hayim Ha-Cohen Rapaport, who had been assigned the burden of refuting the blood libel and the rest of the Frankist–Christian accusations, was an old friend, and Dov Ber, who was fluent in Polish, offered to interpret for him. Most likely it was Dov Ber who came up with the idea of having the rabbi cite one of Ber's favourite sources – the English Catholic Humphrey Prideaux's insistence in his 1716 book that there was no evidence whatsoever that Jews were required by their religion to spill Christian blood. The persistence of the monstrous slander had exercised Dov Ber for some time. A new edition of the viciously anti-Semitic priest and theologian Jacob Radlinski's Polish book *The Truth ... according to Samuel Rabin*, rehearsing all the ancient calumnies, had seen the light of day in 1753 and had become immediately popular. 'The book', Dov Ber wrote, 'abounds in mistakes and shameful falsehoods which are not worth writing down or quoting to reasonable people.' The lunatic lies, Dov Ber said, 'in which they malign and slander the Jewish people and our holy Oral Law ... I read with grief in my heart but I acquired much knowledge of their doctrines ... the fables and miracles in which they believed ... such things which never existed'.[33]

Perhaps, Hayim Ha-Cohen and Dov Ber thought, it was better that the Shabbeteans be excised from the body of Judaism so there should be no confusion between false and true Jews. But that outcome (also the dread of Jacob Emden) had already been anticipated by the Frankists' own eagerness to embrace the cross. The most urgent task was to counter-attack against an apparently Jewish confirmation of the blood libel. An appeal by the rabbis through the papal nuncio in Warsaw along the lines that the Shabbetean heresy was an immoral threat to all natural law and decency, and that the stories of Jewish blood rites were a despicable fabrication, did have effect. Or perhaps it was the intervention of the interpreting wine trader and his impressive breadth of reading which did the trick. For although the Frankists were again judged to be vindicated by the Bishop of Lwów, the blood accusation was declared unproven. Nonetheless the rabbi had to endure the Frankists shouting at him, 'Hayim. Blood for blood!'[34]

The civil war could only have one theatrical ending: a mass apostasy of nearly a thousand Frankists at Lwów Cathedral. Jacob Frank himself received baptism elsewhere, with the king, through a proxy, standing as his godfather. Initially, as with Shabbetai's Muslim years, he was treated with princely largesse, but after questions had been raised about the sincerity of his conversion Frank was taken to Czestochowa, the centre of a cult of the Virgin, whose mystical sanctity he transferred to his daughter Ewa. Others among the Lwów converts were acclaimed and even ennobled. But for the Jews of Poland–Lithuania the fact that the apostasy had taken place voluntarily was a violent body blow. More shocks lay ahead. In 1764 the Council of the Four Lands was abolished. Four years later Cossack troops mutinied once more against the nobility, and slaughtered the Jews of Uman where they stood or ran. 'They filled the whole town with corpses,' a horrified observer wrote, 'the deep well in the market-place was filled with the bodies of dead children. The peasants robbed and killed Jews and their children.'[35]

The mass murder of 1768 was familiar. The spectacle of the mass apostasy at Lwów Cathedral in 1759 was not. The Kabbalist, healer and mystical visionary Israel ben Eliezer – known as the Baal Shem Tov, the Master of the Good Name – who died the following year in 1760 in the Podolian town of Mezhybozhe, was said to have expired of heartbreak as a result. Whether or not this was true, the Baal Shem Tov apparently believed that the excision of the Shabbeteans from the body of Judaism had been an unnecessary calamity; and that they might have been brought back to the fold. He blamed the elders, the rabbis, the council; all of them. If the Jews were to endure, if Judaism was to prosper, it must be less aridly legalistic. The spirit must reign along with the law. The fleshly body, given by the Creator, ought to be embraced with joy, not mortified by ascetic sourness. Quite astonishingly, over the next half-century this belief came to animate a great movement of Jewish revival: Hasidism. The guardians of the rabbinic tradition who had seen off one threat were about to face another, all the more formidable for being immune to any charge of heresy.[36]

III. The Man in White Satin

They were not like other Jews. They were not like other rabbis; some of them were not even rabbis at all. But they had a gift for seeking and finding the divine sparks which had fallen when the primordial vessels shattered and the descending lights had become trapped within the husks of the *qelippot*. There had always been magic mystics among the Jews who apprehended the world and its Creator in secret, profound ways. They could see across immense distances so that the remotest lands were beheld in the neighbouring room. They could exorcise demons who had slid into the body of a woman or a man and taken up lodging there. Once they had expelled those demons from the impotent, he would be virile, and the writhing, barren woman would bear fruit. The irresistibly rank smell of Lilith, poisoned jasmine, would be gone; the same was true of a field which lay year after year obstinately infertile. A house too might have admitted demons through its chimney or the slightest crack in a windowpane.

Before Szmuijlo Ickowitz, the all-powerful cashier of the Radziwills, would cross the threshold of his spanking new mansion in Lithuania he called on Israel ben Eliezer of Mezhybozhe to rid it of any malicious spirits and pronounce it fit for habitation.[37] The Baal Shem travelled many miles to perform that prophylactic exorcism in person, but when such journeys proved impossible he might send an amulet or instructions. Joel, the Baal Shem of Zamosc, likewise instructed a childless husband to take a sword known to have killed a man and, at dawn on a Tuesday or Friday, slice an apple in two. One half was to be given to his wife, the other eaten by himself, after which they would be blessed with fruit. Everything depended on the Baal, the Master, manipulating the letters which formed the names of the Almighty, the Ein Sof, the infinite one, in such a way as to make the rearrangement therapeutic. This was dangerous, forbidden to all but the guardians of esoteric knowledge. So the healers were known as the Masters of the Name, and after his death Israel ben Eliezer, the most renowned and revered of the saintly manipulators, came to be known as the Master of the Good Name, the Baal Shem Tov, or in the way the Jews had with acronyms for the revered dead, the Besht.

Though the Besht became glorified as the founder of the new Hasidism, during his lifetime he was quite unaware of founding anything at all.[38] Such attributes would be left to his disciples and the disciples of the disciples who many decades later would anthologise stories of his wonder-working wisdoms in *Shivhei Ha-Besht* (*In Praise of the Besht*). He had better things to do than seek apostles, though a group of mystics did gather round him in Mezhybozhe. Evidently Israel ben Eliezer felt the weight of the world pressing down hard on the Jews like a grindstone about his neck: the terrible lies of blood sacrifice, the eruption of plagues and wars. What he knew for sure was that his gifts were worthless if they could not somehow help liberate the sparks; bring the Shekhina, the divine female emanation, into the presence of the afflicted Jews to lighten their burden. He felt this not from any grandeur but from a sense of inescapable responsibility, the grave onus of the visionary. Only through the likes of him could *shefa*, abundance, be brought down and poured out as balm for his suffering people.

In 1752 Israel ben Eliezer wrote to his brother-in-law Gershon Kutower (who, five years before, had gone to the Land of Israel) that on the eve of Rosh Hashanah he had made an ascent into the celestial realm.[39] There he had beheld a vast host of souls, belonging to those who were alive and those who were not, thrashing back and forth in uncountable multitudes. He had seen forced converts brought to violent ends and things that gave him great joy, although he could not quite explain the latter. At first he had supposed that this surge of happiness was a sign that he would shortly be departing the earth for the world to come, but he was told, no, he must stay, because those on high took such pleasure in his 'unifications' of the upper and lower realms. Two momentous encounters during the ascent made him understand why he was so transported. The first had been with the Evil Side, satanic Sama'el himself, who had engineered the violent deaths of the converts and who on being asked by the Besht why, said, a little disingenuously (but then he was the Evil Side), so that the righteous would be able to Sanctify the Holy Name through their suicide. The Baal Shem Tov rose higher and higher until, 'step by step', he reached the summit palace of the Messiah. The inevitable question was posed. Why so long, already? 'When your Torah is spread throughout the world,' the Messiah said, 'then I will come' – a not altogether satisfactory answer.

It was not until 1781 that the letter was published as 'The Holy Epistle'. Long before that, the visionary reputation of the Baal Shem Tov had been established by two of his disciples, Jacob Joseph of Polonnoye and Dov Ber ben Abraham of Mezeritch. Hasidic books first saw the light of day in 1776, but it was Jacob Joseph's *Toledot Yakob Yosef* appearing in 1780 which set out the essence of the new temper as he claimed the Besht had wished it. Provided it was engaged in *kavanah* – utter devotion – prayer was ultimately more important than study. The mind is all very well but the soul is the essence; let it be open to God. For remember that God inhabits the whole universe; the merest nook and cranny are brimful of His presence. And since that is the case avoid melancholy and the mortifications of the flesh which bring it on. Do not fast more than the Torah requires. The Shekhina, even in exile, walks in joy not sorrow. Our bodies are not, as some seem to think, prisons for the soul, to be beaten and wasted until its walls are so thin the spirit may break out. That was not it at all, thought the Besht. God gave us bodies for the delight of life. Acceptance, not rejection, of our fleshly selves was the way to blessing.

This was all good news, and there came a time when Solomon Maimon was much in need of it. He had long wished for something deeper from Judaism than a mere calendar of ritual observance. He hungered for beliefs that were philosophically more nutritious than the desiccated fare which was all that the relentless, legalistic scrutiny of the Torah and its innumerable commentaries seemed to offer. ('For example, how many white hairs could a red cow have and still remain a red cow?'[40]) It was then, as he put it in his memoirs, that he 'went on pilgrimage to "M" [the town of Mezeritch]' and beheld the man in white satin, the disciple who had been accepted as the Besht's successor: Dov Ber, the Maggid, the Preacher.

Solomon looked back on his early Hebrew schooling from forty years' distance, in the 1790s, when it had become an article of faith among the *maskilim*, the champions of enlightenment, that education made the man. This had not been his childhood experience in Lithuania. It was all the more galling because the lights of true learning had been glimmering on the domestic bookshelf. But his father meant his son to be a rabbi and frowned on any wayward literature that might distract Solomon from that path. Forbidden books are always irresistible, so whenever he got the chance the seven-year-old stood on a chair and pulled the Hebrew texts from the shelf. The banned items were hardly a call to arms, but they nonetheless made the act of reading a different experience from the wretchedly rote recitation of passages from the Pentateuch which was mostly what went on in the *cheders*, the religious schools. There were histories: the popularised Hebrew edition of Josephus known as the *Josippon*, full of heroic gore; the sixteenth-century Prague scholar David Gans's chronicle which introduced, alongside Jewish events, the happenings of the rest of the world. There was also Gans's book of astronomy and another in the same vein, and it was these which all at once allowed little Solomon to see the stars – not just as astrological patterns and portents but material objects suspended in the sky. And then there were the mathematical calculations in those works, beautiful and ineffably deep, which 'opened a whole new world to me'.[41]

The coming down to earth at his *cheder* in the town of Mir, four miles from the family farm at Nesvizh, was, therefore, all the more dispiriting. His first teacher was a schoolroom sadist who beat his little charges on the slightest pretext and would not hesitate to lay

about the parents too, should they have the temerity to complain. A
second teacher was less of a monster but still conformed to the grim
picture Maimon draws of 'a small smoky hut where the children are
scattered, some on benches, some on the bare earth. The master in
a dirty blouse, sitting on the table holds between his knees a bowl
into which he grinds tobacco into snuff with a huge pestle like the
club of Hercules.' In the four corners of the room, junior monitors
had the boys translate the *chumash* from Hebrew into Yiddish while
looking forward to eating the food they had thieved from the food
bundles brought by the pupils from their homes. Not only were there
no explanations or interpretations, there was no attempt to impart
Hebrew grammar, and no dictionaries from which to build a vocabulary. Minds were being shut down just as they were ready to open up.

Later, when the family fortunes had collapsed, Solomon was forced
to become an accomplice in these pointlessly mechanical exercises,
taking work as a tutor to a Jewish peasant farmer, living in rustic
squalor in a one-room lodging which

> served at the same time for sitting, drinking, eating, study and sleep.
> Think of this room intensely heated and the smoke as is generally the
> case in winter driven back by wind and rain until the whole place is
> full of it to suffocation. Here hangs the foul washing and other dirty
> bits of laundry on poles laid across the room in order to kill the vermin
> with the smoke. There hang sausages to dry while their fat keeps
> constantly trickling down on the heads of people below. Yonder stand
> tubs of cabbages and beets ... in this room the bread is kneaded,
> cooking and baking are done, the cow is milked.[42]

It seemed to Solomon Maimon, thirsty for understanding and knowledge, including self-knowledge, that he had hit rock bottom. In fact
there were worse ordeals ahead of him, including an accumulating
sense of despair that would lead him to attempt suicide – botched,
naturally. But with sausage fat dripping on his scalp, he was ready for
some sort of saving illumination. So he paid attention when an acquaintance spoke to him of a new sect of Kabbalistically inclined Jews (whom
he would misleadingly characterise as a 'secret society', for there was
nothing secret about it). The mysticism of Kabbalah, especially the
sixteenth-century version popularised by Moses Cordovero, the disciple

of Isaac Luria, had not gone away when the number of its followers had dwindled in Safed and disappeared altogether in Tiberias. It may have been an exaggeration for the great scholar of Jewish mysticism, Gershom Scholem, to claim that its printed literature – above all the *Zohar* – swept through Jewish communities in the later seventeenth century especially after the shock of Shabbetai Zevi's conversion to Islam.[43] But there is no doubt that, as Talmudic studies became ever more legalistic and nit-picking, an approach to works that claimed to unlock deeper significance behind the ostensible meaning of words exercised an extraordinary spell. For those stuck in the textual drudgery, or scholastic hair-splitting, it opened the reader to a new way of living. Just looking at Kabbalistic texts – embroidered as they were with cosmic diagrams, anagrams, vortices, webs, musical patterns, the unthreading of words into their constituent letters and sounds and their reworking into magical illuminations – was a heady experience, a kind of literary alchemy which, even if it did not ultimately remake the world as bottomless treasure chest, was a thrilling experiment. But it was entirely possible to be steeped in Kabbalah while not rejecting Talmudic studies. The Kabbalah was first and foremost a cosmology on the ways in which the dynamics of Creation continued to influence earthly experience; the Talmud was about everything else. And yet in the second half of the eighteenth century, the priority given to one or the other represented a definite choice of what kind of Jew one was.

Solomon Maimon, in his late teens sporting 'a stiff enough beard', was not yet sure about this. But he had come to the conclusion that for all its interminable ingenuity, Talmudic exegesis was, literally, pointless; that it proceeded to 'no end'. Though he was himself such an intellectual wanderer, he lived in hope of reaching a happy destination, and that would be the secure, proven knowledge of nature and a grasp of the tools of perception. In this respect he did indeed live up to the examples of his adopted namesake Maimonides and Baruch Spinoza, only less coherent, less muscular in his observations, less confident in his findings. But what he asked of Jewish learning, and at this point failed to discover, was that it help disclose the true nature of things, the things of this world, and that it should not congratulate itself on the mere agility of its performance. He also suspected, not least from his father's urgings, that Talmud study was often pursued mostly as a means to win social respect, honour and office.

Thus, after asking his friend to explain the working principles of the 'secret society' of the 'new Hasidim', Solomon Maimon decided to go see it for himself. He liked the sound of a company that had repudiated the need for relentless fasting, for he had had enough mortification of the flesh to last him a lifetime. And apparently unlike other semi-hidden groups, he was given to understand from the acolyte that 'any man who felt a desire of perfection but did not know how to satisfy it ... had nothing to do but to apply to the superiors of the society and *eo ipso* he became a member'.[44] Solomon was more suspicious of the demand for self-annihilation said to be the condition of receiving a full sense of the sanctity of life. But his friend explained that the real meaning of the verse from 2 Kings 3:15 'when the minstrel played the spirit of God came upon him' was the opposite of what it seemed. It was when the minstrel stopped being the active player and became instead the instrument (a favourite Hasidic analogy) that he received the spirit of divinity. This was the kind of wordplay that made Solomon happy.

As soon as his tutoring term was done, Maimon set off for Mezeritch in Volhynia, where Dov Ber ben Abraham had established the first Hasidic court. After the death of Israel ben Eliezer in 1760, the leadership of the new way had passed briefly to his son, but the weight of the role seems to have been too much, for he resigned and it had then fallen to Dov Ber ben Abraham, as the principal disciple, to assume the role of *maggid*. The Besht had not preached. After his death there were no sermons to publish; just stories of his deeds, going from one place to the next, from one troubled soul to the next. But Dov Ber was seldom on the road. In his youth he was said to have fasted so savagely and so often that it had wasted his body. Certainly a chronically lame left foot made it difficult if not impossible to undertake journeys. So the prospective Hasidim came to him in droves and listened to his sermons, for they were known to be marvels; keys which unlocked hidden meanings, and opened chambers of truth to all who listened. Solomon joined the throng.

Secluded for most of the week in private meditations, the Maggid emerged on the Sabbath to make a dramatic appearance. 'At length the great man appeared in his awe-inspiring form, clothed in white satin. Even his shoes and his snuffbox were white, this being among the Kabbalists the colour of grace.' The Maggid briefly acknowledged all who were there and then set to the meal, which was eaten in disconcertingly un-Jewish silence as if they were monks. After it was finished the man in white broke the silence by beginning to sing, clapping his hand to his forehead while calling on each new arrival by name and identifying their native town even though he had not been alerted to their coming. This was already impressive. When called on, the newcomers responded by shouting out a verse from the Torah to which, in each and every case, the Maggid improvised a perfect mini-sermon, again without having received advance notice of what they might choose. 'What was still more extraordinary was that every one of the newcomers believed that he discovered in the part of the sermon founded on his own verse, something that had special reference to the facts of his own spiritual life. At this we were of course astonished.'[45]

If it was all a stage trick, it worked its spell. But after some time in the company, doubts, however unworthy, began to creep into Solomon Maimon's exacting mind. Could the apparently uncanny fit between the Maggid's impromptu disquisitions and the acolyte's choice of text perhaps have been the result of a little prior research? And there was something about the relentless, obligatory merriment which began to grate. After one of the company had announced that his wife (left behind, as all wives were) had given birth to a daughter, the new father was greeted not with *mazal tovs* but with uproarious laughter and then a joke whipping for having failed to produce a boy. To his credit, this hilarity made Solomon feel sick. 'I would not stay in the place any longer. I sought the superior's blessing, took my departure from the society with the resolution to abandon it forever and returned home.'

The direction of Solomon Maimon's life would turn north and west: to the Enlightenment of Berlin, and to Königsberg, for meetings with Moses Mendelssohn and Immanuel Kant. In between those episodes, he remained a chronic wanderer; and for some time an actual beggar, with a can and worn staff, sleeping rough in his stinking rags, physically and morally degraded, subject to fits of delirium and depression.

If Solomon Maimon imagined that the Hasidim he left behind at Mezeritch would remain an esoteric cult, the next thirty years would prove him wrong. Hasidism spread like wildfire from its hearth in

Podolia and Volhynia, throughout Galicia and Ukraine, penetrating the entirety of Jewish eastern Europe, even Lithuania where it was most adamantly censured by Elijah ben Solomon, the Vilna 'Gaon', in a series of what amounted to Jewish interdicts beginning in 1772, the year of the Maggid's death. This most prodigious conquest of Jewish culture continued into the nineteenth century and knew no bounds, spreading from one end of Jewish Russia to the other, into Balkan Moldavia–Wallachia and then crossing the Atlantic with shtetl emigrants, beginning in the 1880s. Looking across the Hudson River as I write this, I can make out the Hasidic shtetls of Rockland County, New York. Neither the secularism of the twentieth and twenty-first centuries nor even the furnaces of the Holocaust could kill off Hasidism. One of the most astonishing phenomena of post-Holocaust Judaism has been the increase in Hasidic numbers, both inside and outside Israel, to the point where entire temporary towns have had to be constructed at the sites of pilgrimages of devotees to the tombs of the *zaddiks*, the Hasidic patriarchs. In 2014 it was estimated that 50,000 Hasidim (all men), mostly from Israel and the United States, assembled on the eve of Rosh Hashanah at the tomb of their *zaddik* Rebbe Nahman of Braclav, who died at Uman in 1810.

Most non-Jews, for whom one set of sidelocks is much like another, assume Hasidism to be synonymous with observant Judaism, or 'ultra-Orthodox' as it has become anachronistically known. But this is not and has never been the case. Hasidic cosmology owes almost everything to the Kabbalists of Safed – the redemption of the divine sparks of the creation from their entrapment in the base matter of the *qelippot* husks in particular – and this gives the Hasidim of Brooklyn something in common with Madonna Ciccone. But for the Ashkenazim of eastern Europe in the eighteenth and nineteenth centuries, and especially for the young who flocked to its banner in their multitudes, the 'new' Hasidism had specific, practical implications for how they lived their Judaism.

Most essentially it instructed them to set prayer above study. Not that Hasidim were or are against study – in the improvised cloisters by the Western Wall in Jerusalem it's possible to see both activities happening at the same time. But for the early generations of Hasidim it was the total absorption of *kavanah* coupled with the mystical self-dissolution that worried Solomon Maimon, which would enable the apprehension of godly presence throughout the world. When that heightened sensibility was most active, especially during night prayers, the Hasid would experience a trance-like form of exultant joy, a transport compared with which any other earthly experience would be prosaic. Should that ecstatic state recede, it could be restored by kick-starting *kavanah* through rocking, hyperventilated, self-hypnotising utterances; Maimon observed these to be merely 'mechanical' aids, but in fact they were (and are) simultaneously physical and self-dissolving in their power to take the worshipper tripping into out-of-body illumination. As Hasidism evolved, extreme swaying and rocking became controversial. Though it was said to have been recommended by the Besht, Rebbe Simcha Bunim of Przysucha disapproved of it, saying that true *kavanah* required the abandonment of bodily sensations, for the body should be treated as a mere 'bundle of straw' dragged behind the praying soul.[46] But the rockers prevailed and still do, for body motion became spiritual gymnastics, the physical way to generate devotional intensity. Somersaulting, which from the beginning was a standard feature of Hasidic worship, especially on days of rejoicing like Purim and Simchat Torah, has not lasted as well. Shocked critics described the holy acrobatics as 'clowning', while the Hasidim justified turning their rumps in the air not as an act of disrespect but its opposite: the abandonment of worldly vanity before God.

All this was done collectively, the more the merrier since collective engagement – the bliss of the crowd – was at the core of Hasidism and continues to be. It signified a Judaism which rejected the austerity of the solitary penitent, alone with his achingly deprived gut. Jacob Joseph of Polonnoye wrote that

> it used to be thought that the proper service of God was in study, fasting, weeping. When ordinary people saw they could not take up this path they were angered and disappointed thinking they had thus lost eternal life ... and this brought anger and disappointment into the world ... Until the Hasidim realised that this was wrong and taught a correct path, the path of compassion ... One need not devote all one's time to the study of the Torah but one should become involved with other human beings. In that too one can ... fulfil the commandment of being constantly aware of God's presence.[47]

All this, of course, was in sharp relief to the acrobatics of the mind at the core of traditional Talmud Torah studies. Jubilant noise, too, contrasted with the murmur of the study hall (which could, however, rise in contention). Hasidim liked to invoke the exultant music of Psalm 89 and in particular verse 15: 'Blessed is the people that know the joyful sound; they shall walk, O Lord, in the light of thy countenance.' That 'joyful sound' now went well beyond mere singing to sudden bursts of shouted exclamation, and above all to mass rhythmic clapping which first entered the rituals of observant Judaism at this time.

All this happy-clappyness – the spasms of bodily rapture; the enthronement of prayer over study; soul over mind; dream visions over scholastic arguments; the mystical self-effacement; the transports of collective joy – could be witnessed in other popular religious enthusiasms. They were present in the Great Awakening of colonial America, in the fervour of British Methodism, German Protestant Pietism, the sudden blooming of the Russian Old Believers, even in the Sufi revival in Muslim Turkey and Persia, all of which occurred around the same time. Historians of Hasidism have been quick to insist that there is no evidence whatsoever of any direct contacts or exchanges between these different sects. But while this seems true, *something* was evidently going on in the middle and late eighteenth century to produce such closely comparable phenomena. That something was demography. Falling rates of child mortality may well have made for a rise in the number of youths of both sexes comparative to the rest of the population. But since it is known that the Jewish population was increasing at a much faster rate than that of non-Jews, the result was a mass of restive young men: precisely the pool from which the Hasidim drew their rank and file.

There is no way to determine the age stratification of the early Hasidim, but anecdotal evidence from witnesses of the sudden flowering of the sect describes flocks of the young trooping or indeed sprinting (another Hasidic exercise) to the 'courts' of the *zaddiks*. When Hirsch of Zydaczow arrived in a small town, Moses Sambor described 'devotees hoping to catch a holy spark running to greet him ... youths like arrow heads flash by'.[48] So much Hasidic self-expression: the emotional intensity; the belief in visionary revelations; the physical outpourings; the fetish of walking (made to be analogous with the

wandering exile of the divine Shekhina); the estrangement from traditional community institutions whether court, school or *kahal*; the
exhilaration of a new true Judaism, made outside the traditional
order – all obviously fits the classic psychology of youth cultures so
well that it seems perverse not to see it in this light. It was neither
revolution nor rock and roll but the following of Hasidism was without
question a phenomenon of the restless, nomadic, abundant young. It
was precisely because Elijah ben Solomon thought that the future of
Judaism was at stake if impressionable youths could vulgarise the
Kabbalah into a lather of inchoate emotion rather than a disciplined
science, that his denunciations of Hasidism became so ferocious.[49]
Substituting devotion for the analytical study of the law was likewise
a terrible betrayal. There is no doubt that he and other severe critics,
like David of Makow, thought Hasidism was somehow a variant of
Shabbeteanism in the guise of histrionic piety, and should be nipped
in the bud before it flowered into a true heresy. In the year of the
Maggid's death, 1772, the Gaon got the rabbinical authorities in Vilna
to issue what to all intents and purposes was a *herem*, an excommu-
nicating ban.

But the task of marginalising Hasidism as an unorthodox, deviant
cult was made difficult by its absolute attachment to observance. Unlike
the Shabbeteans the Hasidim were not showy violators of the law. If
anything they out-observed the traditionally pious, accusing their slaughterers of lax standards in the sharpness of their blades, for example,
and refusing meat from their butchers. (Given the belief in reincarnation, a dull blade which tore at an animal, rendering it *trayf*, would
prevent its soul-blood, its *nefesh*, from entering another of God's creatures who might turn out to be a Jew![50]) The Hasidim could not be
accused of deviation from the law; just observing it with unruly zeal
and those irritating demonstrations of relentless happiness. It was a sign
of the Vilna Gaon's exasperation that when Rebbe Schneur Zalman of
Lyady came to see him to talk over their differences, Zalman had the
door slammed in his face. 'If someone says something you believe is
incorrect what shall you do?' said the Gaon, explaining his churlishness
later; 'if you continue to speak in a pleasant manner you will have
deceived them because you know in your heart that person is wrong.'[51]

Nor did it help to stigmatise one Hasidic leader when countless
more appeared in their place. They were a moving target. The Baal

Shem Tov died in 1760; the Maggid followed him in 1772, the year of the Gaon's censure. But in 1780 the Besht's other charismatic disciple, Jacob Joseph of Polonnoye (in Volhynia), published the first true Hasidic book, the *Toledot Yakob Yosef*, and the movement – as it now was – became unstoppable. Printers and publishers of Hebrew literature like the enterprising Shapira brothers at Slavuta realised very quickly that to the apparently inexhaustible demand for Kabbalistic works could be added a whole new genre of stories and tales about the saintly founding generation – the Besht and the Maggid – who themselves had published nothing. But to the grief of the conservatives, lore was fast becoming as important as law. In 1814 the *Shivhei Ha-Besht* would canonise the Besht as the founder and anthologise his works and sayings, but it also established the Maggid as his true successor and thus a leadership lineage. Dynasticism became as important for the Hasidim as it was for the Poles.

Oceans of academic ink have been spilled over the timing of Hasidism's rise. Gershom Scholem argued that it was a reaction to the debacle of Shabbetai Zevi, and to the agony of the Cossack massacres of 1648–9. But the century between these events and the beginnings of true Hasidic literature and practice make this an implausibly prolonged period of germination. In response it has been pointed out that Hasidism started at a time of social recuperation. Nor was the Baal Shem Tov a champion of the Jewish poor against the imperious oligarchy of the *kahal*. Mezhybozhe in Podolia where he settled was not a backwater hamlet but one of the largest and most prosperous towns in Jewish Poland; and in his lifetime the Baal showed not the slightest interest in casting himself as the protector of the destitute. If anything he embraced the favour of authority, both Jewish and Polish.

It is, however, possible to over-correct. If the chronology is shifted forward some decades, then it becomes unarguable that Hasidism did indeed take root in painful times. As he himself understood it, grappling with those troubles was the whole meaning of the Besht's mysterious election and his several ascents of discovery. During the last third of the eighteenth century a cascade of troubles struck the million Ashkenazim of Poland–Lithuania. It was not Shabbetai Zevi who shook the confidence of the community but Jacob Frank, since the mass apostasy of his thousand converts in 1759 had been voluntary, a spectacle the Polish Church never let the Jews forget. Nine years later, the massacre at Uman in 1768 was genuinely horrifying, and as the roving presence of Russian Cossack troops began to be a fact of life in terminally beleaguered Poland, violence could be visited on Jewish towns at any time, since that's where the booty lay. The violent disruption of the Jewish world made the poll tax harder if not impossible to collect. By 1763 the Council of the Four Lands owed the Crown 2 million zloty, with annual interest at 200,000. The breakdown of the council's primary function removed the reason for its existence, especially at a time when King Stanislaw Poniatowski was nervous about the loyalty of his nobility, not to mention his predatory, beady-eyed neighbours. A census was taken in 1764 (never a good idea with the Jews, though historians are grateful), and based on its results the government took direct control of tax assessment and collection. With the Council of the Four Lands gone, the hierarchy below them stood exposed as self-perpetuating oligarchies, doing the government's bidding to stay in power. Shtetl revolts demanded election rather than co-option to the *kahal*. In one town, a gang of youths deposed the *kahal* during a synagogue service and staged a mock funeral while they were detained. The rabbi had to call in the local police to restore order, spreading tar on the benches of the offending boys. As the Kingdom–Grand Duchy of Poland–Lithuania itself disappeared, piece by piece, partition by partition, the Jews found themselves divided territorially, first between four states (including the rump Poland) and then after 1797 into three – Prussia, Austria and Russia, each with their own views about how to treat the Jews. The Ashkenazim of Brody, now in what the Austrians called Galicia, and the Ashkenazim of Satanow in Russian Podolia were technically foreigners to each other, an estrangement somewhat mitigated by the copious flow of smuggling in each direction.

The revolutionary and Napoleonic wars, with their tides of invasions and liberations (sometimes the same thing), only accelerated this fragmentation. Polish-speaking 'enlightened' Jews in Warsaw under the command of Berek Josielowicz formed a legion to come to the defence of the city against the oncoming Russian troops of General Suvorov, and put up stiff resistance in their stronghold, the suburb of Praga. It was still possible to believe that French-style emancipation could create a new world of equal rights and patriotic duties for the Jews. As the

Napoleonic state pressed eastwards, apparently unstoppable, creating the 'Grand Duchy of Warsaw', so those hopes were rekindled, notwithstanding all the restrictions and indignities that were known to have been imposed on the Jews of France. But when the rabbis, Hasidic and non-Hasidic, met to talk over the dangerous matters of allegiance, the majority, including Rebbe Schneur Zalman, were resolute that the price of civil rights, French style, would be the loss of Jewish tradition, and put their faith in the tsar. The gamble turned out to be vindicated, though the gratitude was one-way.

The need for allegiance cuts deep, even or especially among Jews, always conscious of their vulnerability. The elaborateness of prayers offered for the Princes of Orange in the Dutch republic, for the Bourbon kings and after them the French republic and the emperor does not undercut their sincerity. The unspoken contract was protection in return for that allegiance. So when a choice of political allegiance in eastern Europe became a hazardous bet, it could instead be given to the protector *zaddik*, the righteous Hasidic patriarch, at once preacher, intercessor, visionary and worker of wonders. Elimelekh of Lezajsk was the first to so describe himself in his *Noam Elimelekh* published in 1798, eleven years after its author's death. In that work, mostly a commentary on the Pentateuch, is an explanation of the role of a *zaddik*: keeper of esoteric truths and cures, illuminator of hidden meanings, but also steward and pastor of a congregation – the indispensable conduit through which an only intermittently understandable design of God could be made available to His people. In Hasidic glosses, a crucial verse from the Book of Habakkuk declaring that a '*zaddik*, a righteous man shall live by faith' was subtly transformed by the alteration of the verb from a personal to a political vocation. The verb *yihyeh* – to live – became *yehyeh* – to revitalise, give life – thus endowing the *zaddik* with the role of bringing life through his faith (*emunah*) to all his followers.[52] 'Life' in the sense of *shefa*, abundance, was exactly what was in short supply at the end of the eighteenth century. The *zaddik*, then, was less a magus than the macroeconomist of happiness, the enabler of life, directing the precious matter to the earthly following. But that still made him, in the words of an anthology of the Maggid's teachings, 'the foundation of the world'.[53]

Described this way, the *zaddik* became the figure around whom new authority over the Jewish community crystallised. The fact that it was always supposed there were to be many (though not too many) *zaddiks* (Elimelekh's brother Zushya of Zanipol was another famed figure) meant that they could provide decentralised leadership over the vast territory of what had been the old homeland. For after 1795 Poland was no more; its remnant had been swallowed up by Russia, and the traditional *kehillah* congregation was under brutal strain.

Early nineteenth-century 'Tales of the Hasidim' literature, the product of the third generation's evangelism, promoted a mythology of homeliness and simplicity inaugurated by the biographies of the Besht. Typical was the story told about the man who, seeing the modesty of Rebbe Zushya's circumstances, slipped a little money into his phylactery bag and found to his amazement that his own supply of cash increased rather than depleted whenever he did this. Upping the ante, he thought that if he could contribute to an even bigger pillar – the Maggid himself – the proceeds might be healthier still. Needless to say when he tried it, the opposite happened. Complaining to Zushya, he was rebuked. When you gave without caring about yourself, you were blessed; when you went seeking a reward, the blessing disappeared.[54] A rich repertoire of these little homilies, parables and anecdotes, often seasoned with a peppery kind of humour, established itself around the several dynasties, along with an iconography of the *zaddiks* whose faces were known from portrait prints. Both the texts and the images were, until the Russian government forbade them, inexpensive so that they quickly became the distinctive folk literature of Hasidism, a populist canon, and in this form they still flourish, in Hebrew and Yiddish, in America, Israel and Europe. That they often resemble the narrative, *aggadic* passages of the Mishnah and the Talmud, rather than the abstract metaphysical speculations of hard-core Kabbalah, is not a coincidence. Whether by luck, instinct or calculation, Hasidic literature made itself earthy as well as heavenly; comforting rather than bullyingly didactic. It winked an eye rather than wagged a finger. And even when it turned to a more teacherly manner, the most artful of the *zaddiks* made sure their message could be easily connected to everyday experience, and could have explanatory force in bewildering times. Nahman of Braclav, for instance, asserted that every soul was constituted from good and evil substances (thus explaining, in a way reminiscent of the very earliest Jewish dualism, the appearance of terrible things in the world). There were those few – the *rasha* – entirely given over to the bad; then there were the vast majority whose lives were the battlefield between good and evil impulses. Only a very small number – the *zaddiks* – were able to draw to themselves the entirely bad matter of the world, and by force of their devotions and their ability to locate the divine sparks could they transcend and transform the base matter into goodness and abundance. Haunted by loss, terror, confusion, the spectre of expulsion, robbery, physical assault, the heroic magnetism of the *zaddik*, the sense of his being a living lightning conductor of immense and imponderable forces, the worker of *miracula* and *mirabile*, miracles and marvels, was bound to have immense appeal.

By the same token, it was exactly the pretensions of the *zaddik* to be 'the foundation of the world' that so enraged its critics, both among traditionalists and the enlightened *maskilim*, the latter trying their utmost to wean Jews from what they dismissed as childish enchantment. But the cult of the practical was not a match for the thrill of the magical-magisterial. Pilgrims continued to come, commit their allegiance and believe they had entered a state of sanctity. Occasionally Hasidic *zaddiks* like Nahman of Braclav actually went to Palestine, at least for a short while, but many of them deliberately cultivated a sense that their courts were little Jerusalems. King David dancing before the Ark was said to be the prototype for their own musical jubilations. The centre of their residence, the *kloyz*, where they gathered followers for study and prayer, was a holy of holies. The court of a great *zaddik* was as close to the Temple as most would get, but it was enough. 'When one comes to Lublin,' wrote an admirer of Yakov Yitzhak Horowitz, the Seer of Lublin, 'one imagines one is in the Land of Israel; the courtyard of the study house is Jerusalem; the study house itself is the Temple Mount; the apartment [of the *zaddik*-Seer] is the vestibule [of the Temple]; the gallery the Sanctuary; and his room, the Holy of Holies. The Shekhina herself speaks from his throat.'[55]

Surrounded by disciples and admirers, followed (literally, in the streets) by awestruck youths, the *zaddiks* of the early nineteenth century could overstep the mark, adopting a holy swagger that would have surprised both the Besht and the Maggid. Israel Friedman, the *zaddik* of Ruzhyn, built a palatial neo-baroque residence; kept a team of four white horses (some said six) to pull his coach; carefully cultivated a princely seclusion, with limited access to his person; and like his ancestor Dov Ber made the most of silent meals. Alexander Bonar said that he travelled in a procession of three carriages with hundreds of smaller carts and wagons and thousands of devotees following in the train. When he stopped at a hostelry on these progresses, star-struck students would be allowed to tiptoe in at the window to gaze upon the *zaddik's* slumbers. The princely style made the *zaddik* enemies, two of whom ended up being murdered. In 1822, Israel Friedman was accused, without much in the way of evidence, of being an accessory to the crime and imprisoned in a Russian jail for nearly two years. When he emerged he crossed the border into the Bukowina corner of Austrian Galicia at Sadagora, where his court was re-established in even greater style, complete with turrets and battlements, the *zaddik's* house in one wing, a grand synagogue at the other. The Austrian authorities quickly came to realise that the service economy which quickly grew up around the Ruzhyner *zaddik's* court had transformed a backwater into a thriving town, and resisted demands from both sides of the border to close it down.

When Leopold von Sacher-Masoch came to Sadagora in 1857, he found the *zaddik's* court in its full splendour, but being who he was paid particular attention to its women.

> We climbed up the stairs, passed an anteroom and found ourselves in a large room where the ladies of the house, the Zaddik's wife and daughters-in-law, his daughters and his nieces, were assembled. I felt as if I had been transported into the harem of the Sultan of Constantinople. All these women were beautiful, or at least pretty; both astonished and amused, they all looked at us with their big, black velvet eyes; they were all dressed in silk morning-gowns and long caftans of silk or velvet, and trimmed and lined with expensive furs: yellow and pink silk, green, red and blue velvet, squirrel, ermine, marten and sable. The women wore headbands with jewels, the girls wore long braids intertwined with pearls.[56]

The red-brick turrets remain, though the seat of the Sadagora rabbis is now in Israel. Christian Herrmann, who is photo-documenting the remains of these communities, reports that the building is surrendering to collapse. No Boris Slobodnyuk is at hand to be the hero of restoration. The *shefa* has moved on.

IV. The Boys

On a cold day in 1835, a young nobleman, illegitimate, but enough of a love child to be called *herz*, the heart of his bad papa, ran into a crowd of small boys in greatcoats. Alexander Herzen was about to start serving a sentence of banishment in Viatka, north-eastern Russia, far from the scene of his crime which had been to attend a concert in which the musician-composer Sokolovsky had, as usual, sung some disrespectful versions about his sovereign majesty, Tsar Nicholas I. To the Third Chancellery, the Sokolovsky concerts were notorious assemblies of seditious rabble-rousers. But they were useful in identifying nuisances who could be dealt with before they became dangerous. Off to Viatka then with the spoiled bastard Herzen.

The twenty-three-year-old student wondered out loud about the gaggle of little boys. They didn't look at all well, half dead in fact, with white lips and blue shadows about their sunken eyes, livid with fever, he thought. There was an officer ushering them along. 'It's an ugly business,' he replied to Herzen's enquiry, 'don't ask; it will break your heart.' And for a moment or two it would.

'You see,' the officer went on, 'they have collected a crowd of cursed little Jew boys of eight or nine years old. Whether they are taking them for the navy or what I can't say. At first the orders were to drive them to Perm, then there was a change and we are driving them to Kazan. The officer who handed them over said it's dreadful, and that's about it; a third were left on the way [the officer pointed to the earth]. Not half will reach their destinations.'

An epidemic? Herzen wondered. 'No, not epidemics, but they just die off like flies. A Jew boy you know is such a frail weakly creature like a skinned cat; he is not used to tramping in the mud for ten hours a day and eating biscuits, being among strangers with no father, no mother or petting; well they cough and cough until they cough themselves into their graves. And I ask you what use are they to them? What can they do with little boys?'

Waiting for the wagons to take them thousands of versts farther on from their homes in the Pale of Settlement, the boys were roughly lined up into ranks. They were 'cantonists' conscripted into military schools until they were eighteen; then obliged to serve another twenty-five years in the Russian army or navy. 'It was one of the most awful sights I have ever seen,' wrote Herzen, wringing his hands, 'those poor, poor children. Boys of twelve or thirteen might somehow have survived but little fellows of eight and ten ... not even a brush of black paint could put such horror on canvas ... these sick children without care or kindness exposed to the raw wind that blows in unobstructed from the Arctic Ocean were going to their graves.'[57] Herzen fell into his carriage and surrendered to a tide of tears.

He would go on to make an entire career as sympathetic underdoggist, and the horror the spectacle of the half-dead little Jews aroused in him was typical of his impulsively humane generosity. But although of the 70,000 conscripts to have been drafted in this way between 1827 and 1854, 50,000 were indeed minors, it was unusual for them to be quite as young as those Herzen describes. Twelve, which was brutal enough, was the statutory age for drafting them into the army, although Michael Stanislawski found at least one case of a five-year-old. The cohort of 1829 included some children whose baby teeth were falling out so even the registration clerks concluded those boys could not have been older than eight.[58] All such extreme minors had the requisite number of years added on their registration forms to bring them up to the statutory twelve.

The tsar (whose death in 1855 triggered an outbreak of Jewish rejoicing) was not a monster but he was certainly an autocratic social engineer. When Russia acquired the lion's share of what was left of Poland–Lithuania in 1797 it also acquired an enormous population of Jews, who by 1815 numbered 1.6 million out of the 46 million total population of the empire. Even though they were now limited to the Pale of Settlement, such an immense population could not, it was thought, be left to form a separate estate within the empire, cut off from the rest of the realm by language and the habits of history. As early as 1802 Alexander I established two 'Committees for the Organisation of Jewish Life', one in Warsaw, one in St Petersburg. Both followed the lead of the Austrian emperor Joseph II's edict of 1789, especially in opening secular state schools to Jewish children, though they stopped short of offering full civil emancipation once the process of social transformation had been completed. When the same proposal had been made during debates in Poland in 1790, one indignant opponent said this couldn't be contemplated until the Jews had

been rid of their notorious leprosy and scabies and managed to approximate actual human beings. The prescriptions set out during Alexander's
time of reforms were the stock answers that had been given every time
some government asked what could be done about the Jews: secular
education, enforced if necessary, alongside a modicum of Jewish religious education, both to be supervised by the state; instruction in the
vernacular language of the fatherland; perhaps the liquidation of the
old form of Jewish self-government, especially its courts. Sometimes,
as had been the case throughout Europe, the proposals came from
the Jews themselves. The leading light of Alexander I's committees,
the Podolian magnate Prince Adam Czartoryski (one of the few Poles
the tsar trusted or at least was charmed by), had discussed all these
matters with Mendel Leffin of Satanow, tutor to his children, whom
he habitually addressed as 'dear Mendel'.[59] Alexander's reforms, had
they been systematically implemented, might have included military
service as had Joseph II's, since it was understood that integral to
being considered a fellow subject were the obligations of serving the
fatherland. In Poland it was agreed that ten years of service would
entitle a Jew to citizenship, an assumption the Russians baulked at.
(Under Nicholas's system no Jew, however long he served, was eligible
to become an officer.)

   But Alexander moved cautiously. The Pale of Settlement, the huge
swathe of territory he assigned for the Jews, stretching from Kiev
province all the way to the Baltic, ought not to be understood as some
sort of holding pen or vast territorial ghetto into which the Ashkenazim
were herded. It simply coincided with the lands in which the Ukrainian–
Polish–Lithuanian Jews had, in any case, been long settled. It is true
that, in deference to the alarm shown by Russian merchants (such as
they were) in Moscow and St Petersburg at the prospect of Jewish
competition, they were prevented from residing in those major cities.
In Warsaw their zone of residence became tighter. But even then there
were significant exceptions. Guild merchants, of whom there were
many, could go to the cities to attend fairs and could stay there for
six months. In other respects, too, Jews under the new Russian dispensation had rights unavailable elsewhere. They could, for example,
become members of city councils within the Pale – a measure which
caused such consternation that numbers were restricted and they were
elected on a list separate from non-Jews.

One piece of social engineering introduced by Alexander was never going to work. In 1804, in response to the predictable muttering that the Jews were reducing the peasantry to drunken beggary through their domination of the liquor industry, an edict was passed banning them from brewing and distilling, and owning taverns or inns in the countryside. Since vast numbers of the Jews made money from that occupation (even when making or selling vodka was not their primary living), the measure, had it been enforced, would have ended much of their livelihood. For a while it looked as though the Jews would be ripped out of a rural world which was all that they had known, generation after generation, and sent into the towns of Podolia and Lithuania where they would become a burden on an already hard-pressed economy. The upheaval, however, proved to be temporary. Many of the Polish and Lithuanian nobles who had been confirmed in their estates after the partitions made it clear that removing Jews from the liquor business would result in massive loss of revenues, to themselves and to the government, since the capital furnished by the monopoly lessees would never be replaced at the same level. Their complaints were persuasive enough to guarantee that though the law of 1804 remained on the books, and was reinforced by another decree in 1817 forbidding any Jews from the liquor trade altogether, both measures went largely unenforced. The Jewish innkeeper, with his vodka still in the cellar, stayed a feature of the scene in the Pale for many generations to come. Even in the late nineteenth century, my maternal grandfather's family in the Lithuanian rural district outside Kowno were, along with log-shlepping, very much in the liquor trade, a calling one of them transferred, first to a Soho pub, and then to the import of pink champagne for bubbly-starved Londoners after the First World War, when they anglicised their name to Strongwater.

Autocratic social planning resumed when Nicholas I succeeded to the throne in 1825. Jews were to be moved out of the villages and pushed into towns in the interior. In 1843, Satanow fell victim to a law expelling Jews from any town within fifty versts (about forty miles) from the borders with Austria or Prussia, ostensibly to crack down on smuggling. For some generations (though not forever) Satanow, sitting on its hill, became a ghost town. Jews had already been ordered to take proper surnames. The aristocratic Decembrist revolt which broke out in the year of Nicholas's accession had convinced the austere

young monarch that all of Russia needed to be imbued with the code
of patriotism, religion and obedience to the tsar. That included the
zhyds, as Nicholas called them. He had no very good opinion of those
people, although he conceded with an air of amazement that they
had been surprisingly loyal during the French invasion of 1812, 'even
risking their lives to help'. Mostly, though, in his diary he reverted to
anti-Semitic clichés. 'They drain the simple folk with their tricks ...
they know how to oppress and deceive the simple folk, taking as
collateral for loans, summer wheat not yet sown ... they are genuine
blood suckers sticking to and exhausting already decaying provinces.'[60]
There were various cures for these social diseases – transferring the
Jews to agriculture (Siberia was originally thought an ideal spot) and
keeping them away from moneylending – but the most likely remedy,
Nicholas believed, would be military service.

He believed he was honouring the memory of his ancestor Peter
the Great, who had also believed in the army as a social school; but
to an even greater degree Nicholas thrilled to the sight of a regiment
on parade, and his dreams were filled with the flash of sabres and the
thunder of cannon. Others who could use a good drilling in the true
ways of Russia – Old Believers, Pietists, Tatars and the like – would
be pressed onto the military matrix too. But first and foremost, not
least because of their vast numbers, the test population had to be the
Jews. The general outlines of the plan which would become law in
1827 he put to a trusted adviser, the head of the Third Chancellery
and thus no bleeding heart, Nicolai Novosiltsev, who to the tsar's
astonishment told him it was unworkable, inhuman and possibly
dangerous in its alienation. Though he hoped that prolonged service
in the army, especially for the young, would make the work of conversion easier, Nicholas was neither so deluded nor so cruel as to see
that as the whole point of the plan. Both he and his father had maintained the Jews in their *kehillot*, governed by the *kahals*, and indeed
had made their freedom of open worship an absolute right. There
was even something about the piety of the Hasidic rabbis which he
did not find entirely offensive. So it was assumed that the teenage
cantonists and indeed the postgraduate soldiers would be allowed to
observe their religion except when it actively interfered with military
duties. Some feasts and holidays could be taken off; Passover meals
could be taken separately with matzot; they could be relieved of some

work on the Sabbath. This is all very well, Novosiltsev responded, but since they are to be sent thousands of versts beyond the Pale, where are they to find kosher meat? Where are the rabbis and cantors to hold and lead services? It was, he concluded, a prescription for despair, and despairing men do not good or loyal soldiers make. Nicholas went ahead anyway.

When the news was made known, mass panic broke out in the shtetls of the Pale. The Apter Rebbe (from Opatow) sat on a high chair, summoning his people to a fast of repentance, for such an oppression (like all the others) could only have come about as a result of the sins of the Jews. Every conceivable possibility of intercession was explored. Could the Jews compound for conscription with a collective tax (the age-old recourse to draconian threats, usually of coerced conversion)? They could not (though individuals were allowed to produce substitutes as long as they were also Jews). Money was collected throughout the Pale anyway, in hopes of bribing whoever might change the tsar's mind. This too was in vain. Parents prepared to hide their children, for was it not said that delivering a child voluntarily to a life away from home and *shul* to the likelihood of their conversion to Christianity was akin to killing them? It was made clear that anyone caught concealing a child would be punished with frightening severity. Commonly it was said that fathers inflicted minor wounds on their own children so that they might escape the draft; but since there were no minimal physical requirements for the service this was also of no avail. Besides, there was only so much a parent would do to his child. As the Jews became resigned to this fate, petitions became more desperate and pathetic. One from Vilna declared 'we beseech you only that our children would not be forbidden to observe the rites of their creed so that their observance would be a means to strengthen their military service'.[61]

The conscription of their children and teenagers has gone down in popular memory as one of the great atrocities inflicted on the Jews, to be added to the enslavement in Egypt, the desecrations of Antiochus IV Epiphanes, the Inquisition. Growing up in the 1950s, if you asked a Lithuanian *zeyde* or *bubba* why they or their parents had come to England at the end of the nineteenth century, they told you 'to escape the *khappers*', the child-snatchers who came in the night to take little boys off to the army and to the baptismal font, even though such horrors were long a thing of the past. As Michael Stanislawski and Yohanan Petrovsky-Shtern have shown, the historical truth is much more complicated and disturbing. The tsar may have had the usual grotesque prejudices about the *zhyds*, but he was not proposing an enforced conversion to the Orthodox Church. The Jewish cadets were certainly to be preached at, and between a third and a half did end up converting, but the new Christian Jews in the army were treated no differently from Jewish Jews in uniform. When Nicholas's minister Kiselev wrote that he hoped the military experience would effect a 'rapprochement' between Russian Christians and Russian Jews and remove 'Talmudic' superstitions, he meant by that to make inroads into what he thought was their separateness, and the mistrust non-Jews had of those strange people. It was the length of their term of service, and above all the removal of children from the wrap-around, Yiddish-speaking world of the shtetl, that made the tsar believe conversion would happen, sooner or later, without the benefit of force.

This hardly makes Nicholas the milk of human kindness, nor was the experience of the cantonist children a picnic. The period of service for Jews was far longer than comparable terms for Old Believers and other non-ethnic Russian conscripts; doubtless because, correctly, the tsar thought them a harder nut to crack. And because Nicholas assumed the message of the gospel would be more likely to work on the impressionable young, the age of conscription was set earlier than for the other groups. The initial experience that sick children in particular had on arrival at their military school could be traumatic. Those thought to be carrying body lice or any other sort of infection might be smeared with sulphur and tar, or even a solution of chicken dung ostensibly for decontamination. When they were sent in the steam or bathhouse they were stuck on the scalding top shelf to kill off the vermin.[62]

But there were also genuinely sympathetic efforts to try and respond to the kind of concerns Novosiltsev had raised. Although there was no sign of them in Herzen's tragic encounter, parents were sometimes allowed to accompany their children on the long, rough journey to the schools. When conditions were very bad, it was Russian officers who reported them, so that the saddened officer Herzen spoke to was very likely not a fiction, both in his compassion and shoulder-shrugging stoicism. Arrangements were put in place, both for the cantonist cadets and serving Jewish soldiers, for the observance of fasts and festivals and even the Sabbath. Rabbis were called to the barracks to lead those services; rooms were set aside for services; candles, wine and *tallit* prayer shawls supplied. Petrovsky-Shtern notes that new Russian words – *sykois* ('Sukkos' – the Ashkenazi pronunciation of 'Sukkot') and *roshachanu* (for the New Year) – appeared at this time, first in the army and navy. In Ekaterinburg, Tula and Tver, synagogues were established for Jewish soldiers (and in Kronstadt for the sailors). In other places an organisation called the Guardians of the Faith (in Białystok, for instance) provided communal rooms for worship and gatherings and, more important, temporary accommodation with Jewish families.

Who, then, was responsible for the selection of all those very young children? The distressing answer is: the Jews themselves, in the form of the *kahals* who were charged with providing the quota of conscripts. Some categories of the community were exempt from conscription: the rabbi and one cantor, plus those whose commercial, industrial occupations could be classified as indispensable. The agriculturalists of Kherson and elsewhere were also protected. But sooner or later, a selection had to be made. It was then that the discussion of the 'trustees' appointed for this dirty work by the *kahal* must have entered their zone of infernal darkness. Someone would have said this is not of our doing, for our sins, this iniquity has been forced upon us, but that is as maybe, now we are duty-bound to think of protecting our people as best we can. And first they would think of those who must not go: young fathers with infants and small children; others with livelihoods the shtetl could not do without. Being human, the families of the *kahal* were not about to ship off their own. Then the finger pointed to those who might conceivably be sacrificed, who were, naturally, the poor, the weak and the young. Sensing the possibility of losing their children, distraught parents would hide them before it was too late, at which point the *khappers*, the kidnappers hired by the *kahal*, would winkle them out, or take them in the dead of night. Israel Itzkowitz, who was just seven when he was taken in Plotzk, describes exactly such a traumatic, violent separation: children thrown a sheepskin jacket, then loaded onto a cart or wagon, one of a long line making up the convoy of boys heading east or north.

Itzkowitz goes on to relate a purgatory of shouting and beatings which, at some point, made the small boy accept baptism. But he would survive the mistreatment to see Nicholas II's successor Alexander II outlaw the conscription of minors, and the return of boys, wherever possible, to their parental homes. Although the Orthodox Church refused to acknowledge such reversions Itzkowitz returned to Judaism and insisted on being treated as a Jewish veteran. The best evidence available suggests that both mortality and conversion rates of the conscripts were less grievous than both Herzen's expectations and Jewish popular memory assume. But still, there were those 50,000 boys: the child soldier – scrawny, scared and coughing inside his sheepskin coat, trying to hoist a rifle on his shoulder and keep it there in drill – was not a myth.

The way of the martinet was not the only way to make Russians out of young Jews. What was meant to be a cultural transformation, largely imposed, was taking place. Jews were henceforth obliged to write commercial, legal and civil documents only in German, Polish or Russian. From 1836 there was a massive exercise in subjecting Hebrew books to state censors (all of whom had to be Jewish converts who could read the language), and the presses of Slavuta and Vilna which had served the whole of eastern Ashkenaz – the innkeeper who still had four or five books on his shelf, the rabbi who had seventy or a hundred, the city merchant who might have had even more – were all arbitrarily shut down. Even appearance and dress were to be regulated. The wearing of skullcaps in public was criminalised, as were other items defined as habitually Jewish. But Hasidic Jews responded by adopting the costume of the Polish-Russian merchant; the black fox-fur *shtreimel* hat worn over the yarmulka, the long belted black coat and white stockings that merchants wore in St Petersburg. This is what they still wear in Jerusalem and elsewhere, imagined as distinctively Jewish dress, which frozen over the generations it has duly become. Long sidelocks and beards were also outlawed but no one thought to employ a scissors police, so that regulation was more or less ignored.

Schooling was the great battleground. There were always actively modernising Jews who were as eager as Russian ministers of education to deny a monopoly of Jewish instruction to the Hasidim. Their mission was not to liquidate traditional Jewish schooling but to carve out room alongside it for the modern knowledge needed to make Jews useful (that word again) subjects of the tsar. The wider Hasidism spread its net, the more determined the champions of an eastern Jewish Enlightenment were to ensure that shtetl children would be exposed to the modern disciplines: Russian language and perhaps German too, mathematics and Russian history. A model school along these lines had been founded in the young port city of Odessa in 1826; another in Kishinev followed, and Riga in 1838. Many of the most zealous champions of the new education had, like Solomon Maimon, made a long cultural journey from the shtetl to Berlin, to drink at the fountain of German reform, and had come to believe it was entirely possible for religious and secular education to share the hours and the space in young boys' minds.

In Sergei Uvarov – Nicholas's minister of education, a classicist by vocation, brilliant and devious – the modernists found an enthusiastic patron and collaborator. The plan was to bring the whole of Jewish education in Russia under the supervision of the state. Henceforth two kinds of teachers would work under the same roof: Jews who would continue to teach religious texts; and either Jews or Christians who would teach the new subjects. Those who wanted to go on to be rabbis could do so, but at seminaries also supervised by the state. Yet generations of Jews in the Pale would now grow up as true Russians, obedient like everyone else to the ethos, coined by Uvarov, of Autocracy, Religion, Nationality.

To accomplish this revolution Uvarov knew he would need well-disposed rabbis to lever open the doors of resistance. There was one obvious candidate for this thankless task: the twenty-three-year-old director of the Riga school, Max Lilienthal, Munich-educated and brimful of confidence if not arrogance. He taught and preached in German and expected Jews to master the tongue of the Enlightenment. After five weeks of close discussion with Uvarov (itself a striking moment of collaboration), Lilienthal was hired to draw up a plan of educational reform. But when he broached it to the rabbis of Vilna, Lilienthal was immediately treated as the agent of the alien state, and his scheme a Trojan Horse for Christian conversion. Going on tour to reassure Hasidic rabbis, he ran into a storm of hatred. In Minsk he was subjected to volleys of abuse, curses and projectiles. Calling on the state to impose measures if they could not be agreed did not help the cause. The Hasidim stayed suspicious; the modernising *maskilim* took offence at his overtures to the traditionalists.

But there were places where his ideas took root: in the 'New Russia' of south-east Ukraine, in Kishinev, and above all in Odessa. There, beyond the old heartland of Hasidism, the new schools stood a better chance of being accepted. Migrants were pouring into these towns, where to the horror of the rabbis, Russian quickly became the language of the classroom, the cafes and the shops, alongside Yiddish. And there was, at last, a school for Jewish girls which taught something more than embroidery. Young men shaved and went to Odessa. Young wives refused to shave their heads and went to Odessa dragging their husbands along. What was going on? The rabbis thundered that 'the fires of hell burn seven miles round Odessa'. But more were listening to the siren song *'lebn vi got in Odes'* – you live like a god in Odessa – and turned their back on the shtetl.

Max Lilienthal had been treated for the most part as not a real rabbi at all, but as an apostate in everything but name. When the education bill was enacted in 1844, he was in Berlin getting married to a fine young woman from a modern-minded family. He wasn't going back to Russia, but he wasn't staying put either. He was looking somewhere else, where perhaps you could be a good German rabbi without having to listen to endless screaming and carrying on that you were leading Jews to the Church, that your name should be blotted out with the heathen; somewhere without all the brickbats and the meshugaas; and that place was called New York.

A M E R I C A N S

I. A House for Uriah; an Ark for Noah

Uriah Phillips Levy was making *aliyah*: his ascent to a holy place. The site of veneration was a house in Virginia sitting atop a low hill five miles east of Charlottesville. It had been designed by its self-taught architect and owner, Thomas Jefferson, to resemble, somewhat, Lord Burlington's villa at Chiswick which in turn had been modelled, somewhat, on Andrea Palladio's Villa 'La Rotonda' outside Vicenza. The owner-architect, generally said to be the most encyclopedically learned man in the Commonwealth of Virginia if not in the entire American republic, would have known all this. Vitruvius' *On Building*, the bible of classical style, was in his library. Accordingly the brick facade was ornamented with a colonnaded, pedimented portico, above which rose a flattened cupola. The portico opened onto a high-ceilinged entrance hall. But instead of the usual gallery of ancestors, the walls had been hung with a variety of Native American objects, many of them sent to Jefferson by the explorers of the western lands, Lewis and Clark. Greeting visitors were elk antlers, mastodon bones and the horns of bighorn sheep. There too were Indian shields, arrows and knives; a Mandan buffalo-hide robe tanned with the juiced brains of the animal, stretched and decorated with scenes from battles between the Mandan and the Sioux, and fine quillwork drawn with the spines of porcupines. True, Houdon's bust of Voltaire smiled down from a pedestal at the pyramid of Cheops modelled in cork. But no one needed informing that this was Jefferson's 'Indian Hall' to understand that the airy room was as much of an American Declaration as the text Jefferson had written in 1776. The Indian Hall was its collector's chamber of curiosities but one which proclaimed the living wonder that was America.

It was a brag but not a vulgar one. Jefferson had carefully positioned the house, called Monticello, not only to catch the summer breezes but also along a fine line between splendour and modesty. It was a republican villa; a retreat where body and mind might work in measured harmony as befitted a retired president who was also still, and forever, educationalist-philosopher-horticulturalist-statesman. The 140 slaves on whom all this studied elegance depended were, with the exception of house servants, lodged well out of sight in 'Mulberry Row' below and beyond the Fruitery. A number of the field hands were lodged still further off on Shadwell Farm.

And now, in 1834, Monticello had become the property (slaves excepted, for they had been sold after Jefferson's death in 1826) of a Jew: Lieutenant Uriah Phillips Levy of the United States Navy.[1] Not everyone in the neighbourhood was overjoyed at this. It was no time at all before muttering about the grasping Jews could be heard in Charlottesville parlours. The poor Jefferson Randolphs, it was said, had been done out of an opportunity to reacquire the house by an odious Levite who had pretended to support them in their efforts while all the time scheming to snatch the property from under their noses at a bargain price. When their own funds fell short, the Israelite had pounced as Jews did. 'Monticello is now owned by a Levy,' one wrote in evident disgust, 'who charges patriotic American Democratic-Republicans 25 cents admission.'

The tale was slander, but it lasted a century and a half. In any case, what Uriah Levy had bought with his $10,000 was no bargain. The house in which Jefferson had mused, farmed, planned his politics, invented his university, received the high-minded, lorded it over his suspicious neighbours, the only place in the world where, he had said, he could be truly happy, was, by 1834, a ruin. When Jefferson had died on 4 July 1826, fifty years to the day after the Declaration of Independence, his estate had been encumbered by a crushing debt of $107,000.

The latest owner was a good-looking, broad-faced, dark-haired man with slickly waxed whiskers and erect military bearing. He took in the broken windows and the partly collapsed roof of the portico. Some of the columns leaned drunkenly at perilous angles. Others had broken entirely, pieces of them lying about in the weedy red dirt, resembling some cautionary print on the fate of empires. Jefferson's stupendous plantings – the beds of berry bushes, situated to catch the warmth from a protecting stone wall – were long gone, as were the fig trees, and experimental cornucopia of new vegetables: asparagus and artichokes, eggplants, both purple and white, broccoli, endive, seakale and sesame (for Thomas Jefferson made his own tahini as well as his own ice cream); also gone, the salsify tubers Lewis and Clark had brought him from their western expedition; the Mexican chilli peppers; and the fifteen types of English peas, an enthusiasm which had triggered the institution of an annual Virginia pea competition to see which of the local growers could be first to bring a sweet harvest to the spring table. The orchard, with its eighteen prize apple varieties (Newtown Pippins, Spitzenburg and Hewes Crab among them), the thirty-eight varieties of peach (Indian Blood Cling, Oldmixon and the rest), had decayed, the trunks turned scaly and worm-eaten. Eden had gone down beneath an ocean of choking weed, its remains strangled by tendrils of wild grape. What the lieutenant saw instead were bolted flags of yellowing corn stalks, also a range of half-dead mulberry trees, their papery foliage drooping in surrender, relics of Monticello's previous owner's futile obsession with silk production.

That first buyer was a Charlottesville druggist and lay preacher, James Turner Barclay, whose other consuming enthusiasms were electricity and the biblical archaeology he believed would bear out the literal truth of scripture. Years after Barclay sold Monticello to Uriah Levy, he would take himself off to Palestine, ride mules and camels along the trails of the Saviour and publish *In the City of the Great King, Jerusalem as it Was, Is and Is to Be*. Its six hundred pages and seventy engravings would supply the small fortune the silkworms had denied him. His own family had judged Monticello the most colossal of white elephants, so when he put it on the market Levy picked it up for $3,000 less than Barclay had originally paid in 1831.

Inside the house glossy beetles scurried through the dust. The shelves of the fabled 'Book Room' lay empty. In 1815 Jefferson had donated his great encyclopedic library to establish the nucleus of the Library of Congress. But when he tried to sell an archive of his manuscripts, there were no takers. A year after his death, in 1827, desperate to pay off at least part of the family debt, his daughter

Martha Jefferson Randolph and the executor of the estate, her son Thomas Jefferson Randolph, had auctioned off anything that might keep creditors at bay. Levy would never own the graceful furniture, much of it designed by Jefferson, though made by his slaves who had also gone under the hammer. (Levy would buy twenty of his own.) Nor would he own the oil portraits of the three Britons Jefferson held to be the greatest minds the world had ever seen, the intellectual godfathers of free America: Francis Bacon, Isaac Newton and John Locke.

Tick-tock. One showy object persisted amid all the echoing emptiness and grime: Jefferson's patent seven-day clock, moved by an assembly of pulleys and iron weights which dropped so low that the inventor had had to cut holes in the floor to accommodate their fall. And in the parlour where he had entertained the mighty of mind and state, as well as the patriotic tourists who made the journey to visit the Sage of Monticello, a handsome parquet floor of beech and cherry lay intact beneath the mantle of dust. It had survived by default since Barclay had judged the wooden tiles not worth the trouble of prising up and selling off.

None of this desolation cooled the warmth of Uriah Levy's emotions as he took possession of the house. For the naval officer, then in his early forties, as for almost all his Jewish co-religionists, the Constitution had made an independent America the first true 'sanctuary' of the modern world. When Washington and Jefferson had visited Newport, Rhode Island, in 1789 campaigning for the adoption of the Bill of Rights, they had been effusively greeted by Moses Seixas as liberators and protectors. Washington had graciously returned the compliment (albeit in the slightly backhanded style of recycling Seixas's own words), celebrating 'a Government which gives to bigotry no sanction, to persecution no assistance'.[2] But it was Jefferson who, as author of the Virginia Statute for Religious Freedom, and thus indirectly of the First Amendment forbidding Congress from any religious legislation, was commonly regarded by American Jews as the second coming of Cyrus the Great. Both during and after his presidency he was the recipient of further garlands and eulogies from elders of the community who understood their American equality to include not just free worship but what had been denied them everywhere else in the world: an unrestricted right to practise whatever occupation they chose, including holding public office. When, in July 1820, Dr Jacob de la Motta sent Jefferson (as well as James Madison) a copy of the flowery discourse he had preached at the opening of the new synagogue in Savannah, the retired president responded by celebrating America's destiny as Emancipator of the Jews. 'It excites in him', Jefferson wrote, 'the gratifying reflection that his country has been the first to prove to the world ... that religious freedom is the most effectual anodyne against religious dissension ... and he is happy in the restoration of the Jews, particularly of their social rights and hopes they will be seen taking their seats on the benches of science as preparatory to their doing the same on the board of government.' What Jefferson meant of course was: educate yourselves so that office may be open to you. But what was widely understood among Jews to be the promise of America was the unrestricted freedom to pursue any work for which their abilities fitted them. Nearly all the states of the Union had, on paper at least, abandoned any sort of religious test for office. Only in Maryland, between 1822 and 1828, had there been an ugly little tussle to ensure equal rights alongside equal duties. Jews, after all, had served the cause of independence in the ranks of the patriot militia. So why should there not be Jewish American soldiers and sailors, Jewish American *officers*?

Uriah Levy's career tested that optimistic proposition. He served on brigs, sloops and schooners, the *Spark*, the *Cyane* and *Gunboat 158*, had steered his vessels through shoals and reefs, storms and battles. He had been captured by the British (a gentle confinement in Ashburton, Devon), had pursued slave traders in the Atlantic and patrolled the Bay of Tunis.[3]

Now he was the self-appointed agent of Monticello's resurrection. Uriah began by making the house habitable. The main well was repaired, the worst of the brambles cleared so that a modest kitchen garden and a rose shrubbery could be planted. The Indian Hall and parlour were repainted and furnished and Houdon's bust of Voltaire, which had somehow escaped the sales, retrieved and cleaned up. Levy tried to bring Jefferson's bedroom, also on the ground floor, back to a recognisable version of what it had been when the mechanical valet helped dress the retired president for the morning. After two years of intensive repairs, Monticello was finally ready for its most exacting inspector: Levy's mother, Rachel. In the spring of 1836 Uriah brought her and his unmarried sister Amelia to the house to install them as custodians while he was away on naval service. There they were, three Jews in the Virginia sunlight: the lieutenant in his high-collared navy coat, the sixty-seven-year-old Rachel, mother of ten, clad in the black silk of the Jewish matron, and her daughter, lame since childhood, all looking over their new mansion.

Amelia would remain unmarried for the rest of her days. Following her mother's death in 1839 she remained at Monticello in the role her brother had assigned her as chatelaine of the house. Rachel, whom Uriah buried at Monticello, had been a great New York beauty in the early years of independence. A portrait attributed to the Swedish painter Adolf Ulric Wertmüller, painted around 1795, eight years after her marriage to Michael Levy, shows her as she might have been dressed for her wedding. A gossamer-light veil falls down her back. On her head she wears a hat decorated with the flowers trailing down the columns of the *huppah* beneath which she had been wed. Her muslin costume is cinched in beneath the bosom with the kind of elaborately embroidered and gem-studded sash commonly seen in the Sephardi communities of Turkey and the Maghreb.

In her own bloodstream Rachel Phillips Levy carried the continuous epic of Jewish wandering. Her great-grandfather Diogo Nunes Ribiero had been a Marrano in Portugal: a court physician with a secret synagogue in the cellar of his house on the Tagus. Like so many Marranos he took one chance too many in his efforts to bring fellow *conversos* back to the religion of their forefathers and was denounced to the Inquisition. Along with his wife and children, one of them Rachel's grandmother Zipporah, Nunes was arrested and thrown into prison where he suffered the usual physical ordeals. Nunes was spared further torture by the kind of intervention it would have been pardonable to think of as biblical. The Grand Inquisitor was suddenly afflicted with crucifying pain brought on by a dangerously obstructed bladder, the torturer tortured. Only Jewish urology could deliver him from the rack. After the successful operation, Dr Nunes and his family were restored to their home by the Tagus River but on condition that two watchmen of the Holy Office would be stationed there at all times to ensure proper Christian conduct. It was house arrest from which, nonetheless, the Nunes family escaped in a gamble of high daring. In 1726 they were invited on board a visiting British vessel for the kind of entertainment common during the heyday of the Anglo-Portuguese Methuen Treaty (port wines for English textiles). What was uncommon was the ship (by prior arrangement, well compensated) abruptly weighing anchor and sailing downstream and off into the Atlantic with both the Jews and their infuriated but helpless guards aboard.

The destination was London where, after undergoing circumcision along with his sons, Diogo Nunes became Samuel Nunez. The elders of Bevis Marks synagogue were at that time involved financially with the scheme of James Edward Oglethorpe to found the new colony of Georgia (initially meant to be populated by freed and reformed convicts), a project which must have stirred the doctor's enthusiasms. In 1733, five months after Oglethorpe himself had gone out with the first colonists, the *William and Sarah* followed with forty-two Jews, all but eight of them Sephardim, the largest group of Jewish settlers destined for America. Among them were the Nunez family. The prospect of Savannah being swamped by Jewish colonists panicked Oglethorpe into forbidding their landing. But with unerring timing, Providence once more intervened on the Jews' behalf by inflicting, simultaneously, outbreaks of yellow fever and the intestinal 'bloody flux' on the fragile colony. Among the victims of the fever was Savannah's only physician, James Cox. As in Portugal, medicine prevailed where supplication could not. Nunez and his party were duly settled and helped smooth the way for a second shipload of Jewish immigrants a few months later. Nunez ministered selflessly to the sick, using Sephardi expertise in tropical medicine, drawn from their long experience of Brazil, West Africa and the Caribbean. Convulsively shivering cases of 'mal-air'ia went to the doctor for treatment with the quinine derived from cinchona, and when that ran out, white dogwood bark. From Nunez they got ipecacuanha as an emetic. Sufferers from asthma and pulmonary conditions received a prescription of datura jimson weed. Those who still despised and abused the Jews were ready enough to take their remedies.

Soon, there were more than enough Jews in Savannah to establish their own synagogue called 'Mikve Israel' after the messianic tract of their hero Menasseh ben Israel, at which point, of course, the congregation divided acrimoniously into Sephardi and Ashkenazi factions. Disunity turned out to be the least of their problems. In 1740 a Spanish force from Florida landed on St Simon's Island in preparation for a descent on Georgia. Suddenly the Inquisition was on their doorstep. The Savannah Sephardim, including the Nunez clan, packed up in haste, removing itself first to Charleston and then to New York where the doctor ended his days peacefully, having seen his daughter Zipporah marry the cantor of the Shearith Israel synagogue, David Machado.

If high rates of infant mortality were a fact of life in eighteenth-century America, the Sephardim did their best to offset it with fruitful multiplication. Rebecca, the daughter of Zipporah Nunez and David Machado, who condescended to marry the enterprising German Jew who had anglicised his name to Phillips, bore him twenty-one children, all but four surviving infancy. The husband, Jonas Phillips, had begun his career working for a Jewish indigo trader in Charleston, and had then moved to New York where he practised as a *shokhet*, a kosher slaughterer, with some mercantile business on the side. He met his match in dark-eyed Rebecca. Marrying into a grand Sephardi clan with a Marrano history made Jonas a Sephardi by adoption, linking him into the golden chain of memory. Rebecca remembered her mother Zipporah (the oral historian of their journeyings) mouthing a silent prayer like the prophetess Hannah, in memory of the victims of the Inquisition when the clock struck a certain hour.

Jonas was not given to hand-wringing lamentation; rather he looked forward to what a Jew might do in this new country. He stopped slitting the throats of chickens and turned to trade. Interest and conviction made him an opponent of the onerous commercial regulations of the British. He joined the non-importation campaign, and when the redcoats occupied New York, persuaded the congregation to close the doors of Shearith Israel synagogue and to move en masse to Philadelphia, where Jonas joined the militia. Many other members of the clan saw service on the Patriot side. Manuel Phillips was an army surgeon; Naphtali one of the paymasters. And when the war was over Jonas wanted to make sure that their commitment was honoured by equal treatment with other citizens of the new republic. When the Constitutional Convention gathered in Philadelphia he sent a message urging it to guarantee 'the natural and unalienable right to worship Almighty God each according to his own conscience and understanding'.

It would be Jonas's grandchildren, though, who would test the further assumption that they might, in any way they chose, be both American patriot and American Jew.

For Uriah, the challenge began when he ran away to sea at the age of ten. This was not what Jewish boys did, especially not in Philadelphia in 1800. A sweetly apocryphal piece of family lore had the cheeky cabin boy telling the captain of the coastal trader that he would have to return home two years later in time for his bar mitzvah. Come home he did, at which point his parents Michael and Rachel made sure that he would at least have a modicum of formal education plus an apprenticeship with a ship chandler. But warehouses were not cargoes. Uriah mooched about the docks, where the masts of anchored merchantmen creaked in the beckoning wind. Eventually he was allowed to attend naval school and learn the principles of seamanship and navigation. Yet when Uriah shipped off again, around the age of seventeen, it was not as most in his class would have supposed, as midshipman, the regular way to become an officer, but along with the deckhands – boatswains and mates – working his way up to sailing master. If you wanted a fellow who would steer you safely through squalls, anticipate the dead calms, pilot a course avoiding reefs and pirates, who worked from the chart in his head as much as one on the table, Uriah the Jewish tar was your man.

Not, however, for everyone on board. For many, Uriah was a double oddity and the wardroom made sure he knew it. He was a sailing master who had ambitions to be an officer; and a Jew to boot. What was more (or so it was said), he had trouble in the mateyness department. If Uriah kept his Jewishness to himself, his shipmates did not. As a Levy he was subjected to a constant undertow of sneering abuse surfacing from an anti-Semitic undercurrent so deep and strong that no constitutional amendment was ever going to dispel it. All the stereotypes of the Jew – touchy, given to pretensions of moral superiority (especially when Uriah mounted a campaign against flogging), giving himself uppity airs, setting himself apart and above the rest – were magnified in the close quarters of an American warship. Levy, it was often said, had a notoriously low boiling point. He was accused of not understanding shipboard custom. In Livorno he had seen Jacob Jackson subjected to one hundred lashes with the cat so that there was nothing much left of him but ripped meat when they cut him

down from the grating. This torment Uriah never forgot, and thereafter could never understand seamen saying they would rather have
their backs in shreds than suffer the indignities Uriah devised as alternative punishments. Especially odious was his 'Flying Horse', a
harnessed contraption which swung the malefactor forty feet up the
mizzenmast for hours on end. The idea was to subject the offender
to mockery, but it was the Jew who caught the edge of ridicule. When
he tarred the backside of a cabin boy and stuck parrot feathers on it
rather than flogging him, Uriah may have thought that the treatment
was akin to, but more lenient than, a classroom birching. But the
backsides of cabin boys were a zone of particular interest in shipboard
life; not to be spoken of or casually exhibited. So the humiliation
imposed by Levy was actually deemed more cruel in its comic display
than if the skin of young John Thompson had been flayed away.
Similarly Uriah's 'Black Lists' bearing the names of offenders and
publicly posted were not received as a sign of benevolent justice.

Uriah's campaign against flogging, ardently pursued in the 1840s,
would eventually result in the abolition of the practice a decade later.
But his expressions of moral abhorrence made enemies among those
who thought there was something unnatural about having to take
orders from a sanctimonious jumped-up Ikey. 'Disagreeable' was a
word commonly used of him. Fights got picked on board and off.
The first and most serious occurred in 1816 when Uriah inadvertently
stepped on the foot of a Mr Potter, then serving on USS *Spitfire*,
during a Philadelphia ball. His apologies, immediately tendered, were
judged insincere and inadequate. Nothing but a duel would satisfy.
Uriah replied to a succession of missed shots from Potter by firing
into the air. But his opponent refused to desist and reloaded. Uriah,
tired of being a sitting duck, took aim in earnest and killed his opponent with his first shot. This was not what was supposed to happen.

Along with the fights came the courts martial, six of them. Most
often Levy was found at fault, removed from duties, discharged
from his commission, and in one case of egregious injustice turned
into a shipboard pariah, eating alone, shunned by everyone else on
board. Another court attempted to have Levy cashiered from the
service altogether as incompetent and temperamentally unsuited
to service in the navy. In every case, however, there were shipmates
who gave opposing testimony exonerating him. Levy, they said, was

a dependable sailing master, an honourable officer and trusted by his crew. Secretaries of the Navy regularly reversed the verdict of the courts martial and ordered the navy to reinstate Levy in his rank and duties. When there was a campaign to obstruct, permanently, his promotion to captain, President John Tyler had to intervene to uphold it.

Even when he was beset by slander and prejudice, Uriah refused to abandon his patriotic conviction that only in America was it possible to be a Captain Levy. He also thought that he had but one man to thank for this gift of emancipation. In November 1832 he wrote to the Philadelphia shipbuilder John Coulter, for whom he had once worked, that

> I consider Thomas Jefferson to be one of the greatest men in history – author of the Declaration of Independence and an absolute democrat. He serves as an inspiration to millions of Americans. He did much to mold our Republic in a form in which a man's religion does not make him ineligible for political or governmental life. A noble man – yet there is no statue to him in the Capitol in Washington. As a small payment for his determined stand on the side of religious liberty I am preparing to personally commission a statue of Jefferson.

During periods of leave brought on by his legal altercations, Uriah Levy travelled in Europe. In Paris he sought out the most admired portrait sculptor of his generation, Pierre-Jean David, known as David d'Angers, who had been teaching at the École des Beaux Arts since 1826. David was nothing if not versatile: supplying classical figures for the pediment of the Panthéon; others imbued with romantic energy for the Arc de Triomphe. He had made a head of Balzac, a full-length figure of Lafayette; who better, then, to fulfil Uriah's dream? Though the story of Lafayette giving Uriah the idea of buying Monticello is apocryphal, the two men may have met, since Lafayette lent Thomas Sully's portrait of Jefferson to David for the sculpture.

Just as it was the Jewish captain who would inaugurate historical preservation in his country with the restoration of Monticello, so he was the first to imagine the rotunda of the Capitol ornamented with figures of the republic's great founders, turning it into an American pantheon. For a project of this importance Levy wanted bronze not marble, a medium which might embody democratic energy rather than the chilly gravity of stone. Uriah made himself felt throughout the making of the statue: remaining in Paris, inspecting David's maquette, ordering a bronzed plaster copy (later presented to the city council of New York, who still have it in their chamber), and overseeing the casting.

He must have been happy with the result; a big improvement on Sully's stiff painting. Though he had trained as a neoclassicist, working for a time in the atelier of Antonio Canova in Rome, David's calling card was romantic sensibility. By posing Jefferson *contrapposto*, he gave the figure a sense of motion, in keeping with the famously restless mind. One hand holds a quill, pointing to the Declaration of Independence held in the other. Levy had every reason to suppose that when he presented the statue to Congress in March 1834, with a suggestion to install it in the rotunda of the Capitol, he would be showered with gratitude.

Awkwardness ensued; polite communications of thanks, but distinctly on the tepid side. There were mixed congressional feelings about a private citizen, a Jew no less, telling them who and how the Founders should be honoured. Eyebrows rose higher when it was noticed that Uriah had had his own name inscribed on the pedestal as the donor of the gift to his 'fellow citizens'. The Speaker wrote to Levy appreciatively but added, somewhat churlishly lest he suppose Congress was beholden, that he had merely anticipated the wishes of the legislature. Representative William Segar of Virginia said that had Congress wished to have such a statue it would 'doubtless have procured one for itself rather than be indebted to any private citizen'. Some thought bronze inferior to marble; others that it was unseemly to have Jefferson honoured before Washington, about whom there was less controversy. Despite all these reservations a joint resolution of both Houses in June 1834 accepted the statue.

Levy had wanted it placed in the rotunda; Congress wanted it installed out of doors in the square just east of the Capitol building. It seems to have been shifted from one site to the other, leaving the rotunda when a statue of George Washington moved in, as if the first and third presidents would not have wanted to share the same space of honour (which may well have been true). In 1847 it was moved away from the Capitol altogether by President James Polk who installed it on the front lawn of the White House, where its surface suffered from the DC climate, and its dignity from the pigeons. During Ulysses Grant's second term it was decided that the statue should be removed from the White House grounds to make way for a fountain, but its fate was so unclear that Uriah's brother Jonas contemplated taking it back. It was not until 1900 during the McKinley administration that the statue was returned to the National Statuary Hall in the Capitol Rotunda, where it remains to this day.

The cool response to the Levy gift, the comings and goings of the Jefferson statue, and the more nakedly hostile comments around Charlottesville on the subject of the Levys as custodians of Monticello, exposed the limits of American liberalism where Jews were concerned. Uriah was called by one local, George Blatterman, 'a Jew of Jews and very unpopular'; others expressed outright disgust that a Jew was the keeper of the Jefferson flame. Similar disappointments and worse could face Jews when they tested the Jeffersonian promise of truly equal citizenship. The pushback was not surprising: a republic of immigrants was bound to stir nativist hostility and certainly not just against Jews but Catholics, Irish, Italians and Poles. The more remarkable thing was that Jews could get so far as to suppose every path was free to them; that the rights to which they were entitled were indistinguishable from anyone else's.

That, at any rate, is what Uriah's older cousin Mordecai Noah believed. He had grown up in Jonas Phillips's crowded household in Philadelphia absorbing his grandfather's conviction that a free America announced a new epoch in the history of the Jews. In a sermonising speech he delivered at the consecration of a newly built Shearith Israel synagogue in New York in 1818, Mordecai echoed his grandfather's practical optimism but added something more oracular. There could be no doubt that the United States was the first truly liberal country in the world: 'the bright example of universal tolerance, of liberality, true religion and good faith'.[4] Pending their restoration to the ancestral land, this hospitality to all faiths, the creation of a country where different religions could live beside each other peacefully, is what made America the 'chosen country' of the Jews.

By 1818, in his thirties, Mordecai had become (at least by his own lights) the unofficial tribune of American Jews. He had done this by deliberately choosing a public and political life; and doing so with a

showy confidence that was also something new in Jewish history. More
often than not, diaspora Jews had told each other that they must
beware of the treacherous reefs of politics and public utterances; that
the best and safest life they could lead was to keep the commandments, get on with business, minister to the sick, look after their poor
and keep a low profile. To do anything else was to expose not just
individuals but the whole community to danger should the wind of
political favour shift, as it invariably did.

But for Mordecai and for his type of Jew, all that was Old World
shuffling and dodging. America was a democracy; to be a properly
patriotic American meant, indeed *required*, active citizenship. Jews had
fought for independence; for their vote. Now they should use it,
unafraid. It was time to make a noise like everyone else in the hurly-
burly republic. And as far as Mordecai and the Phillips circle were
concerned it was Jefferson's Democratic-Republicans who must
command their allegiance. Their opponents, the Federalists, seemed
much colder to the possibility of Jews in the public sphere, let alone
holding elected office. Jews ought to be on the side of 'the People'.

Mordecai was the taken-in orphan (along with his sister Judith) in
the Phillips household, which was always swarming with children.
When the time came to see what he might do with his life, Jonas
thought to make him a model of a Jew who might do something
'useful'. Those who did not like the Jews were always complaining
they congregated in unproductive occupations; very well then, let
Mordecai be a craftsman. Accordingly he was apprenticed to a
Philadelphia wood carver and gilder. But French polish and gold leaf
were not for Mordecai; better, he thought, to shoulder a pedlar's pack
like so many of his co-religionists, walk with or cart a stock of pins
and needles, mirrors, muslins and calicos out on the road.

But what Mordecai really wanted was to be in New York where he
could be close to the gaudy life of the theatre. In New York he hung
around Johns Street hoping for free tickets and began to scribble
juvenile plays. He developed an early sense that American life itself
was a form of social theatre. 'I had a hankering for the national drama,
a kind of juvenile patriotism.' He managed to join a small company;
reviewed plays in the *Trangram or Fashionable Trifler*; and even managed
to get an early play, *The Fortress of Sorrento*, published if never actually
performed.[5] Later when he was better established in the 1820s and 30s,

there would be chest-beating plays of American history, real and invented, featuring the decisive battle at Yorktown; dramas of the wars of independence and 1812, with breeches roles for women like in *She Would be a Soldier*; patriotic fantasies about Greek independence enabled by selfless American assistance.

Mordecai's plays were hardly Shakespeare (everyone's first choice in post-independence America) but that was the point. Bardolatry, he believed, had crushed the independence of the American spirit, imprisoned it within the forms and norms of Old England from which their language and literature should now be liberated. Much the same sentiment animated Noah Webster who composed his dictionary in part to be rid of the burdensome authority of the likes of Dr Johnson and his definitions of what constituted good English.

There was more than one way to make a patriotic show and Mordecai lost no time in exploring any opportunities that came his way. His uncle, Naphtali Phillips, was the editor of New York's leading paper, the *Public Advertiser*, one of a surprising number of Jews, as Jonathan Sarna has noted, who became journalists in the early decades of the republic. Isaac Harby ran a short-lived paper in Charleston for which Mordecai supplied articles in the thin disguise of the Turk 'Muley Mulak' commenting on the wonders of America. And members of the Cardozo and Seixas clans as well as Cohens and Levys all found a livelihood in journalism, just as a century later they would flock to Tin Pan Alley. American Jews were well prepared for the rough and tumble of newspaper life. Many in Mordecai's generation were literate; but it was a street-smart kind of literacy, tuned to tavern gossip, and the punch and counter-punch of local and national politics. And where much of America wanted to find homes and homesteads, their patch of land, the home of the Jews was very often the open road. It was easy enough to take broadsheets and papers in the sales pack, not least because the pedlars understood, perhaps better than Anglo-Scotch or German journalists, that papers were also a storefront, a site to sell things: household goods, fancy clothes, farm tools, patent remedies, pungent opinions and, not least, ribald humour. When in his turn Mordecai became an editor of the *National Advocate*, he would fill its pages with caricatures, jokes and salty stories as well as grey columns of intelligence.

As an unapologetically public Jew, Mordecai was not shy about banging the drum for himself and his people. This too was an American turn. At Shearith Israel (as in Isaac Harby's 'Reformed' synagogue in Charleston), English had been introduced alongside Hebrew in the liturgy, precisely to connect Jews better with their fellow Americans. The pulpit of the Crosby Street synagogue became a place for non-rabbinical speakers like Mordecai to deliver sermons that were more like public lectures, then a major form of entertainment as well as instruction. His 'addresses' were published in Mordecai's papers (for as soon as one failed he founded another). Many were concerned with issues of the day and how the Jews were now to live in the modern world. They inaugurated modern Jewish politics.

Squarely facing the world, American Jews plunged into the public fray, picked sides. In Philadelphia they campaigned for Simon Snyder, whose appeal was in the German community rather than the Anglo. Nationally Naphtali and Mordecai were firmly on the side of the Jeffersonian succession, which meant James Madison and James Monroe. But Mordecai was also enough of a precocious adept in the ways of American politics to know that he could ask for something in return, especially when print hackery and the stage were not quite adequate for making a living.

How about a consulate? The tradition of Jews offering themselves as consuls in far-flung places, responsible for promoting business as well as protecting citizens abroad, went back centuries. They had served Christian and Muslim states as reporters of strategic and commercial intelligence. They were at home in many languages. Cousins and uncles were already residing in useful places. Among Americans the Jews seemed simultaneously cosmopolitan and passion-ately patriotic. Who better, then, to serve the flag abroad? Precociously shameless and never reticent when making a point, Mordecai wrote to Monroe, the Secretary of State, that making him consul would 'prove to foreign powers that our government is not regulated in the appointment of their officers by religious distinction'.

Mordecai first applied for the post at Riga knowing that the great hinterland of Latvian and Lithuanian Ashkenazim lay upriver on the Niemen, but also of course that it was on the strategic frontier of what would be a great contest of military wills between the French and Russian empires. But he was sent instead to a place where his Sephardi connections might do more good: the 'Barbary States' of North Africa. Corsairs operating out of Tunis and Algiers preyed on

American shipping in the Mediterranean. The prizes constituted a major source of revenue for the bey of Morocco and the dey of Algiers; and Americans were taken captive for ransom. During Jefferson's presidency, the conflict had boiled over into a nasty little war between 1801 and 1805. But despite punishing raids by American warships and marines, the corsair rulers were incorrigible and continued to keep American and European captives as slaves. It was known that there was a sizeable population of Jews in the North African ports, the most powerful like the Bacri clan able to exert some influence when they weren't actually profiting from the spoils. Just across the straits the Jews of British Gibraltar, the Cardozos, could provide the necessary introductions.

So in 1813, Mordecai assumed his most showy stage part yet: Yankee Jew at the court of the Pirate Prince (who, in the usual way of things, had just murdered his rival).[6] Mordecai made a spectacular appearance arrayed in 'a coat covered from collar to skirts in gold', bowed deep and kissed the hand of the potentate. But when he was out of the ruler's lair, he discovered something more extraordinary still: a community of 30,000 Jews, about as unlike the frock-coated and hooped-skirt Israelites of New York, Charleston and Philadelphia as could possibly be imagined. These Jews lived in mud houses coated with lime and whitewash in narrow alleys. The doorways of the better off opened onto shady, jasmine-hung courtyards where macaws squawked from hanging branches and lap dogs snoozed on divans. They were tax farmers, minters of coin, suppliers of jewellery to the rulers' inexhaustible appetite for gems. The poorest did what they had done for centuries: hammered copper, stooped over ancient pitted tables to make bracelets and rings, softened hides into slippers then hawked them beside vendors of swivel-eyed chameleons and bright daggers.

Rich or poor, the Jews of Tunis were all obliged to pay the annual *jizya* confirming their inferior tribute status, and were subject to the perennial humiliations. For the Jews there was to be no walking past a mosque, no riding horses, no building of showy synagogues. Brilliant colours were forbidden on their dress. On the street and in the souk the men wore black coats and slippers, the women dark blue. But when Consul Mordecai Noah invited the grandees to celebrate Washington's birthday, they came in sparkling splendour. The plump

women were 'covered with jewels and gold brocades ... their feet
bare' but for 'amber slippers', their tawny ankles encircled with gold
and silver. The young American was dazzled, lost in romantic sympathy
for his Maghrebi co-religionists, for they did things unimaginable in
New York but which seemed survivals of more ancient Jewish customs
and sensibilities. On Friday afternoons before the coming of the
Sabbath, the women would go to their cemetery – fields of unorna-
mented stone, the graves of children proportioned to the littleness of
the lost – and carefully brush away any dirt soiling the tombs. Then
they sat upon the stones and talked with the dead, sighing and
murmuring, fingers fluttering at their breast or palms down towards
their lost loved ones. When the shadows lengthened and it was time
to prepare for the Sabbath, the women would touch their hands to
the stone, and raise them to their lips in farewell.[7]

Just as Mordecai thought his mission was going well, captives
redeemed, a letter arrived from Secretary of State James Monroe.
Instead of the expected appreciation for his services, the note contained
a curt dismissal. When he had been appointed, Monroe explained, it
had not been apparent that being a Jew in such an office, far from
serving to the government's advantage, was in fact a liability, given
the regrettable prejudices and opinions of local rulers. Later, it was
said that there were irregularities in the way Mordecai had accounted
for his consular expenditures. He conceded he had not been above
misunderstanding in such matters but he took the blow as a slight to
his people as well as his pride; a depressing sign that in respect of the
Jews, Americans were less generous than he had assumed.

The grievance spurred him to become irreproachably, unanswerably
American. Back in New York, he wrote and produced more patriotic
melodramas, became the editor of the National Advocate and, in 1820,
city sheriff. Would it not be a fine thing, he opined, only half humorously, if there could be a Jewish president? Mordecai thought and
acted in grandly Solomonic gestures. When an epidemic of yellow
fever hit the city, he opened the prison gates to allow inmates an
escape from what would otherwise have been a certain death sentence,
standing personally responsible for any failure to return once the
danger was over. The humane gesture did not win him popularity at
large, and when he ran for re-election in 1822 the full force of
Judaeophobic invective, mobilised by James Gordon Bennett, the editor

of the *New York Herald*, turned on him. In Bennett's pages he was 'The Jew Noah' or more simply 'Shylock', a member of a degraded, abhorred race who habitually insulted the Saviour and were incorrigibly avaricious. It was unthinkable that even the lowest kind of Christian should be hanged by the order of a Jew! It was a pretty poor Christian, Mordecai replied to Bennett, who wanted so much hanging. But the mud-slinging worked; he lost the election.

For that matter, what Mordecai heard from abroad did not encourage the view that a new age of acceptance was dawning for the Jews. In the thirty-six German states, the Jews were paying the price for having been favoured by liberalising legislation enacted during the Napoleonic ascendancy. Emancipation edicts had been annulled, restrictions on occupations and residence restored. In some states, the old occupations of cattle dealing and peddling were forbidden and Jews were sent to vocational schools to be trained for artisanal work which would mostly be unavailable to them, not least because the guilds were so implacably hostile. In other places the opposite was true and they were subject to the old restrictions, sent back to the roads but limited as to where they were allowed to peddle. In 1819, a wave of violence bore down on them, beginning in Bavaria, spreading to Frankfurt am Main, the Rhineland and even as far north as Hamburg. Known friends of the Jews as well as suspect converts to Christianity were marked men, but as usual the attacks were viscerally indiscriminate, the poorest taking the hardest blows. There were deaths and beatings, the rioters shouting '*Hep hep!*' as they went about their dirty business beneath the impassive gaze of spectators. Students explained that the slogan stood for a cry thought to have been shouted during the Judaeophobic slaughters of the first Crusade: '*Hierosolyma est perdita*' – Jerusalem is lost – which could be taken either as perdition to the Jews or as the determination to retake the holy city. In the Christian revivalist fervour of Romantic Germany, the slogan had a sinister medieval echo.

The ugly hollering carried across the Atlantic, tales of terror arriving with waves of German immigrants. The female poet and writer of hymns for the reform synagogue in Savannah, Penina Moïse, addressed the victims of '*Hep hep*': 'If thou art one of that oppressed race / Whose pilgrimage from Palestine we trace / Brave the Atlantic / Hope's broad anchor weigh / A western sun will gild your future day.' But when

Mordecai was denounced over and again as a Shylock he began to think that 'oppression' could happen even in the great American refuge. He still clung to his grandfather Jonas Phillips's view that America was the Jews' great hope and sanctuary. But perhaps it was time to find a territory, however small, where Jews might govern themselves, an asylum *within* America. He was not alone in this. There were those, often among the Christian 'Restorationist' communities of evangelicals, who wanted a much greater Jewish immigration to the United States. One of them, W. D. Robinson, had published a 'Memoir' in 1819 urging the creation of an expressly Jewish territory somewhere on the western frontier, between the Missouri and the Mississippi. It was patently untrue, he insisted, that the Jews were tribally averse to agriculture. Anyone who read the Bible knew them to be herders and cultivators. 'Convey them to a rich soil, and a smiling climate', remove them from the reach of persecution and they would prove every bit the pioneer. With benevolent help and investment 'we should behold Jewish agriculture spreading through the American forests, Jewish towns and villages bordering the banks of the Missouri and the Mississippi'.[8]

Mordecai was encouraged in his own vision for a Jewish-American territory by enquiries he had received from the German-Jewish *Kulturverein*: the historian-founders of the new discipline of *Wissenschaft des Judentums*, Jewish studies (mostly history, philology and philosophy), among them Leopold Zunz. But in his excitement Mordecai mistook their general curiosity about Jewish-American life as the announcement of a mass migration. A Jewish home needed to be found for this exodus! Seventeen thousand acres of prime land on Grand Island in the Niagara River near Buffalo in upstate New York Mordecai thought would do as a 'place of repose for Israel and Judah' within the United States. To this American ark of refuge would flock the troops of immigrants in their multitudes, and they would unite with Great Lakes Indians whom Mordecai believed were the descendants of the Lost Tribes of Israel. Peace pipes would be smoked in German meerschaum! In 1823 the Congregationalist minister Ethan Smith's *View of the Hebrews* recycled yet again that old story, and he was by no means alone. By 1824 Mordecai had persuaded enough philanthropic enthusiasts to buy 2,555 acres of Grand Island for $10,000. On 15 September 1825 he orchestrated a grandiose ceremony, complete with a Seneca chief, inaugurating the new Jewish-American 'sanctuary'. As the founding father of this moment of hope, Mordecai Noah called the place 'Ararat'.

The proceedings were Mordecai's most extravagant performance. He had planned to reconvene a 'Grand Sanhedrin' of seventy elders, and pending their gathering appointed himself 'Governor and Judge of Israel'. For this he needed a quasi-priestly robe but the best he could come up with was a Richard III costume borrowed from a local theatrical troupe. It was not a good omen. Short of a makeshift temple, Mordecai preached the glories of the day from the pulpit of the evangelical church of St Paul's in Buffalo, promulgating edicts for Jews well beyond Niagara Falls. Ararat was for them all. A census of Jews worldwide was to be taken; a 'head tax' of four shekels levied to defray the costs of Jewish self-government. Polygamy (not a major feature of Jewish life even in Muslim lands) was summarily abolished; literacy in the language of their adopted countries would henceforth be required for both partners in marriage. Ararat sowed a seed but there was no harvest whatsoever. Jewish immigrants (and they were not yet arriving en masse) preferred New York, Philadelphia and Cincinnati to Grand Island. The costs of purchasing the land remained a debt. In short order, the pipe dream of an American Zion by Niagara was abandoned, leaving only a modest cornerstone to commemorate its unfounded optimism.

Mordecai went back to journalism and politics, becoming a supporter of Andrew Jackson and for his pains securing the well-paid post of city surveyor. He flirted with rising nativism, not a seemly position for a self-appointed leader of American Jews. But he had managed to make himself sufficiently famous in American literary life to be mentioned in the same breath as Fenimore Cooper and Washington Irving, and he tried to leverage that renown for the benefit of his people. During the 1830s and 40s he was busy creating benevolent societies, proposing a Hebrew College for the education of young Jews threatened by assimilation, since one of the results of American freedom had been that one in three matches were intermarriages.

Mordecai's repeated message to American Jews, indeed to his co-religionists throughout the world, was that they needed to take charge of their own historical destiny. This collective self-emancipation included the return of the oppressed to their ancient ancestral land, a vision which was already in vogue among Christian 'Restorationists' for whom the physically rebuilt Zion in Palestine was a necessary stop along the way of universal redemption and the return of the Saviour. At the same time as he was adamantly hostile to missionary activity, Mordecai nonetheless presented the Return to Jerusalem, and even the building of a Third Temple, as the common interest of Christianity and Judaism. About the third monotheism of course he had nothing to say. Increasingly he was wrapping himself in the garment of his two names: Mordecai, the rescuer of the Jews from hatred-driven calamity, and Noah the patriarch of a people saved from the deluge.

II. Striking Out

Jews in their multitudes were moving in the opposite direction, west to America not east to Palestine. In the half-century after 1825, the Jewish population of the United States went from five thousand to a quarter of a million.[9] There were demographic oddities: Jewish Cincinnati in the first instance was settled by men from Devon and Hampshire: Portsmouth, Plymouth and Exeter. But by the time Max Lilienthal went there as rabbi in 1855, a long way from his old posting as the herald of reform in Russia, it had become a German-Jewish shtetl boasting the first German-language newspaper for Jewish women, *Die Deborah*. The vast majority of the great mid-century migration came from the thirty-six German states: Bavaria and Württemberg in the south; the small towns and villages of the Rhineland Palatinate like Abenheim near Worms; and further east from the old Polish lands around Posen, which had been returned to Prussia after the Napoleonic Wars; some too from towns like Naumburg in Saxony-Anhalt, and even as far afield as Habsburg Bohemia and Moravia.

'Hep hep' and its aftermath had shaken belief in liberal emancipation. Hopes stayed alive into the 1848–9 German revolutions in which Jews were prominently involved, but when they were crushed, they sailed west. That impulse moved urban Jews to uproot themselves, but the majority of emigrants were not journalists or lawyers but

Dorfjuden, village Jews who peddled or traded in cattle and horses, and they were moved by economic desperation rather than political liberalism, leaving their families behind until they had a better sense of the lie of American land. It was the pressure of rising population, depressed earnings and fewer opportunities in the hungry 1830s and 40s – plus the tightening sense that they would always be bound by petty restrictions preventing them from travelling the distances they needed to peddle, much less do well in the few occupations for which they had been sent to vocational schools (soap-boiling, dyeing, hand-weaving) – which drove the Jews to the ports. Hamburg, Bremen, even Le Havre, Liverpool and, though it was notorious for its tavern swindlers, Rotterdam were their places of embarkation.

Enough of closed doors, barking dogs and bullying policemen! Enough of lonely dumplings bobbing in thin broth on Friday night! *Luft* and *Land* was what they were after: air and space, air to breathe, land to roam, to buy and sell what they could; do what Jews had to to make a go of it. So while, especially in the 1850s, more educated German Jews came to the American cities (particularly the humming ones of the Midwest like Chicago), many of the *Dorfjuden* struck out for the moving frontiers of America: to New Orleans and Montgomery, Alabama, in the South; Louisville and Memphis in the Appalachian states; to the steamboat stations of the western river basins like St Louis; and the most intrepid all the way to Utah and the mining towns of Colorado, Nevada and California. In the days before the railroad, rather than endure the months and the dangers of the western wagon trails, many opted to take the southern route across the fever-struck isthmus of Panama and then ship up the west coast to San Francisco. Enough were drawn by the lure of gold, and stories of towns where a man could start out with nothing and strike it rich, for there to be a substantial community of Jews in San Francisco by the mid-1850s.[10] Naturally, the city had not one but two mutually contentious synagogues, Emanu-El and Shearith Israel, German and Polish respectively, reform-minded and traditional, each with their own *mohels*, *shokhetim*, cemeteries, benevolent associations and, for a while, print journals.

Jews were on the move in America, transplanting the itinerant life they had led in the country towns and villages of the German-speaking world to the American continent. This was a world in which Fanny Brooks (née Bruck) could join the wagon train in 1853 with her husband

(and uncle) Julius, formerly a weaver, tanner and pedlar from Frankenstein near Breslau, hang her clothes out to dry on the sage brush when they got wet fording a river, listen to French songs sung around the campfire, marvel at the oncoming black mass of buffalo one day, and at the impoverished Indians who appeared at some distance from the mule train as it made its ponderous plod, thirteen miles a day, towards Fort Laramie, Wyoming.[11]

The most dramatically intrepid of the wandering Jews was the Baltimore artist Solomon Nunes Carvalho, recruited as photographer by the soldier-explorer John Charles Fremont for what turned out to be his fifth and last disastrous expedition west in the winter of 1853–4. Waist-deep in the snow of the Rockies, Carvalho coated, buffed and mercurialised his daguerreotype plates.[12] Sometimes the company of twenty-two, which included Delaware Indian scouts and Mexicans, would go without food for days on end. Reduced to eating their lamed ponies, Carvalho was so ravenous that he devoured raw liver one morning, cut from the carcass, but baulked at roast porcupine because it looked so much like pork. Privation became so extreme that Fremont made the group take a solemn oath that, however bad things became, they would, at least, forswear eating each other (as was known to have been the case with other expeditions that had come to grief). Carvalho waded through iced-over streams or sometimes attempted to ford the water on horseback, but on one occasion was plunged into the bitterly freezing current for fifteen minutes when his mount sank beneath him. Frostbitten, trudging along on foot, lagging behind the main group, Carvalho seemed to be coming to the end of his rope and his life; he sat himself down on a snowbank, 'my feet resting in the footsteps of those who had gone before me ... I removed from my pocket the miniatures of my wife and children to take a last look at them; their dear smiling faces awakened fires of energy ... I still had something to live for; my death would bring heavy sorrow and grief to those who looked for me alone for support.' When he was at the last extremity he would recite the Psalms. Though suffering from dysentery and scurvy, his fingers split and infected, Carvalho managed to stagger into the Mormon township of Parowan where he was nursed back to health. 'When I entered Mr Heap's house I saw three beautiful children. I covered my eyes and wept for show to think I might

yet be restored to embrace my own.' In Salt Lake City he was
befriended by Brigham Young, who forbore from conversion
attempts. There were long discussions about the Bible and polygamy.
In Los Angeles, where there was a tiny Jewish community, he founded
a Young Men's Hebrew Benevolent Association before returning to
Baltimore where he became a pillar of the Jewish community. His
daguerreotypes of the Fremont expedition were given to the photographer Matthew Brady and, with the exception of a precious few
(including one of a Cheyenne village), were lost in a fire.

Not many Jews went as far as Carvalho to immerse themselves in
deep America. But there were plenty who ventured from the cities,
prompted by disaster at gaming tables or the craving for an overnight
fortune in the gold fields and silver mines. Abraham Abrahamsohn,
who had seen his clothing shop, a booth by the San Francisco docks,
burn to nothing in one of the city's frequent fires, was one of many
who were forced to turn to mining.[13] Set up by a friend from Posen
with pick, shovel, pan, boots and blue woollen shirt, he had no choice
but to 'bite the sour apple' and see if he could make enough from
the mines to be able to return to the city whose music, gambling and
'brown, black-eyed Mexican girls', nosegays at their bosom, had so
bewitched him. Somewhere near Beavertown, Abraham Abrahamsohn
was given an education in western living, narrowly escaping an irate
grizzly who had been sleeping in the hollow oak beside which he and
his nine companions had camped. Coyotes howled and yapped through
the night. He rapidly discovered that the mines were no bonanza and
that the little money from a day's panning was scarcely enough to
buy flour, salt, beef and the liquor needed to keep body and soul
together. Yes, there were moments when Abrahamsohn lay back on
his bed of dirt carpeted with the soft, fragrant needles of the redwoods,
and dissolved into a western epiphany as 'bushy partridges went
clucking through the thickets and larks soared into the lovely blue
heavens'. But the toil was brutal and unrewarding. Carting the ore
rather than digging for it was not much better. 'Oh how I remembered
my confectionery store in Germany.' Three months of this unremit-
ting, back-breaking labour brought him just forty dollars. He gave up.
In Sacramento, he worked for a tailor, then, irked by being asked to
doorknock for mending jobs, set up on his own, doing sufficiently
well to return to San Francisco where he discovered that there were

already Jews making a tidy living as a *mohel*, a fact which astonished
him as in the old country circumcisions were gratis. Though
Abrahamsohn was not the *mohel* who practised the famous triplet
circumcision that caused a great public stir in the papers, he had made
enough in a year or so to switch trades yet again, this time to catering.
For a time, Abrahamsohn swaggered, California-style, as the owner
of a restaurant down at the wharf, furnished with fancy tables and
mirrored walls, the employer of three French waitresses, a Chinese
cook and a dishwasher, until, inevitably, yet another fire destroyed
everything in one hellish conflagration. Passover saved him as, of
necessity, he turned baker and seller of matzot. But Abrahamsohn
had had his fill of the swings and roundabouts of California life, and
there came a day when he heard of Australia as the next golden land,
and made his way to the shipping office for a ticket.

Bitten by the gold bug, Abrahamsohn was a Jew in a hurry. Others
shrugged, took their time, peddled; made do with shlepping buttons
and bows.[14] The immense fortunes that would become (especially
after trading in commercial paper in the Civil War) the businesses
of the Goldmans, the Seligmans and the Lehmans, all began with
a pack full of pins, needles and thread. One man, or family, from
a little shtetl in the Rhineland, Alsace or Bavaria, sought out a
landsman and was set up with the first pack: beside the needles,
mirrors and lace, muslin and soap, a cheap framed print or two:
things that could turn a rickety cabin with a smoky hearth into a
semblance of home. At first the pedlar, with as much as 150 pounds'
worth of goods on his back, walked his territory, minding the dogs,
knocking on doors. If he was persuasive enough and saved a handful
of dollars, a mule and cart or at least saddlebags would relieve him
of the crushing load. The cart could take a bigger variety of goods;
his selling territory would expand. And if this went well he could,
finally, graduate to the horse and wagon which would let him sell
not just stove polish but the stove itself and the housewares the
farmers' wives wanted: chairs and tables, rugs and curtains, stuff
that would make a lonely life out on the prairie or in the mountain
valleys bearable. Thus it was that countless Jews became a familiar
fixture of the American frontier. Their broken English was matched
by that of their customers, the latter accented with Norwegian,

Italian, Polish, a dense Irish brogue. Yiddish met Bayerndeutsch and the two got along enough to make a sale, perhaps to share a cup of weak tea or even a heel of black bread or a slice of *Gugelhupf*. Pedlar and customer knew each other's world of memories: clock towers and strudel. Sometimes, in bad weather especially, if they were lucky, they might find a hospitable customer who would have no qualms about taking the Jewish pedlar in for the night. In the morning the pedlar would make an offer to pay for the kindness and just as often as not would be refused, so a toy or trinket would be left for the farmer's children. Occasionally, the connection made on a peddling circuit might become permanent. Marcus Spiegel, whose brother-in-law was in business in Chicago, had been allotted a territory in the Quaker farmlands of Ohio. At one of the houses he stopped at, belonging to the Hamlins, he fell in love and the feeling was returned with enough warmth for the farmer's daughter, Caroline, to convert to Judaism.[15] During his selling rounds, and later when he served in the Ohio Volunteers for the Grand Army of the Union, Spiegel wrote his 'Yehudi' wife letters of passionate affection, reminding her to keep a Jewish home, make Sabbath and Seder, and take the children to synagogue.

This kind of story could only have taken place in America, where Jewish immersion in the host culture was less bound about by policing and social hatreds than anywhere else in the world, a small miracle which was the result of nearly everyone in the country, other than Native Americans, being of immigrant stock.

Yesterday's pedlar wanted to be tomorrow's shopkeeper. That at least was the common dream, another ambition difficult to realise in the Old World. But America was free of guilds. In its fledgling towns strung across the continent there were no immemorial family rights to be the town baker or the tailor. When newcomers arrived there was already cause for social optimism, as many cousins and uncles and brothers-in-law, who had themselves started with the pack, were now established in retail: sellers of dry goods, coffee, tea, fabric, horseshoes, nails, lumber, seeds and flour. In 1876 Max Lilienthal was asked to officiate at his nephew's wedding in San Francisco and rode the Union Pacific all the way from Cincinnati to the end of the line at Ogden, Utah, before transferring to the Central Pacific for the trip

over the Sierra Nevada.[16] Along the way, through Iowa and Nebraska
and over the Rockies in Wyoming,

> in all the little places [where] we stopped ... we found our Jewish
> brethren ... wherever there is a row of those wooden country stores
> we read on signs the names of our co-religionists – Cohn, Levy and a
> lot of names for Israel are displayed everywhere. I felt sincerely elated
> that wherever you meet them they cling proudly to the faith of their
> fathers. Though secluded in the desert far away from every Jewish
> religious institution they still try to observe as much of Sabbath and
> holidays as they possibly can.

Jews in their dusty overalls greeted him along the route as they would
a great *zaddik* in the old country. His journey became a wide-eyed education in what the Jews, including Lilienthal's own family, might achieve
in the American west. In Sacramento his son Philip, raised to chief cashier
of the Anglo-California Bank, proudly shepherded his father around the
depot and 'introduced me to a crowd of millionaires who had waited in
the depot for the arrival of our train ... a motley crowd of both Jews
and Gentiles'. Riding the bay ferry, Lilienthal made out on the city skyline
the 165-foot-tall twin spires of temple Emanu-El on Sutter Street 'with
the Ten Commandments engraved between them', and for a moment
he believed he was truly arrived at the golden sanctuary. Many others
coming from villages in Bavaria, Posen, Alsace or the Rhineland shared
that vision. By 1870 there were already 10,000 Jews in California.
    Some of them reproduced their lives in Germany but on a bigger,
freer scale. Isaac Stone came from a Bavarian country district but it was
only when he got to California that he could turn dairy farmer and
milk supplier to San Francisco, employing Swiss dairymen to look after
a herd of 175 cows in his range of stables a few miles outside the city.
In the west Jews could multitask in ways unthinkable in the Old World
and even in the cities back east. Mark Strouse, the pistol-packing Jewish
sheriff of Virginia City, the hub of the Comstock Lode in 1862, was
also purveyor of meat to the town and its camps. Offering kosher beef
and poultry did not, however, stop Strouse from owning a hog ranch,
for the west after all was built on bacon.[17] (Jews in the armies of both
sides of the Civil War shared the same camp diet as their Gentile
comrades, which almost always included bacon.) But unobservant Jews

in the west often made room and common cause with the Orthodox. Aaron Fleishhacker, who kept a popular clothing store in Carson City, Nevada, along with his two sons, was not that much of a Jew, if measured by strict Sabbath observance, but those who kept the commandments gathered for prayers in the upstairs room above his shop. Before synagogues were built, those upstairs rooms were usually the place where a *minyan* said their prayers morning and evening.[18]

Rabbis and cantors very often had more than one string to their bow. Daniel Levy, originally from Luxheim in Lorraine, who was reader in the German Emanu-El synagogue in San Francisco and who had been schoolteacher to the Jews of Oran in Algeria (doing a little jail time for attacking Napoleon III), taught in the San Francisco Boys' High School but also emerged as the most articulate and eloquent of San Francisco's tribe of Jewish journalists. The young rabbi Herman Bien, who wore a pistol at his side when he conducted services in Virginia City, was a writer and performer of musicals, not all of which met with success; and was elected to the Assembly in Carson City after Nevada achieved statehood in 1864.[19] The Ashims (or Aschims) were dry-goods salesmen but many other things too: one of them, Baruch 'Barry', was spotted by Samuel Clemens (in the process of becoming Mark Twain) for his proficiency in shorthand transcriptions. He was hired to supply the writer with the proceedings of the Nevada Territorial Assembly on which Twain was supposed to report.

For the boldly inventive, the west provided opportunities for Jews to capitalise on inspired hunches. Against massively entrenched opposition on the part of mine owners and railroads, the engineer Adolph Sutro battled his way to dig an epic four-mile tunnel under the Sierra Nevada to drain the Comstock Lode silver mines of the deep water impeding extraction and removal of the ore. When operational, Sutro's tunnel drained between 3 million and 4 million gallons daily. Eventually more powerful pumping machinery would make the tunnels obsolete, but Sutro saw this in time to sell his share while the going was very good, and turned it into real estate in and around San Francisco. He would end up in the 1890s the first Jewish mayor of a major American city.[20]

The Jewish presence in the mining world of the west produced at least another momentous commercial revolution. It began with a famous job of improvised rough tailoring. In December 1870 the wife

of a bulky, dropsical Nevada miner came to the Virginia City shop of
Jacob Davis (born Jakub Youphes near Riga) complaining that her
husband's work pants were constantly ripping. Davis's main line of
work was wagon covers, tents and horse blankets for the workers
of the Central Pacific Railroad, but he'd been known to knock off the
occasional pair of overalls as well. The fabric for all these jobs was
either the ten-ounce cotton duck twill or the nine-ounce blue denim
supplied to him by Loeb Strauss (now calling himself Levi) in San
Francisco. By his own now canonical account, Davis looked over at
the copper rivets lying around on his workbench, normally used to
secure tenting and wagon covers, and the thought that changed the
look of the modern world stirred. Might the rivets not be used at
pockets and seams for the work clothes? They could and were, and
before long all the railroad workers and miners too wanted them. Davis
made two hundred pairs over the next year and still couldn't keep up
with the demand, nor could his supplier Mr Strauss. In July 1872 Davis
wrote the famous letter asking Strauss to apply for a patent in return
for a partnership in production with a share of all proceeds. An initial
application was rejected by the Patent Office on the grounds that rivets
had already been used in the manufacture of military boots during the
Civil War, but a further application in May 1873 met with success, and
jeans (from the matelot slang for 'Gênes', the French for Genoa, where
blue canvas workclothes had been worn for centuries) arrived.

Going west made Jewish women into businesswomen should the
need arise. Many of them redefined, in distinctively American ways,
just what was meant by *eshet chayil*, held up as the model in the Book
of Proverbs and Jewish tradition.[21] Crossing the Great Plains and the
Rockies on her way to Utah, Fanny Brooks noticed the wagon wives
not just driving the mule trains when it came to their turn, but also,
as a matter of routine, keeping a revolver close by and knowing how
to use it. This, she was surprised but not unhappy to learn, was
expected of the women as well as the men, and she duly followed
suit. Once settled in the west the women often proved to be the more
dependable breadwinner, and in California and other western territories and states applied for licences to trade in their own right. Thus
the capable Caroline Tannenwald ran the Round Tent store at
Placerville, the emporium for all the mining camps and ranches for
miles about. Fanny Brooks became one of the most successful

milliners in hat-crazy San Francisco where there could never be enough silk flowers and flounces, bows, mother-of-pearl studs and sequins and especially ostrich plumes, all loaded onto extravagant brims and crowns. While Emanuel Blochman was running his Torah school for children in San Francisco, and then trying and failing to make a living from, successively, matzo baking, kosher wine-making, dairy farming and editing the *Weekly Gleaner*, his wife Nanette (Yettel) Conrad Blochman was putting challah on the table from her successful millinery store (closed on Shabbat and festivals). When yet another of her husband's ventures failed, Nanette put him behind the millinery counter.[22] Others in the same business like Sarah Loryea knew that there would be a demand for fashionable hats just as soon as silver towns became established, so she opened her shops in Carson City and Virginia City, using the opportunity to sell fancy china and glassware to customers looking for a bonnet. Others discovered a speciality niche in children's clothing and sold knickerbockers and coats alongside the outfits tailored for their mothers. Jewish women also set up as boarding-house keepers, hoteliers and restaurateurs in the silver towns: Matilda Ashim in Carson City, Sara Leventhal and Regina Moch in Eureka. They all needed to be tough in the saloons and careful with the books, but Moch in particular was up to the challenge. In 1879 a fire burned down her hotel and restaurant, taking the life of her husband. Regina grieved, sat *shiva*, and then made sure to advertise the opening of a new establishment within the month.[23]

In many ways it was on Jewish women that America worked its most profound transformations. For the generations coming first from Britain and then from Germany, *eshet chayil* still meant the traditional domestic ideal of 'priestess of the home'. But in some famous cases the conventions expanded into non-stop social activism and became models for a new kind of Jewish life. The opportunities to participate in charitable institutions came more naturally to Jewish women in reform synagogues where the separation of sexes had been replaced by family pews. But the most famous paragon of the new Jewish woman, Rebecca Gratz of Philadelphia, saw Jewish social work as a powerful antidote to the reforming Judaism she feared would be a Trojan Horse for assimilation.[24] The misfortunes of poverty and ignorance she thought made Jews, especially Jewish women, vulnerable quarry for the seemingly benign missionaries. So Gratz became in her own life a champion of social benevolence and education, the Pennsylvania patrician ministering to the *Dorfjuden*.

Gratz could do this because her family were well-to-do: land speculators and merchants; a brood of brothers, many of whom intermarried, a fact which only intensified her resolution. She had all the qualities which would have made her a perfect catch for conversion – she was beautiful, literate, a correspondent and friend of the transatlantic writing world: Washington Irving, Fanny Kemble, Maria Edgeworth, the educationist, and Grace Aguilar, the prolific Anglo-Jewish novelist. Courted socially and personally, she was determined to stay single and single-minded. After nursing her father following his stroke, she helped found a non-sectarian Philadelphia 'Female Association' to assist impoverished women and girls. Orphanages followed, Gratz always at the helm. Before long she became committed to founding similar institutions for Jewish orphans and young women in distress. A Hebrew school was established to educate the young which despite its name gave instruction almost entirely in English and to which she recruited sister-teachers Simcha Peixotto and Rachel Peixotto Pyke, who wrote textbooks for the students.

Resistant to assimilation, conversion and the marriage market, good-looking and stubbornly pious, Rebecca Gratz was a perfect subject for Gentile spinners of the Jewish romance. The best American portraitists – Gilbert Stuart and Thomas Sully – lined up to do her dark-eyed, raven-haired features justice, and some succeeded in making her unattainably beautiful. Although without any foundation in fact, it's not hard to see why a legend arose that Walter Scott modelled *Ivanhoe*'s Rebecca, the first sympathetic portrait of a Jew in English fiction, on the uncompromisingly virtuous and steadfast Gratz.

The romance of the Jewess, both alluringly exotic and somehow intensely American, was strong enough that one cultural celebrity, an actress renowned for qualities other than her social ethics, went so far as to invent a Jewish identity for herself. Adah Isaacs Menken took this new-found allegiance seriously enough to claim Jewish birth, learn Hebrew, and write poems and essays about Jewish culture and history in journals.[25] When she collapsed in Paris at the age of thirty-three, she sent for a rabbi and made sure she would be buried in the Jewish section of the Père Lachaise cemetery.

When she married Isaac Menken, Ada added an 'h' to her first name to make it look more Hebraic. But she had been born in or near New Orleans in 1835, probably as the child either of Catholics or of a free black father and a Creole mother. At various times she claimed her father had been a Marrano Jew. What Adah always wanted to be was famous. For a while she was the best-paid actor in America, though she suspected, rightly, it was not entirely the result of her thespian eloquence. She was exceptionally beautiful, flamboyantly brash, had a go at Shakespeare readings on stage in the South (to mixed reviews), and then took up with the musician Menken who belonged to a wealthy Cincinnati Jewish family of merchants. As her husband, promoter and manager, Isaac took Adah back to Ohio where, to win the affection of her in-laws, she learned the rituals of Judaism and the rudiments of Hebrew. The marriage didn't last but Adah the Jewess did, even through a chain of marriages including to a championship heavyweight boxer. In between husbands, and probably during the marriages too, she had affairs with, among others, Charles Blondin the high-wire artist and Alexandre Dumas *père*, twice her age, thus enraging Alexandre Dumas *fils*. On Broadway she played to packed houses by substituting herself, dressed in flesh-nude costume, for the dummy usually strapped to the back of a horse at the climax of Byron's *Mazeppa*. The confusing fact that she was meant to be playing a male lead, while exhibiting the strongest possible characteristics of womanhood, only added to the excitement. Management claimed that on one night no less than nine generals in the Union Army were in the house to see the apparently nude beauty tied to the horse.

But though she played the publicity game like a harp, cutting her curly hair short and blowing cigarette-smoke rings from her Cupid's bow mouth, Adah was more than just the first Jewish sex goddess. Whitman and Melville encouraged her literary ambitions; Dickens and Swinburne took her seriously, and not all of the hundred poems collected in an anthology she called, with a classically Jewish sense of tragic appeal, *Infelicia* are completely dire. Some have a sensually charged electricity which runs with the free verse of her idol Whitman, breaking into speech exclamations, chants and curses. Even before she got to Paris, where she succumbed to an attack of either cancer or tuberculosis or both, Adah must have known the whole history of the first of the great Jewish stars of the theatre, Rachel, and her own lunge at thespian fame anticipated (though without comparable talent) the ultimate incarnation of histrionic force that was Sarah Bernhardt. In her writing Adah often presented herself as the daughter of suffering Israel; an exterminating angel sent to wreak retribution on the anti-Semites. She succeeded well enough for the great patriarch of American reform Judaism, Rabbi Isaac Mayer Wise, to publish her work in the *Israelite*. But temperamentally she was at the opposite pole of Jewishness from Rebecca Gratz of the Good Works. Adah was bloody-minded, dangerous, almost sinister, burning for a fight on behalf of the Jews and she didn't mind who knew it.

Poetically, there was no top over which Adah would not leap. 'Judith' is an extravaganza of shrieking, operatic sensationalism laced with a heavy dose of Apocrypha-porn; the verse equivalent of nineteenth-century costume paintings, all glinting belly jewels, stained scimitars and ecstatically bulging eyeballs. 'I mix your jeweled heads, and your gleaming eyes, and your hissing tongues with the dust,' she has her gleefully murderous virago proclaim, to the enemies of Israel.

> I am no Magdalene waiting to kiss the hem of your garment.
> It is mid-day.
> See ye not what is written on my forehead?
> I am Judith!
> I wait for the head of my Holofernes!
> Ere the last tremble of the conscious death-agony shall have shuddered,
> I will show it to ye with the long black hair clinging to the glazed
> eyes, and the great mouth opened in search of voice, and the strong
> throat all hot and reeking with blood, that will thrill me with wild
> unspeakable joy as it courses down my bare body and dabbles my
> cold feet!

There is also an unmistakable strain of feminist auto-emancipation running through Adah's writing, one which converged with her Jewishness as the wrath of the doubly mistreated. Perhaps it took flamboyant outriders on the edge of Jewish America to tap into this deep well of latent fury. Ernestine Rose, a German rabbi's daughter, who abandoned all faiths and married out, was in the founding cohort of American feminists, the 'Queen of the Platform'. At one convention, notwithstanding her atheism, she explicitly connected the long-suffering history of women at the hands of a world ruled by men, with the oppressions endured by Jews.

And this, in her own way, was also Adah Menken's refrain. In one of the most compelling of her poems, 'Hear O Israel', the title taken from the first line of the daily profession of faith, the *shema*, she turns almost meditative and the tone becomes biblically repentant, in the manner of the prophets and the wisdom books.

My tears have unto me been meat, both in night and day:
And the crimson and the fine linen molders in the dark tents of the enemy.
With bare feet and covered head do I return to thee, O Israel!
With sackcloth have I bound the hem of my garments.
With olive leaves have I trimmed the border of my bosom.

But in its last cantos, the poem faces outwards, towards the oppressors, gathering itself into a defiant battle cry for her people; one which would echo through the coming century of Jewish catastrophe.

We, the Children of Israel, will not creep to the kennel graves ye are scooping out with iron hands, like scourged hounds!
Israel! rouse ye from the slumber of ages, and though Hell welters at your feet, carve a road through these tyrants!
The promised dawn-light is here; and God – O the God of our nation is calling!
Press on – press on!

Through all the Whitmaniac hyperbole, and despite it coming from the pen of a showgirl with Shakespearean delusions, there is something authentically, ominously modern about the thrashing rage of beautiful Adah Isaacs Menken. By the time she got to Europe in the grand tour of her literary and theatrical self-promotion, a new anti-Semitism was already prowling the culture, inaugurated by the publication of Alphonse Toussenel's *Les Juifs, rois de l'époque* (*The Jews, Kings of the Age*) in 1844. The New World was supposed to have escaped this tenacious disease of the old. But Adah would not have had to look very far in her own America to have noticed signs that the infection had, at some places and times, crossed the ocean.

It was not just at elections that Jewish candidates like Mordecai
Noah could expect to be Shylocked at the hustings. In 1855 a Santa
Cruz lemon grower, William W. Stow, who had become Speaker of
the California Assembly, took exception to the refusal of a single
Jewish trader, Louis Schwartz, to join the petition for Sunday closing
which Stow was hoping to make California law. Stow's exasperation
triggered a vehement diatribe against those he caricatured as economic
and social parasites.

> I have no sympathy with the Jews and would it were in my power to
> enforce a regulation that would eliminate them from not only our
> county but from the entire state! I am for a Jew tax that is so high that
> [Jews] would not be able to operate any more shops. The basis of the
> Republican system is in the Christian Sabbath and the Christian religion.
> The Jews must join the majority. They are a class of people who come
> here only to make money and who leave the country as soon as they
> make money.[26]

Stow had gubernatorial ambitions, and since the political climate of
the 1850s had a strain of 'Know Nothing' nativism about it (anti-
Catholic more than anti-Semitic) he may well have assumed he might
gain some popular clout from his onslaught. If so he was swiftly
disabused by the uproar which greeted his speech, not least from other
Gentile members sitting in the Assembly at Sacramento. They knew
the Jews of San Francisco and Los Angeles, Stockton and Sacramento
not just as small traders and shopkeepers, but as city councilmen,
rabbis who were also teachers and civic luminaries, and not least as
judges like Solomon Heydenfeldt, then sitting as a justice of the state
Supreme Court. None of these people corresponded to the malevolent
portrait of the Jews painted by the Speaker. The *Sacramento Democratic
State Journal* reported that Mr H. P. A. Smith of Marin County said
'he did not believe in laws that were not supported by public opinion
and thought that if the Bill were passed the finger of scorn would be
pointed at it'. But the Stow attack prompted the first passionately
eloquent Jewish American counter-attack on bigotry. In his monthly
magazine *The Occident and the Jewish American Advocate*, Isaac Leeser
– born in Neuenkirchen in the Rhineland, tribune of modern orthodoxy, long-time cantor in Philadelphia, author of *The Jews and the*

Mosaic Law (1833) – associated the cause of the Jews with that of liberal toleration and the Constitution.

> Fanaticism of every kind is now the order of the day; moderate men are not heeded ... and this strange infatuation will run riot for some time ... We can easily imagine that the half educated or those belonging to a particular class of religionists should wish to hurry into all extravagances and endeavour to enact Pharaonic laws even against the children of Israel. It is the nature of the vulgar to hate those who differ from them, but it was not to be expected that a man who from his position as presiding officer of a deliberative assembly should so far forget himself as to utter sentiments so adverse to the spirit of the Constitution under which he was chosen to his position. Such a man is not deserving of being handed down to notoriety and infamy even; utter forgetfulness would be his just due.[27]

Henry J. Labatt, a Sephardi with a Yale law degree, originally from Charleston but the authority on California law as well, addressed the enemy directly in the *Israelite*, which he edited with Rabbi Isaac Mayer Wise. Labatt was also president of the Hebrew Young Men's Debating Society and he now turned his rhetorical artillery on William Stow:

> Mr Speaker occupying the position you do as the head of the House of Representatives you should be loath to disgrace our legislature and our state by flagrant and malicious falsehood ... You say 'they come here to make money and leave'. Are you ignorant of the number of families arriving on every steamer to make California their home? Are you ignorant of the brick synagogues erecting in our large cities for family worship? Are you ignorant of the permanent benevolent societies which extend the hand of charity to their bereaved brethren? ... If you are ignorant of these facts then you are basely ignorant; if not, you have greatly misrepresented facts and you are a disgrace to the House over which you have the dishonour to preside.

The wandering Jews, then, would put down roots as deep as anyone else in a country where they were treated as equals. And far from the odiously shifty characters of Stow's prejudice, Labatt insisted that no group of immigrants were more morally upstanding, and to the list of reprobates from which the Jews were conspicuously absent he added a final category meant to sting the likes of Speaker Stow. 'Have they built grogshops to poison the people? Surely not ... Have they filled your jails or taxed the state with criminal trials? Surely not; they are not robbers, marauders or leading politicians.'

This eruption of Jewish indignation might have been a temporary embarrassment for William Stow, possibly to the point of costing him the governor's office. But in 1858 a further Sunday observance law was passed (without any anti-Semitic speeches). Stow's career prospered. He went on to be one of the political and legal patriarchs of the state, his name still memorialised at a tranquil lake in Golden Gate Park, where swans glide and couples canoodle in the San Francisco mildness.

On the eve of the Civil War there were 150,000 Jews in the United States, or about one half of 1 per cent of the population. As Labatt pointed out at the end of his counter-attack, the unpredictable eruption of Judaeophobia at least had the merit of alerting the Jewish community against complacency. In response to these outbursts of disfiguring prejudice, American Jews first discovered their political voice. B'nai B'rith (literally 'Sons of the Covenant') associations, originally founded in New York in 1843 as a response to Jewish exclusion from Masonic lodges and similar fraternities, now became organisations primed to contest anti-Semitism.

But even the B'nai B'rith could not possibly have anticipated General Ulysses Grant's 'Order 11' in 1862, summarily expelling *all* Jews from his military jurisdiction, the 'Department of Tennessee' covering an enormous swathe of territory extending from Illinois all the way south to Kentucky. The ostensible cause of the order was the violation of the economic war against the Confederacy by smuggling goods, especially cotton, fetching a high price in northern manufacturing cities. Some Jews were involved in this illegal trade but the overwhelming majority of smugglers and black marketeers were, as would one expect, non-Jewish. This, though, was not how the matter appeared in Grant's Order 11, the wording of which immediately brought back, to a people defined by their shared memory, the traumatic medieval expulsions, the brutal mass evictions from Spain and Portugal and, more recent, eighteenth-century acts of forced removal from Prague and Vienna. If commercial treason was being committed against the

Union, the Order implied, it must be the notoriously shady Jews who
were to blame. Or as Grant's Order put it:

> The Jews, as a class violating every regulation of trade established by
> the Treasury Department ... are hereby expelled from the Department
> within twenty-four hours from the receipt of this order. Post
> commanders will see to it that all of this class of people be furnished
> passes and required to leave, and anyone returning after such notifica-
> tion will be arrested and held in confinement until an opportunity
> occurs of sending them out as prisoners.[28]

Grant had been exasperated for some time by what he judged acts
of economic sabotage in the grinding war to break the Confederacy.
There may have been only around five thousand Jews living in and
loyal to the South but some of them, like Judah P. Benjamin, Jefferson
Davis's Cabinet Secretary, were very conspicuous.[29] Some others,
like the poet Penina Moise in Savannah, also remained fiercely loyal
to the South; and many even in the North who, like Isaac Mayer
Wise, were staunch for the Union were nonetheless cool or even
hostile to abolitionism. But when Rabbi Morris Raphall preached a
sermon in New York justifying slavery from the Hebrew Bible, he
was met with an immediate barrage of counter-attacks from anti-
slavery Jews. Some took their protest further. In Chicago, in the
summer of 1853, Michael Greenebaum raised a crowd to stop an
escaped slave being arrested under the infamous Fugitive Slave Act.[30]
For the most determined Jewish anti-slavery campaigners, speeches,
letters to the editor or campaigning for Lincoln's election were not
enough. August (born Anschl) Bondi, who had fought with the
revolutionary Hungarian Student Legion in 1848, came to America
with his family at the end of that year to escape the counter-
revolutionary reaction. In New Orleans he saw slaves manhandled
and clad only in torn coffee sacks; at Galveston it was still worse,
slaves beaten every morning with leather straps. 'I could have married
the most beautiful woman in Texas,' he said, but she was a slave-
owner and 'my father's son could not be a slave driver'. In Kansas,
a free state, he was beaten up and his house burned down by Ruffian
gangs who were in the business of intimidating the state into a pro-
slavery position. Bondi did not take this lightly, joining John Brown's

irregular abolitionist army, attacking and killing twelve Ruffians at
Pottawatomie and taking forty-eight pro-slavery prisoners at the
Battle of Black Jack. When Bondi did marry it was to Henrietta
Einstein, the daughter of a prominent Jewish abolitionist. While
serving in the Kansas Volunteers he greeted the news of the emancipation proclamation Jewishly: 'no more Pharaohs; no more slaves'.[31]
And some Jews who had earlier been neutral, and Democrats rather
than Republicans, turned abolitionist during the war itself. Marcus
Spiegel, who before the war had had no truck with abolition, got
to the point where he changed his mind. 'I am for doing away with
the institution of Slavery,' he wrote to his wife Caroline, 'never
hereafter will I either speak or vote in favour of Slavery ... this is
not a hasty conclusion but a deep conviction.'[32]

In other words the opinions and actions of the Jews divided along
the lines of the rest of the country: another measure of how integrated
they had become with American life. But far more Jewish soldiers
fought for the Union than for the Confederacy, enough for them to
need – and, after some obstruction, to get – their own chaplains.

Whether they were warm or cool to emancipation, the implication
of collective guilt implied by the odious phrase 'as a class' in Grant's
Order horrified American Jews everywhere in 1862, not least because
the guilty were defined as anyone 'born of Jewish parents'. In 1868
when Grant ran for president, he was attacked by Jews with unforgiving memories who urged their co-religionists to vote Democrat,
though many remained loyal to the Republicans. Grant himself
publicly admitted that Order 11 had been an iniquity, and perhaps
under the influence of a remorseful conscience appointed Jews to
official positions like the governorship of Washington Territory and
the governor of Indian Affairs in Arizona.

Grant's guilty conscience was almost certainly bound up with his
realisation that the Jews had been made to pay for his personal animus
against his own father Jesse. Cincinnati – the home of Jews in the
Midwest, the rabbinate of Isaac Mayer Wise and Max Lilienthal – was
the birthplace of Ulysses Grant (not to mention the name of his
horse). But it was also the place where Jesse Grant went into informal
partnership with a Jewish clothing manufacturing family, the Macks,
who were desperately in need of cotton. Father Grant imagined that
a visit to his son's headquarters in company with the Macks might

persuade the general to allow favoured conditions, for which influence he would be duly remunerated. Jesse could not have known that Ulysses had been increasingly vexed by what he had already called 'the intolerable nuisance' of the Jews and had been talking about 'purging the Department' of them. Jesse's uninvited appearance before his son in company with the Macks sent the general over the edge.

Happily, the spectacle of thousands of expelled Jews trooping to the railheads, wagons and boats never materialised. Three days after Order 11 had been made, a surprise Confederate attack overran the Union base in Holly Springs and cut communications, making enforcement of the Order all but impossible for most of the military department. Nonetheless American Jews, who had considered themselves free from the centuries-old oppressions and cruelties of Christian Europe, were not about to tolerate their reappearance in America. Cesar Kaskel from Paducah, Kentucky, in the immediate catchment area of the expulsion, sent President Lincoln a telegram declaring all loyal Jews 'greatly insulted and outraged by this inhuman order, the carrying out of which would be the grossest violation of the Constitution'.

Busy preparing the Emancipation Proclamation, Lincoln did not see Kaskel's telegram, nor did he have any idea about Grant's Order. But he did agree to see Kaskel himself, thanks to the intervention of John Gurley Addison, an ex-congressman who had been defeated for re-election in 1862 but who was a long-time ally of the president. When he took in the substance of the Order, Lincoln expressed his astonished displeasure, and said that if indeed such a thing had been done, it would be immediately revoked. He was as good as his word.

There had not been enough time to discover whether Order 11, having referred to the Jews en masse 'as a class', would apply to the thousands of Jews serving in the Union Army. One of them, Philip Trounstine, an officer in the 5th regiment, Ohio Cavalry (who would later be a fire chief in Denver, Colorado), was so appalled by it that, notwithstanding the annulment, he resigned his commission. But others remained steadfastly loyal to the Union and conspicuously brave. Edward Selig Salomon, born in Schleswig, and a young Chicago lawyer in his twenties, fought with the Illinois 24th Infantry, predominantly German and Hungarian immigrants and ex-1848 liberals and revolutionaries, which included a company made up almost entirely of Jews, paid for by public subscription in the community. At Gettysburg, Salomon had two horses shot from under him, 'the only soldier who did not dodge when Lee's guns thundered', according to General Carl Schurz, 'he stood up, smoked his cigar and faced the cannon balls with the sangfroid of a Saladin'. Salomon succeeded the regimental commander, wounded in action, as lieutenant colonel and went on to face some of the most brutal engagements of the war, at Chattanooga and Lookout Mountain. As president, Ulysses Grant would appoint Salomon governor of Washington Territory.

As the bloody struggle went on, Marcus Spiegel became more adamant about its necessity. In a letter from Louisiana to his brother-in-law Michael Greenebaum in March 1863, and about to join the siege on Vicksburg, Spiegel wrote in terms more passionately patriotic than one could imagine from Jews anywhere else in the world, as though the cause of the Union was axiomatically the cause of their people. As much as he wished he could return home to his wife and children in Ohio, he wrote,

> I do not want it [the war] to close until the enemies of my beloved country are conquered and brought to terms. Men who are so contemptible and unprincipled as to wage war against the best govern-ment in the world and trample under foot the flag that was ever ready to protect you and me from oppression must be taught that though a noble country to live in peaceably, it is a powerful government to rebel against.[33]

As colonel of his regiment, the 120th Ohio Volunteers, Spiegel survived the horrific slaughter at Vicksburg and saw its capitulation, only to suffer a bad wound in the groin from one of his own side's shells during a further attack on Jackson, Mississippi. Lying at the railroad depot at Vicksburg waiting to be taken back to Chicago, Spiegel, who kept photographs of his wife and children with him at all times, wrote to Caroline: 'Home, oh sweet word, oh lovely sounding word … Home where I know my dear wife and children are awaiting me with terrible anxiety and throbbing hearts. Home with all its blessings: there I will soon recover from my fearful wound.' But when he returned to Millersburg, Ohio, he was besieged by both parties, Democrat and Republican, to appear on crutches on their behalf. And as he got better, Marcus was pulled back to the deadly simplicity of the war itself. Towards the end of April 1864 he had a distressing letter from his wife telling him their son had had to have a finger amputated after he had stuck his hand in a printing press. To one of his captains Marcus confessed that he was tortured by the thought that he was 'not doing justice' to his family being away. Though he could not 'leave my boys' in uniform he looked forward eagerly to the day he would come marching home. But on 3 May 1864 on the Red River, his transport boat was ambushed by a large Confederate force. Spiegel took a rifle shot to his abdomen, inevitably fatal because of the certainty of infection. His brother Joseph, himself wounded in the arm, was with Marcus when he died the next day. The news did not reach his wife until sometime in June. In July, she gave birth to a daughter who was called Clara Marcus. In 1865 she moved back to Chicago and lived in the circle of her Jewish in-laws, still the good 'Yehudi', as Marcus had called her.

III. Unplucked

The last summer of American peace, 1860, was also the last time that Uriah Levy stayed in Monticello. He was now Commodore Levy, most recently flagship commander of the United States Mediterranean squadron and master of USS *Macedonia*. Uriah was now sixty-eight years old, but despite some discomfort (most likely due to the onset of Crohn's disease) he felt he had a new lease on life. The spring in his step was the result of marriage to his niece Virginia Lopez, the daughter of his sister Frances. At the time of the union in 1853, Virginia had been just eighteen, while her husband was more than three times her age. For those who had never cared much for Uriah, this unseemly age difference was the last straw. There were mutterings and even the suggestion of legal proceedings to declare the marriage invalid because of improperly close consanguinity. But the grumbling came to nothing. For one last summer, a fine one, before the famously violent storms of autumn bore down on the Commonwealth of Virginia as if in ominous warning of much worse to come, the commodore and his

playful, young fashionista wife, together with the elderly, lame Amelia,
enjoyed Monticello. Jefferson's fruitful garden had never been restored
to anything like its original glory, but an abundance of fleshy roses
scented the warm evenings.

In the autumn, Uriah and Virginia returned to their New York
house in St Mark's Place. Over the years he had been buying up real
estate, and the rising prices which went with the expansion of the
city had made him rich. When he died in March 1862, his estate was
estimated around half a million dollars, which if not in the league
of the Astors and Seligmans still made him a substantial citizen. It
was assumed that his naval days were now definitely behind him, but
when the war began with the attack on Fort Sumter, Uriah made
haste to Washington to assure President Lincoln that he would serve
in any way that might be useful, and that since he had loyally served
the Union since the war of 1812 he was 'not one to abandon it on the
day of peril'.

He was not given the opportunity. But before his death Uriah had
made extraordinary provision for Monticello in his will. It was to be
given to 'the nation' as a Farm School for the sons of naval personnel
who had lost their fathers. Remembering the fate of Jefferson's statue,
he added a rider that should the nation decline the gift then it would
fall to the state of Virginia. Uriah further specified that if neither
Congress nor Virginia wanted it, then it would revert to the synagogues of New York and Philadelphia. In the event it turned out that
none of those parties, including the synagogues, was much interested
in the offer. There was as yet no sense that Jefferson's house (or
anyone else's) was some sort of monument that should be put in
trust for the nation or made socially useful in a way the president
might have approved of. Uriah's own younger brother Jonas would
contest the will for fourteen years before it was declared invalid,
during which time the house once more became a hostel for rats and
spiders. It fell to Jonas's son, Jefferson Monroe Levy, to make
Monticello's restoration his life's work, at the personal cost of a
million dollars.

Whatever Uriah wanted as he lay on his sickbed in New York in
the winter of 1861-2 was in any case moot, since at some point between
August 1861 and the following spring, the Confederate government
declared Monticello the property of an 'enemy alien', subject to

sequestration and sale. Dying when he did, Uriah was spared the shock of Grant's Order 11. But it might not have surprised him, since just a few years before he had himself fought his last, fiercest battle against Judaeophobia.

In 1855 the Department of the Navy decided to review the ranks of its officers to see if any, in particular the more senior personnel, were for whatever reason unfit to hold their commissions. Given that the routes for promotion were clogged up by long-serving officers like Uriah, there was some reason for this. But when the personnel of what became known as the 'Plucking Committee' were revealed, Uriah realised that the five selected captains (out of a board of fifteen) included a number of those who had shown him particular enmity over the years. He knew he would be among those marked, not just for retirement, but for stripping altogether from the navy rolls. And so indeed it fell out.[34]

But Uriah was not going to take the humiliating indignity lying down. The decisions of the Plucking Committee triggered enough of a protest that courts of inquiry had to be established to review its decisions. In pursuit of personal justice, Uriah hired the best legal mind he could find, Benjamin F. Butler, who had served on the state Supreme Court and was then a professor at New York University. When his case came before the court in November–December 1857, Butler and Uriah had an inventory of twenty-six witnesses (including the ex-Secretary of the Navy George Bancroft, better known as a historian) to testify to his seamanship, integrity and energy. Thirteen of the witnesses were officers and men with whom Uriah had served. They also testified that the negative feeling towards Uriah, in particular the attempt to prevent his promotion to captain, had been entirely because he was a Jew, and, to compound matters, because he had risen through the ranks from sailing master.

In the powerfully eloquent statement read to the court by Butler, Uriah associated his own cause with that of the honour of the Republic and the nobility of the Constitution. It began with a ringing declaration, the first of principled appeals to justice and equality in a liberal polity, which would echo in the rest of the world through the remainder of the century and into the next, until moral optimism and social decency would be engulfed by a great epidemic of hatred and, finally, the fires of extermination.

My parents were Israelites and I was nurtured in the faith of my ancestors. In deciding to adhere to it, I have but exercised a right guaranteed
to me by the constitution of my native State and of the United States –
a right given to all men by their Maker – a right more precious than
life itself. But while claiming and exercising this right of conscience I
have never failed to acknowledge and respect the like freedom in
others.[35]

Here Uriah was certainly thinking of the sense he got from those
aboard his ships that there was something indecently unnatural about
having to obey orders given by a Jew.

'At an early day and especially from the time that I aspired to a
lieutenancy and still more after I had gained it, I was forced to
encounter a large share of the prejudice and hostility by which, for
so many ages the Jew has been pursued.' In the mess room aboard
the USS *Franklin* they let him know that as a Jew 'they did not want
to be brought into contact with him ... as an interloper'. The same
bigotry had been used against him in 1824 and 1844, when President
Tyler had intervened once it was shown, as it was now, that the accusation of his unfitness for the service was 'wholly unsupported by
evidence'. Quoting a speech in the British Parliament made by Lord
John Russell in support of the right of Jews to be elected to that
House, in which he had cited the United States as an example of
complete emancipation, he said, 'Little did the author of this generous
tribute to our country suspect that even when he was penning it there
were those in the American navy with whom it was a question whether
a Jew should be tolerated in the service.'

Painting a picture of Jews as exemplary American citizens, Uriah
and Butler concluded:

This is the case before you, and in this view its importance cannot be
overstated. It is the case of every Israelite in the Union ... They are
unsurpassed by any portion of our people in loyalty to the Constitution
and to the Union, in their quiet obedience to the laws and the cheerful-
ness with which they contribute to the public burthens ... how rarely
does any one of them become a charge on your State or municipal
treasuries? How largely do they all contribute to the activities of trade
... to the stock of public wealth! Are all these to be proscribed? And

is this to be done while we retain in our Constitution the language I have quoted? Is this the language to be spoken to the ear but broken to the hope of my race? Are the thousands of Judah and the ten thousands of Israel in their dispersions throughout the earth who look to America as a land bright with promise – are they now to learn to their sorrow and dismay that we, too, have sunk into the mire of religious intolerance and bigotry? And are American Christians now to begin the persecution of the Jews?

There was no doubting the verdict. Uriah Levy was reinstated; and a few months later, in 1858, was given command of the USS *Macedonia* in the Mediterranean squadron. He took his pretty young wife with him who, before they sailed, made it her business to nail a *mezuzah* to the doorpost of the captain's quarters, undoubtedly a first in any modern navy. En route south to the Caribbean and over the Atlantic, the *Macedonia* put in a call at Charlestown Navy Yard next to Boston where the fame of the Jewish captain and his fetching wife had preceded them. A host of luminaries lined up to meet them including Henry Wadsworth Longfellow who, predictably bewitched, gave Virginia and her husband a copy of his 'Psalm of Life'. 'In the world's broad field of battle, / In the bivouac of Life, / Be not like dumb, driven cattle! / Be a hero in the strife!'

The tour of duty in the Med was not exacting. In Genoa and La Spezia there were onshore entertainments where Virginia, a vision in white muslin and silk, flirted with young men at masked balls and Uriah had his portrait painted, full-length, in uniform looking spry. At last, a Levy in epaulettes! History occasionally interrupted the marine promenade. Garibaldi's incursions into Sicily and the armed uprising which set off the rebellion against the Bourbons had made Sicily unsafe enough for Levy to be instructed to evacuate any Americans who needed to leave. Further east, in Ottoman Palestine and Lebanon he was asked to enquire whether the murderers of two American missionaries were being pursued by the Turkish authorities with all the urgency the case demanded. In Beirut he met the British consul at Jerusalem, the remarkable James Finn, who, though a committed missionary with the London Society for Promoting Christianity among the Jews, had made it his personal vocation to give the 10,000 Jews of the holy city (by far the majority of the population) a life that was more than merely praying, Talmud study and dependence on the *halukah*, charity of the diaspora. Finn had bought land outside the city walls to create a training farm he called Keren Avraham where there was also a soap factory. And when he met Uriah Levy in full naval fig he realised he was looking at something extraordinary in Jewish history. 'This Captain Levi [*sic*]', Finn wrote in his journal, 'I had long wished to see, being the only example I ever heard of a Jew commanding a ship of war. He is a fine-looking rosy old fellow aged 69* with strong Jewish features which looked curious, with cocked hat, epaulettes and eagle buttons with abundance of jewellery.' If Palestine was one sort of Promised Land, then America must be another, since 'I have now seen in my time an officer of the Army, Navy and Civil Service of the United States from the Jewish People'.[36]

In mid-September 1859 Uriah Levy, now entitled to be recognised as commodore, rode to Jerusalem. He left no record of what his feelings were on seeing the Western Wall of the Temple courtyard, or moving among the crowds of Sephardi Jews who packed the alleys in the Old City, but one can easily imagine both. What is known is that while there, he gave instructions for carts to be loaded with earth from the area outside the city walls. The *Macedonia*'s log duly shows boxes of soil being taken aboard. Uriah's notion was that they should be brought back to New York and given to his synagogue of Shearith Israel so that dirt from the Land of Israel could be scattered on the biers of the deceased.[37] When Uriah was himself laid to rest in March 1862, handfuls of that dirt must have been thrown onto the body wrapped in its winding sheet within the plain wooden coffin as it lay deep in the New York grave. And even as late as the 1990s, there was still some being used at funerals.

---

* Levy was actually sixty-seven at this time.

MODERNITY AND ITS TSURIS

I. Locomotive Music

Meyerbeer was going on his last train journey. This time he would not be paying the fare.

He had always been a traveller. His mother had given birth to him in a coach *en route* between Berlin and Frankfurt. In his childhood, servants had bundled him into a *stellwagen*, inside of which an odour of black tobacco and yesterday's sausage clung to the leather padding. When the Beers moved into their fine Berlin mansion on the Spandauerstrasse, his tutor – Professor Aaron Wolfssohn, a pillar of the Enlightenment – and his piano teachers, Franz Lausker, Carl Friedrich Zelter and Muzio Clementi, would come to the house. At his mother's soirées, where luminaries of Berlin culture and government held forth on liberty, reason and the needs of the state, Jacob, the wunderkind, with his rosy cheeks and kiss curl, was brought out to perform. Soft applause followed the entertainment. The parents Judah and Amalia, wearing helpless smiles, watched the lad bow, and *schepped naches*. Since the Beers had connections at court, it was not long before Jacob was climbing into the family coach for a performance at Charlottenburg Palace. The composer Louis Spohr remembered one of the recitals given by the 'gifted boy' who, hired for his own concerts, always proved a big draw 'in an overcrowded season'.[1] A few years on, Jacob Liebmann Beer was sent to Darmstadt along with one of his brothers, Heinrich, to be taught composition and organ by the old Abbé Vogler who regularly turned out operas, none of them much admired. There he met Carl Maria von Weber. The two 'brothers', as they would call each other, could hardly wait to improve on Vogler.

Armies marched back and forth through *Mitteleuropa*, halting for mutual slaughter and the odd bit of plunder. Jacob's maternal grandfather Liebmann Meyer Wulff, 'the Croesus of Berlin', had made his fortune from supplying the Hohenzollern monarchs with what they needed – grain, horses, munitions, everything in fact except good generals – to try and keep pace with the monstrously successful French. In 1813, when the cry went up to fight for the Prussian fatherland, Jacob's brother Wilhelm, like many Jews, answered the call. Jacob, nervous of compromising his budding career as a virtuoso pianist (perhaps the greatest in Europe, Weber had said), thought it better to keep out of harm's way. But the decision to stay one step ahead of the recruiting sergeants caused him soul-searching. 'I fear this decision will carry the scorpion's sting that will poison my honour for the rest of my life,' he told Wolfssohn.[2] In Vienna, between Napoleon victorious and Napoleon vanquished, he made the acquaintance of Spohr who thought a great deal of his talent, and Ludwig van Beethoven, who did not. Assigning him the 'large drum' (was this one of the old boy's notorious jokes?), Beethoven complained that Jacob neither hit it hard enough nor on time. Nothing could come of such a person.

Beethoven was wrong. By the time the French wars were staggering to their bloody end, Jacob's reputation as composer as well as virtuoso was already well established. He was in his mid-twenties, dark, dashing and serious. Audiences either went for his Jewish looks or they didn't. He had composed choral works for both synagogue and church but was hankering after the great prize of opera. Off he went on his travels accompanied by a custom-built portable upright piano with his name on its walnut case. 'I go from museum to museum, library to library, theatre to theatre,' he wrote, 'with the restlessness of the wandering Jew.'[3] The newer generations of *diligences* had steel springs solid enough to keep the instrument safe and even to allow the composer to jot down notes as the coach toiled up Alpine passes or shot down into the valleys of Piedmont. Jacob had never seen Italian sunlight, never toasted his face in its warmth, and the happiness kindled his creative imagination. In 1816 he met Gioacchino Rossini for whom opera (and for that matter all music) was made to *delight*, and the serious Ashkenazi and the merriment-maker began a fifty-year friendship of affectionate opposites. In Venice, Cremona, Modena and Rome, 'Giacomo' (as he called himself from 1817) did his best to graft some of that skipping Italian lightness to his passion for grand themes. But what emerged – *Romildo e Costanza, Semiramide riconosciuta, Emma di Resburgo* – were operas that were weighty rather than dancing. Moving forward, Meyerbeer habitually looked back. The opera *Il crociato in Egitto*, which in 1824 gave him an international reputation, featured the last part written for a castrato. But he was something of a musical omnivore and it paid off. Sicilian folk music made its way into his operas alongside *récitatif*. But it was exactly the mash-up of genres, the unblushing over-the-top historical romances, which audiences craved. Multilingual and culturally versatile, Giacomo Meyerbeer, the non-stop traveller, was ready to take on theatre managers from one end of Europe to the other. Librettists in three languages sought him out.

The 'grandes machines' of his operas, featuring love sundered by religious war, zombie nuns rising from the tomb, were as forceful, massively populated and piston-pumping as the trains which now conveyed the rich and successful Meyerbeer from London to Brussels, Stuttgart to Munich, Vienna to Venice, wherever he needed to be. Most often his journeys were the long haul of many days, between Paris, where he had had his great triumph with *Robert le Diable* in 1831, and Berlin, where he was director of court music. Thus it was that Meyerbeer came to know the railway timetables as well as his own musical scores and would get irritable if a delay of the Cologne train meant idling for hours in the sidings at Hanover. One such *Winterreise* halt in January 1855 found Meyerbeer cold and impatient on the four-day journey to Berlin, so that when he got to Potsdam he was obliged to put up at an inn before completing the journey the following evening. Tirelessly productive, tortured by his gut, for all the scrupulous frugality of his diet, he filled the dreary hours by composing a duet. In March he went to Paris, the familiar stations, Hanover, Cologne, Brussels, rolling by; in April east again to be welcomed by the budding lindens of his home city. Minna Mosson, his wife (and first cousin), would be there if she was not taking the waters, for she had no desire to remove herself to Paris for months at a time. June saw a change of direction, north on a newly opened line to Calais to catch the bucking packet boat for Dover. Gagging from the foul crossing and filthy with particles of damp soot clinging to his hair, Meyerbeer caught a fast train which hurtled through the Weald at thirty miles an hour, expeditious enough for him to dress and get to Covent Garden before the curtain rose.

On 6 May 1864 the last locomotive – black engine, black decorations – was waiting at the Gare du Nord to take Meyerbeer's lifeless body home to Berlin. For some time Rossini, also a staple institution in Paris, had been worrying about his friend's punishing work habits, so unlike his own easy-going retirement pottering around the roses of Passy. Meyerbeer would insist on fussing over every last detail: the cast, the sets, the costumes, on taking rehearsals himself. The two composers were both in their early seventies and mortality was no longer just a melody for the cello section. In 1863 Rossini had composed a set of chamber and solo pieces he called, with typically endearing drollery, 'The Sins of Old Age'. The most ambitious piece was the *Petite messe solennelle* which Napoleon III, so the story went, characterised as 'neither petite nor solemn'. Meyerbeer was one of the audience hearing it played for the first time in March 1864 at the hotel of Louise Pillet-Wils, the orchestra of twelve, plus four singers, conducted from the harmonium by an eighteen-year-old prodigy who must have reminded the two old men of their own distant precocity. At the end of it, Meyerbeer, who had stood throughout the performance, shaking with barely contained excitement, flung himself on Rossini, showering him with incoherent, ecstatic congratulations. Much moved, the composer said, in all benevolence, 'Please don't do that, it will harm your health.' Later the two of them walked home along the boulevards while Rossini repeated his counsel of prudent restraint. Meyerbeer brushed off the solicitousness, returning next evening for the second performance. But all the same, he had been thinking of his end. On 8 December 1863 he had added to the daily prayer he himself had composed an additional wish that 'a merciful God grant me a gentle, easy and painless death, free of fear and guilty conscience ... do not let my death be preceded by a long painful illness; may death come softly, quietly and unexpectedly'.[4]

God was listening. In Paris on May Day 1864, Meyerbeer had been rehearsing his endlessly revisited and revised opera *L'Africaine* (which he now called *Vasco da Gama*). He had been suffering from another bout of abdominal discomfort so acute that a doctor was called, who prescribed something and gave Meyerbeer no reason to suppose he would not, as planned, catch the Brussels train the next morning for a short trip. 'I bid you goodnight,' Meyerbeer told the household. The fatal attack must have been sudden. At 5 a.m. he was in severe pain; by 5.40 he was dead.

The following morning, uneasy at the news that his friend was unwell, Rossini went to the rue Montaigne. On being told that Meyerbeer had died he swooned in shock, lying, for a while, unconscious on the floor. The only way for Rossini to cope with his grief was to compose a dirge for pianissimo bass, drum roll and taps over which a choir sang 'Weep weep sublime muse'. Rossini himself would have another four and a half quiet years of suburban peace in Passy before a bout of pneumonia killed him too.

Jewish Orthodox practice required burial within thirty-six hours. But Meyerbeer had grown up in a family of reform-minded Jews who did not always abide by the strictest *halakha*. The instructions Meyerbeer had left about what was to be done with him were as exacting as his stage directions. He was to lie for four days, face uncovered, so that those who wished might pay their respects. This would coincide with the traditional period of visitation, the *shiva*, though with the stipulated seven days abbreviated. Then his body was to be conveyed to the Jewish cemetery in the Schönhauser Allee in Berlin, where he would be buried in the same family tomb as his mother Amalia and beside two of his children who had died in infancy.

His daughters hastened from Baden Baden, and his nephew Julius arrived to help with the public funeral and to put the family imprimatur on any arrangements made by the committee of cultural eminences, including the writer Théophile Gautier, entrusted with the ceremony. *Le tout Europe* mourned. It was commonly felt that the world was suddenly poorer, colder, thinner, for the composer's demise. 'Meyerbeer's death grieved me so much,' Queen Victoria (habitually mantled in widow's weeds) wrote to her daughter Vicky, the Crown Princess of Prussia, adding, 'I do so admire his music and so did darling Papa.'[5] Anyone of fine feeling – sovereigns, princes, kings and emperors, as well as fellow musicians, dramatists and poets – made sure to express their sorrow. Only the passing of Beethoven in 1827 had aroused comparable outpourings of regret. But the obsequies for Meyerbeer would go one better since he would be honoured with not one funeral but two, in each of the great cities, Paris and Berlin, which had been the poles of his long musical life. Nothing like this had been seen in France since the return of the remains of Napoleon in 1840. But there had never been a public ceremony *anywhere* so grand, so prolonged, so officially orchestrated, for a Jew.

It took an hour and a half for the cortège to get to the Gare du Nord from Meyerbeer's house on the rue Montaigne, three miles away. Six black horses pulled the hearse, escorted by a detachment of the Garde Imperiale, helmets plumed, cuirasses burnished, trotting slowly enough that the pall-bearers (who were not bearing anything) – the heads of the Conservatoire and the Opéra, the Prussian ambassador Graf von Goltz – could all hold on to black ribbons attached to the bier without losing their step. Bands, military and operatic, played the slow marches with their instruments muffled. Visitors, unless informed otherwise, would have assumed a great marshal or member of the imperial household had passed away. Up the avenue Montaigne and along the rue Lafayette beat the procession, denied, however, any sort of grand approach since (so the gossips said) the *préfet* who had rebuilt Paris, Baron Haussmann, had discovered his wife was having an affair with the architect of the station, Jacques Hittorff, and in revenge had kept the station entrance obstructed with the dense web of streets which remain to this day.[6]

The new station with its handsome stone facade, which had replaced the more modest building of 1846, was not yet completed. James de Rothschild, the head director of the Compagnie des Chemins de Fer du Nord who was responsible for its monumental scale, had ordered a halt to construction for the funeral of a Jew even more famous than himself.[7] The setting could not possibly have been more magnificent had it been in an imperial palace; in truth this *was* the imperial palace of the new industrial age. Statuesque personifications of station towns on the line – Rouen, Arras, Lille, Boulogne, standing in sculpted masonry niches – were now supplemented with banners bearing the names of Meyerbeer's operas: *Les Huguenots* (popular in Paris, banned for religious reasons in Berlin), *Robert le diable, L'Étoile du Nord*. Inside, the vast train hall flooded with light coming from the tall arched windows which Hittorff had scooped out of the stone facade. Beneath a thrown canopy of glass supported by piers of Glaswegian iron, a multi-tiered catafalque had been erected to receive the coffin. The towering edifice was draped in swathes of black silk embroidered with colossal initial Ms. At each corner of the catafalque, gas-fired funerary torches mounted on iron tripods hissed green flames into the air, the flares reflecting in the glass panels of the roof. Knowing that where his audiences were concerned you could never overdo the stage spec-tacle, it was as if the funeral in the railway station was Meyerbeer's last great production, something he might have called 'Vestibule to Eternity'. Passages from his operas were sung by massed choirs from the Opéra and, incongruously, the cathedral as the procession entered the train hall. Solemn blessings and Kaddish were chanted by three rabbis. Needless to say there were eulogies, five of them, one dignitary after another extolling the dead man's celestial gifts and his unquestionable immortality. The last speech of all was given by the liberal politician and lawyer Émile Ollivier who, with Meyerbeer's double nationality in mind, praised him and his work as binding together those two erstwhile foes, Germany (or Prussia) and France, henceforth musically and politically harmonised. In 1870, as first minister of what had become a constitutional monarchy, it would be Ollivier, artfully ambushed by Otto von Bismarck, who would fatally declare war on Prussia, inaugurating a prolonged period of catastrophe.

In Berlin, the ceremonies were, if anything, even more elaborate. At the Potsdamer Bahnhof, the deceased, plus Perrin from the Opéra and Auber from the Conservatoire who had accompanied the body, were greeted by Prince Georg of Prussia and a host of notables, Jewish and non-Jewish alike. On the day of the formal interment in the Schönhauser Allee cemetery, the king and queen sent carriages (the usual way to be present without actually showing up in person), and the procession down the Unter den Linden was even longer, slower and more grandiose than had been the case in Paris, as if France and Prussia were duelling over who actually had patrimonial rights over Meyerbeer's obsequies.

Bringing the daily traffic of two great European cities to a halt; mobilising the nobility of court and concert house, academies, insti-tutes and operas; the whole sword-clanking, epaulette-heavy, clip-cloppery of the event, all in honour of a dead Jew, was astounding and, to some, appalling. A year before Meyerbeer's bar mitzvah, in 1803, Berlin had been excited by the appearance of *Wider die Juden* (*Against the Jews*), the pamphlet of the lawyer Karl Friedrich Grattenauer, selling some 13,000 copies before it was suppressed by the renewal of censorship. Grattenauer, who only half humorously proposed replacing the circumcision of Jewish male infants with castration, warned his fellow Germans not to be deceived by the ostensibly modern appearance of the 'new' Jews. They might have replaced Yiddish with German, and their long gowns with frock coats, and shaved off their beards, but under the veneer of assimilation they were the same old Jews, bent on grasping wealth and power for themselves and themselves alone and plotting domination.[8]

Meyerbeer was part of a small, wealthy Berliner elite (often with cousins in Vienna) who inhabited a psychologically unstable world which alternated between cultivated display (the mansions, the parks and gardens, the servants, the equipages, the libraries, the salons, the music) and watchful nervousness (the vicious pamphlets, the outbreaks of riots, the audible jokes at their expense cracked by leading lights who had just sat on what they called the '*Judensofa*' of their hosts). In 1812, under a liberalising government, they had been ostensibly freed from restrictions of residence and occupation (always excepting public office) by an edict of emancipation, and granted local citizenship. But with good reason they knew that when the military and political tide turned, that liberalisation could be reversed, not just in Prussia but in many of the other German states, as indeed it was. Seven years after the Prussian emancipation edict, mobs rampaged through German towns smashing Jewish windows and skulls, yelling '*Hep hep, Jude verreck*' ('Jew, die like a beast') or '*Hep hep, der Jude muss im Dreck*' ('Down in the muck with the Jew').

The Jews had done what they were bidden as the condition of their citizenship, abandoning some of the old ways, even in their synagogues. Meyerbeer's grandfather Liebmann Meyer Wulff, the lottery king and military purveyor, had built a private synagogue in his own house in Berlin where he maintained six Talmud students. But his daughter Malka, who became Amalia, and her husband Judah Herz Beer the sugar refiner, had a different kind of private synagogue in mind for the house on the Spandauerstrasse: one in the new style,

with an organ, a tenor cantor, and a choir for which young Jacob
wrote a 'cantatina' as well as sermons in German and prayers for the
welfare of the Prussian royal family. The first organ music to be heard
in a synagogue had originally been performed in 1810 in a school for
poor Jewish children founded by the banker Israel Jacobson in Seesen
in Westphalia.[9] In 1813 Jacobson had moved to Berlin, and made sure
that organ and choral music were performed in his private synagogue.
The new musical services proved so popular that they outgrew the
space Jacobson could offer, which gave Amalia and her husband
the chance to preside uncontested over the new style of Jewish worship.
She also presided over a fine salon where all the Leading Lights sat
on her *Judensofa*: the Humboldts, the Romantic writer-philosophers
Schlegel, Schelling and Gentz, poets like Arnim. The Orthodox saw
this makeover as the antechamber to conversion. They were so horrified by the organ that a petition was got up to the government
protesting that the Beer synagogue violated an ordinance specifying
there should be but one synagogue in Berlin. The petition was
successful and the Jewish vox humana, for the time being, stilled.

Nonetheless Amalia and Judah Beer, with the encouragement of
Wolfssohn, continued to believe a newly reformed Judaism would be
more, not less, likely to keep Jews, starting with their own family,
within the fold of the faithful. When old Liebmann Meyer Wulff
expired in 1811, his grandson the musician had made a solemn promise
to his mother that he would never abandon the faith of his fathers.
He kept the pledge.

The same was not true of the Mendelssohn family. Moses
Mendelssohn's profound conviction that it was possible to live, simultaneously, as a good German and a good Jew, was belied by the pessimism of his children. Only two of them, his daughter Recha and
the eldest son Joseph, remained Jews, a profoundly shocking verdict
on their father's enlightened pluralism. Abraham, Joseph's brother and
partner in the newly founded Mendelssohn bank, waited until their
father had died before baptising his children, including the musical
prodigies Felix and Fanny. Unlike the Beers, Abraham Mendelssohn
and his wife Lea (also from a pious family, the Salomons) listened to
the undertow of malice beneath the polite seeming-acceptance, and
concluded that it was not enough for Jews to shave off their beards
and replace Yiddish with German as their daily tongue if they wanted

to be fully a part of German society and culture. Only abandoning Judaism altogether would do the trick. But even if Abraham's conversion was principally a matter of social convenience, the way he talked about it, not least to his children, seethed with brutal rejection of his father's naive optimism. He would not be so deluded. The children knew, he wrote, 'of the scant value which I place on all [religious] forms. I felt no inner calling to choose for you the Jewish [faith], the most obsolete, corrupt and pointless of all of them, so I raised you in the Christian religion, the purer form accepted by the majority of civilised people.'[10]

Integral to this clean-cut de-Judaisation was a choice of name. The Prussian state had made the taking of surnames a condition of exercising citizenship, and Abraham and his wife wanted their baptised children to adopt something less glaringly Jewish. (He seems not to have thought his own first name a disadvantage.) His wife's brother, Jakob Salomon, had bought a piece of property in Luisenstadt formerly owned and named for a family called Bartholdy and Jakob had added that title to his last name. Now the uncle suggested his nephew and niece do the same. Their father heartily agreed. 'A Christian Mendelssohn is no more possible', he insisted, than 'a Jewish Confucius'. In a long unctuous letter to his children Abraham tried to make the proposal comparable to his father's change of name, mastery of German, and immersion in 'a different community' to the one of immured orthodoxy in which Moses had been born. But Fanny and Felix rejected the analogy. 'Bartholdy', Fanny told her siblings, was 'this name which we all dislike'.[11] And though he was Christian enough to write an oratorio, *Paulus*, around the ultimate Jewish convert, Felix was also devoted enough to his grandfather's memory to ensure a complete seven-volume German edition of Moses' works saw the light of day in 1843–5. Like another convert whom he knew in England, Benjamin D'Israeli, and his teacher Ignaz Moscheles (who had also undergone a conversion of convenience), Mendelssohn knew he would always be taken for a Jew, not least by his ardent admirer Queen Victoria, who described him as 'short, dark and very Jewish-looking'. Less warmly, his friend Robert Schumann remarked to his wife Clara, while congratulating himself for promoting Felix's career, that 'Jews remain Jews'.[12] Music historians have gone back and forth on the strength and depth of Mendelssohn's

Christian convictions or the acceptance of his Jewish origins. Probably, like his friend Heinrich Heine, he was torn. When someone commented that he resembled his distant cousin Giacomo Meyerbeer, Mendelssohn was so put out he made a swift appointment with the barber to correct the impression.

The sloughing off of Jewish identity was a different kind of passion for Felix's aunt Dorothea. Married to the Jewish banker Simon Veit, she led the life of a high-culture salon hostess, but with more independent cultural ambition than Amalia Beer. It was at one of those gatherings that she met and fell hard for the Romantic poet-philosopher and Lutheran pastor's son Karl Wilhelm Friedrich von Schlegel. A year later he published *Lucinde*, a prose hymn to the union of sensual and spiritual love immediately recognised as a portrait of his and Dorothea's relationship. When she left her husband for her lover, Veit was prepared to allow her to keep their two sons on condition she did not marry Schlegel, a condition Dorothea broke and rubbed salt in the wound by converting to Christianity, first in 1804 the Lutheran confession and then, four years later, along with Schlegel, to Catholicism. Crushed beneath this avalanche of pain Simon Veit was concerned, beyond anything, to sustain his family relationship with his sons. Drawing on a tradition, shared by well-meaning Christians and Jews alike, that the two faiths were in fact branches of the same, Veit wrote a letter of astonishing broad-mindedness (or wishful thinking) to his son Philipp on the latter's baptism.

> Let us draw a veil over the event that has come beween us ... I will not stop the two of you ... if religion is illuminated by tolerance; if it should and could go hand in hand with morality, then not only does it not do harm but it might bring us closer to one another, until our religions run practically side by side. Therefore my beloved son as long as we differ in religion but are united in our fundamental moral principles there will never be separation between us.[13]

In his eagerness to avoid father–son estrangement, Simon Veit was echoing the Enlightenment view of a Judaeo-Christian rapprochement in which each party would water down their respective exclusiveness to establish a kind of Jesus-the-Jew common ground. Church and synagogue would thus be of the same family and so would Simon

BELONGING

and his sons. But this was an optimistic delusion. It echoed, somewhat, the friendships established through the indispensability of Hebrew to rabbis and Christian theologians alike. But the latter seldom if ever abandoned their ultimate goal of conversion, and this would be true of nineteenth-century philo-Semites as well. And Christian culture at this time was romantically militant not enlightened and ecumenical. Philipp Veit and Felix Mendelssohn were, in the first instance, Christians of convenience, enabling them both to become pillars of German culture. But they did not so much toy with Christianity as plunge into it, Mendelssohn reviving Bach's sacred music while choir director of the Church of St Thomas in Leipzig and writing his own Christian oratorios as well. Philipp Veit was not only director of the Stadel Gallery in Frankfurt, but also painted two elaborate historical murals for it, one of which was *Art Being Introduced into Germany through Religion*, and the other *Christianity brought to Germany by St Boniface*. Though he had been taught by the complicated, enigmatic Caspar David Friedrich, Veit's formative years were spent with the Nazarene group of painters, including Johann Overbeck whose mission was to restore 'primitive' Christian style and ethos to German history painting.

For the suspicious, though, the converts could never be Christian enough. There were, in the first place, the most glaring cases like Heinrich Heine who, ostensibly Christian, was obsessed with 'Hebraism' and the Jewish identity he had certainly not relinquished with his baptism. For the most relentless Jew-sniffers, those like Veit who pretended to Christian piety were the most dangerous of all, since they constituted a 'caste' within the Church. Under cover of allegiance to their new religion they were secretly engaged in a campaign to turn the tables on missionaries by 'Judaising' Christianity from within. This had been the same argument used by the Iberian inquisitors to hound the *conversos* three centuries before.

As post-emancipation Jews flocked into the gymnasia and the universities, into medicine, law, business, journalism and the theatre, as well as into banking, industry and the railways, from one end of Germany to the other (with the process repeating itself in the Habsburg lands, in Galicia, Bohemia and Hungary alongside Austria proper), so the old/new suspicion intensified. Yiddish-speaking traditionalists migrating to Berlin, Prague and Vienna, Hamburg and Frankfurt, were attacked for their obstinacy and ignorance. But what Wagner called sneeringly 'the cultured Jews' in their frock coats and carriages were assailed even more violently for their laughable, futile, pitiful pretension to be treated as if they were true Germans, or, in fact, normal human beings.

You could always tell a Jew, so Wagner wrote in his essay 'Das Judenthum in der Musik' ('Jewishness in Music'), by the way he or she sounded: 'a croaking, wheezing, buzzing snuffle', 'an entirely inhuman expression'. This was because Jews, being rootless, could have no organic, natural connection with the language of those among whom they pitched their tents. They adopted German, or whichever language it might be, in a functional, mechanical way, but this gross artificiality cut them off from the poetic depths of a culture, the place where its essence, its native music, lay.

Wagner's polemic was published under the pseudonym 'K. Freigedank' in 1850. His targets were the two Jews whom he thought dominated German music, much for the worse: the convert Mendelssohn and the forthrightly Jewish Meyerbeer. Wagner had not always felt this way about the opera composer. A decade before, he had written in neurotically slavish abasement to Meyerbeer, who had championed the young German passionately enough to enable *Der fliegende Holländer* and *Rienzi* to be performed at the Paris Opéra. On New Year's Day 1844, Meyerbeer had thrown a great banquet in celebration of *Der fliegende Holländer* and its composer, and for a while Wagner waxed sycophantic. 'I weep tears of emotion when I think of the man who is *everything* to me, *everything*,' he wrote to Meyerbeer. 'My head and heart are no longer mine to give away; they are your property, my master ... the most that is left of me is my two hands – do you wish to make use of them? I realise I must become your slave, body and soul.'[14] And then again in slightly less unhinged tone: 'May God fill each day of your marvellous life with joy and may you never be burdened with worries ... this is the most fervent prayer of your most dedicated pupil.'

Meyerbeer had been generous in advancing money to Wagner when he needed it, until at some point he decided enough was enough, and this rejection may have turned Wagner from adulation to self-loathing and then to detestation of his erstwhile mentor. He would write to Liszt that he did not actually hate Meyerbeer 'but he disgusts me beyond measure ... This eternally amiable and pleasant man reminds me of the turbid not to say vicious period of my life when he pretended to be my protector; that was a period of connexions and backstairs when we are made fools of by our protectors whom in our hearts we do not like.' Wagner actually confessed there was no real reason for turning against Meyerbeer, only the instinctive sense of dishonesty (on his part at any rate) at the masquerade of friendship. But it seethed within him: 'this rancour is as necessary to my nature as bile is to blood'.[15] Of this welling up of Wagnerian hatred, Meyerbeer, until 1850, could have had no clue.

But then it was not so much Meyerbeer the person as Meyerbeer the symptom which Wagner violently detested: the personification of the 'Judaisation' of music, by which he meant its crass commercialisa- tion. Musical performance had been transformed during Wagner's lifetime. It was no longer, as it had been for centuries, the exclusive preserve of the princely courts and churches who commissioned instrumental and vocal music. In the age of the railways it had become an international business and Meyerbeer was its first and most successful showman. Spacious concert halls in the middle of cities were now built for a paying public which could enjoy what, just a few generations before, had been available only to princes, aristocrats and clerics. To allow instruments to project through these cavernous spaces, traditional instruments had been modified using the materials produced by the industrial world, metals above all. The fortepiano now turned into a grand piano, whose plangent sound would fill every corner of a concert hall through strengthening with an iron frame. String instruments now used fine wires to maximise their acoustics. Many of the instruments were themselves factory-made. The great gush of Romantic music, the force of its sound, had been made possible by machine-tooled modernisation. No matter that Jewish virtuosi like Ferdinand David, who gave the first performance of Mendelssohn's Violin Concerto in E minor in 1845, did so on a Guarneri; his kind would always be associated in the mind of a Wagner or a Schumann as the carrier of a hard-varnished, vulgar modernism.

Though no composer would deploy brass more maximally or turn string sections into melody-armies with more zeal than Richard Wagner, in 1850, even as he sought to emulate and surpass Mendelssohn and Meyerbeer, he let it be known that he hated what music had become, which was, in his swirling mind, a cash dispenser. In the hands of the hucksters of the ear it offered nothing more than meretricious amusement, a distraction from boredom (*Langeweile*). 'What the heroes of the arts, with untold strain consuming love and life, have wrested from the art-fiend of two millennia of misery, today the Jew converts into an art-bazaar' (*Kunstwaarenwechsel* – an art-merchandise market). As gaudy commodity, this Jewish-produced spectacle was gimcrack, its sentimentality contrived. The 'fashion-setter' (Meyerbeer), knowing himself to be incapable of producing true dramatic art, 'composes operas for Paris and sends them touring round the world, the surest means today of earning an art-renown albeit not as an artist'.

As long as princes and bishops had stood sentinel over the integrity of music, there had been no place for the Jews. Likewise the artisan guilds Wagner would celebrate in *Die Meistersinger von Nürnberg* preserved a craft integrity that was at the core of German-ness.[16] The Jewish cash nexus was their destroyer, their deadly enemy. Now that the barriers protecting those traditions had been taken down, and the doors of the Conservatoire opened, a barely baptised Jew like Mendelssohn could masquerade as a Christian and be persuasive enough to pose as the resuscitator of the sublimely spiritual, profoundly German Bach. As a perpetual outsider, the Jew could have no rooted organic connection with the language they mastered functionally, but which cut them off from the tap roots of poetry. So, too, the lack of a true, native, musical tradition meant they could only compose and perform superficially. All the Jews had was synagogue music. And as far as that was concerned, he wrote in 'Judenthum', 'who has not been seized with a feeling of the greatest revulsion, of horror mingled with the absurd, at hearing that sense-and-sound-confounding gurgle, yodel and cackle, which no intentional caricature can make more repugnant'?

If a national culture was sound in itself, Wagner wrote, it would be capable of resisting invasion by the hordes of rootless, parasitical aliens. But this was no longer true of Germany (and perhaps not of anywhere else). The nation had become weak, vulnerable to the occupation of the parasites who battened off its corrupted body. 'When a body's inner death is manifest then outside elements win the power of lodging within it, merely to destroy it. Then indeed that body's flesh dissolves into a swarming colony of insect-life.'

Wagner's biologising of Jew-hatred, his indelible image of them as
the maggoty infestation of a 'worm-befretted carcass', was not entirely
new. It drew on the ancient demonology begun by Manetho of the
Jews as the collectively contagious carriers of infection. But the Jew
recast as invasive foreign body, rejected by healthy constitutions, also
owed much to the zoological morphologies of the nineteenth century.
The most influential of the new wave of Judaeophobes, Alphonse
Toussenel, was a naturalist as well as a political journalist. A child of
western France, he had grown up in Lorraine where the instinct to
identify the Jews with predators and parasites had survived all the
changes of the revolution, in fact had intensified with the new century.
Toussenel's Les Juifs, rois de l'époque, published in 1844, modernised the
idiom by making the usual suspects – railway entrepreneurs, bond-
holders and bankers (Rothschilds above all) – the real sovereigns of
the July Monarchy. The king, Louis Philippe, his governments, the
legislators, and their toadying journalists on the Journal des débats who
whitewashed the scandals, were all in thrall to the insidious power of
Jewish money.

Of course this was standard invective. But three years later in 1847
Toussenel published L'esprit des bêtes. Vénerie française et zoologie
passionelle in which the animal kingdom was classified by its behav-
ioural characteristics, which in turn was imprinted on their anatomies.
Each of the animal types had affinities with humans. Needless to say,
the Jews were characterised exclusively as parasites and scavengers,
feeders on living or dead flesh. Apparently they resembled nothing so
much as a pack of vultures pecking and gobbling at carrion, provoking
horror and disgust. 'The long sinuous flexible neck that allows the
bird to dig deep into the entrails of dead beasts is the reflection of
the conniving and tortuous ways the usurer [read Jew] practises to
ruin his victim and extort the last penny of a worker's purse.' At the
malignant periphery of Romanticism, Jew-hatred was becoming biolo-
gised; the ethno-science of unnaturalism. 'They have clung to us like
leeches', wrote the rabid Jew-hater Georges Mathieu-Dairnvaell in the
1840s; they are 'vampires, scavengers of nature'.

Once ecological-zoological anti-Semitism, with its inevitable corol-
lary of pest extermination, was launched there was no stopping it.
Wagner's hatred fed off it, and in turn he bequeathed to future generations a sense of the physiological uncleanness of Jews, their divorce

from healthy nature. They were, forever, cast as shifty cosmopolitans, only ever at home in urban warrens where they could congregate amid all the other rootless aliens who flocked to the city like rats to refuse. Wagner's early political radicalism, like Toussenel's socialism, led him to associate the Jews with ineradicable, unwholesome practices: speculation designed to fleece and ruin the unwary; loan banking to the state on terms so extortionate that they held the public hostage; exploitative industrial and railway development funded and subsidised by the public purse so that Jews could seize the proceeds. A year before Toussenel's 1844 diatribe, the Young Hegelian Bruno Bauer had published *The Jewish Question*, lamenting the emancipation of the Jews. Only when Judaism itself ceased to exist, wrote Bauer, preferably in a state where all religions had been liquidated, could they take their place with fellow citizens. Bauer could see only two prospects for them: this 'emancipation' which would end their separate cultural and religious existence altogether, or something else which he characterised as '*Vernichtung*', best translated as 'destruction'. It's not necessary to invoke premonitions of Zyklon B or the Einsatzgruppen to see that the treatment of the apparently intractable Jews was already provoking the language of annihilation, and that this lethal hyperbole would, sooner or later, move from the province of words to the realm of deeds.

It then fell to the grandson of the rabbi of Trier, Karl Marx, to make his own contribution, ostensibly as a response to his fellow Hegelian Bauer, to the extremism of Judaeophobic language. Marx took issue with Bauer over the decisiveness of the formal repudiation of religion by the state. Where the Jews were concerned, he argued, it was not the Sabbath service which mattered but how they lived and what they lived for, which was, always, money. In this deep sense, being Jewish was to worship at the golden calf of capitalism: the two habits were one and the same. There were two extraordinary and baleful aspects to Marx's analysis of what it meant to be Jewish. First it was astonishing, especially at a time when the first modern histories – social and religious – of the Jews were being written by the scholars of *Wissenschaft des Judentums*, Heinrich Graetz and Leopold Zunz, that Marx saw what he judged to be reprehensible economic practices, not as the results of persecution and the enforced restriction of Jews to odious occupations, but rather to ingrained and incorrigible habits, so that the usury of the Middle Ages became the vicious banking of the modern age. It was Marx who gave a modern gloss to the ancient libel that Judaism was, in effect, interchangeable with, and nothing more than, the worship of Mammon. Worse still – and ominous for the future – was Marx's echoing of the contemporary commonplace, owned by Judaeophobes of both right and left, that the Jews were hardly in need of emancipation since they were the masters of the modern age. 'The Jews have [already] become emancipated in so far as Christians have become Jews.'

Paris in the mid-1840s, the time and place of publication for Toussenel, Bauer and Marx, was the fountainhead of modernised Jew-hatred. Even as Meyerbeer and Mendelssohn were enjoying their triumphs, the poisoned stream flowed freely to the young radical Richard Wagner. Later, his wife Cosima recalled him wanting a piece-by-piece *Vernichtung* of the Jewish world: first outlaw the celebration of their festivals, then close their presumptuous, ostentatious synagogues, and at some point get rid of them altogether by mass expulsion from German land.

One answer to this invective, in France, Germany and elsewhere in Europe, was, in all senses of the term, simply to make progress. By fits and starts, the doors of *lycées*, gymnasia, universities were opened to the Jews. Then the barriers which had long been raised in medicine were at last extended to the law. When medicine became more specialised, Jews colonised its new provinces: ophthalmology, respiratory diseases (for which in industrial Europe there was a never-ending flow of patients). Culture opened up. They were actors and – especially like the internationally famous Rachel – actresses, as well as great virtuoso performers such as Joseph Joachim and Anton Rubinstein, and as the daily newspaper became an urban staple, Jews published and wrote for them as well. Professions like engineering and industrial chemistry which were too new to have restrictions in place, and which depended on the supply of scientifically inspired talent, put no obstructions in the way of qualified Jews, of whom by the second generation of the nineteenth century there were many. Emerging from Jewish districts (though those remained with great synagogues at their centre), Jews felt the quickening pulse of metropolitan life and knew how to multiply the traffic: with hotels, department stores, pleasure gardens, concert halls and theatres. In one respect

Wagner was right. Jews like Fromenthal Halévy and Jacques Offenbach were ashamed neither of their instinct for entertainment nor of the money to be made by serving it up. Poring through the records the Nazis were horrified to discover that Johann Strauss had, all along, been a heavily disguised Jew, but we, on the other hand, should not be surprised. Likewise the Jews became in short order purveyors of urban comfort: of gas lighting and house heating, of fabrics and furniture, corsets and curtains, hats and haberdashery. They were the impresarios of modern life.

But they were also – and for those who were hostile to what they thought of as the Jewish invasion of modern life, most conspicuously – bankers: the new 'feudal lords' of the world in Toussenel's account with the Rothschilds as supreme sovereigns. In that view, the nominal occupant of a throne, be they Hohenzollern or Habsburg, Bourbon or Orléans, was sovereign in name only. It was the dynasty which funded their armies, their apparatus of state who truly ruled. Once, the Jews had provided gold or horses; now they reigned over the bond markets, lending, as they chose, to prop up autocrats or underwrite constitutional monarchs like Louis Philippe, whose governments in turn would award contracts for mines or railways. It was a simple thing, then, to refresh ancient prejudices for the modern age. The medieval usurer morphed into the high-hatted banker who by supplying or withholding funds could actually control the destinies of states, whether waging war or making peace. They were the Arnsteins and Eskeles, Biedermanns, Bleichröders and Hirschs. But it was always the Rothschilds, whose fortunes were in fact tied up with their international presence, in London, Paris, Vienna, Frankfurt and Naples, who could be represented as owing allegiance first and foremost to their own dynasty. Their habit of consolidating business alliances through marriages within the clan only reinforced this suspicion. When Rothschilds from all over Europe assembled for a grand family wedding in one of their spectacular houses, with invitations issued to the great and the grand of the non-Jewish as well as the Jewish establishment, the whole immense social performance avidly reported in the press, the impression of a new ruling class, just two generations removed from the ghetto, was unavoidable.

For the vast majority of Jews the sudden, prodigious rise of the Rothschilds was nothing but a source of shared pride and hope. But there were also thoughtful souls for whom the enthronement of the new lords of finance needed to be accompanied by an attention to social ethics. Generations of rabbis like Marx's grandfather in Trier had pointed out again and again the weight of ethical obligations in social and economic conduct enshrined in the Talmud. But Karl Marx the pamphleteer and polemicist inhabited a different kind of temper from Karl Marx the systematic philosopher, and the first Marx would have been undeterred by accusations that when he defined Judaism as gold-madness, he was giving ammunition to Jew-haters. If Jews wanted to uphold economic justice, then let them abandon Judaism.

Not all Jewish social philosophers felt this way. Two of them who were also businessmen, and who for a time worked with and for the Rothschilds, took a quite different view. But then, they were Péreires, the descendants of the Jacob Rodrigues who had spent his life trying to return the deaf to the company of humanity, and so they were drawn to projects that would turn hard economics into social benevolence.[17] Jacob Rodrigues had died in 1780. His son Isaac made himself the champion of the Péreire Method, keeping old Jacob's 'secret' hidden even as the treatment of the deaf passed it by. Revolutionary violence and the damage done by endless war to the fortunes of the Bordeaux Sephardi mercantile community made a victim of Isaac Péreire too, although it was an epidemic which carried him off, just days before his second son was born to his wife Henriette. That boy, named Isaac for his dead papa, and his elder brother Émile would devote their lives to making capitalism and the industrial future the common 'property', as they put it, of all classes. That they got very rich while preaching and practising socially conscious banking reinforced, if anything, their conviction that they were on the right track to a more just economic future; one which would pre-empt the inevitability of class war.

Fatherless, Émile and Isaac Péreire grew up in a struggle for survival, dependent on the kindness of other Bordeaux Jews and kin. Their mother, evidently a commercial innovator herself, made an attempt to keep body and soul together with a discount haberdashery store, Au Juste Prix. But the business failed and her clever boys, the slight handsome Émile and the affable Isaac six years his junior, were sent to Paris to make their own way helped by Péreire uncles, aunts and cousins. There was spiced rice, girl cousins with silk ribbons hanging from their black curls, half-remembered Ladino songs; a feeling for Sephardi family, amid the obscurantist Jesuitical gloom imposed by the Restoration governments. Napoleon's Consistoire, the state-authorised governing institution for the Jews, had been retained during the Restoration but after 1815 Jews had been locked out again from being either students or teachers at the elite schools of higher education.

One cousin, Olinde Rodrigues, felt particularly aggrieved by the exclusion. A beneficiary of the kind of scientific and engineering education introduced by the Napoleonic schools, he had hoped to spend his life as an advanced mathematician. When the government reaction precluded this, the natural course for Olinde was to turn his gift with numbers to banking, where Jews like the Fould family (the father Jewish, the son a convert of convenience) and James de Rothschild had already done well. But Olinde, like Émile and Isaac, was in his twenties and was avid for a social vision which went beyond floating bonds and counting profits. He became secretary to the Comte de Saint-Simon who had dreamed up just such a vision of a new world of modernity. Saint-Simon's philosophy united the two spheres of human activity commonly assumed to be irreconcilable: religion and technology. Instead of industry and science being the inevitable instruments of man's degradation, Saint-Simon wanted them harnessed for universal social amelioration. This, he thought, would come about not through the independent action of individuals acting first and foremost in their own individual self-interest, as Adam Smith and the Scottish economists had proposed, but through the alternative principle of 'association'. Association was in fact not far from the governing ethic of Smith's *The Theory of Moral Sentiments*, the work he most cherished. But in Saint-Simon's hands the idea of social association had practical application. It argued for the creation of banks and instruments of credit open to working people, small traders and all manner of economic agents, high and low. Thus capital – especially inherited capital, otherwise tied up in funds that were 'idle' (*oisif*, Saint-Simon's most damning word) and destined to subsidise and perpetuate unproductive indolence – would now be unlocked for all those who wished to put it to work. Workers high and low would be thus connected in a unified community of the industrious. Not long before he died in 1825, Saint-Simon elaborated his stirring philosophy in *Nouveau Christianisme*, almost certainly dictated to his young Jewish secretary, Olinde Rodrigues. The old Christianity had failed the egalitarian sympathies of its founder. As a result it had become obsolete. The only true religion now was one which would harmonise technology with the universal wants of productive man. It was an alternative to both socialism and capitalism and, all things considered over the next two centuries, not quite so naive or utopian a philosophy as textbooks invariably assume.

Olinde Rodrigues had seen the light, and even while he was spending his days in the bank, he was preaching the new gospel to his cousins. Isaac especially became a wholehearted convert. After the patriarch-count died in 1825 a group of his followers, many of them engineering graduates of the *hautes écoles*, set about publicising Saint-Simonian views, giving lectures, establishing journals to promote the philosophy. The Péreires became active journalists and commentators on both economics and politics in the most widely read liberal newspapers of the day, the *Globe* and the *National*. Increasingly Émile and Isaac saw themselves as a new kind of socially and ethically aware capitalist. Such consciousness did not preclude working, as Émile did, for James de Rothschild. On the contrary, Émile may have harboured fancies that he could convert the bank from within; at any rate create something different not only from the bond-market-driven Rothschilds but also the grandees of the *'haute banque'* like Jacques Laffitte and Casimir Perier who dominated both the financial market and, after the revolution of 1830, the governing elite of Louis Philippe's 'July Monarchy'. A beginning was made with a small investment bank funded by debentures.

The Péreires stayed Jews; though not observant Jews, as their dismayed mother quickly noticed when she came from Paris to stay with her sons, swiftly returning in high kosher dudgeon back to Bordeaux. There's no pleasing some mothers, even when the brothers professed themselves unapologetically true to their religion. Isaac had strayed furthest, committed as he was to Saint-Simon's economic unitarianism, and was already its most zealous apostle delivering the gospel in public lectures. In all likelihood Henriette heard the *Christianisme* and not the *Nouveau*. But conversion never occurred to either of the brothers Péreire. Émile insisted that while he was not much of a synagogue-goer he would remain Jewish and bring his children up the same way. Isaac, who for a while at any rate shared the Saint-Simonian rejection of marriage as a form of institutionalised bondage for wives, nonetheless ended up marrying his Sephardi cousin Rachel Laurence Fonseca. When their mother was dying at Auteuil in 1827, both her sons sat beside the deathbed, holding Henriette's hands and reciting, along with her, the *shema*.[18]

In 1832 everything changed. For two years cholera raged through much of France; funerals were where one made new friends. At one such mournful event burying a young Saint-Simonian, Émile and Isaac Péreire met a group of engineering graduates from the École des Ponts et Chaussées whose shared obsession was railways. Five years earlier the very first iron railroad, fourteen miles long, had come into operation in the south-east stretch of the upper Loire. But its purpose was confined to carrying coal, sand, gravel and lime from the mines at Saint-Étienne to a depot at Andrézieux-Bouthéon. The railway carts were horse-drawn and no thought was given to steam traction much less a passenger line. When the Manchester–Liverpool line, carrying goods and passengers, opened in 1830 the French engineers thought again. In 1832 the head of the Department of Bridges and Highways, Baptiste Alexis Legrand, set out a scheme of Saint-Simonian vision: an ambitious network of rail radiating out from Paris, connecting the capital with major cities like Lyons and Rouen, perhaps even as far as Marseilles. Calculations of time and distance would be revolutionised. For the first time a true national market would be possible in France.[19]

The Péreires considered how long it had taken to transport men and goods (the wines of the Médoc but also the French colonial wares which their family had traded) from Bordeaux to Paris, and saw the future. A first line – between Paris and Saint-Germain-en-Laye, thirteen miles away – was proposed, as much as a pilot demonstration of the viability of passenger transport as anything else. While the engineers, in Napoleonic style, assumed this would be a state-run enterprise, the Péreires had an eye on a partnership between private capital and government. The state would provide land for the routes and fund costs of construction and rolling stock; they themselves would then operate the business. It sounded crassly profiteering but Émile thought of the multitudes who would find work; and more multitudes whose lives would be transformed by this new kind of transport. Railways would create just that mass 'association' Saint-Simonians envisaged. Should the brothers make a franc or two, that was no sin either. The Péreires estimated that 5 million francs would take care of the project, but James de Rothschild, for whom government debt was the only sure thing, was deeply sceptical. With the exception of the enterprising Salomon in Vienna, who was the prime mover in Kaiser Ferdinand's Nordbahn (along with the usual Jewish suspects the Arnsteins and Eskeles), the Rothschilds were railway sceptics. In England, the centre of the boom, Nathan Rothschild took no part at all in the early investments. When James was finally drawn into the Paris/Saint-Germain scheme it was the prospect of making money from appreciated stock rather than any visionary macroeconomic transformation which held most appeal.

The Péreires got a warmer reception elsewhere: from Adolphe d'Eichthal (whose family had started out as Seligmanns), and the Foulds, some of them like Benoît still Jewish, some like Achille not. And as business and economic journalists they promoted their own scheme shamelessly in the liberal press of the July Monarchy. This in turn found friends in the Chamber of Deputies betting that the scheme would be a success. Land for the route was acquired. Ground was broken for the Paris terminus on a site between the rue Saint-Lazare and the place de l'Europe where Émile occupied an improvised office made of planking, suspended over the works so he could inspect its daily progress. The whole business became a marvel. Forty thousand workers were hired; the project came in before time and under cost. By now the great banks were paying attention. On 24 August 1837 Queen Marie-Amelie formally opened the line at a ceremony for six hundred. Two days later, when the line opened for regular traffic, 18,000 passengers took the twenty-minute ride out to Saint-Germain (or rather to Le Pecq a couple of miles away, since the gradient in the centre of town had defied the engineers; it would be another ten years before that problem was solved), the high hats and frock coats, the bonnets and crinoline skirts all jammed together for their suburban excursion. The Péreires liked to think that social pleasure was not irreconcilable with profit and that the union of the two would remake Paris. They were not altogether wrong. That August day had the atmosphere of a fete rather than a journey.

The effect of PSG was spectacular. Friends and enemies alike of the railways announced that a new era had begun. Heinrich Heine, then in Paris, declared the moment comparable only to the discovery of

America or the invention of the printing press for world-historical importance. Popular songs were written hymning the marvel of the line; a
pasteboard train appeared on stage at the *variétés*. To the monied classes,
Péreire's balance sheet looked promising. In six months the running
costs of the PSG had fallen to less than half of gross revenues. Viability
engendered competition. James de Rothschild now managed to crack
a thin smile when railways were mentioned, but it disappeared when,
in alliance with the Péreires for an extension line out to Versailles, he
found himself in a bidding war with the Foulds. Heine, who had named
Émile 'the Pontifex Maximus of the railways', now compared the
contending 'rail rabbis' with the rival schools of Hillel and Shammai
quarelling over the Torah at the dawn of rabbinic Judaism. The Chamber
of Deputies was more cynically Solomonic in its judgement. Not
wanting to short-change the handouts, the legislature and the government awarded contracts for *two* lines to be built. The Péreire–Rothschild
line was to run out to Versailles on the Right Bank, the Foulds with
their partners the Seguins on the Left. That was one line too many.

Then came the accidents. On Sunday 8 May 1842, the 5.30 p.m. from
Versailles was returning to Paris carrying 770 passengers. They were
travelling from a public fete thrown by the king in the park of Versailles.
The *grandes eaux* had all been switched on, the fountains playing along
with the music. In anticipation of a crowd wanting to return to Paris,
the Company of the Right Bank line had laid on eighteen carriages
pulled by two locomotives. This turned out to be a bad idea. A few
minutes after the train left Bellevue station, the axle tree of the leading
locomotive broke. The second locomotive drove into the stationary
one, riding up over its body, killing the stoker-engineer, the Englishman
Mr George. Carriages piled into the back of the second locomotive.
Both were now on fire, throwing flames into the wooden cars, setting
them alight. Because a passenger had committed suicide by throwing
himself out of a carriage the previous year, the company had locked
the doors of all the carriages (a practice also adopted by the Great
Western in England, as the *Railway Times* complained). At least forty
passengers were killed, the majority by being burned alive. The inferno
was so fierce that body parts were found scattered over the wreckage,
most of them unidentifiable. One of those whose remains were identified was a national hero: the explorer-navigator Jules Dumont d'Urville,
who had crossed the Antarctic Circle just three years before. His skull

was identified both by a doctor who had served on his ship the *Astrolabe* and by a phrenologist-sculptor who had taken a recent cast. Cries of the casualties were said to be heard for miles. The National Guard arriving on the scene did what it could, and the horrified king opened the chateau to the victims.

Just a few months before, the Chamber of Deputies had debated a charter governing the expansion of the railways. In the spirit of the times, the state would provide land, subsidies and rolling stock while private syndicates (like the Rothschild–Péreire and the Fould–Seguin) would operate the lines which, as hostile commentators like Toussenel pointed out, suited the private companies very well indeed. The way he put it, though, was that the state – funded by taxes from the people – took up the burden while the Jews took the profits.

Hostility and accidents did not slow down the race. The Péreires had in mind a great national network, reaching to their home town of Bordeaux and south-east to Marseilles, and to Lyons. James de Rothschild thought a northern line to Belgium and the Channel ports, linked to the Channel ferries, was a more urgent priority, connecting the crucial points of the industrial heartland of north-western Europe. It was calculated that it would take a mere fourteen hours to get from Paris to London (including the Channel crossing). In June 1846, an immense gala occasion for six hundred of the July Monarchy's most resplendent *notables* was held to celebrate the opening of the Nord. Three months later, a driver en route to the Channel coast took his engine to twice the approved speed, reaching about forty-five miles an hour. Crossing a viaduct in the Pas-de-Calais near the village of Fampoux, the train derailed, sending carriages plunging into a deep-water marsh. Fourteen people lost their lives in the wreck. A journalist from the *Revue du Nord* wrote of smashing the glass in his coach window to escape and trying to extract drowning fellow passengers, to no avail.

Of course there were Geneva Protestant bankers like the Hottinguers prominently involved in railway development, and Catholics too, but the most infuriated writers laid the latest catastrophe almost exclusively at the door of the Jews. Toussenel, the socialist Pierre Leroux and, the most toxic of all, Georges-Marie Mathieu-Dairnvaell, whose pamphlet *Histoire édifiante et curieuse de Rothschild Ier, roi des Juifs* (*Edifying and Curious History of Rothschild the First, King of the*

Jews) sold 60,000 copies in a matter of weeks after the Fampoux disaster, all blamed the Jews in much the same way. (You can still order Mathieu-Dairnvaell's venomously anti-Semitic tract from Amazon's French site, courtesy of Hachette, and doubtless many who enjoy this kind of thing do. When I last checked there were still '*aucun commentaire client*'.) Concerned only with profit, they had cut safety corners. In decent countries like Prussia, the state regulated and ran the railways; not in France, where a corrupt regime had become the pawn of the Rothschilds and the rest of the 'tribe of Judah and the tribe of Benjamin'. Aside from the disasters, the Jewish railways (Toussenel called them exactly that) subjected their second- and third-class passengers to carriages fit only for the transport of livestock to the butcher, the worst of them open to rain and freezing cold. Apocryphal stories circulated of men found frozen to death in the wagon-car. And yet however callous the Jews' exploitation of the railways, Toussenel wrote, when a new line opened the Chamber of Deputies chorused 'Glory be to the Jews' and the credulous people followed them in their cry.

For centuries the Jews had been vilified and persecuted as incorrigibly obscurantist: standing apart from the rest of humanity, locked into their own impenetrably antisocial rabbinic ways. Now they were attacked for the opposite reason: for emerging all too quickly into the rest of society, casting themselves as the ushers of modernity. The socialist Pierre Leroux did not just declare that their emancipation had been inadvisable, but actually dangerous, 'the most reprehensible of all the vices committed by our society'. In common with many others of the left as well as the right, he wanted to lock them away again in their urban prisons. What a mistake Napoleon had made when he tore down the ghetto gates and walls!

The timing of Jewish emancipation had been terrible for its beneficiaries, albeit not of their choosing. For it came about exactly when Enlightenment cosmopolitanism, the universal brotherhood, that short-lived little flame, had burnt out. By the second quarter of the nineteenth century, resistance to the dominion of the machine took the form of a militant cult of history, religion, nature and nation, against which the Jews seemed to personify the opposite: a people – a dynasty like the Rothschilds – indifferent to borders, a race who were everywhere and nowhere since now they could not be reliably identified by marks on their clothing, not at any rate until Wagnerian ears picked up their ugly, comical wheezing, croaking and snuffling. Now they had mastered the perpetuation of their ancient viciousness by disguising it as modern practice. Leroux saw banking as a latter-day form of crucifixion.

And in the railways they had found the perfect instrument of their dominion. For the railways were, after all, against nature. They murdered space; turned the serene contemplation of landscape into a mad whirl, a 'kaleidoscope'. Travel, said Ruskin, dulled in exact proportion to its velocity, and the railways did nothing except turn humans into 'living parcels'. By contracting time and killing distance, they scrambled a sense of being *somewhere*. When Heine famously described his being able, courtesy of the railways, to smell the Berlin lindens while still in Paris and sense the North Sea crashing on his doorstep, his excitement kept company with dismay and fearfulness.[20] The railways made you ill, jangled your nerves so that you would have to seek remedy from the inevitable Jewish doctor round the corner. Railways had robbed people of consoling intimacy with their beasts of burden: no more stroking the mane of Dobbin the carriage horse. No one stroked the face of the iron horse which had replaced it. Some critics complained that carriages were unsociable, a space in which men were constantly taking out their watches on the fob to check whether the train was or wasn't on time, where the stations themselves were dominated by giant clocks that glared at the passengers as they scurried off to work. Others complained that second-class carriages in particular were altogether *too* social, or at any rate too close for comfort, obliging one to inhale the fetid garlic breath of a fellow traveller or try and stop up one's ears against the snore of a sailor lost in drunken sleep.

The world was going to hell. Obviously, it was all the fault of the Jews.

II. 'We are one people'

It was just another beheading in Fez. A Jewish girl, from Tangier, seventeen years old and, as everyone noticed, exceptionally beautiful, who, so the *qadi* said, had received the message of the Prophet but then wilfully turned her back on him. Death was the penalty for such apostasy but the sultan of Morocco had, in his compassion, given her a last chance to reconsider, ordering the executioner to cut her with his scimitar just deep enough that a flow of blood would persuade her to change her mind. But the blade had no effect. The girl was unrepentant, calling out the *shema* as the stroke fell. The girl's father collected the severed head and torso for burial, paying the required fee to the sultan.

Some months later, in 1835, the writer Eugenio Maria Romero, who had heard something of the tragedy, sought out the girl's brother in Gibraltar.[21] In a small room of a house on one of the backstreets at the lower end of the Rock, the brother told Montero the whole story. The Christian was so moved by what he heard that he crossed the Mediterranean to Tangier to listen to Simcha and Haim, the girl's grieving parents. Then Romero set the whole tale down and published it two years later.

The girl's name was Sol Hatchuel, the bearer of sunlight. After an argument with her parents (and what seventeen-year-old does not have those) she stormed out of the house to visit an Arab friend on the same street, for there was no Jewish *mellah* (quarter) in Tangier as there was in Marrakech or Fez. It was Sol's familiarity with her Muslim neighbours that had worried the parents and had been the cause of the argument. The anxieties turned out to be well founded. When Sol complained bitterly about her mother and father, the friend suggested that perhaps she might begin a new life as a Muslim, especially honoured for embracing the true faith. Alarmed, Sol protested this was too high a price and in any case she never meant to imply alienation from her faith. But the fatal seed had been sown. Being a great source of merit to have brought a convert into the fold of the faithful, the friend reported to the pasha of Tangier that a conversion had actually taken place. Sol was brought before him, indignantly and then tearfully protesting that nothing of the sort had happened; that she would remain loyal to the religion of her forefathers forever. So obstinate was she that she had to be imprisoned, her distraught parents kept at bay, and then taken to Fez, strapped to a mule, to be questioned, cajoled and threatened by the sultan of Morocco himself, who spelled out graphically the consequences of an apostasy. To the last,

Sol insisted that there could have been no apostasy since there had been no conversion. But she was not believed and her life's blood poured out onto the dusty straw of the Fez medina.

For the Jews of Morocco, Sol had died for *kiddush hashem*, sanctifying the name like the medieval martyrs of the Crusades and the slaughtered of the Inquisition's autos-da-fé.[22] *Qissat* laments in Judaeo-Arabic and Hebrew were made in her memory, and her grave became a site of pilgrimage, more remarkably, for some Muslims who treated Sol with reluctant admiration. For Romero – according to Marc Rey, who repeated the story in his *Souvenirs d'un Voyage au Maroc* – her beheading had been shocking evidence of the barbarism and backwardness of the Arabs of the Maghreb. Algeria was already a French colony although it would not be until 1882 that Morocco would follow.[23]

But no one in Europe, Jewish or otherwise, seemed to notice the fate of Sol Hatchuel, much less turn her story into a cause célèbre. Romero's hundred-page history went untranslated and then out of print. In Rey's *Souvenirs* it was just another anecdote to feed the excitement of blade-sharp exoticism. Any number of painterly romancers, excited by the combination of soft bodies, naked throats and bared swords in Delacroix's *Death of Sardanapalus*, looked for comparable stories in the Levant and the Maghreb. One of them, Alfred Dehodencq, went one better than most of his studio-bound orientalists by actually living in Morocco for some years after 1853.[24] There he painted Sol, her shirt open at throat and neck, a scarlet-clad swordsman leaning manically over her while the bloodthirsty mob wait for the coup, roll their eyes and shake their hands in the ways thought typical of the souk and the medina.

But in 1834 frock-coat Jewry was not paying much attention to tarboosh Jewry whose condition, apart from the occasional murder, was in any case shocking. The vast majority lived in poverty, ignorance and especially fearfulness. There exists today a romance of Jewish life in the Islamic world, imagined as one of neighbourly harmony, irremediably altered by the rise of Zionism and the creation of Israel. It is true that in cities like Cairo, Alexandria, Baghdad and Aleppo, at the end of the nineteenth century and into the twentieth, a Jewish middle class, much of it identified with the forces of modernisation, lived a culturally vibrant life alongside Muslim and Christian co-citizens. But this was the creation of colonial modernising, and the Jews paid a heavy price for their identification with empire. For centuries before that, the mass of Jewish poor in Syria, Egypt, Palestine and the Maghreb states lived a back-alley life, hammering metalwork or selling brightly woven textiles and leather goods. In so far as their children were educated at all, it was in religious schools, the *cheders*, where they were taught to recite the Torah by rote much as their Arab peers chanted passages from the Quran. Those same children had to get used to being spat on in casual encounters with Muslims in the street, and showered with stones whenever it amused anyone to do so. The Jews of the Muslim world were still more or less legally powerless, prohibited from testifying on their own behalf in a Muslim court (the only place they might get redress against assault or robbery). Even in the relatively tolerant Ottoman world, sudden reversals of fortune – the disposal and judicial murder of the latest Jewish moneylender and banker – could trigger violence. Public executions brought on mob rampages in the Jewish quarters, and sometimes wholesale massacres against which Jews were defenceless since they were still forbidden to carry any kind of weapon. When insulted in the street, they were to lower their heads in meek acceptance and be prepared for degrading humiliations when they paid the annual *jizya* tribute tax.

An edict was passed (although later rescinded) in the Persian city of Hamadan, banning them from eating fresh fruit (as distinct from the overripe and flyblown), and from leaving their houses during rain and snow, since the Jews, being impure, might carry some of that contaminated rainwater to the doors or even the persons of the Faithful.[25] Jewish women were *forbidden* to cover their faces so that they would be automatically identified as immodest, virtually as prostitutes. If a Jew dared to appear in the streets at all during the sacred Shi'a period of Muharram he or she could be instantly killed for their blasphemous temerity. During festive periods they could be thrown into tanks for the fun of it. At such moments there were always 'fireworks and Jews' for the amusement of the populace. In 1836 the English traveller Edward Lane reported from Palestine that Jews were 'held in the utmost contempt and abhorrence by Muslims in general ... they scarcely ever dare to utter a word in response to abuse or when they are reviled or beaten unjustly by the nearest Arab or Turk ... for many a Jew has been put to death upon a false malicious accusation of uttering disrespectful words against the Kuran and the Prophet'.[26]

But history was stirring to bring together, as yet very tentatively, the eagerly modernising Jews of Europe and America with their 'backward' (the universally used term) brethren and sisters in the Muslim world. Steamboats, port development, those railways with lines extending already from Vienna to the Balkans, made for tentative connections, as did the opening of bank and shipping offices. When bad things happened in one place, enterprising Jews found another to pitch their stalls. Leaving Baghdad in the wake of one anti-Jewish riot, the Sassoons fetched up in British Bombay. Beginning in the 1820s and 30s, European Jews who had seen their own communities branch out from anciently impoverished occupations – pawnshops and old clothes – into schools which added secular 'useful' instruction to religion, and then into the new universities which did not require a religious test, wanted some of the same for the Jews of the east.

The more intrepid made their way to Palestine, not least because Christian evangelicals were setting the pace, discussing the 'Restoration' of the Jews to their ancestral land as a precondition of their mass conversion and the Second Coming of the Saviour. It was known that there were thousands of Jews in Jerusalem, Safed and Tiberias, the vast majority living in ignorance and indigence, depending on *halukah*, while they attended forever to their Talmud studies. If those Jews could somehow be brought into the modern world without compromising their religion, would they not be better able to withstand the missionaries?

That was on the mind of Moses Montefiore, businessman and sheriff of London, when he first visited the Holy Land with his strong-minded wife Judith in 1829. En route, in Cairo and Alexandria, the Montefiores were appalled by the squalor they encountered and began to dream of a social transformation. A terrifying earthquake in 1837 which destroyed Jewish Safed and Tiberias, houses breaking apart, the wreckage tumbling down the Galilean hillside, imposed its own more urgent priorities. Those who had not been buried beneath the rubble were now without food or shelter, and sleeping on rush mats in the open. Disaster relief, called for in synagogues all over Europe, was another moment when the Jews of two utterly different worlds recognised that, nonetheless, they belonged to the one community. And in London, Paris, Berlin, Vienna and New York they began to realise that when bad things happened to them they were not necessarily without friends in the Gentile world.

One such very bad thing unfolded in the winter of 1840. On 5 February in Damascus, where there was an anciently settled community of five thousand Jews, a Capuchin friar, Tomasso, together with his Muslim servant went missing.[27] He was reported to have been last seen in the Jewish quarter, and suspicions were raised, followed by accusations from the Christian community that the men had been abducted and murdered so that their blood could be used for Passover matzot. The blood libel never slept for very long. Three of the community's rabbis were arrested, put in chains and beaten, to 'an extreme that their flesh hung in pieces', in an attempt to extract a confession that blood was used in Passover rituals, 'to which they replied that if such had been the case many Jewish proselytes would have published the fact'.[28] Six hundred Jewish houses were summarily demolished in the vain hope of finding the remains of the missing priest. A Jewish tobacconist said to have been a witness to the ritual murder was arrested, and flogged so severely to extract (in vain) a confession that he died of his ordeal. The Jews who came for his body had the greatest difficulty in purifying it for burial because the shredded flesh simply fell away from the bones. A barber was the next to be subjected to merciless treatment. Thorns and reeds were pushed under his nails, his feet flogged and his back flayed with hippo-hide whips; his beard was set alight, lit candles pushed up his nostrils and his genitals twisted to bursting point. In this case, a 'confession' was extracted to the satisfaction of the governor Sharif Pasha. But the Passover murders and blood drainage were always supposed to be the work not of individual Jews but a communal conspiracy, so the elderly Rabbi Antebi was the next in line, held in and under freezing water, and when he surfaced gasping for breath, smashed in the face; after which his genitals were crushed with rocks. Inconveniently, the rabbi refused to confirm the libel and asked instead for death. Another rabbi, Yusuf Lignado, died after ten days of being beaten on the soles of his feet, though it took only one relentless session of this bastinado torture to kill the sixty-year-old gatekeeper of the Jewish quarter.[29] Seventy Jews were imprisoned and violently assaulted, some of them children. A mother was told that her children aged from five to twelve would be killed unless she confessed. Yet when the French consul Ratti Menton

referred to the events as an 'appalling affair' he meant the abduction
and the likely involvement of Jews in the crime.

But then, a remarkable thing happened in the form of righteous
Gentiles, the most influential of whom was the Austrian consul in
Damascus who, in contrast to his French counterpart, was horrified
by the mistreatment and incredulous at the allegations, especially
when it had been reliably reported that the friar and servant had been
seen very much alive leaving the city on foot. The Austrian consul in
Cairo was alerted and he duly sent a sceptical report back to the
government in Vienna where Chancellor Metternich was on friendly
terms with his banker Salomon Rothschild. Salomon lost no time
writing to his brother James, the honorary Austrian consul in Paris,
and James began to orchestrate a public campaign of outrage in the
press. The lawyer and liberal politician Adolphe Crémieux, whose
family had originally been from Carpentras, wrote an article of
eloquent indignation in the *Journal des débats*, knowing full well that
the Judaeophobes, both ultra-Catholics and socialist enemies of the
'Jew bankers', would immediately raise a hue and cry against the
power of the Israelites.

On 5 May 1840, Crémieux participated in a meeting of the Jewish
Board of Deputies at its headquarters in Park Lane, London, to plan
a systematic campaign to demand the release of Jewish prisoners, the
withdrawal of libellous accusations and the protection of the community. A conscious decision was taken, very much in line with Crémieux's
own politics, that this was a moment to align the cause of the Jews
with the cause of liberalism everywhere.

The men who took this momentous step were the grandees of the
Anglo-Jewish world: Mocattas and Goldsmids, Cohens and Levys,
Montefiores and of course Rothschilds. Most of them were liberally
inclined Whigs for the good reason that ten years earlier it had been
the Tories, including the ungrateful Duke of Wellington, when prime
minister, who had dragged their feet over the final step in political
emancipation: the opening of Parliament to Jews through the waiver
of a Christian profession of faith. It had been the rising star of their
party, Thomas Babington Macaulay, who had made his impassioned
maiden speech on Jewish emancipation. They were also both the
champions and beneficiaries of a social liberalisation which was
galloping through traditional British institutions. After the part the

Rothschilds had played in financing the defeat of Napoleon (largely by smuggling gold to the European theatres of conflict) the City warmed to the Jews. Moses Montefiore, who had been a Rothschild employee and partner, was elected one of only two sheriffs. Stories, more affectionate than sneering, rapidly circulated of Moses arriving in his sheriff's robes carrying a kosher chicken or his favourite dish of cold boiled beef. There were other new points of entry: David Salomon was admitted to the Bar without the Christian oath requirement; University College and its school opened to Jews; St Paul's, City of London and King Edward's School, Birmingham, followed.

More important than these institutional openings was an informal social convergence, sometimes made through those who had formally left the religion but made no secret of their origins (pointless in any case) even as they embedded themselves in the heart of British culture. Isaac D'Israeli, who had stormed out of synagogue, thought out loud as he baptised himself and his son that ultimately Judaism and Christianity were pretty much the same religion, so what difference did a sprinkling at the font really make? Once Christian, Benjamin famously smelled opportunity in Scott's romance of the Jewess in *Ivanhoe* to inaugurate a whole literary industry of the Noble Semitic-Exotic, beginning with a daily look in the mirror and extending to Eva the charismatic Jewess of *Tancred*, who draws her infatuated Christian into the depths of Hebrew mystery in the Holy Land so that he would receive an epiphany with an angel on Mount Sinai.

But popularity was not conditional on conversion. The domestic romances of Grace Aguilar, unapologetically Jewish, were the best-sellers of early-Victorian England. Jewish musicians and actors, including the irresistible French Rachel, had ardent followings. On the grounds of Gunnersbury, Nathan and Lionel's country estate, vast flocks of game birds dropped to Rothschild guns. Just as *le tout Paris* wanted to be at the parties at James de Rothschild's Château de Ferrières, the same held true for fashionable society in England. Anthony Rothschild complained bitterly that 'all we have these days are stinking balls'. A Rothschild or a Salomon wedding was itself an immense society occasion, reported in drooling detail in the *Illustrated London News*. And some sort of threshold was crossed in 1845 when Eliza Acton's popular cookbook *Modern Cookery for Private Families* included a section on 'Foreign and Jewish Cookery'. Reflecting the circles in which non-Jews met the Jewish elite, most of the dishes were Sephardi, especially those featuring 'pounded almonds and rich syrups' which declared 'their Oriental character'. Though it probably wasn't a good idea to describe 'Jewish smoked beef' as 'possessing the fine flavour of a really well-cured ham', Acton loved the almond puddings, Portuguese '*chorissa*' sausage with rice and the fish fried in 'fresh olive oil' that the Sephardi Jews had brought to Britain. 'The Jews have cold fried fish much served at their repasts,' she wrote, conjuring up a picture of Victorians at *kiddush*, and recommended that plaice, sole, brill and turbot could all be fried as well as the salmon of her recipe 'and arranged in a symmetrical form around a portion of larger fish or by themselves'.[30]

Of course, there was still poverty, illiteracy, begging and borrowing away from the Jewish finery of Islington, Stamford Hill and Mayfair (to which the English Rothschilds finally moved from New Court in the City). But there was also the beginning of a genuine Anglo-Jewish middle class, feeling itself at home in Britain and who, from 1841, had their own weekly organ of opinion, the *Jewish Chronicle*.

So when a grand meeting of protest against the atrocities in Damascus was called for at Mansion House, there was no doubt that it would be packed, as indeed was the case, nor that there would be vocal friends of the Jews to say their piece. The most passionate of all was the Irish 'Liberator', the great orator of Catholic emancipation, Daniel O'Connell. 'Every feeling of humanity,' O'Connell roared, 'is contradicted by the foul, the murderous charge ... was there a being so degraded as to believe that they [the Jews of Damascus] made human blood a part of their ceremonies ... was not the Hebrew exemplary in every relation of life ... was he not a good father, a good son?' With only the egregious exception of *The Times*, which opined that it was for the Jews now to prove their innocence, the entirety of the British press followed in denouncing not just the cruelty in Damascus itself but anyone so bigoted and credulous as to believe the ancient slander.

The response was encouraging enough for the Board of Deputies to send a delegation to the Foreign Secretary, Lord Palmerston, to have the government support a mission to the ruler of Egypt, Muhammad Ali, under whose jurisdiction Syria had fallen, and perhaps to the sultan himself (the seventeen-year-old Abdulmecid). Palmerston had his own strategic reasons for an eastern overture and at one point even envisaged a Jewish return to Palestine as the seedbed of a Britain-friendly modernisation of the region. But there was also no doubt that his anger at both what had transpired in Damascus and especially French collusion in the charges was genuine.

With the blessings of the British government, Montefiore and Crémieux embarked on their mission. Although in the classic ways of Jewish grandees they fell out over just who was leader and who deputy – Sir Moses assuming lordly airs, and Crémieux fuming that his thunder had been stolen – the mission was an astonishing success. The formidable old conquistador Muhammad Ali received them warmly (again with his own political and military interests in mind) and ordered the immediate release of the Jewish prisoners. In Constantinople the meeting with the grand vizier Recid Pasha proved to be even more dramatic. Just a year before, the young sultan, guided by the vizier, had issued the 'Tanzimat' edicts, making over the notori-ously arbitrary and absolutist Ottoman state into a liberal model: life, property and liberty guaranteed. The approach of Crémieux and Montefiore allowed Recid Pasha to show an even more liberal face to the world. There had been other outbreaks of blood-libel persecutions, notably in Rhodes where a mob attacked the Jewish quarter, and this minor eruption of hatred allowed the sultan to issue a formal denun-ciation of the monstrous slander as a gross falsehood. 'We cannot permit the Jewish Nation (whose innocence of the crime alleged against them is evident) to be vexed and tormented upon accusations which have not the least foundation in truth.'[31] A further firman gave Jews equal rights with all other subjects of the Ottoman Empire, freed from the tribute tax and any remaining restrictions on residence or occupation. It was extraordinary that only ten years after the 40,000 Jews of France were formally emancipated by the revolution of 1830, a comparable transformation had come about at the other end of the Mediterranean. There were even hints that the Ottoman government might look with favour on Jewish immigration and economic develop-ment in Palestine. None of this, though, would preclude the Syrian minister of defence, Mustafa Tlass, publishing in 1983 his own book on the Damascus affair, *The Matzah of Zion*, in which the blood libel was assumed to be a universally accepted truth.

*

The wheels of liberal Europe turned, sometimes for good and sometimes for ill. Jews were caught up in the revolutions of 1848, sometimes as heroes and sometimes as targets. Crémieux joined the provisional government of the Second Republic as minister of justice while angry crowds ransacked some of the Péreire and Rothschild railway depots. The minister who hated capital punishment looked on in fatalistic horror as the guns of the bourgeois National Guard mowed down the uprising of the workers in June of that year. Émile and Isaac Péreire, who still occasionally gave lip service to their old Saint-Simonian ideals, now made the project entrepreneurial rather than idealistic, sensing in Prince President Louis Napoleon – shortly to declare himself emperor – a disciple, as indeed he was. In 1852 they opened the Crédit Foncier for agricultural property loans, and later in the same year their most famous and innovative creation, the Crédit Mobilier, an investment bank floated by public subscription.[32] To Saint-Simonian purists the bank betrayed its principles by failing to lend to genuinely small enterprises, instead raising capital for Grand Projects, including ever more railway lines, to Toulouse and into Spain in the south-west, and the great railway of the Nord, all the way to Belgium and on through Germany to Berlin, the line Meyerbeer rode over and again.

Think of Second Empire Paris and you think of Baron Haussmann and the creation of the *grandes boulevardes*, clearing a brutal path through the old *quartiers* of the artisans. But this was also a Paris made by the Péreires, who created their enormous department store, the Grand Magasin du Louvre, employing 2,400 staff, and near it the Grand Hôtel de l'Europe, with its endless banqueting rooms and steam-powered elevators. The brothers thought themselves not a bit inferior to the Rothschilds and bought themselves a huge country estate just down the road, so infuriating Baron James that all he cared about henceforth was to see them laid low. That would indeed happen, mostly through overreach when they took their railway and industrial enterprises deep into central Europe (colliding with another branch of the Rothschilds). And Paris would itself fall, catastrophically, in 1870, to a Prussian army financed by yet another Jewish banker, Gerson Bleichröder.

For the growing number of Jew-haters, including Wilhelm Marr who in 1879 was the first to coin the term 'anti-Semite' as the principle around which a new political force should be organised, all this was irrefutable evidence of the Jewish conquest of Europe. The modernity they were selling was a shoddy bill of goods: vulgar, commercial opera; tawdry geegaws in their department stores; the railways which contemptuously rode over ancient, noble boundaries of language, territory and nation. Everything sacred, beginning with the Holy Church itself, was captive to their vicious greed.

The counter-attack of Christian, nationalist tradition, whether coming from the vitriolic pen of Louis Veuillot, the editor of the Catholic paper *L'Univers*, took the Jewish carriers of modernity somewhat by surprise, at least in its violent, vehement intensity. They had assumed that sooner or later the forces of ancient bigotry would have to yield to modern reason, utility, an urban, even cosmopolitan way of being in the world; Paris one day, Cologne the next.

Often enough, though, self-congratulation was pulled up short by fear and dismay. 1858 ought to have been a year of triumph for the liberal hopes of Jews. Lionel de Rothschild had been elected to Parliament three times, the first in 1847, as member for the City of London, but on each occasion the House of Lords had frustrated disability bills passed in the Commons which would have allowed him to be seated without having to take a Christian oath. Finally, in the summer of 1858 the Lords agreed that each of the two Houses of Parliament might have their own form of oath, so that Rothschild was able to swear 'on Jehovah' and take his seat as the first practising Jewish member of the House of Commons.

But for every such advance there was always a stinging reminder of the helplessness of Jews, even when it came to protecting the sanctity of their families against kidnapping in the name of conversion. In the first week of June 1858, in the city of Bologna, then part of papally ruled Emilia, the police of the local inquisitor barged into the house of a Jewish shopkeeper, Momolo Mortara.[33] They had come, they said, for his six-year-old son Edgardo, whom, they had been reliably informed, had been secretly baptised by a former servant, Anna Morisi. Despite the frantic desperation of the mother, Marianna, Edgardo was torn from her arms. When the distraught parents went to see the local inquisitor, they were told that once a child had been baptised he could not remain in a Jewish household to be brought up in that false religion. He would be taken to the House of Catachumens, instituted for the lodging and instruction of converts, and would be kindly treated. Now his mother was the Holy Church and his father the Pope.

Such Christian abductions of Jewish children in Italy, while not exactly commonplace, were not rare either. In 1817 a three-year-old had been taken from her parents in Modena. Saporini d'Angei was seven when she was taken; Pamela was just *nineteen months* when she was torn from the arms of Venturina and Abram Maroni in 1844. In every case, it had been Christian house servants, often working only a few days or weeks for their employers, who claimed to have performed the baptism that became a licence for kidnapping. This gave the Church the opportunity, especially in the Mortara case where it found itself on the defensive, to claim that it was once again the fault of the Jews for hiring Christians in their homes despite the official ban on their employment. This indeed had been the case off and on since the bull *Cum nimis absurdum* in the sixteenth century. But as there were many who needed the work, the Church had generally looked the other way. This opened an opportunity for any women (and it was always women) who bore a grudge or believed that by baptism they were saving a Jewish child from damnation, guaranteeing a place in heaven instead, to perform the sprinkle.

It was the tiny Jewish community of Bologna itself which made sure that the Mortara abduction did not remain local. It was they who persuaded Momolo to go over the head of the local inquisitor and write directly to Pope Pius IX via his Secretary of State, Cardinal Giacomo Antonelli. Canon law, they discovered, expressly forbade baptism without the consent of parents. Though the appeals won Momolo a heartbreaking meeting with his captive son in the house of Catachumens, they fell on deaf ears in the Vatican.

At the deceptively liberal beginning of his pontificate Pius IX had actually relieved the Jews of Rome of some of the most appalling of their humiliations: the Jew races during carnival when old and young were pelted with abuse and rotten fruit, and the obligation to listen to conversionary sermons in their own synagogues. For these mercies Pius regarded himself as 'the friend of the Jews' who were now showing outrageous ingratitude by such gestures of protest.

But just as the strategic interest of the European powers in the future of Turkey and the Middle East allowed the Damascus-affair protesters to join their cause with a larger one, so the fate of one small Jewish boy lit a fire of angry debate over the temporal power of the Pope. The personality of Pius IX, who had gone from liberal hero to pillar of reaction, aggravated the arguments which broke out in almost every western country. To the secular, self-consciously modernising politicians pushing for Italian unification, especially in the kingdom of Sardinia, papal rule over territories far from the Vatican was a monstrous anomaly. Had there been no inquisitor in Bologna, the unnatural violation of the sanctity of the family exemplified by the abduction of Edgardo would never have happened. Riding a wave of visceral anti-Catholicism in America, Rabbi Isaac Mayer Wise in Cincinnati actually claimed the conversion of the Mortara boy was just a pretext for the Pope and his 'soulless lackeys', the Jesuitical inquisitors, to enforce their power.[34] Even in Catholic France, Napoleon III, facing his own ultra-Catholics, was outraged at the barbarism of abductions. Not long after he received the information from his ambassador to the Vatican, the emperor went to meet the prime minister of the Sardinian kingdom, Camillo Cavour, to plan the military strategy which would break the Austrian protection of the status quo in Italy and create a new Italian kingdom, one in which the papacy would be reduced to a spiritual power. Bologna would fall to the Risorgimento army in 1860 although the Papal States would not disappear until ten years later, the same year in which the doctrine of Papal Infallibility was decreed. On hearing that news, William Gladstone declared that as a result Catholics had lost 'their moral and mental freedom'.

The outrage over Edgardo Mortara once again turned a wrong inflicted on the Jews into the cause célèbre of international liberalism. Unlike the Damascus affair, however, there was no happy ending. When the leaders of Rome's Jews went to see the Pope they were treated to an abrasive dressing-down for presuming to air their imagined grievance to the rest of the world. What an act of ingratitude to someone who had done so much for the *ebrei*! The taking to task gathered intensity. Newspapers like *La Civiltà Cattolica* railed, predictably, against the effrontery of Jewish money; the sinister dealings of secret Jewish power. Lest people forget what Jews were capable of, the paper pointed to a gruesome murder in Hungarian Moldavia, where the body of a child had been found with multiple mutilations and puncture wounds. Yet again the bloodthirsty matzo-baking Jews were accused. Jews and synagogues were attacked by mobs with the assumption of guilt remaining well after the boy's uncle confessed to the crime in Budapest.

Momolo Mortara, though ruined psychologically and financially by the tragedy, never abandoned hope of his son returning to the bosom of his Jewish family. He travelled through Europe, to give heart-breaking speeches which moved the high-hatted elders of Jewry to tears. In London he spoke to the Board of Deputies, inspiring the septuagenarian Montefiore to make a personal mission to Rome. But the Vatican, Pharaoh-like, had hardened its heart and all Montefiore got were stories of how contented the boy was with his new religion and the tender care of his Holy Father. Barred from seeing Pius, Montefiore was received by Cardinal Antonelli with frosty indifference.

In Paris Momolo stirred Isidore Cahen to conclude there had to be some international organisation which would work for the defence of Jews. Cahen was himself a well-nigh perfect personification of the central conviction of Jewish liberalism: that taking a full part in national culture would not weaken a loyalty to Judaism. His father Samuel had grown up in Mainz and had become the French Moses Mendelssohn by producing a multi-volume French translation of the Jewish Bible, with Hebrew on the facing page along with commentaries. In 1840 he founded the *Archives Israélites*, a monthly journal which published scholarly and literary reflections on matters of Jewish history and religion in French, much as Ludwig Philippson's *Allgemeine Zeitung des Judenthums* did in German.

Growing up in the emancipated generation, Isidore could shine at the Collège Charlemagne, and then at the École Normale, while all the time pursuing his deep scholarship in rabbinics. Appointed to teach philosophy at the Catholic Lycée Napoléon-Vendée, he was removed from his post by disgruntled ultras who evidently thought it unfitting for an observant Jew to be in such an institution. Cahen moved into journalism, writing for *Le Temps*, but the Mortara case would have had a personal resonance for him. And in 1860 in conjunction with the businessman and social reformer Charles Netter, Cahen founded the Alliance Israélite Universelle, the name of which he had dreamed up two years earlier at the height of the crisis.

The name itself was a gesture of defiance against all the Judaeophobes who were busy unmasking international Jewish conspiracies against

Christian Europe. Turning the accusations on their head, the Alliance had the temerity to declare that Jews were indeed one people, but that their solidarity in no way compromised their loyalty to the countries of their adoption.[35] The international cause of the Jews was not the creation of a Rothschild empire of money, but the cause of humanity, decency and toleration. For Netter and Cahen, who were joined in 1864 by Adolphe Crémieux, the Alliance also had a social and educational mission to fit Jews for the modern world without weakening their traditions. Schools were opened, the first, significantly, in Tétouan in Morocco in 1862, and then others concentrated in the welcoming environment of modernising Turkey.

The founding of the Alliance was, then, doubly momentous. It connected, at last, the Jews of liberal Europe with the millions in the Islamic world and in Balkan countries like Romania, where an impoverished and undereducated Jewish population faced brutal oppression. And it turned its face bravely out to the world against the oncoming of new persecutions. Here is what its founding statement announced:

> If dispersed to all corners of the globe and mixed with the nations you remain attached with your heart to the ancient religion of your fathers however weak the link ... if you detest the prejudices from which we still suffer, the lies which are repeated ... the calumnies which are fomented ... If you believe that the most ancient and spiritual of religions must keep its place and fulfil its mission, must take its place and manifest its vitality in the great movement of ideas at work in the world ... If you believe that a great number of your co-religionists overwhelmed by centuries of misery can recover their dignity as men conquer their dignity as citizens ... If you believe that it would be an honour for your religion, a lesson for the peoples of the whole world, progress for humanity, a triumph for truth and universal reason to witness the living force of Judaism ... If finally you believe that the influence of the principles of 1789 is all-powerful, that the example of peoples who enjoy absolute religious equality is a force ... then Jews of the entire world come ... give us your cooperation, work everywhere for emancipation and progress, support all those who suffer because of being Jews.

Fine words. But Edgardo Mortara would grow up a Jesuit, the blood libels would claim victims every few years in the Middle East, and in

Europe Sir Moses Montefiore, a hundred years old, would die in his house at Ramsgate, strongly conscious his work had been only half accomplished. So what did those words mean for the Jewish future?

III. The Calling of Moses

Moses Hess had noticed something funny about the way the *Augsburger Allgemeine* referred to Meyerbeer. Whenever the composer was mentioned, the paper added parenthetically '(actually Jacob Meyer Lippman [*sic*] Beer)'. This brought back painful memories to Hess. He had grown up in the Rhineland, in the ancient city of Bonn, so had felt moved to compose music for Nikolaus Becker's 'Die Wacht am Rhein' ('The Watch on the Rhine'), the great anthem of patriotic resistance to the French. But Becker had spurned his effort, letting him know that it was quite out of the question for a Jew to be composing music which had to spring from the breasts of German patriots.[36]

As if he needed reminding! Hess's youth had been a struggle between the pulls of Judaism and Germany. His father had gone the assimilationist way, departing Bonn for Cologne when Moses was only five, making money from sugar refining, the same business, albeit on a smaller scale, that had served Meyerbeer's father so well. Moses had been left in the care of his maternal grandfather, a rabbi whose tears whenever the destruction of Jerusalem and the Temple were mentioned, the boy remembered with the deepest emotion. He would search forever for his own temple of the spiritual and ethical life, but not where rabbinics and the Talmud led him. Trapped inside peda-gogical narrowness he came to hate his Talmud teachers, describing them as '*Unmenschen*', unnatural men.

Instead he found socialism, which somehow he believed was a perpetuation of the Jewish way, or at any rate the way of Baruch Spinoza, one of Hess's philosophical heroes. His first book was an excited but incoherent attempt to set Spinoza within a humane Jewish tradition, rather than as the deist who had forthrightly rejected pretty much the entirety of Judaism. Spinoza's cosmic Creator, set free from the narrowness of rabbinic rules, was the kind of Jew Hess himself wished to be, and in his enthusiasm he made his hero also stand against barren individualism. Improbably, Spinoza, the ultimate outsider, became in the Hessian imagination the personification of the social and communal life.

Where else to go with such stuff but vanguard journalism? Hess became one of the editors of the *Rheinische Zeitung*, where he ran into the grandson of the rabbi of Trier, the son of the baptised Heinrich Marx, Karl. It was an uncontainable epiphany – the agitated, warm-hearted, terminally well-meaning Moses falling for the uncompromising, arrogant, supremely self-assured, scientifically-historically correct Hegelian. Moses was undone. Marx was 'the greatest, the only real philosopher living now … Dr Marx is my idol … Voltaire, Lessing, Heine and Hegel all combined'. The infatuation survived Marx using many of Hess's own ideas and writings, rather than the other way round, especially for the *Communist Manifesto*. It had been Hess, not Marx, who had first articulated the idea that money was the religion of the modern age, one which doomed its millions of devotees to lives of barren alienation. 'Money is human value expressed in numbers, the mark of our slavery.' A revolutionary Exodus was needed. Given his background, Hess truly meant it when he described capitalism as a kind of fetishistic cult, a Golden Calf – in effect the opposite of the Judaism in which he had seen a code of ethics. Marx took this and flipped it, making religion a kind of sneering metaphor, and identifying it, notoriously and exclusively, with the Jews.

Hess pottered about in socialist journalism, sustained by a modest inheritance he had received from his sugar-refining papa. Strange and stranger books appeared from his mind and pen: world-historical effusions tracing the Jewish ethos all the way back to biblical times, through the Roman destruction to the diaspora, endeavouring always to make it somehow an alternative to the mechanistic spirit which had consumed Europe. He boarded the same trains as Meyerbeer between Paris and Germany, but not in the same class. The life of the wandering Friend of the Workers was his, moving between Basel and Brussels, Cologne, Geneva and Zurich and back to Paris again; preaching in word and print his ethically saturated version of communism.

Then, feeling the dirty wash of Jew-hatred foul the world he was living in, Hess did something powerful. Most of his publications had hidden his first name. He had been 'M. Hess', 'Moritz Hess' or 'Maurice Hess'. Now that he was thinking more deeply and compulsively about the fate of the Jews, he declared 'I shall adopt my biblical name, Moses', adding, with characteristic weirdness, 'I regret only that I am not called Itzig.'

Judaism, he now thought, especially if stripped of its crippling narrowness (particularly its abhorrence of intermarriage; he himself had married a Catholic), *was* in essence the world-ethic. Sustained by morally righteous traditions, Judaism and Hebrew Jewish culture was the antidote to individualism, for 'nowhere does Judaism tear the individual away from the family, the family from the nation, the nation from humanity, humanity from the organic and cosmic creation, and that creation from the Creator'. Judaism understood Spinozistically *was* the golden chain of human connection.

And from this interior illumination came the book which astounded everyone who thought they knew Hess, who patronised his eccentricities, condescended to him as the endearingly incoherent frothing uncle figure of communism. The book was called *Rome and Jerusalem*, to which Hess added the significant subtitle '*The Last National Question*'.

It saw the light of day in Leipzig in 1862, and there is no doubt that the Mortara case and the gathering force of modernising Jew-hatred played a part in Hess's new outpouring. For he had come to the conclusion that the liberal experiment in integration and assimilation had failed; that whatever his or her legal position within a political society, the Jew was doomed to be thought of, always and everywhere – and notwithstanding how fine his French, German or English might be – as a stranger, a misfit, an alien presence. The answer to the ills and sufferings which resulted from that ingrained hostility was not the one which the Alliance had given: schoolwork which would fit Jews better for the modern world, education, agricultural settlements and the like. The answer was to understand first and foremost that the Jews constituted a *nation*. Whether they were observant in their religious practices or not, as long as something inside them moved to the sound of the shofar and the words of the *aggadah*, the consciousness of carrying through all the centuries of their dispersion and persecution the secret of survival as Jewish *spirit*, then they were this nation. And the nation needed political and institutional realisation if Jews would ever be free to be Jews. This national self-determination need not necessarily uncouple them from proper loyalty to the countries in which they lived. But it did require a place where the reborn national spirit could take shape, and there was only one place possible as the crucible of this regenerative transformation: Palestine.

And so Moses lifted up his eyes from the innumerable charters of workingmen's liberation, and saw, dimly, Jerusalem glimmering from afar.

TURNING POINT

I. The Disappointment of Hayyim Hibshush[1]

A calamity! The trunks of M. Joseph Halévy had failed to arrive in
Sana'a, causing their owner such acute distress that he became ill and
took to his bed. Escaping from a band of marauders during the journey
to al-Hiraz, he had entrusted the baggage to a servant who had assured
him he would bring it to Sana'a. But of course the man had disappeared, leaving Halévy without money, clothes, books, cascara,
magnesia, parasol or sturdy boots which might resist the snakes and
scorpions abounding in the desert hills. He meant to be the first
European Jew to penetrate deeply into the interior of Yemen. But all
he possessed now, other than the clothes he stood in, were letters
from the chief rabbi of Aden introducing him to the 'sheikhs' and
rabbis of the many towns and villages where Jews, mostly impoverished, had lived for centuries. Some of those Jews traced their origins
back to the Himyarite Empire of the fifth century which had converted
to Judaism, so that for 150 years, the most powerful state in Arabia
had been Jewish.[2] Halévy was in Yemen to locate and copy inscriptions
from that ancient pre-Islamic culture.

Halévy was still in his state of prostration when Hayyim Hibshush
first encountered him in person. Hibshush was a coppersmith but one
learned enough to be interested in inscriptions written in a language
other than Arabic. In his modest way he too was a collector of mysterious inscriptions. The villagers who lived with these broken
fragments guarded them jealously. Though their meaning was
obscure, the potters and shepherds knew that removal of the stones
would bring evil down on those from whom they had been taken, by

whatever means. So Hayyim Hibshush allayed local suspicions by claiming he needed the inscriptions for their magical-alchemical healing properties. The truth, however, was that Hibshush – who looked just like a devout Yemeni Jew, with *simanim*, the long corkscrew sidelocks – thought of himself in the tradition of Maimonides as a sceptic of superstitions, and an anti-Kabbalist, one of the Generation of Knowledge, later known in Yemen as the 'Dor Deah'.[3]

The foreigner Halévy would be an ally. Hibshush would offer himself as his dragoman: guide, interpreter, amanuensis, finder of safe routes to the northern wadi town of Najran which was Halévy's prime destination. Accordingly he sent the stricken Frenchman a letter enclosing, by way of credentials, a copy of one of his inscriptions. The tactic worked; he was hired. Hibshush now tried to make the best of Halévy's misfortunes. Was it not the case that the professor was always going to assume the guise of a Jerusalem rabbi wandering the country to collect alms from his co-religionists? Very well then, if he was supposed to be a beggar, now he would look the part.

Joseph Halévy needed little instruction. He was an oriental orientalist born in Ottoman Adrianople, on the ancient Eurasian frontier, north-west of the Bosphorus. As his cleverness flowered he had moved north and west, first to Bucharest, then to Paris where the study of the more obscure languages of the region was well established. In this year of 1869 he was forty-one years old and already something of a master of tongues, dead and alive, in Arabia and the Horn of Africa. Two years earlier the Alliance Israélite Universelle had sent him on an exploratory mission to Abyssinia to the Falasha people around Gondar and Tigray province to see whether their claim to be Jews had any justification. The primary role of the Alliance was to 'regenerate' communities of far-flung Jews, especially those in Muslim lands stretching from the Ottoman Empire to the Maghreb territories which had fallen under French control. Regeneration began with an education in the languages and skills needed in the modern world. But the Alliance was also becoming interested in making contact with the remotest communities (and there were Jews in Azerbaijan, Afghanistan and Ethiopia) and returning them to the great global tabernacle of Jewish solidarity. This yearning to gather in the scattered tribes, to understand Jews and Judaism as much more than a European culture, had been going on for centuries, each generation producing its messianic geographers. But now those ancient urges dovetailed with the explorations of ethnographers and linguists, with modern, scientific speculations about the evolution of human cultures and the spreading tree of their languages, and they delivered the new explorers by railway and steamship to their fields of discovery.

Halévy was one of those fieldworkers. He knew Amharic and Ge'ez, the ancient language in which much of the Falasha liturgy and ritual was chanted. He was learned in the pan-continental dispersion of the Jews, preoccupied by the question of whether a common core of beliefs lay beneath dramatically different cultural expressions. He amused the rabbis of Aden and Sana'a by telling them of Falasha incredulity that a white man could also be a Jew, an experience which would be repeated in one of the remoter villages in Yemen. But he misled his hosts by telling them he had 'come to seek his brethren'; Halévy's mission in Yemen was not, in the first instance, Judaeo-ecumenical. It had a much narrower, scholarly goal. The Académie des Inscriptions et Belles-Lettres had commissioned him to collect the stone and bronze inscriptions already known to be scattered throughout the country, but which had been reported to survive in fine specimens in the towns and wadis of the north-east. It was there that the Himyarite kingdom had had its strongholds, but the Sabean language (associated in the minds of Jews and Muslims alike with the queen of Saba or Sheba) was many centuries older: pre-Arabic and pre-Hebraic. Hayyim Hibshush would be invaluable, not only because he seemed to know just where to find inscribed stones, often used to support crumbling mud-brick walls, but because his family were descended from the al-Futayhi, one of the four great Jewish Arabian clans tracing their presence in Yemen to centuries before the Islamic conquest.[4] For all this pedigree and local knowledge, Halévy might still have regarded Hibshush as a coppersmith with pretensions, but to the communities in and around Sana'a, Hayyim Hibshush was a learned *mori*, a teacher, not to be trifled with by foreigners even if they were Jewish.

Hibshush was also resourceful. With the scholar prostrate, he offered to begin the quest at the town of Ghaiman, just four hours away from Sana'a. He would copy as many inscriptions as he could find, and then return in the hope that the professor had recovered sufficiently for them both to embark on their expedition in the opposite direction, to the north. In Ghaiman, 'where every stone cried out "I am two thousand years old"', the local Jews – silversmiths, dyers, weavers and tanners – were eager to show Hibshush their inscriptions, embedded in the half-ruined town walls, since they believed that 'evil spirits' lay within the incomprehensible letters. Once deciphered and brought to light, the characters would be purified of their dark power and 'an end to Israel's sufferings' would follow. Hibshush would be their deliverer. Unbeknown to Halévy, Hibshush's anti-Kabbalism was responding to a contemporary urgency. In 1865, four years before Halévy's arrival, a false redeemer calling himself Shukr Kuhayl, whose wonder-working cult had attracted multitudes of ecstatic believers, had been decapitated as an impostor in the main square of Sana'a, his head impaled on one of the town's gateways.[5] But such was the incorrigible desperation of Yemeni Jews for a saviour that when three years later, in 1868, one Judah ben Shalom, probably a potter or cobbler, announced that thanks to the prophet Elijah *he* was the resurrected and reassembled Messiah, he too won a mass following. Knowing that Yemeni Jews, even those in small villages, were in the habit of memorising chunks of the Bible, the two pseudo-Messiahs quoted passages from the prophets and the Wisdom Books heralding their appearance. There were differences between the two editions of the redeemer, though. Unlike the original model, who had wandered the communities as a mystic preacher living in ascetic poverty, Shukr Kuhayl II (as Judah was now known) recalled the organisational genius of Nathan of Gaza, establishing cells of apostles in many of Yemen's communities who levied tithes for the support of the Messiah. This provided a princely manner of life. The richest of all the communities, in Aden, was said to have sent him the entirety of its synagogue treasury.[6]

All this – the establishment of fund-raising circles in Egypt, Bombay and Baghdad; the dissemination of a spurious calendar for the end of time; the orders for mass repentance prior to the Great Redemption – would have dismayed Hayyim Hibshush. He took his cue from his hero Maimonides, who had similarly given himself the role of disabusing the credulous. That campaign against false Messiahs had taken place seven hundred years earlier, but in Yemen time collapsed in on itself and everything that had happened was still happening. Hibshush's battle plan was to strip the inscriptions of any esoteric mana even as he claimed he could decode their healing qualities.

But he had to be discreet. There was always the possibility that local Muslims on their guard against messianic disturbances among the Jews might suspect that he was part of the problem rather than the solution. It was best not to attract attention. In Ghaiman, disguised as a seller of snuff, Hibshush co-opted his wife in a system of secret signs. She would carry a basket on her head, while in the company of women collecting saltpetre for the making of gunpowder. Lowering the basket would be the signal that an inscription was present, and that the coast was clear for Hibshush to go about his copying. At Zugag he had to be even more furtive, scribbling inscriptions on the back of his hand with a straw and then transcribing them later behind closed doors. He was already feeling himself in a strange land. But that didn't stop him from taking a quick look inside the local mosque, a folly which would have got him killed had he not persuaded the irate Muslims that he knew the location of ancient buried treasure.

Very much a Sana'a Jew, Hibshush was disconcerted by local customs. At Muhsuna, one of the daughters of his hosts removed her trousers to wash them in the same bowl in which they had all just eaten supper and for that matter in which bread dough was kneaded. In these parts, he remembered, to remark that a man 'wore the trousers' was to accuse him of effeminacy.

Back in Sana'a, he was happy to see that Halévy had risen from his divan. But even without the telltale encumbrances of baggage, Hibshush was anxious about the unwelcome attention they might attract. This was a bad time for the Jews in Yemen. The gross humiliations to which they were habitually subjected had grown more brutal, the curses louder, the casual physical assaults now including small children as targets. There were famines, outbreaks of the plague, rumours (well founded) of a coming attack by the Turks, who in fact conquered the Yemen in 1873. Such difficulties, needless to say, were laid at the door of the Jews. Hibshush later wrote that 'the troubles were so extreme as to become almost intolerable'. Emigration to Palestine, which would gather force in the 1880s, had already begun. To test the foreigner's resolve, Hibshush told Halévy of another 'Ashkenazi' visitor who had been subjected to a rain of stones and, still worse, a dead cat. Bruised and affronted the Ashkenazi had had the temerity to throw the cat back at his tormentors, an offence which could have earned him corporal or even capital punishment had not the imam before whom he was taken found the whole incident amusing. It was a close call but Halévy, as Hibshush would discover, possessed surprising reserves of disciplined courage and seemed unmoved by the prospect of similar indignities. Very well then, but Hibshush insisted that Halévy dress like a Yemeni Jew: a long *quftan*, the heavy woollen *shamlah* serving as both shawl and night blanket, and the peculiar kind of *quffaya* headdress known as the *lijjah*, a cap 'stiff as wood' with the brim striped in black and white. At all costs he must not appear mysterious.

As soon as his identity was revealed in the privacy of a local synagogue and word got around, the local Jews – and there were many, five hundred at al-Madid alone – wanted to meet the Ashkenazi. Hibshush explained to him that it was generally believed that the European had come to find the tribe of Dan, thought to be riding the hill country of the north, the outlier Israelites who would lead him to the rest of the Lost Tribes of Israel. But all that Halévy wanted was to gather as many Sabean inscriptions as he could so that he could lay the foundations for systematic scientific study back in the Paris academies. To that end he was spectacularly successful. By the time the expedition concluded in 1870, he had acquired 685 inscriptions (although as Hibshush later observed, he somehow forgot to give credit to his copyist for all his labours).

Turning their heads from the spray of sand kicked up by the hot winds, swatting away the biting flies, the two men plodded along on their donkeys, riding side-saddle: the only way permitted to Jews. Occasionally the asses were replaced by camels lent, as a special favour, by local Jews. Hibshush hated the camel ride so much that he often took to walking in his bare feet instead, and was surprised that the European seemed not to feel such discomfort. Thickly woven saddle cloths, the crimson dye darkened with dust, hanging over the animals' flanks did not give enough relief to the sore behind. So Hibshush was grateful when at al-Ghail, even after he had embarrassingly interrupted a Jewish householder while she was washing her hair, the woman was kind enough to massage his aching legs with melted butter, and give him a pot of grease for his hair and face.

Appearing in the villages of the upland Jauf, they were surrounded by boys and young men, whooping as they ran beside the animals. Many wore *simanim*, more heavily oiled than Hibshush's own, swinging at their cheeks. Around Sana'a this was less a matter of observing the Torah's prohibition on 'shaving the sides of the head' and more from compliance to the Muslim demand that Jews look distinctive enough to identify them for public degradation. For the same reason Jews were forbidden from wearing any kind of headgear that would cover up those identifying sidelocks. Upcountry to the north of Sana'a, though, relations between the tribes and the Jews were less hostile and the peltings and jeering less relentless. There, country Jews could interpret the biblical commandment as forbidding only the close *shaving* of the sides of the head, thus allowing the odd scissor-trim of beard and locks. What a boon.

The arrival of the pseudo-beggar, Joseph Halévy, led by Hibshush, eyelids painted with kohl to improve, as everyone believed, the vision, invariably caused a stir in the little synagogues of the wadis. Was he another herald of the Messiah? The 140-year-old man at al-Milh, his beard still dark and his frame massive, certainly believed so and told his little pupils. Or at the very least was he someone who might act as their interlocutor with European co-religionists? For the unification of the Jews of the world, somehow, somewhere, was seen in communities as far apart as India and Galicia as the condition of their redemption. Paradoxically, then, the mission of the emissaries and teachers of the Alliance Israélite Universelle, which was to bring 'backward' Jews into the world of modern liberal instruction, was actually flipped by those on the receiving end, to mean the imminence of a mystical communion of all Israelites (sometimes including those elusive Lost Tribes). The Alliance had not yet come to Yemen, but from Palestine, Egypt and especially the Baghdad–Aden–Bombay trading connection, local rabbis had heard of the works of Sir Moses Montefiore and the Rothschilds. So Joseph Halévy could be the messenger who would connect them with the grand Jews and with the great happenings which were apparently taking place far beyond the desert and the sea. It was time Europe knew of their misfortunes, sufferings and ardent hopes. They too looked to Jerusalem even if the direction of their prayers was north-west.

The professor was largely impervious to this tragic fervour and to any kind of role as carrier of the word from Yemen. He just got on with his work while trying not to offend those who might be helpful. Halévy would follow Hibshush to the little whitewashed prayer houses of the weavers, leatherworkers, potters and silversmiths. Even a place scarcely more than a village like Nihm had four synagogues, and it would give offence if he neglected any one of them. In the oasis of Khabb where the Jews wore swords decorated with silver inlay (they were, after all, the silversmiths of Yemen), he was especially solicitous. On Shabbat he sat and ate the breakfast *kubaneh* bread which had been sitting in its stone pot over smouldering ashes. This was not so bad; at the end of the meal there was always turbid coffee of a richness unimaginable in Paris or even Turkey, and a dish of fresh dates from the palms of the wadi. The cattle got the pounded pits.

Every so often, dressed as he was, Halévy would be asked to give responsa as if he were a real rabbi. In Khabb he was asked to adjudicate a case in which a man claimed a bride whom he said had been betrothed to him when he was four years old. The girl's family repudiated the betrothal and swords were drawn before the pseudo-rabbi calmed everyone down. In green Najran, where the date palms were so dense that the sun could hardly be seen through their spiny foliage, at the house of his hosts he wondered out loud about a girl whose face, unusually, was veiled. He was told she was awaiting execution for becoming pregnant while unmarried. Dismayed, he asked the girl, whose name was Sai'dah, how this had come about, and she replied that she had been visiting the house of a sick man to help his wife with household chores. During the brief period when her father left her at the house, six young men, known to the family, had come to spend the night and one of them had forced himself on her. She had been too ashamed to cry out and the result of the assault lay stirring in her swelling belly. The sad story prompted Hibshush, not altogether helpfully, to tell the tale of a famed Jewish beauty who had resisted the assault of a sharif by locking him up in a small chamber. Before the tribal lords gathered in judgement, she had made an impassioned speech, declaring that such wicked behaviour had been unknown since the Jews had first come to Yemen. Judgement was given against the malefactor, although the penalty hamstrung his mare rather than the assailant. According to Hibshush, Halévy was moved by Sai'dah's tragic story but not so moved that, after their party had departed, he bothered to return, much less discover what had become of the doomed girl.

Hibshush was beginning to think that Halévy's passion for the people of his country was confined to the long dead. He had been misled by Halévy's profession that he had 'come to seek his brethren', for as the journey had progressed his curiosity had waned and his impatience with the importunate grown. There were altogether too many sleeve-tuggers.

Back in Paris Halévy lost no time publishing his findings in the *Journal Asiatique* and the *Bulletin de la Société de Géographie*. In a separate essay he described the state of ruined castles and mosques and the lie of the land. In 1879, on the strength of his work in Abyssinia and the Yemen, Halévy was appointed professor of Ethiopic Languages in the École Pratique des Hautes Études, and became librarian of the Société Asiatique. Such feathers in the cap of a Jew from Adrianople.

Hayyim Hibshush did not forget or forgive what he took to be ingratitude compounded by indifference. For himself he would live with the professor's failure to mention his own part in the recovery of the Sabean inscriptions. It was the betrayal of his fellow Yemeni Jews that he found intolerable when they had opened their doors to the foreigner, given him money, food and hospitality. In 1892 he published an open letter expressing that disappointment. When Halévy had appeared, he had kindled a hope that at last there would be someone who could adequately represent the ordeals of Yemeni Jews to the co-religionists in Europe who, after all, professed to take an interest in their welfare. He was supposed to have been the ambassador of their sorrows, the agent by which their fortunes and misfortunes would become part of the destiny and history of the Jews. And he was also meant to be a guardian against messianic heresies. Judah ben Shalom, 'Shukr Kuhayl II', had eventually been unmasked and undone; funds had dried up and he ended his life in poverty and then in prison in 1878, but this was no thanks to the likes of Halévy. The scholar had not even made good on what Hibshush had most hoped for: the sending of teachers to bring the Jews of Yemen into the community of the enlightened while not forsaking their traditions. Shame on him. Had not the Alliance declared that the Jews were one people?

Only up to a point, it seemed. But then how were the Yemeni Jews to know that the man they had believed could be their emissary, protector and champion 'would undoubtedly forget them in his heart and leave them with their hopes dashed'?

II. The Domes of the Semites

In the last decades of the nineteenth century there was a good deal of holding fellow Jews at arm's length. In Vienna, Budapest, New York, Paris and London, Jews in high hats and decent tailoring flinched when they saw the beards and *kapotes*, the *shtreimels* and sidelocks advancing down the street. Did they belong to the same family, really? The incoming *Ostjuden*, loud in their Yiddish, bulky in their manners, shouty and finger-jabbing, were sometimes an embarrassment to the waistcoated and crinolined Jews who spoke German, English, French, Magyar, Russian, and read Pushkin and Schiller. In 1864, when the Prussian government summarily expelled Polish Jews from the country, the principal organ of Berlin Jews, the *Allgemeine Zeitung des Judenthums*, looked the other way and held its tongue. No one wanted to endorse the gross caricatures of the anti-Semites but when they were in Leopoldstadt and Whitechapel the opera-box Jews flinched at the whiff of garlic and herring. The uncouthness of the *Ostjuden* might reflect badly on the better sort of Jews who had laboured so hard and so long for social respectability and legal emancipation. Now all that was put in jeopardy by the 'backwardness' of the newcomers. In a futile attempt to staunch the flow, the Board of Guardians in London (the body established to help relieve the poor) announced it would assist only immigrants who had already lived in Britain for six months. In no circumstances would it provide cash, unless the money was to be used to send the new arrivals back to their place of origin. 'We beseech every right-thinking person among our brethren in Germany, Russia and Austria,' the Board said, 'to place a barrier to the flow of foreigners, to persuade these voyagers not to venture to come to a land they do not know.'

The appeal, coming as it did from the comfortably settled, fell on deaf ears. Jews were on the move. When were they not? But from the 1870s the migrations were epic. Ashkenazi Jews were uprooting themselves by the millions – over 2 million alone from Russia and Poland between 1880 and 1914 and 150,000 from Romania. There was every kind of reason: renewed, vicious nativist assaults; a multiplication (in this modern nineteenth century) of ritual-murder accusations; demographic pressure in the territories of the Pale; sheer grinding destitution for which there seemed no hope of betterment. Where once there had been three, four, five mouths to feed there were now ten, eleven, twelve. Who knew why the infants were surviving, even in shtetls where the water was foul and the coughing bloody, and even though cholera had not entirely abated? Epidemics (diphtheria, scarlatina, tuberculosis) and famine ravaged the Pale yet still the babies came and more of them made it past weaning. Economic dislocation added to the pressure to leave. In Galicia, after the abortive Polish uprising of 1863, aristocratic estates were punitively broken up by the Russian government. Jews who had had a long (if uneasy) mutual relationship with the *szlachta* gentry and nobility, lending the nobility what was needed to maintain their impossibly ostentatious style of life and receiving in return tax farms, leases and liquor monopolies, now lost those dependable sources of income. At the other end of the social scale, peasants who had been customers for their boots and blouses on market days were moving to factory towns. It was no longer a sure thing to load a cart on Sunday morning and come back to the shtetl on Friday with enough money to put challah on the Shabbat table. There was more taking in of laundry, odd jobs sewing by the women and girls. Food became more meagre: herring, cabbage, a heel of dry bread. A few kept animals but the cows' milk was watery, the goats bony and the chickens so many bundles of grimy feathers. Why not go, then? What and who was there to stay for: the *rebbe* who still rolled his eyes to heaven and promised the Messiah would, without fail, show up some day soon; the yeshiva boys bobbing and dipping until visions swam before their closed eyes? Did anyone believe the one *maskil* in the village with his newspaper, his trimmed goatee, his tarry cigarettes and his quotations from Lermontov, when he droned on that enlightened days were just round the corner?

There would come a morning when it all got too much. Voices were raised; hollow-chested children in their patched hand-me-downs cowered in the corner while their parents bludgeoned each other with shouted recriminations: 'Dreamer!' 'Always with the dreamer! So what do you want? God will provide!' 'Look at your children! Skin and bone! It's you who should provide, not God!' But factories in Lwów and Cracow and Warsaw and Kiev were turning out cheap clothes, boots and shoes, which meant no one needed old ones mended. Into those factories and sweatshops went the Jews to be cutters, pressers, seamstresses, buttonhole makers, cigar or cigarette rollers; into the miserable, brick-faced, airless backstreets and tenements, twenty of them working in small, stifling workshops, dawn to night, going back to tiny rooms with five others, some sleeping on the floor, babies crying all night.

If Cracow, Vilna or Lwów were too forbidding, Vienna, Berlin, Warsaw, Prague and Budapest seemed to promise a different life; beyond them, Amsterdam and London; and still further away the 'Goldeneh Medinah' or 'Golden Country' of New York, Cincinnati, Chicago, Boston, where a man came home for the Sabbath and emptied a bill-fold full of dollars. So the carts got under way, cockeyed wheels rolling drunkenly on the rutted roads. Trains rattled past, loaded up with boys in *tzitzits* whose sidelock *payes* flew up when they stuck their heads out of the window, ducking to avoid a clip round the ear from Papa, sisters hanging on the bulky woollen skirts of their mothers. Beside them, or piled up at the back of the car, roped together, were pots and pans, mattresses and pillows, boxes stuffed with the Good Sabbath dress, the all-important hats, and other essentials for a Jewish life wherever it would be led: candlesticks; a Havdalah box; a Hanukkah lamp; a single silver *kiddush* cup, chased or even filigreed Polish-style; a Passover Seder plate.

Way stations, especially Brody, the frontier town between Polish Galicia and Austria–Hungary, were packed to bursting with Jews departing from Ukraine or Bessarabia. The 15,000 native Jews, swamped by migrants, turned difficulty to opportunity by servicing the unending flow of travellers, while their own bourgeoisie, the families who had been brokers and small bankers, moved off elsewhere, to Budapest, Berdichev or Odessa. Carts choked the streets. In the inns of Brody (this was also true of exit ports like Hamburg and Rotterdam), shady characters made empty promises over a glass of plum brandy. In smoky wooden rooms klezmorim played without being asked; a *badkhan* might try a joke; a Romanian would produce a pack of cards. But things could go hard with the migrants. In 1882 an appeal was launched in London to help out the 23,000 Jews said to be hungry in Brody.

If they didn't die in Brody, on they went: to Vienna, where the Jewish population rose from 10,000 in 1810 to 175,000 a century later; and to Budapest, called 'Judapest' by those who didn't care for the 150,000 Jews who made up one in three of the population by the 1880s.

Cities like Warsaw and Berlin, where the Jewish population went from just 36,000 in 1871 to 144,000 thirty years later, were transformed by this oncoming tide of the poor.

They came from the goose-gaggle life, from Lithuania and east Galicia, from wonder-working Hasidic courts, tumbledown oil-lit cottages, unpaved lanes, sooty taverns, rattletrap day markets; from *cheders* where the *melamed* loved his switch as much as the Mishnah and both more than his pupils; from the *shir* and the *schrei*, the songs and the shrieks, on they came to the alien universe of the humming metropolis: horse trams and boulevards, gaslight and glass-fronted department stores (many of them, in Berlin anyway, owned by Jews – Tietz and Wertheim), to the parks patrolled by policemen sporting waxed whiskers and polished truncheons, to the alleyways filled with painted whores and ragged flower girls, to the ponds and fountains, theatres and wine cellars, the wheeling waltz and the brassy oompah. Such shocks they had, none more startling than to discover that these were towns where Jewish girls were better educated than Jewish boys, whole rows of them lined up on the benches of the medical schools, paying attention to anatomy spelled out in graphic detail, or bent over books at the public libraries for days on end; girls, for whom it was no longer enough to sew, cook, pray, wait for the *shadkhan*, the marriage brokers, to bring them a husband and then deliver little Jews into the world to confound the inevitable persecutors. And not just girls: women, wives who had had enough of being extolled as *eshet chayil*, prized above rubies. Enough with the rubies already! New Jewish women wanted none of such verbal *schmeckerei*. What they did want was learning – science, art, philosophy, mathematics, all devoured in greedy, ecstatic, liberating gulps of intellectual oxygen. Disconcerted newcomers could see these girls who still, apparently, called themselves Jews, hair pinned up, a wayward curl hanging from their broad-brimmed hats, laughing on the street as they walked arm in arm, sprawled on park benches flirting with overdressed swells, or (God forbid) *alone* in mirror-walled cafes, rustling the newspapers (also owned by Jewish publishers like Mosse and Ullstein) while they nibbled the *kuchen* and tried (not too hard) to evade the glances of admirers.

Would the university, the opera house, the cafe and the theatre take them from Judaism forever? Not if the new type of metropolitan synagogue could help it. The synagogue was now far more than simply a house of prayer and study. It was the hub of urban Jewish micro states, a complete governance covering anything and everything a Jewish body and soul could possibly want. For centuries, Jewish self-government had meant rabbinical courts, arbitrating disputes about property, wills, marriages and divorces, licensing and inspecting slaughterers and circumcisers, keeping a watchful eye on funerals and burial grounds. In the Pale, the traditional, autonomous *kahal* had been abolished by order of the state; and in the rest of Europe, the beneficiaries of emancipation (1861 and 1867 in the Austro-Hungarian Empire, 1871 in Germany), the magnates of modernity, had taken over communal leadership; some of them, *nokh* – the first Jewish barons and *Ritters* – had taken over commercial leadership: industrial entrepreneurs like Emil Rathenau (first to see the light, literally, and it was electrical, and had a future); shipowners like Albert Ballin whose Hamburg–Amerika line treated the masses of Jewish emigrants like human beings rather than livestock; bankers naturally, Deutsche, Dresdner and Mendelssohn; and at one stage down the ladder socially, doctors, engineers, newspaper editors and publishers like Leopold Sonnemann of the *Frankfurter Zeitung*, and a few (the Germans resisted) professors. They did so in a style which would, as they hoped, make them seem a natural extension of the liberalising state, rather than a doubtful enclave within it. They were the ones who emphasised the importance of prayers offered to royal and princely sovereigns during the Sabbath morning service – and who often, at that crucial moment following the Reading of the Law, top-hatted, delivered it ceremoniously as if coming straight from court.

In place of the omniscient rabbi came the Board, meeting weekly in committee rooms at the synagogue: Boards of Deputies (in the British case) keeping a watchful eye on hostility and with authority to make representations to the government when necessary; Boards of Guardians to distribute food to the impoverished. Whether this paternalism was supposed to extend to the incoming masses of eastern Jews, or whether it was 'local-born first' was often a source of contention. But once established, such institutions were often driven by the momentum of their own hospitality, even if those who did the giving were inclined to put city space between themselves and the poor. Uptown cleansed its conscience by going downtown with money, time and compassion. So hospitals, homes for the 'incurable', and soup kitchens multiplied as did agencies offering start-up help for tailors, carpenters, shoemakers, and money to rent tools and materials. Most important of all were the schools that would equip children, who otherwise would have had only the rote learning of the *cheder*, for work in the modern, not necessarily Jewish world: trade schools, technical schools, even agricultural schools, schools teaching languages, maths and the natural sciences, literature and history. The transformations those schools wrought were profound. For as long as many could remember, what Jews did was study the Torah and the Talmud, butchered kosher meat, peddled, sold old clothes, tailored, made shoes, lent money; for as long as anyone could remember Jewish women helped around the house and cooked until they had a husband and house of their own. With the new learning they could do anything: journalism, chemistry, poetry, even soldiering. And still, come Friday night, if they wished they could walk to synagogue and welcome in the Sabbath bride.

Nothing spoke more optimistically about the place Jews might have in the metropolis than the new mega-synagogues, monumental in scale, often flamboyantly showy in design, standing conspicuously in the centre of cities, staking a claim to be as much a part of the modern European townscape as museums, opera houses, town halls and cathedrals. For once, Jewish visibility was not imposed as a means of insult and victimisation. It was engineered by the Jews themselves as a sign of cultural self-confidence. When the elders of the Neue Synagogue in Berlin noticed that it was hard to see the enormous golden dome (modelled on the Brighton Pavilion) from the other side of the Oranienburger Strasse, they had the builders set it forward even though it meant that it would crown not the main interior but the vestibule.[7] The grandiose Tempio Maggiore in Florence got over this problem by having both a copper dome of a size rivalling Brunelleschi's on the cathedral of Santa Maria del Fiore and a half-cupola over the entrance.[8] The Jewish bourgeoisie of this brief period of collective elation went dome-happy. Two onion domes evoking Russian or Greek Orthodox churches surmounted slender towers on the front of the unapologetically enormous Dohany Street Synagogue in Budapest, built to accommodate three thousand, and the effect was so satisfying that it was immediately copied in the spectacular Central Synagogue in New York and in the Great Synagogue at Pilsen (Plzeň) in Czech Moravia. Though numbering just two thousand in 1880, the community in Pilsen thought nothing of embarking on its own onion-domed towers a full sixty-five feet high, which would have made the building a good way taller than the nearby cathedral of St Bartholomew. It was only when the Jews of Pilsen agreed to lower their towers by twenty feet that the project was allowed to proceed.

Two domes weren't enough for the Jews of Turin, who doubled the number by placing one at each corner of the building: an astonishing striped hybrid of Venetian-Gothic, Renaissance and Russian Orthodox. The dominant impression, though, was what the nineteenth century liked to call 'Moorish', meaning quasi- or not-so-quasi-Islamic. Both the triple horseshoe-arched doorways through which one entered the Great Synagogue in Turin and the Ajimez windows above it, divided by a slender mullion, were unmistakably reminiscent of a mosque. In many of the most colourfully grandiose synagogues built in the 1860s and 70s, including my own, the West London Synagogue on Seymour Place, the Ark is set in a niche canopied by a half-cupola, very much in the style of the *mihrab* where it encloses the *qibla* indicating the direction of prayer.

At first sight 'Moorish Revival' seems an odd choice of vernacular for communities yearning so much to be part of the European cultures where, at last, they enjoyed equal rights, especially since a favourite complaint of the anti-Semites was that however western their appearance, the Jews were at heart an unassimilable oriental 'Semitic' people with no true place among the Christian nations. But at the same time, in Britain and to some extent central Europe, the Jews were being romanticised by philo-Semites for precisely the same reason. Literary personifications of the Jews were invented as a spiritual aristocracy in contrast to the mercenary utilitarianism and especially the empty-headed horse-and-hound vanities of the landed classes. (This was especially ironic since it was exactly at this time that the great Jewish magnates, led by the Rothschilds, were getting an education in estate management, the breeding of thoroughbreds, and the social calendar of hunts and balls.) But in place of the usual caricatures of the pedlar and the petty criminal, the knuckle-cracking miser and the greasy pawnbroker, Jewish Wanderers began to appear in fiction, romantic in their difference, endowed with the peculiar dignity born of the displaced. Disraeli created a whole genre of novels featuring

Zion-longing, morally elevated Jews who cast a spell over the blond Gentiles, sometimes in the Holy Land itself.[9] Dickens replaced the grotesque crook Fagin of *Oliver Twist* with the saintly Mirah and her father in *Our Mutual Friend*. Most memorably, George Eliot's *Daniel Deronda* chronicled an odyssey of self-discovery by a figure whose decent instincts and moral severity as much as his un-English complexion identified him as the latest edition of the eternal Jew, sanctified rather than degraded by his wanderings, and with a magnetic needle quivering, always, in the direction of Jerusalem. That figures like Augustus Melmotte in Anthony Trollope's *The Way We Live Now* continued to give a Jewish caste to speculative commercial villainy and Shylockian self-destruction only made the alternative ideal – of Jews dwelling in a universe of spiritual grace, their hearts eaten by yearning for Zion – all the more attractive. The Victorians were actually going to the Holy Land as pilgrims, archaeologists and photographers in some numbers, and while many were startled to see the impoverished conditions in which the Jerusalem and Galilean Jews lived, going to the Western Wall of the Second Temple unfailingly moved them. Thoughts of the rebirth of Zion came to Christians at the same time as they did to Jews.

So it was not surprising when architects like Ludwig von Förster, who built the Leopoldstadt Temple and the Dohany Street Synagogue, co-opted their dreams of the First Temple in their design, and the twin towers of the Vienna synagogue were given the names of Jachin and Boaz which, according to Josephus, were the names of the twenty-seven-feet-high bronze columns in the porch of the Solomonic Temple.[10] When the cornerstone was laid for the Vienna temple, it included a parcel of soil from the Holy Land. Zion was already being rebuilt (if a little Moorishly) in Vienna, Berlin, Paris and London.[11]

But, since mishmash was kosher, there was nothing to stop the same synagogues being equally influenced on the interior by the spatial conventions of Christian cathedrals. While the focal axis of churches was down the length of a nave to the altar, often set at the centre of the crossing, the place where the heart of Christian mysteries and rituals were performed, Jewish mystery was concentrated on the Torah: its housing in the Ark and its reading on the *bimah*. Traditionally, those two sites were physically separated, and the procession of carrying the scrolls moving from Ark to reading desk. But almost all the synagogues designed in the second half of the nineteenth century moved the *bimah* to a place directly in front of the Ark, so that both were reached by broad flights of steps. The procession carrying the Sefer Torah, both before and after the reading, now wound itself round the aisles and through the entire space of the synagogue, men and boys crowding towards the mantled scrolls to touch them with the fringes of their prayer shawls and then to their lips.

At the end of the Jewish nave, the raised dais became a stage, a spotlit focus of vision. The same thought was given to visibility and acoustics as would have been the case for theatres and opera houses. Two of the architects of the Florence temple were in fact engineers (the third, Marco Treves from an old Venetian Jewish dynasty, was the only Jew). Modern Jews used modern materials, but always to deepen the experience of communal worship, of an ingathering of sensibilities. Iron was used for columns because it was strong enough to be load-bearing while still slender in dimensions, minimising obstruction of vision. The same industrial materials used both below and in the ladies' galleries opened up their sight lines and it became routine to drop any kind of grille screening them off from view.

Sound was even more important. For the first time in Judaism, two kinds of vocal performance structured the liturgy and the service: that of the preaching rabbi, of whom mastery of rhetoric as well as textual learning was expected, and the melodiously emotive force of the cantor and chorus, leading a great swell of music through the lofty space. Both speech and song now rose upwards from the theatrical *bimah*, directed as much towards the women in the gallery as the men below, inviting them into the liturgy. Unheard of hitherto, women could now join in the responses during the *kedusha* of the Amidah prayer; sing along with the joyfully closing 'Ayn Keiloheinu'. A newcomer from a Galician or Lithuanian shtetl, accustomed to a service that was all chanted prayer with a leading rabbinical speed-gabble, finding himself in these vast, ornately decorated interiors, now exposed to Judaic sacred opera with its highly stylised alternations of speech and song, would have felt himself to be in the presence of an entirely alien religion, with only the Hebrew of the *shema* and the Amidah and readings from the Torah to remind him this was a Jewish service at all.

But who were all those men in top hats sitting in their panelled box at the front of the congregation as if they were lords of the Jews?

Was social grandeur rather than holy learning now supposed to be
the criterion for respect? And how could that man, in his peculiar
beret-like headgear, call himself a rabbi when his chin was shockingly
smooth? In the Leopoldstadt Temple, from 1856, that particular rabbi
would have been Adolf Jellinek, originally from Moravia, a yeshiva
boy who had had both an intensely religious and, at Leipzig, an ambi-
tiously secular education which included a speciality in oriental
languages like Arabic and Persian.[12] Jellinek was a one-man bridge
between warring camps of the Orthodox and the Reformers; a scholar
of *midrash* and Kabbalah but also a virtuoso of formal rhetoric,
deployed to magnetic effect in his sermons, which were so enthralling
that a collection of two hundred of the best became one of the great
publishing successes of nineteenth-century Jewish Vienna. Jellinek was
the complete modern rabbi, refusing to modernise for the sake of it,
leery of the more radical reformism of Abraham Geiger, a defender
of the Talmud without being enslaved to it. Where he thought tradition was indefensibly archaic or inhumane he would let go of it. The
custom of *helitzah* – which, in order to release a brother-in-law from
the obligation of marrying his dead brother's widow, required her to
throw a shoe at the potential new husband – was abandoned. For
Jellinek this was not true Judaism at all, which he understood *historic-*
ally rather than as a phenomenon forever adrift in time.

In the tradition of Maimonides, Jellinek also led a public life beyond
rabbi and teacher, standing, albeit unsuccessfully, in elections for the
Lower Diet of the Austrian Parliament in 1861. He was demonstratively
loyal to the fatherland at the same time as he was uncompromisingly
Jewish, and thus exactly the kind of Jew the emperor Franz Joseph
had in mind when he repeatedly denounced anti-Semites. The respect
shown to Jellinek was all the more remarkable since his brother
Hermann had been condemned and executed at the age of twenty-
five for his part in the Hungarian Revolution of 1848–9. That Adolf
could become an eloquent advocate for the abolition of capital punishment for political offences and not suffer any consequences himself
says something about his standing with the liberal governments and
in particular with the emperor.

But then the Jellineks were a one-family embodiment of what was
possible in liberalised *Mitteleuropa*.[13] One of Adolf's sons became a
professor of international law at Heidelberg; another had a chair of

philology (a Jewish speciality) at Vienna. But a third, Emil, may have taken his cue for life from his uncle Moritz who had made money from pioneering Vienna trams (still very much in service today). It was apparent early on that Emil Jellinek was not much interested in a scholarly much less a religious life. Constantly in trouble in school, he was then fired from a job working for a railway company (secured through family connections) when he was discovered organising nocturnal locomotive races. Sent to Morocco in some minor diplomatic capacity he discovered that Fez, Tangier and Tétouan were more to his taste, and so was the African-born Sephardi Rachel Goggmann Cenrobert, whom he married. Rachel and Emil decided to give their daughter the pretty name of Mercedes. Four years later Rachel died, and Emil returned to Europe to sell insurance and equities on the Côte d'Azur, his clientele drawn from the very well-to-do who were just discovering the Riviera. He called the house he built with his proceeds the Villa Mercedes. On the Côte d'Azur Emil became intrigued by a motorised four-seat carriage and its inventor Wilhelm Maybach. Emil sought out Gottlieb Daimler, named the development team 'Mercedes', changed his own name to E. J. Mercedes, and began to design racing cars with Maybach. By 1909 he was producing six hundred Mercedes cars a year, a future his fretful rabbinical father could not have anticipated.

As he became unstoppably successful Emil Jellinek gave up Judaism. But his family, above all his father, had made their mark on the Jews and the Judaism of Vienna. The other half of the Temple duo was no less imposing than Rabbi Jellinek. The cantor Salomon Sulzer's collection of synagogue music, the *Shir Tzion*, published in two volumes in 1840 and 1866, and adopted by cantors from Leipzig to San Francisco, may have done more to shape the whole experience of Ashkenazi worship than any other work in the nineteenth century. It was Sulzer who made certain moments of the service – Ki Mitzyon, Hashiveinu, Aleinu, the *kedusha* of the Sabbath Amidah – points of high musical drama, punctuated with bursts of choral grandeur, and clearly designated places for the whole congregation to respond. But Sulzer's music – the refutation of Wagner's crude dismissal of cantorial singing as so much melismatic wailing – reached beyond its immediate congregation to the larger musical world of Vienna. Schubert had composed a beautiful 'Tov Lehodot' for the Seitenstettengasse synagogue but it was Franz Liszt, no friend of the Jews, who after a visit to hear Sulzer sing wrote of 'an overwhelming spiritual and aesthetic experience ... one seemed to see the psalms floating aloft like spirits of fire'.

Coming to hear Sulzer, the great organ and the massed choir of the temple was one reason for Jews who had moved out of Leopold-stadt, as the *Ostjuden* moved in, to return. The liberal reforms of the empire, the gymnasium and university education of Vienna's more modern-minded Jews, also made them seek some distance from the pickle barrels and the little tailoring shops. Those who did busi-ness with the government – lawyers as well as bankers – moved to the Innere Stadt, the old heart of Vienna now encircled by the Ringstrasse. But Sigmund Freud's father Jacob – born in Moravia, a textile merchant in Vienna, learned in German culture; mostly a Rosh Hashanah and Yom Kippur Jew – settled down with his third wife, Sigmund's mother, in Alsergrund where there had been a Jewish cemetery since the sixteenth century. Incorporating parts of the university, Alsergrund became the home district of the Jewish busi-ness and professional classes. By 1880 two-thirds of the gymnasium students were Jewish and you could scarcely walk the streets of an evening and not hear someone practising Beethoven.

Back in Leopoldstadt, traditionally garbed Jews from Galicia and the Pale opened their own little house-synagogues, the *shtiblach*, as they did in Stepney and Whitechapel, the Bowery and Delancey Street, and in Berlin's Scheunenviertel district, a tenacious world of custom, Galicia in the big city. There they could say the Amidah as they always had: a quick run of the eighteen blessings just briefly interrupted by a half-shouted *kedusha* in the reader's repetitions. No sermons, no great cantorial oratorios for them. The grandiloquent service in the temple (or for that matter in the Seitenstettengasse synagogue where Jellinek moved in 1865) would have seemed no more truly Jewish to them than High Mass in St Stephen's Cathedral. Nonetheless, during the most solemn moments of the religious year – on Rosh Hashanah or Kol Nidrei, when 'all Israel' was said to stand before God's judge-ment – even if just out of curiosity, some of them did crowd into the big space and then the ideal of Kol Israel, a single people, became real. So that at the Great Synagogue on Duke Street in London, or the spectacular Eldridge Street Synagogue in downtown New York, in the synagogue on the rue Notre-Dame-de-Nazareth in Paris, all of them drenched in light and flooded with song, the imploring prayers which conducted Jews to self-scrutiny, the chants and songs making up the storehouse of common memory, bound together the living and the ghosts of Jews long dead, with bright, expectant children standing beside their parents.

If the interiors of the great metropolitan synagogues were designed to give Jews a sense of their solidarity, especially in the face of anti-Semitic hostility, the outward grandeur of the buildings was directed towards Gentile society.[14] This unapologetic claim to a visible place in the civic world of Europe had begun majestically in Amsterdam two centuries before, but the synagogues of the 1670s had been a striking exception. Mostly, facades were discreetly hidden away; even in Amsterdam where their roofs were certainly visible, the bodies of the buildings were enclosed by a courtyard wall. When much of the Dutch design was transposed to London at Bevis Marks in 1701, the London *parnassim* made sure to site it within a courtyard away from the street. Two centuries later, the building plan was eloquently more confident: towering facades right to the street, or even more grandly set back with a garden court entrance, and only light railings as obstruction. (These days, of course, the fencing is fortified by concrete barriers, metal detectors and heavily armed security guards.)

But the metro-synagogues in their glory days were meant to hold their own with cathedrals. They had to be fit to receive chancellors, prime ministers, princes and kings, as indeed they often did. The inauguration of the Neue Synagogue in Berlin in 1866 was attended by Otto von Bismarck in the company of his friend and banker, Gerson (now) *von* Bleichröder, whose funds had made possible the wars by which Prussia led German unification. In London, the Prince of Wales and (more dubiously) the emperor of Brazil were visitors to the Central Synagogue in Great Portland Street. Before his suicide in the love nest at Mayerling, the Crown Prince Rudolf was a friend of the charismatic and learned Adolf Jellinek. Most dramatically Emperor Franz Joseph proclaimed that 'I will tolerate no *Judenhetze* [persecution of Jews] in my empire'. A few years later he would diagnose anti-Semitism as 'an illness which has spread now to the highest circles'.

One of the emperor's most forthright criticisms of the anti-Semites had come in 1882, which perhaps was why Jellinek thought his visitor

from Odessa, Dr Leon Pinsker, was overdoing it when he prophesied
that anti-Semitism, sooner or later, would make life intolerable for
Jews in Europe. This, Jellinek felt, was news from Russia. Tsar
Alexander III was not the decent Franz Joseph. But he would have
known perfectly well that there was good reason to turn pessimistic
in the German lands as well. The crowning moment of acceptance
when Gerson von Bleichröder had been summoned to Versailles to
manage the indemnity extracted from vanquished France was not a
reliable predictor of the future. Back in Charlottenburg, Adolf
Stoecker, the court chaplain to the kaiser, preached regularly on the
Christ-killing infamy of the Jews and the alien character which would
make them forever strangers to Germans, incapable, short of mass
conversion, of ever being truly integrated into the body of the nation.
The emancipation of the Jews had been a terrible mistake. Now was
the time to reverse it.

Jew-hatred burned through Europe. The financial crash of 1873,
especially disastrous in central Europe, was blamed on the Jews, just
as the collapse of the Crédit Mobilier in France was characterised as
another act of fraud perpetrated on the persons of Christians by those
criminal Jews the Péreire brothers. In 1879, the ex-radical, anarchist
and atheist Wilhelm Marr, three of whose four wives had been Jewish,
published a pamphlet, *Der Weg zum Siege des Germanenthums über das
Judenthum* (*The Way for the Victory of Germanness over Jewishness*), the
operatically Wagnerian title of which said it all. (Wagner himself had
republished his polemic in 1869, this time under his own name,
obsessing over the power of Jewish money to boycott his operas or
defame his reputation.)[15] There was a strong social element to Marr's
polemic. In his vision 'Judenthum' was as much the destructive ethos
of modern commercial life that had ripped the heart out of the traditional world of German artisans, as it was any kind of racial epithet.
The sacrifice of craft to the Moloch of modern industry was the result
of that alien presence in German life which Marr called 'Semitism',
and the only known antidote was its opposite. As a result his polemic
was instantly popular to anyone fearing the dislocations of the modern
world, selling 20,000 copies in its first run and going into eleven
editions. Even more lethally, the epigram coined by the journalist Otto
Glagau, *'Die soziale Frage ist die Judenfrage'* ('The social question is the
Jewish question'), recruited all those alienated by the corrosions of

Commodore Uriah Levy in uniform, 1858.

Portrait of Rebecca Gratz
by Gilbert Stuart, 1802.

Adah Menken in an exotic costume
(possibly as the Tartar Mazeppa), ca. 1862.

Lieutenant colonel
Edward Selig
Salomon.

Portrait of the 12-year-old Giacomo
Meyerbeer, 1802.

Meyerbeer in the last years of his life.

Portrait of Amalia Beer
by Johann Karl
Kretschmar, 1803.

The Synagogue on Oranienburger Strasse, Berlin by Emile Pierre Joseph de Cauwer, 1865.

View from the front of Tempio Maggiore Israelitico (Great Synagogue).

Busts of Isaac (left) and Jacob Émile Péreire (right) by Antoine Samuel Adam-Solomon.

Still from the Georges Méliès film *L'affaire Dreyfus*, 1899.

Portrait of Alfred Dreyfus.

Front page of Clemenceau's *L'Aurore*, 13th January 1898, with Émile Zola's essay of indictment.

The cover of the intensely anti-Semitic *La Libre Parole*, 17th November 1894. The caption reads: 'Fruitless soaping: Jews, for us in France, only blood can get out a stain like that.'

Doctored photograph purporting to show Herzl meeting the Kaiser at Mikveh Israel. The meeting did take place but the shot was bungled so the print was reconstructed from an entirely different image of Herzl, superimposed beside the mounted Kaiser.

Commemorative postcard from the first Zionist Congress in Basel, 1897.

Theodor Herzl with the Zionist delegation on board the ship *Imperator* on the way to Palestine, October 1898.

modern life to the cause of anti-Semitism. The Jews, he wrote, were 'hated strangers who are nowhere at home and lack all feeling for the *Volk* wherever they live'.[16]

The Jews of the cities had taken a bet on modernity, but now they were faced with a self-consciously archaic, rural-Teutonic and mythic attack in which the part they were assigned was that of subhuman goblins whose elimination, one way or the other, was the precondition not just of a flourishing German future but of its very survival. Only one side could win this war to the end, Marr made clear, and the purpose of his work was to sound the battle cry and ensure it would not be Aryan Germans who would be the vanquished race. Not long before his death in 1904 Marr had a sudden and complete change of heart, publishing his *Testament of an Anti-Semite* and publicly asking forgiveness from the Jews. It was too late. His League of Anti-Semites had created a new kind of political party and the toxin had been released into the bloodstream of German nationalism. Paul de Lagarde, Germany's most eminent scholar of oriental languages, described anti-Semitism as 'the mainstay of our national movement ... the most essential expression of genuine popular conviction'. It was this equation of anti-Semitism with political engagement, a tonic against bourgeois complacency, which would be so deadly to the people most associated with middle-class urban materialism. Put another way, anti-Semitism was the way to restore national health. To be vigorously German, then, rather than just paying lip service to the national ideal, meant being robustly, forthrightly anti-Semitic.

There was something about the new anti-Semitism which lent itself to catchphrases which stuck. The stickiest and deadliest was '*Die Juden sind unser Unglück*' ('The Jews are our misfortune'), and the fact that it was coined by someone hitherto unknown as an anti-Semite and ensconced in two of the highest institutions of the new German Empire – the University of Berlin and the Reichstag – made the epigram even more lethal. Heinrich von Treitschke was the author of the multi-volume history of Germany, and so not just widely respected but in some ways treated as the personification of the new nation, a role he was not shy of embracing. It was as the oracular seer of the new identity that he undertook to review the eleventh and last volume of Heinrich Graetz's *History of the Jews*. In some ways their works were parallel productions but such an assumption would have horrified Treitschke, who chose to make them profoundly anti-thetical. In the last section of his review in the *Preussische Jahrbücher*, a monthly review of politics, and elaborated the next year in his pamphlet *Ein Wort über unser Judenthum* (*A Word about Our Jews*), Treitschke made anti-Semitism intellectually respectable for anyone devoted to the cause of the nation. There was a pretence, or at least an affect, of holding his nose at the coarseness of popular anti-Semitism, which he managed to blame on authors like Johann Eisenmenger whom he wrongly identified as Jewish (a common libel). But at the same time as deploring its crudeness, Treitschke congratulated the ordinary people of Germany for their healthy aversion. They had sensed what was poisoning the country, and the necessity of purging it from the national bloodstream if its history was to go forward. If you were an ardently patriotic Jewish German newspaper editor, businessman, lawyer or especially a professor, you might be able to write off Wilhelm Marr and Otto Glagau as gadfly journalists. But the hatred of Treitschke came as a violent shock, and to those who wanted to take stock of it, an awful warning.[17]

Treitschke wrote from the heart of the Reich. But pan-Germanists beyond its borders like Ernst Vergani could be even more deranged in their insistence that the excision of Jews was the paramount condition for the reborn nation. Vergani – who had grown up in Lwów where Jews made up a third of the population, and who had insisted that the issue between Germans and Jews was 'racial, a matter of blood ... and can only be decided by blood' – was being only partly facetious when, in the Austrian legislature, he called for bounties to be given to those who shot Jews like game. The biologising of Jew-hatred, first spelled out in Alphonse Toussenel's book, had come on apace with the arrival of race theory and even epidemiology. Paul de Lagarde wrote of the 'de-Judification' (*Entjudung*) of Germany, an excision from the body politic. It was a simple matter of national health. Since the Indo-Germanic race and the Jews were biologically incompatible, the latter had to be 'crushed like vermin. Trichinella and bacilli could not be negotiated with; trichinella and bacilli could not be nurtured; they must be destroyed as quickly and thoroughly as possible.'

As pathological as these sentiments were, they only became politically incendiary through the work of Georg Ritter von Schönerer.

Schönerer could glory in his inherited title only because his father had been ennobled for his contribution to the railways of the Austro-Hungarian Empire. And it may well be that Schönerer Senior's work for and with the Viennese Rothschilds was one of the sources of the son's resentments, especially after the financial crash of 1873. But it was then that Georg first turned to the soil, studied agronomy, patronised the peasants, and began to grumble about those responsible for the disaster, including the reprehensible Jews. Nonetheless, for a while Schönerer collaborated with Jewish liberal politicians like Viktor Adler who were at least as enthusiastic about pursuing an aggressive German nationalism. With the arrival of Russian Jews fleeing the pogroms of 1881, Schönerer moved sharply to the far right and brought two forms of traditional Jew-hating into modern politics: the hostility of peasants and artisans who thought that Jews had destroyed their world, and that of Christianity which had never abandoned its ancient revulsion for Christ murderers.[18] As the enemies of Aryans and Christians, Schönerer wanted not just to reverse the emancipations but to place Jews under 'special laws'. In person he was too gruff and grim to be the charismatic leader of a mass movement, but he succeeded in getting the first expressly anti-Semitic politicians elected to the Austrian legislature. Most ominously it was Schönerer who made a war against the Jews, as he put it, 'a basic pillar of the national idea', describing the anti-Semitic crusade as 'the greatest national achievement of this century'. There was nothing that Adolf Hitler, born around this time in 1889, would end up saying which had not been anticipated in the writing and speeches of these first vehement German-nationalist anti-Semites.

None of this could have been missed by Adolf Jellinek. In 1881 he had become editor of the weekly paper which best represented the concerns and opinions of Vienna's liberal Jews, *Die Neuzeit*. It had been in existence for twenty years, the brief heyday of Austrian liberalism, and was thought to be the vehicle for Jellinek's hopeful belief in the interdependent future of the empire and its Jews. Its co-founder and previous editor, Simon Szanto, was a fierce adversary of what he thought of as retrograde orthodoxy, and his collaborator Leopold Kompert, through his fiction about the Bohemian ghettos, was the medium (often sentimental) by which the Jews of Alsergrund and the Innere Stadt could flatter themselves that they understood the world of the *Ostjuden* without having to get too close to its social reality.

Nothing written by Marr or de Lagarde, or said by Schönerer, gave Jellinek enough reason to change the generally optimistic tone of *Die Neuzeit*. It was a German contagion and would lose its force in the multinational empire of the benevolent Franz Joseph. But there was another writer in Vienna in whom Jellinek had taken a personal interest, and he had an altogether darker view of what the future held for Jews in central Europe, and for that matter everywhere else. Like Dr Pinsker, Peretz Smolenskin was from Odessa, had been brought up Orthodox and had turned to the Haskalah, but instead of contenting himself with European languages had become obsessed with the idea of giving Hebrew a new life, of turning it into a genuinely modern vernacular. After Smolenskin moved to Vienna in 1868, Rabbi Jellinek had helped him found the periodical *Ha-Shahar* (*The Dawn*), which both championed and embodied this momentous rebirth. As hostility towards the Jews of Vienna kept pace with their worldly and educa-tional success, Smolenskin began to lose faith in the victory of the *Menschenfreundlichkeit*, the fraternal universalism preached by *Die Neuzeit*. 'Do not listen to the words of those who glorify this era as a time of human justice and honest opinion,' he told his student followers. 'It is all a lie!' As long as Jews were in denial about their own collective existence as a nation, so they would be hostage to the fickle goodwill of states and empires, any of whom could be infected with the anti-Semitic strain.

Jewish students in the Austrian universities, especially Vienna, who had been excluded from the *Burschenschaften* fraternities, paid attention to Smolenskin's dark but inspiring theme. When they were the target of some of the most vicious abuse, they understood full well that anti-Semitism was, especially, a young person's ideology. Under Smolenskin's guidance, three of them – Moritz Schnirer, Reuben Bierer and Nathan Birnbaum – formed a reading group based on the premise that the Jews had a national as well as a religious history. Until the Jews embraced their own national self-determination they would be, as they had been for centuries, everyone's punchbag. In 1883 the trio founded the first Jewish student fraternity, Kadimah. It was Smolenskin who came up with the name, loaded with a double meaning: 'forward' and 'eastward'. What was in the east was not Odessa; it was Zion. It was one of the co-founders of Kadimah, Nathan Birnbaum, who would later coin the term 'Zionism'.

So when, in March 1882, Leon Pinsker, the author of an anonymous booklet saying much the same as Smolenskin, came calling on Adolf Jellinek, the rabbi had a good idea of what he was going to be told and assumed an expression of resigned patience. Pinsker's father, a scholar, had been a good friend of Jellinek's over many years. Now here was the son, himself middle-aged, a grey-beard, lecturing him on the indifference of the Viennese Jews to the plight of the Russian refugees; or if not that exactly, then their willed slowness to draw the right pessimistic conclusions, and to *do* something other than perform the usual acts of charity. Dr Pinsker was going to ask him to support the settlement of Jews in agricultural colonies, a place where they could be free to make their own lives with ploughs and hoes. Baron Maurice de Hirsch was already doing this in Argentina; but, really, kosher gauchos? Jellinek was doubtful. However, it was the bigger idea at the back of it, a giving up on Jews in the city, which weighed on him. Now that there was fighting to be done against the anti-Semites he was not one to give up. One imagines competitive sighing descending on the men in the apartment, with their cakes and tea. Pinsker broke a silence oddly, as if the rabbi needed reminding who he was: 'I visited you here with my father.' (This had been nearly twenty years before, in 1864.) And then with a note of dramatising self-consciousness: 'I'm perfectly aware I look distraught and melancholy and bear the traces of great sorrow on my face ... but you seem to have changed too, not in your outward appearance but your spiritual personality.' Pinsker implied that the change he saw was not altogether for the better. What was it – complacency? resignation? What was he going to give him: that guff about Jews being at home wherever they were, good patriots of their respective fatherlands? God knows, even in Russia they had tried, he, Leon, had tried, served loyally and bravely in the medical corps at Crimea. It made no difference. Jews would always be treated as alien invaders of someone else's fatherland. What Jews needed was *their* homeland! Pinsker's voice rose:

a piece of earth where we can live like humans. We are tired of being driven like animals, outcast by society, insulted, robbed and plundered; we are sick of having constantly to fight back the outrage rising inside us ... against the abuses and torments inflicted on us by upper and lower sorts of people alike ... I tell you with all the power of my soul

> we want to be a people, to live on our own national land, to make our
> communal and political institutions ... to found a state however small
> ... help to find a territory for us where we persecuted Russian Jews
> can live as a free people.

But Adolf Jellinek had spent his life arguing against those enemies of
the Jews who insisted they thought of themselves as a separate nation,
apart from the country in which they lived. To agree with that premise
was, as he told Pinsker, to abandon the principles he had held and
promoted for more than thirty years; the rock on which Jewish rights
had been built. He acknowledged to Pinsker that this was a worrying
time but told him his fears were exaggerated, that organised anti-
Semitism – the 'poisonous plant grown on the banks of the Spree'
(in Berlin) – had no deep roots in the soil of history, and thus was a
passing phase.

. Really? said Pinsker. Let me tell you about Odessa.

III. Sweet Odessa

... love child of the marriage between Black Earth and Black Sea, high
cliffs and deep water, *Odessa*, the sibilant word pushed gently out
between the teeth, a name so soft it didn't even sound Russian, no
surprise since it had been 'Hacibey' to Tatar and Turk, and only
baptised Greek Odyssos by the German empress of Russia Catherine
the Great when her Spanish-Irish Neapolitan general José de Ribas
took it from the Ottomans in 1792.[19] There was not much Russia in
this part of New Russia. The first governor of the place the locals
liked to call 'little Paris' was the French Duc de Richelieu, and the
architect who gave the city its hundred-foot-wide boulevards and grand
limestone public buildings was the Swiss-Sardinian Francesco Boffo,
a name so irresistible that when Yankel Adler, the kid boxer, found a
gang of street toughs, 'pavement roamers', to run with, they had to
call themselves the 'Boffi'.

You could be a new kind of Jew in Odessa, a place where everyone
smoked in the streets and Jewish girls were bat-mitzvahed by the

open-minded (if non-Russian-speaking) Rabbi Dr Shimon Arieh Schwabacher.[20] Welcome to the Talmud Torah of the future: Mishnah in the morning, metalwork in the afternoon, when the rabbi, sleeves rolled up, did a little light welding before the Mincha prayers. 'Learn the crafts,' he would say, 'become artisans!' Enough with the pawn-shops and the boxes of old clothes. Plane, file, burnish! The Jews did; even today you can find manhole covers with the word 'Trud', the name of the Odessa Jewish Artisans Association, many of them graduates of Dr Schwabacher's workshops, stamped on the pretty iron lid. A rabbi for a new age was Dr Schwabacher, so his appre-ciative congregation thought. So what if his Russian was non-existent. They could get by with Yiddish, and besides, his German sermons were a nice excuse to take a snooze or a smoke. The doctor-rabbi was a cultivated man who could, if asked, recite in French, Polish, Italian. What more could you ask for? At the big, beautiful Brody synagogue with its choir of angels, Arieh Schwabacher was a reason-able rabbi, assailed by unreasonable enemies who arrogated to them-selves rights of judgement.

So indeed they did. In Lithuania and in the yeshivot of Berdichev and Zhitomir, Schwabacher was denounced as the usher to ruin; the hastener of the disappearance of the Jews. Hands were wrung when yeshiva *bokhurim* hightailed it south to the fleshiest of fleshpots, which, during the desperate Lithuanian famines of the late 1860s, they did in ever increasing numbers. Peachy Odessa was waiting. Denouncing it as 'Babylon' or 'Sodom' only reinforced its magnetic pull. The rabbis fulminated that it was lit by the fires of hell, but who cared when carts made it through the moral inferno with boxes of French silk, Italian wine and Belgian lace. At last there were dockland Jews. The opening to the sea got rid of that age-old feeling Jews had, even when it was not literal, of being walled-in.

The runaways from the shtetls filled their bellies and turned their faces to the sun. Why should a Jew not warm his *kishkes* where and when he could? When the poet Yakov Fichman got on the train he 'stood nearly the entire night at an open carriage window breathing in the fragrance of the vast, dark, southern steppe'.[21] Winter left early by the Black Sea. On May Day the whole city took time off, the acacia hung out their yellow cords of blossom and a Jew could open up his nostrils, take a pull on the heady perfume, before promenading down

Deribasovskaya Street, or down the two hundred steps of Boffo's Gigantskaya, pausing on one of the nine landings to twirl his cane and look out at the rippling sea, the first that many Jews had ever set eyes on. Even on cloudy mornings the soft waves were dusted with silver light.

Jewish life *sounded* differently in Odessa. Martinet *melameds* of the *cheder*, swishing their switches as they made boys parrot the *Shulkhan Arukh*, had been replaced by schoolteachers of the 'Russian Schools' in waistcoats; and for the girls, strong-minded young women in broad-belted dresses and pinned-back hair recited Pushkin and Shakespeare to the class. Melisma had given way to the mass choir and organ of the Brody synagogue, founded to accommodate Jews from that Galician border town who wanted a modern – four-cupola, two-gable – affair, which they duly got, standing on the fashionable Pushkinskaya Street. Its cantors taught opera and lieder, and at Pesach Piotr Stolyarsky's music academy students (like the Oistrakhs) were on their way to becoming Jewish Paganinis.

By 1870 there were 50,000 Jews in Odessa, one in four of the boom town's population; twenty years later, 130,000, a third of the city, and not the kind of Jews who flapped around in long black *kapotes* and heavy beards, but Jews who had their chins and cheeks shaved close and anointed with eau de cologne until their skin shone, Jews who waxed the tips of their moustaches before they set off for the boule-vards in their shiny patent shoes; boatered Jews, panama-hatted Jews, Jews for whom, thanks to Alexander Tsederbaum's weekly *Kol Mevasser* (originally folded as a supplement into his Hebrew paper *Ha-Melitz*), Yiddish had become, sensationally, the language of politics, literature, *poetry!*[22] But if it was a rule in your little group of readers, writers and shouters that you did all this in Russian, then you'd read Tsederbaum's *Rasvet* (*The Dawn*). Having urged Russification for years, it was typical of the officials to be unsure, when it came, that it was Good for the Jews and for everyone else. When Tsederbaum applied to the censors, he was initially only given licence for a Yiddish- not a Russian-language publication, and had to press harder and longer before it was granted in 1858. But it always proved a tougher sell for its publisher than the Yiddish and Hebrew journals, lasting just three years, though it was succeeded by the *Vestnik russikh evreev* (*The Herald of the Russian Jews*).

You could be a beach Jew in Odessa, fill your lungs with ozone out at Langeron, or the pleasure park at Arkady, then take a clifftop stroll past the dachas of the big shots, the Ephrussis and the Brodskys, peering over the walls to marvel at the shrubbery. So Jewish gardening was not just potatoes! Any number were habitués of the Public Library with its 150,000 volumes. It was a home from home for Jewish girls and women, who could prop their elbows on the reading tables, push their glasses up the bridge of their nose and get stuck into Chernyshevsky, Pisarev, Lavrov and Tolstoy. Theatre Jews (which was most of them) got their first sight of Yisroel Gradner's outrageous talents, the face-pulling comedy alternating with the tear-jerking honey-dark voice, at Akiva's restaurant where Abraham Goldfaden's Yiddish company, fresh (he said) from triumph in Bucharest, emerged from behind a drawstring curtain to do one of their farces. When Goldfaden moved to more exalted quarters at the New City Theatre, there were full-on plays like *Schmendrick*. At curtain time the cast was rewarded with a bedlam of happiness, hands clapping till they hurt.

On summer nights there were plays and music on Langeron beach; klezmer on the water, or performances at the big wooden theatre on Kuyalnitzky Liman. Who could go home after the show? Time for brandy and coffee at Fankoni, Italian pastries at Zambrini or down into Gambrinus beer hall on Deribasovskaya Street where Sedner Perel, 'Sasha the Fiddler', played like a madman and all the rough-necks from Peresyp roared and belched and threw themselves on the tavern girls. Or if you hankered for a sweeter end to the evening you could walk in the direction of the nearest *sharmanka* street organ, programmed with slow, lilting waltzes, Odessa-style, the kind that let you take your girl for a gentle sway under the stars. Those who were already four sheets to the wind found themselves, without quite meaning to, in shadier territory deep in grubby Moldavanka at Josja Feldman's whorehouse on Glukhanka, the 'Deaf Street' full of alley rats with cocked ears, some of them the foot soldiers of the female con artist Sonka 'Golden Hand', lurking in alleys and doorways, waiting for the purses and watches of obligingly sloshed johns. Those who woke with pounding heads and lighter purses could nurse the damage at Isaac Solomonievich Isakovich's baths where, if they had seventy kopecks left, they could pull on a hookah and down a shot of healing Turkish coffee.

In all this urban carnival, Jews were constantly rubbing shoulders with the rest of Odessa: Greeks, Albanians, Germans, Armenians, Azerbaijanis, Poles, Italians, Turks, Georgians, the odd Russian here and there. Though there were some obviously Jewish districts, there was nowhere purely Jewish; even down in the shacks of Moldavanka, poor Jews had neighbours who were stevedores. All Odessa shopped at the same 'English' department stores, or in Primoz market; took the same horse trams; listened to the same music.

Never confuse neighbours with friends. None of this proximity, the sharing of districts, the common experiences of work and play, made the slightest difference when every twenty years it was time once more to attack the Jews.

An out-of-towner coming into a pogrom-struck city – Kiev, Elizavetgrad or Odessa – would have been met by a snowfall of feathers, lying on the streets, blown into the water, hovering on the marine gusts, the insides of what had been ripped apart: pillows, bolsters, cushions, the comforters of the Jews; the first target of their assailants who stabbed and tore and hacked at them before moving on to the hard furniture and glass and crockery and then on to the householders caught at home or running for their lives. Then your nostrils would pick up the stink of burnt-out houses, the wooden shacks of the poorest the easiest to set alight. So what with the feathers and the scorch, the town smelled like singed, plucked goose. But it was the Jews who had felt the butchery just round the corner, while children, away from their hand-wringing elders, ran around picking bits and pieces from the debris.

Kiev in May 1881 was four days of terrorising hell; the poorer Jewish houses in Podol and Pobskaia down near the Dniepr smashed, burnt and plundered (while those of the local sugar barons like Israel Brodsky up on the heights getting such police protection as was available). Most of those Jews, Yiddish-speaking, often dressed in the traditional garb, were more obvious targets of the *zhid*-haters. But Odessite Jews discovered in the most painful way that dressing like everyone else and speaking Russian was no protection. In fact, Odessa – which in many ways was a model for a new, integrated kind of Jewish life – suffered more regularly from mass violence than almost anywhere else in the Russian Empire. So much for cosmopolitanism.

Economic resentments were part of the reason (as they were in Kiev). When the Jews began to move into Odessa in the 1790s, liberated from the occupational restrictions prevailing in the rest of the Pale, the Greek community of merchants bridled at competition in the grain trade, the business that made serious money. After the Napoleonic Wars a grain shortage in western and central Europe was made good by supplies from the black earth of Ukraine, which in short order became the granary of Europe. Enormous quantities of rye and wheat came to the port city on plodding caravans of ox carts before being shipped out from the harbour to destinations primarily in the west. With their international connections, especially in port cities like Livorno and London, the Jews had a ready-made onward-trading network, one to rival the Greeks', and capital resources on a Rothschildian scale which the Greeks, despite their own commercial diaspora, couldn't match. Hence the swiftly rising fortunes of the Ephrussis, the Rafaloviches and (yet again) the Brodskys. They in turn filled their offices with co-religionists: sorters, weighers, quality inspectors, warehouse clerks. Together they made up a whole community of import/export harbour Jews just as they did in Bombay and Livorno.

Maritime competition did not go down well with the Greeks, many of them dockers and sailors but also, anciently, merchants and chandlers. Competition became envy; envy could, if a cause presented itself, turn into violence. Such causes were almost always a dangerously volatile mix of religious and national feelings. When the patriarch of Constantinople, Gregory V, was made an 'example' to the Greeks who had risen in revolt in 1821, his executed corpse thrown into the Bosphorus, Greek communities all over the Aegean and Levant mourned and raged and looked for someone they could blame and on whom they could exact retribution. In Odessa, the Jews with their kin all over the Ottoman were treated as quasi-Turks, villains of convenience, and were set on accordingly. Gangs of Greek sailors and stevedores reached for their clubs, axes and iron bars. Rumours of church blessings on the assaults only made matters worse.

There were only three thousand Jews in Odessa in 1821, yet there were synagogues enough to sack. But the principal targets (as they had been in all Judaeophobic violence since the Middle Ages) were homes and belongings. It was easy enough to storm and burn, to inflict the terror of the smashed-in door, the shattered glass, the ripped

featherbed, the looted silverware, though what was being destroyed
in these early 'pogroms' (the Russian word for a devastation or a ruin,
hitherto associated with invading armies) was an idea: the notion that
the Jews could have homes somewhere; that they might have their
share of domestic peace; that they could be *seated* in the furniture of
their lives. One of the most common occupations for Jews in Odessa,
right up until the mass murders inflicted by Romanians and Nazis in
the war, was that of furniture makers: carpenters, cabinetmakers,
French polishers – the suppliers of ease and comfort. So the breaking
of chairs, the stabbing of sofas, the wrenching of table legs, was a
way of telling the presumptuous Jews that they would never be able
to sit down in their houses and even in cosmopolitan, sun-warmed
Odessa feel themselves safe.

Intermissions between pogroms grew shorter. The next outbreak
was thirty-eight years on, in 1859, when a blood-libel story triggered
the violence; once again with some connivance by rogue clerics in
the Greek Church and fomented by the Greeks of the dockyards. By
this time, especially after the Crimean War, the grain barons had
established themselves as some of the most powerful (and showy) in
the city. But as in Kiev, their grand houses on Pushkinskaya and
Deribasovskaya were the ones which got most protection.

Twelve years later, in 1871, it happened again, when Easter and
Passover were close enough to generate maximum Christian antipathy,
almost as if Jews were shamelessly celebrating the crucifixion all over
again with their Paschal meals and rejoicings. Rumours that the Jews
had stolen a cross mounted on churchyard fencing for some sort of
ritual desecration, a mockery of the Passion, was the trigger for
violence. Greek and Russian Orthodox Churches were sufficiently
alike in their rituals and liturgy for them to share a common enemy,
and this time, when the axes hacked at the homes, the clubs also
rained down on Jewish bodies, any men daring to defend homes or
families. Beating up Jews, leaving them bloody, mutilated, or in six
cases dead, making sure the children were screaming with terror, now
became part of the pogromnik assault. Synagogues big and small,
dispersed across Odessa, became targets, and since the informal Jewish
trade guilds – from butchers and tailors to metalworkers and clerks
– each also had their own little synagogues, there was no shortage of
places to desecrate and burn. The standard attack always involved

slashing and tearing the Torah scrolls before dumping them on an improvised bonfire. This time, the attacks happened in rich districts and poor, on Pushkinskaya Street where the Brody synagogue stood as well as in Moldavanka; Jewish stalls knocked over in Primoz market; the bathhouses smashed up.

Sympathy in non-Jewish Russia was limited. For there was an additional element now enriching the stew of hatred: conspiracy theory. The instigator was (as had been the case in eighteenth-century Lwów) a converted Jew, Jacob Brafman, who turned the *kahal*, the governing body of Jewish communities, abolished by the tsarist government in 1844, into sinister cells of secret Jewish organisation. The *kahal* was said to live on as an underground plot against church, state and all Christians everywhere. Brafman had offered his services to the tsarist government as a spy on his former co-religionists, claiming the usual secret underground knowledge. When the paranoia about revolutionaries undermining the regime gathered force, the sense that the Jews were an incorrigibly estranged, dangerously subversive element in Russian society became a standard mindset in certain quarters of the government. The charge of 'separateness', a staple accusation directed against religious Jews, was neatly transferred to revolutionaries and became tantamount to treason. The fact that the Jews were notoriously literate, studious not just in the Talmud (which had once functioned as the same text of satire and subversion in Christian demonologies) but also now in secular disciplines, with a strong presence in journalism and political and philosophical literature, only intensified this police paranoia. Where once their esoteric religious texts had been the scripture of subversion, now it was their immersion in, and propagation of, anarchism and socialism that marked them out as enemies of Mother Russia and the world beyond. Brafman pointed to the international meddling of the Alliance Israélite Universelle, ostensibly to protect Jews from persecution, but actually to act as the institutional front for the international conspiracy, as the most obvious proof of his argument. It was natural, then, that when one of the revolutionaries involved in the assassination of Tsar Alexander II, Gesya Gelfman, was identified as a Jewish woman, the violent death of the sovereign could, at the popular level, be characterised as the fruit of a malevolent Jewish plot. 'The Jews killed the tsar' was the wildfire rumour among peasants who believed his

successor Alexander III was a friend of the landlord class in cahoots
with the Jews. The fact that the new tsar surrounded himself with
famous anti-Semites and characterised the Jews as 'repulsive' economic
predators made no difference.

A wave of pogroms broke out around Easter/Passover 1881, often
again with some sort of quasi-religious detonator so that the murdered
Christ and the murdered tsar became one and the same victim of
you-know-who. In towns like Elizavetgrad, the first of the serious riots
began in a Jewish-owned tavern where a fight broke out between a
drunk and the landlord, the former charging into the street shouting
the *zhidy* were trying to kill him.[23] Liquor was the explosive. Russian
Easter was a week's celebration with much heavy drinking and free
time for crowds; vodka and brandy were among the first things looted
from a smashed-up Jewish inn. Particular social groups were the shock
troops: artisans who hated Jewish market vendors, and railroad
workers who believed Jews stole baggage from unsuspecting travellers
while they had to make do with long hours and low wages. Since
they could get on trains at any time, it was easy enough for them to
find their way to trouble. Then there were out-of-town peasants who
had come to Elizavetgrad or Kiev for Easter and who belonged to an
ancient 'death to the Jews' culture.

It was once thought that the Russian government must have insti-
gated the pogroms as a way of redirecting antipathy for the countless
social ills affecting Russia. But there is no evidence of government
collusion. On occasions – in 1859 in Odessa, for example – the violence
might have been much worse had not Cossack troopers intervened
and arrests been made. And in 1881, police and troop dispositions
made by the local governor, notwithstanding his own anti-Semitism,
contained the violence. No one died in Odessa that year, as they did
in Kiev and Elizavetgrad.

There is, however, plentiful evidence of slow or shaky response.
Often local police forces were inadequate in a situation which many
predicted would get out of control. Elizavetgrad had just forty-seven
police for its population of 43,000, so order depended on the presence
of troops, who in this case had been sent off at exactly the wrong
time. But even if soldiers were present, their orders usually were not
to use firearms against the mobs. That, and the relatively lenient
punishment of the rioters, signalled to incendiaries in other towns

that the authorities were winking at the violence against the Jews even when that was untrue.

Sometimes, too, Jews on the receiving end noted a kind of chilly indifference on the part of the authorities amounting to grim satisfaction. The general attitude was that the Jews had brought it on themselves by their cupidity and greed. When Rabbi Schwabacher went to see the governor of Odessa, Count Kotzebue, after the pogrom of 1871 to complain about the lack of police protection, he was given a brusque dressing-down and told that the Jews had 'started it'. Alexander III himself subscribed to these economic myths. While regretting the pogroms, the tsar predicted violence would continue as long as the Jews did not mend their evil ways. If any Jew living in the areas of south Russia terrorised by the pogroms of 1881 and 1882 expected much in the way of security they were quickly disabused by Alexander III's new minister of the interior, the hearty anti-Semite Count Nikolai Pavlovich Ignatiev. Ignatiev had had a long military and diplomatic career and it had not escaped his attention that Russia had been robbed of the fruits of its victory over the Turks in the war of 1877–8 by the arbitration of the Jew Disraeli. 'His' people needed restraining, correcting.

Even before the wave of pogroms abated in 1882 (though there were a few outbreaks in 1883 and 1884) Ignatiev had issued 'Temporary Regulations' (which became near permanent) for the Jews, which continued to punish them for their own misfortunes. For more than half a century their woes had been blamed on their obstinate separateness. The abolition of the *kahal*, its replacement by state-appointed institutions and the creation of Russian Schools were meant to bring them into the world of non-Jewish Russia, and under Alexander II it had done its work only too well. Now it was the Jews' invasiveness which, as in the German-speaking lands, was said to be the problem. The Regulations were meant to contain if not reverse that. Rural Russia was to be locked off again; back to the shtetls with them! No more free settling in the countryside wherever they chose, even if they were in the commercial and educational classes approved under Alexander II. There were altogether too many educated Jews getting up to mischief, so ferocious quotas were set on their numbers in high schools and universities and in the professions. Jewish doctors were forbidden to hire Christian orderlies, and to appease one of the prime grievances of the rioters, there was to be no more Sunday trading.

The police now had the power to detain those who were where they were not supposed to be, and they used it. Night raids broke open Jewish apartments in Moscow and St Petersburg, and hammered on the doors of shtetl houses to determine that the Jews were in their properly registered location. In the end, even this failed to satisfy the reactionary urge to de-Judaise urban Russia. The presence of Jewish merchants and artisans in St Petersburg, and especially the ancient capital Moscow, was somehow an intolerable indecency to guilds and the Orthodox Church. The head of its Most Holy Synod (the highest lay office), Konstantin Pobedonostsev, was eager to remove them. The disaster was, as usual, timed for Passover, late March 1891. Of Moscow's 30,000 Jews, 20,000 were to be expelled; almost all its working artisan population plus shopkeepers and merchants were arbitrarily deemed desirable. The decree became known on the morning following the first Seder as Jews were assembling for synagogue. The tragic variation on the exodus fell hard on them. Different groups were to be deported in phases depending on how long their residence had been; last in, first out. But the uprooting, the panic selling of property – movable and immovable – the liquidation of assets, with the Church looking on in satisfaction, seemed not so much an Egyptian tale as a replay of the expulsion from Spain. Families, livelihoods, lives were broken by it. To add another twist of cruelty, those who were unable to sell off everything in time to comply with police orders were arrested in their houses and packed into common prisons, where some of the aged perished. Despite their total destitution and exposure to the bitter cold, the last category of deportees – those who had lived in the city twenty or thirty years – fled to the freight cars at Brest station rather than risk being taken to prison. Dressed in rags, women and small children trembled in terror and died of hypothermia. In a further irony, the governor of Moscow had decided to suspend the deportations until the worst of the cold had passed but his order came too late for many of the victims. Newspaper stories kindled the usual expressions of indignation and regret from Vienna to Washington, where President Harrison and Congress conveyed their abhorrence to the Russian ambassador (while regretting it should darken the normally cordial relations between their countries). But it was Alphonse de Rothschild's declining to subscribe to the latest issue of Russian government bonds which made the authorities have second

thoughts. Pressure from the Rothschilds of course only confirmed to
anti-Semites their conviction that Jews were extortionists.

In any case, many Russian Jews did not need this latest misery to
persuade themselves that the dream of civil equality, of living alongside other Russians, was just that. Some thought this would be the
case until there was revolutionary alteration in the country. To have
a Jewish life you needed to be rich enough and powerful enough to
be indispensable even to Russians who hated you. So the people who
aroused the most resentment, whose very success made old families
and the Orthodox Church speak of a 'Jewish conquest', were the last
people to feel the blade edge of oppression.

Whoever said life in Russia was fair? Or for that matter life anywhere?
Not Moshe Leib Lilienblum.[24] Odessa had made him free but, as he
bitterly recorded in a memoir written when he was thirty, free to be
unhappy. But then Lilienblum was one of the ancient line of virtuosi
of *tsuris*, poets of misery. The memoir was called *Sins of Youth*, and
was written just a year or two after his arrival in Odessa in 1869, on
the invitation of the enlightened, so that he might escape persecution
as a religious reformer in Lithuania. With no sense of irony at all
Lilienblum divided his still youthful life into 'Chaos', 'Heresy' and
'Despair': the first when, as an Orthodox yeshiva boy (and later its
teacher), he had begun to doubt the very existence of God. Worse,
those doubts ate at him most deeply on the solemn occasions of
the ritual calendar – Rosh Hashanah and Yom Kippur! He donned the
shroud of woe like a man born for it: there was the wife, betrothed
to him when they were still more or less children; the children she
had borne to a loveless marriage. Forced to live with his in-laws,
Lilienblum's claustrophobia was now doubled, the strangling grip of
the Talmud tightened by the suffocation of his domestic life.

He began to murmur against the Talmud even as he dived more
deeply into its sixty books as if he had missed something, the nugget
of wisdom which would make sense of everything. But the bright
gem eluded him. The Kabbalah of the Hasidim seemed even more
wilfully esoteric, if not actually nonsensical. Still the question gnawed
at Moshe Leib Lilienblum as it had so many other distracted Jews for
a thousand or so years: how could God make the universe from
nothing; from, please, 'a *word*'? Why had he been given the faculty
of reason if not to worry over such matters, before which the work

of every day and especially his teaching in the yeshiva shrank into
paltry insignificance? The dog of doubt sunk its teeth into his shins
and would not let go. Murmuring to himself became verbalising to
friends and then in writing to the whole of Wilkomir, the shtetl; and
for his honesty he was made instant pariah: hooted at in the streets
by children; his own children bullied and ostracised; denounced on
the Sabbath. Anguished that this stifling, unthinking conformity was
losing Jews altogether, and that if certain changes were made to strictures that were not even in the Torah, they might remain Jews,
Lilienblum was castigated yet again. It was in vain that he protested
that he himself could hardly have been more orthodox in the ways
of his life; that he never touched cheese until six hours had elapsed
following a meal of meat! He was met with the laughter of hating
disbelief. It was unbearable.

The reforming publications reached Odessa where he found sympathisers in the Society for the Promotion of Enlightenment among
Odessa Jews, from whom he received an invitation to teach. It had
been a relief but also bewildering. Being Lilienblum he soon felt the
loss of Wilkomir more acutely than the joy of escape. The shtetl
wraparound which had all but suffocated him he now missed like an
old blanket. The weather was warm but the society cold. Pleasure
eluded Lilienblum; he barely went through the motions. He yearned
for what he had once hated: the closeness of people he knew well.
You went your own way in Odessa; dropped off in its world like a
passenger from a horse tram. Co-editing Tsederbaum's journals was,
somehow, not family. His brain was full of notions but the deeper
part of Moshe Leib Lilienblum was empty. 'My heart is wood,' he
wrote, 'I am twenty-nine and old age has already overtaken me. I have
given up the idea of living a vital life. My eyes are heavy with
weeping ... I am a failure.'

But then, as if it was good for something, the big *tsuris* called
Pogrom showed Lilienblum the way. Amid the flying trash, murderous
din and crowds of unsheltered Jews, stumbling glassy-eyed through
the streets, he came to a bleak conclusion: houseless meant homeless
meant hopeless. While the madness was raging he saw a woman
'ragged and drunk dancing in the streets shouting "this is our country,
this is our country"'. 'Can we say the same,' he asked rhetorically,
'without the dancing, without being drunk? We are aliens not only

here but in all of Europe for it is not our fatherland ... we are Semites among Aryans, the Shem among the sons of Japhet, a Palestinian tribe of Asia in the European land.' This 'orientalism' was the very complaint some of the anti-Semites voiced when they saw another synagogue dome on their streets. The government was apparently 'collecting data on Jewish activities which harmed natives. We, then, are not natives.' Better to embrace the difference with fortitude and pride 'than dream that we will become children of the European nations, children with equal rights [for] what can be more fatuous?'

Elsewhere in the city Dr Leon Pinsker was coming to the same painful conclusion. Though they were not yet close, it is unlikely that Lilienblum and Pinsker had not heard of each other; but they came to what was not yet called Zionism by different routes and through different worlds. Lilienblum was so steeped in rabbinic Judaism that even when he was trying furiously to shake it off, the tradition clung to his self-interrogating habits of thought. The Pinskers were long-established Odessites. Leon's father had taken the family south from the shtetl of Tomaszow (in what is now Belarus) when he was offered a post at the new Hebrew school teaching both Jewish and non-Jewish subjects. It gave him the chance to pursue his owlish, scholarly passions: the medieval Karaites and the vocalisation of Assyriac. Educated in that broad-minded curriculum, and with opportunities finally opening up, Leon was destined for – what else? – the law or medicine; he tried the first, and settled on the latter. As a young physician he did everything he could to demonstrate his patriotic selflessness. In 1848–9 he volunteered to work directly with cholera patients, at real risk to his own life; six years later during the Crimean War he was courting even greater peril working in the lethal typhus-stricken wards of the Russian army.

If anyone had reason to assume that his Jewish and Russian identities were unproblematically twinned, it was Pinsker; yet the pogroms and the tepid attitude of authority to both prevention and correction taught him this was not so. He also came to the shocking realisation that the optimism of the Society for the Promotion of Enlightenment among Odessa Jews was all idle piety. The truism that hatred would dissipate with education, and with easy social familiarity between Jews and non-Jews, was a vain comfort. Anti-Semitism was not an anachronism destined to disappear with the conquest of modernity;

it *was* modernity, as up-to-date and future-friendly as electricity and the railway.

This was because it was a psychic disease, one capable of infinite mutation. Pinsker the diagnostician observed a moral metastasis eating through the body of modernity. Better than almost any other Jewish commentator on anti-Semitism, he understood how ancient phantasies cohabited with modern habits; and the particular madness, 'a demonopathy', he identified was the fear of ghosts, zombies. The Jews walked through the fears of the non-Jewish mind as alien beings, neither wholly alive nor satisfyingly dead; both there and not there; mercurial, slippery, immune to exorcism through banishment, conversion or any number of brutal bashings. Worse, they kept coming back as successes, masters of the modern world; hobgoblins of capitalism. The Jews themselves were not without responsibility for this phobia because they refused to gather themselves into a physically recognisable national existence, an entity which would command respect. Instead they left their destiny in the hands of the Almighty, stuck forever in the waiting room for an appoinment with a Messiah who never showed up. Meanwhile the blows rained down on their heads. But 'if we are ill-treated, robbed, plundered, outraged we do not defend ourselves, worse still we look upon it almost as a matter of course ... if a blow is dealt we soothe it by rinsing our burning cheeks with cool water; if we receive a bloody wound we apply a bandage ... what a pitiful figure we cut'.

It would always be thus as long as the powers thought of the Jews as so many individuals rather than the nation they were; always they would be treated like beggars or refugees, 'and where is the refugee to whom a refuge may not be refused?' The Jews were the world's perennial refugee, manhandled or granted civic crumbs from the table as it suited those who had absolute power over them. The response was first to rouse the dormant spirit of collective existence and then to give it institutional reality. The foundations for such a national rebirth were, he thought, already in place. It was just a matter of convincing the grandees of Vienna, Paris, Berlin, Frankfurt and London that they needed to move from charitable relief, educational projects and the periodic mobilisation of public opinion when yet another hideous blood libel came to light, towards a forthright, international organisation for the dispersed Jewish nation. Let the anti-Semites rail that this was the age-old Jewish conspiracy revealing its true colours; they would do that anyway. What was urgently needed was to give the Jews who had lived forever in the ethereal world of abstractions, an earthier, material existence. What was wanted was a homeland.

With these revolutionary principles circling inside his head, Leon Pinsker decided to go on the road and set them out before Jews who mattered in the great capitals. That was when he knocked on the door of Rabbi Dr Adolf Jellinek even as another wave of pogroms was erupting in southern Russia around Easter/Passover 1882. His cool reception in Vienna was dispiritingly repeated in Berlin and Frankfurt. In Paris, where anti-Semitic literature was blooming with poisonous virulence, he had a more sympathetic hearing from the chief rabbi Zadoc Kahn, who wanted to introduce him to the one man who might turn Pinsker's notions into working reality: Baron Edmond de Rothschild. Oddly, and perhaps because he was already so discouraged by meetings with rich Jews who failed to share his zeal, Pinsker did not wait around for another.

It was only in London that he found someone who took what he was saying, his call to *action*, seriously: Arthur Cohen, Liberal Member of Parliament for Southwark. Despite the name, Cohen was from the cream of the Anglo-Jewish 'Cousinhood', the nephew of Sir Moses Montefiore, around whom it was impossible not to be interested in the fate of Jews in Palestine. Cohen was also president of the Board of Deputies, so all in all the kind of British Jew likely to greet Pinsker with lukewarm sympathy but no more. But Arthur Cohen was neither parochial nor complacent. His father Benjamin, City merchant and broker, had sent him to a Frankfurt gymnasium for his schooling and afterwards to the only college freely accepting Jews, University College London. But Benjamin thought nothing except Cambridge could possibly be good enough for his son, who showed an aptitude for mathematics. Two colleges refused him before Prince Albert prised open the gates of Magdalene on Arthur's behalf, a favour which embarrassed the young man. At Cambridge, rowing and hunting took him away from advanced calculus, and in 1852 he became president of the Cambridge Union. The result was that Arthur was placed as just Fifth Wrangler in his examinations, a grievous blow to Pa. But what bit further into Arthur's own equanimity was that he was forced to wait until the Cambridge University Act of 1856, which did away with an oath to the Church of England, before he was allowed to graduate.

Two years later Lionel de Rothschild took the oath as an incoming Member of Parliament on the Old Testament with the words 'So help me Jehovah'. Arthur, who was also related to the Rothschilds, was himself elected in 1880, following the wave of Liberal success which ended the government of the most famous (albeit baptised) Jew in Europe, Benjamin Disraeli. And in 1882 Cohen listened to the gaunt, worn figure of the doctor from Odessa, and without the raised eyebrows, the armchair fidgeting or the diplomatic ahems to which Pinsker had become depressingly accustomed. Cohen, who might have considered himself a living example of why a Jewish homeland was gratuitous, thought Pinsker right; so right, in fact, that he urged him to publish his opinions as soon as possible.

Back in Odessa with this one decisive encouragement to sustain his convictions, Pinsker wrote and published *Auto-Emancipation*.[25] Its anonymity was curiously at odds with the clarion-call forthrightness of the message, though the doctor who always felt himself ailing (he had another nine years of life) wanted to uncouple the man from the message, and avoid any dominant role in the movement he was committed to launch. A charismatic leader, he often said, was needed; but he was not that person.

Moshe Leib Lilienblum did not agree. Reading *Auto-Emancipation* was akin to an epiphany for him; a dramatic statement of all the arguments that had been tumbling around his fevered mind. Nor did anyone else who got their hands on a copy think it less than revolutionary. In New York the wealthy Sephardi poet and essayist Emma Lazarus, moved by the news coming from south Russia, responded ardently to the burning eloquence of the writing. 'For the living the Jew is a dead man, for the natives an alien and a vagrant, for property owners a beggar, for the poor an exploiter, for patriots a man without a country.' Nudged by Lilienblum, Pinsker emerged from anonymity, accepted his fame as a mission, moved into an office with his new comrade-in-arms (the address marked today with a small plaque), and from there set about organising a movement they called with biblical flourish Hovevei Zion, the Lovers of Zion.

Two years later, on 6 November 1884, the first Congress of the Jews assembled in the Polish-Silesian town of Katowice. Naturally, the delegates all expressed their love for Zion by arguing with each other. Pinsker gave the opening and closing addresses, still genuinely reluctant to assume any kind of leadership. Somewhere, he thought, there was a Moses waiting in the wings.

It was all very well to love Zion, and to send Jews to till its soil, but where was it exactly? In *Auto-Emancipation*, Pinsker spoke of the desperate need for a refuge, in particular for Russian Jews who were facing the bitterest and most unrelenting hostility. He did not, he wrote, have any expectation of course that the whole of the world's Jews would emigrate to the self-governing homeland, and the territory itself could be a mere patch of land, just enough to give protection and self-respect. Thus modestly defined it could be an autonomous territory within the United States (though somewhat bigger than Mordecai Noah's Ararat); or perhaps a province of Ottoman eastern Anatolia? But for most of the Lovers, Zion could only have one possible location and that was 'Eretz Yisroel', the place where language and collective identity had been formed; where kings of Israel and Judah might have disappeared out of sight but never out of mind; where in fact there was already a Jewish majority in Jerusalem.

It was not, as is often claimed, the first Zionists who spoke of Palestine as empty, 'a land without people for a people without land'. That was the comment of an American missionary earlier in the nineteenth century. But it is true that even if you look very hard amid all these passionate, desperate yearnings for Zion, you will not find, anywhere at all, the word 'Arab'.

IV. Qatra, 1884

Winter sun rose on the village at the foot of Tel Qatra. The usual chorus began: roosters, donkeys, goats, an occasional dog. At the edge of the village, where arable fields took over from olive groves, a mule and an ox were being tethered to a light-yoked plough. Inside the houses the first tea of the day was brewing: comfort against the season's chill.

The Shephelah where Qatra stood was the region of low hills dividing the coastal plain of Palestine from steeper, rockier, limestone Judaea. Its cube-houses were all grey, and greyer still after winter rain when the rudimentary streets turned muddy. Downstairs: a hearth, a bed, sometimes a goat; upstairs, a rug and a bigger, better bed. It was a village of fellahin, tenant-cultivators; families, in the case of Qatra, who had come earlier in the century from Libya. The whole region, indeed the whole of Palestine, was full of Arab immigrants, many of them descendants of Ibrahim Pasha's army, who had conquered the country on behalf of Muhammad Ali, the Khedive of Egypt, in the 1830s. After the conquest was complete in 1841, many of the military families were settled in Palestine. The majority were native Egyptian but there were also Maghrebi Arabs from Algeria and Morocco, Circassians and Bosnians. At the same time, there was some immigration from Syria and Lebanon, including Druze and Christians. The assumption that, before the arrival of Jews in the nineteenth century, Arab Palestine was a place of timeless continuity, the same indigenous people immemorially inhabiting the same villages and cultivating the same plots of ancestrally inherited land, overlooks all these shifts of population. Beduin tribes (also in many cases ex-soldiers) – called (unfairly) by settled fellahin 'creators of the desert' – fought with cultivators and still more fiercely with each other. Every so often Beduin would descend on village pasture with flocks of camels, letting them graze and challenging the locals to take them on. Pitched battles broke out over pasture and water. Once their camels had grazed the pasture down to the barest stubble, the Beduin would break camp and move on, leaving the fellahin wringing their hands.

As everywhere in this part of the world, there were ruins. The villagers of the Shephelah, where every hill seemed to have its *khirbet*, had become accustomed to seeing Europeans, and the odd American, dismount, poke and peer at the fallen stones, take a trowel or a little shovel to the surrounding dirt, then kneel down and sift a handful through their fingers. A tripod would appear with extending legs, then the massive camera, while another of the group pulled drawing materials from a flat canvas bag, found a flat stone to sit on and made sketches; yet another would be busy with survey instruments, pacing out preliminary measurements. Most of these busy pink men in their pressed khaki shorts and long socks came with guides from Jaffa or

Ramle. But sometimes they tried out their own Arabic, spoken slowly and flatly, unlike the galloping run of the Libyan- or Egyptian-accented vernacular. After 1858, when a new Turkish land law required registration of titles, another class of surveyors from Jaffa, Jerusalem and Haifa appeared with their own surveying instruments. The fellahin knew that registration would be followed by taxation, as was exactly the case. Everything that could be taxed would be: livestock, crops, houses, even beehives.

But nothing prepared the villagers of Qatra for the latest arrivals. At twilight on the second day of Hanukkah, two Russian Jews, self-described Lovers of Zion, walked into the middle of an empty field south of the village, their arms loaded with twigs. Setting them on the ground, they arranged them into two small pyramids, each one signifying a day of the festival. Once lit, the twin bonfires became an outsize Hanukkah lamp flaring up into the evening sky. A few days later they were joined by seven more student types including, briefly, Israel Belkind, who two years before in January 1882 in Ukraine had brought a group of fourteen Kharkov University undergraduates to his house, and with the solemnity only twenty-year-olds in search of a mission can muster, had formed them into a phalanx of pioneers. No self-respecting group of this kind could be without an acronym, and after fishing about in the Bible they settled on a verse from Isaiah: *Beit Ya'akov Lechu Ve'nelcha* (House of Jacob come, let us go). Thus, by a slight twist of acronym, they became the 'Bilu'. Pinsker's stirring utterance had not yet been published in Odessa but the pogroms of 1881 had thrown sparks over many other communities and they bloomed from one end of the Pale to the other, from Kovno to Kherson, with ardent little flames.

Romancing the land, by which was meant actual physical soil, was not unique to these young Jews. The wheat fields of Russia were thick with bespectacled idealists hearkening to Chernyshevsky or Tolstoy, bent on redeeming the country and themselves with scythe and sickle, and fraternising with the long-suffering peasantry. In a half-hearted attempt to wean the incorrigibly urban Jews from their addiction to petty commerce, the Russian state in its socially evangelical mode had established agricultural colonies for Jews in Kherson province not far from Odessa, with mixed success. So Jews could hoe and harrow, milk and thresh. More influential on the Bilu were the majestically eloquent appeals from two rabbis, one Ashkenazi and one Sephardi, Zvi Hirsch Kalischer and Yehuda Alkalai, both in Hebrew, the reborn language of redemption, both preaching a return to the soil of Israel. Once established, the Lovers of Zion in Odessa acted as a kind of clearing house for the emigrants, and it was from Odessa, after another cycle of pogroms reinforced their convictions, that the Bilu sailed to Zion.

So there they were, nine Jewish peasants, shivering together in a wooden shack, nursing blisters and swatting away the insects, their hands raw from pulling up esparto and wild alfalfa, briar and nettle.[26]

It was not quite what had been anticipated; a little short on the olives and vines and not much sign of milk and honey. The original fourteen Biluim, including the owlish Belkind (who it quickly transpired was not cut out for the Jewish peasant life), arrived in the summer of 1882: prime mosquito season; the insect which would have almost as much of a decisive effect on the fate of Zionism as the words of Leon Pinsker. An agricultural school, Mikveh Israel, established in 1870 by the Alliance Israélite Universelle on a modest patch of land south of Jaffa, was waiting to receive its first cohort. It was managed by Charles Netter, one of the few men in this early chapter of Jewish farming in Palestine to combine steely resolution with practical wisdom.[27] After learning which end of a plough was which, off the Biluim went to Rishon LeZion, its name (First in Zion) jumping the gun, as the very first settlement was actually Motza, established in 1854 in the hill country outside the walls of Jerusalem. Though the land in these earliest farms was leased to groups, each cultivator was responsible for his own plot. That had been the idea of Zalman David Levontin, a religious Jew from Mogilew. Moved by the plight of refugees from the pogrom-struck cities, Levontin had promoted a scheme for land purchase, and with a promise of investment from a wealthy uncle he had travelled to Palestine in the summer of 1882 to execute the plan. Six refugees and ten other settlers moved into Rishon LeZion. Almost immediately the settlement was compromised by bitter disputes as to whether it ought to be run from Jerusalem or by the settlers themselves. But the quarrels were as nothing compared to the impossibility* of finding adequate supplies of water. Within a few months, it was obvious the farmers at Rishon LeZion were unlikely to make a go of it. Eaten alive by malarial mosquitoes, not to mention horseflies and sand leeches, unable to produce even a minimal harvest of wheat or barley, reduced to surviving from plates of potatoes and radishes, Rishon was abandoned less than a year after it was initially occupied.

Help was needed, and where else to find it if not from a Rothschild? One in particular, Baron Edmond – the youngest son of the railroad and banking founder of the Paris end of the dynasty, James – was said to have an interest in the replanting of Palestine with Jews.[28] Through the mediation of the chief rabbi Zadoc Kahn and Netter, deputations of the desperate made their way to the great house on the rue Laffitte for an audience with the formidable magnate. They included a rabbi from Brody, Shmuel Mohilewer, who reported to the baron on the dire situation in his own town, crowded as it was with fugitives from the pogroms. Mohilewer treated the great baron as though he were a *resh galuta*, a leader of the exile (which was not far off the truth), and secured support for the transplantation of a group of families from Rozhany in Poland. But the most effective impact on Edmond was made by Joseph Feinberg, a Zion Lover chemist working for the Zaitsev Sugar Company in Odessa. Feinberg had waited but a few weeks after the arrival at Rishon LeZion before judging it would fail without immediate help. Edmond saw this not as a sign of premature pessimism but the anxiety of a practical man who understood that Zion would need more than Love if its crops were to grow. It needed investment so that sand could be stabilised, wells dug and – a Rothschild obsession – Australian eucalyptuses planted to fix the sand.

Edmond was willing to provide the needful, but on condition that the settlers agreed to be managed by men Edmond judged to have what it took, technically, to make these seedling communities take root. He also saw that the transplantation of refugees from persecution could be badly handled from Odessa. A boatload of refugees from Romania had been denied landing by the Turkish officials and were reduced to sailing up and down the coastline with almost no food and less sanitation before getting a mercy landing at Jaffa, where they were promptly locked up. When they got to their promised patch of land, it was the usual mix of rock and swamp. This all needed better management, Rothschild thought, but it also needed grandeur of vision. With a modicum of investment why should Palestine not produce the kind of things he himself valued: wine, silk, perfume? Once, the Bible made clear, Israel and Judah had been thick with vineyards. Why should they not reappear?

Intensive western agriculture – irrigation, crop rotation, iron-yoked ploughs that turned the soil rather than just raked furrows into it with a single metal spike, manuring and even steam-driven combines – had actually been first introduced into Palestine by American evangelicals from Maine and Pennsylvania, and, still more improbably, by the German Order of the Templars, all of whom had a messianic interest in seeing the Holy Land blossom into fruitfulness. The Templars managed to create colonies near Jaffa and Haifa, build flour mills and lay down paved roads. But with the experiment, as usual, came unsupportable debt and near collapse; Edmond de Rothschild, though, had his own characteristic notions of what modern Jewish farming might yield, and the willingness to fund the great experiment, even if it went into the red.[29] Cadres of European-trained specialists were dispatched to see if the country was right for wine, silk and even perfume. Sericulturalists came from Padua, *jardiniers* from the Horticultural School at Versailles, oenologists who had put in time at Rothschild chateaux in the Médoc, and hydraulic engineers from the École des Ponts et Chaussées. It was all very Napoleonic, with the emperor of cultivation back in Paris or at the chateau at Ferrières, impatiently waiting results, berating anyone he thought was obstructing success, threatening to pull funds if 'insubordination' against his managers compromised the accomplishment of the 'experiment'. For many of the immigrants – from Poland and Romania as well as Russia – the addition of Gallic-Jewish dressing-downs on how they lived and worked, in addition to plagues of yellow fever, malaria and the terrible eye disease trachoma carried by the sandflies, was altogether too much, and they departed, back to Europe, or to Jerusalem (where Israel Belkind became a teacher), or to an early grave. Charles Netter himself died at the end of 1882 from malaria. By the time that Rishon LeZion became independently viable in the 1890s, both its major founders, Levontin and Feinberg, had returned to Russia.

But there were some who stuck it out, even as the vines withered (disastrously when phylloxera and mildew struck in the early 1890s) and the worms fell off the mulberry trees (though the trees themselves endured). At Qatra, the little Jewish colony called itself Gedera and stayed put. The Arab village watched the odd determination of the Jews to rent ploughs and draught animals from them, and to toil over the land themselves, with bemused suspicion. This was not what Jews did; they wouldn't last. But when the first stone houses were built at Gedera it was apparent they meant to stay, and then what the Jews were doing lit up arguments in the village. The angriest said that land had been taken, and they had been robbed of the use of it. Legally this was untrue. The parcel of land which became Gedera had reverted to the Turkish government when the village disclaimed the property a few years earlier. That disclaimer had been made to avoid liability for a murder which had taken place within the boundaries of the parcel. Moving the village limits of Qatra shifted responsibility away from their doorstep while they carried on, as usual, using it for grazing. The legal vacancy allowed the Turkish authorities to reassign the land to the neighbouring village of Mughar which in turn sold it to the French consul in Jaffa, a M. Polivierre. Finally, the consul had sold it to Yechiel Michal Pines, who had come to Palestine as an agent for the Montefiore Foundation.

Faithful to the spirit of Montefiore, Pines wanted to remake Palestinian Jews as artisans and farmers, and in Jerusalem romantically created a society for 'The Return of Craftsmen and Smiths'. When, in 1882, he encountered Eliezer ben Yehuda, whose life was devoted to the recreation of Hebrew as a daily vernacular tongue, Pines saw the outlines of what a reborn Jewish society in Palestine might be and what it might sound like. But even as he made himself patron and protector of the Lovers of Zion and jumped on the opportunity to buy that plot of land south of Qatra, he was not oblivious to Arab sensibilities. Where he could, Pines tried to find land compensation for villagers who felt that, despite lots being legitimately bought, they had had working property taken from them. Sometimes Pines succeeded and calmed an inflamed situation down; sometimes, as at Qatra, he did not.

What unfolded, as the first Jewish villages appeared in Galilee, the coastal plain of Samaria and the Shephelah, was not a case of an unbroken agriculture disrupted by colonial intrusion. The ecology of Palestine in the second half of the nineteenth century was unstable and, in many parts of the country, deteriorating.[30] The great event of the century had been the earthquake of 1837, with its epicentre in Galilee. Ruined villages had been abandoned and depopulated. Deforestation had had an even more dramatic impact. Until the 1840s, much of the Sharon Valley had been covered with a Mediterranean dry oak forest. A century later most of it had been denuded for char-coal and lime kilns. Timber taken by the Turkish state for the construc-tion of railways took more of the oaks. Upland topsoils eroded; nearer the coast, the line of sand dunes advanced into previously cultivable land. Drifting dirt clogged natural water flows, creating stagnant ponds and marshes where there had been running brooks and rivulets. Different incoming populations treated these changes in their own ways. The Arab el Damair tribe of Egyptian Beduin who had come to the region with Ibrahim Pasha moved to the edge of the Huzera swamp where they raised water buffalo and cut reeds in the manner of the marsh Arabs of Mesopotamia.[31]

Environmental degradation created commercial opportunity. When villagers chose not to register their land use with the Turkish author-ities for fear of taxation, they produced legal vacancies which were instantly filled by opportunistic buyers from Jaffa and Jerusalem but also much further away in the region. A class of absentee landlords arose in the area, almost entirely Christian and Muslim Arabs, who then leased their properties to those who would bring improvements – drainage and irrigation above all – and with it dramatic capital appreciation. Enter, in the first place, those Americans and German Templars, followed not long afterwards by the Jews.

Thus the fellahin, partly by their own doing and partly by circum-stances completely beyond their control, had beome tenants of land-lords who had never lived or farmed in their plains, hills and valleys. To begin with just who was selling and who buying – effendi, Turk, French consul or Jerusalem Jew – was a matter of utter indifference to those who ploughed fields, scattered seeds from their opened fists, tended and grazed sheep and goats, so long as they could get on with providing a subsistence for their families and village. But these belt-and-braces young men were not Jerusalem Jews and were impervious to ancient, sacrosanct customs. Customary convention prescribed that those who had sown and harvested a summer crop were then entitled to follow with a winter crop; and the stubble fields after harvest were always theirs for grazing. But both local officials and Jewish farmers had new, office-paper versions of rights. Even at this early stage, hostilities erupted. The Jews drove grazing animals from their land, or even confiscated them as a 'lesson'. Infuriated Arab villagers responded with violent attacks, smashing up cabins, and physically attacking men and women. The situation was made worse by the refusal of the settlers to take up the customary offer of 'protection' from Arab watchmen, preferring instead to defend themselves. Armed Arabs then made the Jews experience first-hand the cost of denying themselves that protection. In both the grazing wars and the watchmen rejection, then, Arab sensibilities were already confused, dismayed and wounded by what they encountered. 'They are up in arms,' the local Lovers of Zion agent wrote to Pinsker in Odessa, 'for how will they sustain themselves?' It was a good question.

In the late spring of 1887, Edmond de Rothschild's yacht anchored off Port Said. He had come to inspect the results of his 'experiment' though the journey had been kept, or so he thought, a secret. In all the correspondence about his trip he insisted he be referred to as 'REB' (a reversal of the initials of Baron Edmond de Rothschild) as if that would fool anyone, or if for that matter anyone cared. The Ottoman governor, Rauf Pasha, it is true, had banned all Jewish immigration after 1882, with the exception of Turkish subjects moving around the empire, but even they were forbidden to own land outright. So purchases had to be made through local surrogates. Edmond was concerned not to jeopardise what was in any case a precarious foothold, but he exaggerated the offence that would be taken by his presence. For the Turks in Jaffa, Jerusalem and the Galilee, as for much of the rest of the world, the appearance of a Rothschild was an event and an opportunity, whatever they might have said behind his back and after he had departed.

Since it humoured him, the pretence of incognito was kept up. From Jaffa, the baron in his panama hat and impeccable tropical suit travelled with his long-suffering wife Baronne Adelaide, in a closed carriage despite the broiling heat, the first *khamsin* sirocco of the season blowing burning grit against its windows. In Jerusalem the baron, like all the grand philanthropists, expressed his dismay at the poverty and ignorance of the religious, at their degrading dependence on *halukah* charity, and voiced the usual social pieties about Useful Trades and Crafts. He did Jewish tourism: the optimistically identified Tomb of Rachel, a site of pilgrimage, especially for childless women; and the Western Wall which, naturally, Edmond attempted to buy.

When he visited the settlements, the baronial side got the upper hand. At Rishon LeZion – which he had been told had become a nest of rebellion – he delivered imperious lectures to the farmers and ordered Joseph Feinberg, who he thought had misled him at their Paris meeting, out of the village. When Feinberg demurred, Edmond told him he was henceforth 'a dead man'. Feinberg would later reply that he had duly reported to the pearly gates only to be turned away as still living. 'There must be some mistake,' Feinberg told the angels, 'Baron Edmond has declared me dead so surely I am.' It was outrageous enough for the autocratic philanthropist to crack a smile and retract the sentence of expulsion. By the time Edmond returned in 1893, Feinberg, like many others, had left of his own accord.

The land bought for the Romanians at Samarin had become the village of Ekron, named for an ancient Canaanite and Philistine town but then speedily renamed Zikhron Ya'aqov (Memory of Jacob) for Edmond's father James. There he found much to please him: a row of neat stone houses, pantiled and whitewashed as if in Languedoc or Provence, each with a small barn for tools and draught animals. Vines were growing and surviving; a bottling plant had been built, and at the centre was an ornamental fountain, pure Rothschild style. Guided by his manager Elie Scheid, Edmond threw a banquet for the Arab villagers and their sheikh in celebration of their part in the hamlet's success. For that one evening, Jew and Arab exchanged smiles and stories as the stars came out in the darkening sky.

V. The Gadites Return

Horatio Spafford had every reason to call his little group of immigrants to Jerusalem 'the Overcomers'. He and his wife Anna had endured the afflictions of Job, if not worse. A successful lawyer, Spafford had invested in Chicago real estate only to see that investment go up in flames when a large part of the city burned down in 1871. Two years later Anna and their four children departed for an exciting European vacation. After some real estate business was seen to, Horatio would join them. But in mid-passage the *Ville du Havre* was struck and sunk by a British vessel. Anna was picked up, unconscious, clinging to a spar. All four of her children were lost. From Cardiff she telegraphed her husband piteously: 'SAVED ALONE. WHAT SHALL I DO?'

It was a rhetorical question. Anna Spafford bore more children, yet their lives seemed cursed by precariousness, the boy, Horatio Junior, dying at four of scarlet fever. It was enough to make them abandon the Presbyterian Church but not hope. Instead the Spaffords would do good works in the Holy Land in the hope of hastening the Second Coming. Horatio quit the Chicago law firm and along with the two surviving children and thirteen adults emigrated to Palestine to realise their utopian Christian mission. Lodgings were rented inside the Old City close to the Damascus Gate from where the 'American Colony' served soup and vegetables to the destitute.[32]

Around Passover 1882, on one of their evening walks, Horatio and Anna came across a group of families, camped in open fields outside the city walls. They were in a pitiful condition: covered in sores and flies, many emaciated, all of them squatting beneath bits and pieces of cloth which served as primitive tents. At first sight they appeared to be Arabs, and indeed spoke a thickly accented Arabic. But the long, oiled corkscrew sidelocks of the men, the unusual headdresses, long heavy wool skirts and silver bracelets of the women suggested otherwise. With the help of an interpreter the Spaffords learned these were Yemeni Jews. Believing the Appointed Time had come, their remnant of the tribe of Gad must make its way to Jerusalem in preparation for a messianic moment. The devotion and the ordeal were as old as the diaspora. They had walked from their Yemeni villages across Arabia to a port on the Red Sea where for an extortionate price they were given passage to Aqaba. Other Jews had warned them not to attempt the journey but they were in the grip of belief. The Torah was in their heads, every line of it memorised.

But this was of no help when they got to Jerusalem. The religious of the city brusquely rejected their claim to be Jews at all. How could that be possible, given the colour of their skin, the barbaric way they dressed and spoke? Desperate and destitute, they camped either in the fields where the Spaffords found them or in the rock-cut caves near the Mount of Olives and the Kidron Valley, amid tombs from the days of the Hasmoneans and the Romans. But on Shabbat they recited the Torah, since no one could take away their sacred memory. Even when they heard their Hebrew, the religious inside the Jewish quarter referred to the Yemenites as 'Arab Jews'. It was not meant as a compliment.

Yet the Overcomers who had once been Presbyterians believed in the 'Gadites', took them in, fed first the children, then the adults. For the guardians of orthodoxy inside the Old City walls this only confirmed the prejudice that these people could not possibly be Jews, since they ate from Christian tureens.

The Gadites stayed. Their scribes wrote the holy books from their heads. One of them whom the Spaffords loved, crippled to the point where he could not use either hand, wrote holding the goose quill between his toes. Hundreds, then thousands, followed the first cohort. By 1900 Yemenite Jews were fully 10 per cent of the Jewish population of Palestine. They built synagogues and began to recover the ancient skills of silver- and goldsmithing. They turned what had been a temporary shelter in Siloam into Kfar Hashiloach, their own village, with a religious school for the boys. For better or worse they became a fixture on the itinerary of travelling photographers specialising in the peoples of Palestine. The usual commonplaces followed: how beautiful the women were; how charming the children; how picturesquely exotic the long-bearded elders and rabbis; how wild the music; how spicy the food; who would have thought such noble types could be Jews? And eventually they ended up in large numbers on the land where the two Russian boys had lit their bonfires: Gedera.

Back at the American Colony, an elderly Yemeni rabbi did what he had to do: compose a *mi sheberach* blessing. 'He who blessed our fathers Abraham, Isaac and Jacob, bless, guard and keep Horatio Spafford and his household and all those that are joined with him for he showed mercy to our children and little ones. Therefore may the Lord make his days long in righteousness ... in his and our days may Judah be helped and the Redeemer come unto Zion and let us say Amen.'

16

SHOULD IT BE NOW?

I. The Jew in the Movies

The movies, the proper ones with characters and a plot, began, of course, with the story of a mistreated Jew. The script had everything: hero in manacles, bravely loyal wife, resolute brother, mustachioed bounder, a gunshot, a suicide. A happy ending, sort of. And it was all true, mostly.

Wherever a Palace of Varieties boasted one of Thomas Edison's Kinetiscope projectors, Alfred Dreyfus was box office. After the turbaned psychic, the dog acts, the gowned soprano with the fine embonpoint, after the leering comedian, a screen was rolled to centre stage, lights went dark, the clatter and whirr of a projector started up and there he was. Hurriedly, a superior officer has the young captain write something down and then he triumphantly arrests a thunderstruck Dreyfus. The hand matches that of a note with details of manoeuvres found in the wastebasket of the German military chargé d'affaires in Paris by a cleaning lady-cum-agent sent to snoop. *TRAHISON!* Offered a gun to blow his brains out rather than face disgrace (this bit they made up), our hero indignantly rejects the weapon along with the unjust charge. In another one-minute reel, now alas lost, he is 'degraded' in the courtyard of the École Militaire. His sword (half sawn through the previous day to make sure the ritual goes according to protocol) is snapped across the knee of a warrant officer. (On the actual day, 5 January, this officer was chosen from the largest, tallest men available to make the traitor look shrunken by villainy.) Epaulettes (likewise half unthreaded) are ripped from his military coat. Now he is just a treacherous Jew, naked in his infamy. He has lost the trappings of dignity but not its essence. Then look again (and you can, on YouTube), there he is, the solitary prisoner of Devil's Island, walled in by an eight-foot-high palisade. He is being shackled to his iron bed, struggling against this additional torment, though to no avail. But wait! All is not lost! The loving wife, the determined brother, a famous writer, are all working tirelessly for his vindication. Military skullduggery is at work. There has been forgery. The cover-up is exposed; a second court martial is granted. Now see Dreyfus land on the Breton coast in the midst of a violent storm for his date with destiny! Love smiles after the scowling tempest. After four years of separation husband and wife are reunited in tearfully conjugal embrace. But, *attention*, villainy stalks the streets. BANG! (a silent one). A puff of smoke. The gallant lawyer for the defence, Maître Labori, has been shot in the back by a dastardly assassin, yet bravely lives on to fight in court. When the journalists hear about this, a brawl breaks out between pro- and anti-Dreyfus reporters. The trial, held in a Rennes *lycée*, opens (a double reel, this). What a farce! The military judges, sitting at their high bench, deliver a face-saving conviction which makes no sense at all. Dreyfus is once more declared guilty but with 'extenuating circumstances'. Really? Instead of a life sentence to solitary on Devil's Island he is to serve a mere ten years. Our hero is led away again to prison. No! This will kill him. This *cannot* be the end?!

Audiences from one end of Europe to the other, but also on both sides of the Atlantic, anywhere music halls, variety palaces, fairgrounds could show cinematographic reels, watched agog, as the 'real life' drama unfolded before their eyes. Barely two years after the invention of the cinematograph, Georges Méliès had already fully understood the instant appeal of movie-journalism. It was not just having history replayed before you with an animated vitality against which no painting or photography could compete. Kino-news put you right there at the scene; Kino-news told you what was important. In 1897 and 1898 in his studio at Montreuil, Méliès had filmed reconstructions of the sinking of the USS *Maine* which had been the pretext for the Spanish-American war, and staged engagements from that same conflict. The battle formula was so popular that he followed it with skirmishes from the frontiers of the Raj: wily Pathans with dazzling teeth popping up from behind pasteboard pinnacles, Kipling style. For more local interest he produced scenes from the Franco-Prussian war of 1870. But then in 1899, Méliès inaugurated the genre which would become a staple of the cinema: the injustice drama.

Méliès's twelve one-minute-fifteen-second Dreyfus films would be as much a work of personal conviction as shrewd commercial showmanship. He had been converted to the urgency of the cause by his cousin Adolphe who belonged to that half of France convinced that the judgement of Dreyfus for passing military secrets to the Germans had been a judicial outrage. The accusation began in blunder, but then as the truth became known, including the identity of the real traitor, the business had rapidly deteriorated into a cover-up followed by a criminal frame-up. The handwriting on the document found by a French spy in the wastebasket of the German military attaché in Paris did not match that of Dreyfus, whatever the military authorities said. Thanks to a comparison published two years later in the press, anyone with eyes in their head could see that it was instead identical to the hand of someone else. The real traitor, Major Ferdinand Walsin Esterhazy, had an expensive mistress habit which needed funding wherever and however he could get the money. Dreyfus, independently rich (though with a racehorse habit), did not. Esterhazy was discovered to have ridiculed France and its soldiers; Dreyfus was a compulsive stickler for patriotic duty. One of them had been going down in the world and the army; the other had been coming up. The conviction made no sense, unless the army assumed that a Jew attached to its general staff was, by definition, such an anomaly that sooner or later he must be revealed as a traitor.[1]

Though caught out by the glaring evidence of Esterhazy's guilt, the army brass refused to admit its mistake, much less any wrongdoing. What, after all, was the life and liberty of a jumped-up Jew, incapable of true allegiance to his country, beside the honour of their sacrosanct institution? The high command stuck to its guns. When the head of the intelligence section of the general staff, Lieutenant Colonel Georges Picquart (an Alsatian, like Dreyfus), had discovered the identity of the real traitor and refused to suppress it, in spite of his own anti-Semitism, he was not commended for perseverance. He was first banished to Tunisia, and when he persisted he was arrested, accused of divulging military secrets.

The conspiracy of injustice unravelled of its own accord. To ensure that Dreyfus's guilt was unarguable, Major Hubert-Joseph Henry of the Statistics Section of the War Office had forged a second letter, the *petit bleu*, incriminating Dreyfus by name. But, as Picquart discovered, Henry had botched the job, patching the 'letter' from glaringly different pieces of paper. It was child's play to expose the forgery. Henry was arrested and thrown into prison, where he first confessed and then cut his throat. Playing for high stakes, his name now revealed in the Dreyfusard press, Esterhazy demanded a court martial to clear his name, reassured in advance that it would acquit, which it did.

But all efforts to shut the case down, to keep Dreyfus languishing on Devil's Island, confined to his hut and its four-metre-square fenced patch, eaten alive by tropical diseases, failed. In November 1897, France's most famous novelist, Émile Zola, joined the fray, publishing two articles on the case. The first was headlined 'A Judicial Error', the second an appeal to the Youth of France. Zola was turning the case of a single miscarriage of justice into the trial of democratic decency and justice. On 13 January 1898, Georges Clemenceau filled the front page of his newspaper, *L'Aurore*, with Zola's lengthy letter to the president of the republic, Félix Faure. The text was an explosive arraignment of the 'guilty men'. The minister of war and the army command were indicted by Zola for obstruction of justice. It was solely because he was a Jew, Zola wrote, that Dreyfus had been identified as the traitor, and only because of the curse of anti-Semitism that the charge had any credibility. It was Clemenceau who came up with the idea of the giant headline thrown over his front page, roaring 'J'Accuse ... !'

On that single day Clemenceau sold 300,000 copies of his newspaper. Zola had thrown down the gauntlet, goading his enemies to prosecute for criminal libel. The following month he got his wish amid scenes of such pandemonium and uproar that they shook even the star author, who was duly found guilty and sentenced to a year of prison. Violent anti-Zola and anti-Semitic riots broke out in seventy towns and cities around France.[2] In Nantes three thousand rioters sacked property, threatened the local rabbi and beat up store owners; in Angers, thousands went on a rampage for several days in a row.[3] There were similar outrages in Lyons, Dinant, Dijon and Avignon. The most violent assaults took place in Oran and Algiers where the virulent anti-Semite

Max Régis stirred up a full pogrom against the Jewish community of the city. A huge crowd marched through the streets of the city chanting

> *À mort les Juifs*
> *À mort les Juifs*
> *Il faut les pendre*
> *Par leurs pifs*

> Death to the Jews
> Death to the Jews
> They must be hanged
> By their snouts

Later that year, when the founder of the Anti-Semitic League of France, Édouard Drumont, was in financial trouble, Régis ensured that he was elected deputy for Algiers to the Legislative Assembly. Modern anti-Semitism now flowed into traditional Islamic disdain for Jews and Judaism and stayed in the bloodstream of Maghrebi culture with lingering, malevolent power. Zola appealed the verdict against him but after his final effort was rejected he exited the country in haste before he could be escorted to prison, appearing at Victoria Station in London on 19 July. Months were spent in exile before he returned. Better a grey suburban winter in Upper Norwood, with Sir Arthur Conan Doyle as neighbour, than incarceration.[4]

Zola's crusade was not the start, but the consummation, of the campaign to vindicate Alfred Dreyfus, whose wife Lucie and brother Mathieu had never for a moment doubted the captain's innocence. For a year or so after the traumatic public degradation in January 1895 they had done what they could to keep the case open through conventional channels. In 1896, Lucie had written to the Chamber of Deputies requesting revision. When that line of approach went nowhere Mathieu enlisted the anarchist Jewish writer Bernard Lazare, who was the first to publish the obvious but as yet unspoken truth: that it was entirely Dreyfus's Jewishness which had made him the scapegoat for another's treason.

> He is a soldier but he is a Jew and it is as a Jew he was prosecuted.
> Because he was a Jew he was arrested, because he was a Jew he was

tried, because he was a Jew the voice of justice and truth could not be heard in his favour, and the responsibility for the conviction of this innocent man falls entirely on those who provoked it by their vile excitations, lies and slander. Because of those men such a trial was possible, because of them the light could not penetrate. They needed their own Jewish traitor to replace the classic Judas, a Jewish traitor who could be called to mind every single day to cover an entire race with shame.[5]

This was no more than the truth. The journalist and novelist Maurice Barrès had cheerfully admitted that 'I need no one to tell me why Dreyfus committed treason. That he is capable of treason I conclude from his race.'[6]

Others began to join the battle on Dreyfus's behalf. They included non-Jews like the politician Auguste Scheurer-Kestner, all the more telling because, like Dreyfus, he came from Alsace, now annexed to Germany and, over many generations, home to the kind of Judaeophobia which assumed a Jew incapable of patriotic loyalty. But the whole history of the Dreyfus family had been one long affirmation in the promise of the revolution's emancipation, in an unproblematic identity as Frenchmen and -women of the Israelite religion. After the annexation of 1870, Alfred's father had moved his textile business and the family home into France when it would have been easier to stay put in the new Germany. Those Jews who joined the cause of Alfred's exoneration likewise all shared a passionate belief that they belonged fully to France. Joseph Reinach, a parliamentary deputy for Digne, was the editor of the intensely patriotic La République française; his brother, the archaeologist Salomon, despite being called 'a dirty little Jew from Hamburg' by Drumont, was co-founder of the École du Louvre. Their friend the chief rabbi Zadoc Kahn was a pillar of integration.

So as the case against Dreyfus began to fray, the question became bigger than the treatment of the Jew; rather a matter of 'what was France': its ancient traditions or its republican principles? On this matter of national identity, the country divided, making enemies of friends, alienating former comrades-in-arms and families. Edgar Degas, who since boyhood had been a close friend of Daniel Halévy, became a violent anti-Dreyfusard who had his maidservant Zoé read to him every morning at breakfast from the anti-Semitic papers.

Camille Pissarro, Jewish himself but who had drawn caricatures of the shady world of finance, became a champion of Dreyfus along with his son Lucien. Claude Monet, Félix Vallotton, Mary Cassatt and Édouard Vuillard were pro; Pierre-Auguste Renoir, Jean-Louis Forain and Paul Cézanne all bitterly anti. Writers stopped talking to each other except in abusive polemics. Charles Péguy, Anatole France and the Jewish Marcel Proust, who wrote for *La Revue Blanche*, all rallied to Dreyfus, while Maurice Barrès and Léon Daudet were virulently hostile.[7] For one side, the sacred honour of traditional institutions, above all the army, was the supreme good, and they united behind the poet Paul Déroulède's Ligue des Patriotes. For the opposing side, articulating its credo in the publications of the Société des Droits de l'Homme, France was the revolution – equal rights of citizens to republican justice – or it was nothing. 'It is a crime', Zola had written in his great rodomontade, 'to poison the minds of the humble, ordinary people, to whip reactionary and intolerant passions into a frenzy while sheltering behind the odium of anti-Semitism. France the great and liberal cradle of the rights of man will die of anti-Semitism if it is not cured of it.'

It was one of the battles between fellow writers which had caught the imagination of the first docudrama maker. In 1898 at the height of the Zola furore, the British Mutoscope and Biograph Company decided to convert the polemical duel between the abrasive, anti-Semitic Henri Rochefort and Émile Zola into an actual fight. Actors playing the parts of Zola and Rochefort thrust and lunged at each other with rapiers, their blades clashing to an inconclusive end. Never mind that the duel (unlike the real duel between Georges Clemenceau and Drumont) never happened: the film could still be billed as *réalité*.

But it was the explosive news of Dreyfus's return to France in the summer of 1899 for a second trial before a military court at Rennes which turned the Affair into a media revolution. Dreyfusards like Georges Méliès, who had begun his own career as a caricaturist, noticed that anti-Semites had made the most effective use of the popular end of publishing: Gothic caricature with its full array of monsters and victims. In those papers and magazines, the collapse of the Catholic bank, the Union générale, founded expressly to liberate finance from what was said to be the stranglehold of the Rothschilds, was laid at the door of you-know-who. 'The Jews killed the Union générale' ran the truism. Six years later a comparable collapse of the Panama Canal Company, ruining some 800,000 investors, was also said to be the fault of a global conspiracy of Jewish financiers. In fact Cornelius Herz and Baron Jacques Reinach had not been directors but they had been the money conduit to the Legislative Assembly which authorised the floating of the company. Far more non-Jewish than Jewish actors were involved in the debacle. But what difference did that make? Reinach's suicide was taken as a confession of Jewish guilt.

The great impresario of mass-market anti-Semitism, Édouard Drumont, had published his *La France Juive*, luridly illustrated, in the aftermath of the Union générale fiasco. It was an *omnium gatherum* of all the venerable motifs of Judaeophobic hatred: Christ killers, economic vampires, subhumans, masters of France, reptiles dripping with slime and engorged with their victims' blood. The book sold 100,000 copies in its first year, far and away the best-seller of the century, went through a hundred reprints and was translated into foreign-language editions all over the world. Long before *Mein Kampf*, *La France Juive* was the invitation to an extermination.

He did not have things all his own way. In 1892, two years before the Dreyfus case, Drumont had already warned that any Jewish officer in the army was bound, sooner or later, to turn traitor. But there were three hundred such officers in the French army and some took it personally, challenging their traducer in exactly the way it was claimed Jews were too weak and too cowardly to think of: a duel. On 1 June 1892, André Crémieux de Foa, one of the Crémieux dynasty, whose rise in French public life symbolised the success of emancipation, fought Drumont with sabres. After wounds were inflicted on both parties the duel was stopped. Dissatisfied with the outcome, Drumont had a surrogate, the Marquis de Morès, fight another Jewish officer, Armand Mayer, on the Île de la Jatte. Morès was in his own right an extraordinary figure who had gone to the United States to repair his depleted aristocratic fortunes. A cattle-farming venture in North Dakota did well enough, but when he tried vertical integration of the business, slaughtering and packing directly, and was thwarted by the great Chicago packers, he blamed his failure, of course, on the Jews who ran the American economy. Back in France his goal was to rebrand the nobility as warriors who would take on the Jews. The least he could do, then, was to fight the upstart immanently treacherous

Jew officer Armand Mayer. It was not a fair fight as Mayer's arm was already injured before the duel began, but conscious of predictable imputations of cowardice, Mayer absurdly went ahead. Within five seconds Morès's weapon had penetrated Mayer's lung and spinal cord and he died in hospital that evening. Morès was arrested for homicide, tried and of course acquitted. The chief rabbi of Paris Zadoc Kahn presided at the funeral, but more astonishingly, tens of thousands – some said 20,000, some 100,000 – came for the obsequies, in an evident demonstration of solidarity against the anti-Semites.

For a while it seemed that Drumont and his cause were on the defensive, his journal *La Libre Parole* in financial trouble. Dreyfus, then, was a godsend. The journal broke the news of a guilty party being a Jew, and then for years afterwards went to town on Jews as constitutionally incapable of loyalty. 'I've been telling you for eight years that Jews are traitors,' he crowed. The text of *La Libre Parole* was now luridly illustrated with the entire bestiary of anti-Semitic grotesques: a giant Jew-spider trapping France in his foul and hairy web; the vampirical Jew sinking his fangs and talons into the helpless body of his French victims, the hook-nosed, blubber-lipped monster drooling over his prey. Drawing on ancient Christian demonologies of the Jews as Lucifer's accomplices, the Jews were turned into satanic conspirators. Their Sabbaths were occult; their books, full of spells and murderous stratagems; their perpetual prey, the lives of Christian innocents. The cover of *La Libre Parole* for 7 November 1894, sixteen days after Drumont had identified Dreyfus as the 'traitor', features two Jews vainly trying to wash blood from their hands and clothes. The caption reads: 'Jews, for us in France, only blood can get out a stain like that.'[8] The phantasmagoria chimed perfectly with the *fin de siècle* taste for the horrific macabre: monsters walking among us, dressed in waistcoats and spats. There was also a strong scatological strain in the cartooning. When he wasn't drawn as a pig, Zola was very often represented naked from the waist down on the toilet while clutching a little doll of Dreyfus. In another image the pig Zola, in the business of fouling himself, smears excrement on the map of France.[9]

'*J'Accuse*' redressed the imbalance of sensation, somewhat. But the tone of the Dreyfusards was sententious. They specialised in lofty appeals to civic decency, the eternal spirit of the revolution. Many of their earliest appeals were delivered in the pages of newspapers and journals catering to the enlightened and thus with modest circulations, although after a while illustrated magazines like *Le Sifflet* competed for mass attention with its opposite number *Psst*. For the most part Dreyfusard polemics were too fastidious to deliver shock images, except when they had a go at clerical obscurantism and when the army cover-up became too nefarious to miss.

Like much of France, Georges Méliès had been initially unmoved by the fate of Dreyfus, though the spectacle of the Jewish officer retaining his dignity during the monstrous degradation at the École Militaire was an extraordinary drama. But after his cousin Adolphe had persuaded him of Dreyfus's innocence, he made the one-minute shorts which lent the cause the persuasive power of popular entertainment, not least because the films could be bought individually or as a whole set. One way or another the Jews and the movies were destined to come together.

Méliès shot *L'Affaire Dreyfus* during August and September 1899 in his custom-built studio with its internal glass walls, at Montreuil, on the outskirts of Paris. He used newspaper photographs as the basis for his dramatised reconstructions, and cast a local ironworker as the imprisoned hero on the strength of his resemblance to Alfred Dreyfus rather than any particular talent for acting. Halfway through filming, the ironworker's jaw blew up from a sudden dental abscess which meant that Méliès was only able to film the good side of his face. Nonetheless, the little scraps of films, shot as they were on giant 68mm format, are brilliant in their dramatic immediacy. Méliès scarcely had to exaggerate anything to deliver gripping action history. He himself played the part of Maître Labori, one of Dreyfus's two defence lawyers at the trial, and the intended target of the pistol-packing assassin at Rennes. The films had everything the people's theatre craved: conjugal tenderness, wicked conspiracy, inhuman incarceration, an impenetrably stoic star. And unlike theatre, the films could, and did, travel. From San Francisco to Odessa they played and played. When there was a great protest meeting in Hyde Park at the transparently absurd verdict of the second trial, it was because the crowds would have learned about Dreyfus from the movies.

The Dreyfus craze went intercontinental. One of Louis Lumière's photographers, Francis Doublier, recalled in his memoirs that he had been travelling in Ukraine in 1898 when he realised that the audience for his talk on the Dreyfus Affair at Zhitomir (heavily Jewish) had a passion to see the plot played out on screen. The obliging Doublier faked a spectacle using some old shots of soldiers, pretending they were part of the Dreyfus story, but inevitably there was a local know-all pointing out that some of the scenes (the degradation), purportedly shot live, had taken place before the first movie cameras had become available in late 1895.

The thirst for on-screen Dreyfus was not going to be satisfied by Méliès alone. At about the same time Charles and Émile Pathé began their own filmed docudrama reconstructions. In 1907 they revisited the story with a film which had the advantage of being able to include Dreyfus's vindication and ceremonial reinstatement as an officer in the army, taking place on the same parade ground of the École Militaire that had witnessed his degradation twelve years earlier. More revolutionary still, the first authentic on-the-spot newsreel was made by the French branch of the British Mutoscope and Biograph Company, which decided to put actuality, not actors, before the public.

The Breton city of Rennes, the site of the retrial, was packed with journalists and photographers from all over the globe. The daily walk of Lucie, together with Mathieu Dreyfus, to see Alfred in his pre-retrial confinement gave a determined Mutoscope cameraman a precious opportunity for human-interest filming. But the cinematic holy grail was a shot of Dreyfus himself. Fearing that the sight of the prisoner – much emaciated and aged by his ordeal on Devil's Island – would generate public sympathy, the military authorities had covered the windows of his cell with wooden slats. Should a determined cameraman attempt to film Dreyfus's brief turns for exercise, they covered the space with a tarpaulin. Undeterred, and deaf to the pleas of Lucie and Mathieu to leave the family alone, the most intrepid of the cameramen, a M. Orde, who had been carting his enormous Biograph camera around the streets of Rennes, organised the erection of scaffolding high above the rooftop of a house facing Dreyfus's place of confinement. For a brief moment he was rewarded with the glimpse the whole world wanted of the tragic hero.

And what did those flickering images beyond the blue smoke of the projectors reveal? Why, that Dreyfus was just a man like any other. He didn't even seem to look that Jewish. Despite readily available photographs, the countless caricatures of the 'traitor' had altered his appearance to conform better with the anti-Semitic stereotype. All Jews, it was well known, had hooked noses, so the cartoon Dreyfus was equipped with one. But *this* man, the Jew in the movies – and in the welter of half-tone photographs circulating around the globe – had a rather refined nose to go with his studious, solemn demeanour and pince-nez. This affirmation of ordinary humanity was just as well, since the period following Zola's trial and the forger Henry's suicide had seen an outbreak of anti-Semitism which went well beyond the usual stereotypes towards a modern pathology. On the lookout for opportunities to sway public opinion, Drumont had had the clever idea of turning Henry's widow into a grieving woman, every bit as faithful and wronged as Lucie Dreyfus, whose steadfastness had become a legend for the other camp. He got an unexpected gift when Scheurer-Kestner went a step too far, suggesting that Henry had not only been a party to the cover-up but a treacherous co-conspirator of Esterhazy's. Drumont was then able to launch a public appeal for a 'Monument Henry': a fund to support the widow and pay any legal costs to clear the dead man's name.

The 'Monument Henry' quickly drew 25,000 subscribers. Drumont published their names, organised by social class or profession – the Church, the aristocracy, the army and so on – along with any comments they cared to make in addition to pledging money. Those comments are an inventory of dehumanising abuse against the Jews, often called by their anti-Semitic slang '*youtres*' or '*youpins*'. The demonisation was so violent that the pro-Dreyfus poet Pierre Quillard reprinted them verbatim in his own journal as a way of provoking horror and shame in the undecided public. In keeping with the new vocabulary of anti-Semitism there was the usual biological-zoological-bacteriological colouring to the abuse. Jews were 'cosmopolitan vermin', 'the phyl-loxera of commerce', monkeys, snakes, vultures, festering microbes, walking contaminants. France had to be protected from such parasitical contagions, by evicting them en masse from the country. Once they had been forced to wear yellow clothes and rounded up they could be packed off to their 'precious Judaea', the Sahara or to Devil's Island. Someone had better be organising a mass mobilisation of carts needed for their deportation. Or, if the logistics proved too complicated, they could just be destroyed, physically, wherever they could be found.

Just how the filthy *youtres* would be disposed of invited a rich variety
of suggestions. Their mouths could be sewn up, their eyes gouged
out, their noses slit or smashed, their teeth knocked in. They could
be dunked in boiling oil, laved with acid, turned into mincemeat,
white sausage (*boudin blanc*), tripe, pâté, or shredded into dog food (if
any self-respecting hound would eat them). They could be bled, flayed,
guillotined, burned alive in glass furnaces, poisoned with strychnine
or rat poison, their skins could be tanned and made into military
drums, boots or parchment to write on. Since they were so fond of
music, their guts could string cellos and violins. One proudly self-
identifying anti-Semitic medical student wanted Jews, rather than
'some innocent rabbit', to be vivisected for his anatomy classes; but
another wrote that their hides were too tough and their smell too
nauseating for this to be practical. 'I wouldn't harm a fly,' wrote
another, 'but I do say "death to the Jews".' A proud mother wrote that
she would see to it that her five-day-old daughter Germaine grew up
to be an anti-Semite. In the section for the armed services a self-
identified group of officers, stationed on the borders of the *patrie*,
reported that it 'impatiently awaited orders to try out the latest artillery on the hundred thousand Jews poisoning the country'. The clergy,
led on by the anti-Semitic order of the Assumptionists and their journal
La Croix, preserved, at the diocesan level, a more decorous tone. But
further down the social scale there were *curés de campagne* (country
priests) who didn't at all mind 'ardently wishing for the extermination'
of the Jews, to which they often added that other bugbear of Catholic
paranoia, the Freemasons. 'Extermination' was a term which appears
with unapologetic frequency in almost all of the categories: the
'nobility', law, medicine, schools and universities, and of course among
writers. One 'Michelon of Tours' exclaimed that 'to see the last *youtre*
breathe his last will cause us to expire with sheer pleasure'. Others
said that they were offering donations not just to the unfortunate
widow and the monument but to 'buy rope to hang all the Jews'.

Pierre Quillard evidently felt that by republishing all this outpouring
of deranged hatred he could sway the undecided into recoiling from
it, joining the party of decency. He was wrong. The exposure merely
reinforced the malicious glee. A monstrously bloated infection
ruptured the fragile membrane of civility, and began to foul the body
politic of the modern age.[10]

II. A Curtain Rises

Was this what it took, the victimisation of a bespectacled captain seen on screen, to make the story of the Jews the story of humanity? A single grainy photograph of the degradation survives, shot from behind spectators who have their faces pressed to the courtyard railings. This makes spectating the subject of the picture as much as the degradation itself. Maurice Barrès, the author of *The Cult of Me* and the editor of *La Cocarde* (*The Cockade*), characterised the spectacle as more exciting than witnessing an execution by guillotine. The object of that excitement, of course, had to be the degraded Jew, and the thrill of seeing it refreshed the ancient tradition of watching Jews laid low: the autos-da-fé; the witch burning in Mantua; the 'Games of the Jews' in Rome; all good for a yell and a cackle. A writer for the British Photographic Society, commenting on the picture and understanding the potential of vicarious, malevolent excitement for the new medium, called the print 'prosecution by photograph'.[11] This, of course, did not prevent it from travelling, even though a French ban on taking pictures of such public events ensured it would not be printed in the country where it most counted.

In 1895, after Dreyfus had been locked away on Devil's Island, the case went quiet. No one outside the army's judiciary knew that he had been convicted without seeing what was said to be an incriminating 'secret dossier'. Late in 1896, with the publication of Bernard Lazare's eloquently infuriated pamphlet, however, the case began to turn into the 'Affaire'. Once Zola joined the campaign a year later, the whole business became universalised, going beyond the Jews to become a cautionary prophecy of what the oncoming century might have in store. Was there a fight coming between democratic decencies and visceral prejudice, between reason and passion, justice and tribal solidarity? Zola certainly thought so, going so far as to declare that the very survival of the Third Republic turned on recognising and correcting the indecency of anti-Semitism. Enemies, like Édouard Drumont, of course, felt precisely the opposite: that France, if not all Europe, would perish if the Jews were not dealt with – curbed, removed, eliminated. At stake for the antagonists was the character of the modern nation state: what might emerge from the atrophy and eventual collapse of the dynastic empires? Would successor nations be grounded in ethics or ethnicity, tribal romance or constitutional principle? Would they be shaped by Enlightenment assumptions of the equality of citizens or the mystical communion of race, blood, geography and memory? In one poignant letter from the imprisoned Dreyfus to his wife, he expressed bewilderment that the Enlightenment, whose emphasis on reason he had honoured all his life, should have been so brutally set side. The general contention was broader than 'can the Jews be truly French?' (or German or Russian or British). The argument turned into a debate about roots, an argument in which the wandering, cosmopolitan Jews, habitually accused of rootlessness, were bound to be on the defensive. The monarchist *ultra* Léon Daudet insisted that Dreyfus, whatever he said, was 'not French' and this presumption extended to anyone naively believing in his innocence. Barrès drolly conceded Zola's sincerity in defending Dreyfus, but only because that transparency exposed the awkward fact that Zola was not actually French at all. Barrès himself had been born in the Auvergne but his family was from Lorraine, from the eastern frontier departments lost to Germany in 1870 and which were still theatres of cultural war. A barrier, he wrote, separated him and Zola. 'What is that barrier? It is the Alps ... because his father and the line of his ancestors were Venetian. Émile Zola thinks like a deracinated Venetian.'[12]

In the minds of ultra-nationalists like Barrès, geography and history were a matter of indifference to the Jews. Their only homeland was the realm of money. Wandering wherever it beckoned, they sought each other out. Ergo, a Jew was incapable of patriotism, which presupposed a deep-rooted attachment to a particular country. Dreyfus's crime, then, had been to wear the uniform when he was biologically incapable of embodying the loyalty it symbolised. If, at the very moment of his disgrace and in the loudest voice he could command, Dreyfus protested his unbroken allegiance to the fatherland and the army, this was read by the likes of Barrès as just another sign of the Jewish capacity for masquerade. The mask, behind which lay the countenance of the monster, was a favourite theme of anti-Semitic caricaturists.[13]

But when they saw him on that grey winter morning of 5 January 1895, not everyone thought Dreyfus was masked. His stoicism during the degradation as the crowd shouted 'Judas' and 'Death to the Jews'

seemed unforced and, in fact, what was expected of military composure. Dreyfus's sobriety wrong-footed anti-Semitic expectations. Jews,
even when they were not traitors, were supposed to be hyper-nervous,
gesticulating, agitated. Where, then, was the remorseful, broken creature slumped in humiliation? And why wasn't Dreyfus crying instead
of remaining visibly dry-eyed throughout the fifteen-minute ordeal?
Aggravatingly, Dreyfus refused to play the part of the overawed degen-
erate. He carried his head high, defying orders to remain decently
mute, voicing his innocence and loyalty to France and the army. On
leaving the parade ground under guard, passing a group of spectators
hissing 'Judas', Dreyfus even had the temerity to say, 'I *forbid* you to
insult an innocent man.'

Dreyfus's stoicism forced unsympathetic spectators to switch tack
and treat his *lack* of emotion as a sign of abnormality. Léon Daudet
described him as 'a rigid puppet' before reverting to Toussenel's
zoology of abuse: 'a weasel'. Or, could he have been made of stone?
The reporter for *Le Matin* described him, not flatteringly, as 'a living
statue'. 'Does he feel anything? Is he even conscious?' Others attributed
the inhuman self-mastery to Dreyfus's 'Germanic' character. For
Barrès, Dreyfus's 'ashen' complexion, the 'colour of treason', gave
him away, for it was the pallor of the 'debris of the ghetto'. Others
thought they detected a slight limp. Neutrals, though, responded
differently to Dreyfus's extraordinary composure. One of them, the
Paris correspondent of the Vienna paper the *Neue Freie Presse* (edited
by the Jews Moritz Benedikt and Eduard Bacher, but studiously unpar-
tisan), wrote that, on entering the courtyard, 'Dreyfus marched like
a man convinced of his innocence' and that the 'strangely resolute
attitude of the degraded captain ... made a deep impression on many
eye-witnesses'.[14]

Four years later in 1899, that same journalist, Theodor Herzl, would
insist that the Dreyfus case had been his dark epiphany, the moment
that he became a Zionist. But this may have been a case of back-
projection on his part. As Jacques Kornberg and Shlomo Avineri have
noticed, the case featured barely at all in his diaries and correspondence at the time.[15] But that, of course, is true for many of the fiercest
Dreyfusards who, before Bernard Lazare launched his barrage at the
army, had no inkling of the depth of the conspiracy, nor of the anti-
Semitism which drove it. Herzl actually met Lazare in the autumn of

1896, was very favourably struck by him, and in November, well in advance of public opinion, wrote in his diary that it was likely that Dreyfus was, in fact, innocent.[16]

Much historiographical heat has been spent on whether it was Paris or Vienna, Dreyfus or the demagoguery of the anti-Semitic Christian Social Party, which contributed most decisively to Herzl's Zionist epiphany. But the two scenarios aren't mutually exclusive. Between 1893 and 1895 he was often travelling back and forth between the two cities. Some of the reasons were personal. His bitterly unhappy marriage to Julie Naschauer, the teenage daughter of a wealthy distributor of drilling and drainage machinery, wells and pumps, had disintegrated quickly. Herzl wanted a divorce, but to spare the children they separated rather than formally ending the marriage. In 1892 Julie moved to Paris, as did Herzl's parents. His Vienna world thus came to him, and with it, increasingly dismaying news of the rise of mass anti-Semitism. Temperamentally and intellectually Herzl mistrusted democracy, believing it a gift to demagogues able to exploit uneducated people who, from 1895, had the vote. What was unfolding in Vienna, where anti-Semitism moved from verbal to physical violence, only reinforced his pessimism. There were outbreaks of window smashing, shop burning and random physical attacks on the street. Herzl had personal experience of it when on leaving a tavern he was shouted at as a bloody Jew. Karl Lueger, about to be vice burgomaster of the city, and his Christian Socials had campaigned on a platform of repealing emancipation and ultimately expelling the Jews from the empire. This is what the peasants, artisans and small shopkeepers who blamed the Jews for any economic hardship wanted to hear. As anti-Semitic rhetoric caught fire, Liberals who had been the champions of Jewish emancipation refrained from any criticism of anti-Semitism lest the protest lose them votes – much good it did them.

For Herzl this was deeply chilling. He had already come to the conclusion that emancipation had failed. Its promise had been that, as the obstacles on education, residence and occupation fell away, as Jews became more fully integrated into liberal society, so the root causes of anti-Semitism – the concentration of Jews in the world of money, their separation from their fellow citizens – would also disappear, and with them, Judaeophobia. Enlightenment would banish the remnants of ancient paranoias about Christ killers, child murderers, and the rest. But none of this had happened. Blood-libel accusations recurred every few years. In 1882 the Jews of Tiszaeszlar in Hungary were accused of killing a local girl whose body was found in a river. Her mother blamed the Jews, they had killed her for the blood everyone knew Jews needed to bake Passover matzot, and the charge was repeated by politicians in the Hungarian House of Deputies who called for the expulsion of Jewish members from the legislature. Fifteen members of the local community were accused of ritual murder on the strength of a 'confession' extracted from a five-year-old Jewish boy. When the prisoners were acquitted and the charges found baseless, anti-Semitic riots broke out in Hungarian towns, including Herzl's boyhood home of Budapest.

But it was the modern predicament of assimilated Jews which most exercised Herzl. The more such Jews integrated themselves into business and professions, the more hatred they provoked. Liberals like his editors at the *Neue Freie Presse*, or modern rabbis like Zadoc Kahn and Moritz Güdemann, Jellinek's successor in Vienna, were deluding themselves. Short of some drastic act of collective transformation, anti-Semitism would never go away. So, in 1893 Herzl proposed in the pages of the weekly journal of Vienna's Defence Association Against Anti-Semitism, and in all seriousness, the most drastic change he could think of: a negotiation with the Pope to bring about the wholesale conversion of Austrian Jews. Moreover, this was not to happen piecemeal, or secretively, but deliberately staged as a great public drama. There would be a procession in broad daylight to St Stephen's Cathedral where a mass baptism would take place. Only then would the promise of assimilation, something Herzl evidently longed for, be realised. It would be, he wrote, 'a reconciliation' not a capitulation. In a perverse way, Herzl thought of a conversion which was self-willed, not coerced, as an act of Jewish empowerment.

Was he crazy? Was the sacrifice of martyrs precisely to avoid such a fate of no concern to him? Did he not repeatedly say how moved he was by two millennia of Jewish endurance? But Herzl had had enough of sacrifice, of the *kiddush hashem*, the sanctification of the name which was just, he supposed, a euphemism for collective suicide. Rather, live. In 1893 his own attachment to Judaism was minimal. He was not a synagogue-goer. Hebrew was a closed book. Intermarriage, he believed, might be another good way to blunt the edge of anti-Semitism. Nonetheless the pull of Jewish identity was strong and written into his family history. The Herzls had originally been Loebs or Lobls, the root of which was '*lev*', Hebrew for heart, hence the Germanisation. Their ancestral town was Semlin in Serbia, now a north-western district of greater Belgrade and nondescript except, in the earlier half of the nineteenth century, for one powerful presence: the Bosnian Sephardi rabbi Yehuda Alkalai, who devoted much of his life to preaching the mass return of Jews to Palestine.[17] Alkalai was in Semlin from 1825, at the same time as Herzl's paternal grandfather Simon, first as teacher and then as rabbi, and although he wrote initially in Ladino, it seems inconceivable that the Lobls/Herzls would not have been aware of his presence and fame. Alkalai's belief, set out in 'The Third Redemption' and considered a Kabbalistic heresy by the Orthodox, was that a Jewish return need not wait for the appearance of the Messiah but could be its precursor, and that since, according to his scanning of the messianic calendar, the auspicious era was to begin in 1840 (and last a century before realisation), such work should begin at once. There were, of course, other proto-Zionists in his generation, Moses Hess and Rabbi Zvi Kalischer, but unlike Alkalai neither had actually been to Jerusalem. Alkalai had studied there as a youth, and when he envisioned the restoration of Jews, he thought in terms of practical settlement, especially agricultural, as well as a religious rebirth. A startling number of Herzl's own propositions, set out in *The State of the Jews* in 1896, were exactly anticipated by Alkalai half a century earlier, including a Land Bank to acquire arable property, a Jewish Joint Stock Company, an organisation of Jewish notables as trustees, and an offer to help modernise the Ottoman economy and communications. But Alkalai was adamant that the language of Jewish restoration had to be Hebrew, while Herzl, who knew little or none, thought such an idea quaintly oriental and assumed if there was to be a dominant tongue it must be the true language of civilisation: German.

Just how Jewish Herzl was when, following the traumatically sudden death of his sister from typhoid at the age of nineteen, the family moved from Budapest to Vienna is questionable. Though they lived a short walk from the enormous reform temple on Dohany Street, his mother and father were not regular service-goers. Young Theodor was sent to a Jewish elementary school where the headmaster was a published scholar, but he seems to have had an informal 'confirmation' at home rather than a synagogue bar mitzvah. And much of his experience of being Jewish, both in Budapest and Vienna, was likely to have been negative: yelled insults in the schoolyard, snickering at the gymnasium. After the Vienna Stock Exchange crash of 1873 he would have heard the usual attacks on the Jews (especially the Rothschilds) for bringing about the disaster, even though the stockbroker Jakob Herzl was one of its many Jewish victims.

None of this, however, made the young Herzl lose faith in the possibility that he could be another successful, upwardly mobile Jew. At Vienna University, where he studied law, he joined the debating union, the Akademische Lesehalle, then embattled between Austrian loyalists and increasingly strident young German nationalists.[18] Although its statutes were supposed to keep the club neutral, it invited the arch anti-Semite Georg von Schönerer to give speeches more than once. Herzl was also admitted to one of the university fencing clubs, 'Albia'. Entry was conditional on an initiating bout which would produce the required scar of honour on the student cheek, an exercise for which Herzl practised long and hard, but he thought he gave a poor account of himself. It was enough, though, to get the needed nick. It would have been possible for Herzl to have joined one of the duelling *Korps* like 'Danubia', more loyal to the multinational empire, and thus more populated by Jewish students. But Herzl chose the more aggressively Germanising Albia, with its casual anti-Semitic joking. He himself was known, surely ironically, as 'Tancred Prince of Galilee', a specimen of that oddity, the tall, handsome Jew, who would be a source of entertainment for the sheer peculiarity of it. So for a while Herzl played the part, strutting around in the Albia blue cap and sash, swinging his black cane with the ivory handle. He drank with the lads, fornicated with girls, suffered hangovers and doses of the clap. But even while putting on a good show, the man who declared himself to be 'a German Jew from Hungary' and was doing his best to be neither, began to torment himself for bad faith. In the German nationalist fraternities an assembly was organised to memorialise the recently deceased Richard Wagner. Herzl had nothing against Wagner – quite the opposite, he was an enthusiast – but he claimed the event had descended into rank anti-Semitism and resigned from Albia, turning in his blue cap and sash. Jacques Kornberg has noticed that in fact the Wagner event featured speeches that were much more German nationalist and not especially anti-Semitic, at least no more than had generally been the case during Herzl's years of membership. But Herzl, listening to his own inner voice, made it anti-Semitic enough for him to leave the corps.

Departure from Albia did not signal a sudden attachment to Jewish self-defence. The next years were spent practising law, first in Vienna, then in Salzburg, but all the while hankering for the literary life he assumed intellectuals of Jewish origin but German sensibility should lead. Back in Budapest he and his sister had founded a literary maga-zine they called *Wir* (*We*) and increasingly Herzl cast himself as a writer. He was torn between novels, journalism and the theatre, but hoped somehow to try his hand at all three genres. He abandoned the law, and began to write in earnest while living the life of the boulevardier dandy. There were trips to Heidelberg and Paris, summers with his parents at lakeside spas, the odd essay published in papers and magazines. And there were girls. In the way of things diagnosed by his literary doctor friend Arthur Schnitzler, they were either working girls, society courtesans, or the opposite, young, sometimes very young, adolescents whom he extolled as creatures of tender purity. In 1889 he married one of them, Julie Naschauer, with predict-ably disastrous consequences.

Then there were the plays: light comedies, speedily tossed off, of an innocuous and forgettable kind, but audience-friendly enough to get performed; operettas without the music or dancing. Herzl's consuming ambition was to have one of his plays produced at Vienna's prime house, the Burgtheater. Failing that he was happy enough to have them receive performances in Berlin as well as Vienna.

But on the same day that Alfred Dreyfus was led away under arrest, 21 October 1894, Herzl, in what he described as a kind of creative delirium, began work on a drama the purpose of which was polemical rather than entertainment. *Das neue Ghetto* (*The New Ghetto*) featured a great deal of speechifying from the front of the stage and an unhappy, assimilated, upwardly mobile Jewish lawyer called Jacob Samuel, not wholly dissimilar from the author. His dreams of being completely accepted are sabotaged by his brother-in-law's shady dealings with the usual wastrel aristocrat, Schramm. It all ends badly. Jacob's non-Jewish best friend dumps him, a rejection from which he never recovers, and inevitably he is on the fatal short end of a duel with Schramm. (Herzl is *obsessed* with duelling.)[19] In his diary, begun in the spring of 1895, in which Herzl embraced what he called the *Judensache*, the cause of the Jews, he dated his awareness of the futility of assimilation to the shock of reading Eugen Dühring's ferociously anti-Semitic treatise *On the Jewish Question* fourteen years earlier. Dühring's book argued that the fundamental racial difference dividing Jews from Aryans could never be harmonised, however much the former put on a veneer of culture. Coming as it did from a self-described 'realist' and 'socialist' professing to believe (like Adam Smith!) that social bonds were generated by instinctive moral sympathy, a quality from which Jews were excluded, Dühring's denunciations made Herzl see all his Germanising as a dead end. 'As the years went by the *Jewish Question* bored into me, tormenting me and making me very miserable.'[20]

It was, however, only in 1894–5 that a solution to this bitter predicament began to crystallise in Herzl's mind. Nothing short of the establishment of a state for the Jews, a place where they might control their own destinies and where being Jewish would be a badge of honour rather than shame, could give them self-respect. When he began to outline the plan – to himself and to prospective Jewish magnates like Maurice de Hirsch – Herzl was only dimly aware (if at all) of the many Zionist predecessors like Moses Hess, Leon Pinsker and the Hovevei Zion. Pinsker had died in Odessa in 1891 and when, five years later, Herzl got round to reading *Auto-Emancipation*, he professed astonishment that they shared so many ideas.

What Herzl did not share with either the Lovers of Zion or for that matter with Alkalai was their practical gradualism, the strong sense that, to begin with, seeds should be planted in Palestinian soil (literally as well as metaphorically) and that a Jewish society, different from its mostly religious presence in Jerusalem and Galilee, had to take root before there could be any question of political nationalism. Herzl was as uninterested in Judaeo-Palestinian incrementalism as he was in Jewish liberal incrementalism in Europe. Both, he thought, were doomed to disappointment and were no answer for the urgency of the times. Jews were being beaten up, their houses and shops burned, smashed up. Before long there would be killing, of that he was sure. What Herzl also added to proto-Zionist writing was a conviction, surely born of his familiarity with anti-Semitic remarks about getting rid of the Jews, that mass emigration could be sold to the great powers. This instinct was not just tactical but natural for Herzl. As an assimilated Jew who had courted every kind of non-Jewish audience, and had even flirted with mass apostasy, he did still want there to be some sort of 'reconciliation', a convergence of historical interests if not destinies. Zionism had to be seen to be as good for non-Jews as well as Jews. When he told the kaiser that his solution would 'drain' excess Jews from Germany, why should he not be believed? When he told the Turkish sultan Abdul Hamid that in return for permitting a return to Palestine, Jewish money would liberate his empire from the European Debt Control Commission, he imagined the sultan jumping for joy.

He was going to make everyone happy! For only when the Jews who really wanted to be Jews left Europe for their homeland could the Jews who didn't want to be Jews rest assured of the success of their assimilation. What evidently Herzl did not believe in was the kind of diaspora pluralism which offered the hope of living a fully Jewish life outside a Jewish nation state. Such myopia, he thought, was asking for trouble. When he bumped into Moritz Güdemann, the Vienna rabbi who became an outspoken opponent of Zionism and who asked Herzl (with an air of facetious disingenuousness) to 'explain' Zionism, he commented that the rabbi pontificated to him about the Jewish 'mission' to be dispersed through the world, of refusing to abandon the fight against anti-Semitism at home. All that, Herzl believed, was sanctimonious self-deception, a recipe for mass suicide under the guise of liberal pieties.

He had had enough of low-profile meliorism. The Herzl of 1895 wanted to take his talent for drama out of the theatre and into the chambers of the powerful, but most of all to the clamorous, terrified Jews themselves. A big piece of him was Wagnerian and Nietzschean, for he fervently believed that unanticipated, undreamt-of change would only happen through some willed act of consciousness-raising. Herzl now cast himself as the dramaturge of a Jewish-national awakening. Time was spent in front of the mirror studying the look, rehearsing his part. Costume and body language were as important for politics as for any stage actor. First impressions counted, and he meant to confound assumptions of the powerful about how a Jew spoke, walked, dressed, laughed. Herzl himself spoke a quasi-Prussian

Hochdeutsch, with no traces of the Yiddish he despised but neither with the lilting softness of Austrian or Hungarian accents. This too was a choice.

His idol at this time was Otto von Bismarck, whom he believed personified national accomplishment through the force of personal conviction and a flair for the dramatic. Such was Herzl's admiration for the Iron Chancellor, now in metal-fatigue mode, retired and powerless, that he wrote to him seeking sympathetic support for Zionism. Reply came there none. This could hardly have been a surprise. Their positions were absurdly disparate, but since Bismarck's unification had been funded by his Jewish banker Gerson von Bleichröder, Herzl wondered why some of that same money could not now be applied to the Zionist project. With or without Bismarck, Herzl's priority was High Chutzpah: the imaginative audacity which would bowl over the naysayers and electrify the masses. Herzl believed that the coming age of mass politics, of shouting in the streets, would, for good or ill, turn on such lightning-struck conversions. The new politics was old religion, vulgarised. Its currency was revelation not reason. Conventional liberalism, whether Jewish or Gentile, with its painstaking calculus of gains and losses, its twitchy nervousness that temerity was a vote-loser, was doomed to give way to the more adrenalin-driven charismatics of the mass age. If the Jews did not take the plunge into these dangerous, turbulent waters, they would be engulfed in the breaking tide.

All this – amounting to a blueprint for the creation of a modern Jewish national identity – Herzl scribbled down in a fever of conviction. But he began the diary which recorded his conversion to historical vocation, to the cause of the Jews, the *Judensache*, with an entry of self-dramatising solemnity.

> For some time past I have been occupied with a work of infinite grandeur. At the moment I do not know whether I shall carry it through. It looks like a mighty dream. But for days and weeks it has possessed me beyond the limits of consciousness; it accompanies me wherever I go, hovers behind my ordinary talk, looks over my shoulder at my comically trivial journalism, disturbs and intoxicates me.[21]

Pursuing the multimillionaires who could make the project live or kill it stone dead, Herzl anticipated what he knew would be their scepticism, patronising comments about its impracticality, condescension towards a typical intellectual who (unlike them) was innocent of the cold facts of monied power. So he wrote and wrote, at least as much in self-clarification and rehearsal as for the edification of prospective patrons.

Target number one was Baron Maurice de Hirsch, who had used his fortune to fund the Alliance Israélite Universelle, and the Jewish Colonisation Association, which brought Jews from Russia and Romania to Palestine, but also to the United States, Brazil and Argentina where Hirsch hoped to transform them into farmers and cattle ranchers. With what would become his trademark cheek, Herzl wrote to Hirsch more or less telling him he was wasting his time and money. He needed to think bigger. He knew that the baron would think him a fantasist, building castles in the sky, but 'Believe me, the policy of an entire people, particularly when it is scattered over the earth, can be carried out only with imponderables that float in thin air. Do you know what went into the making of the German Empire? Dreams, songs, fantasies and black-red-and-gold ribbons – and in short order. Bismarck merely shook the tree which the visionaries had planted. What? You do not understand the imponderable? And what is religion? Consider, if you will what the Jews have endured for the sake of this vision over a period of two thousand years.'[22]

All the memorandum-writing was cut short by a note from Hirsch himself letting Herzl know he would be in Paris for a few days at the beginning of June and would be able to receive him 'at home' at 2 rue de l'Élysée.

This sounded like a domestic address albeit in the richest district of Paris – it had once been owned by Émile Péreire. Nothing quite prepared Herzl for the scale of the establishment. 'It is a palace,' he wrote in his diary, still awestruck, after the meeting on 3 June. He was not exaggerating. Hirsch had amalgamated three houses on one side and two on the other to make something stupendous, but which at the same time made him the choice target of critics of the Jewish nouveau riche. Drumont had a fine old time with 2 rue de l'Élysée, noting that the ceremonial staircase was so immense that an entire regiment could ascend without much crush. In fact Hirsch's wealth was not at all nouveau, though it was very Jewish. He and his wife both came from a long line of *Hoffuden*. His grandfather had been ennobled as banker to the king of Bavaria, his mother was a Wertheimer, and his father had expanded the business under Louis Napoleon to a colossal scale. Maurice himself had gone into railways, copper and sugar, and laid the financial foundation for the Orient Express on which three years later Theodor Herzl would travel into history. When Herzl met him in Paris he was worth a cool hundred million francs.

In theory Herzl despised philanthropy, but when he walked through the endless enfiladed rooms, over floors of white marble, past mirrored doors imitating the Galerie des Glaces at Versailles, the palace which was the neighbour of Hirsch's own Château de Beauregard, he surrendered to the magnificence. '*Donnerwetter!*' Such unexpected good taste! He peered at the pictures; his fingers brushed the gilded arms of rococo chairs. Perruqued flunkeys peered snootily at him. He became self-conscious about his dress; a frequent occurrence. All of which set him on edge and prone to overreact. When the baron made his entrance from the billiard room he gave the impression that only a brief audience would be granted before he departed. The self-appointed champion of the Jews was not having this. Before beginning his remarks, Herzl said, he would like to be assured that he would get at least an hour of the baron's time, otherwise the conversation was pointless and it would be a waste of time for both of them. This was the kind of audacity which either got the attention of the powerful or it didn't; more often it did. Herzl's appearance – the curly Assyrian beard, the flashing eyes, the sheer *bigness* of his presence, weighty and dramatically supported on his tall frame – made an immediate impression. But much must have turned on the tone of his voice, and of that, other than it being pitched deep and low, there seems to be no record, though phonographic wax cylinders had been available for about ten years.

Hirsch was rewarded for agreeing to hear Herzl out by being told 'you are a Jew of big money; I am a Jew of the spirit', and that he was pouring money down the drain. If undiplomatic it was true that the scheme was an uphill battle. Property owners in Argentina had refused to sell fertile and well-watered pampas, forcing the Jewish settlers onto land so arid it killed crops, livestock and hope. Plagues of locusts and a multitude of diseases laid waste to the colonies so that by 1895, many of the six thousand or so settlers had migrated to cities like Buenos Aires.[23] Those who stayed were in constant need of refinancing. Worse, Herzl said, even well-intentioned philanthropy on a grand scale perpetuated the morally crippling condition of *schnorrerism*: the hands-out beggary, the self-hatred of those who had to do the *schnorrering*, the inevitable bitterness between those who gave and those who took. Instead he would propose a plan which would replace dependence with dignity, collective pride and self-reliance. It started with the axiom that the Jews, wheresoever they might be, constituted a single nation. Given a place in their ancestral home to make that national consciousness concrete, then like every other people on the face of the earth they would command respect, beginning with their own. How could Hirsch not support such a proposition? But the *sine qua non* was sufficient financing to persuade the sultan that it was in his interest to permit and encourage such a home in Palestine. In return, a Jewish fund would take the pressure off the crushing burden of the Ottoman debt, thus restoring his proper sovereignty. As a bonus, the Zionist project would be a dynamic motor of modernisation for the moribund Ottoman Empire. All those doctors, chemists and engineers would do the trick!

Should Hirsch subscribe to the scheme he need have no fear that Jewish mass migration would create chaos, or deliver the Jews to socialism and anarchism, both very much on the minds of everyone in France of the 1890s with bombs going off. On the contrary such a migration, carefully managed, would be a prophylactic against revolutionary disorder for it would happen step by step and would be governed by the administration of a 'Society of Jews'. Herzl himself would take responsibility for establishing such a governing body for this transformation, but then would step aside. Nor should the baron worry that the whole scheme was meant to serve some misplaced messianic instinct on the part of Herzl himself.

So what did he think? Interrupting Herzl's torrential flow only occasionally, Hirsch agreed with him about the unfortunate effects of philanthropy, the balefulness of *schnorrerism* which seemed to be as corrosive in Argentina as in the poorer districts of Vienna or Paris. But there the meeting of minds came to an end. The national scheme was dangerous utopianism; it would compromise the standing of French Jews, open them to accusations of double allegiance at the very time that prejudice was becoming regrettably popular. Goodbye. Descending Hirsch's regiment-sized staircase Herzl was, predictably, seized by *esprit de l'escalier*, thinking of all the things he ought to have said to reinforce his case. He then set them out in jottings, fragments, some formed into supplementary letters to Hirsch, many more to himself. *His* plan was not whimsical, it was practical for 'I do not care to look like Don Quixote'; the Jews would not yet see how it must work because 'they are not yet desperate enough'; Argentina was 'a petty solution', and on and on.

As the Paris spring turned to summer, and hopes of Hirsch being the great enabler faded, Herzl thrashed around, writing to Bismarck, 'big enough to moderate or cure me', but then inevitably going to Hirsch's rivals, the Rothschilds. He would make 'an address to the Rothschilds', to their family Council, and it would begin by puncturing the complacency of the rich, persuading them that anti-Semitism was not a minor disfigurement of the modern age, it was at the black heart of the present and future. Crazily he wrote and wrote, over cassoulet in the Taverne Royale, and the more he wrote, the more shockingly prophetic he became, seeing the future through a glass darkly but with icy clarity. For Zionism to take hold, he scribbled, 'We shall have to sink lower, shall have to be even more insulted, spat on, mocked, whipped, plundered and slain ... we must finally end up at bottom, rock bottom. What appearance this will have, what form, I cannot surmise. Will it be a revolutionary expropriation from below or a reactionary confiscation from above? Will they chase us away? Will they kill us? I have a fair idea it will take all these forms and others.'[24] In France, Drumont's vile outpourings had left Herzl in no doubt that in a crisis the first objects of popular rage would be bankers and Jews, which in the Rothschilds' case made them prime targets. His vision widened, again with shocking prescience. 'In Austria the people will let themselves be intimidated by the Viennese rabble and deliver up the Jews. There you see the mob can achieve anything once it rears up. It does not know this yet but the leaders will teach it. So they will chase us out of these countries and in the countries where we take refuge they will kill us.'

There was only one salvation. Home.

This was the germ of what would become *Der Judenstaat*, which Herzl began to write towards the end of 1895, 'morning to night', an exercise he said 'would be torment if it were not also bliss'. Getting to the Rothschilds was harder than getting to the sultan, but in the meantime he fished elsewhere.

London opened its doors, up to a point. The chief rabbi Hermann Adler (later an opponent) sent him to the banker, broker and MP for Whitechapel, Samuel Montagu, Baronet since 1894, a committed Lover of Zion. Herzl sat between two bulky brokers in Montagu's City office and then dined with him at home on kosher food brought by three liveried footmen, white gloves dishing out the kugel. Montagu, born Montagu Samuel, the son of a Liverpool watchmaker, told Herzl he felt more 'Israelite than Englishman' and would go and live with him in Palestine, but Herzl, while charmed by his ebullient host, suspected this might have been shmooze and, as time would prove, he was right.[25] Montagu passed him to the Montefiores who introduced him to Lucien Wolf who connected him with the Henriques who wrote to the Arthur Cohens. And so on, albeit nary a Rothschild in sight. Pretty soon Herzl came to realise how divided the Anglo-Jewish upper crust was on Zionism. The clans disagreed with their own relatives. Francis Montefiore was an ardent Zionist; the rest of the family, despite (or possibly because of) Sir Moses' involvement in Palestine, were hostile. The 'gros legumes' as Herzl called them (sometimes 'big shots') were bound to oppose an idea which presupposed the failure of the very emancipation they had fought so long and hard for and which had, in the end, triumphed. Now they could be whatever they chose – judges, mayors, MPs, university men, surgeons, dog breeders, steeplechasers, antiquaries – and could live wherever they wished. One of their own in all but nominal form had been a great prime minister; the *present* prime minister was married to a Rothschild! In the Indian Raj dynasties like the Sassoons, on the run from a vengeful ruler in Baghdad, had landed, taken root and put their stamp on imperial Bombay, transforming the metropolis. There was a whole class of Jew-wallahs. Now, were they supposed to put all that achievement in jeopardy, expose themselves to the accusation of divided loyalties, for the sake of Jews facing the odd pogrom? They gave when asked, didn't they? They made sure that the distressed of Ukraine and Moscow, from where Jews had been summarily expelled in 1891, were taken care of, the outrages publicised, ambassadors upbraided, letters written to *The Times*. East London was now chock-a-block with poor Jews; the Jew-haters, like Arnold White and his high-bred crony Lord Dunraven, were speaking about an alien flood: bringers of disease. Parliamentary commissions about the aliens had been instituted. So it was no time to be raising doubts about absolute loyalty.

Confronted with coolness, Herzl took warmth where he could get it: in Kilburn and Cardiff. In north-west London he visited the writer Israel Zangwill, who had become famous as 'the Dickens of the Ghetto' after the success of his novel, *Children of the Ghetto*. Zangwill had been educated at the Jewish Free School in Spitalfields and then at University College London, so he was the creative link between literary London and poor immigrant Jews of the East End, bohemian-*heymisch*. Herzl took one look at the eruption of books and papers on Zangwill's desk and took to him, though he also thought Zangwill's notion of a Jewish race was belied by the fact of his 'long Negroid nose' and 'woolly hair', not at all like the Herzl he saw in the mirror.

In Cardiff, Herzl discovered a still more unlikely phenomenon: Colonel Albert Goldsmid, born in Poona, whose whole life, since discovering his hidden Jewish identity, was an exercise in demonstrating one could be a sahib for the Raj and a forthright Jew to boot. He was the counter-Dreyfus, living evidence that in late-Victorian Britain, unlike France, it was possible to be an officer, a gentleman, a Jew and a Zionist and not be target practice for the anti-Semites, not while Arnold White was kept at arm's length anyway.

Goldsmid picked Herzl up at the railway station, put him in a dog cart and took him to 'The Elms' on the bosky outskirts of town. There he opened with a well-practised but invariably dramatic line: 'I am Daniel Deronda.' Like George Eliot's hero, he too, along with his baptised wife, had embarked on a journey of discovery. Circumcised, he had become an Orthodox Jew, and then an ardent supporter of Pinsker's Hovevei Zion, establishing outposts in Britain which, in the scouting spirit, Goldsmid called 'Tents'. When the issue of Argentina or Palestine as a preferred home for the Jewish state came up, Goldsmid had no doubt and spoke from experience. He had travelled through Palestine with Laurence Oliphant, who had gone there to buy land for Jewish agricultural settlements in Galilee, but he had also worked in Argentina for Hirsch's horseback colonists and left in disappointment. Herzl was gratified to hear that for Goldsmid there was not a moment's doubt about Palestine as the only authentic destination for the Jewish home. If either of them spoke of the Arabs at their meeting, history of course does not record it. The strain of orientalist romanticism embraced by both Oliphant and Goldsmid presupposed that the modernising project inaugurated by the settlement of Jews would somehow be shared by Arabs as well as Jews, that the tide of money and technical skills would lift all boats. There was much talk of 'regeneration' of both the land and the peoples.[26] And of course to someone like Goldsmid, who thought of himself as a benevolent imperialist, it didn't hurt that, with Russia and Germany circling the enfeebled body of the Ottoman Empire like sharks scenting blood, Zionism could assist British strategic interests in the region lying so crucially between Egypt and India.

Herzl got on so well with the colonel that he felt, as he wrote in his diary, almost brotherly about him. But he was, like Zangwill, small fry compared to even the 'midget millionaires' whom he hoped would fund the project. At a dinner organised by the 'Maccabeans', a cultural-cum-social organisation, he could feel coolness, as damp as the London drizzle, which all but put out his fire. It didn't help that he spoke mostly in German (with a translator) or in French. Dr Herzl looked the part but he didn't sound like it. And he himself felt he had come away empty-handed. As for assistance from government types, he remained steadfast in his belief that there would be only one power which could really persuade the Ottoman sultan to allow Jewish settlement, and that was Imperial Germany, still his lodestar.

At the end of 1895 Herzl returned to his writing desk. A hundred-page manifesto, tract, treatise, promotional booklet, whatever one might call it, would perhaps be more persuasive than going cap in hand to the moneybags. He would, at last, get a readership among the Jewish middle classes, and maybe their collective enthusiasm would get the venture off the ground. Herzl did not mean to alienate the millionaires in whom he still had hope. One day they would see not just that the principles he set out were the only ones which could save the Jews for whom the future was dark and getting darker, but also that he had thought through all the concrete details, from how numbers would be transported to Palestine, how land would be acquired, how the government of the sultan would be brought round. Everything, of course, except what the indigenous population living in Palestine might think of such a scheme.

Thus was *Der Judenstaat* brought into the world. Though the title is habitually known in English as *The Jewish State*, Jacques Kornberg is right to point out that this is, in fact, a mistranslation of what Herzl actually had in mind, which was much more like 'The State of the Jews'. The difference was, and is, important. A Jewish state presupposes the political realisation of either Torah Judaism or some less straightfor-wardly religious notion of Jewish ethos. That, indeed, was very much the ideal of Alkalai, and later 'cultural Zionists' like Ahad Ha'am. It was suffused through the centuries with the ancient tradition of messianic redemption. But though his name would, in eastern Europe and Russia, come to be spoken of in that way, Herzl, for all his self-regarding obsession with charismatic leadership, repudiated any such pretensions. His state for the Jewish nation was to be a more worldly, matter-of-fact entity, a place where, at last, Jews could live whichever way they wanted, speak whichever language came naturally to them (though he would prefer it be German), a country where the hetero-geneity of the Jews, not their uniformity, could be protected and celebrated. When he heard from a Jewish doctor in Jerusalem about Kurdish Jews, Yemeni Jews, Mountain Jews from Baku, Jews of all kinds and colours, he was exhilarated.

Which is not to say that Der Judenstaat is a prosaic document. Much of it is the pure political theatre one would expect from its author. Herzl begins defensively as if knowing – correctly – that critics, especially the rabbis (most of whom were horrified by his plan), would stigmatise Zionism as a heresy, the brainchild of an assimilated Jew cut off from tradition. It was a truism of that tradition that a reborn Jewish state was conditional on the appearance of the endlessly awaited Messiah. And Herzl, self-evidently, was no Messiah. So he was at pains to present Zionism as the awakening of the 'slumbering idea' of return and the recreation of the Jewish state, something that was constant through the centuries of dispersion. A little later he reiterates 'the Jews have dreamed this kingly dream through all the long nights of their history. "Next year in Jerusalem" is our old phrase. It is now a question of seeing whether that dream can be converted into a living reality.'[27]

But the dramatic core, the heartfelt cry, of the early pages of the book is his answer to 'why now?' And that answer is the shattering force of modernised anti-Semitism, its morphing from ancient demon-isation into resentment at the emancipated; the lose/lose predicament of the Jews.

We have honestly endeavoured everywhere to merge ourselves in the social life of surrounding communities and to preserve the faith of our fathers. We are not permitted to do so. In vain are we loyal patriots, our loyalty in some places running to extremes; in vain do we make the same sacrifices of life and property as our fellow citizens; in vain do we strive to increase the fame of our native land in science and art or her wealth by trade and commerce. In countries where we have lived for centuries we are still cried down as strangers and often by those whose ancestors were not yet domiciled in the land where Jews already had experience of suffering. The majority may decide which are the strangers; for this as in every point which arises in the relations between nations is a question of power. I do not here surrender any portion of prescriptive right when I make this state-ment merely in my own name, as an individual. In the world as it now is and for an indefinite period, might prevails over right. It is useless therefore for us to be loyal patriots as were the Huguenots who were forced to emigrate.

Herzl then ends the famous passage with the perennial 'plea of the Jews' – 'If we could only be left in peace' – and follows it with his clear-eyed, ominous prophecy: 'But I think we shall not be left in peace.'[28]

Der Judenstaat, still only in its Introduction, then takes a dramatic, unanticipated turn. Herzl turns sociologist. Smarting from the cold-ness of Hirsch and the London grandees, he attacks the assimilated and the well-to-do, first for their nervousness about Zionism imperil-ling their status as local patriots, but more seriously for the pathetic inadequacy of their philanthropy faced with the crisis of millions. When he restates his primary article of faith, freshly discovered for the Vienna dandy-feuilletonist and playwright, 'we are one people', it is an accusation against those 'civilised' Jews who held their noses at incomers from the shtetls. The social reality was an immense upheaval, a tide of the despairing, the terrorised and the wretched, away from the brutality and hatred with which they were increasingly faced in the modern world. 'Anti-Semitism increases day by day and hour by hour.' The patrons of small-scale emigration and colonisation, he implies, were doing it as much for their own convenience as out of the kind-ness of their hearts and a concern for the welfare and survival of all

Jews. 'I do not think that this or that man took up the matter merely as amusement, that they engaged in emigration of poor Jews as one indulges in horse-racing. The matter was too grave and tragic for such treatment. These attempts were interesting in that they represented on a small scale the practical forerunners of the idea of a State for the Jews.' But most of those projects were, he judged, failing, and what the times called for – a wholesale transplantation of a nation – would never be accomplished as the project of any single multimillionaire, however philanthropic.

The stodgy middle of *Der Judenstaat* then faces down all the practical objections and explains, in relentless detail, how they might be overcome (a responsibly managing organisation run by his Society of the Jews, a bank, the improvements in modern communications which now make the previously unthinkable possible, the complaisance of governments eager to be shot of impoverished Jewish migrants, the relief for assimilated Jews for the same reason, and so on). The tenor throughout is, in a Herzlian way, as patrician as those whose assumed superiority he attacks. It is certainly anti-revolutionary. There would be no chaos, no anarchy, no violence. Mistrusting the fickle credulousness of the masses whose welfare is his professed concern, Herzl has misgivings about democracy. His preferred constitution for the new state is 'aristocratic republicanism' along the lines of the old Republic of Venice. But the guardians of the Jewish state will take care of the workers. This is just as well since the vanguard emigrants would be the unskilled labouring class who would create the infrastructure of the country: railways, roads, bridges and canals, irrigation and new cities. They would be protected by the institution of the seven-hour day, and its paramount importance would be imprinted on the national flag, which was to feature neither a menorah nor the hexangle Star of David but seven golden stars on a field of white, 'symbolising our pure new life'.

Once the working stiffs had got the infrastructure in place, the new state would be ready to receive the professionals: the scientists and engineers, the doctors and lawyers, the writers and professors, artists and musicians, all those who had felt themselves thwarted by the disappointments of emancipation, accused by the anti-Semites of colonising the culture of their home countries. No vanguard feminist, Herzl graciously thought that 'the daughters of our middle classes will then marry these ambitious men'.[29]

The experimental spirit around which the new state would be built would, along with the seven-hour day, make it not just an ark of refuge for the persecuted but a 'model state' accomplished for the 'common good of humanity' as much as for the Jews. This was Herzl's moving (if naively ecumenical) conclusion. In his idealistic assumption that there could be a fit between Gentile states wanting to get rid of surplus Jews, aggravated by the overreach of the emancipated, and what, objectively, the Jewish masses urgently needed, Herzl was reflecting all the contradictory desires and obsessions of his own tumultuous personality. The piece of him that yearned to be more Jewish summoned up the ancient biblical notion of the 'light unto the nations'. Once the immediate emergency had been taken care of, the ethical nationalism he was trying to invent for the Jews would be instituted. When he encountered the usual expressions of amused disbelief, Herzl turned to his inner conviction that everything which seemed destined for conflict could in fact be harmoniously resolved. Even anti-Semitism. If people say, well, this state of yours will be a long-drawn-out business, 'In the meantime, Jews in a thousand different places will suffer insults, mortifications, abuse, blows, depredations and death. No; if we only begin to carry out the plans, anti-Semitism would stop at once and for ever ... For it is the conclusion of peace.'[30]

III. On the Street of the Prophets

A long summer Sunday evening in Whitechapel, July 1896: pickle barrels, smoked-fish sellers and hand-me-down stalls were still doing brisk trade. Everything and everyone who could be was out of doors – it was much too hot to stay at home. For those who didn't mind a little *shvitz* for the sake of higher things, Commercial Road handbills were advertising a 'Mass Meeting' that evening at the Jewish Workingmen's Club in Great Alie Street. The audience would be addressed by Dr Herzl, recently returned from meetings with the government of the sultan. An hour before the speeches, with the sun hanging over smoky Whitechapel, a crowd of Jews converged on the club. Around its doors there was a lot of shouting as people found each other in the throng. Elbows were fully armed, orderly queuing not being East End style. There were women there too, as the club – no drinking, no gambling – was one of the few places of its kind to encourage them to get out of the buildings and come to its offerings. It even had cycling clubs for both sexes. Jews on bikes, now there was a revolution.

It wasn't that hard to get an audience for Herzl. To the horror of the Judaeophobes, by 1890 one in three residents of Whitechapel was a Jew. The post-pogrom influx from eastern Europe was blamed for swamping the tailoring and shoemaking trades and pushing down wages with sweatshop labour. The vast majority of East End Jews were poor or very poor, and were said by the enemies of the 'alien invasion' to be carriers of diseases, steeped in crime. But when the social statisticians looked and counted they found a different story. The Jews were not vectors of any maladies; in fact their life expectancy was longer than any other city population in similar economic circumstances. They were seldom drunk and even more rarely in trouble with the police. Of course there were always bad apples. But given that they lived in desperately crowded spaces – six hundred to an acre in the heart of Whitechapel and Stepney – they got on as best they could. Their East End was not Ripper Town, it was Rebbe Town.

They were avid for learning. There was the Jewish Free School in Spitalfields to provide it, but also Toynbee Hall, and the talks given at Great Alie Street on premises squeezed in between the three synagogues on that one lane. So there they were, streaming to the club from down the road in Stepney and up the other way from Spitalfields; from Mile End and Bethnal Green and Dalston. They came from the Four Per Cent Industrial Dwellings, the Charlotte de Rothschild Dwellings, some even from the Poor Men's Temporary Shelter founded by 'Simcha Becker' Simon, the baker of black bread and beigels. And some, who were hardly workingmen at all, drawn by the excitement of hearing Herzl, had come in trams from the middle-class synagogues of Maida Vale, Kilburn and Hampstead.[31]

Herzl was astonished at the sea of faces greeting him; less astonished at the noise they were making before his talk got under way. Since neither Goldsmid nor Montagu, his erstwhile friends, would do it, the meeting was called to order (in so far as this was possible) by the *haham*, the chief rabbi of the Sephardi community, Moses Gaster from Bevis Marks in the City. For all the many times Herzl had apostrophised 'the Jewish people', had invoked them against the timidity, and as he saw it cowardice, of the big shots and bankers, had threatened to 'move the masses', they were for him mostly an ideological abstraction, a figure of speech. There was nothing abstract about this lot.

Herzl wished that Montagu, Goldsmid or the dignified literary Maccabeans had been there to see and feel the press of expectancy in that jam-packed hall. From the briskness of their communications, they seemed to have cooled towards him and his cause. Herzl knew why. It was because of the criticisms he'd made of the Hovevei Zion and the paralysing prudence of their philanthropists. But then what were their 'Tents', however goodly, compared to Whitechapel on a Sunday night?

The happiness was timely because the immediate impact that *Der Judenstaat* had made in Britain had been a serious disappointment. The essence of the booklet had first seen light of day the previous January in an English summary prepared for the *Jewish Chronicle*, notwithstanding the editors of the paper opposing its central idea. Letters had been invited by the paper but precious few had been received. A mere five hundred copies were printed of the first full English translation, published in May. (The German original was three thousand, not a big run.) When Herzl enquired about British sales, he was told that, given the hostility towards most Jewish institutions, bookshops had taken just two hundred. When he was feeling gloomy, Herzl brooded that the work he had hoped would set the Jewish world alight had turned out to be a damp squib. Only the students of Kadimah and the other Jewish clubs in Vienna seemed to appreciate what he'd done and gave him standing ovations when he appeared before them. He drank in the praise of the young.

Their cheers, rather than the *ts-ts* disapproval of the rabbis and the rich, were a better guide to what was going on after the appearance of *Der Judenstaat*. Something oracular had in fact taken place, though not in the manner discernible to a Viennese writer, accustomed to the culture of press reviews. But it happened where Herzl badly needed it to happen: in the east. At the 1947 commemoration in Israel for the Jubilee of the first Zionist Congress, Chaim Weizmann, who in 1896 had been a young student of chemistry at the Technische Hochschule in Berlin, explained how Herzl's idea of a state for the Jews had got out to the people. Once the Yiddish and Russian editions of *Der Judenstaat*, all published in the late spring and summer of 1896, had been digested, branches of the Hovevei Zion and other more recently formed Zionist groups sent travelling explainers into the towns and shtetls of Galicia, Lithuania and Black Sea Ukraine to give improvised talks about what the book signified; who Dr Herzl was; what a 'Congress' might be; what indeed Zionism wanted. The response was instantaneous, as it had been for other messianic moments over the centuries: dry kindling waiting for the spark. Weizmann recalled that, following his explanations in a shtetl near Pinsk, probably his home town of Motol, he'd asked a little old man whether he'd understood anything of what he'd said. The man replied, 'No, but one thing I do understand: if all this wasn't true you wouldn't have come all this way to tell us.'

Despite the mordant sarcasm of Ahad Ha'am congratulating Dr Herzl on discovering the Jews and their sorrows, there had been a *Judenstaat* effect, just as when American colonials read the Declaration of Independence and understood, at the most basic level, what had to be fought for; or in Ireland when Daniel O'Connell gave voice to the oppressed (at one point Herzl said he wanted to be the Parnell of the Jews); or in India when Gandhi spoke and walked. It was the nimbus around the idea of a state for the Jews, a place where *being* a Jew was the norm rather than a problem, which cast its glow through Jewish Europe.

Hence all those upturned faces at the Workingmen's Club in Whitechapel, all the expectancy from people who, under the spell of that idea, had turned from being unwanted 'aliens' back into actual human Jews. Herzl was not the Messiah – he bristled at the folly; if he could redeem Jerusalem, it wouldn't be any time soon, but *dayenu*, what he was promising sufficed: a place where the shout of 'Jew' would be an exclamation of honour and pleasure, and not one of terror and abuse; a place where one could have any kind of nose (he was still preoccupied with that), any colour beard, bandy or bow legs and no one would vilify either; a place of common dignity. Any Jew could understand that; no Jew could think about it without a little bump of joy. Who cared about the trepidation of the big shots? As

Zangwill (with whom Herzl had become close) said, the Orthodox like Montagu 'ask us to pray for a return to Jerusalem three times a day and when we actually plan to do just that they all shrink in fear'.

The euphoria in Great Alie Street only made Herzl brood more bleakly on everything he had failed to achieve. What could he tell the crowd? Usually he wrote out a careful speech. This time, not expecting such numbers, he had decided to improvise from just a few scribbled paragraph headings. He put the best face on it he could. What had happened in Constantinople at the Yildiz Palace still distressed him. He had been led by his powerful, amiable go-between, the Polish diplomat at the Austrian embassy in Constantinople, Baron Philip Nevlinsky, to believe that he would get a personal audience with the sultan. But he never got further than a succession of conversations with the aged grand vizier, Kamil Pasha. The vizier himself was receptive to the idea of a Jewish fund which would free the embattled Ottoman state from the iron grip of the Debt Control Commission. And he knew the sultan felt the same way. But when the matter had been raised directly, Abdul Hamid had been adamant: Herzl and whoever of the Jews was behind him can hang on to their millions. Palestine, or any part of it, was not his to yield; it belonged to the people of Turkey who had fought and died for it.

Despite the disappointment, Herzl had not abandoned hope of persuading the Ottoman government to allow mass Jewish migration to Palestine. Everything depended of course on the willingness of the barons of capital to play their part, and, for the moment, most of them were hostile to Herzl's dangerous utopianism. Just a week after the Whitechapel meeting, Herzl met Baron Edmond de Rothschild in his offices on the rue Laffitte. He did not then know that the man he still thought of as a friend and supporter, Albert Goldsmid, had betrayed him. Herzl had asked Goldsmid to warm up Baron Edmond with a letter of introduction and endorsement. Goldsmid had indeed written to Rothschild, but instead of support, issued a warning against 'the wild man' and his wild fancies. After discovering this, Herzl referred to Goldsmid as a 'traitor'.

Even without knowing of the betrayal, Herzl went into the meeting fists up: defensive, combative, assuming the worst. His attitude was probably aggravated by having to go through a preliminary audition with the vice president of the Alliance, Narcisse Leven, before being ushered into the baronial presence. When they finally faced each other, it was an encounter of physical opposites: Herzl – big, dark, imperious; Edmond – foxy, trim, elegant, cerebrally sharp-witted, 'an ageing youth' with 'quick, shy movements' dressed in 'a white waistcoat which flapped about his thin body'. Edmond heard Herzl out – he had already digested the essence of his plans from the mandatory pre-submitted text – and then he responded predictably in much the same tone as the sceptical, practical Hirsch. The announcement of a nation state was dangerously premature; it would jeopardise work that was being slowly but steadily done by ringing alarm bells in Constantinople; that one had to build from the bottom up, in material, concrete ways. Even if everything that Herzl was promising about the willingness of the powers to go along with the plan and thousands of poor east European Jews descended on Palestine, how could that country itself possibly cope? How would they earn a living, be materially sustained? Edmond had a point, but delivered it with a sharp little epigram: 'One's eyes shouldn't be bigger than one's stomach.' This prompted Herzl to embark on one of his grand locutions about the Power of Ideas, ending in what to Rothschild's ears sounded like a threat: 'You were the keystone of the entire scheme. If you refuse, everything I have fashioned so far will fall into pieces. I shall then be forced to do it a different way. I shall begin a mass agitation.'[32] Edmond declined support and Herzl wrote him off, never seeing him again. It would take a very different approach from a very different Zionist, Chaim Weizmann, to bring Edmond back to the project of a Jewish national home.

This was a classic case of 'the aristocracy getting too aristocratic'. But it was surely the startling contrast between the warmth of the Whitechapel crowd and the coldness of the French-Jewish patrician, as well as the feeble response to Der Judenstaat, and the obstacles put in his way by the Hovevei Zion, that made Herzl think concretely about some sort of 'National Assembly' for Zionism. Such a gathering would be alive with human immediacy, not just print on the page, and it would gather Jews from all over the wide world of their struggles and suffering.

Herzl was not the originator of the plan. In 1893, there had been an attempt by the Union of Russian Jewish Scientists led by the Zionist student Leo Motzkin to have a meeting of representatives from towns and shtetls across Russia and Poland, but lack of funds and leadership made it impossible to realise. But when *Der Judenstaat* began to circulate in Hovevei circles in Russia, Romania and Bulgaria, whether as print or in lecture and discussion meetings, it made the cells of the Lovers of Zion receptive to some sort of unifying gathering. In March 1897, a preliminary meeting of representatives from Austria, Germany and Russia was held in Vienna, approving the plan for a congress on the condition that the Jews of eastern Europe would be fully represented in the assembly.

It would, however, have a distinctly German accent (not least the language of its proceedings). For political as well as cultural reasons Herzl assumed the congress would be held in a major German city, probably Munich. With both France and Britain dragging their feet, he had become more and more committed to Kaiser Wilhelm II emerging as the great enabler and protector of the Zionist cause. This was less quixotic than it may seem in retrospect. All his life Herzl had been a German romantic. Writing *Der Judenstaat* by day, he went to performances of *Tannhäuser* in the evening. And the spring of 1896 had opened new German possibilities. William Hechler, chaplain to the British embassy in Vienna, had discovered *Der Judenstaat* on the tables of a bookstall and treated the moment as divine intervention. Hechler was bilingual, as close to an authentic Anglo-German as could be imagined. His father was an active missionary among the Jews in both England and Germany, with the goal of hastening the Second Coming of the Saviour through their conversion. But in the old tradition going back to the humanist popes and the Dutch Hebraists, that conversion was not to be won by coercion, nor was it an absolute precondition of the Second Coming. What was imperative, though, for both father and son Hechler, was the *return* of the Jews to the Holy Land and the building of a Third Temple (Hechler Junior thought at 'Bethel' rather than Jerusalem).[33]

Hechler sought Herzl out for a meeting early in April. It changed everything. Even before Herzl got to the apartment overlooking the Schillerplatz, he heard organ music pumping out into the spring air. On the fourth floor he found a pink-faced bearded gentleman in a room, lined floor to ceiling with books, all of which, according to Herzl, were Bibles. It became plain, quite quickly, not least from Hechler's excited display of his maps of Palestine, a model of

Solomon's Temple à la Templo, and elaborate calculations of the timing of the Second Coming (a major event was predicted for 1897 or 1898), that he treated Herzl as a providentially delivered prophet. The commandments he was living by were the restoration of the people of Israel to Palestine and the even more important decree 'love the Jews'. He himself had gone to Russia in 1882 following the pogroms, and, witnessing the horrific consequences, had had no trouble obeying that commandment. Hechler had met Pinsker, taken up with the Lovers of Zion and had even attempted to have a letter from Queen Victoria delivered by the British ambassador in Constantinople to the sultan, recommending the return of the Jews to Palestine. Horrified at the crazy reverend, the ambassador wouldn't hear of it. Hechler admired the slow progress made in the agricultural settlements but he knew how brutal it was to make arable land out of the rocks and the swamps. Yellow fever and malaria – and their outlier, exhausted despair – were taking a heavy toll. Settlers were filling graves, leaving for the towns, returning whence they'd come or looking up passages to America. But now here was Herzl's messianic plan for a *Judenstaat* (the chief rabbi of Sofia, Dr Reuben Bierer, had actually declared him the Messiah) which expedited the sacred timetable in exactly the way Hechler prayed for each and every day. With saintly glee he took out a capacious overcoat to show Herzl an inside pocket big enough to hold the map of Palestine they would take with them when they rode through the Holy Land together.[34]

Herzl went from embarrassment to enchantment. Such was Hechler's effusiveness and determination that he almost came to believe in his own providential election. There were so many convergences! William Hechler had been tutor to the children of Frederick I, the Grand Duke of Baden, the kaiser's uncle. The Grand Duke had been so enthusiastic for the creation of the Second Reich that he had been in the Hall of Mirrors at the moment of its founding following the defeat of France. As a result the Grand Duke had been preserved in all his powers and territories under the new imperial regime and was personally close to the kaiser. Hechler offered to go to Berlin (at Herzl's expense), or to Karlsruhe, the Grand Duke's schloss, wherever was necessary, to gain a hearing for Herzl from the kaiser. With the Grand Duke it worked. Come to Karlsruhe, Hechler wrote; come quickly. In a state of nervous excitement, on 23 April

Herzl showed up at the schloss and went into raptures at the Gothic Teutonry, the whiskered guards, the timbered halls, the flagons of hale and hearty hospitality, the princely charm and genuine enthusiasm of the old *Grossherzog* who promised to work wonders with his imperial nephew. Herzl kept pinching himself. This was something, was it not? The mighty of the world listening to a Jew.

But as Herzl seemed to have a door opening to the seats of power in Germany, those of German Jewry were shutting as fast as they could against him and any plan for a congress. Zionists were renegades, a danger to everything that had been achieved by emancipation. When the Munich community, led by their rabbis, heard that their city was the preferred venue for the congress, it was made clear that Zionists would not be welcome there. For both political and religious reasons all the major communities of central and western Europe were brought into line. Sardonically Herzl called them 'the Protest Rabbis'. They included Hermann Adler in London and the disingenuously bewildered Moritz Güdemann in Vienna.

Not all the Orthodox felt this way. Aaron Marcus, rabbi of Podgorze, near Cracow, had written promising to bring millions of Hasidim round. David Farbstein, a Warsaw rabbi who had joined one of the earliest organisations of religious Zionists (thus against the grain of the overwhelming rabbinical consensus), was a passionate enthusiast. While remaining involved in religious life, Farbstein studied law, successively, at the universities of Berlin, Zurich and Berne, which gave him his doctorate in 1896. When the initial calls for the congress were going out in the late spring and summer of 1897, it was Farbstein who came up with the possibility of Basel. The idea struck a chord with Herzl because he was much given to invoking the example of the Swiss Confederation whenever the language of the Jewish state was raised as a contentious issue. Sceptical of a Hebrew renaissance, probably because he was so unfamiliar with it, Herzl repeatedly said he wanted a language that would face the future rather than the past, one which would immediately connect the Jewish state with the wider world. He had no idea of the elastic, powerfully modern tongue appearing in Ahad Ha'am's literary and political journal *Ha'Shiloah* every month. He wrote off Yiddish as an even less desirable option even though it was not only the vernacular of the millions of Jews most likely to respond to a call to emigrate, but had also undergone a spectacular rebirth in every genre of literature and journalism. For Herzl, like Moses Mendelssohn before him, nothing could be nobler than German, but by the time he wrote *Der Judenstaat* he wanted a country in which any and all languages might comfortably coexist, in short a Jewish Switzerland (which has four).

Switzerland also had a reputation for hospitality to political movements, though Zurich was full of the socialists and communists with whom Herzl and the Zionists would have to compete for allegiance. Basel was chosen partly for not being Zurich but also as a crossroads city on the Rhine, accessible to delegates from all over Europe, albeit at their own expense. Farbstein was put in charge of locating a suitable venue in the town; the first place he found, a variety theatre, was certainly not that. When Herzl was told the backdrop for the acrobat acts couldn't be changed, he told Farbstein to look elsewhere. The Stadt Casino, which in spite of its name was mostly used for concerts, was the best option. Including the galleries it could seat over a thousand, which since the congress was expecting two hundred delegates could have been embarrassing, but Herzl, correctly as it turned out, expected to fill it with public attendees and the press. The hall, acoustically friendly to Brahms and Beethoven, had the solemnity he was looking for. All his old stage-management instincts came into play, as Herzl planned the event from the Hôtel Les Trois Rois overlooking the Rhine. Later he would pose for the artist and photographer Ephraim Lilien, leaning on the balcony, staring moodily above the great river as if communing with history, the leonine, Assyrian profile of 'Tiglath-Pileser' (as Zangwill called it) looking like 'the beautiful sombre face of a kingly dreamer'. It became the first great Zionist icon: the portrait of the new Moses, summoned from princely assimilation to take hold of the destiny of the Jews. Herzl's saturnine intensity spoke of what he had written in his diary: 'my life is over; world history begins'.

The thespian in him knew that epic moments required careful theatrical planning, perfect visual atmospherics. The delegates, coming from far and near, need not bring frankincense and myrrh to the Hôtel Les Trois Rois; it was enough they come with the solid gold of their commitment. But that enthusiasm had to be clad in dignity. Even though humid Basel was sweltering in the dog days of August, nothing less than formal dress would do. Most of the delegates were not really a white-tie-and-tails crowd so the Basel rental establishments did good business. Max Nordau, who, Herzl thought, should surely have known better, had brought only a frock coat, and as a star speaker of the opening session had to be hastily recostumed. There were other crucial visuals. A photograph of the Stadt Casino taken at the time shows two flags hanging over the entrance, both featuring two blue stripes on an empty white field. The white was for the purity of the mission; the blue stripes recalled the Bible's prescription for *tzitzit* and *tallit*, fringe garment and prayer shawl, the visible signs of daily absorption in the Torah and God's will. The Karaites, with their insistence on the exclusive authority of scripture, had preserved blue, but when the Talmudist rabbis failed to agree on exactly *which* blue God and Moses had in mind – sky, marine, indigo? – they went to consensual black. Herzl, Nordau and the rest had had enough of the picayune *pilpul*, the scholastic nitpicking of exile. Back to essentials. Blue it would be. Inside the hall was another flag, the six-pointed Star of David within which was featured a lion of Judah, like the twin lions said to guard the Holy of Holies and preserved symbolically in synagogue decorations all over the world. Something was coming together for the iconography of Zionism. For the moment, the accents of blue and gold helped dress up the dun interior of the casino with its buff paint, cane chairs, stifling red curtains and green baize of the balcony tiers where leaders and speakers would sit.

But more important than the way it all looked was who was there: not just the 197 delegates from Odessa, The Hague, Berlin, Cologne, Baltimore, Algiers, Jerusalem, New York, London, Minsk, Jassy, Stockholm, Grodno, Białystok, Brussels, Belgrade and the rest, but the crowds from non-Jewish Basel, Zurich and Berne – students, professors, schoolteachers, businesspeople – who had bought tickets in advance and lined up around the street for good seats; also the world's press, the *Frankfurter Zeitung*, *The Times*, *L'Écho de Paris*, the *New York Herald* and the rest, filing their reports telegraphically back home. Whether the rabbis and the stay-at-homes liked it or not, the congress had instantly become a world event. It had what Herzl had hoped for: political electricity. How wrong, how timid, how small-minded Samuel Montagu had been when he sent a letter to Herzl urging him to stay away since the Jewish and a Jewish homeland would only be settled by an agreement of the great powers or 'by a leader in whom the Jews have confidence'.

For Montagu that leader was clearly not Theodor Herzl. But the vast majority of the delegates to the congress, even those who had misgivings about Herzl's grand patrician style, felt differently. They saw someone the like of whom they had never seen before. He emitted something they couldn't quite put their finger on, but it had, as one of them said, a radiance to it. Somebody, for this was a literary and scriptural bunch of Jews, must have thought of the light on the countenance of Moses as he descended from Sinai after being in the presence of God.

The feeling was reciprocated. Herzl was deeply moved as he saw Jews in all shapes and sizes coming into the Braunschweig restaurant 'where the food is quite bad' right off the trains, from Frankfurt, Ekaterinoslav, Amsterdam, wherever it was, 'caked with coal dust, sweaty from their journey, full of intentions – most of them with good ones, a few with bad'.[35] Fraternity was immediate. Berthold Feiwel from Brno – who had organised a Zionist circle, Veritas, in 1897, and who became a close friend of Herzl's – threw himself into this spirit of exuberant Jewish togetherness. 'Upon arrival,' he wrote in his notes, 'we were a proper stately assembly. What excitement incurred when another "Baseler" was discovered and introduced to the rest! A heartfelt brotherly handshake and a joyful getting to know each other.'[36] Herzl recalled even more intense emotions. 'We embrace and kiss each other. We do not know each other yet. But we know we are brothers ... Hugging and kissing we tell each other our names. And after we hear those names we kiss again ... *Ivri anokhi*. We are Hebrews.'

It was this sense of belonging, no matter where they came from or what version of politics or religion they upheld, which finally made Herzl's profession of faith in *Der Judenstaat* – 'we are a nation, one nation' – something more than an empty piety, for it rested on a community of ideas. In March he had said that the intention of such a congress would be to 'put the Jewish nation on its feet and give it its first expression'. That he had accomplished before anyone had even spoken.

First at the podium was the oldest delegate, Dr Karpel Lippe of Jassy, a Lover of Zion but one who immediately conceded that the Katowice Conference had not done enough. Now after '1,800 years of persecution' Jews were met to make a change in their shared fate.

Speaking second, Herzl, only thirty-seven at the time but timelessly big with seriousness, spoke in soft, subdued tones as was his wont, the depth of his voice reinforcing the gravity of what was being said. The word he used over and again was 'home'. 'We are here,' he told the delegates, 'to lay the foundation stone for the home that is destined to be a safe haven for the Jewish people.' Zionism, he said, 'is a homecoming to the Jewish fold even before it is a homecoming to the Jewish land'. 'We the children who have come home' have found in the condition of the family much misery, much to redress. And he then went on to lay out the intolerable predicament posed by growing anti-Semitism. It was not just the Jews who were helpless to prevent terrible happenings but governments answerable to popular elections. If they defended the Jews they would incur the rage of the masses; if they stood merely neutral, they would leave the Jews defenceless. The only answer was to recreate the nation and to bring it to safety. But the homeland had to be secured in international law, and, given the relentless rise of persecuting anti-Semitism, how could it not be? He offered uplifting reassurance to anyone listening in the world beyond Basel: that Zionism would be peaceful, would care for the downtrodden, and would be a gift to humanity as well as the Jews. It should not be construed as any sort of belligerence. 'With enlightenment and comfort go forth from this Congress. Let everyone find out what Zionism really is, Zionism rumoured to be a thousand-year wonder is a moral, humanitarian movement directed towards the long-yearned-for goal of our people.'

Though the speech was a modest text, when Herzl finished, a storm of cheering, foot stamping, hat and handkerchief waving erupted in the hall. On being elected president by acclaim, a second wave engulfed the gathering in its dress suits and ties. Buttons burst, throats were made hoarse, more than the usual crying broke out. Herzl himself, inexpressibly moved behind his Assyrian beard, refrained from bowing as he did at curtain calls 'so as to keep things from turning into *cabotage* [showtime]'. At that moment he had left the boards of the stage and become something else entirely. One hardened reporter, spellbound, surrendered to the vision that he was seeing 'a scion of the House of David risen from the dead, clothed in legend and fantasy and beauty'.

Max Nordau, the physician and writer, an assimilated Jew who had turned to Zionism after the Dreyfus Affair, followed Herzl and gave what was, rhetorically, the more powerful and much darker speech, returning to the introductory theme of *Der Judenstaat* that Zionism was the fruit of thwarted emancipation. But Nordau treated the problem historically and philosophically. The trouble was that emancipation had been granted as a matter of political logic rather than sentiment; not to redress the dehumanising outrages inflicted on Jews for hundreds of years but merely in accordance with the abstract principles of the French Revolution. By insisting on the dissolving, or even disappearance of Jewish identity within a monolithic nation of citizens, the bestowers of legality had set impossible barriers for the emancipated Jew to overcome. The result was a kind of social over-exertion and the seeding of a new, racial enmity along with the endurance of the old hatreds. Jews trapped in the post-emancipation world had thus 'lost the old Ghetto' where at least solidarity had brought them together, but in this new world, 'the land of his birth is still denied to him as a home ... his countrymen recoil from him when he wishes to associate with them. This moral misery is worse than the physical one ... and so he dashes his head against the thick ice crusts of hatred and contempt which form over his head.'

Herzl was too frantically busy during the three days to make his usual copious, vivid diary entries. But he does tell us that, when he got to the dais, after acclamation as president, the first thing he saw was a letter from his son Hans. 'I was greatly moved.' When he got back to the presidential seat after the speech, 'I wrote Congress postcards to my parents, my wife and each of my children, Pauline, Hans and Trude. This is the first act of childishness I have committed in the two years since the movement began.'[37]

On the second day of the congress (and after much debate) the 'Basel Programme' proclaimed the goal of Zionism to be the creation of the national home in Palestine, secured by public law. To that end, farmers, artisans and manufacturers were to be encouraged to emigrate and settle; the unity of the Jewish people was to be worked for; national consciousness raised and, where necessary, the support of the powers sought. But the pithiest summary, at least of Herzl's own state of mind at the end of it all, was the famous sentence written in his diary, at once egotistical and not entirely false: 'At Basel I founded the Jewish State.' Then he added: 'if I said this out loud today I would be answered by universal laughter. Perhaps in five years and certainly in fifty everyone will know it.' To anyone worrying unduly what the implications of state creation by declaration might be, Herzl added the qualification that it was the *idea* of it that he had inaugurated. But that was foundational. All states, he argued, begin with such ideas, for 'a state even when it has territory is always an abstraction'. At Basel, he wrote, 'I created this abstraction which as such is invisible to the vast majority of people. And with infinitesimal means I gradually worked the people into the mood for a State and made them feel they were the National Assembly.'[38] He had not made a Jewish nation; but had he succeeded in making it conceivable?

Perhaps only one of the 197 'Baselers' thought emphatically not, but then his diamond-sharp intellect was as forceful as Herzl's and by his own lights a lot less sentimental. The essayist Ahad Ha'am, born Asher Ginsberg, who had taken the pen name 'One of the People' when he started writing for the Hebrew press in the late 1880s, described his feelings on returning to Odessa from the congress as those of 'a mourner at a wedding'.[39] But then he felt he had much to grieve about. He resented what he considered to be Herzl's ignorant criticisms of the long, painfully earned achievements of the Hovevei Zion; his taking the credit for bringing Jews back to collective life. 'To hear him one would think that a genius had suddenly discovered the Jewish people still alive and that it needed to be informed of that fact.'[40]

As the founding editor of the Hebrew monthly *Ha'Shiloah*, he felt that the Germanising of the congress not just in language but in ethos had taken nascent Zionism further and further away from its core, which ought always to be Judaism. What had those white ties and tails to do with Judaism, or for that matter Nordau's disquisitions on the French Revolution? He believed himself, with good reason, to come from the eastern heart of Jewish culture, though his development was anything but Orthodox. His father had leased a farm near Berdichev and Ha'am spent eighteen years in the countryside as a working farmer. He stayed observant but also critical of mystical Hasidism and of any metaphysical cloudiness. But his sense of what it meant to farm made him gnash his teeth when he heard Herzl go on about Zion as if it were just an abstraction. He had made two trips to Palestine, in 1891 and 1893, when all his suspicions of mismanagement of the Hovevei Zion settlements, their dependence on philanthropic injections of capital, their abasement before baronial governance, their reliance on Arab labour, were confirmed. So that when he saw the effect Herzl had on the congress, he thought he was watching a Jewish Cagliostro, a bogus magician casting a spell on the impressionable. The enchantment was doubly deceptive: about the true Judaism and the true Palestine. In his caustically grand way, Ahad Ha'am had a point about the content-free quality of Herzl's notion of 'Jewishness' defined more by how the Gentiles felt, for ill or good, than by the core of Judaism itself. But the counterpoint is that for all his devotional eloquence and penetrating intellect, Ahad Ha'am also was unclear about what true Judaism was, for the simple reason that at least since Maimonides this had not been an agreed truism. It was not pure Torah or the Karaites would be right. It was not unexamined Talmud (not that that was a monolithic work) or Maimonides would be wrong. It could not accommodate the reforming Judaism by which millions now defined themselves as Jews. But all that Ahad Ha'am knew was that it was richer, weightier, more serious than anything the irreligious Herzl was offering, which was Jewish secularism, and that for the Jews to be reborn as a nation, they needed to find Judaism first. Thus an enmity, a civil war, was seeded at the very birth of Zionism. It has yet to be reconciled.

And there was, for Ahad Ha'am, another fly in the ointment of Herzl's balm for the afflicted, and that was his unrealistically imperial vision of what the Great Powers, especially Germany, could or couldn't deliver to the Middle East. Unlike Herzl, his visits had given him a better grip on its geostrategic realities and the competing appetites of predator-inheritors of the Turkish Empire than one might suppose from a sometime farmer-Hebraist. Herzl's vision might work if the whole region of which Palestine was the centre could somehow be left to its devices. But that was inconceivable. Much more likely was that for the foreseeable future it would be a cockpit of violence, and Palestine not in the kaiser's or the sultan's gift to bestow.

For the moment, Herzl was too busy to notice any of this, least of all from a stinging critic and inconvenient adversary like Ahad Ha'am. Delegates were being sent off home to organise local branches of what would be the World Zionist Organisation, to begin fund- and consciousness-raising. But the 'National Assembly' had made Herzl think statesmanlike thoughts, and he was acutely conscious that if the momentum of the movement he had created was not to stall, he

needed a breakthrough on the diplomatic front. The Grand Duke of
Baden, after assuring Herzl that he could sway the kaiser, had gone
mysteriously silent. But in September 1898, things began to move
again and very fast. Herzl was summoned to Mainau Island in the
Bodensee, the Grand Duke's summer place. He arrived while birds
were dropping to German guns, painfully aware he was not dressed
for shooting; not the right boots, not the green loden, not really the
right way with the dogs. But the news was good. Herzl had actually
written independently to the kaiser in June. Now, according to
Frederick, Wilhelm was close to accepting the idea of a German
protectorate for the Jews, subject of course to the sultan coming round
to the idea. As it happened, the kaiser was planning to travel to
Jerusalem in October, ostensibly for the consecration of the German
Church of the Holy Redeemer. Should Herzl not consider going at
the same time?

Two weeks later Herzl saw the German ambassador in Vienna, the
Prince of Eulenburg, shrewd, shifty and secretly gay, and the German
foreign minister, Bernhard von Bülow, clever and undisguisedly hostile.
Then in Amsterdam in the first week of October, Herzl had a message
from the German consulate confirming everything: the kaiser was
favourable to the protectorate and wished to meet with both Dr Herzl
and a delegation in Jerusalem to discuss the matter further. A delegation? Who could he take with him? Herzl had hoped for heavyweights
like Nordau but he refused outright. Instead Herzl turned to the next
tier of potential leaders: two from Cologne, the lawyer Max
Bodenheimer and the businessman David Wolffsohn. Wolffsohn had
come from the world of Lithuanian orthodoxy, had been sent to
Memel and had begun his career with firms run by religious Jews. He
was the link to their world, and after reading Der Judenstaat he went
directly to Vienna to see Herzl and to offer whatever he could to make
the dream real. The deputation was completed by Moritz Schnirer,
who as a medical student in Vienna had been one of the founders of
Kadimah, and the Russian engineer Joseph Seidener, whom Herzl
thought could speak of the technical expertise the Jews would bring
to the transformation of Palestine.

So there they were, five Jews on a train, the Orient Express in fact,
on their way to Constantinople for a meeting with the emperor of
Germany. Almost belatedly Herzl had realised the paramount

importance of seeing the kaiser before they were all in Palestine and before Wilhelm met the sultan. He needed to do everything in his power to make sure that the kaiser would raise the matter of the Jews with the sultan.

Eulenburg seemed to have arranged things. In Constantinople Herzl waited restlessly for the audience. The meeting was so delayed that in desperation he had to write directly to the kaiser explaining that unless it happened soon he would miss the only ship which could put him in Palestine to coincide with the kaiser's visit. Finally the summons came to present himself at the Yildiz Palace. Situated in Besiktas on the shores of the Bosphorus, designed by an Italian architect as a variation on a Lake Como/Swiss chalet resort, the pavilions which made up the compound, all gables and arched windows, were, for the sultan Abdul Hamid, more pleasurable and more defensible than residing in the heart of the city. The Sala pavilion had been built by the sultan expressly as a residence for visiting potentates, the kaiser above all, and, fine carpenter that he was, Abdul Hamid kept on making extensions he could supply with his own furniture and enormous rugs woven by teams of sixty weavers. Herzl had been bidden to the Sala for 4.30, and as usual had spent time considering exactly how he should be properly dressed for the momentous encounter, breaking in the pair of 'delicate' grey gloves of which he was especially proud. But, of course, he was made to wait. And wait. Three-quarters of an hour after the appointed time he was ushered up the enormous staircase, at the top of which the kaiser's aide-de-camp Count von Kessel said in the proper way 'Count von Kessel' and clicked his heels. Feeling foolish as soon as he had done it Herzl parried 'Doktor Herzl' and clicked his back. Then he caught a glimpse of the empress who vaguely nodded to him before disappearing through a door, and suddenly there he was, facing the kaiser dressed in the dark uniform of a Hussar. The first thing that struck Herzl was that Wilhelm seemed embarrassed by his withered arm, to which a watch was strapped and this somehow made him instantly more sympathetic. One couldn't help but notice when the good arm was extended in a handshake. But the second thing was his eyes: 'great sea-blue eyes', his 'truly imperial eyes' about which Herzl writes with the almost unhinged infatuation of a lover. 'I have never seen such eyes', 'magnificent eyes, he looks at you squarely and strongly'.[41]

'Heart pounding', Herzl summarised the letters he'd sent; what he hoped for from the kaiser. There was no disagreement; it seemed Wilhelm wanted that too, but as the kaiser held forth, a tone entered the conversation that was all too familiar to Herzl, and it was not exactly friendly. If Herzl had known the substance of a letter Wilhelm had sent to his uncle the Grand Duke in late September he would have been even more shocked at the outright cynicism. While the kaiser expressed his abhorrence of the excesses of anti-Semitism rearing up in Germany and Austria, the Zionist plan was primarily useful to him in getting rid of unwanted Jews while creating a semi-colony of Germany right in the heart of the Ottoman Empire, all funded by the Jews. What was there to dislike about such a scheme?

'There are elements of *your people*,' the kaiser said, 'whom it would be quite good to settle in Palestine. I am thinking for example of Hesse where there are usurers at work.' This too Herzl had heard before, and his hackles rose notwithstanding the spell of the sea-blue eyes. Bülow chimed in with the ingratitude of the Jews towards the Hohenzollern dynasty to whom they had every reason to be eternally grateful: all those Jewish reds and revolutionaries. Zionism, said Herzl, is an alternative to the appeal of socialism.

And then, this being late 1898, the talk turned to Dreyfus, and slightly to Herzl's surprise it became clear the court thought the Jewish officer entirely innocent, though the reasons were more to do with how the kaiser felt about the absurd, corrupt, republican French. Wilhelm had heard that the general staff had embezzled funds, that Dreyfus had been offered money to keep quiet about it, spurned the offer and thus was framed. Somehow Herzl moved it all back to how loans would be mobilised to free the sultan from his debts, adding 'it all seems completely natural to me' and hearing the kaiser respond 'And to me too!' At which point, Herzl tells his diary, he imagines being in a magic forest where a fabled unicorn appears, and at some point that happens and the unicorn speaks and says, genially, 'I am the fabled unicorn.' His Viennese contemporary Dr Freud might have said something about that horn, possibly triggered by the spiked *Pickelhaube* helmet the kaiser wore on parade and his habit of always riding white stallions. But what the unicorn actually said was: 'Tell me what I am to say to the sultan.' 'A chartered company under German protection,' Herzl instructed, 'and he grandly gave me his hand which is strong enough for two, squeezed mine good and hard and went out through the centre door.'

A week later, the five unsuitably dressed Jews were sailing on a calm and glittering sea towards Palestine. From Constantinople to Alexandria, comfortably aboard the *Imperator Nikolai II*, stopping at Smyrna, where Herzl noticed the mix of Sephardi and Ashkenazi Jews, then on to Piraeus with an excursion to the Acropolis which impressed Herzl less than the engineering feat of the Suez Canal. At Alexandria they had to change vessels to the small and crowded steamer, the *Russiya*. At some point on the voyage, the camera which David Wolffsohn had bought expressly for the trip was brought out and they all posed for a shipboard photo. Since a standing European in the picture has his head cut off by the edge, it's possible that Wolffsohn took the snap, which explains just four seated Zionists. Or else someone altogether different took the picture including an inadvertently beheaded comrade. The four are seated directly on the boards of the deck; two of them, including Bodenheimer, are dressed in bulky worsted and bow ties despite the sweltering heat of the eastern Mediterranean. Herzl, at the front of course, and ever the natty dresser, has a jaunty quasi-nautical peaked cap on, skipper of the band. He also seems to be holding a collapsible telescope, attached to a leather strap thrown over his shoulder.

But the most telling feature of the photograph is also the one that none of the texts which invariably include it as illustration comment on. The Jews are not alone. They sit among five Arabs, who had come along with them all the way from Constantinople. They are traditionally dressed, one not looking at the camera but with a profile as striking as Herzl's. Two are stroking their chins thoughtfully, perhaps bemusedly. Their expressions are neither ingratiating nor hostile but also not indifferent to what is happening. How could they be? Given everything that had to happen to set up such a photo, the group can't possibly have been accidentally composed. The mix, so at odds with the usual assumptions about the invisibility of the Palestinian Arabs to Zionists, and Herzl's blind spot in particular, has to have been consciously arranged. In fact, though it was certainly low on the agenda of difficulties in realising the dream of the national home, the reality of the Arab population was not at all ignored, romantic though the Zionists might have been about a future of cooperation and fraternity.

Two reporters set out the issue of coexistence with the Arabs, or the difficulty thereof, as plainly as they could. Exactly aware he could be accused, especially by his enemy Ahad Ha'am, of vague invocations of a fantasy Palestine, Herzl sent Leo Motzkin there a few months before to report on material conditions, including the local population. Motzkin's account was full of thorns and brambles – the usual troubles with the settlements and the baronial governance – but also the incontrovertible fact of the Arab population. The other reporter was Ahad Ha'am himself; following visits in 1891 and 1893, he was uncompromising in setting out the problems ahead for any scheme of mass migration. 'Truth from the Land' painted a dire portrait of settlers demoralised by their dependence, insisting on the necessity of a gradual organic development of a Jewish society in Palestine before any schemes of mass population transfer could be thought of, and the setting of deep roots, both agrarian and spiritual, and self-generated rather than the product of some sort of international power play or the philanthropy of western bankers. But most directly of all, Ha'am pointed to the fact that most cultivable land was already being worked by the local population. For the moment, he said, landowners were content to sell to Jews for tidy sums, for the population was sparse. But should there come a time when that Jewish presence was substantial and seemed threatening, no Zionist should be under any illusion that they would not be fiercely resisted.

Ahad Ha'am thought that Herzl, in his fancy suits and with his deracinated German attitude to everything, had no answer to this near insuperable problem. But Herzl himself believed that in his obsession with things spiritual, the deep core of Judaism he accused western Jews of ignoring, Ha'am was forgetting the other side of their character, the one which dwelled in modernity, technology, secular science, all of which were not only compatible with a true Jewish life but were realms of knowledge in which Jews had excelled and pioneered. The technology of the present and future, especially that of hydraulic engineering, would make Ha'am's view of what was cultivable and what was not small-minded, unimaginative and unrealistic. Earlier in 1898 Herzl had been in Holland and there two sights struck him with emotional force. One was the sight of three little Jewish boys in Amsterdam, in the Jodenbuurt, the Jewish quarter where the two great synagogues stood, the two bigger boys holding the hands of the littlest one, triggering in Herzl a sense of how they might grow up as Jews when and if the national home were to be realised. The second sight was the Dutch countryside for which he had a special fondness, since it seemed to him the example par excellence of what human ingenuity and resourcefulness could do with an impossibly unpromising physical habitat. If the Dutch could make the lush polders arise from the waters of the inland seas, then anything was possible for the Jews in a land of swamp and desert. Four years later, in 1902, Herzl published his futuristic novel *Altneuland* (*The Old New Land*) in which, in 1923, a group of travellers return to the Palestine they had first encountered in 1902 (the descriptions of which are closely autobiographical). The 1923 chapters feature a Palestinian Arab, Reshid Pasha, who is the optimised version of Jewish–Arab reconciliation and who has nothing but praise to lavish on the coming of Zionism, for its improvements have lifted all boats, made the local population incomparably better off. Herzl made sure to contrast the brotherly feeling between the Palestinian Arab and the liberal-minded, morally driven head of the 'new Village' with the politician Geyer who preached an exclusive nationalism and who insisted that jobs, land, prosperity should be for Jews only. Ahad Ha'am was not impressed by the sentimental wishful thinking and turned the full force of his critical artillery on the book which he found childishly preposterous.

Two visions of how a Jewish life could be lived in Palestine confronted each other, two visions of how Jews and Arabs could or would live in one land. Jerusalem or Tel Aviv; spiritual or secular. The two visions refused to marry up, to agree on what constitutes a truly Jewish life. They still do.

Onward sailed Theodor Herzl with his dreams, his politics, his Germanophilia, his self-deception, his self-possession and, increasingly, his palpitating Viennese heart. Every so often he would have the doctor, Moritz Schnirer, take his pulse which, under stress, would shoot up to an unhealthy 108. It didn't help that the five of them were sharing a cabin in the stifling heat, so Herzl spent most of the night sleeping on deck under the stars. But as the first light leaked into the sky on the morning of 26 October, everything, absolutely everything seemed well. Peering as hard as he could over the bow of the *Russiya* he made out what he called 'the Jewish coast'.

If he experienced a great surge of emotion at the sight it barely gets registered in the diaries; he is too busy making sure they safely disembark under the suspicious eyes of the Turkish police. At the Jaffa dockside there are also German police allowing the five pith helmets to insist they are there in accordance with the kaiser's instructions. It works. But in the dusty waterside melee, Herzl went out of his way to perform a small act of kindness. Aboard the *Russiya* he had encountered a Romanian Jewish woman who was going to 'Jeruscholajim' (as Herzl spelled it) to find her gravely, possibly terminally, ill daughter.[42] She was terrified that travelling under a Romanian passport the Turks would not allow her to disembark. Herzl approached the wife of one of the French journalists who had been fellow passengers and arranged that the woman could pose as her maid. It worked; mother and daughter could be reunited.

Over the next few days they did lightning tours of the Jewish settlements. At Rishon LeZion, supported by Baron Edmond, where, to Herzl's eye, the colonists lived in fear of the administration, they were shown the wine cellars, the austere living quarters. There was a little recital 'which, unfortunately, was only well intentioned', then a speech which tried to reconcile their respect for Herzl with their deference to the baron and which, Herzl meanly observed, was no better than the attempt to harmonise the violin and the lute in their concert. The village of Rehovot, the following day, he liked better. They were treated to a galloping charge by young Jewish riders on Arab ponies. Just imagine, Herzl wrote, those who at home would be trouser salesmen could be transformed here into Jewish cowboys!

The next morning at the training farm run by the Alliance, everyone was waiting for a promised visit of the kaiser himself. Herzl boasted, smugly, that they would see the two of them exchange greetings. There was some incredulousness but around nine, a cloud of dust was kicked up by a troop of Turkish cavalry, and when it settled, there indeed was the kaiser on his white stallion, the spiked *Pickelhaube* on his head which, when combined with the dust veil, gave him a look like the Saracens in illustrated history books for the young. Herzl had a line of schoolchildren burst into 'Heil dir im Siegerkranz' ('Hail to thee with the victor's garland') sung to the tune of 'God Save the Queen'. Cheered, the kaiser leaned down and shook Herzl's hand with his good arm while jaws gratifyingly dropped. An exchange of shattering banality ensued. Kaiser: 'Very hot. But the country has a future!' Herzl: 'It's still sick.' Kaiser: 'Water! That's what it needs, lots and lots of water.' Herzl: 'Yes, Your Majesty: irrigation, massive irrigation.' Kaiser: 'Still, it has a future, eh?' Off he went in the red dust cloud while the children sang out another chorus.

That afternoon, later than they had hoped, the five boarded the train to Jerusalem. The line from Jaffa had been the prize project of the swashbuckling Sephardi entrepreneur Yosef Navon, born in Jerusalem, educated in Marseilles, builder of Jerusalem's Mahane Yehuda district, named for his brother. Though as an Ottoman subject and a persuasive projector Navon secured the concession, which was also supposed to extend to Gaza and Nablus, he had trouble finding the capital to build it and had sold it to a French lighthouse contractor for a million francs. The Jaffa–Jerusalem section, cutting through the steep grades of the Judaean hills, was operational but notorious for delays. The five pith helmets broiled as they waited and then broiled some more aboard the packed coaches. 'Torture,' said Herzl, who was feeling ill, sweating with some sort of fever and worrying about his pulse. It didn't help that they arrived well after sunset, with Jerusalem seen 'by moondust', and the Kaminitz Hotel was some distance. Herzl wanted to be driven, but the faces on the rest of the company made it clear they were going to have to walk to avoid violating the Sabbath.

The majority of Jerusalem's population at that time, some 70,000, were Jews, but not the kind of Jews Herzl had in mind as the future of the national home; as unlike his *Heydad*-hollering Jewish cowboys as it was possible to be. Everywhere there were *schnorrers*, beggars, so many at the Wailing Wall that any emotional response to the remains of the Temple was impossible, try as he might to summon it up. Everywhere were sleeve-tuggers and the religious in their heavy coats and fur hats who depressed him. He did at least some of the tourism: a swift stride down the Via Dolorosa in defiance of Orthodox mutterings that any Jew who did so would be plagued with dire consequences; climbed the Mount of Olives; visited the 'tombs of the Kings' in the valley of Kidron which had once been owned, at the height of their powers, by the brothers Péreire.

But what Herzl wanted more than anything was word from the kaiser's encampment on the Street of the Prophets, of a time for the fateful audience. It didn't come. The kaiser and his retinue were seen entering the Old City, only thanks to a large hole which had to be blasted in Suleyman's beautiful walls at the Jaffa Gate so the mounted entourage could pass through. His Imperial Majesty duly consecrated the Church of the Holy Redeemer. They were two tourists, each impatient in their own way. As the delay grew, Herzl felt physically worse and worse, and began to panic. The other four were even more demoralised; perhaps it had all been a wild goose chase; perhaps they were just pawns in some sort of international power game of which they were only dimly aware. That was not altogether wrong. It got worse when William Hechler, who had come to Jerusalem, rushed to tell them that France had declared war on Britain and that the kaiser was leaving forthwith for Berlin. It took some hours to dismiss that story as specious. Herzl tried to keep spirits up by giving orders on how they were to dress for the imperial occasion and inspecting their limited wardrobes. Bodenheimer's top hat was ridiculous; his cuffs kept falling down at the ends of his sleeves. Disaster!

Finally, a summons came for Herzl to present himself at the German consulate where he was briskly condescended to by a young official who handed him a radically amended version of the address to the kaiser he had sent in advance. The core of it – the protectorate, the national home, the Chartered Company – much of this had gone in Eulenburg's or Bülow's deletions. Dejection weighed on Herzl, but there would, at least, be the endlessly awaited Jerusalem meeting, the object of all his hopes and plans for years. Germany would be the maker of a new Jewish life. What would Moses Mendelssohn have thought, what would Richard Wagner?

On the morning of 2 November, the five made their way to the grand encampment on the Street of the Prophets, a little beyond the Damascus Gate of the Old City. There were triumphal arches, flags with the imperial colours. The aide-de-camp Count von Kessel, who had met Herzl at the top of the staircase of the Sala pavilion in Constantinople, reappeared and ushered them into the tent where Wilhelm stood, dressed in grey field boots, and 'oddly', Herzl thought, with a riding crop in his good hand. The pleasantries of Constantinople were replaced by formal exchanges, clearly according to Bülow's advice: nothing about the protectorate, words only about the development of Palestine. It needed, said the kaiser uncontroversially, 'water and shade' and then there 'would be room for everyone'. The work and technology of the immigrants would be a stimulus for the Arabs. 'Water,' the kaiser kept saying, 'water and trees, water and shade.' 'We can supply the country with it,' Herzl volunteered. 'It will cost billions, but it will yield billions.' At which the kaiser, reverting to form, slapped his thigh with the riding crop and chuckled, 'Well, money is what you have plenty of ... More money than any of us.' Bülow chipped in, 'Yes, the money which is such a problem for us, you have in abundance.' The hilarity spread, with a distinct undertone of malice. Nothing had changed.

Hydraulics to the rescue. Herzl brought Seidener into the conversation; the talk moved to hydroelectric power, to the Jordan, to what might be envisaged for the future, and just before the kaiser did one of his looks at the watch on his withered arm and signalled it was all over, Herzl hastily attempted to say something about a new Jerusalem, the one he had conjured up in his mind's eye as he climbed the Mount of Olives.

That had been his only true Jerusalem epiphany. He had stood there, looking towards the Dead Sea and the dark rose Mountains of Moab, the purple wilderness beyond. Then he looked back at Suleyman's golden walls, at the pack of buildings crowded in the Old City, and what had to be done came to him all at once. The ancient city should be cleared of traffic, of hucksters, of dirt, of disease. It would be made a realm for walkers alone, pilgrims, worshippers of each and every religion. No one would rule but everyone and their sacred places would be looked after. It would be a Jerusalem of communion for all faiths and for the faithless too.

But beside it, outside the limestone walls, the Jews would build a completely new city: harmoniously designed using the apricot-hued stone of the old. It would have tree-lined avenues, parks, modern schools, theatres – perhaps performing, who knows, his plays. It would be shady, fragrant, civilised, peaceful. Just want it enough and it would be no dream.

And that odd sensation he felt in his heart from time to time, along with a shortness of breath, that little catch and jump, the allegretto of his beating pulse? Well, it was hilly, this Jeruscholajim. It was nothing really; Schnirer had said not to worry, so it was nothing. All would be well.

UNAUTHORITATIVE GLOSSARY OF HEBREW AND YIDDISH TERMS USED IN *BELONGING*

aggadah

post-biblical Jewish teaching and literature (like the Talmud) is divided into legal prescriptions and their explanations, *halakha,* and, as the rabbis like to say, 'everything else'. Everything else is *aggadah*: homiletic stories, tales and lore; legends, free interpretations, pointless nitpicking, meaningful nit-picking, gossip and reports of miraculous events. In yeshivot it is a truism that *halakha* is heavyweight and *aggadah* is what professors of narrative theory teach on their courses. But if you think that the *aggadah* history of the gnat which flew up the nose of the Emperor Titus, and lodged there for seven years eating at his brain until the conqueror of Jerusalem perished is mere idle fable, that's your problem. Not to be confused with the Haggadah (see below), the book used for the Passover Seder, though come to think of it, since most of the Haggadah is *aggadah*, but not vice versa, go ahead and be confused anyway.

aliyah

lit. an ascent, used to describe emigration to the Land of Israel and more specifically the Temple since Jerusalem sits on its hills. But following the destruction of the Temple used also for participation in synagogue service – 'going up' to the Ark of a synagogue or the reading desk

	(see *bimah* and *tevah*) or a more honorific duty like opening or closing the doors of the Ark, or carrying the Sefer Torah scroll to the congregation.
Amidah	lit. standing. The eighteen-blessing core of thrice-daily prayers (morning *shaharit*, afternoon *minhah* and evening *maariv*), recited in silence, and standing, though heavy bobbing, swaying and dipping from the knees (*dukhaning*) is the norm. The deeper the bob the *frummer* (more devout) you'll feel – or at least look. Every Jew has their own favourite *berakha* (blessing) of the eighteen, and the closer, with its invocation of peace, gets an extra nod left and right, along with a backward shuffle and final bob.
anusim	forced converts, secretly practising Judaism, initially referring to Ashkenazim, then to Sephardim, but also used for converts to Islam like the Mashadi Jews of Persia, forced to become Muslims in 1839 and only permitted to practise Judaism openly in 1925. A blood-libel accusation in 1946 triggered an emigration to Israel and the 1979 Islamic revolution intensified the exodus. Twenty thousand Mashadi Jews now live in Israel.
Ashkenazi	in the narrow sense Jews from the Germanic world, but broadened to include those from eastern Europe, in fact anyone other than those tracing roots to Spain and Portugal, to the Maghreb and Levant. Confusingly, there have been and are plenty of Ashkenazi Jews in Mediterranean countries like Italy but it's safe to say anyone whose mouth waters at the prospect of cold poached minced carp crowned with a little yarmulka of boiled carrot can only be Ashkenazi.
badkhan	stand-up entertainer, hired to perform at weddings and other festive occasions, and not only Jewish ones. *Badkhanim* were reported at celebrations of Polish and Ukrainian magnates; their jokes have (as far as I know) been lost to history, though it's a reasonable assumption that a fair number of them must have featured mothers and/or soup.
Beit Din	lit. House of Justice. Jewish religious court consisting of three members, one of whom has to be fully conversant with *halakha*, licensing kosher slaughterers, marriages; ruling on divorces, sometimes arbitrating disputes over wills and even civil litigation. And thus very busy.

bimah	reading desk raised on a dais in Ashkenazi synagogues (for Sephardi usage, see *tevah* below). Traditionally located in the centre of the synagogue and often railed off with finely wrought or turned railings or balustrades. In the nineteenth century, in imitation of church altars, the *bimah* was often moved to the eastern Ark end of the synagogue where it became the focal point for the cantorial leadership of prayers and the recital of sermons.
bokhur	boy or lad, both before and after bar mitzvah. Often used in conjunction with religious students as 'yeshiva *bokhurim*'.
brit milah	lit. covenant, but meaning circumcision normally carried out on the eighth day of a male infant's life though a ritual which *anusim* returning to Judaism underwent in adulthood. Exodus 4:25 supplies a weirdly violent origins narrative when, en route back to Egypt to liberate the Hebrews, Moses is subjected to an attack on his life by God. The assault is forestalled by his wife Zipporah's seizing a stone, cutting the foreskin of their son and throwing it at his feet with the declaration 'surely thou art a bridegroom of blood to me'. As gestures of identification go this was a bit much but it seemed to do the trick for the notoriously unpredictable Jehovah.
chazzan	synagogue cantor, relatively unimportant or even insignificant in ultra-Orthodox communities but a great feature of nineteenth- and twentieth-century synagogues from Russia to the United States. My childhood *chazzan*, the Rev. Tashlitzky, taught me my bar mitzvah portion, steering me through the cantillation while simultaneously training his dachshund to bark impressively every time an '*omeyn*' (amen) was called for.
cheder	Hebrew school mostly for children before bar mitzvah and bat mitzvah age; traditionally teaching *siddur*, the daily and weekly prayer book, *chumash*, the Pentateuch, then moving on to some of the rabbinical commentaries like Rashi's. I briefly taught *chumash* to restive nine-year-olds but never managed to come up to the high standards of the formidably charismatic Mrs Cohen who could burn you with a glance or the tenderly witty Sammy Kramer. 'You know why he was called the prophet Isaiah, boys? Because one eye's higher than the other' (accompanied by eyebrow hike).

chevrah   circle of friends or comrades; used for reading or political circles in diaspora, but invested with specifically Zionist ethos once the movement got going in earnest in the later nineteenth century.

chokhem   lit. wise one, but often used for clever clogs, applied to precociously smart boys not especially reticent about showing off their learning. Talmud *chokhems* are the envy of the yeshiva.

cholent   the one-pot Ashkenazi dish designed for Sabbath observance. It's a violation of the prohibition on work to turn an oven on or off, but nothing prevents an observant Jew from carrying a pot of stew to a baker's oven and leaving it there overnight cooking slowly so that it can be collected for the Sabbath dinner. A hearty, power-packed dish, it characteristically includes beef, lamb or mutton, beans or barley – parboiled before adding to stew – and a bed of sturdy veg – carrots and turnips, onions and potatoes – which, if the hospitable oven is slow and low enough, will coagulate into a toothsome mush, flavoured with the meat juices. Sabbath worshippers (my father for example) enduring long *derashot* (see below) have been known to get testy and take it personally if kept from their *cholent*. Sometimes it's served with the glutinous equally long-reduced and caramelised pot of carrots called *tzimmes*. WARNING! the combined effect of the two dishes rules out any sudden movement for at least twenty-four hours, at risk of severe cardiac stress.

chumash   Pentateuch printed as a book (rather than the Torah scroll). May include rabbinical commentaries on the same page.

cohanim   priests. You can still be a *cohan* without being a Cohen but not vice versa. In the most solemn services the *cohanim* go to the Ark (or the *bimah*), pull the prayer shawl over their heads and formally bless the congregation. Mere Israelites (me) aren't supposed to look, on pain of something terrible but unspecified, so naturally I always did and do.

converso   Jew forced to convert by the Inquisition; known in the Iberian world as 'New Christian' or reprehensibly as 'Marrano' (swine) and constantly subject to well-founded suspicion that they were secretly practising Jews.

derasha	sermon, but more properly disquisition on a particular text or verse from the Torah, from which an artful rabbi will spin more general and universal issues resonating in Judaism, opening up lines of questioning (often, in the Talmudic style, left unresolved).
devekut	lit. 'clinging fast to God'. The trance-like state of total absorption achieved in concentrated prayer.
emunah	unconditional faithfulness to God and the core tenets of Judaism. God is in the habit of setting extreme tests of *emunah*, ordering the sacrifice of one's son for instance or the Job routine.
eshet chayil	'woman of worth' ... for her price is above rubies; much controversy over whether (in view of the jewellery metaphor) we are talking about gem valuation and a nice little dowry or some more generalised measurement of virtue. General agreement though about preciousness of the paragons.
Gemara	rabbinical commentary on the Mishnah, forming the second part of the Talmud and thus a commentary on a commentary. The Gemara can be tough going for the less Talmudically minded especially (as in my case at the age of twelve) when the Gemara teacher has the habit of administering a crisp blow to the back of the head if he suspects his charges of not giving the matter their full and undivided attention.
gerush	exile. Jews can get the feeling wherever they are.
groyse makhers	big shots; movers and shakers, usually shiny-shod, sharp-suited and with a slight swagger in their walk. If they say 'shaaa' to silence your synagogue prattle you usually heed the order. But also used tenderly by mothers for their big boys (from age of about five).
hacohen hagadol	the high priest of the Temple; the only person admitted to the Holy of Holies innermost sanctum on the Day of Atonement.
Haggadah	Passover service book, the only item of the liturgy meant expressly for home use, copiously illustrated, though managing to tell the Exodus story with no mention whatsoever of Moses, probably the result of rabbinic allergy to any sort of charismatic quasi-secular leadership.
Hasidim	a term often but inaccurately used as a synonym for Orthodox or ultra-Orthodox Jews; or still less accurately for anyone dressed in That Hat and sporting long *payes*

and beard. Hasidim are specifically followers of the mystical teachings of the *zaddikim* of the eighteenth and nineteenth centuries, often associated with the Baal Shem Tov. See chapter 12.

Haskalah — the eighteenth-century Jewish 'Enlightenment' (sustained into the nineteenth) which sought to reconcile Judaism with the practice of rational enquiry, and thus make common cause with non-Jewish rationalists.

Havdalah — lit. 'division' – as in that between the Sabbath rest and the working week; the very beautiful ceremony formalising the end of the Sabbath; and involving a particular kind of braided candle, sometimes multicoloured, whose flame is extinguished in a glass of wine; also a decorative spice box in the form of a silver tower complete with bell and little pennant at its top. Havdalah spice boxes are among the most exquisite of Jewish ritual objects and are found in their appropriate decorative vernaculars everywhere from Ethiopia and Yemen to the Ukraine and the fine silverware makers of London.

herem — excommunication or ban imposed by Jewish governing bodies, though in cities like Amsterdam (see chapter 7) often invoked to persuade the errant back to conformity than actually executed. When carried out, extreme in its ostracism.

huppah — canopy extending over bride and groom in wedding ceremony (see *nissuin* below) and symbolising the home they will make together. In modern ceremonies, especially in synagogues, the *huppah* poles may be fixed to the floor, but the idea of a Jewish home is anything but stationary real estate so it's always seemed better to me when the *huppah* is free-floating, held aloft at each corner, the poles wound round with flowers and foliage.

Kabbalah — see volume 1 and chapter 4: the literature and teaching of esoteric mystical Jewish cosmology first set out in the *Sefer Yetzirah*, the *Book of Creation*, dealing with God's creation of the universe and ascribed variously to Abraham and to Rabbi Akivah but first described in the thirteenth century at roughly the same time as the appearance of the second fundamental text, the *Sefer haZohar*. In both, the concept of the *sefirot*, the ten divine emanations, were set out, perpetuated and elaborated in Lurianic Kabbalism in the sixteenth century. In addition, the *Sefer Yetzirah* proposed a complicated numerology based on the twenty-two letters of the Hebrew alphabet from which the world had been brought into being. So, crazy, but very beautiful.

Kaddish — the mourners' prayer, written in Aramaic and entirely without reference to death, but instead an extended glorification of the Almighty. The duty of the mourner is to say Kaddish at thrice-daily services for a year following the death of a parent, child or spouse.

kahal — the self-governing body of autonomous Jewish communities (see chapter 12) mostly in the Russian Pale of Settlement.

kapote — the long robe-like garment or coat now the uniform of ultra-Orthodox Jews but in no way ordained by any kind of commandment; simply the habitual dress of Jews, especially merchants in eighteenth-century Poland and Russia and frozen into an identifying costume. Not to be confused with *kompote*, which is a dish of stewed dried fruit commonly eaten during the weekdays of Passover. Obviously you never want to get *kompote* on your *kapote*.

kashrut — the dietary laws specified in the Torah and elaborated in the Mishnah and Talmud (see volume 1).

kavanah — lit. devotion: unequivocal emotional surrender to prayer.

kedusha — the most intense sacred passage of the Amidah (see above); embodying the 'Holy holy holy is He' chant, at which point congregants raise themselves on their toes three times.

kest — the obligation of a bride and groom's families to support the couple after marriage if necessary. In the Ashkenazi world this often involved a young couple living with one or other family so in effect supported by an extended kinship network. The institution has been invoked as one of the possible reasons for a low Jewish infant mortality rate compared to the rest of the population.

ketubah — because they are often richly decorated and read out at wedding ceremonies, *ketubot* are sometimes mistaken for 'marriage licences' or even romantic formalisations of the union akin to Christian exchanges of vows. In fact they are rather cold-blooded legal documents, written and read (lengthily) in Aramaic, much closer to a prenuptial contract, inheriting from both biblical and Talmudic prescriptions the obligations of the parties. Those of the groom are specified as the obligation to provide shelter, sustenance and sexual union. Often there are also provisions for the assignment of property in the event of the death of one of the parties and other dry-eyed matters. But they may be the only such legal documents to be written in high calligraphic style and ornamented with all kinds of colourful flourishes.

kiddush hashem   lit. 'sanctification of the name' (see volume I), martyrdom, either enforced by persecutors or suicidally enacted to avoid forced conversion. Always distressing and unforgivably horrible when extended to family members including children.

kishkes   guts; generally meaning intestinal fortitude but not excluding testicular varieties. So can women have *kishkes*? Please – what do you think? *Kishka* is also a traditional Ashkenazi dish made of cooked vegetables – yes, those carrots, onions, celery ride again – mixed with matzo meal and chicken fat and made into sausage-like form before being baked.

klezmorim   secular musicians hired to play at festivities, weddings in particular, and in a distinctive style with drone and wailing wind instrument and/or string instrument which by the nineteenth century was usually a fiddle. Klezmorim are often assumed to come from the Polish–Ukrainian–Lithuanian heart of the Pale and klezmorim are documented performing for non-Jewish Polish aristocratic celebrations in the eighteenth century. In fact, both their repertoire and the distinctive combination of instrumental sounds originated in the Balkan borderlands between the Ottoman and south Slavic worlds, hence the unmistakable Romany influence. The skirls and flourishes of fiddle and clarinet are the most famous signatures of the klezmorim, but some of us love, more than anything, the solemn *niggun* slow marches accompanying the warm-up to weddings and which have always seemed to me the Jewish equivalent of the slow jazz marches of black New Orleans. The music of the klezmorim became 'klezmer' when it was shipped across the Atlantic, producing recording stars like ... and hits like 'Roumania' and ... The music all but died out after the Second World War but has undergone a spectacular revival in recent years.

Kol Nidrei   the service of the eve of the Day of Atonement; arguably the most deeply affecting moment in the entire Jewish calendar. Lit. 'all vows', a formula which, perverted by anti-Semites, was held to mean that Jews allowed themselves the repudiation of all contracts when in fact the reference is to the merciful suspension of promises made between Jews and their Almighty Maker. Some congregations say a preliminary prayer beginning 'All Israel Stands Before You', and since synagogues, especially those in non-ultra-Orthodox communities, are usually packed with congregants who may only make an appearance at the New Year and Day of Atonement, the sense of communal kinship with Jews across the world is at its strongest.

ma'amad   the governing body of some Sephardi congregations, most famously of Amsterdam.

maggid   from the same root as *aggadah* (a 'telling'): a preacher but in the storytelling vein, so historically often itinerant; given to preaching homilies from everyday life, legends and parables. In the mystical tradition, though, the *maggid* looms much larger as someone in touch with deep revelation, sometimes involuntary as with spells of automatic writing or inexplicable utterances; even a periodically miraculous worker of wonders.

Marrano   lit. 'swine': the odious name applied by Christians to the *conversos* (see above) they suspected of secret adherence to Jewish observance; subsequently adopted by those reverting to Judaism as a collective badge of pride.

maskilim   practitioners of and believers in the Haskalah (see above).

megillah   literally a story, especially in a single scroll, such as the scroll relating the Book of Esther, read at the minor but exuberant festival of Purim. More freely meaning a long story – about absolutely anything – trouble with the neighbours, a funny thing happening at the kosher butcher's, someone running off with someone he shouldn't, the *gantze megillah*, the whole story, usually so characterised by a listener who doesn't really want to hear it.

melamed   teacher, in *cheder* or sometimes yeshivot, or simply a learned person; in any event, deserving of respect.

menorah   often, but inaccurately, used to describe the eight-branched candlestick or candelabrum celebrating Hanukkah, which is in fact the hanukkiah; the menorah being the *seven*-branched candelabrum which stood in the Jerusalem Temple and which is the most ancient visible symbol of Jewish religious and communal identity, appearing on the coins of the Hasmonean monarchy and on synagogue floors.

meshugaas	Yiddish: craziness; meshuggener: crazy person, liable to be prone to meshugaas, which can also spread infectiously amid institutions. Basically anyone who incomprehensibly, and despite all your best efforts to bring them round to a reasonable point of view, still doesn't agree with you.
mezuzah	Scroll-shaped case containing passages from the Torah, attached to the doorpost of a home, identifying the residents as Jewish and also as faithful to the tenets of Judaism. As per usual, the style and size of the *mezuzah* (conventionally small) represents a fine negotiation between inconspicuousness and self-declaration. There are, however, countless examples of spectacularly decorated *mezuzot*.
midrash	texts interpreting the Hebrew Bible; the earliest dating from the second century; some learned and interrogatory but some fanciful and folkloric elaborations on scripture often derived from oral tradition. In contemporary Judaism, especially in the reform movement, used to characterise any kind of interpretative engagement with both scripture and commentary.
mikvah	purification bath or pool, in the first instance for menstruating women who are required by *halakha* to cleanse themselves *before* immersion. All manner of mikvahs can be found at ancient Jewish sites, including one just outside the walls of the Second Temple by Robinson's Arch; another medieval mikvah, now in the Jewish Museum in London, was discovered during excavation on a building site. Contrary to many assumptions, men can and do use the mikvah, on the eve of Yom Kippur, for example, and some of the more religious on every Shabbat, though male use is customary rather than prescriptive. A mikvah can't just be a body of walled-in water but must be connected to a flowing stream, and according to *halakhic* prescription must be capable of holding at least two hundred gallons.
minyan	the ten adult males required as a minimum for daily prayers. Yes. I know.
mi sheberach	one of the most touching prayers in the Jewish liturgy because, aside from the opening invocation 'may He who blessed our fathers Abraham, Isaac and Jacob' etc., essentially improvised to call for a little help from the Almighty

for those in need of it, usually and especially the ill but in fact anyone and any community in a state of suffering or distress.

Mishnah	the earliest (late first or second century AD) rabbinical commentary on the Torah, the foundation stone of the much larger Talmud. See volume 1 for an account of its writing.
mitnagdim	rabbinical opponents of both the Haskalah and Hasidism (see chapter 12).
mohel	ritual circumciser (see *brit milah* above).
nasi	lit. 'prince'; sometimes used for figures who might turn out to be the Messiah; after all, someone has to.
nebbish	Yiddish for milquetoast or at any rate mediocrity.
nefesh, neshama	elements of the soul, thought of sometimes as almost physiological though enduring after the expiry of the rest of the body.
nissuin	the second act in a Jewish wedding, of which the first is the *kiddushin*, betrothal. *Nissuin* marks the beginning of the couple's married life together.
ohel	lit. 'tent' – a canopy or other structure over the tomb of a prominent or eminent figure; revered sage or *groyse makher* (see above).
parnas, *parnassim* (pl.)	officer of the board of governors of a Sephardi community.
parokhet	synagogue Ark curtain; originally the multicoloured 'veil' hanging before the Holy of Holies in the Jerusalem Temple. Made from fine materials, usually silk or velvet, and often richly embroidered.
payes/peyot	sidelocks worn by Orthodox Jews in compliance, as they read it, with scripture requiring that … (see *simanim* below).
pilpul	hair-splitting debates over fine meaning of scriptural and rabbinic texts like the Talmud. An art in itself though also prone to scholastic aridity and thus not always used flatteringly.
pisher	Yiddish for a drip. You can work out the implications. The entirety of diaspora history, some Jews think, is embodied by the successive name changes of Maurice Lafontaine of Paris who had once been Moritz Spritzwasser of Leipzig but had started out in life as Moyshe the Pisher from Motol. At least his trajectory was upwards.

qelippot   the husks or shells in which, according to Kabbalistic literature, the divine sparks are imprisoned. The work of *tiqqun* or healing is to liberate those sparks and thus reunify creation. Sometimes *qelippot* has been used as a general term for evil, or at any rate the obstruction of good.

rebbe   colloquial for rabbi, but since there is no Jewish equivalent of ordination may just be a term for teacher. 'Rebbe' or 'reb' can thus be conferred as a term of respect on any learned member of the community, even a *groyse makher* (see above).

resh galuta   chief of the exile; a term apparently first coined in the Babylonian exile and certainly used for the chief notables responsible for representing the medieval Jewish community in cities like Cairo and Baghdad. Later used honorifically to mean any grandee speaking to governments on behalf of the Jews – Moses Montefiore for instance.

rimmonim   lit. pomegranates; but also the name for finials, often but not invariably silver, that slip over the wooden posts supporting the Torah scrolls. They may indeed be pomegranate-shaped, but evolved into a variety of decorative forms including bell towers and crowns. *Rimmonim* were described by scripture ornamenting the costume of the high priest and they appear on coins of the Hasmonean kingdom of Judah. A tradition claims that the number of its seeds corresponds to the 613 positive commandments in the Torah. No one is counting.

Romaniot   Jews living in and whose culture was formed by the medieval Byzantine empire and who remained in its cities and island territories following the Ottoman conquest (see chapter 4).

ruakh   'breath' but also 'spirit': residing not just in the body but the soul, along with *neshama* (see above).

schnorrer   beggar. Can be used as noun or verb; an attitude as well as an occupation. You can be a millionaire and still be a *schnorrer.*

sefirot   in Kabbalah, the ten divine emanations (see chapter 4).

Sephardi   lit. Jews of Spanish and Portuguese origin, but commonly used to describe any non-Ashkenazi (see above) Jews. Latterly, especially in Israel, Jews from the North African Maghreb, the Middle East (Syria, Iraq, Lebanon and the Yemen), as well as communities from Ethiopia and India, are called 'Mizrachi' ('from the East'). True (i.e. Spanish–Portuguese) Sephardim have a rich literature and oral tradition (including songs) in the Judaeo-Spanish language, Ladino.

Shabbat	Hebrew for the Sabbath; 'Shabbes' in Yiddish.
shadkhan	matchmaker.
shamash	synagogue officer, akin to a verger or sexton, charged with custody of the physical fabric of the building but also its daily material needs – available prayer books, candles and so on. In reform synagogues, boxes of yarmulkes and *tallits* provided for worshippers. Also used as a name for the 'extra' candlestick on the hanukkiah used to light the others.
Shavuot	the Feast of Weeks, Pentecost.
shefa	in Kabbalah another divine emanation and more loosely understood in, for example, Hasidism as the divine 'flow' from the ineffable to the earthly world.
Shekhina	divine presence, first mentioned in the Dead Sea Scrolls and in rabbinic literature, often as a female force, and sometimes connected with the Shabbat bride. More generally the resting place of divinity, and thus an element of holy fire and warmth within a married home.
sheytl	wig worn by ultra-Orthodox married women, required to shave their heads.
shiva	full seven days of mourning following a death; of profound importance in Jewish life as it enables friends and extended family to visit with the bereaved, attend prayers, and offer comfort and reminiscence. Mourners during the week of *shiva* sit on low chairs in rooms with covered mirrors.
shokhet	ritual slaughterer of animals intended for consumption according to Jewish dietary laws of kashrut. Rabbinically licensed or by a Beit Din. Absolute sharpness of blades was required to minimise any possibility of animal suffering about which there was much debate among the Hasidim.
shtadlan	professional negotiator and intercessor on behalf of a Jewish community with non-Jewish authorities, nobles, government officials and the like, especially in Poland and central Europe in the sixteenth to eighteenth centuries. *Shtadlanim* were hired for being well connected, having the linguistic fluency, social or business connections, and being seen in the Gentile world as men of substance and authority. They were not, however, above mobilising 'gifts' (bribes really) to grease the wheels of their negotiations, passing on the responsibility of raising sums (or objects) to the communities who had called on them.

shtreimel	fur-trimmed, broad-brimmed hat, sometimes with raised crown; another item borrowed from standard Polish merchant costume of the eighteenth century and turned into an obligatory item for the ultra-Orthodox. Often seen covered with a plastic sheath in Jerusalem's rainy season.
shul	Yiddish for synagogue.
Shulkhan Arukh	lit. 'Set Table'; the compilation of laws and observances governing Jewish life written by Joseph Karo in the sixteenth century; periodically revised and very much part of modern Jewish instruction in the *cheder*.
shvitz	sweat – noun and verb.
siddur	daily prayer book.
simanim	the oiled and spectacularly curled hanging sidelocks worn by Yemeni Jews (see chapter 15).
sukkah	the tabernacle, in which Jews dwell and eat during the eight days of the autumn festival of Sukkot; characteristically decorated with fruit and greenery hung from a fretwork roof open to the sky, an opportunity especially for children.
taschlikh	the purification ritual.
tefillah	prayer.
tefillin	phylacteries: two small leather boxes containing passages from the Torah, one connected to leather straps bound around the arm, making, on the fingers, the letter *shin* for the permitted euphemistic name of the Almighty; the other set on the brow, worn for the daily morning service (except on Shabbat) as required (more or less) by Deuteronomy 6:8 so that the commandments would be bound on hands and head.
tevah	the raised, often railed dais for reading the Torah in Sephardi synagogues (see *bimah* for Ashkenazi version.) Usually separate from the 'ark' holding the Sefer Torah, and this gets complicated since the Hebrew word is used just twice in the Torah; once for Noah's Ark, and once for the basket in which the child Moses was placed in the Nile to spare him the death to male Hebrew children ordered by the Pharaoh, and which in some translations is also rendered as 'ark'. So the *tevah,* in either version, is a place of safety – and where could be safer than a reading desk?
thummim	together with *urim*, objects set on the breastplate of the high priest and used to obtain oracles. But what were they *precisely*? No one has a clue.

tiqqun	see *qelippot* above: in Kabbalah, a reparation of the universe, so a big deal; now used in a more touchy-feely way to mean 'healing', especially of the riven contemporary world. Nice idea.
trayf	non-kosher food; especially fish without fins and scales, animals missing either a cloven hoof or a ruminant stomach, 'creeping' things – but Leviticus and Deuteronomy aren't always in total conformity about definitions. Leviticus for example deems locusts (if crunchy) flying creatures and thus kosher while Deuteronomy takes a harder line about their creepiness and deems them definitely *trayf*.
tshuva	lit. 'return'; signifying also repentance, and still more generally a coming back to the fold of a Jewish life.
tsuris	troubles. Not all of Jewish history.
tzedaka	lit. 'righteousness' but in Jewish social practice the giving of charity; a perfectly beautiful conflation.
tzimtzum	the Great Contraction (in Lurianic Kabbalah) when the Ein Sof, the One without End who had filled the entirety of the universe, withdrew leaving a void in which the worlds of matter might be formed.
yachad	see volume 1: the community at Qumran known from the Dead Sea Scrolls.
yeshiva	Jewish seminary, institution of higher Jewish learning.
yizkor	memorial prayer for parents or children said on festival holy days and the high holy days.
Yom Kippur	Day of Atonement.
zaddik	saintly eminence, especially in the Hasidic world.

NOTES

Chapter 1

1. Eldad the Danite, in Elkan Nathan Adler, *Jewish Travellers in the Middle Ages* (New York, 1987), 14. For the Sambatyon and the tradition of the Tribes: Zvi Ben-Dor Benite, *The Ten Lost Tribes: A World History* (Oxford, 2009), 86ff; Hillel Halkin, *Across the Sabbath River: In Search of a Lost Tribe of Israel* (New York, 2006), 96ff.

2. Eldad, in Adler, 13.

3. The letter is in Franz Kobler, *Letters of Jews Through the Ages, Volume One – From Biblical Times to the Renaissance: A Self-portrait of the Jewish People* (New York, 1952), 311.

4. Abrahamo Peritsol (Abraham Farissol), *Itinera Mundi Sic Dicta Nempe Cosmographia [Iggeret Orhot Olam]*, trans. Thomas Hyde (Oxford, 1691), 151. Hyde was professor of Arabic and Hebrew at Oxford and head librarian at the Bodleian. His translation, made with the help of Rabbi Isaac Abendani, was based on a manuscript lodged in the library which predated the first published 1586 Venice edition. Hyde accepted there could be such a river as the Sambatyon and its general whereabouts not far from the Ganges or 'River Gozan', while remaining heavily sceptical about the accounts of its behaviour. Marvin J. Heller, *The Seventeenth Century Hebrew Book*, 2 vols (Leiden, 2011), 1177. On Farissol's geography, and the influence of messianic impulses: David B. Ruderman, *The World of a Renaissance Jew: The Life and Thought of Abraham ben Mordecai Farissol* (Cincinatti, 1981), 131–43.

5. David Ha-Reuveni's own extraordinary account is in Adler, 251–328. The manuscript disappeared from the Bodleian at some point after 1867, the year in which Y. Y. Cohen used tracing paper to copy the entirety of its content by hand. The provenance is dependable enough to have convinced most scholars, in particular Aharon Zeev Aescoly, *Sippur David HaReuveni* (Jerusalem, 1993), of its authenticity. On David

and Solomon Molkho: Moshe Idel, *Messianic Mystics* (New Haven, 1998), 144–52; Harris Lenowitz, *Jewish Messiahs from Galilee to Crown Heights* (Oxford, 1998), 103–25; Yirimiyahu Yovel, *The Others Within: Split Identity, the Marrano and Emerging Modernity* (Princeton, 2009), 205–8; Matt Goldish, 'Mystical Messianism: From the Renaissance to the Enlightenment', in Frederick E. Greenspan (ed.), *Jewish Mysticism and Kabbalah: New Insights and Scholarship* (New York, 2011), 120–3; Miriam Eliav-Feldon, 'Invented Identities and Credulity in the Age of Prophecy and Exploration', *Journal of Early Modern History*, 3:3 (1999), 203–32; Moti Benmelech, 'History, Politics and Messianism: David ha'Reuveni's Origin and Mission', *Association of Jewish Studies Review*, 35:1 (April 2011), 31–60.

6.   Lenowitz, 103.

7.   Others followed: the 'Canton' synagogue, also facing the piazza of the Gheto Novo, in 1532; the 'Levantine' in 1541; the 'Italian' in 1572; and the 'Ponentine' (Spanish–Portuguese) in 1580. On the foundation of the ghetto and the relationships between the Jewish community and the government of the republic: Robert C. Davis and Benjamin Ravid (eds.), *The Jews of Early Modern Venice* (Baltimore, 2001), especially the essays by David Malkiel and Benjamin Ravid; Brian Pullan, *The Jews of Europe and the Inquisition of Venice, 1550–1670* (Oxford, 1983). Riccardo Calimani, *The Ghetto of Venice* (Milan, 1985), is still in its way a narrative classic.

8.   Katrin Kogman-Appel, 'Illuminated Bibles and the Rewritten Bible: The Place of Moses dal Castellazzo in Early Modern Book History', online academia.edu, 2, 1–18; Avigdor Shulvass, *The Jews in the World of the Renaissance* (Leiden, 1973), 240–1. On the history of the 'Warsaw Codex' and for a facsimile, Mendel Metzger, 'Le pentateuque en images de l'ancienne collection Wolf de Dresde et de la communaute juive de Berlin – Codex 1164 de l'Institut historique juive de Varsovie', in Kurt Schubert (ed.), *Bilder-Pentateuch von Moses dal Castellazzo, Venedig 1521: Vollständige Faksimile Ausgabe im Original Format des Codex 1164 aus dem besitz Judisches Historisch Instituts Warschau* (Vienna, 1986), 119–31.

9.   Diane Wolfthal, 'Remembering Amalek and Nebuchadnezzar: Biblical Warfare and Symbolic Violence in Two Images in Italian Renaissance Yiddish Books of Customs', in Pia Cuneo (ed.), *Artful Armies, Beautiful Battles: Art and Warfare in Early Modern Europe* (Leiden, 2002), 203.

10. Benmelech, 42ff.

11. See Simon Schama, *The Story of the Jews: Finding the Words, 1000 BCE–1492 CE* (London, 2013), 415ff.

12. Lenowitz, 115–16.

Chapter 2

1. Samuel Usque, *Consolation for the Tribulations of Israel*, ed. and trans. Martin A. Cohen (Philadelphia, 1964), 198a. On Usque in Ferrara and the reception of *conversos* there, see Renée Levine Melammed, *A Question of Identity: Iberian Conversos in Historical Perspective* (Oxford, 2004), 112–14.

2. The details come from the extraordinary 'Regimento' written in Spanish and prepared for the travellers, dated 1544, published in Aron Di Leone Leoni, *The Hebrew Portuguese Nations in Antwerp and London at the Time of Charles V and Henry VIII: New Documents and Interpretations* (Jersey City, 2005), 185–8, to which this account is much indebted.

3. Usque, 208.

4. Ibid., 75.

5. For Gracia and Reyna Benveniste, known for most of their lives as Beatriz de Luna or Beatriz Mendes and Brianda Mendes: Cecil Roth, *Doña Gracia of the House of Nasi* (Philadelphia, 1947); much more recently and more firmly based on archival research, Andrée Aelion Brooks, *The Woman Who Defied Kings: The Life and Times of Doña Gracia Nasi* (St Paul, 2002); Marianna D. Birnbaum, *The Long Journey of Gracia Mendes* (Budapest, 2003). Aron Di Leone Leoni's archival research (see above, n. 2) is constantly refining what we know of the career of the two sisters.

6. S. D. Goitein and Mordechai A. Freidman (eds.), *Indian Traders of the Middle Ages: Documents from the Cairo Geniza* (Leiden, 2007).

7. Herman P. Salomon and Aron Di Leone Leoni, 'Mendes, Benveniste, de Luna, Nasci: The State of the Art (1532–1558)', *Jewish Quarterly Review*, 88: 3/4 (Jan–Apr, 1998), 135–211.

8. This is Cecil Roth's speculation in *Doña Gracia*, but as Aron Di Leone Leoni points out it remains conjecture.

9. The first historian to reveal this undercover world of Jews in Tudor England was Lucien Wolf, 'The Jews in Tudor England', in his *Essays in Jewish History* (London, 1934). Also see Edgar Samuel, 'London's Portuguese Jewish Community 1540–1573', in Randolph Vigne and Charles Littleton (eds.), *From Strangers to Citizens: The Integration of Immigrant Communities in Britain, Ireland and Colonial America 1550–1750* (Brighton, 2001).

10. Samuel, 239.

11. Ibid., 240.

12. Howard Tzvi Adelman, 'The Venetian Identities of Beatrice and Brianda de Luna', *Nashim: A Journal of Jewish Women's Studies and Gender Issues*, 25 (Autumn 2013), 10–29.

13. Ibid., 15. Adelman has radically and convincingly overthrown the long-standing version of the respective characters of the two women.

14. Alice Fernand-Halpern, 'Une grande dame juive de la Renaissance', *Revul de Paris*, 36:17 (1929), 148; Jacob Reznik, *Le duc Joseph de Naxas; contribution à l'histoire juive de XVIe siècle* (Paris, 1936), 49; Brooks, *Woman Who Defied Kings*, 176.

15. Adelman, 21.

16. Aron Di Leone Leoni, 'Gli ebrei sefardisti a Ferrara da Ercole I a Ercole II. Nove ricerche e interpretazione', *Rassegna Mensile di Israel*, 52 (1987), 407–18.

17. Melammed, 115.

18. R. Segre, 'La tipografia ebraica a Ferrara e la stampa della Biblia', *Italia medievale ed umanistica*, 35 (1992), 305–32.

19. Kenneth Stow, 'The Burning of the Talmud in 1553 in the Light of Sixteenth Century Catholic Attitudes towards the Talmud', in Stow, *Jewish Life in Early Modern Rome: Challenge, Conversion and Private Life* (Aldershot, 2007), 1–25.

20. Usque, 47.

21. See Simon Schama, *The Story of the Jews: Finding the Words, 1000 BCE–1492 CE* (London, 2013), 368–73.

22. Usque, 52.

23. Maria Teresa Guerrini, 'New Documents on Samuel Usque, the Author of the *Consolaçam as Tribulaçoens de Israel*', *Sefarad revistas*, 61:1 (2001), 83–9.

24. Usque, 229.

25. Guerrini, 84–5.

26. Usque, 227.

27. Ibid., 243.

28. Ibid., 231.

29. Ibid., 230.

Chapter 3

1. The description of Leone's ideal theatre and staging, including his discussion of optics and the effects of light both in the auditorium and on stage, is taken from his *Quattro Dialoghi in Materia di Rappresentazioni Sceniche*. I have used the edition by Ferruccio Marotti (Milan, 1968). Leone's whole approach represents a radical redefinition of what theatre *was*, away from Renaissance humanists' concern to reinstate the classical aesthetics of Aristotle and Plato, towards the empirical practice of stagecraft, leaning heavily on optics, and the illusion of the stage as an extension of the real world. His was a forward-facing Renaissance dramaturgy.

2.   There are good introductions to Leone and his work by Alfred S. Golding in *A Comedy of Betrothal (Tsahoth B'dihutha D'Kiddushin)* (Ottawa, 1988), 16ff; and Donald Beecher and Massimo Ciavolella (trans.), *The Three Sisters* (Ottawa, 1993). Many aspects of Leone's own works and career, as well as the Mantuan culture in which he flourished, are in Ahuva Belkin (ed.), *Leone de Sommi and the Performing Arts* (Tel Aviv, 1997). The PhD dissertation of Wendy Sue Botuck, 'Leone de Sommi: Jewish Participation in Italian Renaissance Theatre' (UMI reprints, 1991), is also a pioneering and exceptionally valuable work of scholarship. There is as well a vivid account (the first in modern Jewish historiography in any detail) in the lovely and readable book by Cecil Roth, *The Jews in the Renaissance* (Philadelphia, 1959), 243–69.

3.   As readers of Volume 1 of *The Story of the Jews* will know, I don't believe that the entirety of Jewish cultural history should be explained as response to trauma, but the history of Jewish public performance begins with the realisation that the popularity of the Esther plays with Gentiles offered an opportunity to overturn stereotypes of Jews as victims or malignant conspirators. However, the manner in which Jews were represented in plays like *The Jew of Malta* and *The Merchant of Venice*, performed in theatres from which they were missing as actors, suggests this liberation from stereotype had some way to go. If only there were a contemporary performance history of *The Merchant of Venice*! See John Gross, *Shylock: Four Hundred Years in the Life of a Legend* (London, 1993).

4.   David Kaufmann, 'Leone de Sommi Portaleone (1527–92): Dramatist and Founder of a Synagogue at Mantua', *Jewish Quarterly Review*, 10 (April 1898), 455–61.

5.   Anna Levenstein, 'Songs for the First Hebrew Play *Tsahut bedihuta dekidushin*, by Leone de' Sommi (1527–1592)', MA dissertation (Case Western Reserve University, January 2006), 85–141.

6.   Botuck, 282.

7.   Ibid., 281.

8.   Ibid., 283.

9.   Ibid., 287.

10.   Don Harrán, 'Madama Europe, Jewish Singer in Late Renaissance Mantua', in Thomas J. Mathiesen and Benito V. Rivera, *Festa Musicologica: Essays in Honour of George J. Buelow* (Stuyvesant, 1995), 197–232.

11.   There is a lively debate among scholars as to whether the primary thrust of *Cum nimis absurdum* was conversionary or punitive. It seems to me that it could have been both at the same time. Roberto Bonfil, *Jewish Life in Renaissance Italy*, trans. Anthony Oldcorn (Berkeley, 1994), 71, argues that the imposition of the ghetto in Rome was a

'compromise', preferable as in Venice to outright expulsion. This begs a big issue and seems to me excessively counter-intuitive. The Jewish population in Venice was much less deeply rooted in ancient places of residence when the ghetto there was established. In the case of Rome it did not preclude acts of expulsion elsewhere in the papal territories as the painful experience of 1569 demonstrated. On the foundation and character of the Roman ghetto, see Kenneth Stow, *Theater of Acculturation: The Roman Ghetto in the 16th Century* (Seattle, 2001).

12.   Don Harrán, 'The Levi Dynasty: Three Generations of Jewish Musicians in sixteenth-century Mantua', in Giuseppe Veltri and Gianfranco Miletto (eds.), *Rabbi Judah Moscato and the Jewish Intellectual World in Mantua in the 16th and 17th Centuries* (Leiden, 2012), 167–99.

13.   Ibid., 179–80.

14.   On Jewish musicians and composers, see Donald C. Sanders, *Music at the Gonzaga Court in Mantua* (Plymouth, 2012), 108–12; Shlomo Simonsohn, *History of the Jews in the Duchy of Mantua* (Jerusalem, 1977), 669–77; Roth, *Jews in the Renaissance*, 283ff.

15.   On Colorni, see Rabbi Giuseppe Jare, *Abraham Colorni: Ingegnere di Alfonso II d'Este* (Ferrara, 1891); Cecil Roth, 'The Amazing Abraham Colorni', in *Personalities and Events in Jewish History* (Philadelphia, 1953) 296–304. Lately there has been a minor and very welcome Colorni industry of archival research and interpretation. See in particular Ariel Toaff, *Il prestigiatore di Dio – Avventura e miracoli di un alchemista ebreo* (Milan, 2010); and the important article by Daniel Jutte, 'Trading Secrets: Jews and the Early Modern Quest for Clandestine Knowledge', *Isis*, 4 (December 2012), 665–86.

16.   Simonsohn, 33; L. Carnevali, *Il Ghetto di Mantova* (Mantua, 1884), 13.

Chapter 4

1.   Cecil Roth, *The Duke of Naxos of the House of Nasi* (Philadelphia, 1948), 43.

2.   Nevra Necipoglu, *Architecture, Ceremonial and Power: The Topkapi Palace in the Fifteenth and Sixteenth Centuries* (New York, 1991), 69ff.

3.   Minna Rozen, *A History of the Jewish Community in Istanbul: The Formative Years, 1453–1566* (Leiden, 2006), 208–9.

4.   For the earlier history of such defamations in the Christian world, see Simon Schama, *The Story of the Jews: Finding the Words, 1000 BCE–1492 CE* (London, 2013), 307–10, 363–5.

5.   Cecil Roth, *Doña Gracia of the House of Nasi* (Philadelphia, 1947), 84.

6. Hans Dernschwam, *Tagebuch einer Reise nach Konstantinople und Kleinasien (1554–1555)*, ed. F. Babinger (Munich, 1923), 290.

7. Aleida Paudice, *Between Several Worlds: The Life and Writings of Elia Capsali: The Historical Works of a 16th-Century Rabbi* (Munich, 2010), 99–127.

8. Joseph Hacker, 'The Surgun System and Jewish Society in the Ottoman Empire during the Fifteenth to the Seventeenth Centuries', in Aron Rodrigue (ed.), *Ottoman and Turkish Jewry: Community and Leadership* (Bloomington, 1992), 1–65.

9. Ibid., 32ff.

10. For numbers and the difficulties of the two communities, Esther Benbassa and Aron Rodrigue, *The Jews of the Balkans: The Judaeo-Spanish Community 15th to 20th Centuries* (Oxford, 1995), 9–29; also Walter Weiker, *Ottomans, Turks and the Jewish Polity: A History of the Jews of Turkey* (New York, 1992), 40–1.

11. Sanford J. Shaw, *The Jews of the Ottoman Empire and the Turkish Republic* (New York, 1991), 79. See also Alfred Rubens, *A History of Jewish Costume* (New York, 1967), 40ff.

12. The synagogue existed – with an unusual *tevah* reached by galleries – until 1655 when a massive earthquake destroyed it; it was subsequently rebuilt as a near replica of the original.

13. Rozen, 78.

14. Roth, *Naxos*, 31.

15. Benjamin Arbel, *Trading Nations: Jews, Venetians and the Early Modern Eastern Mediterranean* (Leiden, 1995), 22ff. Arbel makes this multiplication of Castros quite clear, finally explaining why an 'Abraham Castro' is identified as having converted to Islam yet *also* identified as 'the Jew'. One did; one didn't. On Jewish tax farmers, see H. Gerber, 'Jewish Tax Farmers in the Ottoman Empire', *Journal of Turkish Studies*, 10 (1986), 143–54.

16. An effort has been made to argue that the Jerusalem walls were constructed as a precautionary measure against the possibility of a latter-day Crusade for the Holy Places. But it seems wildly unlikely that an administration as intelligently informed as Suleyman's would have mistaken the usual Habsburg bluster for actual strategic intent.

17. Abraham David, *To Come to the Land: Immigration and Settlement in Sixteenth-Century Eretz-Israel*, trans. Dean Orden (Tuscaloosa, 1999).

18. Lawrence Fine, 'New Approaches to the Study of Kabbalists in 16th-Century Safed', in Frederick E. Greenspan (ed.), *Jewish Mysticism and Kabbalah: New Insights and Scholarship* (New York, 2011), 91–111.

19. Benbassa and Rodrigue, 39.

20. Roth, *Naxos*, 126–9.

21. Ibid., 126–7; David, 18–19.

22. *The Diary of Master Thomas Dallam 1599–1600, Early Travels and Voyages in the Levant,* Hakluyt Society (1893), 68–74; Lisa Jardine, *A Point of View,* BBC Radio 4, December 2007; Jerry Brotton, *The Sultan and the Queen: The Untold Story of Elizabeth and Islam* (London, 2016).

23. Susan Skilliter, 'Three Letters from the Ottoman "Sultana" Safiye to Queen Elizabeth I', in S. M. Stern (ed.), *Documents from the Islamic Chanceries, First Series* (Cambridge, MA, 1965), 184ff; on the *kiras,* see Leslie Peirce, *The Imperial Harem: Women and Sovereignty in the Ottoman Empire* (New York, 1993), 223–6, and *idem,* 'Gender and Sexual Propriety in Ottoman Royal Women's Patronage', in D. Fairchild Ruggles (ed.), *Women, Patronage, and Self-Representation in Islamic Societies* (Albany, 2000), 53–68.

Chapter 5

1. Leone Modena, *The Autobiography of a Seventeenth-Century Venetian Rabbi: Leon Modena's 'Life of Judah',* trans. and ed. Mark R. Cohen, notes by Howard Tzvi Adelman and Benjamin Ravid (Princeton, 1988), 111.

2. Raphael Patai, *The Jewish Alchemists* (Princeton, 1994), 340.

3. Ibid., 401.

4. Ibid., 350.

5. Modena, 212.

6. Ibid., 112.

7. Ibid., 93.

8. Ibid., 91.

9. Joanna Weinberg, 'Preaching in the Venetian Ghetto: The Sermons of Leon Modena', in David B. Ruderman (ed.), *Preachers of the Italian Ghetto* (Berkeley, 1992), 110ff.

10. On ghetto tourism, Eva Johanna Holmberg, *Jews in the Early Modern English Imagination: A Scattered Nation* (Farnham, 2011), 35–7.

11. Thomas Coryate, *Coryat's Crudities* (London: Printed by W[illiam] S[tansby] for the author, 1611), 233.

12. Samuel Purchas, *Purchas, His Pilgrimage* (London, 1613), 165; Holmberg, 77.

13. Brian Pullan, *The Jews of Europe and the Inquisition of Venice, 1550–1670* (Oxford, 1983), 165.

14. Coryate, 233; see also Pullan, 159.

15. The Guercino, for example, was commissioned in 1627 in Ferrara by Cardinal Magalotti *at the same time* as he instituted a ghetto in that hitherto freest and most tolerant of Italian city states. The *Esther* was supposed to celebrate his 'clemency'. See Shelley Perlove, 'Judaism and the Arts in Early Modern Europe: Jewish and Christian Encounters', in

Babette Bohn and James M. Saslow (eds.), *A Companion to Renaissance and Baroque Art* (Oxford, 2013), 53ff.

16. Sarra Copia Sulam, *Jewish Poet and Intellectual in Seventeenth-Century Venice: The Works of Sarra Copia Sulam in Verse and Prose*, trans. and ed. Don Harrán (Chicago, 2009), 201. See also Howard Tzvi Adelman, 'Jewish Women and Family Life Inside and Outside the Ghetto', in Robert C. Davis and Benjamin Ravid (eds.), *The Jews of Early Modern Venice* (Baltimore, 2001), 146ff.

17. On Sarra's vocal and musical performances, Don Harrán, 'Doubly Tainted and Doubly Talented: The Jewish Poetess Sara Copio (d. 1641) as Heroic Singer', in Irene Alm, Alyson McLamore and Colleen Reardon (eds.), *Musica Franca: Essays in Honor of Frank A. D'Accone* (Stuyvesant, 1996), 367–410.

18. Pellegrino Acarelli, *Debora Ascarelli, poetessa* (Rome, 1925).

19. Carla Boccata, 'Lettere di Ansaldo Cebà, genovese, a Sara Copio Sullam, poetessa del ghetto di Venezia', in *Rassegna mensile di Israel*, 40 (1974).

20. Copia Sulam, 122–3.

21. Ibid., 227.

22. Ibid., 159.

23. Ibid., 138.

24. Ibid., 207.

25. Ibid., 182.

26. Ibid., 183.

27. Ibid., 270; the subsequent exchange is 271–348.

28. Ibid., 314.

29. Ibid., 317.

30. Ibid., 228.

31. Ibid., 254.

32. Ibid., 266.

33. Ibid., 514.

34. Don Harrán, '"Dum Recordaremur Sion": Music in the Life and Thought of the Venetian Rabbi Leon Modena (1571–1648)', *Association for Jewish Studies Review*, 23:1 (1998), 17–61; *idem*, 'Jewish Musical Culture: Leon Modena', in Davis and Ravid (eds.), 211–30; on Rossi: *idem*, *Salomone Rossi: Jewish Musician in Late Renaissance Mantua* (Oxford, 1999); Joshua R. Jacobson, 'Defending Salomone Rossi: The Transformation and Justification of Jewish Music in Renaissance Italy', *IRis* (Music Faculty Publications, Northwestern University, October 2008), 85–92.

35. Modena, 24–5. See also Don Harrán, 'Tradition and Innovation in Jewish Music of the Later Renaissance', *Journal of Musicology*, 7:1 (Winter 1989),

107–30; Paul Nettl and Theodore Baker, 'Some Early Jewish Musicians', *Musical Quarterly*, 17:1 (1936), 40–6.

36. Miraculously, Obadiah Ha-Ger's score of the hymn to Moses was found among the countless manuscripts preserved in the Cairo Geniza. Norman Golb, 'The Autograph Memoirs of Obadiah the Proselyte of Oppido Lucano', Convengno Internazionale di Studi, Giovanni-Obadiah da Oppido: proselito, viaggiatore e musicista dell'età normanna (online proceedings), Oppido Lucano, March 2004.

37. Israel Adler, *La pratique musicale savante dans quelques communautés juives en Europe aux XVIIe et XVIIIe siècles*, 2 vols (Paris, 1996); *idem*, 'The Rise of Art Music in the Italian Ghetto: The Influence of Segregation on Jewish Musical Praxis', in A. Altmann (ed.), *Jewish Medieval and Renaissance Studies* (Cambridge, MA, 1987), 321–64.

38. Modena, 117.

39. Ibid., 120.

40. Ibid., 121.

41. Published (in Hebrew) as *The Songs of Solomon: Psalms, Songs and Hymns which have been set to music for 3, 4, 5, 6, 7, and 8 voices by Salomone Rossi, resident of the holy congregation of Mantua. In order to praise God and to sing His exalted name. Something new in the land* (Venice, 1623).

42. On the experience and history of the prayer, Leon Wieseltier, *Kaddish* (New York, 1998).

43. Leone di Modena, *Historia de Riti Hebraici* (Paris, 1638); Simone Luzzatto, *Discorso circa il stato de gl'Hebraici et in particolar di morandi nell' in citta di venezia* (Venice, 1638).

Chapter 6

1. The inscriptions were written on three stone stelae, dated 1489, 1512 and 1663. The last of these had an additional inscription added on the reverse. The later the inscription the more likely it was to claim the most ancient myth of origins (in this case all the way back to the Chou dynasty). Tiberiu Weisz, *The Kaifeng Stone Inscriptions: The Legacy of the Jewish Community of Ancient China* (Lincoln, Nebraska, 2006). See also: Chen Yuan, 'A Study of the Israelite Religion in Kaifeng', in Sidney Shapiro (ed.), *Jews in Old China: Studies by Chinese Scholars* (New York, 2001), 15–45; Michael Pollak, 'The Revelation of a Jewish Presence in Seventeenth Century China: Its Impact on Western Messianic Thought', in Jonathan Goldstein (ed.), *The Jews of China, Vol. 1: Historical and Comparative Perspectives* (Armonk, 1999), 50–70; Irene Eder, 'Kaifeng Jews

Revisited: Sinification as Affirmation of Identity', *Monumenta Serica Institute*, 41 (1993), 231–47; Donald Leslie, *The Survival of the Chinese Jews: The Jewish Community of Kaifeng* (Leiden, 1972).

2. The presence of Kaifeng Jewish artefacts in Canada is largely due to the presence of Anglican-Canadian missionaries in the region in the nineteenth and twentieth centuries. Bishop William White, who lived in Kaifeng, published a pioneering three-volume survey, *Chinese Jews* (Toronto, 1942).

3. Weisz, 6–7.

4. Xu Xin, *The Jews of Kaifeng, China: History, Culture, Religion* (Jersey City, 2004), 84.

5. Fook Kong-wong and Dalia Yasharpour, *The Haggadah of the Kaifeng Jews of China* (Leiden, 2011).

6. Michael Pollak, *Mandarins, Jews and Missionaries: The Jewish Experience in the Chinese Empire* (New York, 1983), 293.

7. Weisz, 10.

8. Pollak, 71ff.

9. Ibid., 71.

10. Ibid., 72.

11. Ibid., 328.

12. S. D. Goitein and Mordechai A. Freidman (eds.), *India Traders of the Middle Ages: Documents from the Cairo Geniza* (Leiden, 2007).

13. Peter Mark and José da Silva Horta, *The Forgotten Diaspora: Jewish Communities in West Africa and the Making of the Atlantic World* (Cambridge, 2011).

14. Peter Mark and José da Silva Horta, 'Catholics, Jews and Muslims in Early Seventeenth Century Guinea', in Richard L. Kagan and Philip D. Morgan (eds.), *Atlantic Diasporas: Jews, Conversos and Crypto-Jews in the Age of Mercantilism 1500–1800* (Baltimore, 2009), 177.

15. Ibid., 178–9.

16. Ibid., 23.

17. Jonathan Schorsch, 'Mosseh Pereyra de Paiva: An Amsterdam Portuguese Jewish Merchant Abroad in the Seventeenth Century', in Yosef Kaplan (ed.), *The Dutch Intersection: The Jews and the Netherlands in Modern History* (Leiden, 2008), 63–85.

18. J. B. Segal, *The History of the Jews of Cochin* (London, 1993), 40.

19. Ibid., 41.

Chapter 7

1. *Letters of Queen Henrietta Maria including her private correspondence*, ed. Mary Anne Everett Green (London, 1857), 63–5.

2.   David Humphrey, 'To Sell England's Jewels: Queen Henrietta Maria's Visits to the Continent, 1642 and 1644', online, *E-rea, Revue électronique d'études sur le monde anglophone* (2014); *idem*, 'A Chronicle of the "Three Brothers" Jewel between 1623 and *c.* 1644', *Jewellery Studies*, 12 (2012), 85–92.

3.   Pierre l'Ancre, *L'incrédulité et mescréance du sortilège plainement convaincue* (Paris, 1622); Harry Melnick, *From Polemics to Apologetics: Jewish–Christian Rapprochement in 17th-Century Amsterdam* (Assen, 1981), 24–5.

4.   Ibid., 29.

5.   Marsha Keith Schuchard, *Restoring the Temple of Vision: Cabalistic Freemasonry and Stuart Culture* (Leiden, 2002).

6.   This is the great theme of Miriam Bodian's fine work, *Hebrews of the Portuguese Nation: Conversos and Community in Early Modern Amsterdam* (Bloomington, 1997). See also Daniel M. Swetchinsky, *Reluctant Cosmopolitans: The Portuguese Jews of Seventeenth-Century Amsterdam* (Oxford, 2000). And on the ambiguous attitudes of the Sephardim to further waves of incoming impoverished Jews, Tirtsah Levie Bernfeld, *Poverty and Welfare among the Portuguese Jews in Early Modern Amsterdam* (Oxford, 2012).

7.   Menasseh ben Israel, *The Hope of Israel*, trans. Moses Wall (1650), ed. Henry Mechoulan and Gerard Nahon (Liverpool, 1987), 25.

8.   Noah H. Rosenbloom, 'Discreet Polemics in Menasseh ben Israel's Conciliador', *Proceedings of the American Academy of Jewish Research*, 58 (1992), 143–91. On Menasseh, Cecil Roth, *A Life of Menasseh ben Israel* (New York, 1945); and the many illuminating essays in Yosef Kaplan, Henry Mechoulan and Richard H. Popkin (eds.), *Menasseh ben Israel and his World* (Leiden, 1989), especially Mechoulan, 'Menasseh ben Israel and the World of the Non-Jew', 83–97.

9.   For some general but powerful reflections on this issue, Yosef Kaplan, 'Gente Política: The Portuguese Jews of Amsterdam vis-à-vis Dutch Society', in Chaya Brasz and Yosef Kaplan (eds.), *Dutch Jews as Perceived by Themselves and Others* (Leiden, 2001), 21–40.

10.   Adri Offenberg, 'Jacob Jehudah Leon (1602–1675) and his Model of the Temple', in J. van den Berg and Ernestine G. E. van der Wall (eds.), *Jewish–Christian Relations in the Seventeenth Century: Studies and Documents* (Dordrecht, 1988), 95–115; *idem*, 'Dirk van Santen and the Keur Bible: New Insights into Jacob Judah (Arye) Templo's Model Temple', *Studia Rosenthaliana*, 34 (2004), 401–22; Gary Schwartz, 'The Temple Mount in the Lowlands', in Yosef Kaplan (ed.), *Dutch Intersection: The Jews and the Netherlands in Modern History* (Leiden, 2008), 111–21.

11.   Richard I. Cohen, *Jewish Icons: Art and Society in Modern Europe* (Berkeley, 1998), 31–2; Michael Zell, *Reframing Rembrandt* (Berkeley, 2002), 20. Zell reminds us that, in the light of court archives recording Jacob being

summoned for violent acts inflicted on his wife, his surname may have
been a misnomer.

12. Johannes Buxtorf, *Synagoga Judaica* (*Juden-Schul*) (Basel, 1603), trans. and
     ed. Alain Corre, online.

13. Offenberg, 'Jacob Jehudah Leon', 99.

14. Helene Rosenau, *Vision of the Temple: The Image of the Temple in Judaism
     and Christianity* (London, 1979); Tessa Morrison, 'Shifting Dimensions:
     The Architectural Model in History', in Mark Bury, Michael Ostwald,
     Peter Downton and Andrea Mina (eds.), *Homo Faber: Modelling Architecture*
     (Melbourne, 2007), 142–57.

15. Hartlib Papers (Sheffield University online), 3/3/12A 33B, 1646.

16. Bodian, 22–5.

17. Ibid., 23.

18. Melnick, 13.

19. For more details of these Dutch narratives and the Hebraic–Israelite
     analogy, Simon Schama, *The Embarrassment of Riches: An Interpretation
     of Dutch Culture in the Golden Age* (London, 1987), 82ff; for the Sephardi
     martyrologies, Bodian, 80–1.

20. Jonathan I. Israel, 'The Intellectual Debate about Toleration in the
     Dutch Republic', in C. Berkvens-Stevelinck, Jonathan I. Israel and J. H.
     M. Posthumus Meyjes (eds.), *The Emergence of Tolerance in the Dutch
     Republic* (Leiden, 1997), 3–36; Miriam Bodian, 'The Portuguese of
     Amsterdam and the Status of Christians', in Elisheva Carlebach and
     Jacob J. Schachter (eds.), *New Perspectives on Jewish–Christian Relations:
     In Honor of David Berger* (Leiden, 2012), 340–2.

21. Henrietta de Bruyn Kops, *A Spirited Exchange: The Wine and Brandy Trade
     Between France and the Dutch Republic in the Atlantic Framework, 1600–1650*
     (Leiden, 2007), 254.

22. Jessica Vance Roitman, *The Same but Different? Inter-cultural Trade and
     the Sephardim 1595–1640* (Leiden, 2011), 252ff. Roitman argues, to my
     mind persuasively, that Sephardi commercial networks were less endog-
     enous and exclusive than has sometimes been argued, and as often
     depended on partnerships that went well beyond the Sephardi commu-
     nity.

23. Menasseh ben Israel, *De Problema Creatione XXX* (*Thirty Problems of
     Creation*) (Amsterdam, 1635); prefatory poems by Caspar Barlaeus;
     F. Blok, 'Caspar Barlaeus en de Joden: De Geschiedenis van een epigram',
     Nederlands archief voor kerkgeschiedenis, 58: 1 (1977), 85–108.

24. Swetchinsky, 235.

25. For Jews on the Bourse, Jonathan Israel, 'The Amsterdam Stock
     Exchange and the English Revolution of 1688', *Tijdschrift voor Geschiedenis*,
     ciii (1990), 412–40.

26. See Simon Schama, *The Story of the Jews: Finding the Words*, 1000 BCE–1492 CE (London, 2013).

27. Eric Nelson, *The Hebrew Republic: Jewish Sources and the Transformation of European Political Thought* (Cambridge, MA, 2010), 18–19.

28. Ibid., 110.

29. Simon Schama *Rembrandt's Eyes* (London, 1999), 622–4; and *idem, The Embarrassment of Riches*, 115–21.

30. On Rembrandt's treatment of Jewish subjects, Steven Nadler, *Rembrandt's Jews* (Chicago, 2003), 42–103.

31. Mechoulan, introduction to Menasseh, *The Hope of Israel*, 63.

32. D'Andrade brought a notary in to witness his complaint. Rembrandt proposed submitting the issue of 'likeness' to a panel appointed by the artists' Guild of St Luke but only after the merchant had paid the balance owing in full. The upshot of the dispute is not, alas, known.

33. The account of the suicide is given by Philip van Limborch as an introduction to da Costa's autobiography, which came into his hands and which he published in 1687 as *Exemplar humanae vitae*, appended to his account of theological discussions between himself and a 'learned Jew', Isaac Orobio de Castro, *De Veritate Religionis Christianae Amica Collatio cum Erudito Judaeo*. The autobiography together with the introduction was translated into English in 1740 as *The Remarkable Life of Uriel da Costa*. An almost contemporary verification was supplied by the Lutheran cleric Johann Muller, who also owned a copy of the autobiography and described the circumstances of the suicide in his *Judaismus oder Judenthum* just four years later (Hamburg, 1644). The most authoritative summary of da Costa's dramatic life is the introduction to H. P. Salomon and I. S. D. Sassoon (eds.), *Uriel da Costa's Examination of Pharisaic Tradition* (Leiden, 1993), 1–24.

34. Talya Fishman, *Shaking the Pillars of Exile: 'Voice of a Fool', an Early Modern Jewish Critique of Rabbinic Culture* (Stanford, 1997). See also Ellis Rivkin, *Leon da Modena and the Kol Sakhal* (Cincinnati, 1952).

35. We owe our knowledge of the text to H. P. Salomon's discovery of one of the only two surviving copies in the Royal Library in Copenhagen. H. P. Salomon, 'A Copy of Uriel da Costa's *Exame das tradicoes phariseas*', *Studia Rosenthaliana*, XXIV (1990), 153–68.

36. Steven Nadler, *Spinoza: A Life* (Cambridge, 1999); Don Garrett (ed.), *The Cambridge Companion to Spinoza* (Cambridge, 1996); Geneviève Brykman, *La Judéité de Spinoza* (Paris, 1972); see also Rebecca Newberger Goldstein, *Betraying Spinoza: The Renegade Jew who Gave us Modernity* (New York, 2009); Susan James, *Spinoza on Philosophy, Religion and Politics* (Oxford, 2012); Yirimiyahu Yovel, *Spinoza and Other Heretics: The Marranos of Reason* (Princeton, 1989).

37. By some accounts Morteira is said to have pleaded with Spinoza to abandon his 'terrible heresies', and it was only after failing that he accepted the *herem* would be inevitable. Jonathan I. Israel, 'Philosophy, Commerce and Synagogue – Spinoza's Expulsion from the Amsterdam Portuguese Jewish Community in 1656', in Jonathan I. Israel and Reinier Salverda (eds.), *Dutch Jewry: Its History and Secular Culture, 1500–2000* (Leiden, 2002), argues, plausibly, that by this stage Spinoza, through acts of calculated temerity, was virtually challenging the community to bring on his excommunication.

38. Odette Vlessing, 'The Excommunication of Baruch Spinoza and the Birth of a Philosopher', in Israel and Salverda (eds.), 141–72, argues that Spinoza's financial manipulations were more likely than any kind of philosophical audacity to have brought on the *herem*, but the text of the excommunication refers to 'atrocious heresies', so however poorly received, his social tactics hardly seem the breaking point.

39. Israel, 133–5.

40. Nadler, *Spinoza*, 120.

41. Y. Kaplan, 'The Social Function of the Herem in the Portuguese Jewish Community of Amsterdam in the 17th century', in J. Michman and T. Levie (eds.), *Dutch Jewish History: Proceedings of the Second Symposium on the History of the Jews in the Netherlands, November 28–December 3* (Tel Aviv–Jerusalem, 1982), 111–55.

42. I. S. Revah, *Spinoza et Juan de Prado* (Paris, 1959); *idem*, 'Aux Origines de la Rupture Spinozienne', *Revue des Études Juives*, 123 (July–December 1964), 359–431.

43. On the *Tractatus*, Steven Nadler, *A Book Forged in Hell: Spinoza's Scandalous Treatise and the Birth of the Secular Age* (Princeton, 2011); and the essays in Yitzhak Y. Melamed and Michael A. Rosenthal (eds.), *Spinoza's Theological-Political Treatise: A Critical Guide* (Cambridge, 2010).

44. On Spinoza's complicated relationship with the Maimonidean tradition, David Biale, *Not in the Heavens: The Tradition of Jewish Secular Thought* (Princeton, 2011), 16–32.

45. 'The Relation of Antony Montezinos', trans. Moses Wall, in Menasseh ben Israel, *The Hope of Israel*, reprinted in Lucien Wolf, *Menasseh ben Israel's Mission to Oliver Cromwell* (London, 1901: reprinted Cambridge, 2012). See also Richard H. Popkin, 'The Rise and Fall of the Jewish Indian Theory', in Kaplan et al. (eds.), *Menasseh ben Israel and his World*, 63–8; Benjamin Schmidt, 'The Hope of the Netherlands: Menasseh ben Israel and the Dutch Idea of America', in Paolo Bernardini and Norman Fiering (eds.), *The Jews and the Expansion of Europe to the West, 1450–1800* (New York, 2001), 86–106; Ronnie Perelis, '"These Indians Are Jews!": Lost Tribes, Crypto-Jews and Jewish Self-Fashioning in Antonio de

Montezinos' *Relación* of 1644', in Kagan and Morgan (eds.), *Atlantic Diasporas*, 195–211.

46. Ben-Dor Benite, *The Ten Lost Tribes* (Oxford, 2009), 155ff.

47. Andre Neher, *Jewish Thought and the Scientific Revolution of the 16th Century: David Gans* (Oxford, 1985), Vol. II, 3–4.

48. Diego de Landa, *Relacion des las Cosas de Yucatan*, online (n.p.). Landa's book on the Maya was first published by Charles Etienne de Boubourg, *Relation des choses de Yucatande Diego de Landa* (Paris, 1864); see also William Gates (trans. and ed.), *Yucatan Before and After the Conquest* (New York, 1937; reprinted 1978).

49. The detail of their dress comes from a letter written by Montezinos to an Italian correspondent called Elias Péreire who may or may not have been of the same family as the wealthy Pereyra of Amsterdam. Jonathan Schorsch has published the copy in the Indiana University Lilly Library, with commentary in *Swimming the Christian Atlantic: Judeoconversos, Afroiberians and Amerindians in the Seventeenth Century* (Leiden, 2009), 505–13. Schorsch rightly says the additional details described in the letter make the Montezinos story if anything even more fantastic. See also Perelis.

50. Menasseh, *The Hope of Israel*, 18.

51. On the link between excitement about 'Jews in America' and readmission to England, Albert Hyamson, 'Lost Tribes and the Influence of the Search for Them on the Return of the Jews to England', *Jewish Quarterly Review*, 15:4 (July 1903), 640–76.

52. Grant Underwood, 'The Hope of Israel in Early Modern Ethnography and Eschatology', in Shalom Goldman (ed.), *Hebrew and the Bible in America: The First Two Centuries* (Waltham, MA, 1993).

53. Ismar Schorsch, 'From Messianism to Realpolitik', *Proceedings of the American Academy of Jewish Research*, 45 (1978), argues strongly that the Montezinos story had little or nothing to do with Menasseh's motives in seeking readmission, although *The Hope of Israel* and the *Vindiciae Judaeorum* emphasise the global extent of the dispersion precondition of messianism.

54. Menasseh ben Israel, *Vindiciae Judaeorum* (n.p., 1656), in Wolf, *Menasseh ben Israel's Mission to Oliver Cromwell*, 105–47.

55. Menasseh ben Israel, *Humble Addresses* (1655), in Wolf, 75–103.

56. On Moses Wall (whose father was also called Moses), Noel Malcolm, 'Moses Wall, Millenarian, Tolerationist and Friend of Milton', *The Seventeenth Century*, 27: 1 (Spring 2012), 25–53.

57. David S. Katz, 'Menasseh ben Israel's Christian Connection: Henry Jessey and the Jews', in Kaplan et al. (eds.), *Menasseh ben Israel and His World*, 116–38; also Katz, *Philo-Semitism and the Readmission of the Jews*

to England, 1603–1655 (Oxford, 1982); on the mission to England see also Cecil Roth, *A Life of Menasseh ben Israel* (New York, 1945).

58. Roth, 51; John Sadler, *The Rights of the Kingdom* (n.p., 1649).

59. Edgar Samuel, 'Oliver Cromwell and the Readmission of the Jews to England in 1656', in *idem, At the End of the Earth: Essays on the History of Jews in England and Portugal* (London, 2004), 180.

60. Susanna Akerman, 'Queen Christina and Messianic Thought', in David S. Katz and Jonathan I. Israel (eds.), *Sceptics, Millenarians and Jews* (Leiden, 1990), 142–60.

61. For Williams's radical tolerationism: Edmund Morgan, *Roger Williams: The Church and the State* (New York, 2007); John Barry, *Roger Williams and the Creation of the American Soul* (New York, 2012); Simon Schama, *The American Future: A History* (London, 2008), 152–71.

62. Whether the king took any action is not known.

63. Yosef Kaplan, 'Political Concepts in the World of the Portuguese Jews of Amsterdam during the Seventeenth Century: The Problem of Exclusion and the Boundaries of Self-Identity', in Kaplan et al. (eds.), *Menasseh ben Israel and his World*, 50–1.

64. Wolf, 83. Don Patinkin, 'Mercantilism and the Readmission of the Jews to England', *Jewish Social Studies*, 8:3 (July 1946), 161–78.

65. Wolf, liii.

66. Menasseh ben Israel, *Vindiciae Judaeorum*, 2.

Chapter 8

1. *A New Letter from Aberdeen in Scotland sent to a Person of Quality wherein is a more full account of the Proceedings of the Jews than has hitherto been published* (London, 1665), quoted in Gershom Scholem, *Sabbatai Zevi: The Mystical Messiah 1626–1676* (Princeton, 1973), 348–9.

2. Ibid., 345.

3. Ibid., 340–1.

4. Ibid., especially 15–66. 'Lurianic' Kabbalism does indeed have a strong purchase on the diaspora and the Jewish yeshivot of Palestine and Egypt in this period, but there was also fierce resistance to it in the Rabbinate, both Sephardi and Ashkenazi, and the masses of Jews who became Shebbatians were certainly not all adepts of its rarefied cosmology and metaphysics. It seems to me that it was precisely when, in its Hasidic incarnation in the eighteenth and nineteenth centuries, it found a simplified vernacular that a dilute Kabbalism morphed into a genuinely popular mass movement.

5.   Scholem, 206.

6.   Matt Goldish, *The Shabbetean Prophets* (Cambridge, MA, 2004), 64–5.

7.   Scholem, 124.

8.   Simon Schama, *The Story of the Jews: Finding the Words, 1000 BCE–1492 CE* (London, 2013), 267–8, 348.

9.   Robert Alter, 'Shabbetai Zevi and the Jewish Imagination', *Commentary*, 43:6 (June 1967), 66–71.

10. Goldish, 120–1.

11. Ibid., 491.

12. Scholem, 519.

13. Ibid, 520.

14. David J. Halperin, *Sabbatai Zevi: Testimonies to a Fallen Messiah* (Oxford, 2012). This is the best source book for contemporary accounts, and letters both pro and con.

15. *The Memoirs of Gluckel of Hameln*, trans. Marvin Lowenthal (New York, 1932), 46–7.

16. On the de Hooghe circumcision print, and the representation and demand for prints of Jewish life, Steven Nadler, *Rembrandt's Jews* (Chicago, 2003), 58ff.

17. Sergey R. Kravtsov, 'Juan Bautista Villalpando and Sacred Architecture in the 17th Century', *Journal of Architectural Historians*, 62: 3 (September 2005), 327.

18. Yosef Kaplan, 'For Whom did Emannuel de Witte Paint his Three Pictures of the Sephardi Synagogue in Amsterdam?', *Studia Rosenthaliana*, 32 (1998), 133–54.

19. Gary Schwartz, 'The Temple Mount in the Lowlands', in Yosef Kaplan (ed.), *Dutch Intersection: The Jews and the Netherlands in Modern History* (Leiden, 2008), 112ff, points out that architectural elements of the Temple were also incorporated into Dutch church architecture in Haarlem by the most celebrated of contemporary architects, Jacob van Campen.

20. Adri Offenberg, 'Jacob Jehudah Leon (1602–1675) and his Model of the Temple', in J. van den Berg and Ernestine G. E. van der Wall (eds.), *Jewish–Christian Relations in the Seventeenth Century: Studies and Documents* (Dordrecht, 1988), 107.

21. Ibid., 109.

22. Tessa Morrison, *Isaac Newton's Temple of Solomon and his Reconstruction of Sacred Architecture* (Basel, 2011).

23. H. W. Robinson and W. Adams (eds.), *The Diaries of Robert Hooke 1675–1680* (London, 1935), 179.

Chapter 9

1. Amos Elon, *The Pity of It All: A Portrait of the German-Jewish Epoch* (London, 2004), 29.

2. Alexander Putik, 'Prague Jews and Judah Hasid: A Study on the Social, Political and Religious History of the Late Seventeenth and Early Eighteenth Centuries', *Judice Bohemiae*, 38 (2003), 72–105; 39 (2004), 53–92; Samuel Krauss, 'Die Palastinasiedlung der polnischen Hasidim und die Wiener Kereise im Jahre 1700', *Abhandlung zur Erinnerung an Hirsch Perez Chajes* (Vienna, 1933; reprinted. New York, 1980), 51–94.

3. Selma Stern, *The Court Jew: A Contribution to the History of the Period of Absolutism in Europe* (Philadelphia, 1950); Michael A. Meyer (ed.), *German Jewish History in Modern Times, Vol. 1, Tradition and Enlightenment 1600–1780* (New York, 1996), 104–26; Vivian B. Mann and Richard I. Cohen (eds.), *From Court Jews to the Rothschilds: Art, Patronage and Power 1600–1800* (New York, 1997).

4. Michael Graetz, 'Court Jews in Economics and Politics', in Mann and Cohen (eds.), 27–44.

5. The false imprimatur was Konigsberg.

6. In fact the original Jewish Historical Museum of Vienna opened its doors in 1898 while the city had an anti-Semitic mayor and was the first such public museum of its kind anywhere in the world. On fine arts and architectural patronage, Richard I. Cohen and Vivian B. Mann, 'Melding Worlds: Court Jews and the Arts of the Baroque', in *From Court Jews to the Rothschilds*, 97–131.

7. Rachel Wischnitzer, *The Architecture of the European Synagogue* (Philadelphia, 1964), 155; Carol Krinsky, *Synagogues of Europe: Architecture, History, Meaning* (Cambridge, MA, 1985); Saskia Coenen Snyder, 'Acculturation, Particularism and the Modern City: Synagogue Building and Jewish Identity in Modern Europe', PhD dissertation (University of Michigan, 2008), 56–8.

8. Richard I. Cohen, *Jewish Icons: Art and Society in Modern Europe* (Berkeley, 1998).

9. 'Ritual Art', in Cecil Roth and Bezalel Narkiss, *Jewish Art: An Illustrated History* (Jerusalem, 1971).

10. Vivian Mann, 'Jewish Display Silver after the Age of Exploration', *Early Modern Workshop: Jewish History Resources, Vol. 4, Jewish Consumption and Material Culture in the Early Modern Period* (2007), online.

11. Cohen, 101–12.

12. Aubrey Newman, 'The Expulsion of the Jews of Prague in 1745 and British Foreign Policy', *Transactions and Miscellania* [Jewish Historical Society of England], 22 (1968–9), 30–41; William Abeles Iggers (ed.),

The Jews of Bohemia and Moravia: A Historical Reader, trans. Wilma Abeles Iggers, Kaca Polackova-Henley and Kathrine Talbot (Detroit, 1992), 31–8.

13. *Notes on the Diplomatic History of the Jewish Question*, Lucien Wolf (ed.), Jewish Historical Society of England (London, 1919), 9.

14. Franz Kobler, *Letters of the Jews Through the Ages* (London, 1952), 597.

15. For the most recent commentary, Moshe Halbertal, *Maimonides: Life and Thought* (New York, 2013), 277–368.

16. Solomon Maimon, *An Autobiography*, trans. J. Clark Murray (Chicago, 2001), 195.

17. Ibid., 193–6.

18. Menahem Schmelzer, 'Hebrew Printing and Publishing in Germany 1650–1750: On Jewish Book Culture and the Emergence of Modern Jewry', *Leo Baeck Institute Year Book*, 33 (1988).

19. Steven N. Lowenstein, 'The Jewish Upper Crust and Berlin in the Enlightenment: The Family of Daniel Itzig', in Frances Malino and David Sorkin, *Profiles in Diversity: Jews in a Changing Europe, 1750–1870* (Detroit, 1998), 182–205.

20. Steven M. Lowenstein, *The Berlin Jewish Community: Enlightenment, Family and Crisis 1770–1830* (Oxford, 1994). The classic survey of the subject is Jacob Katz, *Out of the Ghetto: The Social Background of Jewish Emancipation, 1770–1820* (Cambridge, MA, 1973), 40–78.

21. David Ruderman, *Jewish Thought and Scientific Discovery in Early Modern Europe* (New Haven, 1995).

22. There were just twenty-five Jews studying in five German universities in the first half of the eighteenth century. Shmuel Feiner, *The Jewish Enlightenment* (Philadelphia, 2004), 3. On medical study and the Gumpertz family, G. Freudenthal, 'New Light on the Physician Aaron Salomon Gumpertz: Medicine, Science and Early Haskalah in Berlin', *Zutot: Perspectives on Jewish Culture*, 3 (2003), 66–77.

23. John M. Efron, *Medicine and the German Jews* (New Haven, 2001).

24. Noah Efron, *Judaism and Science: An Historical Introduction* (Westport, 2007), 150; the portrait is reproduced in Shmuel Feiner and Natalie Naimark-Goldberg, *Cultural Revolution in Berlin: Jews in the Age of the Enlightenment* (Oxford, 2011), 14. On Raphael Levi's attack on rabbinical anti-Copernicanism, Jeremy Brown, *New Heavens and New Earth: The Jewish Reception of Copernican Thought* (New York, 2013), 146–67.

25. Feiner, *Jewish Enlightenment*, 22.

26. Ibid., 29–30.

27. Ibid., 18.

28. Jacob Emden, *Megilat Sefer: The Autobiography of Rabbi Jacob Emden (1697–1776)*, trans. S. B. Leperer and M. H. Wise (Baltimore, 2011), 177. On Emden and the temptations of flesh, Shmuel Feiner, *The Origins of Jewish Secularization in Eighteenth-Century Europe*, trans. Chaya Naor (Philadelphia, 2010), 51–4.

29. Ibid., 179.

30. David Sorkin, *Berlin Haskalah and German Religious Thought: Orphans of Knowledge* (London, 2000); idem, *The Religious Enlightenment: Protestants, Jews and Catholics from London to Vienna* (Princeton, 2009).

31. Hugh Barr Nisbet, *Gotthold Ephraim Lessing: His Life, Works and Thought* (Oxford, 2013), 157.

32. Alexander Altmann, *Moses Mendelssohn: A Biographical Study* (Oxford, 1973), 41. Despite recent criticism, this exhaustive study of the man and his work still holds up extraordinarily well. The more recent literature on Mendelssohn is considerable. See, for example, Allan Arkush, *Moses Mendelssohn and the European Enlightenment* (Albany, 1994); David Sorkin, *Moses Mendelssohn and the Religious Enlightenment* (Berkeley, 1996); Dominique Bourel, *Moses Mendelssohn: La naissance du judaïsme moderne* (Paris, 2004); Michah Gottlieb, *Faith and Freedom: Moses Mendelssohn's Theological-Political Thought* (Oxford, 2011).

33. Gad Freudenthal, 'New Light on the Physician Aaron Solomon Gumpertz: Medicine, Science and the Early Haskalah in Berlin', *Zutot: Perspectives on Jewish Culture*, 3 (2003), 66–77; idem, 'Aaron Solomon Gumpertz, Gotthold Ephraim Lessing and the First Call for the Improvement of Civil Rights of Jews in Germany (1753)', *Association of Jewish Studies Review*, 29:2 (2005), 299–353.

34. Robert Liberles, *Jews Welcome Coffee: Tradition and Innovation in Early Modern Germany* (Waltham, MA, 2012).

35. On Mendelssohn's 're-Jewing' of Spinoza, Adam Sutcliffe, 'Quarreling over Spinoza: Moses Mendelssohn and the Fashioning of Jewish Philosophical Heroism', in Ross Brann and Adam Sutcliffe (eds.), *Renewing the Past, Reconfiguring Jewish Culture: From al-Andalus to the Haskalah* (Philadelphia, 2004).

36. Jonathan Karp, 'The Aesthetic Difference: Moses Mendelssohn's *Kohelet Musar* and the Inception of the Berlin Haskalah', in Brann and Sutcliffe (eds.), 93–115.

37. Edward Breuer and David Sorkin, 'Moses Mendelssohn's First Hebrew Publication: An Annotated Translation of *Kohelet Mussar*', *Leo Baeck Institute Yearbook*, 48:1 (2003), 3–23.

38. Gottlieb, 15.

39. Altmann, 92.

40. Ibid., 93.

41. Ibid., 209.

42. Ibid., 219.

43. Ibid., 220.

44. Ibid., 251.

45. Ibid., 428–9.

46. Paul Mendes-Flohr and Jehuda Reinharz, *The Jew in the Modern World: A Documentary History* (Oxford, 2010), 78.

47. Altmann, 466–7.

48. Moses Mendelssohn, *Jerusalem, or On Religious Power and Judaism*, trans. Allan Arkush, with an introduction by Alexander Altmann (Hanover, NH, 1983), 551–2.

49. Ibid., 550.

50. Ibid., 138.

51. Shmuel Feiner, 'Moses Mendelssohn's Dreams and Nightmares', in Lauren B. Strauss and Michael Brenner (eds.), *Mediating Modernity: Challenges and Trends in the Jewish Encounter with the Modern World* (Detroit, 2008), 268. Feiner notes that the experience was so traumatic that Mendelssohn repressed it, communicating it only to a young Catholic admirer, Peter Weinkopp, in July 1780.

52. Ibid., 269.

Chapter 10

1. Pierce Egan, *Boxiana, Or Sketches of Ancient and Modern Pugilism: From the Days of the renowned Broughton and Slack to the Championship of Cribb* (London, 1829), 258. Simon Schama, 'The King's Pugilist: Daniel Mendoza (1764–1836)', in Franklin Foer and Marc Tracy (eds.), *Jewish Jocks: An Unorthodox Hall of Fame* (New York, 2013).

2. Egan wrote that 'no pugilist ever stopped with greater neatness' – the ultimate compliment.

3. Thomas Fewtrell, *Boxing Reviewed* (London, 1790), compared Mendoza's guard to Humphreys' and John Jackson's, and concluded that while it might have been the least aesthetically appealing, it was the most effective.

4. Daniel Mendoza, *The Memoirs of the Life of Daniel Mendoza*, ed. Paul Magriel (London, 1951).

5. Michael Stanislawski, *Autobiographical Jews: Essays in Jewish Self-Fashioning* (Seattle, 2004), 32–54 (on Gluckel and R. Asher of Riechshofen).

6. Egan, 280.

7. Daniel Mendoza et al., *The Art of Boxing including The Six Lessons of Mendoza for the Use of His Scholars* (London, 1789).

8. The novelist was Charles Johnstone. *The History of John Juniper, Esq. alias Juniper Jack* (London, 1781), Vol. 1, 265. Frank Felsenstein, *Anti-Semitic Stereotypes: A Paradigm of Otherness in English Popular Culture, 1660–1830* (Baltimore, 1999), 230.

9. Ibid., 124.

10. Ibid., 150.

11. Todd Endelman, *The Jews of Georgian England, 1740–1830: Tradition and Change in a Liberal Society* (Ann Arbor, 1999), 114.

12. Felsenstein, 72–3.

13. Ibid., 92.

14. Ibid., 111.

15. Ibid., 102.

16. See, for instance, the heroic pose adopted in #195, the mezzotint by 'WL' printed by J. Robineau and captioned 'DANIEL MENDOZA, the most SCIENTIFIC BOXER ever KNOWN', reproduced in Alfred Rubens, *Anglo-Jewish Portraits: A Biographical Catalogue of Engraved Anglo-Jewish and Colonial Portraits from the Earliest Times to the Accession of Queen Victoria* (London, 1935), 78 and facing. Rubens lists another twenty such engravings, a small sample of the immense abundance featuring Mendoza and his legendary bouts. Even the most aggressively anti-Jewish images such as *The Triumph* (1788), celebrating a victory of Humphreys', represented as an archetype of British manhood, carried on a chair held by (among others) the Prince of Wales, and with blood pouring from the mouth of the loser, forbore from the usual grotesque caricatures although his seconds (including a rabbinical figure) predictably feature the hooked nose. By 1789, another print (Rubens, 196) was able to declare 'The Christian pugilist proving himself unequal to the Jewish hero'.

17. Egan, 255.

18. Endelman, *Jews of Georgian England*. See also David S. Katz, *The Jews in the History of England, 1485–1850* (Oxford, 1994); Cecil Roth, *A History of the Jews in England* (Oxford, 1941), 211–53; Rubens.

19. Gedalia Yogev, *Diamonds and Coral: Anglo-Dutch Jews and Eighteenth-Century Trade* (London, 1978), 102–3.

20. Ibid., 141–2.

21. Ibid., 187–8.

22. Katz, 258.

23. The Hi-Fi Hymn Book's (YouTube) recording of 'The God of Abraham Praise' will make Oliver's debt to Lyon's 'Yigdal Elohim Chai' – still

the melody most used in British synagogues – immediately and gloriously clear.

24. David Conway, *Jewry in Music: Entry to the Profession from the Enlightenment to Richard Wagner* (Cambridge, 2012), 82ff.

25. Lucien Wolf, 'Astley's Jews', *Jewish Chronicle*, 26 May 1893.

26. Jacob Decastro, *The Memoirs of J. Decastro, Comedian* (London, 1824).

27. Rubens, 377.

28. Edgar Samuel, *To the Ends of the Earth: Essays on the History of the Jews of England and Portugal* (London, 2004), 31.

29. Ibid., 315.

30. Ibid., 266ff.

31. Ibid., 267.

32. P. J. P. Whitehead, 'Emanuel Mendez da Costa (1717–91) and the Conchology or Natural History of Shells', *Bulletin of the British Museum (Natural History)*, Historical Series 6 (1977), 1–24.

33. Endelman, *Jews of Georgian England*, 263.

34. Todd Endelman, *Radical Assimilation in English Jewish History, 1656–1945* (Bloomington, 1990), 16.

35. Ibid., 130.

36. Ibid., 36.

37. In the earliest versions of the rhyme, in *Tommy Thumb's Pretty Song Book* (London, 1744), 'Shoreditch' is 'Fleetditch', which would also have had resonance for the City Jews. The same is true for other chimes – beginning with 'White Chapple' (rhymed with 'two sticks and an apple') and Aldgate.

38. The deliciously sinister 'here comes a candle to light you to bed … here comes a chopper to chop off your head' was a nineteenth-century addition along with schoolyard play actions.

39. Endelman, *Jews of Georgian England*, 250.

40. Samuel Taylor Coleridge, *Table Talk* (London, 1884), 104; Betty Naggar, 'Old Clothes Men: 18th and 19th Centuries', *Jewish Historical Studies*, 31 (1988–90), 173.

41. On the old-clothes walks, Naggar, 172; on the later history, Adam D. Mendelssohn, *The Rag Race: How Jews Sewed their Way to Success in America and the British Empire* (New York, 2015), 18–36.

42. Eliza Acton, *Modern Cookery for Private Families* (London, 1845); chapter 32 has a whole section on Jewish food; her chapter on 'foreign cooking' is the first to contain a recipe for frying fish in olive oil, exactly in the style of the Mediterranean Jews. She specifies allowing the fish to cool before serving and 'garnishing with foliage'.

43. There were evening sales too. Benjamin Silliman, an American visitor in 1805, reported that 'at evening they repair to Wapping where a grand display is made of every species of apparel in every stage of

decay'. Cited by R. D. Barnett, 'Anglo-Jewry in the Eighteenth Century', in V. D. Lipman (ed.), *Three Centuries of Anglo-Jewish History: A Volume of Essays* (London, 1961), 61; Benjamin Silliman, *A Journal of Travels in England, Holland and Scotland*, 3 vols (New Haven, 1820), I, 270–1.

44. Endelman, 184–5.
45. Naggar, 176–8.
46. George Bryan, *Chelsea in the olden and present times* (London, 1869), 155–7.
47. Mendoza, *Memoirs*, 20.
48. Mendoza et al., *The Art of Boxing*, 18.
49. Ibid., i–ii.
50. Mendoza, *Memoirs*, 14–15.
51. Ibid., 16.
52. Ibid., 23.
53. Egan, 102, makes a great deal of Humphreys' 'genteel appearance and behaviour'.
54. Mendoza, *Memoirs*, 26.
55. Egan, I, 78.
56. Mendoza, *Memoirs*, 30.
57. Mendoza et al., *The Art of Boxing*, 10.
58. Mendoza, *Memoirs*, 40–54.
59. Ibid., 44.
60. Ibid., 49.
61. Egan, 293.
62. Ibid., 221.
63. Ibid., 265–6.
64. Mendoza et al., *The Art of Boxing*, xi.

Chapter 11

1. Frances Malino, *The Sephardic Jews of Bordeaux: Assimilation and Emancipation in Revolutionary France* (Tuscaloosa, 1978).
2. David Cesarani (ed.), *Port Jews: Jewish Communities in Trading Centres, 1550–1950* (London, 2002); and see in same work for the concept of 'Port Jews' coined by Lois Dubin, David Sorkin, 'Port Jews and the Three Regions of Emancipation', 31–46; Lois Dubin, 'Trieste and Beyond', 47–59.
3. Richard Menkis, 'Patriarchs and Patricians: The Gradis Family of Eighteenth Century Bordeaux', in Frances Malino and David Sorkin (eds.), *Profiles in Diversity: Jews in a Changing Europe, 1750–1870* (Detroit, 1998), 11–45.

4. 'Observations remarquables sur deux enfants sourds et muets de naissance a qui l'on apprit à articuler le son', *Journal des Scavans* (Paris, 1747), 435–7.

5. Jonathan Ree, *I See a Voice: A Philosophical History of Language, Deafness and the Senses* (London, 1999), 143–4ff; Harlan Lane, *When the Mind Hears: A History of the Deaf* (New York, 1984); J. R. Péreire, *Observations sur les sourds Muets et sur quelques endroits* (Paris, 1768); on Péreire and his sources and antecedents, Ernest La Rochelle, *Jacob Rodrigues Péreire, premier instituteur des sourds et muets en France, sa vie et ses travaux* (Paris, 1882); Marjoke Rietveld-van Wingerden and Wim Westerman, '"Hear, Israel": The Involvement of Jews in the Education of the Deaf', *Jewish History*, 23 (2009), 43–4; Jean-René Presneau, *L'éducation des sourds et muets, des aveugles et des contrefaits au siècle des lumières, 1750–1789* (Paris, 2010), 124–7.

6. Ibid., 165.

7. *Mercure de France*, August 1749, 159; *Histoire de l'Académie Royale des Sciences* (1749), 183.

8. Ronald Schechter, *Obstinate Hebrews: Representations of Jews in France, 1715–1815* (Berkeley, 2003), 144ff.

9. Voltaire, *Oeuvres Complètes* (Paris, 1879), Vol. VII, 'Mélanges', 439–40; Arthur Hertzberg, *The French Enlightenment and the Jews* (New York, 1968), 300–1.

10. For an interesting comparative discussion of the experience and challenges of citizenship and Jewish allegiance in France and America, see Frederic Cople Jaher, *The Jews and the Nation: Revolution, Emancipation, State Formation and the Liberal Paradigm in America and France* (Princeton, 2002), especially 59–102.

11. Adrian Seville, 'La nouvelle Combinaison du Jeu du Juif: un intrigant jeu de des, imprimé du VIIIe siècle', *Le Vieux Papier* (Paris, April 2012), 433–44; also in Thierry Depardes (ed.), 'The Rothschild Collection of Board Games at Waddesdon Manor', in *Proceedings of XIIIth Board Games Studies Colloquium* (Paris, 2012), CD ROM, 91–127.

12. In eighteenth-century French *'subtiliser'* had the deliberately ambiguous meaning of stripping away, removing things for the sake of purification! As such, it was much used in the soft-porn literature of nuns and priests, immensely popular in Ancien Régime France.

13. Hertzberg, 289.

14. Hell was also *bailli* in his district; in effect the representative of local justice.

15. Margaret O'Leary, *Forging Freedom: The Life of Cerf Berr of Medelsheim* (Bloomington, 2012), 134.

16. Isidore Loeb, 'Un baron juif au XVIIIe siècle', *Annuaire des archives Israelites* (1885–6), 136.

17. O'Leary, 242.

18. Ibid., 253–4.

19. Ruth Necheles, 'L'émancipation des Juifs 1787–1795', in Bernard Blumenkranz and Albert Soboul (eds.), *Les Juifs et la Révolution française: Problèmes et aspirations* (Toulouse, 1976), 77.

20. Hertzberg, 341.

21. Paul Mendes-Flohr and Jehuda Reinharz, *The Jew in the Modern World: A Documentary History* (Oxford, 2010), 124.

22. *Opinion de M. l'évêque de Nancy, député de Lorraine sur l'admissibilité de Juifs à la plénitude de l'état civil et des droits de citoyens actifs* (Paris, 1789), 3–4.

23. Frances Malino, *A Jew in the French Revolution: The Life of Zalkind Hourwitz* (Cambridge, MA, 1996), 88–9.

24. Ibid., 94.

25. Berr Isaac Berr, *Lettre d'un Citoyen* (Nancy, 1791).

26. Zosa Szajkowski, 'Sephardic Jews in the French Revolution', in *The Jews and the French Revolutions of 1789, 1830 and 1848* (New York, 1970), 440ff. Furtado's story was related in an evidently extraordinary diary while he was under cover, 'Memoires d'un patriote proscrit', the original of which has been lost but which has survived in a manuscript copy made by the bibliophile Ernest Labadie and bought by the Bordeaux municipal library in 1943 after the Germans had overrun the Vichy zone!

27. Szajkowski, 451; Ernest Ginsburger, *Le comité de Surveillance de Jean-Jacques Rousseau/Saint-Esprit de Bayonne* (Paris, 1934), 98–100.

28. Szajkowski, 815.

29. H. Tribout de Morembert, 'Les Juifs de Metz et de Lorraine', in Blumenkranz and Soboul (eds.), 100.

30. Ibid., 101.

31. Federica Francesconi, 'From Ghetto to Emancipation: The Role of Moisè Formiggini', *Jewish History*, 24:2–3 (2010), 331–54. On the Italian Jews in the 1790s, Geoffrey Symcox, 'The Jews of Italy in the Triennio Giacobino, 1796–1799', in David N. Myers, Massimo Ciavolello and Peter Reill (eds.), *Acculturation and its Discontents: The Italian Jewish Experience Between Exclusion and Inclusion* (Los Angeles, 2008), 307–29.

32. Cecil Roth, *History of the Jews of Italy* (Philadelphia, 1946), 406ff.

33. Robert C. Davis and Benjamin Ravid, *The Jews of Early Modern Venice* (Baltimore, 2001), vii.

34. Mendes-Flohr and Reinharz, 146.

35. The Pitigliano synagogue is still very much as it was in the eighteenth century, as is much of the whole town. Though the community was

all but wiped out during the last war, no one interested in Jewish Italy should miss it.

36. Simon Schwarzfuchs, *Napoleon, the Jews and the Sanhedrin* (London, 1979), 24.

37. Schechter, 227.

38. Ibid., 202ff.

39. Schwarzfuchs, 50.

40. Mendes-Flohr and Reinharz, 153.

41. Ibid., 156.

42. Ibid., 159.

43. 'Erlebenisse von Gabriel Schrameck', in Max Grunwald, *Die Feldzuge Napoleons* (Vienna, 1931), 238–42; also F. Raphael, 'Les Juifs d'Alsace et la Conscription', in Blumenkranz and Soboul (eds.), 35–8.

Chapter 12

1. The practical archivist of Polish wooden synagogues is Moshe Verbin who devoted himself to creating exquisite wooden models of the lost buildings, *Wooden Synagogues of Poland from the 17th and 18th Centuries* (Herzliya, 1990); see also the architectural historian Thomas Hubka, *Resplendent Synagogue: Architecture and Worship in an Eighteenth Century Polish Community* (Waltham, MA, 2003), which traces the history and his magnificent project of building a replica of the handsome, painted synagogue of Gwoździec, built in 1731. For their fate at the hands of the Nazis and their local sympathisers, Robert Bevan, *The Destruction of Memory: Architecture at War* (London, 2006).

2. For these cemeteries, see the superb photographic archive shot by David Goberman, collected in Goberman with contributions by Gershon Hundert and Robert Pinsky, *Carved Memories: Heritage in Stone from the Russian Pale* (New York, 2000). The hares of Sataniv (Satanow), along with many other stones and the Great Synagogue, then only very partially restored, were photographed by Jeremy Pollard and Hugo McGregor on the film shoot for the BBC series *The Story of the Jews* in November 2012.

3. An extraordinary exception were the Sephardi tombstones at Ouderkerk outside Amsterdam, and in the Dutch Caribbean colony of Curaçao, where in the early eighteenth century the tombstones of the merchant elite were carved with a full cast of characters from biblical stories corresponding to the deceased: the grave of Mosseh Mordechay Senior at Ouderkerk was illustrated with scenes from the book of Esther, for instance. See Rochelle Weinstein, *Stones of Memory: Revelations from the*

Cemetery in Curaçao: The Sculptured Tombstones of Ouderkerk and Curaçao in Historical Context (American Jewish Archives, 1992).

4. Israel Bartal, 'Imagined Geography: The Shtetl, Myth, and Reality', in Steven T. Katz (ed.), *The Shtetl: New Evaluations* (New York, 2007), 179–93.

5. The richest work of revision along these lines based on a prodigious trove of primary sources is Yohanan Petrovsky-Shtern, *The Golden Age of the Shtetl: A New History of Jewish Life in Eastern Europe* (Princeton, 2013).

6. In 1765 there were 1,365 poll-tax-paying Jewish households in Satanow, which translates to around four thousand souls.

7. Dov Ber Birkenthal, *The Memoirs of Ber of Bolechow (1723–1805)*, trans. and ed. M. Vishnitzer (Oxford, 1922), 33.

8. Petrovsky-Shtern, 97.

9. On the *splaw* freight trade, M. J. Rosman, *The Lords' Jews: Magnate-Jewish Relations in the Polish-Lithuanian Commonwealth during the Eighteenth Century* (Cambridge, MA, 1992), 95ff.

10. Petrovsky-Shtern, 103.

11. Yohanan Petrovsky-Shtern, '"You will find it in the Pharmacy": Practical Kabbalah and Natural Medicine in the Polish–Lithuanian Commonwealth', in Glenn Dynner (ed.), *Holy Dissent: Jewish and Christian Mystics in Eastern Europe* (Detroit, 2011), 21–85.

12. Revd William Coxe, *Travels Into Poland, Sweden and Denmark, Vol. 1* (London, 1784), 270; Gershon David Hundert, 'The Importance of Demography and Patterns of Settlement for an Understanding of the Jewish Experience in East-Central Europe', in Steven Katz (ed.), *The Shtetl: New Evaluations* (New York, 2007), Project Muse, 31.

13. Solomon Maimon, *An Autobiography*, trans. J. Clark Murray (Chicago, 2001), 6–7.

14. Glenn Dynner, *Yankel's Tavern: Jews, Liquor and Life in the Kingdom of Poland* (Oxford, 2013), 26.

15. Petrovsky-Shtern, *Golden Age of the Shtetl*, 221.

16. Birkenthal, 190.

17. Gershon David Hundert, *Jews in Poland-Lithuania in the Eighteenth Century: A Genealogy of Modernity* (Berkeley, 2004), 5–6.

18. Andrew Alexander Bonar and Robert Murray M'Cheyne, *Narrative of a Mission of Inquiry to the Jews for the Church of Scotland* (Philadelphia, 1839), 267. Their description of Brody, 'it seemed wholly a Jewish city', is one of the most vivid of the period. The occupational spread of the Jews extended to being masons and plumbers. Bonar and M'Cheyne were especially struck by seeing notices at the post office printed in Hebrew (almost certainly Yiddish) as well as Polish and German.

19. Adam Neale, *Travels through some parts of Germany, Poland, Moldavia and Turkey* (London, 1818), 146.

20. Ibid., 147.

21. Hundert, 'The Importance of Demography ...', in Katz (ed.), 34.

22. Petrovsky-Shtern, *Golden Age of the Shtetl*, 106.

23. Ibid., 133.

24. Dynner, 33–5.

25. David Assaf, *Untold Tales of the Hasidim: Crisis and Discontent in the History of Hasidism* (Waltham, MA, 2010), 97–119.

26. Ibid.

27. On the multipurpose functions of the taverns, Dynner, 17–20.

28. Maimon, 25–6.

29. Ibid., 85–6.

30. Adam Kazmierczyk, 'Jews, Nobles and Canon Law in the 18th Century', academia.edu (2014).

31. Hundert, *Jews in Poland-Lithuania*, 45; see also J. Goldberg (ed.), *Jewish Privileges and Charters of Rights in Poland-Lithuania in the Sixteenth to the Eighteenth Centuries: Critical edition of Original Polish and Latin Documents with introduction in English* (Jerusalem, 1985).

32. Antony Polonsky, *The Jews in Poland and Russia, Vol. 1, 1350–1881* (Liverpool, 2010); also Hundert, 'The Importance of Demography ...', in Katz (ed.), 31–2; Raphael Mahler, *Hasidism and the Jewish Enlightenment: Their Confrontation in Galicia and Poland in the First Half of the Nineteenth Century* (New York, 1998), 171ff.

33. Nancy Sinkoff, *Out of the Shtetl: Making Jews Modern in the Polish Borderlands* (Providence, 2004), 30.

34. Chimen Abramsky, 'The Crisis of Authority within European Jewry in the Eighteenth Century', in Siegfried Stein and Raphael Loewe (eds.), *Studies in Jewish Religious and Intellectual History* (Tuscaloosa, 1979), 16.

35. Hundert, *Jews in Poland-Lithuania*, 17.

36. Although the terms of the *herem* excommunication issued in Vilna in 1772 and Cracow in 1786 came very close to making that charge.

37. Hundert, *Jews in Poland-Lithuania*, 143.

38. Moshe Rosman, *Founder of Hasidism: A Quest for the Historical Baal Shem Tov* (Berkeley, 1996 and 2013). On new approaches to almost all aspects of Hasidism, textual and social, see the essays in Ada Rapoport-Albert (ed.), *Hasidism Reappraised* (Oxford 1996).

39. Ibid., 99ff; on the ascent and the history of the 'Holy Epistle' recording it, Rosman, 106–7, 111ff.

40. Maimon, 28.

41. Ibid., 26ff.

42. Ibid., 146.

43. Gershom Scholem, *Major Trends in Jewish Mysticism* (New York, 1946).

44. Maimon, 164.

45.   Ibid., 168–9.

46.   Mahler, 289.

47.   Hundert, *Jews in Poland-Lithuania*, 193.

48.   Raphael Mahler, 'Hasidism and the Jewish Enlightenment', in Gershon
      David Hundert (ed.), *Essential Papers on Hasidism: Origins to Present*
      (New York, 1991), 373–429.

49.   Eliyahu Stern, *The Genius: Elijah of Vilna and the Making of Modern
      Judaism* (New Haven, 2013), 83–114.

50.   In return the Vilna Gaon in 1784 prohibited the observant from buying
      any meat slaughtered by a Hasidic *shokhet*! The matter of the blades
      became a huge issue in the *mitnagdim*–Hasidic battles.

51.   Stern, 26.

52.   Sinkoff, 150–1.

53.   Moshe Idel, *Hasidism: Between Ecstasy and Magic* (Albany, 1995), 203.

54.   Martin Buber, *Tales of the Hasidim*, 2 vols. (New York, 1972), I, 238-9; Ada
      Rapoport-Albert, 'Hasidism after 1772: Structural Continuity and Change',
      in Rapoport-Albert (ed.), *Hasidism Reappraised*, 97.

55.   Assaf, 98.

56.   Leopold Ritter von Sacher-Masoch, *A Light for Others: And other Jewish
      Tales from Galicia*, ed. Michael O'Pecko (Riverside, CA, 1994), 7.

57.   Alexander Herzen, *My Past and Thoughts*, trans. Constance Garnett,
      (Berkeley, 1973), 170; Michael Stanislawski, *Tsar Nicholas I and the Jews:
      The Transformation of Jewish Society in Russia 1825–1855* (Philadelphia, 1983),
      27; see also Yohanan Petrovsky-Shtern, *Jews in the Russian Army: Drafted
      into Modernity* (Cambridge, 2009).

58.   Stanislawski, 26.

59.   On the Czartoryski–Leffin relationship, Sinkoff, 50ff.

60.   Petrovsky-Shtern, *Jews in the Russian Army*, 34.

61.   Ibid., 53.

62.   Ibid., 108.

Chapter 13

1.   For the Levys and Monticello, Marc Leepson, *Saving Monticello: The Levy
      Family's Epic Quest to Save the House Jefferson Built* (New York, 2003);
      Melvin I. Urofsky, *The Levy Family and Monticello 1834–1923: Saving Thomas
      Jefferson's House* (Charlottesville, 2001).

2.   For a full account of the visit to Newport and the response of the
      Jews there, Simon Schama, *The American Future: A History* (London,
      2008), 161–5.

3.   For Levy's naval career, Ira Dye, *Uriah Levy: Reformer of the Antebellum
      Navy* (Gainsville, 2006).

4. Jonathan D. Sarna, *Jacksonian Jew: The Two Worlds of Mordecai Noah* (New York, 1981), 54–5; also Michael Schuldiner and Daniel J. Kleinfeld (eds.), *The Selected Writings of Mordecai Noah* (Westport, 1999); Isaac Goldberg, *American Jewish Pioneer* (Philadelphia, 1936).

5. *The Fortress of Sorrento* (1808) can be found in Jules Chametzky et al. (eds.), *Jewish American Literature: A Norton Anthology* (New York, 2001), 57–69.

6. Mordecai M. Noah, *Travels in England, France, Spain and the Barbary States in the Years 1813–14 and 15* (New York, 1819).

7. Ibid., 312.

8. W. D. Robinson, *Memoir Addresses to Persons of the Jewish Religion on the Subject of Emigration to and Settlement in One of the Most Eligible Parts of North America* (London, 1819); Charles P. Daly, *The Settlement of the Jews in North America* (New York, 1893), 92–6.

9. For the German immigration, Hasia Diner, *A Time for Gathering: The Second Migration, 1820–1880* (Baltimore, 1995).

10. Ava F. Kahn (ed.), *Jewish Voices of the Gold Rush: A Documentary History 1849–1880* (Detroit, 2002).

11. Ibid., 111–18.

12. S. N. Carvalho, *Incidents of Travel and Adventure in the Far West with Colonel Fremont's Last Expedition across the Rocky Mountains* (New York, 1857).

13. Kahn (ed.), 72–80.

14. Hasia Diner, *Roads Taken: The Great Jewish Migrations to the New World and the Peddlers Who Forged the Way* (New Haven, 2015).

15. Jean Powers Soman and Frank L. Byrne (eds.), *A Jewish Colonel in the Civil War: Marcus M. Spiegel of the Ohio Volunteers* (Lincoln, NB, 1994), 5ff.

16. Kahn (ed.), 141–4.

17. Ibid., 81.

18. John P. Marschall, *Jews in Nevada: A History* (Reno, 2008), 21–2.

19. Ibid., 28–37.

20. Ibid., 76–9; see also Robert E. Stewart and M. F. Stewart, *Adolph Sutro: A Biography* (Berkeley, 1962).

21. Jacob Marcus, *The American Jewish Woman: A Documentary History* (New York, 1981).

22. Kahn (ed.), 267–9.

23. Marschall, 97–8.

24. For Gratz and a characteristic selection of her letters, Chametzky et al. (eds.), 44ff; see also David Philipon (ed.), *Letters of Rebecca Gratz* (Philadelphia, 1929); Dianne Ashton, *Rebecca Gratz: Women and Judaism in Antebellum America* (Detroit, 1997).

25. There is an excellent critical introduction to Menken and her poetry in Chametzky et al. (eds), 86–7; see also: Paul Lewis, *Queen of the Plaza: A Biography of Adah Isaacs Menken* (New York, 1964); Wolf Mankowitz, *Mazeppa: The Lives, Loves and Legends of Adah Isaacs Menken* (New York, 1982).

26. Kahn (ed.), 405, 409–11.

27. Lance J. Sussman, *Isaac Leeser and the Making of American Judaism* (Detroit, 1995).

28. Jonathan D. Sarna, *When General Grant Expelled the Jews* (New York, 2012), *passim*.

29. Jonathan D. Sarna and Adam Mendelsohn (eds.), *Jews and the Civil War* (New Haven, 2010); Jonathan D. Sarna and Benjamin Shapell, *Lincoln and the Jews* (New York, 2015).

30. Morris U. Schappes, *A Documentary History of the Jews in the United States, 1654–1875* (New York, 1971), 312–15.

31. For August Bondi, Schappes, 252–364; Bondi's papers, with a vivid description of the battles at Black Jack and Powattomie, are in the American Jewish Historical Society.

32. Soman and Byrne (eds.), 316. Spiegel made it clear he was 'in favor of doing away with slavery'.

33. Ibid., 261.

34. Dye, 207ff.

35. Schappes, 376–83.

36. Dye, 232–3; James Finn, *Journal* (16 September 1859), quoted in Beth-Zion Abrahams, 'Historical Notes: Some Early American Jews: From a British Unpublished Diary', in *American Jewish Archives Journal*, 33:2 (1981), 210–12.

37. Dye, 233.

Chapter 14

1. Conway, *Jewry in Music*.

2. Heinz and Gudrun Becker, *Giacomo Meyerbeer: A Life in Letters*, trans. Mark Violette (London, 1983), 29.

3. Ibid, 33.

4. *The Diaries of Giacomo Meyerbeer, Vol. 4: The Last Years (1857–1864)*, trans. and ed. Robert Ignatius Letellier (Madison, 2003); Conway, *Jewry in Music*.

5. Becker, 43.

6. Not for long, however, since the Gare du Nord – grimy, chaotic and sometimes dangerous, with unspeakably awful food, shamed by the

splendour of St Pancras at the other end of the Eurostar line – is about to undergo large-scale renovation along with the forecourt.

7. On the Rothschilds and railway finance: Niall Ferguson, *The World's Banker: The History of the House of Rothschild* (London, 1998); Melanie Aspey, 'Making Tracks: Promoting the Rothschild Archive as a Source for Railway History', in Ralf Roth and Gunter Dinhobl (eds.), *Across the Borders: Financing the World's Railways in the Nineteenth Century* (Aldershot, 2008), 3–12. In the same volume, Christophe Bouneau, 'The Pereires' International Strategy for Railway Construction in the 1850s and 1860s', 13–24. See also Kurt Greenwald, 'Europe's Railways and Jewish Enterprise: German Jews as Pioneers of Railway Promotion', *Leo Baeck Institute Yearbook*, XII (1967), 163–209.

8. Jonathan M. Hess, *Germans, Jews and the Claims of Modernity* (New Haven, 2002). Christian Ludwig Paalzow, lawyer to the Prussian Supreme Court (Kammergericht), had already argued that the presumptuous grandeur of the Jewish elite – the Itzigs, Levys, Wulffs and Beers – was evidence of the plot for world domination.

9. Tina Fruhauf, *The Organ and its Music in German Jewish Culture* (Oxford, 2009), 28–9.

10. Jeffrey S. Sposato, *The Price of Assimilation: Felix Mendelssohn and the 19th Century Anti-Semitic Tradition* (Oxford, 2006), 16ff.

11. Ibid., 26.

12. Ibid., 4.

13. Ruth Gay, *The Jews of Germany: A Historical Portrait* (New York, 1992).

14. Thomas S. Grey, 'Wagner admires Meyerbeer (*Les Huguenots*)', in Thomas S. Grey (ed.), *Richard Wagner and His World* (Princeton, 2009), 335–46. Wagner described *Les Huguenots* as the 'pinnacle' of opera. Richard Wagner, *Selected Letters of Richard Wagner*, trans. S. Spencer, ed. S. Spencer and B. Millington (London, 1987), 68–9. See also Milton E. Brener, *Wagner and the Jews* (Jefferson, NC, 2006); Leon Poliakov, *The History of Anti-Semitism, Vol. III: From Voltaire to Wagner*, trans. Miriam Kochan (Philadelphia, 1968), 429–57. Conway, *Jewry in Music*, 258–61, identifies Theodor Uhlig, a violinist in Dresden and a champion of Wagner's, as the originator of violent attacks in reviews on the 'Jewish School' of music and was certainly the source for Wagner's derision of Jewish synagogue babble. Conway is perhaps less convincing about Wagner's recycling of Uhlig's invective as merely opportunistic in 1850.

15. J. S. Shedlock, 'Wagner and Liszt Correspondence', *Proceedings of the Musical Association (1887–1888)*, 131.

16. On artisan enmity to the Jews, Shulamit Volkov, *The Rise of Popular Antimodernism in Germany: The Urban Master Artisans, 1873–1896* (Princeton, 1978).

17. Helen M. Davies, *Emile and Isaac Pereire: Bankers, Socialists and Sephardi Jews in Nineteenth-Century France* (Manchester, 2014).

18. Ibid., 45–6.

19. The classic account of the revolutionary impact of the railways on culture as well as economy is Wolfgang Schivelbusch, *The Railway Journey: The Industrialization of Time and Space in the Nineteenth Century* (Oxford, 1979).

20. Ibid., 44, 58–9.

21. Eugenio Maria Romero's drama about the story is *El Martirio de la Joven Hachuel* (Gibraltar, 1837).

22. Juliette Hassine, 'The Martyrdom of Sol Hatchuel: *Ridda* in Morocco in 1834', in Michael M. Laskier and Yaacov Lev (eds.), *The Convergence of Judaism and Islam: Religious, Scientific and Cultural Dimensions* (Gainesville, FL, 2011), 109–25.

23. M. Rey, *Souvenirs d'un Voyage au Maroc* (Paris, 1844).

24. His memoirs were edited by Gabriel de Seailles, *Alfred Dehodencq: Histoire d'un coloriste* (Paris, 1885).

25. Martin Gilbert, *In Ishmael's House: A History of Jews in Muslim Lands* (New Haven, 2010), 121–3; Mark Cohen, 'Islam and the Jews: Myth, Counter-Myth, History', in Shlomo Eshen and Walter Zenner (eds.), *Jews Among Muslims: Communities in the Pre-Colonial Middle East* (Basingstoke, 1996), 50–63; Bernard Lewis, *The Jews of Islam* (Princeton, 1984).

26. Abigail Green, *Moses Montefiore: Jewish Liberator, Imperial Hero* (Cambridge, MA, 2012), 69.

27. Jonathan Frankel, *The Damascus Affair: 'Ritual Murder', Politics and the Jews in 1840* (Cambridge, 1997); Green, *Montefiore*, 133ff.

28. 'A Plea for Aid in the Damascus Affair' (PRO 195/162), in Norman A. Stillman, *The Jews of Arab Lands: A History and Source Book* (Philadelphia, 1979), 393–4.

29. 'Report on the Treatment of Jewish Prisoners in the Damascus Affair', (PRO, FO 78/405, 32–4), in Stillman, 397; see also Frankel, 41–4.

30. Eliza Acton, *Modern Cookery for Private Families* (London, 1845); also ed. Jill Norman (London, 2011), 605–7.

31. Stillman, 401.

32. Davies, *Emile and Isaac Pereire*, 112–34.

33. David I. Kertzer, *The Kidnapping of Edgardo Mortara* (New York, 2008); Green, *Montefiore*, 258–82.

34. Ibid., 125; Max B. May, *Isaac Mayer Wise: The Founder of American Judaism* (New York, 1916), 271.

35. Aron Rodrigue, *French Jews, Turkish Jews: The Alliance Israélite Universelle and the Politics of Schooling in Turkey, 1860–1925* (Bloomington, 1990); André Chouraqui, *Cent Ans d'Histoire: l'Alliance israelite universelle et la renaissance juive contemporaine 1860–1960* (Paris, 1965).

36. On Hess, see Shlomo Avineri, *Moses Hess: Prophet of Communism and Zionism* (New York, 1985); Isaiah Berlin, 'The Life and Opinions of Moses

Hess', in Henry Hardy (ed.), *Against the Current: Essays in the History of Ideas* (Princeton, 1979).

Chapter 15

1. Hayyim Hibshush, *Travels in Yemen: An Account of Joseph Halévy's Journey to Najran in the year 1870, written in Sana'ani Arabic by his Guide Hayyim Hibshush*, ed. S. D. Goitein (Jerusalem, 1941); Halévy's own version: 'Voyage au Nadjran', *Bulletin de la Société de Géographie*, VI (1873), 5–31, 241–73, 581–606, and XIII (1877), 466–79. On Yemeni Jewish history, Joseph Tobi, *The Jews of Yemen: Studies in their History and Culture* (Leiden, 1999). Hibshush was sometimes known as Habshush.

2. See Simon Schama, *The Story of the Jews: Finding the Words, 1000 BCE–1492 CE* (London, 2013), 231–235.

3. Bat Zion Eraqi Klorman, *The Jews of Yemen in the 19th Century* (Leiden, 1993); *idem*, 'The Attitudes of Yemenite Rabbis towards 19th Century Jewish Messianic Figures', in *Proceedings of the 10th World Congress of Jewish Studies* (Jerusalem, 1990). *Dor Deah* originally referred to the generation that had actually witnessed the Exodus first-hand, but from 1912 it became applied in Yemen to all those opposed to mysticism and fatalism and offshoots of Kabbalism in the region.

4. The others were the al-Uzayri, the al-Marhabi and the al-Bishari.

5. On the messianic movements in later nineteenth-century Yemen, see Tobi, 48–84.

6. Bat Zion Eraqi Klorman, 'Muslim and Jewish Interactions in the Tribal Sphere [in Yemen]', in Michael M. Laskier and Yaacov Lev (eds.), *The Divergence of Judaism and Islam: Interdependence, Modernity and Political Turmoil* (Gainesville, FL, 2001), 133; *idem*, *The Jews of Yemen in the Nineteenth Century: A Portrait of a Messianic Community* (Leiden, 1993); Harris Lenowitz, 'Shukr Kuhayl II reads the Bible', in Leonard J. Greenspoon and Bryan F. Lebau (eds.), *Sacred Texts, Secular Times: The Hebrew Bible in the Modern World* (Omaha, 2000), 245–66.

7. Carol Krinsky, *The Synagogues of Europe: Architecture, History, Meaning* (Cambridge, MA, 1985), 265–70; Richard I. Cohen, 'Celebrating Integration in the Public Sphere in Germany and France', in Michael Brenner, Vicki Caron and Uri R. Kaufmann (eds.), *Jewish Emancipation Reconsidered: The French and German Models* (London, 2003), 63–7.

8. Ibid., 348–51.

9. Adam Kirsch, *Benjamin Disraeli* (New York, 2008), is the best account of Disraeli's Jewish self-consciousness notwithstanding his baptism.

10. Flavius Josephus, *Antiquities of the Jews*; 1 Kings 7, 15.

11. Krinsky, 187–93.

12. On Jellinek, Robert S. Wistrich, *The Jews of Vienna in the Age of Franz Joseph* (Oxford, 1989), 112ff, and 238–69.

13. On the higher echelons of liberal Jewish Vienna, the extraordinary family biographies assembled in Georg Gaugusch, *Wer Einmal War, Das Judische Grossburgertum Wiens 1800–1938, A–K* (Vienna, 2011), *L–R* (Vienna, 2016). On Berlin, the excellent catalogue for the opening exhibition of the Berlin Jewish Museum, Andreas Nachama and Gereon Sievernich (eds.), *Judische Lebenswelten: Katalog zur Ausstellung Judische Lebenswelten*, 2 vols (Berlin, 1991).

14. On this spatial relationship, see Richard I. Cohen, 'Urban Visibility and Biblical Visions: Jewish Culture in Western and Central Europe in the Modern Age', in David Biale (ed.), *Cultures of the Jews*, Vol. 3, *Modern Encounters* (New York, 2002), 10–74.

15. Jacob Katz, 'German Culture and the Jews', in Jehuda Reinharz and Walter Schatzberg (eds.), *The Jewish Response to German Culture: From the Enlightenment to the Second World War* (Hanover, 1985), 89.

16. Shulamit Volkov, *The Rise of Popular Antimodernism in Germany: The Urban Master Artisans, 1873–1896* (Princeton, 1978), and for some general reflections, *idem*, *Germans, Jews and Anti-Semites: Trials in Emancipation* (Cambridge, 2006).

17. On Treitschke, George Mosse, *The Intellectual Origins of the Third Reich* (New York, 1964), 200–2; Fritz Stern, *The Politics of Cultural Despair: A Study in the Rise of the Germanic Ideology* (Berkeley, 1961).

18. For Schönerer and the beginnings of modern anti-Semitic politics, Peter Pulzer, *The Rise of Political Anti-Semitism in Germany and Austria* (revd edn, London, 1988), 142–55; Robert Wistrich, *A Lethal Obsession: Anti-Semitism from Antiquity to the Jihad* (London, 2010).

19. Steven J. Zipperstein, *The Jews of Odessa: A Cultural History, 1794–1881* (Stanford, 1986); Patricia Herlihy, *Odessa: A History, 1794–1914* (Cambridge, MA, 1986); Charles King, *Odessa: Genius and Death in the City of Dreams* (New York, 2011); one of the most vivid portraits of Jewish Odessa is Vladimir Jabotinsky's novel, *The Five: A Novel of Jewish Life in Turn-of-the-Century Odessa*, trans. Michael Katz (Ithaca, 2005).

20. Jarrod Tanny, *City of Rogues and Schnorrers: Russian Jews and Myths of Old Odessa* (Bloomington, 2011), tries very hard to deconstruct a 'mythology' of a heterodox, diverse, relatively open-port metropolis, a place where Jews could be educated in modern knowledge, work at occupations closed to them elsewhere in the Russian empire. But on the whole he ends up confirming exactly this character of the city, albeit with literary helpings of criminal romance culminating in Isaac Babel's Benya Krik.

21. Steven J. Zipperstein, 'Remapping Odessa', in *Imagining Russian Jewry: Memory, History, Identity* (Seattle, 1996), 80.

22. Alexander Orbach, *New Voices of Russian Jewry: A Study of the Russian-Jewish Press of Odessa in the Era of the Great Reforms, 1860–1871* (Leiden, 1980).

23. John Doyle Klier, *Russians, Jews and the Pogroms of 1881–2* (Cambridge, 2011); see also the essays in Jonathan Dekel-Chen and David Gaunt (eds.), *Anti-Jewish Violence: Rethinking the Pogrom in Eastern Europe* (Bloomington, 2010).

24. On Lilienblum, Michael Stanislawski, *Autobiographical Jews* (Seattle, 2004), 54–68; for the flavour of the memoir, see the long extract in ChaeRan Freeze and Jay M. Harris (eds.), *Everyday Jewish Life in Imperial Russia: Select Documents, 1772–1911* (Waltham, MA, 2013), 353–67.

25. Shlomo Avineri, *The Making of Modern Zionism: The Intellectual Origins of the Jewish State* (New York, 1981), 73–82.

26. In the short term this was not a good idea. The esparto grass in particular did the work of stabilising shifting coastal sand.

27. For the early history of the settlement and its tortured relationship with Jewish philanthropy, Ben Halpern and Jehuda Reinharz, *Zionism and the Creation of a New Society* (Oxford, 1998), 59ff. See also Shmuel Ettinger and Israel Bartal, 'The First Aliyah: Ideological Roots and Practical Accomplishments', in Jehuda Reinharz and Anita Shapira (eds.), *Essential Papers in Zionism* (New York, 1996), 63–93.

28. Simon Schama, *Two Rothschilds and the Land of Israel* (London, 1978).

29. Ran Aaronsohn, *Rothschild and Early Jewish Colonisation* (Lanham, MD, 2000).

30. Ruth Kark and Noam Levin, 'The Environment of Palestine in the Late Ottoman Period', in Daniel E. Orenstein, Alon Tal and Char Miller (eds.), *Between Ruin and Restoration: An Environmental History of Israel* (Pittsburgh, 2013), 1–29; Gad Gilbar (ed.), *Ottoman Palestine 1880–1914: Studies in Economy and Society* (Leiden, 1990).

31. Arieh L. Avneri, *The Claim of Dispossession: Jewish Land Settlement and the Arabs, 1878–1948* (Efal, 1982), 82–3.

32. The Colony grew despite Horatio's death in 1888 from malaria. A substantial house was bought outside the city walls in Sheikh Jarrah district which turned into the American Colony hotel, today still decorated with photographs of the Spaffords and still serving the best breakfast in Jerusalem.

Chapter 16

1. The literature on the Dreyfus Affair is immense and never stops growing. In my view the best of all books and the most readable is Ruth Harris,

The Man on Devil's Island: Alfred Dreyfus and the Affair that Divided France (London, 2010); for up-to-date debates, Maya Balakirsky Katz (ed.), Revising Dreyfus (Leiden, 2013); also Michael Burns, France and the Dreyfus Affair: A Brief Documentary History (Boston, 1998); and for the longer family history before and after, idem, Dreyfus: A Family Affair, 1789–1945 (New York, 1991). On the dilemmas of French Jews during the Affair, Michael Marrus, The Politics of Assimilation: A Study of the French Jewish Community at the Time of the Dreyfus Affair (New York, 1971); Paula Hyman, The Jews of Modern France (Berkeley, 1998); Phyllis Cohen Albert, The Modernization of French Jewry: Consistory and Community in the Nineteenth Century (Hanover, NH, 1977). See also the magisterial Jean-Denis Bredin, The Affair: The Case of Alfred Dreyfus, trans. J. Mehlman (New York, 1986); and for recent reflections on resonance, Louis Begley, Why Dreyfus Matters (New York, 2009). On the imagery and iconography of the Affair, see the superb Jewish Museum exhibition catalogue, Norman Kleeblatt (ed.), The Dreyfus Affair: Art, Truth and Justice (Berkeley, 1987). For those who can't get enough Dreyfus there is Robert Harris's excellent novel An Officer and a Spy (London, 2014), but for a contemporary passionately Dreyfusard literary satire, see the great Anatole France, Penguin Island (1908).

2.   Ruth Harris, 125–7; Pierre Birnbaum, The Antisemitic Moment: A Tour of France in 1898, trans. Jane Moore Todd (New York, 2003); Stephen Wilson, Ideology and Experience: Anti-Semitism in France at the Time of the Dreyfus Affair (Rutherford, NJ, 2003).

3.   Birnbaum, 233–6.

4.   Michael Rosen, The Disappearance of Émile Zola (London, 2017).

5.   Nelly Wilson, Bernard-Lazare: Antisemitism and the Problem of Jewish Identity in Late Nineteenth-Century France (Cambridge, 1978); Ruth Harris, 77.

6.   Bredin, 28, see also 295–6.

7.   Linda Nochlin, 'Degas and the Dreyfus Affair: A Portrait of the Artist as Anti-Semite', in Kleeblatt (ed.), 96–116; and Susan Rubin Suleiman, 'The Literary Significance of the Dreyfus Affair', in Kleeblatt (ed.), 117–39.

8.   Ibid., 196.

9.   V. Lenepveu, 'Le Roi des porcs', from that artist's Musée des horreurs (1900), the most elaborately lurid of the anti-Semitic personifications also featuring Dreyfus himself, complete with hooked nose and a serpent's body from which a multitude of snakes emerged. Kleeblatt (ed.), 244, 246.

10.   Stephen Bottomore, 'Dreyfus and Documentary', Sight and Sound (Autumn 1984); also Luke McKernan's fine Bioscope blog, alas no longer active but kept as an archive, thank you, Luke: 'Lives on Film: Alfred Dreyfus' (three consecutive blogs) with illustrations. On Méliès, John

Frazer, *Artificially Arranged Scenes: The Films of Georges Méliès* (Boston, 1979); Jacques Malthête, *L'Oeuvre de Georges Méliès* (Paris, 2008).

11. Bottomore, 291.

12. Maurice Barrès, *Scènes et doctrines du nationalisme* (Paris, 1920), 40; Zeev Sternhell, *Maurice Barrès et le nationalisme français* (Paris, 1973).

13. On Dreyfus's body language during the degradation: Christopher E. Forth, *The Dreyfus Affair and the Crisis of Manhood* (Baltimore, 2004), 21–60; Venita Datta, 'The Dreyfus Affair as National Theatre', in Balakirsky Katz (ed.).

14. Theodor Herzl, 'Die Degradation des Capitäns Dreyfus', *Neue Freie Press* (Vienna, 6 January 1895).

15. Jacques Kornberg, 'Theodor Herzl: A Re-evaluation', *Journal of Modern History*, 52:2 (June 1980), and *idem, Theodor Herzl: From Assimilation to Zionism* (Chicago, 1993); Shlomo Avineri, *Herzl's Vision: Theodor Herzl and the Foundation of the Jewish State* (London, 2013); Amos Elon, *Herzl* (New York, 1975), is as one would expect a lively read but now a little dated; Ernst Pawel, *The Labyrinth of Exile: A Life of Theodor Herzl* (New York, 1989), is the most sardonic and sceptical of the biographies, at the opposite pole from the classic excessively uncritical Alex Bein (1934), but Pawel's artfulness somehow misses the core of his subject.

16. *The Complete Diaries of Theodor Herzl*, ed. Raphael Patai, trans. Harry Zohn (New York, 1960), 5 vols.

17. On Alkalai: Raymond Goldwater, *Pioneers of Religious Zionism* (New York, 2009); Arthur Hertzberg, *The Zionist Idea: An Historical Analysis and Reader* (New York, 1976), 102–5; Shlomo Avineri, *The Making of Modern Zionism* (New York, 1981).

18. Kornberg, 32ff.

19. For an excellent and very detailed reading, Kornberg, 67–71.

20. Herzl, *Diaries*, I, 4.

21. Ibid., I, 3.

22. Ibid., I, 27–8.

23. Ran Aaronsohn, *Rothschild and Early Colonization in Palestine*, trans. Gila Brand (Jerusalem, 2000); Judith Noemie Freidenberg, *The Invention of the Jewish Gaucho: Villa Clara and the Construction of Argentine Identity* (Austin, Texas, 2009).

24. Herzl, *Diaries*, I, 131.

25. Cecil Bloom, 'Samuel Montagu and Zionism', *Jewish Historical Studies*, 34 (1994–6), 17–41.

26. Barbara W. Tuchman, *Bible and Sword: England and Palestine from the Bronze Age to Balfour* (New York, 1956).

27. Theodor Herzl, *The Jewish State* (New York, 1946), 82.

28. Ibid., 76.
29. Ibid., 129.
30. Ibid., 156.
31. On Jewish London and early Zionism: Geoffrey Alderman, *Modern British Jewry* (Oxford, 1958); Daniel Gutwein, *The Divided Elite: Economics, Politics and Anglo-Jewry, 1882–1917* (Leiden, 1992); Stuart Cohen, *English Zionists and British Jews: The Communal Politics of Anglo-Jewry, 1896–1920* (Princeton, 1982).
32. Simon Schama, *Two Rothschilds and the Land of Israel* (London, 1978), 145–7.
33. On Hechler and the Christian Zionists: Gerhard Gronauer, '"To love the Jews": William H. Hechler (1845–1931), der christliche Förderer des politischen Zionismus', in Berthold Schwarz and Helge Stadelmann (eds.), *Christen, Juden und die Zukunft Israels* (Frankfurt am Main, 2009); Shalom Goldman, *Zeal for Zion: Christians, Jews and the Ideal of the Promised Land* (Chapel Hill, 2008); Victoria Clark, *Allies for Armageddon: The Rise of Christian Zionism* (New Haven, 2007).
34. Herzl, *Diaries*, I, 311ff.
35. Ibid., II, 579.
36. Quoted in Michael Berkowitz, *Zionist Culture and Western European Jewry Before the First World War* (Chapel Hill, 1996), 17.
37. Herzl, *Diaries*, II, 580.
38. Ibid., II, 581.
39. On Ahad Ha'am, David Vital, *The Origins of Zionism* (New York, 1980), 187; also a brilliant essay by Hillel Halkin, 'What Ahad Ha'am Saw and Herzl Missed', *Mosaic* (October 2016), online.
40. Halkin.
41. Herzl, *Diaries*, II, 727–8.
42. Shlomo Avineri, 'Theodor Herzl's Diaries as Bildungsroman', *Jewish Social Studies*, 5:3 (1999), points out that Herzl spelled Jerusalem this way only during his brief trip to Palestine; Herzl, *Diaries*, II, 738–9.

FURTHER READING: A SHORT(ISH) GUIDE FOR THE GENERAL READER

There is a vast, complex and exhilarating literature of scholarly writing on Jewish history between the Renaissance and the turn of the twentieth century, but few narratives for the general reader. Exceptions are the pleasingly idiosyncratic Melvin Konner, *Unsettled: An Anthropology of the Jews* (New York, 2003), and Howard M. Sachar, *A History of the Jews in the Modern World* (New York, 2006). Paul Johnson's *A History of the Jews* (London, 1987) covers four millennia and is still a wonderful read. Many of the books of Cecil Roth on any number of topics covered in this volume are now sadly out of print, but it's worth hunting especially for *The History of the Jews of Italy* (Philadelphia, 1946), *The Duke of Naxos of the House of Nasi* (Philadelphia, 1948), *The Jews in the Renaissance* (Philadelphia, 1959) and *A History of the Jews in England* (rev. edn, Oxford, 1978). The classic work on emancipation and its challenges is Jacob Katz, *Out of the Ghetto: The Social Background of Jewish Emancipation, 1770–1870* (Cambridge, MA, 1973; 2nd edn, Syracuse, 1998).

For particular aspects of Jewish culture and history, Ruth Wisse, *Jews and Power* (New York, 2007); Amos Oz and Fania Oz-Salzberger, *Jews and Words* (New Haven, 2013); Amos Elon, *The Pity of It All: A Portrait of the Jews in Germany, 1743–1943* (London, 2003); Ruth Gay, *The Jews of Germany: An Historical Portrait* (New Haven, 1992); Riccardo Calimani, *The Ghetto of Venice* (Milan, 1995); Mozes Heiman Gans's enormous, spectacularly illustrated *Memorboek: A History of Dutch Jewry from the Renaissance to 1940* (Baarn, 1977); Nils Roemer, *German City, Jewish Memory: The Story of Worms* (Waltham, MA, 2010); Todd M. Endelman, *The Jews of Britain, 1656–2000* (Berkeley, 2002); Hasia Diner's *A New Promised Land: A History of Jews in America* (Oxford, 2000) and *The Jews of the United States, 1654–2000* (Berkeley, 2004); Jonathan D. Sarna (ed.), *The American Jewish Experience* (New York, 1997).

For art and architecture in this period, Richard I. Cohen, *Jewish Icons: Art and Society in Modern Europe* (Berkeley, 1998); on synagogues, Carol Herselle Krinsky, *Synagogues of Europe: Architecture, History, Meaning* (New York, 1985). Those interested in the eloquence of synagogue design might want to consult two fine websites: the Foundation for Jewish Heritage and Centre for Jewish Art of the Hebrew University's Synagogue Mapping Project, which pays special attention to synagogues in need of restoration primarily in Europe (though the project hopes to extend its work to Iraq and Syria); and the glorious Synagogues360 offering online tours of synagogues throughout the world from Kerala to South Carolina.

The eloquently beautiful little meditation by the medieval historian Yitzhak Baer, *Galut*, written as darkness closed in fast in 1936 but published in an English translation by Robert Warshaw in the momentous year of 1947, is one of the jewels in the treasury of Jewish writing. On the same subject, a plangent essay by Yosef Hayim Yerushalmi, 'Exile and Expulsion in Jewish History', in Benjamin R. Gampel (ed.), *Crisis and Creativity in the Sephardic World, 1391–1648* (New York, 1997), and the same author's tour de force, *Zakhor: Jewish History and Jewish Memory* (Seattle, 1982).

David Biale (ed.), *The Cultures of the Jews* (New York, 2002), is an essential collection of essays reflecting new historical thinking, available either in one big volume from biblical antiquity to the present or, for the later period, Vol. 3, *Modern Encounters*. For the earlier period, David Ruderman, *Early Modern Jewry: A New Cultural History* (Princeton, 2010). The most important work on Jews in the early modern world is Jonathan I. Israel, *European Jewry in the Age of Mercantilism, 1550–1750* (Oxford, 1985); see also Richard L. Kagan and Philip D. Morgan (eds.), *Atlantic Diasporas: Jews, Conversos and the Crypto-Jews in the Age of Mercantilism, 1500–1800* (Baltimore, 2009); Jacob Katz, *Jewish Emancipation and Self-Emancipation* (New York, 1986); and Michael Meyer, *The Origins of the Modern Jew: Jewish Identity and European Culture in Germany, 1749–1824*. On writing about personal and religious odysseys, Michael Stanislawki, *Autobiographical Jews: Essays in Jewish Self-Fashioning* (Seattle, 2000). Although Yuri Slezkine's *The Jewish Century* (Princeton, 2004) is located more or less 1850–1950, it is one of the most stimulating books ever to have been written on Jewish – or for that matter any – history.

More specialised works are

On the Renaissance: Hillel Halkin, *Across the Sabbath River: In Search of a Lost Tribe of Israel* (New York, 2002); David B. Ruderman, *The World of a Renaissance Jew: The Life and Thought of Abraham ben Mordecai Farissol* (Cincinnati, 1981); idem, *Jewish Thought and Scientific Discovery in Early Modern Europe* (Detroit, 2001); idem (ed.), *Preachers of the Italian Ghetto* (Berkeley,

2002); Aron di Leone Leoni, *The Hebrew Portuguese Nation in Antwerp and London at the Time of Charles V and Henry VIII* (Jersey City, 2005); Andrée Aelion Brooks, *The Woman who Defied Kings: The Life and Times of Doña Gracia Nasi* (St Paul, 2003); Ahuva Belkin (ed.), *Leone de Sommi* (Tel Aviv, 1997); Robert Bonfil, *Jewish Life in Renaissance Italy*, trans. Anthony Oldcorn (Berkeley, 1994); Kenneth R. Stow, *Jewish Life in Early Modern Rome: Challenge, Conversion and Private Life* (Aldershot, 2007); Elisheva Carlebach, *Palaces of Time: Jewish Calendar and Culture in Early Modern Europe* (Cambridge, MA., 2011); Robert C. Davis and Benjamin Ravid (eds.), *The Jews of Early Modern Venice* (Baltimore, 2001); Brian Pullan, *The Jews of Europe and the Inquisition of Venice, 1550–1670* (Oxford, 1983); Sarra Copia Sulam, *Jewish Poet and Intellectual in Seventeenth-Century Venice: The Works of Sarra Copia Sulam in Verse and Prose*, trans. and ed. Don Harrán (Chicago, 2009); Don Harrán, *Salomone Rossi, Jewish Musician in Late Renaissance Mantua* (Oxford, 1999).

On the Sephardi world: Esther Benbassa and Aron Rodrigue, *Sephardi Jewry: A History of the Judeo-Spanish Community, 14th–20th Centuries* (Berkeley, 1995); Benjamin R. Gampel (ed.), *Crisis and Continuity in the Sephardi World* (New York, 1999); Yirimiyahu Yovel, *The Other Within: Split Identity and Emerging Identity* (Princeton, 2009); Jessica Vance Roitman, *The Same But Different? Inter-cultural Trade and the Sephardim, 1595–1640* (London, 2011); Renée Levine Melammed, *A Question of Identity: Iberian Conversos in Historical Perspective* (New York, 2004).

On the Kaifeng Jews: Michael Pollak, *Mandarins, Jews and Missionaries: The Jewish Experience in the Chinese Empire* (New York, 1984); Jonah Goldstein, *The Jews in China*, Vol. 1 (New York, 1999); Xu Xin, *The Jews of Kaifeng, China: History, Culture and Religion* (Jersey City, 2003); Tiberiu Weisz, *The Kaifeng Stone Inscriptions: The Legacy of the Jewish Community in Ancient China* (New York, 2006).

On the Dutch Jews: Jonathan I. Israel and Reinier Salverda (eds.), *Dutch Jewry: Its History and Secular Culture, 1600–2000* (Leiden, 2002); Miriam Bodian, *Hebrews of the Portuguese Nation: Conversos and Community in Early Modern Amsterdam* (Bloomington, 1997); Tirtsah Levie Bernfeld, *Poverty and Welfare Among the Portuguese Jews of Early Modern Amsterdam* (Oxford, 2012); Steven Nadler, *Rembrandt's Jews* (Chicago; 2003); Michael Zell, *Reframing Rembrandt: Jews and the Christian Image in Amsterdam* (Berkeley, 2002). On Spinoza: Don Garrett (ed.), *The Cambridge Companion to Spinoza* (Cambridge, 1996); Steven Nadler, *Spinoza: A Life* (Cambridge, 1997); *idem*, *A Book Forged in Hell: Spinoza's Scandalous Treatise and the Birth of the Secular Age* (Princeton, 2011); Susan James, *Spinoza on Philosophy, Religion and Politics* (Oxford, 2012); Rebecca Newberger Goldstein, *Betraying*

Spinoza: The Renegade Jew Who Gave Us Modernity (New York, 2006); Peter Vlaardingerbroek (ed.), *The Portuguese Synagogue in Amsterdam* (Zwolle, 2012).

On Shabbetai Zevi: The classic, monumental work is still Gershom Scholem, *Sabbatai Sevi: The Mystical Messiah, 1626–1676*, trans. R. J. Zwi Werblowsky, with an introduction by Yaacob Dweck (Princeton, 1976; new edn Baltimore, 2009), but see also, especially for Nathan of Gaza, Matt Goldish, *The Sabbatean Prophets* (Cambridge, MA, 2006); David Joel Halperin, *Shebbetai Zevi: Testimonies to a Fallen Messiah* (Berkeley, 1996); Pawel Macjieko (ed.), *Sabbatian Heresy: Writings on Mysticism, Messianism and the Origins of Jewish Modernity* (Waltham, MA, 2017); Ada Rapoport-Albert, *Women and the Messianic Heresy of Shabbetai Zevi, 1666–1816* (Liverpool, 2015); on Frankism, Pawel Maciejko, *The Mixed Multitude: Jacob Frank and the Frankist Movement, 1755–1816* (Philadelphia, 2011).

On Germany and the Haskalah: Vivian B. Mann and Richard I. Cohen (eds.), *Court Jews: Art, Patronage, Power* (New York, 1996); Shmuel Feiner, *The Origins of Jewish Secularization in Eighteenth-Century Europe*, trans. Chaya Naor (Philadelphia 2010); David Sorkin, *The Religious Enlightenment: Protestants, Jews, and Catholics from London to Vienna* (Princeton, 2011); *idem, The Berlin Haskalah and German Religious Thought: Orphans of Knowledge* (London, 2000); *idem, Moses Mendelssohn and the Religious Enlightenment* (London, 1996); Michael A. Meyer, *The Origins of the Modern Jew: Jewish Identity and European Culture in Germany, 1749–1824* (Detroit, 1967); Alexander Altmann, *Moses Mendelssohn: A Biographical Study* (Oxford 1998); Allan Arkush, *Moses Mendelssohn and the Enlightenment* (New York, 1994); Michah Gottlieb (ed.), *Moses Mendelssohn: Writings on Judaism, Christianity and the Bible* (Waltham, MA, 2011); *idem, Faith and Freedom: Moses Mendelssohn's Theological-Political Thought* (Oxford, 2011); Shmuel Feiner and David Sorkin (eds.), *New Perspectives on the Haskalah* (Oxford, 2004); Shmuel Feiner and Natalie Naimark-Goldberg, *Cultural Revolution in Berlin: Jews in the Age of Enlightenment* (Oxford, 2011); Jacob Katz, *Exclusiveness and Tolerance: Studies in Jewish–Gentile Relations in Medieval and Modern Times* (Oxford, 1961); H. M. Graupe, *The Rise of Modern Judaism: An Intellectual History of German Jewry, 1650–1942*, trans. John Robinson (Huntington, NY, 1978); Deborah Hertz, *Jewish High Society in Old Regime Berlin* (New Haven, 1988); Hannah Arendt, *Rahel Varnhagen: The Life of a Jewess*, ed. Liliane Weissberg, trans. Richard and Clara Winston (Baltimore, 1997).

On Britain, France and the Atlantic World: David Cesarani (ed.), *Port Jews: Jewish Communities in Cosmopolitan Maritime Trading Centres* (London, 2007); Paolo Bernardini and Norman Fiering (eds.), *The Jews and the Expansion of*

Europe to the West, 1450–1800 (Oxford, 2001); Lois Dubin, *The Port Jews of Habsburg Trieste: Absolutist Politics and Enlightenment Culture* (Stanford, 1999); Gedalia Yogev, *Diamonds and Coral: Anglo-Dutch Jews and Eighteenth-Century Trade* (London, 1978); Francesca Trivellato, *The Familiarity of Strangers: The Sephardic Diaspora, Livorno and Cross-cultural Trade in the Early Modern Period* (New Haven, 2009); Todd Endelman, *The Jews of Georgian England: Tradition and Change in a Liberal Society* (Philadelphia, 1979); V. D. Lipman, *Three Centuries of Anglo-Jewish History* (Cambridge, 1961); Frances Malino, *The Sephardic Jews of Bordeaux: Assimilation and Emancipation in Revolutionary and Napoleonic France* (Alabama, 2003); idem, *A Jew in the French Revolution: The Life of Zalkind Hourwitz* (Cambridge, MA, 1996); Arthur Hertzberg, *The French Enlightenment and the Jews: The Origins of Modern Anti-Semitism* (New York, 1968); Ronald Schechter, *Obstinate Hebrews: Representations of Jews in France, 1715–1815* (Berkeley, 2003); Zosa Szajkowski, *Jews and the French Revolutions of 1789, 1830 and 1848* (New York, 1970); Frederick Jaher, *The Jews and the Nation: Revolution, Emancipation, State Formation and the Liberal Roads in America and France* (Princeton, 2002); Michael Brenner, Vicki Caron and Uri R. Kaufmann (eds.), *Jewish Emancipation Reconsidered: The French and German Models* (London, 2003); Frank Felsenstein, *Anti-Semitic Stereotypes: A Paradigm of Otherness in English Popular Culture, 1660–1830* (Baltimore, 1995).

On Eastern Europe and the Pale: The classic characterisation of the shtetl is Mark Zborowski and Elizabeth Herzog, *Life is With People: The Culture of the Shtetl*, with a foreword (remarkably) by Margaret Mead (New York, 1952). But our understanding of the reality of the shtetl has been transformed by a wealth of brilliant, archivally grounded recent histories: Antony Polonsky, *The Jews in Poland and Russia: A Short History* (Oxford, 2013); Chimen Abramsky (ed.), *The Jews in Poland* (Oxford, 1971); Israel Bartal, *The Jews of Eastern Europe, 1772–1881*, trans. Chaya Naor (Philadelphia, 2005); Gershon David Hundert, *The Jews of Poland-Lithuania in the Eighteenth Century: A Genealogy of Modernity* (Berkeley, 2004); Yohanan Petrovsky-Shtern, *The Golden Age of the Shtetl: A New History of Jewish Life in Eastern Europe* (Princeton, 2013); Glenn Dynner, *Yankel's Tavern: Jews, Liquor and Life in the Kingdom of Poland* (Oxford, 2013); Nancy Sinkoff, *Making Jews Modern in the Polish Borderlands* (Providence, 2004).

The classic essay on the rise of Hasidism is found in Gershom Scholem, *Major Trends in Jewish Mysticism* (New York, 1946), but there has been a great recent flowering of work on the subject; see Ada Rapoport-Albert (ed.), *Hasidism Reappraised* (Oxford, 1996); Moshe Idel, *Hasidism Between Ecstasy and Magic* (New York, 1995); Glen Dynner, *Men of Silk: The Hasidic Conquest of Polish Jewish Society* (Oxford, 2008); David Assaf, *Untold Tales of Hasidism: Crisis and Discontent in the History of Hasidism* (Waltham, MA, 2010); Moshe Rosman, *Founder of Hasidism: A Quest for the Historical Baal Shem Tov* (Oxford, 2007);

Eliyahu Stern, *The Genius: Elijah of Vilna and the Making of Modern Judaism* (New Haven, 2013); Michael Stanislawski, *Tsar Nicholas I and the Jews: The Transformation of Jewish Society in Russia, 1825–1855* (Philadelphia, 1983); ChaeRan Y. Freeze and Jay M. Harris (eds.), *Everyday Life in Imperial Russia: Select Documents, 1772–1914* (Waltham, MA, 2013).

On nineteenth-century America: Morris U. Schappes (ed.), *A Documentary History of the Jews in the United States, 1654–1875* (New York, 1971); Marc Lee Raphael (ed.), *The Columbia History of Jews and Judaism in America* (New York, 2008); Jonathan D. Sarna: *American Judaism: A History* (New Haven, 2004); *idem, Jacksonian Jew: The Two Worlds of Mordecai Noah* (New York, 1981); *idem, When General Grant Expelled the Jews* (New York, 2012); Jacob R. Marcus (ed.), *The American Jewish Woman: A Documentary History* (New York, 1981); Ira Dye, *Uriah Levy: Reformer of the Antebellum Navy* (Gainesville, 2006); Marc Leepson, *Saving Monticello: The Levy Family's Epic Quest to Rescue the House That Jefferson Built* (Charlottesville, 2001); Hasia Diner, *Roads Taken: The Great Jewish Migrations to the New World and the Peddlers Who Forged the Way* (New Haven, 2015); Ava F. Kahn (ed.), *Jewish Voices of the California Gold Rush: A Documentary History* (Detroit, 2002); Jeanne E. Abrams, *Jewish Women Pioneering the Frontier Trail: A History in the American West* (New York, 2006).

On modernisation and liberalism: David Conway, *Jewry in Music: Entry to the Profession from the Enlightenment to Richard Wagner* (Cambridge, 2011); Heinz and Gudrun Becker, *Giacomo Meyerbeer: A Life in Letters*, trans. Mark Violette (London, 1983); Robert Letellier, *Diaries of Giacomo Meyerbeer*, 4 vols (Madison, NJ, 1999–2004); Niall Ferguson, *The World's Banker: The History of the House of Rothschild* (London, 1998); Claude Collard and Melanie Aspey (eds.), *Les Rothschild en France au XIXe siècle* (Paris, 2013); Helen M. Davies, *Emile and Isaac Pereire: Bankers, Socialists and Sephardi Jews in Nineteenth-Century France* (Manchester, 2015); Jerry Z. Muller, *Capitalism and the Jews* (Princeton, 2010); Abigail Green, *Moses Montefiore: Jewish Liberator, Imperial Hero* (Cambridge, MA, 2010); Adam Kirsch, *The Making of Benjamin Disraeli* (New York, 2008); Aron Rodrigue, *French Jews, Turkish Jews: The Alliance Israelite Universelle and the Politics of Schooling in Turkey, 1860–1925* (Bloomington, 1990); Jonathan Frankel, *The Damascus Affair: 'Ritual Murder', Politics and the Jews in 1840* (Cambridge, 1997); David Kertzer, *The Kidnapping of Edgardo Mortara* (New York, 1998); Keith H. Pickus, *Constructing Modern Identities: Jewish University Students in Germany, 1815–1914* (Detroit, 1999); Michael Meyer (ed.), *German-Jewish History in Modern Times: Integration and Dispute 1870–1918* (New York, 1978); Robert S. Wistrich, *The Jews of Vienna in the Age of Franz Joseph* (New York, 1989); Steven E. Aschheim, *Brothers and Strangers: The East European Jew in Germany and the German Jewish Consciousness, 1800–1923* (Madison, 1982);

Jehuda Reinharz and Walter Schatzberg (eds.), *The Jewish Response to German Culture from the Enlightenment to the Second World War* (Hanover, NH, 1988); Steven Zipperstein, *The Jews of Odessa: A Cultural History, 1792–1881* (Stanford, 1985); Jarrod Tanny, *City of Rogues and Schnorrers: Russia's Jews and the Myth of Old Odessa* (Bloomington, 2011); Norman A. Stillman, *The Jews of Arab Lands: A History and Source Book* (Cambridge, 1979); Reeva Spector Simon, Michael Menachem Laskier and Sara Reguer (eds.), *The Jews of the Middle East and North Africa in Modern Times* (New York, 2002).

On anti-Semitism and early Zionism: Robert Wistrich, *A Lethal Obsession: Anti-Semitism from Antiquity to the Global Jihad* (London, 2010); Leon Poliakov, *The History of Anti-Semitism, Vol. III: From Voltaire to Wagner*, trans. Miriam Kochan (Philadelphia, 2003); George L. Mosse, *The Crisis of German Ideology* (New York, 1965); Shulamit Volkov, *Germans, Jews and Antisemites: Trials in Emancipation* (Cambridge, 2006); *idem, The Rise of Popular Antimodernism in Germany: The Urban Master Artisans, 1873–1896* (Princeton, 1978): Peter Pulzer, *The Rise of Political Anti-Semitism in Germany and Austria* (revd edn, London, 1988); Jonathan Dekel-Chan, David Gaunt, Natan M. Meir and Israel Bartal (eds.), *Anti-Jewish Violence: Rethinking Pogroms in Eastern European History* (Bloomington, 2010); I. Michael Aronson, *Troubled Waters: The Origins of the 1881 Anti-Jewish Pogroms in Russia* (Pittsburgh, 1990); Ruth Harris, *The Man on Devil's Island: Alfred Dreyfus and the Affair that Divided France* (London, 2011); Jean-Denis Bredin, *The Affair: The Case of Alfred Dreyfus*, trans. Jeffrey Mehlman (New York, 1986); Michael Burns, *France and the Dreyfus Affair: A Documentary History* (Boston, 1988); *idem, Dreyfus: A Family Affair, 1789–1945* (New York, 1991); Michael Marrus, *The Politics of Assimilation: A Study of the French Jewish Community at the Time of the Dreyfus Affair* (Oxford, 1981); Louis Begley, *Why the Dreyfus Affair Matters* (New Haven, 2009); Shlomo Avineri, *The Making of Modern Zionism: The Intellectual Origins of the Jewish State* (2nd edn, New York, 2017); *idem, Theodor Herzl and the Foundation of the Jewish State* (London, 2008); Jacques Kornberg, *Theodor Herzl: From Assimilation to Zionism* (Bloomington, 1993); Simon Schama, *Two Rothschilds and the Land of Israel* (New York, 1978); Ran Aaronsohn, *Rothschild and Early Colonization in Palestine*, trans. Gila Brand (Jerusalem, 2000).

LIST OF
ILLUSTRATIONS

Section One

Mid-sixteenth-century pen-and-ink copy of illustration from Moses of Castellazzo, *The Building of the Tower of Babel*, Picture Bible, 1521. Facsimile of the Bilder-Pentateuch von Moses dal Castellazzo Codex 1164. © Kurt and Ursula Schubert & Family.

The banner of Solomon Molkho. From the collections of the Jewish Museum in Prague: Jewish Museum in Prague Photo Archive.

Interior of Balat synagogue in Istanbul, Turkey. Photo by Izzet Keribar. Getty Images.

The Ten Sefirot of the Kabbalah, from *Portae Lucis* (Augsburg, 1516) by the Jewish convert to Christianity Paolo Riccio. © culture-images/Lebrecht Music & Arts.

Frontispiece portrait from Leone Modena's *Historia de'riti hebraici*, 1638. Courtesy of the Library of the Jewish Theological Seminary, RB420:13.

Tombstones in the Jewish cemetery on the Lido, Venice. © Tim Kirby.

Spanish–Portuguese ('Ponentine') synagogue, Ghetto Vecchio, Venice, enlarged by the workshop of Baldassare Longhena, c.1635. Photo by Michael Calimani.

Poster promoting Templo's reconstruction of Solomon's Temple. Bibliotheca Rosenthaliana, Special Collections of the University of Amsterdam.

Engraved portrait of Menasseh ben Israel by Salom Italia, 1642. Courtesy of the Library of the Jewish Theological Seminary, PNT G1885.

Yakov ben Abraham Zaddik, colophon self-portrait etching, from Abraham Goos, *Map of the Holy Land*, Amsterdam 1620–1. © culture-images/Lebrecht Music & Arts.

Photograph of interior of Paradesi synagogue, Cochin, Kerala, India. Photo by Joel S. Berkowitz.

Portrait of Dr Ephraim Bueno, etching by Rembrandt van Rijn, 1647. Musée de la Ville de Paris, Musée du Petit-Palais, France / Bridgeman Images.

Moses with the Tablets of the Law by Rembrandt van Rijn, 1659. Gemäldegalerie, Staatliche Museen zu Berlin, Germany / Bridgeman Images.

Detail of map of Amsterdam by Balthasar Florisz van Berckenrode, 1625, showing the district of Vlooienburg. Rijksmuseum, Amsterdam.

The Inauguration of the Esnoga in 1675 by Romeyn de Hooghe. Courtesy of the Library of the Jewish Theological Seminary, B(NS) OV71.

Sephardi Family Circumcision Scene by Romeyn de Hooghe, 1668. Rijksmuseum, Amsterdam.

Portrait of a Young Jew by Rembrandt van Rijn, 1648. bpk / Gemäldegalerie, SMB. Eigentum des Kaiser Friedrich Museumsvereins / Christoph Schmidt.

Section Two

Shabbetai Zevi. Bibliotheca Rosenthaliana, Special Collections of the University of Amsterdam.

The human body as a house, from Tobias Cohen's medical encyclopaedia, *Ma'aseh Tuviyah*, Venice, 1708. Wellcome Library, London.

A New Year's postcard from the late nineteenth century showing the Hurva Synagogue in Jerusalem. © A. Andrusier / Lebrecht Music & Arts.

Portrait of Samuel Oppenheimer by Johann Andreas Pfeffel. Private Collection / Bridgeman Images.

Moses Mendelssohn, engraving by Daniel Chodowiecki, 1792. Photo © Tarker / Bridgeman Images.

Portrait of Moses Mendelssohn by Anton Graff, 1773. Deutsches Historisches Museum, Berlin, Germany. © DHM / Bridgeman Images.

Dr Ralph Schomberg by Thomas Gainsborough. © The National Gallery, London.

Moses Mendelssohn's eyeglasses, *c.*1751–1800; Courtesy of the Leo Baeck Institute, New York. Photo by Jens Ziehe.

Portrait of Daniel Itzig. ART Collection / Alamy Stock Photo.

Portrait of Isaac Daniel Itzig. L-GEM 90/2/0): Isaac Daniel Itzig, Berlin, 1777, oil on canvas, 58 x 48 cm; Israel Museum, Jerusalem. Permanent Loan to the Jewish Museum Berlin. Photo by Jens Ziehe.

Ark curtain. KGT97/1/0: Torah curtain, Berlin, 1774–1775, silk linen, embroidered, 210 x 145 cm. Purchased with funds from the Stiftung Deutsche Klassenlotterie Berlin. © Jewish Museum Berlin. Photo by Jens Ziehe.

John Braham as Prince Orlando by Thomas Woolnoth, 1828. © culture-images / Lebrecht Music & Arts.

The English boxing champion Daniel Mendoza, etching by James Gillray, *c*.1788–95. Photo © Granger/Bridgeman Images.

Rag Fair by Thomas Rowlandson, London, *c*.1800. Royal Collection Trust © Her Majesty Queen Elizabeth II, 2017/Bridgeman Images.

The Game of the Jew, eighteenth-century French board game. Private Collection/Archives Charmet/Bridgeman Images.

Rabbi Israel ben Eliezer. © culture-images/Lebrecht Music & Arts.

Ark of Satanow Great Synagogue. Photo by Ruth Ellen Gruber.

'Chasing hares' tombstone from the cemetery at Satanow. Photo by Christian Herrmann.

Section Three

Commodore Uriah Levy in uniform, 1858. Courtesy of US Naval Academy Museum.

Portrait of Rebecca Gratz by Gilbert Stuart, 1802. © culture-images/Lebrecht Music & Arts.

Adah Menken, *c*.1862. Photo by Hulton Archive/Getty Images.

E. S. Salomon, State Library Photograph Collection, 1851–1990, Washington State Archives.

Portrait of Giacomo Meyerbeer as a 12-year-old boy, by Friedrich Georg Weitsch, 1802. akg-images.

Giacomo Meyerbeer. © Lebrecht Music & Arts.

Portrait of Amalia Beer by Johann Karl Kretschmar, 1803. Stadtmuseum Berlin, reproduction: Oliver Ziebe, Berlin.

The Synagogue on Oranienburger Strasse, Berlin by Emile Pierre Joseph de Cauwer, 1865. bpk.

View from the front of Tempio Maggiore Israelitico (Great Synagogue), Florence. © 2017 Manuel Cohen/Photo SCALA, Florence.

Busts of Isaac and Jacob Émile Péreire by Antoine Samuel Adam-Solomon. Photo © Tallandier/Bridgeman Images.

Still from the Georges Méliès film *L'affaire Dreyfus*, 1899. Star Film/Collection Christophel/ArenaPAL.

Portrait of Alfred Dreyfus. DEA/A. DAGLI ORTI, De Agostini Picture Library/Getty Images.

Front page of *L'Aurore*, 13 January 1898. Bridgeman Images.

La Libre Parole, 17 November 1894. © Leemage/Lebrecht Music & Arts.

Doctored photograph purporting to show Theodor Herzl meeting Kaiser Wilhelm II at Mikveh Israel. Central Zionist Archives.

ACKNOWLEDGEMENTS

To a large degree this is a story about Jews telling stories and I realise, not for the first time, that my appetite for tales was the legacy of the first practitioners I encountered, my mother and father, who never stopped telling them, except to eat, sing, argue and, only at the point of vocal exhaustion, sleep. The stories would promptly begin again at breakfast. Many, though not all, of those stories involved Jews – on the rivers of Lithuania, the docks of Smyrna, the streets of Brooklyn and Whitechapel, but also much further afield in places where our family had for a while fetched up – Valparaiso, St Louis, Johannesburg, Sydney, Harbin and, as my mother insisted, on the wagon train west across America. (As the reader will have discovered this was not entirely out of the question.) The stories were populated by unlikely, richly described characters, a surprising number of whom (the white witch Mime Xenia and the firebrand test pilot Johnny de Havilland for instance) turn out to have been real. Thanks to my father's unpredictable commercial fortunes everyone and everything was forever in motion and commotion and suitcases, nattily monogrammed for my father, were never far away. So I expect some of the sense that Jewish history is a gazetteer annotated by announcements of weddings, scandalous runaways and oncoming assaults, comes from this yeasty brew of narratives cooked up most supper times. If I have overdone it, Trudie and Arthur are certainly not to be blamed and are in any case long beyond noticing, though sometimes I do wonder.

There are others, also gone from the world too soon, who were friends and abetters of this history, and who listened sympathetically to its meanderings, above all Lisa Jardine whose merriment, intellectual and personal, I miss every single day; also Christopher Hitchens who, on discovering very belatedly that he was himself Jewish, ordered me to hurry up with the words; Svetlana Boym, who walked me round Petrogradsky, talked to me of Soviet Jews, usually with a touch of mischievous whimsy; and Cyril Sherwood who was a walking encyclopedia of everything but especially of everything Jewish. With the late, great historian Robert Wistrich I shared Jewish history when we were eleven years old in Golders Green and Kilburn, nineteen years old in Cambridge and sixty something in Yemin Moshe in Jerusalem. It grieves me more than I can say that he is not around to give me the benefit of his critical wisdom. Other friends have lent an ear of encouragement even when what they were hearing could have made little or no sense at all: Andrew Arends, Chloe Aridjis, Clemence Boulouque, Jan Dalley, Celina Fox, Julia Hobsbawm, Suzannah Lipscomb, Rabbi Dame Julia Neuberger, Elena Narodzanki, Clara Sanabras, Jill and Robert Slotover, and my friend and television agent Rosemary Scoular. Charlotte Sacher and I shared a long, fog-shrouded filming odyssey into the world of the shtetls and the great metropolitan communities of Jews in Europe and America five years ago during the production of The Story of the Jews for BBC2. That whole extraordinary experience shaped some of the thinking running through this volume and I am also grateful to Janice Hadlow, Hugo McGregor, Tim Kirby, Kate Edwards, Julia Mair and Ella Bahair, all of whom, in their different ways, made it happen, and to Georgette Bennett, Leonard Polonsky and Howard and Abby Milstein who made the PBS broadcast of the Story of the Jews possible.

I owe a great debt of gratitude to my agents Michael Sissons of PFD in London and Michael Carlisle of Inkwell in New York for reassuring publishers who expected a one-volume history and who will end up getting three, none of them especially on the slim side. But my heroic publishers, Stuart Williams at The Bodley Head and Dan Halpern at Ecco in New York, have been generous and patient enough to keep faith with the project in spite of warnings by the gloomy preacher of Ecclesiastes that 'of the making of books there is no end'. At Bodley Head I'm grateful to David Milner, for his scrupulous editing, and to Katherine Fry for copyediting; also to Douglas Matthews for the index, Sally Sergeant and Alison Rae for proofreading; Caroline Wood for picture research; the brilliant, resourceful Anna-Sophia Watts; Joe Pickering for publicity; to Rowena Skelton-Wallace and Graeme Hall; to Nick Skidmore for pinyin consultation; to Lily Richards and Matt Broughton for the jacket design which so perfectly embodies the spirit of the volume. At Ecco, thanks to Emma Dries for her kind help, and to Miriam Parker and Martin Wilson; and to Allison Saltzman for the cover design.

Dan Herron at PFD was heroic enough to take on the thankless task of sorting inconsistencies and omissions in the notes for which this historian is deeply grateful. He is not responsible for any blemishes and blunders which will surely remain.

None of this could have happened without the unflagging help of Griselda Murray-Brown, Jennifer Sonntag and especially Marta Enrile Hamilton, all of whom have kept the runaway Schama express more or less on the rails.

Stella Tillyard has been a kind listener when the Story of the Jews seemed all too much and yet not enough and has been a warm-hearted enthusiast of the whole project from its genesis. My literary agent and dear friend Caroline

Michel has gone way beyond the professional call of duty by reading every chapter almost as soon as it emerged from the keyboard-pounding hand of the author, and has made editorial suggestions which have invariably made the book better. The whole work is unthinkable without her impassioned encouragement. That the book could and should speak to common concerns of humanity without ever diluting the distinctiveness of Jewish history has been the constant conviction of Alice Sherwood, who thought up the perfect title, who has read and listened to all the tales and the arguments and who has been along for the journey every step of the way.

My family, especially Ginny who has coped with endless comings and goings with unlimited supplies of kindness and good humour, as well as Chloe and Mike, Gabriel and Chieh, have all taken the usual tantrums, distractedness and general meshugaas of the author in their loving stride.

Belonging has been written during a time of catastrophic uprootings around the world but there is no antidote to historical pessimism as potent as the smiles of small grandchildren for whom delight in the world is second and indeed first nature. So this book is dedicated by their zayde to Moses and Franklin who, as they grow, will see that they too belong to this story.

New York, 2017

INDEX

Irving, Washington, 501, 512
Isaac, Levi, 438
Isaacs, Daniel, 343
Isaacs, Lewis, 342
Isabella I of Castile (the Catholic), Queen
    of Spain, 54
Isaiah the Reprover, Master, 247
Isakovich, Isaac Solomonievich, 607
Islam: Jews and, 558–60
Israel: dispersion, 214–15; *see also* Palestine
Israelites *see* Lost Tribes of Israel
Isserles, Moses, 278
Italia, Salom, 163
Italy: refugee Jews in, 11; David Ha-Reuveni
    returns to, 23; Jewish theatre in, 70,
    244; Jews admitted to medical schools,
    71; Jews expelled from cities and terri-
    tories, 80; Shabbetai Zevi's followers
    in, 244; anti-Jewish laws under Pius VI,
    410; Jewish repression lifted under
    Napoleon, 411–13; Christian abduction
    of Jewish children, 568–9
Itzig, Daniel, 278–9
Itzig, Isaac Daniel, 279
Itzkowitz, Israel, 477–8

Jackson, Andrew, 501
Jackson, Jacob, 488
Jackson, John, 357
Jacob ben David of Naples, 71
Jacobins (Amis de la Constitution), 397, 401,
    404, 407
Jacobson, Israel, 537
James I, King of England (James VI of
    Scotland), 120, 134, 160, 228
Jefferson, Thomas: drafts statute of tolera-
    tion, 311; Monticello home, 481–5;
    portrait sculpture, 491–3
Jellinek, Adolf, 594, 597, 601–4, 619
Jellinek, Emil *see* Mercedes, E.J.
Jellinek, Mercedes, 595
Jellinek, Moritz, 595
Jereboam, General (fictitious), 233
Jerusalem: Suleyman rebuilds walls, 98–9;
    Dome of the Rock, 99; Jewish popula-
    tion, 99, 690; Solomon's Temple, 141,
    160–1; Judah Ha-Hasid arrives with
    followers, 262–3; James Finn's reforms,
    527–8; Uriah Levy visits, 528; Kaiser
    Wilhelm visits, 683, 689–90; *see also*
    Palestine
Jessey, Henry, 223, 225–6; *The Glory of the
    Salvation of Jehudah and Israel*, 216

Jesus bar Sirach, 145
Jesus of Nazareth: Jews blamed for killing,
    143, 379; Montalto denies being
    Messiah, 159
Jewish Chronicle (weekly), 564, 669
Jewish Colonisation Association, 657
Jews: expelled from Spain and Portugal, 4;
    life in Venice, 6–10, 119–20; and circum-
    cision of converts, 54; and theatre,
    68–70, 72–8; and classical learning, 70;
    admitted to medical schools in Italy, 71;
    culture and learning, 71–2; betrothal
    and marriage, 74–5; Pope Paul IV's bull
    against, 79–80, 96, 261, 568; expulsions
    from Italian cities, 80; as physicians to
    Ottomans, 90; in Jerusalem, 99; reli-
    gious services, 119; women's qualities,
    121–2; music, 129–31, 133; criminal
    gangs, 134; Modena and Luzzatto write
    on, 134; in China, 137–48; blamed for
    killing Jesus, 143, 379; in India, 148–51,
    154–5; in West Africa, 153–4; find refuge
    in Netherlands, 163–4; martyrs' books,
    174; historical mistreatment, 177–8;
    granted citizenship rights in
    Amsterdam, 180; gambling, 182, 244; as
    stockbrokers, 182; Mendelssohn on
    continuing prejudice against, 207–8;
    and blood libel accusations, 228–9, 257,
    308, 449–50, 561, 565, 569–70, 650;
    Eisenmenger demonises, 261; as finan-
    ciers and moneylenders, 264–70, 327,
    416, 418; Protected (*Hofjude*), 270, 280;
    Maria Theresa expels from Bohemia
    and Moravia, 272–5; Voltaire dispar-
    ages, 278, 290, 312, 373–5, 389;
    Enlightenment (*Haskalah*), 281, 291; in
    medicine, 281–3, 328; effect of emanci-
    pation, 290–1; Lessing and Gumpertz
    propose full civic rights for, 290; accept
    Jesus's teachings, 299; and Joseph II's
    Edict on Tolerance, 304–5; granted
    education rights, 305; and liberal
    pluralism, 310; performers, 325–6, 439;
    converts accepted into English society,
    327–8; beards, 334; campaign for French
    citizenship, 379–94, 416–19; as agricul-
    turalists, 382, 623–4; granted French
    citizenship (1791), 396–400; under
    French Revolution régime, 400–6; and
    intermarriage, 417–18; traders and
    merchants in eastern Europe, 430–1,
    435–6; command of languages, 431;

Paiva, Mosseh Pereyra de, 155
Palestine: conquered by Ottomans, 98; new
    town at Tiberias, 102–4, 107; Napoleon
    in, 414; earthquake (1837), 560, 626;
    Palmerston proposes Jewish return to,
    565; emigration to, 580; Victorians visit,
    592; as Zion, 621, 655–7; Arabs in, 622,
    627–9, 687–8; early Zionist settlements,
    623–7, 629–32; intensive agriculture in,
    626; ecology, 627; land ownership, 628;
    Christian immigrants, 631; Herzl visits,
    686–92; see also Israel; Jerusalem;
    Zionism
Palgrave, Sir Francis (formerly Meyer
    Cohen), 360
Palgrave, Francis Turner, 360
Palmerston, Henry John Temple, 3rd
    Viscount, 564–5
Panama Canal Company, 640
Pangu (cosmic giant), 145
Panigarola, Francesco, Bishop of Asti, 118
Paradesi synagogue, Cochin Old Town,
    India, 148–9, 151, 155
Paris: Jews petition for rights, 386–7; Jews
    excluded from civic status, 396; Jews
    granted citizenship, 397; insurrection
    (1792), 401; falls to Prussians (1870), 566;
    synagogue, 597; see also France
Parnell, Charles Stewart, 670
Pastorini, Pastorino, 59
Pathé, Charles and Émile, 643
Paul III, Pope, 42, 56
Paul IV, Pope, 56, 68
Pearce, Henry 'Hen' ('the Game
    Chicken'), 358
Péguy, Charles, 639
Peixotto, Simcha, 512
Pelham, Henry, 317
Peña, Hayyim, 241
Penso de la Vega, José: Confusion de
    Confusiones, 182
Pentateuch: polygot, 95
Péreire, Émile, 548–52, 566, 598
Péreire, Henriette, 548, 550
Péreire, Isaac, 548
Péreire, Isaac the younger, 548–52, 598
Péreire, Jacob Rodrigues (formerly Francisco
    Antonio Rodrigues), 362–9, 373–5, 400,
    404, 548
Péreire, Rachel Laurence (née Fonseca), 551
Perel, Sedner ('Sasha the Fiddler'), 607
Pereyra, Abraham, 236, 240, 245, 249
Perez de Maltranilla, Captain Miguel, 201

Perier, Casimir, 550
Pessoa, Abraham, 181
Peter, Hugh, 216
Peter I (the Great), Tsar of Russia, 474
Petrarch, 55
Petronius, 68
Petrovsky-Shtern, Yohanan, 476–7
Petter, Nicolas, 345
Philadelphia: Constitutional
    Convention, 488
Philadelphia, Jacob, 325
Philip II, King of Spain, 108, 113, 175
Philip IV, King of Spain, 173
Philippson, Ludwig, 570
Phillips, Jonas, 488, 493–4
Phillips, Manuel, 488
Phillips, Naphtali, 495–6
Phillips, Rebecca, 488
philosophes, 292, 368–9, 373, 382
physiocrats, 382
Picard, Moyse, 407
Picquart, Lieut. Col. Georges, 635–6
Piedra gloriosa de la estatua de
    Nebuchadnesar, 186
Pilsen: Great Synagogue, 590–1
Pina, Jacob, 201
Pinehas, Rabbi, 146
Pines, Yeciel Michal, 627
Pinsker, Leon, 598, 602–4, 617–21, 629, 654,
    674; Auto-Emancipation, 620–1, 654
Pinto, Daniel, 186
Pinto, Isaac de, 374–5
Pires, Diego see Molkho, Solomon
Pires, Diogo ('Pyrrhus Lusitanus'), 46–9
Pissarro, Camille, 639
Pissarro, Lucien, 639
Pitigliano: Jewish settlers, 80
Pius IV, Pope, 80
Pius V, Pope, 80–1
Pius VI, Pope, 409–410, 418
Pius IX, Pope, 568–70
Place, Francis, 318
Plautus, 68
Plica polonica (disease), 432
Pobedonostsev, Konstantin, 614
Podolia, Poland, 445–7
Polacco, Daniel Levi, 411–412
Polak family, 402
Poland–Lithuania: Cossack pogroms (1648),
    188, 219, 241, 451, 465; cases of blood
    libel, 308; synagogues destroyed and
    despoiled by Nazis, 424; fortress syna-
    gogues, 425; Jewish population and

786 BELONGING

Sanudo, Marin, 25

São Tomé (island), 62, 153

Saralvo, Joseph (born Gabriel Henriques), 54, 181

Sarmiento, Jacob de Castro, 329

Sarna, Jonathan, 495

Sarphati, Rabbi Aaron, 244, 252

Sarphati, Joseph, 11, 13

Sasportas, Jacob, 240–1, 244–5

Sassoon family, 560, 661

Satanow (Sataniv), Ukraine, 425–30, 445, 449, 465, 473

Savannah, Georgia, America, 487

Scandinavia: absence of Jews, 215

Scheid, Elie, 630

Schepperus, Cornelis, 33

Scheurer-Kestner, Auguste, 638, 644

Schlegel, Karl Wilhelm Friedrich von, 539

Schnirer, Moritz, 602, 688, 692

Schnitzler, Arthur, 653

Scholem, Gershom, 235, 239–40, 457, 464

Schomberg, Sir Alexander, 336, 331

Schomberg, Elizabeth (née Crowcher), 330–1, 334

Schomberg, Isaac, 328–9, 336

Schomberg, Meyer (earlier Meyer Löw), 328–30; Emunat Omen (The Profession of a Doctor), 336

Schomberg, Rachel, 329

Schomberg, Ralph, 329–31, 334, 336

Schönbrunn palace, Vienna, 273

Schönerer, Georg Ritter von, 600–2, 652

Schott, Gerhard, 258

Schrameck, Gabriel, 420–2

Schubert, Franz: 'Tov Lehodot', 595

Schumann, Clara, 538

Schumann, Robert, 538, 542

Schurz, General Carl, 522

Schwabacher, Rabbi Shimon Arieh, 605, 613

Schwartz, Louis, 516

Scott, Sir Walter: Ivanhoe, 512

Sefer Torah, 180

Sefer Yetzirah (Book of Creation), 72, 100, 364

sefirot (ten emanations), 100, 102

Segar, William, 492

Segonio, Carlo, 184

Seguin family, 553

Seidener, Joseph, 683, 692

Seixas, Moses, 484

Selden, John, 120

Seligman family, 506

Selim I, Ottoman Sultan, 98

Selim II, Ottoman Sultan ('the Sot'), 88–9, 105, 438; death, 108–9

Seneca, 68, 373

Senegal: Jewish community, 153; Portuguese Jews in, 153

Sephardim: in Ferrara, 53; in Ottoman Turkey, 94, 96, 104; in Jewish histories, 96; in Amsterdam, 162, 164, 166, 175–6, 219, 253; patronise Rembrandt, 187; re-education in Judaism, 192; contacts in England, 218; migrate to North America, 219, 487–8; traders' link with England and Netherlands, 219; Menasseh recommends in England, 222, 226; in Bordeaux, 362, 369–70, 373, 395–6; differences with Ashkenazis, 374–5, 487; and claims to French citizenship, 386, 419; in French Revolution, 403; as bankers, 548–9; cooking, 564

Serlio, Sebastiano, 66

Serrão, Manuel, 35

Serrarius, Peter, 234, 249

Serwouter, Johannes, 177

Sesso, Salomone da, 83

Seven Years War (1756–63), 278, 296

Sforim, Mendele Moykher, 429

Shabbeteans see Zevi, Shabbetai

Shaftesbury, Anthony Ashley Cooper, 3rd Earl of, 280, 296

Shakespeare, William, 6

Shandur, Avraham, 112

Sharif Pasha, 561

Sheba (or Saba), Queen of, 578

Sherwood, Mrs (of Bowl Yard, London), 343

Sheshet ben Isaac ben Joseph, 43

Shimon bar Yochai, 100–1

Shivhei Ha-Besht (In Praise of the Besht), 453, 464

Shlomo, Rabbi of Chelm, 284

Sholem, Gershom, 235

shtetl: life in, 428–9, 435, 445; revolts, 465

Shukr Kuhayl II (Judah ben Shalom), 579, 584

Shulkhan Arukh, 22, 120, 166, 198, 229, 235

siddurim (prayer books), 55

Sieniawska, Elzbieta, 443

Sièyes, Abbé Emmanuel Joseph, 395

Sifflet, Le (magazine), 642

Sigismund III, King of Poland, 105, 432

Simchat Torah (Rejoicing of the Law), 180

Sintzheim, Rabbi David, 387, 417

Six, Jan, 187